HUMAN RESOURCES MANAGEMENT

Canadian Edition

Andrew J. Templer
University of Windsor

R. Julian Cattaneo
University of Windsor

David A. De Cenzo
Towson State University

Stephen P. Robbins
San Diego State University

John Wiley & Sons, Inc.
Toronto • New York • Chichester • Weinheim • Brisbane • Singapore

Canadian Cataloging in Publication

Main entry under title:

Human resources management

Canadian ed.
Includes bibliographical references and index.
ISBN 0-471-64303-3

1. Personnel management.   I. Templer, A.

HF5549.H85 1998   658.3   C98-932965-8

Production Credits
Acquisitions Editor: John Horne
Publishing Services Director: Karen Bryan
Developmental Editors: Karen Staudinger, Margaret Williams
Marketing Manager: Carolyn Wells
Copy Editor: Focus Strategic Communications
Proofreader: Focus Strategic Communications
Designer: Interrobang Graphic Design Inc.
Cover Design: Fizzz Design Inc.
Cover Photo Credit: Robert Shepherd/Masterfile
Printing and Binding: Tri-Graphic Printing Limited

Printed and bound in Canada
10 9 8 7 6 5 4 3 2 1
John Wiley & Sons Canada, Ltd
22 Worcester Road
Etobicoke, Ontario M9W 1L1
Visit our website at: www.wiley.com/canada

Preface

Welcome to the first Canadian edition of our human resources management text. We're glad you're taking the time to read this preface and get a better overview of the book. We'll use this section to address three important things: what this book is about, important in-text learning aids, and who (besides the authors named on the cover) was instrumental in the book's development.

ABOUT THE BOOK

When we began discussing how to prepare the Canadian edition, we set a number of goals for ourselves. Our primary goal was to write a text that addressed the most critical issues in human resources management (HRM) for Canadians. Over the past decade, management practice has gone through some dramatic changes. These changes include increased workforce diversity, downsizing, re-engineering, total quality management (TQM), outsourcing, and the rediscovery of the importance of satisfying the customer. All of these changes have implications for HRM. For example, as more organizations re-engineer their processes, many full-time employees have been replaced with part-time, temporary, and contract workers. A contingent workforce presents new challenges for HRM in areas such as training, career development, and motivation. Societal and organizational change means that traditional HRM practices also need to change. A text for the dawn of the twenty-first century must reflect these changes while presenting the fundamentals of HRM. We have tried to achieve this delicate balance, presenting the basic HRM functions of finding, training, motivating, and keeping people, while also discussing the new world of HRM.

Strategic HRM

The importance of HRM to an organization's strategic planning process continues to gain recognition as more organizations try to ensure that they have the right people at the right time. This trend reinforces our belief that HRM is the responsibility of all managers in an organization and not just that of specialists in the human resources department. Thus, we have written this book for all students of business administration, who must know the basics of HRM.

HRM Professionals

At the same time, we are acutely aware of another trend in the practice of HRM—increased professionalization and the need to identify competencies that practitioners of HRM must possess. The Canadian Council of Human Resources Associations (CCHRA), in partnership with Human Resources

Development Canada (HRDC), has developed the National Capabilities Project to establish national standards for the generalist HR professional. These developing standards are reflected in the requirements for the Certified Human Resources Professional (CHRP) designation offered by provincial HR associations, and we have worked to ensure that our book meets these requirements.

A "De-Jobbed" World

One of the most far-reaching trends from an HRM perspective is the disappearance of jobs. Not only are jobs being transferred to countries where the cost of labour is low and reduced through downsizing, but the whole notion of jobs as we know it seems to be changing. Global competition, restructuring, and a contingent workforce have all had an impact. The trend is to define the workplace not in terms of jobs but in terms of competencies that workers must have. What will HRM be like if the organization is "de-jobbed"? We attempt to answer that question in a number of places in the text.

Research and Practice

In a dynamic and applied field like HRM, it is important for a text to reflect the current status of research and practice. Our book does so, with particular emphasis on the research and practical applications that are most relevant to the Canadian environment. In addition, we have endeavoured to present this material in a way that makes it easy for the student to understand. We've used three themes to integrate important current issues throughout the text: **International HRM**, **Ethical Decisions in HRM**, and the role of **HRM in the "De-Jobbed" Organization**. These will be found either as sections in selected chapters or as highlighted boxes.

HRM Skills

We also recognize that in HRM job success depends on practical skills. Therefore, we've included **HRM Skills** in many of the chapters in the text. These presentations provide a step-by-step basis for handling particular aspects of HRM. For example, in Chapter 3, we describe the steps you should follow to protect your organization from sexual harassment charges. As well, every chapter includes the profile of a person involved in the HR issues covered in that chapter, with an invitation to Meet that person. Furthermore, we have included two appendices that focus on students' specific needs: "Making a Good Impression—Writing the Résumé" and "The Critical Meeting—Improving Interview Skills."

LEARNING AIDS

Material

Our teaching experience has led us to conclude that a text becomes highly readable when the writing is straightforward and conversational, the topics flow logically, and the authors make extensive use of examples to illustrate concepts. These factors guided us in developing this text. Students and instructors who use our other texts regularly comment on how clearly we present ideas. We think that this book, too, is written in a clear, concise, and conversational style. Furthermore, our classroom experience tells us that students understand and remember concepts and practices most clearly when they are illustrated with examples. So we've used a wealth of examples to clarify our ideas.

Each chapter of this book is organized to provide clarity and continuity. Each chapter opens with a real-life vignette. **Learning Objectives**, which identify specifically what the student should know after reading the chapter, are stated on the title page of each chapter and are reviewed in the **Summary** section. There is also a **Key Terms** section at the end of each chapter, and these terms are defined in both the margins and the end-of-book glossary.

Have you had students tell you that they do the reading assignments and think they understand the material, but still don't do well on the exam? We have also had this experience and know that many students have too. We decided, therefore, to do something about it in the form of a **Testing Your Understanding** section at the end of each chapter. The questions in this section are designed to help students determine if they understand the chapter material. In most cases, questions link directly to the learning objectives. These questions have been specifically written to challenge students' critical thinking and generally require some application of the chapter's content.

Each chapter also includes an **Experiential Exercise** and a **Case Application**. These exercises and cases have been selected to reinforce material in the chapter. Furthermore, each case is based on a HRM situation that a real Canadian organization actually face.

Supporting Material

This book is supported by a comprehensive learning package that will help instructors create a motivating environment and that provides students with additional tools for understanding and reviewing major concepts. The *Instructors Resource Guide* developed by Vicki Kamen, Colorado State University, and Canadian adapter Vivien Clark, Wilfrid Laurier University, provides many useful items, including sample syllabi, learning objectives, key concepts, chapter overviews, chapter outlines, lecture suggestions, review and discussion questions, media resources, and an additional case per chapter.

The *Testbank*, developed by Trudy Somers, Towson State University, and Canadian adapter Joan Condie, Sheridan College, consists of approximately 1800 multiple-choice, true/false, and completion questions categorized by level of difficulty, text-page reference, and learning objective. The *Testbank* is available in paper and in a computerized version called MICROTEST.

A set of full-colour transparency masters highlights key concepts and figures found in the text and is available in PowerPoint format.

The Website for *Human Resources Management*, Canadian Edition, can be accessed at <http:www.wiley.com/canada/templer>. The site includes direct links to online resources that are mentioned in the text as well as updates on important developments in HRM, particularly in Canada. The site also links to resources such as the Websites of HRM professional associations and aims to help both instructors and students find HRM-related material on the Internet. Instructors can download PowerPoint slides directly from the site's **Instructors' Resource Centre**. Students can test their knowledge and get immediate results through the site's online testing feature in the **Students' Resource Centre**.

ACKNOWLEDGEMENTS

Getting a finished book into the hands of a reader requires the work of many people. The authors do their part by developing an outline, researching topics, and keyboarding sentences into their computers. But that only starts the process. Many other people contribute to the making and marketing of a textbook. We'd like to recognize just a few of the people who contributed to this text.

In particular, we would like to thank our graduate assistants, Brad Bossence and Anil Risbud, for their energy and dedication in tracking down references, examples, and research articles. We are also grateful to the contributing authors who provided some critical materials under very tight deadlines: Chapters 3 and 4 were written by Gerard Seijts, University of Manitoba; Chapter 15, by Allen Craig, Smith Lyons; Chapter 17, by Kenneth Wm. Thornicroft, University of Victoria; and the "Meet" boxes by Elizabeth d'Anjou. The assistance of Allan Jarvis of the HRPAO in facilitating interviews is also gratefully acknowledged.

Of utmost importance are our reviewers. Our Canadian reviewers gave us great feedback and provided substantial insight. The book you have before you is a much better learning tool because of our reviewers'. We cannot thank them enough and hope that they see the benefits of their work. Specifically, we wish to recognize the following people who reviewed our proposal:

Edward G. Fisher,
   University of Alberta

Robert J. Oppenheimer,
   Concordia University

John D. Hart,
   Humber College

R.A. Rodgers,
   Southern Alberta Institute of Technology, and

M. Nummelin,
   Conestoga College

P.H.J. Wilson,
   Vanier College.

We would also like to thank the people who reviewed our manuscript:

J. Ronald Edmonds,
   University of Saskatchewan

Alec J. Lee,
   Camosun College

Anne Harper,
   Humber College

Gloria Miller,
   St. Francis-Xavier University

Brian Harrocks,
   Algonquin College

M. Nummelin,
   Conestoga College

Cheryl Harvey,
   Wilfrid Laurier University

R.A. Rodgers,
   Southern Alberta Institue of Technology, and

Leeann Henry,
   Sheridan College

Diane White,
   Seneca College.

Brad Hill,
   St. Lawrence College

A book doesn't appear automatically on bookstore shelves. It gets there through the combined efforts of many people. For us, these people are part of the outstanding publishing team at John Wiley & Sons Canada, Ltd: John Horne, Acquisitions Editor; Karen Bryan, Publishing Services Director; and Developmental Editors, Karen Staudinger and Margaret Williams.

We also have some individual acknowledgements. Andrew wishes to thank his friends at HRPAO for their assistance and the ongoing support of the four special women in his life, Mary, Alison, Deborah and Jennifer.

Julian recognizes the continuing support of his wife, Vivian, without whom none of this would make any sense, and children Ben and Jessica, who continue to make him proud. Also, a word of thanks is in order to the institution of the academic sabbatical, which relieved him of onerous administrative tasks just at the moment when the book's demands started to exceed his capacity to respond to them; and a very special thanks to CBC's Radio Two.

Brief Contents

Contents

HRM COMPETENCIES

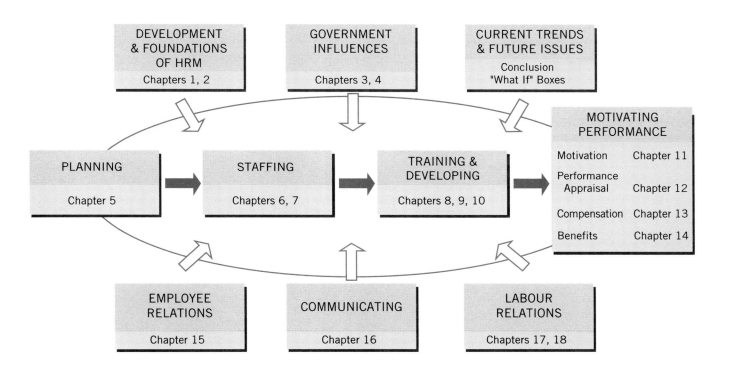

DEVELOPMENT & FOUNDATIONS OF HRM

Chapters 1, 2

GOVERNMENT INFLUENCES

Chapters 3, 4

CURRENT TRENDS & FUTURE ISSUES

Conclusion
"What If" Boxes

MOTIVATING PERFORMANCE

Motivation	Chapter 11
Performance Appraisal	Chapter 12
Compensation	Chapter 13
Benefits	Chapter 14

PLANNING

Chapter 5

STAFFING

Chapters 6, 7

TRAINING & DEVELOPING

Chapters 8, 9, 10

EMPLOYEE RELATIONS

Chapter 15

COMMUNICATING

Chapter 16

LABOUR RELATIONS

Chapters 17, 18

Chapter One

INTRODUCTION TO HUMAN RESOURCES MANAGEMENT

LEARNING OBJECTIVES

AFTER READING THIS CHAPTER, YOU WILL BE ABLE TO:

1. Discuss the importance of human resources management.
2. Describe what is meant by the term human resources management.
3. Explain what environmental influences affect human resources management.
4. Describe how management practices affect human resources management.
5. Discuss the effect of labour unions on human resources management.
6. Outline the components and the goals of the major functions of human resources management.
7. Explain how human resources management practices differ in small businesses and in an international setting.

Claire Somas had a real sense of achievement as she began her third week as manager of human resources and administration at Ester Enterprises. She was pleased she had decided to complete her certification in human resources management (HRM) after graduating, and that she had taken up the invitation to speak on managing people for success at a lunch meeting of the Chamber of Commerce. It was after this meeting that she met Edwin (Ed) Esterhuizen, the founder of Ester Enterprises, a small company set up to modify tools and equipment for left-handed users. Ed was preparing to take on a wider range of products and invited her to join Ester to advise him on getting the most from the people. So Claire felt quite excited as she reflected back after just three weeks as Ester's first human resources manager. Her position also included responsibility for such administrative departments as shipping and food services.

As a "lefty" himself, it was while Ed was employed in a drafting office that he discovered how difficult it was to use equipment designed for right-handers—scales on rulers were upside down, and drawing arms and paper supports were uncomfortably placed, to name a few. He decided to start his own business modifying drafting equipment, but he quickly expanded into a range of office equipment and workshop implements for what seemed to be an untapped market across North America. He was bidding on a half-million dollar contract to supply left-handed workstations for a large engineering consulting firm with offices across Canada. He felt sure he could deliver on this contract because he now had someone who could make it easy to plan for the right people to get the new work done.

Claire had spent her first week meeting the fifty-three people who worked at Ester, finding out what her job involved and how her boss thought the human resources and administration parts of her job would fit together. She found that her daily HRM reality was rather different from those large organizations that could afford full-time HRM specialists and which had mostly been the focus of her studies at university. She spent a good part of her second week organizing the coffee service and chip wagon for Esters. Then, in her third week, she was reading up on all she had learned in her HRM courses on interviewing and hiring in preparation for evaluating the hiring suitability of the three applicants that her boss had sent to her for employment.

As she sat at her desk, Claire reviewed her to-do list for the morning. Firstly, she had to evaluate the results from the three applicants on a battery of mechanical aptitude tests. Secondly, she had to suggest a training program for employees to operate the new left-facing blade-sharpening machine Ed had found at a recent tools exhibition. Perhaps most importantly, she had to prepare for periodic visits to the plant by the provincial health and safety inspector.

While completing her plans for the morning, she came upon the scribbled note from her boss: "Claire, am finalizing our bid for the workstations. Could you let me know what personnel costs to include in the bid by 11 o'clock this morning?" While this did upset her previous plans, Claire was enthusiastic about being involved in a project of such obvious importance to the future success of the company.

As she revised her morning plans yet again, the phone rang. It was the shipping supervisor. "Ms Somas, we forgot to include the product information sheets to accompany the big order that leaves this morning for Vancouver. Please, can you find some quickly? The truck drivers arrive in two and a half hours."

Claire realized she had to set some priorities among the various tasks she had to complete that day. Some of the less urgent things could be left for her secretary to organize, and the most urgent ones, she would have to see to herself. She knew it was important to leave time for the most important activities, even if they were not immediately required. After all, she had stressed the importance of including human resources in the ongoing planning process of all companies in her own address to the Chamber of Commerce.

Introduction

When you reflect for a moment on Claire Somas's position, you can see that Ester could not achieve any of its objectives without someone able to look after human resources. Claire may seem very busy, perhaps even overloaded, but this is not at all unusual in Canadian organizations—particularly in smaller companies in which the HR manager may have all types of pressures and other responsibilities with which to contend. What is a company like Ester without its employees—some buildings, some equipment, and some impressive dreams in the head of the founder? If you removed the employees from such varied organizations as the BC Lions football team, the CBC, Scouts Canada, or your local town's parks board, what would you have left? Not much. It's people and their contribution—not buildings or equipment—that make an organization. This is expressed well by John Di Sebastiano, national sales manager and acting general manager for Lanier Canada, who says: "Happier and more motivated employees will do a better job for you. It's common-sense management. We want people to be proud of where they work."[1]

This point is one that many of us take for granted. When you think about the millions of organizations that provide us with goods and services, any one of which might employ you during your lifetime, how often do you explicitly consider that these organizations depend on people to make them operate? Only under unusual circumstances—such as when you get put on hold for an eternity on a company's toll-free customer-service line or when a major corporation is sued for a discriminatory HRM practice—do you recognize the important role that employees play in making organizations work. But how did these people come to be employees in their organizations? How were they selected? Why do they come to work on a regular basis? How do they know what to do in their jobs? How does management know if the employees are performing adequately? And if they are not, what can be done about it? Will today's employees be adequately prepared for the technologically advanced work the organization will require of them in the years ahead? What happens in an organization if a union enters the picture?

We will draw on some examples from larger organizations because they are the ones with the resources to employ a range of human resources management specialists. But as Claire Somas in our chapter opener demonstrates, HRM is equally important in the small- and medium-sized organizations that employ the majority of people in Canada. In smaller organizations, HRM may not be as sophisticated and may not even be the sole responsibility of its manager, but it plays no less an important role in the company's success. As you read through the text, you will be continuously reminded to consider how particular practices can be applied to small- and medium-sized organizations in both the profit and non-profit sectors in Canada.

HRM Is Part of Management

We have seen that the answers to a number of key management questions lie in the field of human resources management. Yet HRM does not exist in isolation; instead, it is best viewed as that part of management that deals with people at work. So, before we attempt to understand how an organization should manage its human resources, let's briefly review the essentials of management.

Management The process of efficiently getting activities completed with and through other people.

Planning A management function focusing on setting organizational goals and objectives.

Organizing A management function that deals with what jobs are to be done, by whom, where decisions are to be made, and the grouping of employees.

Leading A management function concerned with directing the work of others.

Controlling A management function concerned with monitoring activities.

Management is the process of efficiently achieving the objectives of the organization. To achieve its objective, management typically requires the coordination of several vital components that we call functions. The primary functions of management that are required are **planning**[2] (i.e., establishing goals), **organizing** (i.e., determining what tasks need to be completed to accomplish those goals), **leading** (i.e., ensuring that the right people are on the job with appropriate skills and motivating them to levels of high productivity), and **controlling** (i.e., monitoring activities to ensure that goals are met). When these four functions operate in a coordinated fashion, we can say that the organization is heading in the right direction towards achieving its objectives. Three elements are common to any effort to achieve objectives: goals, limited resources, and people.

In any discussion of management, one must recognize the importance of setting goals. Goals are necessary because activities undertaken in an organization must be directed towards some end. For instance, your goal in taking this class is to build an understanding of HRM and, obviously, to pass the class (see the memo to students). There is considerable truth in the observation, "If you don't know where you are going, any road will take you there." The established goals may not be explicit, but if there are no goals at all, there is no need for managers.

Limited resources are a fact of organizational life. By definition, economic resources are scarce; therefore, managers are responsible for their allocation. This requires not only that managers be effective in achieving the established goals, but that they be efficient in doing so. Managers, then, are concerned with the attainment of goals, which makes them effective, and with the best allocation of scarce resources, which makes them efficient.

In summary, managers are those who work with and through other people, allocating resources, in the effort to achieve goals. They perform their tasks through four critical activities: planning, organizing, leading, and controlling.

TO: Students reading this book

FROM: Julian Cattaneo and Andrew Templer

SUBJECT: How to get the most out of this text

All authors of a textbook generally include a preface section that describes why they wrote the book and what's unique about it, and then thank people for the role they played in getting the book completed. Well, we're no different. We did that, too. But it has become crystal clear to us that two things are common about a book's preface. First, it's usually written for the professor, especially one who's considering selecting the book. Second, students don't read the preface. That's unfortunate, because it often includes information that students would find useful.

As authors, we listen to our customers, and many of ours have told us that they'd enjoy some input from us, but placed where they can find it—not buried in the preface. So, we've written this memo. Its purpose is to provide you with our ideas about the book, how it was put together, and more importantly, how you can use it to better understand the field of HRM and do better in this class!

This book was written to provide you with the foundations of HRM. Our underlying theme is that HRM matters to *all* employees in *all* organizations. We draw many examples from large organizations because these are the ones with the resources for comprehensive HRM practices that are characteristically highlighted by the media. We work very hard, however, in helping you apply HRM principles to the smaller Canadian businesses where most of you will be employed. Whether you intend to work in HRM or not, most of these elements will affect you at some point in your career. Take, for example, the performance appraisal. Although you might not currently be in a position to evaluate another individual's work performance, if you are working, you're more than likely to have your own performance appraised. Consequently, it's important for you to have an understanding of how it should work and the potential problems that may exist.

We began Part I of this book with the chapter you are now reading. The emphasis in Chapter 1 is to provide you with an overview of HRM, its approach, and its cast of characters. From there, we move to more global issues surrounding the HRM function. The environment in which HRM operates is changing rapidly, so we want you to get a feel for what is happening in the business world today and what implications that presents for HRM. Next, we need to turn our attention to the laws that affect HRM activities. Much of how HRM operates is guided by legislation and court decisions that prohibit practices adversely affecting certain groups of people. Without a good understanding of these laws, an organization's performance can suffer, and the organization can be vulnerable to costly lawsuits. Part I ends with a discussion of employee rights and a look at some ethical concerns influencing HRM.

Parts II to V provide coverage of the fundamental activities that exist in HRM. Part II explores the staffing function, with discussions on strategic human resources planning, recruiting, and selection. Part III addresses means for orienting, training, and developing employees. Part IV, the motivation function, reviews several areas designed to get the maximum effort from workers. Then, in Part V, we look at ways for management to keep high-performing employees.

Much of the discussion in Part II to V reflects typical activities in an organization that is not unionized. When a union is present, however, many of these practices might need modification to comply with another set of laws. As such, we reserved the final two chapters, Part VI, for dealing with labour-management relations.

While we are confident that the six parts will provide the fundamentals of HRM, a book has to offer more. It should not only cover topics (in an interesting and lively way, we hope), it should also assist in the learning process. It should be written in such a way that you can understand it, it keeps your attention, and it provides you with an opportunity for feedback. We think we've met each of these goals. Of course, only you can be the judge of our claim. But let's look at how we arrived at our conclusion.

To be understandable and lively means that we need to communicate with you. We make every attempt in this text to have it sound as if we were in front of your class speaking with you. Writing style is important to us. We use examples, whenever possible, from a range of actual Canadian companies so you can see that what we talk about is happening in the real world. In the past, people using our books have indicated that our writing style did help hold their attention. But the communication connection, albeit critical, is only half of the equation. The ultimate tests for you are: Does the book help you do well on exams? Does it help prepare you for a job?

We start every chapter with learning objectives. We view these as the critical learning points because they present a logical flow from which the material will be presented. If you can explain what is proposed in each learning objective, you'll be on the right track to understanding the material. But memory sometimes fools us. We read the material, think we understand it, see how the summaries directly tie the learning objectives together, then take the exam and receive a grade that is not reflective of "what we *knew* we knew." We have given a lot of thought to that issue, and we think we've come up with something that will help—putting a feedback test in the book. Let's explain.

The typical textbook ends each chapter with a set of review questions. Unfortunately, your tests rarely look much like the review questions. Exams, for the most part, emphasize multiple-choice questions. So, we've replaced the review questions with a set of test questions. These questions are actual ones that we've used to test our students' understanding of the material. If you can correctly answer these questions, then you're one step closer to enhancing your understanding of HRM. Recognize, of course, that these are only a learning aid. They help you to learn but don't replace careful reading or intensive studying. And don't assume that getting a question right means you fully understand the concept covered. Why? Because any set of multiple-choice questions can only test a limited range of information. So don't let correct answers lull you into a sense of false security. If you miss a question or don't fully understand why you got the correct response, go back to the corresponding pages in the chapter and reread the material.

Learning, however, goes beyond just passing a test. It also means preparing yourself to perform successfully in tomorrow's organizations. You'll find that organizations today require their employees to work more closely together than at any time in the past. Call it teams, horizontal organizational structures, matrix management, or something else. The fact remains that your success will depend on how well you work closely with others. To help model this group concept for you, we have included a dozen class exercises in this text. Each of these experiential learning efforts is designed to highlight a particular topic in the text and give you an opportunity to work in groups to solve the issue at hand.

One last thing. What can you take out of this course and use in the future? Many business leaders have complained about the way business schools train their graduates. Although business schools have made many positive contributions, one critical component appears lacking—practical skills. The range of skills you need to succeed in today's business environment is increasing. You must be able to communicate, think creatively, make good and timely decisions, plan effectively, and deal with people. In HRM, we have an opportunity to build our skills bank. As you go through this text, you'll find a dozen or more practical skills that you can use on your job. We hope you give them special attention, practise them often, and add them to your repertoire.

If you'd like to tell us how we might improve the next edition of this book, we encourage you to e-mail us at: templer@uwindsor.ca [Andrew Templer] and rjcatt@uwindsor.ca [Julian Cattaneo].

The Importance of Human Resources Management

Prior to the mid-1960s,[3] personnel departments in organizations were often perceived as the "health and happiness" crews.[4] Their primary activities involved planning company picnics, scheduling vacations, enrolling workers for health care coverage and other benefits, and planning retirement parties. That has certainly changed during the past three decades, particularly in large organizations. Federal and provincial laws have forced employers to adopt new requirements on hiring and employment practices. Jobs have changed, becoming more technical and requiring greater skills. Job boundaries are becoming blurred. In the past, a worker performed a specific job in a specific department, doing particular tasks with others who did similar jobs. Today's workers are just

HR staff discuss HRM practices in the organization that must be designed to deal with such issues as globalization, downsizing, changing skill levels, corporate restructuring and diversity.

as likely to find themselves working on project teams with various people from across the organization. And, improved workforce productivity is more important than ever with the new global competition. Even in smaller organizations, this has resulted in the need for HRM specialists trained in psychology, sociology, organization, work design, and law. Federal legislation requires organizations to hire the best-qualified candidate without regard to race, religion, colour, sex, or national origin, and someone has to ensure that this is done. Employees need to be trained to function effectively within the organization, and someone has to oversee this. Once hired and trained, the continuing personal development of each employee has to be provided by the organization. The work environment must be structured to induce workers to stay with the organization, while simultaneously attracting new applicants. Of course, the responsiblity for carrying out these activities lands on the shoulders of human resources professionals.

What's in a Name?

A constant theme of this book is the changing nature of HRM. This includes a growing professionalism and a new respect for the field, new resources, new skills, and even new names.

Today, professionals in the human resources area are vital elements in the success of any organization. Their jobs require an unprecedented level of sophistication,[5] and not surprisingly, their status in the organization has also been elevated.[6] Even the name has changed. Although the terms *personnel* and *human resources management* are frequently used interchangeably, it is important to note that the two connote quite different aspects.[7] Personnel seems to suggest the employee welfare roots of the field and is often termed personnel administration. On the other hand, human resources management places much more stress on the managerial and strategic focus of the field today. This difference holds true even in small organizations with no full-time specialists in which HRM activities are part of the overall organizational strategy. In a large organization, the human resources department head may be a vice-president with an assured position at the executive board level.

Companies today recognize the importance of investing in people through whom organization goals are met. For instance, according to Gay Mitchell, executive vice-president at the Royal Bank of Canada, their investments of over $100 million on various learning interventions, "are a crucial investment in preparing our employees to adjust to dramatic changes under way in the financial services industry."[8] The HRM function also has to adjust to dramatic change. Michael O'Brien, executive vice-president at Toronto-based Sunoco, Inc., puts it this way: "We've got a responsibility to ensure that we're helping people build their own competencies so they can move as the organization moves. It's a very different role than it has been in the past…and we're looking to the HR department to lead us through that."[9]

One of the most significant developments is the growth of professional accreditation in HRM in Canada. The first legally recognized designation, the certified human resources professional (CHRP) in Ontario, is likely to be followed by similar legislation in other provinces. At the time of writing, the Canadian Council of Human Resources Associations (CCHRA), together with Human Resources Development Canada, were working on the competencies and skill elements that might go into a Canada-wide professional designation. Many colleges and universities help prepare HRM professionals by offering the educational course component towards certification in the field. The CHRP, however, is made up of a number of other components as well (see "HRM Skills").

Human Resources Management: A Closer Look

Human resources management is the part of the organization that is concerned with the "people" dimension. It is a staff or support function, and its role is to provide assistance in HRM matters to line employees or those directly involved in producing the organization's goods and services. Every organization is comprised of people. Acquiring their services, developing their skills, motivating them to high levels of performance, and ensuring that they continue to maintain their commitment to the organization are essential to achieving organizational objectives. This is true regardless of the type of organization—government, business, education, health, recreation, or social action. Getting and keeping good people is critical to the success of every organization.

HRM consists of four functions: *staffing, training and development, motivation,* and *maintenance.* In less academic terms, we might say that HRM is made up of four activities: getting people, preparing them, stimulating them, and keeping them.

When one attempts to piece together an approach for human resources management, many variations and themes may exist. However, when we begin to focus on HRM activities as being subsets of the four functions, a clearer picture arises (see Figure 1-1). You will notice that labour relations is placed outside the main circle of HRM. This is to emphasize the key role it plays in all areas of HRM. Of course, in unionized organizations, labour relations would also be a key part of employee relations, in the *maintenance* phase of the profession. Before we take a closer look at each component—*staffing, training and development, motivation,* and *maintenance*—let's look at the external influences that affect the HRM processes.

Human Resources Management Function in the organization concerned with the staffing, training and development, motivation, and maintenance of employees.

The External Influences

The four HRM activities don't exist in isolation. Rather, they are highly affected by what is occurring outside the organization. It is important to recognize these environmental influences because any activity undertaken in each of the HRM processes is directly or indirectly affected by these external elements. For example, when a company downsizes its workforce, does it lay off workers by seniority? If so, are an inordinate number of minority employees affected? Although any attempt to identify specific influences may prove insufficient, we can categorize them into four general areas: *dynamic environment, governmental legislation, labour unions,* and *management thought.*

Environmental Influences Those factors outside the organization that directly affect HRM operations.

Dynamic Environment It's almost a truism that the only thing that remains constant during our lifetimes is change, and that we must prepare ourselves for events that will have a significant effect on our lives. HRM is no different. Many events help shape our field. Some of the more obvious ones include globalization, workforce diversity, changing skill requirements, corporate downsizing, Total Quality Management (TQM), re-engineering work processes, decentralized worksites, and employee involvement. Although these topics are the focus of Chapter 2, let's look at them briefly now.

Meet

Nancy Hancock
Recruiter, Human Resources
Jasper Park Lodge

Nancy Hancock had always wanted to live in Jasper, a ruggedly beautiful town on the edge of the Rocky Mountains. While studying business at the Northern Alberta Institute of Technology, Ms Hancock was especially interested in her human resources class. She had also taken a course on the hospitality industry at night school. So when a position opened up in human resources at the scenic Jasper Park Lodge, she saw it as the perfect opportunity to combine several of her interests.

Eight years later, she has no regrets. In two and a half years as the human resources secretary, her duties expanded from administrative work and pre-screening applicants to include running a newsletter and participating in the staff activities committee. She was promoted to human resources coordinator, where she played a greater role in hiring—doing interviews and reference checks—as well as creating safety reports and looking after the employee benefits program.

Then, in 1994, she moved into her current position of recruiter. She is responsible for staffing most of the hotel's seven hundred positions with capable, committed employees. These include about one hundred temporary workers hired each summer, many of whom are college students in hospitality or business programs. "We want staff who can really make a difference in a guest's stay," she explains.

"It takes a special kind of person to work in human resources," says Ms Hancock. "You need a lot of stamina and energy. You have to be pretty outgoing—you have to like to talk! Integrity is also very important because you need to respect the confidentiality of employee information. You need to be organized and able to plan ahead. And you need a teamwork attitude. "You even need to be a bit of a salesperson since you are selling your organization to potential employees just as they are selling themselves to you." It's a demanding environment, but a rewarding one. "I think it would be difficult," she laughs, "if you didn't love the job."

Globalization reflects the worldwide operations of many businesses today. We are no longer bound by continents or societal cultures. Take the motor industry, for example. Can you imagine some of the people issues involved in the merger of Chrysler and Daimler-Benz, or the purchase of Rolls-Royce by Volkswagen? Think of some of the challenges facing HRM in the resulting merged companies, such as integrating different cultures, histories, and training and selection programs. Homogeneity of employees and their needs no longer exist. Our work today is more complex, requiring employees with sophisticated skills. Without them, many employees will lack the basic abilities to perform successfully in tomorrow's organizations.

Corporate downsizing, Total Quality Management, and re-engineering all relate to one another. As the world changed, Canadian companies had to compete harder to maintain their leading industrial status. This meant doing things differently, and in an effort to become more productive, organizations downsized to create greater efficiency by eliminating certain jobs. Of the remaining

 **HRM** *Skills*

What skills and competencies are necessary for successful performance in HRM? As mentioned earlier, this particular question is presently being investigated by a joint project of the Canadian Council of Human Resource Associations (CCHRA) and Human Resource Development (HRD) Canada. The eventual outcome is likely to be a national certification in HRM. For the moment, we direct your attention to the requirements for the certified HR professional (CHRP) of the Human Resources Professionals Association of Ontario (HRPAO).[10] Three components to the CHRP are: education, professional experience, and code of ethics.

1. **Educational**: This comprises two elements:

   Academic Courses: The first part of this entails the completion of eight academic courses.

   Tier 1 four required courses are: finance and accounting; labour economics, introductory human resources management, and organizational behaviour.

   Tier 2 four optional courses are drawn from the following specialization areas: training and development, compensation and benefits, human resources planning, health and safety, industrial relations, and human resources research and information systems.

   Comprehensive Exam: After completing the above courses, the educational component is completed by the successful completion of a comprehensive provincial exam (CPE).

2. **Professional Experience**: This component entails the successful completion of a specified number of years in HRM practice at a professional and managerial level.

3. **Code of Ethics**: An ongoing component of the CHRP is the adherence to a code of ethics. This is particularly important in a field which impacts upon the actual life experience of so many individuals in an organization. The code includes such things as: adherence to relevant by-laws and regulations, confidentiality, moral behaviour, community and employer support, commitment to human rights, and the promotion of human resources development.

jobs and work processes, such quality initiatives as Total Quality Management and ISO 9000 certification look at ways of improving job effectiveness. By continuously improving on methods, techniques, processes, and the like, companies make constant efforts to better what they produce. But what if what they produce, even if it's better, still doesn't satisfy the customer? In those cases, re-engineering is necessary. Where TQM looks at new and improved ways of producing goods and services, re-engineering looks at starting the processes over again from scratch. That is, instead of improving on an existing product, the organization analyses what should be done and how they should do it. Searching for answers is not constrained by current business practices.

Decentralized worksites are quickly becoming part of many organizations. With the technologies that are available (personal computers, fax machines, modems, etc.), work that once had to be done on the company premises may now be more cost-effectively handled from the employee's home. Lastly, employee involvement looks at how employees' work lives are changing. Involved employees now have more control over their jobs. Certain activities, such as goal setting, were once the sole responsibility of managers, but employee involvement now permits participation.

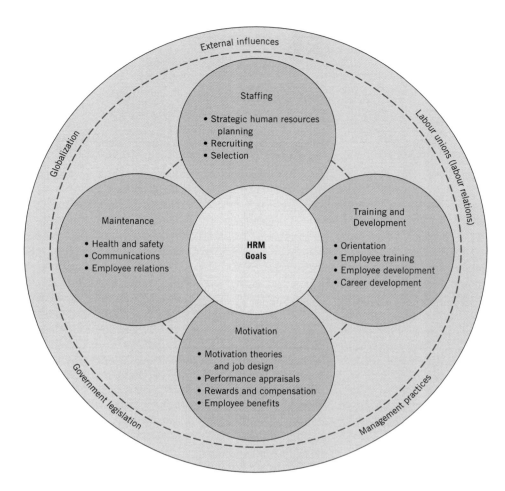

Figure 1-1
Human Resources
Management Approach

Government Legislation There are an enormous number of government regulations and laws which have widespread influence on the HRM field. It is now easier for many employees to take several weeks of unpaid maternity leave to be with their newborn children and return to their jobs without loss of seniority. Although some employers see the negative effects these leaves have on the work flow, government legislation has given employees the right to take this leave. Laws supporting this and a multitude of other employer actions are important to the HRM process and may cost employers if ignored. Not even senior government departments can ignore this. For example, the Department of National Defence was ordered to compensate a hearing-impaired woman, Monica Koeppel of Winnipeg, the sum of $13,063 for forcing her to answer the telephone as part of her job duties.[11] Through this action, a human rights tribunal showed that it had found that the employer had failed to accommodate her disability. An important area of legislation deals with discrimination in employment. Figure 1-2 summarizes the prohibited grounds of discrimination across Canada. We'll explore this critical area in depth in Chapter 3.

Labour Unions Labour unions were founded and exist today to assist workers in dealing with the management of an organization. As the certified third-party representative, the union acts on behalf of its members to secure improvements

Prohibited Grounds of Discrimination

Jurisdictions	Dependence on Alcohol/Drugs	Race	National/Ethnic Origin	Color	Nationality/Citizenship	Religion	Age	Sex	Pregnancy/Childbirth	Marital Status	Criminal Conviction	Mental Disability	Physical Disability	Ancestry	Political Beliefs	Family Status	Sexual Orientation	Harassment	Civil Status	Language	Source of Income	Social Origin	Social Conditions	Creed	Place of Residence	Place of Origin
Federal	•	•	•	•		•	•	•	•	•	•	•			•											
Alberta		•		•			•	•	•	•	•	•	•	•							•		•			
British Columbia		•		•		•	•		•	•	•	•	•	•		•							•			
Manitoba	•	•	•	•	•	•	•		•		•	•		•	•	•		•								
New Brunswick	•	•	•		•	•	•		•		•	•			•	•							•			
Newfoundland	•	•	•		•	•	•		•		•	•	•			•				•	•					
Nova Scotia	•	•	•		•	•	•		•		•	•			•			•					•			
Ontario	•	•	•	•			•	•	•	•	•	•	•		•	•	•				•		•			
Prince Edward Island	•	•	•		•	•	•		•		•	•	•								•					
Quebec	•	•	•		•	•	•	•	•	•	•	•	•		•		•	•	•	•		•				
Saskatchewan	•		•	•	•	•	•		•		•	•		•	•		•						•			
Northwest Territories	•		•	•		•	•		•		•	•		•						•	•	•				
Yukon Territory	•	•	•		•	•	•	•	•	•	•	•	•	•		•	•				•					

In Alberta discrimination on the basis of pregnancy is deemed to be discrimination on the basis of sex. In Ontario, Manitoba, Nova Scotia and the Yukon discrimination on the basis of pregnancy is included in discrimination on the basis of sex.

**Harassment is banned on all proscribed grounds of discrimination except in New Brunswick and Nova Scotia where it only refers to sexual harassment.*

Source: 1996 Canadian Master Labour Guide, CCH Canadian Limited.

Figure 1-2
Prohibited Grounds of
Discrimination

in wages, hours, and other terms and conditions of employment. Another critical aspect of unions is that they promote and foster what is called a grievance procedure, or a specified process for resolving differences between workers and management. In many cases, this process alone constrains management from making unilateral decisions. For instance, a current HRM issue is the debate over employers' ability to terminate employees whenever they want. When a union is present and HRM practices are spelled out in a negotiated agreement, employers cannot fire for unjustified reasons. Because of the complexities involved in operating under the realm of unionization and the special laws that pertain to it, we will defer that discussion until Chapters 17 and 18 when we will explore the unique world of labour relations and collective bargaining. Canadian HRM differs significantly from that in the US and is more like that in Europe, with its much higher level of unionization.[12] About 30 per cent of the workforce in Canada is unionized, compared to less than half that in the US. In addition, almost half of all employees in Canada are covered by the provisions of collective agreements. Thus, many non-union employees are affected by union-negotiated agreements. Beyond that, the spillover effect means that non-union employees often look at what those in the unionized workforce gain through contract negotiations and demand parity. To maintain a non-union status, then, HRM practices must be comparable to those where unions exist.

Management Thought Early theories of management that promoted today's HRM operations.

Scientific Management A set of principles designed to enhance worker productivity.

Hawthorne Studies A series of studies that provided new insights into group behaviour.

Management Thought   The last area of external influence is current **management thought**. Since the inception of the first personnel departments, management practices have had a major influence in the evolution of today's HRM operations. Much of the emphasis has come from some of the early, and highly regarded, management theorists. Four individuals specifically are regarded as the forerunners of HRM support: Frederick Taylor, Hugo Munsterberg, Mary Parker Follet, and Elton Mayo.

Frederick Taylor, who is often regarded as the father of **scientific management**, developed a set of principles to enhance worker productivity. By systematically studying each job and detailing methods to attain higher productivity levels, Taylor was the pioneer of today's human resources practices. For instance, Taylor advocated that workers needed appropriate job training and should be screened according to their ability to do the job (a forerunner of skill-based hiring). Hugo Munsterberg and his associates made suggestions to improve methods of employment testing, training, performance evaluations, and job efficiency. Mary Parker Follet, a social philosopher, advocated people-oriented organizations. Her writings focused on groups as opposed to the individuals in the organization. Thus, Follet was one of the forerunners of today's teamwork concept with its emphasis on group cohesiveness. But probably the biggest advancement in HRM came from the works of Elton Mayo and his famous Hawthorne studies.

The **Hawthorne studies**, so named because they were conducted at the Hawthorne Plant of Western Electric just outside Chicago, ran for nearly a decade beginning in the late 1920s. They gave rise to what today is called the human relations movement. The researchers found that informal work groups had a significant effect on worker performance. Group standards and sentiments were more important determinants of a worker's output than the wage incentive plan. Results of the Hawthorne studies started the trend which led to many of the paternalistic programs that human resources managers have instituted in their organizations. There have been some criticisms of the original methodology of these studies, but their impact on HRM cannot be denied. For example, we can point to the advent of employee benefit offerings, safe and healthy working conditions, and the concern by every manager for human relations as stemming directly from the work of Mayo and his associates at Hawthorne.[13]

In more modern times, we can see the influence of management practice affecting HRM in a variety of ways. Motivation techniques that have been cited in management literature, as well as W. Edwards Deming's influence on Total Quality Management to enhance productivity, have made their way into HRM activities. Writers such as Tom Peters and Ed Lawler emphasize employee involvement, teams, re-engineering, TQM, and the like. Implementing these will ultimately require the assistance of HRM professionals.

Now that you have a better picture of what affects this field, let's turn our attention to the functions and activities within HRM. These are *staffing, training and development, motivation,* and *maintenance.*

Staffing

Although recruiting is frequently perceived as the initial step in the staffing function, there are a number of other prerequisites. Specifically, before the first job candidate is sought, the HR specialist must embark on strategic human resources planning (SHRP). This area alone has probably fostered the most change in human resources departments during the past fifteen years.

We can no longer hire individuals haphazardly. We must have a well-defined reason for needing individuals who possess specific skills, knowledge, and abilities that are directly likened to specific jobs required in the organization. The critical question then becomes: How do we know what jobs are critical? The answer to that question lies in the SHRP process. No longer does the HR manager exist in total isolation or, for that matter, in a purely reactive mode. Not until the mission and strategy of the organization have been fully developed can human resources managers begin to determine their human resources needs.

Specifically, when a company plans strategically, it determines its goals and objectives for a given period of time. These often result in structural changes being made in the organization. In other words, these changes foster changes in job requirements, reporting relationships, how individuals are grouped, and the like. As such, these new or revised structures bring with them a host of pivotal jobs. It is these that HRM must be prepared to fill.

As these jobs are analysed, specific skills, knowledge, and abilities are identified that are essential to be successful. The importance of this cannot be overstated, for herein lies much of the responsibility and success (or failure) of HRM. Through the job analysis process, HRM identifies the essential qualifications needed for a particular task. Not only is this sound business judgement since these jobs are critically linked to the strategic direction of the company, but it is also well within the stated guidelines of major employment legislation. Additionally, almost all activities involved in HRM revolve around an accurate description of the job. One cannot recruit without knowledge of the critical skills required, nor can one appropriately set performance standards, pay rates, or invoke disciplinary procedures fairly without this understanding.

Employment Legislation Laws that directly affect the hiring, firing, and working conditions of individuals.

Once these critical competencies have been identified, the recruiting process begins. Armed with information from SHRP, we can begin to focus on our prospective candidates. When involved in recruiting, HR specialists should be attempting to achieve two goals: to obtain a large enough number of applicants to give human resources and line managers more choices, while simultaneously providing enough information about the job so that only those who are qualified will apply. Recruiting, then, becomes an activity designed to locate potentially good applicants, conditioned by the recruiting effort's constraints, the job market, and the need to reach members of under-represented groups such as minorities and women.

Once applications have come in, it is time to begin the selection phase. Selection, too, has a dual focus. It attempts to thin out the large number of applications that arrive during the recruiting phase and ultimately to select an applicant who will be successful on the job. To achieve this goal, many companies use a variety of steps to assess the applicants. The candidate who successfully completes all steps is typically offered the job, but that is only half of the equation. HRM must also ensure that the best prospects accept the job offer and remain on the job afterwards. Accordingly, HRM must communicate a variety of information to the applicant such as the organization culture, what is expected of employees, and any other information that is pertinent to the candidate's decision-making process.

Once the selection process is completed, the staffing function has come to an end.[14] The goals, then, of the staffing function are to locate competent employees and get them into the organization. When this goal has been reached, it is time for HRM to begin focusing its attention on the employee's training and development.

Training and Development

While HRM professionals pride themselves on being able to identify those candidates who are best qualified, the fact remains that few, if any, new employees come into an organization and immediately become fully functioning, 100 per cent performers. First, employees need to adapt to their new surroundings, and orientation is a means of doing this. While it may begin informally in the late stages of the hiring process, the thrust of orientation continues for many months after the individual begins working. During this time, the focus is to orient the new employee to the rules, regulations, and goals of the organization, department, and work unit. Then, as the employee becomes more comfortable with his or her surroundings, more intense training can occur.

Reflection over the past few decades tells us that, depending on the job, employees often take a number of months to adjust. Does that imply that HRM has not hired properly or that the staffing function goals were not met? On the contrary, it indicates that intricacies and peculiarities involved in each organization's positions result in jobs being tailored to adequately meet organizational needs. Accordingly, HRM plays an important role in shaping this reformulation of new employees so that within a short period of time, they will be fully productive. To accomplish this, HRM embarks on four areas in the training and development phase: *employee training, employee development, career development* and *organization development*. It is important to note that employee and career development are more employee centred, whereas employee training is more job centred and designed to promote competency in the new job. Organization development, on the other hand, focuses on system-wide changes. While each area has a unique focus, all four are critical to the success of the training and development phase. We have summarized these four in Figure 1-3.

At the conclusion of the training and development function, HRM attempts to reach the goal of having competent, adapted employees who possess the up-to-date skills, knowledge, and abilities needed to perform their duties successfully. If that is attained, HRM turns its attention to finding ways to motivate these individuals to exert high energy levels.

Training employees comes in many forms. In this seminar, the facilitator works with employees discussing the latest methods the company will employ in its redesigned work process. By helping employees learn the skills, the company helps itself building a talented workforce.

Employee Training:	Employee training is designed to assist employees in acquiring better skills for their current job. The focus of employee training is on current job skill requirements.
Employee Development:	Employee development is designed to help the organization ensure that it has the necessary talent internally for meeting future human resource needs. The focus of employee development is on a future position within the organization for which the employee requires additional competencies.
Career Development:	Career development programs are designed to assist employees in advancing their work lives. The focus of career development is to provide the necessary information and assessment in helping employees realize their career goals. However, career development is the responsibility of the individual, not the organization.
Organization Development:	Organization development deals with facilitating system-wide changes in the organization. The focus of organization development is to change the attitudes and values of employees according to new organizational strategic directions.

Motivation

Motivation is one of the most important, yet probably the least understood, aspects of the HRM process. Why? Because human behaviour is complex. Trying to figure out what motivates various employees has long been a concern of behavioural scientists. However, research has given us some important insights into employee motivation.

First of all, one must begin to think of motivation as a multifaceted process—one that has individual, managerial, and organizational implications. Motivation is not just the behaviour the employee exhibits, but a compilation of environmental issues surrounding the job. You can think of an individual's performance in an organization as a function of two factors: ability and willingness to do the job. Thus, from a performance perspective, employees need to have the appropriate skills and abilities. This should have been accomplished in the first two phases of HRM by correctly defining the requirements of the job, matching applicants to those requirements, and training the new employee on how to do the job.

But there is also another concern: the job design itself. If jobs are poorly designed, poorly laid out, or improperly described, employees will not perform to their capability. Consequently, HRM must look at the job. Has the latest technology been provided in order to permit maximum efficiency? Is the office setting appropriate (properly lit and adequately ventilated, for example)? Are the necessary tools readily available for employee use? For example, if an employee prints on a laser printer throughout the day and the computer is networked to a printer two floors up, that employee is going to be less productive than if they had a printer that was more conveniently located. Office automation and industrial engineering techniques must be incorporated into the job design. Without such planning, the best intentions of managers to motivate employees may be lost or significantly reduced.

Once the measures have been taken to ensure that jobs have been properly designed, the next step in the motivation process is to understand the implications of motivational theories. Some motivational theories are well known by most practising managers, but recent motivation research has given us new and interesting theories about what motivates people at work. (We'll look at these in Chapter 11.) Performance standards for each employee must also be set. While no easy task, managers must be sure that the performance evaluation system is designed to provide feedback to employees regarding their past performance while simultaneously addressing any weaknesses the employee may have.

A link must be established between employee compensation and performance. The compensation and benefits activity in the organization must be adapted to, and coordinated with, a pay-for-performance plan.

Throughout the activities required in the motivation function, the efforts all focus on one primary goal: to have those competent and adapted employees, with up-to-date skills, knowledge, and abilities, exerting high energy levels. Once that is achieved, it is time to turn the HRM focus to the maintenance function.

Maintenance

The last phase of the HRM process is called the maintenance function. This phase is sometimes also referred to as *governance* or *quality of work life and security*. Maintenance may sound rather plebeian to you, but as the name implies, the objective of this phase is to put into place activities that will help retain productive employees. When one considers how job loyalty of employees has declined in the past decade—brought about in part by management responses to leveraged buyouts, mergers, acquisitions, downsizing, changing family requirements, and increased competition[15]—it is not difficult to see the importance of maintaining employee commitment. To do so requires some basic common sense and some creativity. HRM must work to ensure that the working environment is healthy and safe; caring for employees' well-being has a major effect on their commitment. HRM must also realize that any problem an employee faces in his or her personal life will ultimately be brought into the workplace. Employee assistance programs, such as those that help individuals deal with stressful life situations, are needed. Such programs provide many benefits to the organization while simultaneously helping the affected employee.

Communication Programs HRM programs designed to provide information to, and receive feedback from employees.

In addition to protecting employees' welfare, it is essential for HRM to operate appropriate communications programs in the organization. These allow employees to know what is occurring around them and to vent their frustrations. Employee relations programs should be designed to ensure that employees are kept informed and to foster an environment in which employees are heard. If time and effort are expended in this phase, HRM may be able to achieve its ultimate goal of having competent employees who have adapted to the organization's culture, with up-to-date skills, knowledge, and abilities, who exert high energy levels, and who are willing to maintain their commitment and loyalty to the company. This process is difficult to implement and maintain, but the rewards warrant the effort.

HRM Departments

All organizations, even the smallest ones, carry out each of the major HRM functions described above. But the way they do this varies depending on their size and resources. In this next section, we describe the way HRM is organized around different departments to make it easier for you to see how the various functions are covered. In larger organizations, we typically find four distinct departments within the HRM area: *employment, training and development, compensation and/benefits*, and *employee relations*. Reporting to a vice-president of human resources, managers in these four areas have specific accountabilities. Figure 1-4 is a simplified organizational chart of an HRM department, with some typical job titles and a sampling of what these job incumbents earn.

Employment Department

The main thrust of the employment department is to promote the activities of the staffing function. Working in conjunction with line managers (either in compensation, in benefits, or in the accounting office), the employment department embarks on the process of recruiting new employees.[16] This means advertising the job correctly to ensure that the appropriate skills, knowledge, and abilities are being sought. After sorting through résumés or applications, the employment specialist usually conducts the first weeding out of candidates who do not meet the requirements. The remaining applications are then reviewed by the line manager, who then tells the employment specialist which candidates to interview. This initial interview is another step in the hiring process, and understanding what the line manager needs in an employee, the employment specialist begins to further whittle down the list of prospective candidates. During this phase, those candidates who appear to best fit the needs are scheduled to meet with the line manager for another interview.

It is important to note that it is not the employment specialist's role to make the hiring decision but rather, to coordinate the effort with line management. Once the latter has selected its candidate, the employment specialist usually makes the job offer and handles the routine paperwork associated with hiring an employee.

Training and Development Department

This department is responsible for a multitude of activities regarding training and developing employees. The training that occurs may be job-specific or more developmental in nature. In either case, the aim of the training is to enhance the personal qualities of the employees which will improve organizational productivity the most. More importantly, the training and development department can help individuals and organizations cope with change. Changes that occur in an organization come in many forms. It can be a cultural change where the philosophy, values, and ways of operating are changed by top management. For instance, changing from a production focus of producing whatever the company wants and selling it to the public, to a marketing focus whereby what is produced and sold is contingent on consumer demand, requires a new organizational orientation.[17] A change may also occur in the organization's structure, which can result in lay-offs, new job assignments, team involvement, and the like. This, again, requires new orientations by the organizational members. We may also see

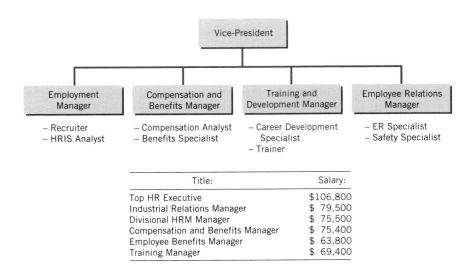

Title:	Salary:
Top HR Executive	$106,800
Industrial Relations Manager	$ 79,500
Divisional HRM Manager	$ 75,500
Compensation and Benefits Manager	$ 75,400
Employee Benefits Manager	$ 63,800
Training Manager	$ 69,400

Figure 1-4
Sample HRM Organizational Chart (and average salaries of selected HRM positions in large firms). [In small and medium sized firms, one individual may perform duties in several areas.]

Salary Figures Source: KPMG Executive Compensation Report 1995/1996 (KPMG, Toronto: 1996). Figures are for salary element only and reflect a correction to allow for cost of living increase 1996 to 1998.

changes in procedures or policies where employees must be informed and taught to deal with such occurrences. For instance, a growing concern of companies has been to implement policies to stop sexual harassment from occurring in the organization. Not only must employees understand what constitutes sexual harassment, they must also become more sensitive to issues surrounding a diverse workforce. Training and development often lead this charge.

In another area of training and development, we find the activities surrounding career development. Training and development specialists are responsible for counselling employees, helping them to make better choices about their careers, and finding ways to achieve those desired goals.

Compensation and Benefits Department

This department[18] is often seen as dealing with the most objective areas of a subjective field. As the name implies, compensation and benefits is concerned with paying employees and administering their benefits package—by no means easy tasks. First of all, salaries are not paid on a whim; rather, dollar values assigned to specific positions come from elaborate investigations and analyses. These investigations run the gamut from simple, logical job rankings (i.e., the position of president of a company should be paid more than the position of a maintenance engineer) to extensive, in-depth analyses. Once these evaluations are complete, job ratings are statistically compared to determine the relative worth of each job to the company. External factors such as market conditions, limited supply, and the like may affect the overall range of job worth. Additionally, analysis is conducted to ensure that there is internal equity in the compensation system. This means that as job rates are set, they are determined on such dimensions as skill, job responsibility, effort, and accountability—not by personal characteristics, such as gender, or age that may be suspect under employment law.

On the benefits side of the equation, much change has occurred over the past decade. As employees benefits have become significantly more costly, the benefits administrator has the responsibility of piecing together a benefits package that meets the needs of the employees, while simultaneously being cost-effective to the organization. As such, much effort is expended searching for lower-cost products, such as health insurance, while concurrently maintaining or improving quality. Various new products are often reviewed, such as flexible benefits programs and utilization reviews, to help in benefit-cost containment.

The benefits administrator also serves as the resources information officer to employees regarding their benefits, helping employees prepare for their retirement, looking for various pay-out options, keeping abreast of recent tax law changes, or helping executives with their perquisites.[19] This gives this individual a great deal of responsibility and high visibility in the organization.

Employee Relations Department

The final element in our scheme of HRM operations is the employee relations department. This is the department that handles relationships between employees and management in both unionized and non-unionized settings. Employee relations (ER) has a number of major responsibilities. In Canada, the term industrial relations is sometimes used to reflect the greater role of unions and the close link between employee and labour relations. There is, however, a distinction between employee relations and labour relations. While the two are structurally similar, labour relations involves dealing with labour unions. As such, because other laws apply, some of the techniques in employee relations may not be applicable. For instance, in a unionized setting, a specific grievance procedure might be detailed in the labour-management contract and might involve the union, management, and the alleged wronged employee. In a non-union environment, a similar procedure may exist, or the grievance may be handled one on one. While these may be subtle differences, the fact remains that labour relations requires a different set of competencies and understanding. Because of the importance of labour relations in Canadian HRM, many companies employ specialist labour relations managers.

In the non-union setting, however, employee relations specialists perform many tasks. As mentioned earlier, one of their key responsibilities is to ensure that open communications permeate the organization. This is done by fostering an environment in which employees are able to talk directly to supervisors and settle any differences that may arise. If needed, employee relations representatives can intervene to assist in achieving a fair and equitable solution. ER specialists are also intermediaries in helping employees understand the rules. Their primary goal is to ensure that policies and procedures are enforced properly and to permit a wronged employee a forum to obtain relief. As part of this role, too, comes the disciplinary process. These representatives are in place to ensure that appropriate disciplinary sanctions are used consistently throughout the organization.

In addition to its communications role, the employee relations department is responsible for additional assignments. For example, the department might collect and tabulate statistics and document them in the company's employment equity plan. This material is updated frequently and made available to employees on request. Part of responsibilities the employee relations department is to ensure safe and healthy worksites. This may range from casual work inspections to operating nursing stations and coordinating employee assistance programs. However involved, the premise is the same—to focus on those aspects that help make an employee committed and loyal to the organization through fair and equitable treatment and by listening to employees.

Lastly, there is the fun side of employee relations. This department is responsible for company outings, athletic teams, and recreational and recognition programs. Whatever they do under this domain, the goal remains to have programs that benefit the workers and their families and make them feel part of a community.

Conclusion

Although we have presented four generic areas of HRM, we would be remiss not to recognize the evolving nature of HRM in today's organizations. As organizations change structures (to reflect global competition and other factors), there has been a movement away from centralization of functional areas towards more self-contained units. In companies where strategic business units or market-driven units dominate,[20] an HRM professional may be assigned to these units to handle all the HRM operations. While a headquarters HRM staff remains to coordinate the activities, the HRM representative is expected to perform all the HR functions. Accordingly, the movement towards generalist positions in HRM appears to be on the rise. In general, it is estimated that on average in the US, one HRM specialist serves the needs of one hundred employees. In Canada, because of the smaller size of most companies, fewer HRM specialists are employed, and so the overall average is more like one HRM specialist to 150 employees.

Another trend is towards assigning part of the HRM task to specialist groups either located inside the organization (*shared services*) or outside (*outsourcing*).[21] In large organizations such as Bell Canada or General Motors of Canada, companies that are geographically dispersed are finding it more cost-effective to share their HRM services among the divisions. Under shared services, each location is staffed by a few generalists who handle routine local matters such as recruiting, policy implementation, grievances, and employee training. Organization development, compensation and benefits, and other specialized services are handled by a staff at a centralized location. Each division, then, shares these services offered by the centralized unit and uses only what it feels is necessary. As such, each location gets specialized care as needed, without the cost of having full-time staff. In smaller companies, without large HRM functions, the outsourcing of HRM activities to third parties that specialize in HR activities is more likely to occur. This is the source of much of the recent growth in HR consulting companies and is often the most efficient way of providing HR services in small business.

Shared Services Sharing HRM activities among geographically dispersed divisions.

HRM in a Small Business

As we mentioned earlier, the discussion about the four departments of HRM refers to situations where there are sufficient resources available for functional expertise to exist in each of these areas. That, however, is not always the case. For instance, in a small business operation, the owner-manager may perform these activities. In other situations, such as Claire Somas's in our chapter opener, small-business human resources departments are staffed with one individual and (possibly) a secretary. Such individuals are forced, by design, to be HRM generalists.

Irrespective of the unit's size, small-business HRM managers must be able to perform the four functions of HRM properly and achieve the same goals that a larger department does on a smaller scale. The main difference is that they are doing the work themselves without benefit of a specialized staff. In such cases, there may be a tendency to use outside consultants to assist in HRM activities. For instance, benefit administration may be beyond the capability of the small-business person. In that case, benefit administration may need to be contracted out.

Effective HRM requires that individuals keep abreast of what is happening in the field. This is especially true of keeping current on legal issues. For example, the application of pay equity legislation to small business in Ontario has changed several times in the past few years. Accordingly, the small business may be exempt from many laws affecting other employment practices. Being aware of this information can save the small business time and money. There are many advantages as well as disadvantages for the small-business HRM manager. Often, they feel less constrained in their job. That is, the bureaucratic hierarchy of larger organizations is often absent in the small business. Furthermore, some small-business HRM managers use this arrangement to their advantage. For instance, in recruiting efforts, a selling point to attract good applicants might be the freedom from a rigid structure that the small business offers. Consequently, the small-business HRM manager may be in an advantageous position. In fact, isn't it ironic that the movement towards self-contained business units having their own human resources generalists closely resembles the small-business set-up? Maybe this back-to-basics movement indicates, in part, that HRM in the small-business enterprise may better facilitate HRM goals.

HRM in a Global Market Place

As a business grows from a regional to a national one, the human resources management function must take on a new and broader perspective. As a national company expands to a global one—first with a sales operation, then to production facilities, and finally to fully expanded operations or to international joint ventures—the human resources function must adapt to a changing and far more complex environment. Reflect again on the challenge of creating a congruent HRM policy for DaimlerChrysler workers both in Windsor, Ontario and Stuttgart, Germany.

All the basic functions of domestic HRM become more complex when the organization's employees are located around the world, and additional human resources management activities that would be considered overkill or intrusive in a domestic operation are often necessary. This is partially because of the increased cultural adaptation required of Canadian executives and their families abroad.

When a corporation sends its Canadian employees overseas, it takes on responsibilities that add to the basic HRM functions. For example, the staffing and training and development functions take on greater importance. Not only are organizations concerned about selecting the best employee for the job, they must also be aware of the entire family's needs. Many individuals who take international assignments fail because their spouses or families just can't adjust to the new environment. Furthermore, the relocation and orientation process before departure may take months if foreign language training is included (as it should be), and it should involve not just the employee, but the employee's entire family. Details such as work visas, travel, and household moving arrangements, and family issues such as the children's schooling, health care, and housing, all must be provided for.[22] Administrative services for the expatriate employees also must be available once they are placed in their overseas posts. All these additional functions make international human resources management a very costly and complex undertaking.

A Cautionary Note

It should be clear to you that the field of HRM is undergoing dramatic change, a point we develop further in Chapter 2. To give you the clearest introduction to HRM, we have presented a traditional model of the field in which the HRM function provides the different activities listed in Figure 1.1. Recent research,[23] has criticized this traditional model as being an oversimplification, and the point is made that the actual structure of the HR contribution to an organization is often quite different. The detail of this criticism is beyond the scope of an introductory text. Just take note that HR strategy is becoming sufficiently closely aligned with overall business strategy that HR and organization objectives are becoming quite interwoven.

Study Tools and Applications

Summary

These summaries relate to the Learning Objectives identified on p. 1.

After having read this chapter, you should know:

1. Human resources management is responsible for the people dimension of the organization. It is responsible for getting competent people, training them, getting them to perform at high levels, and providing mechanisms to ensure that these employees maintain their productive affiliation with the organization.

2. Human resources management is comprised of the staffing, development, motivation, and maintenance functions. Each of these, however, is affected by external influences.

3. Environmental influences are those factors that affect the functions of HRM. They include the dynamic environment of HRM, government legislation, labour unions, and management thought.

4. Management practices affect HRM in a number of ways. As new ideas or practices develop in the field, they typically have HRM implications. Accordingly, once these practices are implemented, they typically require the support from HRM to operate successfully.

5. Labour unions affect HRM practices in a variety of ways. In a unionized situation, HRM takes on a different focus—one of labour relations as opposed to employee relations. Additionally, what occurs in the unionized sector frequently affects the activities in organizations that are non-union.

6. The components of the staffing function include strategic human resources planning, recruiting, and selection. The goal of the staffing function is to locate and secure competent employees. The training and development function includes orientation, employee training, employee development, organization development, and career development. The goal of the development function is to take competent workers, adapt them to the organization, and help them to obtain up-to-date skills, knowledge, and abilities for their job responsibilities.

7. The components of the motivation function include motivation theories, appropriate job design, reward and incentive systems, compensation, and benefits. The goal of the motivation function is to take competent, adapted employees, with up-to-date skills, knowledge, and abilities, and provide them with an environment that encourages them to high-level performance. The components of the maintenance function include safety and health issues and employee communications. The goal of the maintenance function is to take competent, adapted employees, with up-to-date

skills, knowledge, abilities, and high energy levels, to maintain their commitment and loyalty to the organization.

8. In large HRM operations, individuals perform functions according to their specialization, but such may not be the case with the small-business HRM practitioner. Instead, they may be the only individual in the operation and thus, forced to operate as an HRM generalist. In an international setting, HRM functions become more complex and typically require additional activities associated with staffing, training, and development.

Key Terms

communication programs	management
controlling	management thought
employment legislation	organizing
environmental influences	planning
Hawthorne studies	scientific management
human resources management	shared services
leading	

EXPERIENTIAL EXERCISE:

Getting Acquainted

Beginning a new semester is associated with excitement, but also anxiety. There are new friends to be made and new frontiers to be crossed. But one of the more basic issues that face us is what is expected in this class. By now, you probably have received a course syllabus that provides some necessary information about how the class will operate. No doubt this information is important to you and is designed to help you plan your semester. But there is another side to that equation—giving your instructor some indication of what you want/expect from the class. Some information can serve a useful purpose for your instructor, so you'll need to answer some questions.[24] First, take out a piece of paper, write your name at the top, then respond to the following:

1. What do I want from this course (other than a passing grade)?
2. Why is this "want" important to me?
3. How does information covered in this course fit into my career plans?
4. What is my greatest challenge in taking this class?

When you have finished answering the questions, team up with several class members (preferably two or three others who you do not already know) and exchange papers. Get acquainted with one another using the responses to the four questions above as an ice-breaker. Then, as your professor goes around the room, introduce your team (each member introduces another team member), and share your group's responses to these questions with the class and your instructor.

CASE APPLICATION:

It Pays to Know at Scotiabank[25]

Many organizations devote considerable resources to customer surveys. They believe that what customers think directly affects what they will purchase and how they will respond to the organization. The HR function in these same organizations often also puts a lot of time and money into employee surveys, but is this additional effort worthwhile, and is there any relationship between the two kinds of surveys? Does it make any difference to the business success of an organization to find out what its employees think? Scotiabank set out to find out the answer to these questions by specifically linking their annual customer and employee surveys.

Pam LaPalme, vice-president of Scotia Service, believed that it was employees' confidence in the services they offered that was the key driver of customer satisfaction. She pointed out that the ongoing assumption was that, "if employees are happy, they will serve their customers better." However, this had never been tested.

For a long time, Scotiabank has had two parallel surveys:

- In the first place was a survey of more than 800,000 customers to isolate those factors that had the greatest impact on overall satisfaction with the bank. In terms of the results of this survey, managers were accountable for improving their results over time, with their survey ratings forming part of their performance appraisal report, driving both base pay and incentive compensation.

- In the second place, Scotiabank also surveyed its eighteen thousand employees' attitudes towards such issues as management responsiveness, communication, teamwork, working conditions, and development.

LaPalme's innovation was to combine and analyse the results from the two surveys, based on a sample of 370 branches, to find out which employee attitudes had the greatest impact on customer service. The interesting finding was that there was a clear relationship. Customer service was linked to self-perceptions of quality and service, pay and benefits, and performance management. If employees felt positive about the quality and service they delivered to customers, they were more confident in their own ability to meet customer needs, which resulted in increased customer satisfaction. In addition, if employees felt they were fairly compensated for the work they did, they reflected this satisfaction to their customers.

It became useful to everyone in Scotiabank to know *both* what employees and customers were thinking. Surveys from both the HRM and marketing areas of the bank were important and a source of competitive advantage to the bank.

Questions:

1. Even before the customer survey was linked to the employee survey, what evidence is there in Scotiabank that they already used the customer survey to assist them in their HRM?
2. How important was LaPalme in bringing about the linkage between the two surveys? What does this tell us about the role of top management in HRM effectiveness?
3. The case mentions some of the key relationships between the two surveys. Can you think of any other items you would like to survey in the years ahead and how would you expect them to relate to each other?

How well did you fulfil the learning objectives?

1. Organizational efficiency is expressed as
   a. planning for long-range goals.
   b. making the best use of scarce resources.
   c. goal attainment.
   d. meeting deadlines.
   e. rewarding and recognizing time-saving activities.

2. When a compensation director reports on successful cost containment with a new health care package, the primary management function being performed is
   a. planning.
   b. organizing.
   c. leading.
   d. controlling.
   e. delegating.

3. All of the following are typical responsibilities for the human resources management professional except
   a. training employees to function effectively within the organization.
   b. hiring the best-qualified candidates.
   c. establishing working conditions that are conducive to retaining the best workers.
   d. providing for continued personal development of employees.
   e. evaluating the performance of managerial employees.

4. Which statement is most likely to be true of Claire Somas, a top-level human resources professional in a smaller corporation?
   a. She would have worked her way up from a clerical job.
   b. She would have a narrow and well-defined interest.
   c. She would have been vice-president of marketing or finance before getting this assignment.
   d. She would be aware of the strategic importance people have in the attainment of organizational success.
   e. None of the above are true of Claire Somas.

5. A vice-president of human resources of a medium-sized provincial government department regularly retains the services of labour lawyers when recruiting employees. What external influence most prompted this action?
   a. Government legislation.
   b. Workforce diversity.
   c. Labour unions.
   d. Management thought.
   e. Restructuring the corporation.

6. What point is made in the external influences section of the text?
   a. Human resources managers need to be aware of their ability to exert influence outside of their organizations on the surrounding community.

   b. Human resources managers need to be aware of external factors because all human resources management activity undertaken is either directly or indirectly influenced by these factors.
   c. Human resources management goals affect the motivation function, which affects legislation.
   d. Human resources management goals affect the development function, which influences management practices.
   e. Human resources management goals affect the staffing and training and development functions, which influence both management practices and labour unions.

7. Elton Mayo's Hawthorne studies contributed which principles to management practices?
   a. Informal work groups have a significant effect on worker performance.
   b. Wage incentive plans are the most important influence on work group productivity.
   c. Employees who receive training for job skills they already possess are less motivated than other employees.
   d. Union workers are less productive than non-union workers.

8. Which one of the following statements best reflects why labour unions were founded?
   a. To satisfy a social belonging need in workers.
   b. To assist management in hiring and firing workers.
   c. To act on behalf of workers to secure favourable terms and conditions of employment.
   d. To preserve guild ancestries.
   e. To offer an alternative career path for workers.

9. A human resources manager in a medium-sized manufacturing firm sets his pay scale in accordance with local prevailing union rates. Why would he do that if his company is non-union?
   a. Grievance procedures can occur in any organization.
   b. It is the influence of the spillover effect.
   c. Negotiated agreements are binding by geographical area.
   d. Comparable wages are a good way to get his company in the union.
   e. He balances the high wages with lower benefits.

10. Which one of the following best describes the selection process?
    a. It assesses probable job success of applicants.
    b. It reaches members of under-represented groups, such as minorities and women.
    c. It builds a large applicant pool.
    d. It provides remedial skill training when necessary.
    e. It matches goals and objectives to structural changes of the organization.

11. System-wide development functions are part of
    a. employee orientation.
    b. employee training.
    c. organization development.
    d. career development.
    e. employee development.

12. The major objective of the maintenance function is best stated as
    a. retaining productive employees.
    b. reducing grievance procedures and lawsuits.
    c. maintaining recruiting costs.
    d. supporting employee wellness centres.
    e. keeping pay scales in line with geographical peers.

13. What is the difference between employee relations and labour relations?
    a. Labour relations deals with unskilled workers. Employee relations deals with highly skilled, technical workers.
    b. Labour relations deals with hourly workers. Employee relations deals with salaried workers.
    c. Labour relations deals with manufacturing workers. Employee relations deals with clerical workers.
    d. Labour relations deals with unionized workers. Employee relations deals with non-union workers.
    e. Labour relations deals with foreign workers. Employee relations deals with Canadian workers.

14. What are the differences between human resources management in a large and a small business?
    a. There is no difference. The activities are the same, just on a grander scale in a larger organization.
    b. Small businesses can afford to hire only specialists.
    c. Small businesses need only employment department activities and, therefore, hire only recruiters.
    d. Small businesses usually have generalists who perform a variety of HRM tasks.
    e. Small businesses do not need any human resources management professionals.

15. How important is human resources management to an organization?

    a. Human resources management is expendable, the first functional area to be cut in hard times.
    b. Human resources management is important only for social action and public sector organizations.
    c. Human resources management is important only for manufacturing sector organizations.
    d. Human resources management is important for all organizations that want to get and to keep good people.
    e. Human resources management is important only for small companies. Large organizations have professional managers to provide needed support for employees.

16. Mary is a human resources consultant hired by a large manufacturing firm to find out why so many new employees were leaving within their first six months of employment. She suggested a formal orientation program. Why?
    a. Mary probably specializes in orientation programs.
    b. Orientation helps new employees adapt to their new surroundings.
    c. Orientation programs provide a "halo effect" for even the worst organization that usually lasts at least six months.
    d. Orientation helps to build the applicant pool.
    e. Training is a necessary first step for all employees.

17. Why is the maintenance function important to an organization?
    a. Commitment from good employees contributes to organizational success.
    b. Most home-based problems an employee faces will not affect job performance.
    c. A safe and healthy work environment maintains OSHA standards.
    d. Organizational loyalty is an old-fashioned idea.
    e. It is not important. Maintenance is the only human resources management function that is optional.

Chapter Two

HRM IN A DYNAMIC ENVIRONMENT

LEARNING OBJECTIVES

AFTER READING THIS CHAPTER, YOU WILL BE ABLE TO:

1. Describe how globalization affects human resources management practices.
2. Identify the significant changes that have occurred in the composition of the workforce.
3. Explain the implications of human resources management on the changing workforce composition.
4. Discuss how changing skill requirements affect human resources management.
5. Describe what is meant by corporate downsizing, and identify its effect on human resources management.
6. Describe what is meant by Total Quality Management and ISO 9000, and identify the goals of these quality initiatives.
7. Discuss the re-engineering and restructuring phenomena and the role HRM plays in the re-engineered organization.
8. Describe the contingent workforce and its HRM implications.
9. Discuss the implications of telework on HRM practices.
10. Define employee involvement, and list its critical components.

If there is one thing we can confidently predict for the practice of HRM in Canada in the new century, it is the continuation of dramatic change. The turmoil in global stock markets and changing work patterns are just more dramatic examples of the world of change around us. No organization will be immune to change. All will have to learn to cope with it, and HRM must play a key role in this dynamic environment. As an illustration of the reality of change, consider the case of Eaton's, one of the oldest and most trusted retail operations in Canada.[1]

The observer might have been forgiven for assuming that a company of this stature, which had successfully weathered all that the past 128 years had to bring, might be able to avoid the turmoil facing smaller and newer competitors in the field. Far from it. On February 27, 1997, the troubled company won court protection from its creditors and announced, just a few weeks later, that it would be forced to close almost a third of its stores. The critical issue was how to handle this downsizing in a way that would leave the company in a more effective position to face the changing environment of the late nineties and particularly, what role HRM could play in the process.

According to Glenn Quarrington, Eaton's vice-president of human resources management, one of the biggest challenges has been to set employees straight about sensationalized news reports that virtually predicted the failure of the entire company. "We're having to do an enormous job of correcting information with employees because it's so badly represented in the media." In an environment in which employees were already concerned about their future, HRM had a particularly crucial role to play.

Key to HRM's communication effort has been a cascading process of channelling information from senior managers through to store managers and down to employees. According to Quarrington, the key principle is that "our people need to know first. We don't want them hearing about it from anybody else." Eaton's has set up e-mail chat groups and anonymous bulletin boards for employees to find out what they wish to know without having to identify themselves. In addition, head office has made a practice of delaying major announcements out of Toronto until 4:00 p.m. so that employees on the west coast hear them directly from the company first rather than on a central Canadian media broadcast.

Another key role of HRM has been in keeping morale high and people focused on work during change management. Quarrington has been particularly aware of the importance of setting up activities at which employees can vent their feelings and sort out their anxieties. The company has also found that short-term goals, set daily or weekly rather than over longer terms, are useful motivators in times of uncertainty for employees.

For the HR function, the Eaton's restructuring has brought a split focus. On the one hand, it has meant trying to prepare for an uncertain future in the stores targeted for closure and, on the other hand, continuing longer-term HR development in those stores which will continue to operate. This has entailed a level of flexibility and customizing of services that was not typical of earlier HR practices in the company. The overriding ethic of all the HRM practices in the restructuring is treating all employees as valued people important to the company. Early on in the change, Eaton's promised that all employees affected by any store sale or closure would be treated fairly and offered assistance. In particular, Eaton's promised to try to find people jobs with new tenants if stores were sold.

Introduction

As we briefly noted in the last chapter, the world of work is rapidly changing. The global economy is experiencing a level of turmoil unprecedented since World War II sparked off by the so-called "Asian Crisis". Even as little as a decade ago, the times were calmer than they are today, but that doesn't mean that we didn't experience change then. On the contrary, we were then, as we are today, in a state of flux. It's just that today, the changes appear to be happening more rapidly and affecting more and more organizations in Canada. While our opening example illustrates a large company (Eaton's) under change, do not think that smaller companies are any less affected. In fact, smaller companies, particularly those that are run by an owner-manager, may be especially vulnerable to change because of the breadth of issues the owner has to cover. You can probably all think of a small company that has almost faced extinction when a founder retired but did not make arrangements for someone with equivalent motivation and skills to take over.

As part of an organization, then, HRM must be prepared to deal with the effects of the changing world of work. For HRM, this means understanding the implications of globalization, workforce diversity, changing skill requirements, corporate downsizing, Total Quality Management, re-engineering, the contingent workforce, telework, and employee involvement. While more immediately obvious in large companies, each of these impacts of change affect HRM in smaller organizations, and so we should look at how they are affecting HRM goals and practices.

Globalization and Its HRM Implications

Back in 1973, with the first oil embargo, Canadian businesses began to realize the importance that international forces had on profit and loss statements. The world was changing rapidly, with other countries making significant inroads into traditional North American markets. Unfortunately, Canadian businesses did not adapt to this changing environment as quickly or adeptly as they should have. The result was that our businesses lost out in world markets and have had to fight much harder to get in. Only by the late 1980s did Canadian businesses begin to get the message, but when they did, they began to improve production standards aggressively, focusing more on quality (we'll look further at this issue later in this chapter) and preparing employees for a globalized workplace. It is in this latter area that human resources will have the biggest effect.

●

Global Village The world considered as a single interdependent community linked by telecommunications.

What Is the Global Village?

The global village is a term that reflects the state of businesses in our world. The rise of multinational and transnational corporations[2] places new requirements on human resources managers. For instance, human resources must ensure that the appropriate mix of employees in terms of knowledge, skills, and cultural adaptability are available to handle global assignments.

In order for human resources to meet this goal, they must train individuals to meet the challenges of the global village. First of all, workers must be able to gain a working knowledge of the language of the country in which they will work. The importance of understanding the local language cannot be overstated. This explains why Canadian Airlines International has opened an International Accelerated Language Centre (IALC).[3] According to Spence Mikituk, manager of employee training and development, it seemed an obvious requirement to teach employees the languages spoken in the places to which Canadian Airlines flies. The airline has now taken this further and expanded the IALC to help executives improve their skills in foreign languages as well as knowledge of the local cultures. There have been too many examples of embarrassing situations and lost business because executives and level managers were unprepared. For example, during the Mandarin language course at the Canadian Airlines learning centre, employees were taught the correct protocol for toasting a dinner host for visitors to China. (It is important for guests never to raise their glasses higher than that of their host.) Accordingly, before any organization sends any employee overseas, human resources should ensure that the employee can handle the language and cultural niceties of the location.[4]

Language requirements are just the starting point in communication programs for employees. Abroad, people with specific skills, entering an organization may speak very little English and will need assistance in learning the language, and more. That is, even though foreign-born employees may learn English as a second language, HRM must ensure that all communication is understood. To achieve that, companies have moved towards multilingual communications—anything transmitted to employees should appear in more than one language to help the message get through. While there are no hard and fast rules in sending such messages, some people are better at it than others. Canadians, of course, are more sensitized to language issues than are citizens of unilingual jurisdictions such as the United States or the United Kingdom. Canadian bilingualism requires that companies operating nationally be prepared to communicate effectively in English and French. This flexibility can stand organizations in good stead as they expand in Spanish-, Chinese-, or Russian-speaking markets.

An illustration of the increasingly global nature of management and communications is the engineering consulting company Golder Associates. Though based in Calgary, their president, Hal Hamilton, argues that in practice, his office is the world. The company has no formal corporate headquarters. Its nine-member management team is distributed throughout eight cities in Canada, the US, Italy, and Australia. As Hamilton puts it: "Our clients transfer their people around the world. Our management team should be able to function in the same way."[5]

In addition to the language, human resources must also ensure that workers going overseas understand the host country's culture. Every country has different values, morals, customs, and laws, and accordingly, people going to another country must have exposure to those cultural issues before they can be expected to work effectively. It is also equally important for human resources managers to understand how the host society will react to one of these mobile employees. For example, although Canadian laws guard against employers discriminating against individuals on the basis of such factors as race or religion, similar laws do not exist in other countries. Consequently, cultural considerations are critical to the success of any global business.

Although it is not our intent here to provide the scope of cultural issues needed to enable an employee to function competently in another country, we do want to recognize that some similarities do exist (see Table 2-1). Research findings allow us to group countries according to such cultural variables as status differentiation, societal uncertainty, and assertiveness.[6] These variables indicate a society's means of dealing with its people and how the people see themselves. For example, in an individualistic society, people are primarily concerned with themselves and their own family, whereas, in a collective society people care for all individuals who are part of their group. Thus, a strongly individualistic Canadian manager may not work well in a Pacific Rim country where collectivism dominates. Accordingly, flexibility and adaptability are key components for managers going abroad. It will be critical, then, for those in human resources to have an understanding of the working conditions and social systems globally so that they can counsel management on decisions and issues crossing national frontiers.

TABLE 2-1   Countries Sharing Similar Cultural Environments

Latin American	Central European
Peru	Switzerland
Mexico	Austria
Argentina	Germany
Colombia	
Chile	**Latin European**
Venezuela	Portugal
	Spain
Anglo-American	Italy
New Zealand	Belgium
South Africa	France
United States	
Australia	**Nordic**
United Kingdom	Norway
Ireland	Finland
Canada	Denmark
	Sweden

Source: Adapted from Simcha Ronen and Allen I. Kranut, "Similarities Among Countries Based on Employee Work Values and Attitudes," *Columbia Journal of World Business* (Summer 1977), p. 94.

HRM must also develop mechanisms that will help individuals from a variety of cultures work together. As background, language, custom, or age differences become more prevalent, there are indications that employee conflict will increase. HRM must make every effort to acclimatize different groups to each other, finding ways to build teams, and thus reduce conflict. HRM must make a real effort to bring different types of employees together and build into the performance appraisal systems reward systems that value diversity. For instance, Levi Strauss & Co. (Canada), has developed a value system that includes the recognition of the importance of diversity, but more importantly, requires that employees meet "aspirational goals" based on Levi's value systems.[7] Of course, HR programs to bring multicultural employees together should not be limited to employees who grew up in Canada. Employees who came to Canada from other countries (an increasingly important group of workers) may bring with them their own biases toward individuals from other countries, and that also can be problematic. For instance, while initiatives have been under way to bring about peace in the Middle East, the deep division between Israel and its surrounding Arab neighbours continues. Accordingly, requiring workers from these two areas to work together could create an uneasiness that must be addressed.

Cultural Environments

Cultural Environments The attitudes and perspectives shared by individuals from specific countries that shape their behaviour and how they view the world.

Understanding cultural environments is critical to the success of an organization's operations, but training employees in these is not the only means of achieving the desired outcomes. Companies such as Northern Telecom, Canadian Pacific, RTZ, and Hewlett-Packard are dealing with this issue by hiring nationals in foreign countries in which they operate.[8] What that has meant to these corporations is a ready supply of qualified workers who are well versed in their home country's language and customs. This recruiting has other benefits, too. When the foreign nationals and employees of the "home" company are mixed together, there is a spillover training effect. While working closely with one another, individuals learn informally the differences that exist between them and their two cultures. The Mars company, for example, builds on this informal development by providing formalized training that focuses on the "major differences that lead to problems."[9]

HRM also will be required to train management to be more flexible in its practices. Because tomorrow's workers will come in a diversity of colours and nationalities, managers will be required to change their ways. This will necessitate managers to be trained to recognize differences in workers and to appreciate— even celebrate—those differences. The various requirements of workers because of different cultural backgrounds, customs, or work schedules must all be taken into account.[10] An increasingly important part of what HRM professionals do is the provision of training to assist employees in adapting to co-workers from other cultures and to make the most of the growing diversity in the workforce.

Workforce Diversity

Forty years ago, the role of human resources management was much simpler. In the 1950s, the Canadian workforce was strikingly homogeneous, consisting primarily of white males employed in manufacturing. They had wives who stayed at home, tending to the family's two-plus children. Inasmuch as these workers were alike, "personnel's" (as it was called) job was certainly less complicated. These workers were recruited locally, and, in fact, new employees were often related to a current worker. Because those workers all shared the same interests and needs, personnel's responsibility was to get them in the door, sign them up, tell them about the standardized benefit program, and plan the company's annual Christmas party. Then, when the time came, it was HRM's responsibility to purchase the traditional gold watch, have it engraved, and present it to the employee at a gala event in honour of the employee's retirement. But times have changed, and so has the new workforce. By the year 2000, fewer than one-third of the workforce will be white males.[11]

Much of the change that has occurred in the workforce is attributed to the passage of legislation in the 1960s prohibiting employment discrimination. Based on such laws (we'll look at discrimination legislation in the next chapter), avenues began to open up for female and minority applicants. These two groups have since become the fastest-growing segment in the workforce, and accommodating their needs has become a vital responsibility for human resources managers. In the first place, women are participating in the labour market at the highest levels in history, actually dominating many of the employment categories in the fast-growing service and information sectors. In addition, visible minorities who represented slightly less than 10 per cent of the Canadian population in 1991, are projected to be over 17 per cent by 2001.[12] In 1981, one million Canadians had a first language other than French or English. Within a decade, this had risen to four million—15 per cent of the population. Of the approximately half million who could speak neither official language, 28 per cent spoke Chinese as a first language, 15 per cent Italian, and 11 per cent Portuguese.[13] Furthermore, during this time, birth rates in Canada began to decline. The baby boomer generation had already reached its apex in terms of employment opportunities, which meant that as hiring continued, there were fewer baby boomers left to choose.[14] And as globalization became more pronounced, Central American, Eastern European, Asian, and other immigrants came to North America and sought employment.

The future is anybody's guess and trying to predict the exact composition of our workforce diversity is no exception, even though we do know it will be made up of males, females, Whites, Blacks, Latin Americans, Asians, Aboriginal Peoples, the disabled, homosexuals, heterosexuals, and the elderly. Nonetheless, we can get a pretty good idea of what is to come by looking at the data from Statistics Canada and the federal census, and especially the statistics kept by Employment and Immigration Canada (see Figure 2-1). Canada's population is increasingly becoming multi-ethnic, urbanized, and older. The so-called traditional White male is rapidly becoming the exceptional employee in the Canadian workplace of today. For more detail on Canadian demographic trends, refer to the interesting analysis in the Canadian best-selling book, *Boom, Bust and Echo.*[15]

Workforce Diversity The varied personal characteristics that make the workforce heterogenous.

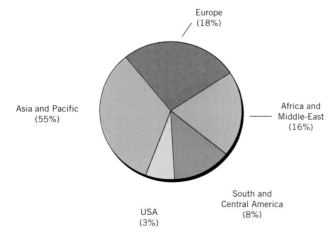

Source: A Stronger Canada, Employment and Immigration Canada: 1998 Annual Immigration Plan. Ottawa: 23 October, 1997.

Figure 2-1
Immigrants to Canada by Source Area, 1994-1996.

The Implications for HRM

As employees from diverse ethnic backgrounds become the dominant element within the workforce, HRM will have to change its practices to attract and retain this diversity. This makes excellent business sense since it is estimated that the spending power of minorities in Canada is over $76 billion,[16] and customers are much more supportive of an organization in which they find people like themselves.[17] The organization's benefits package contributes to supporting diversity. An illustration of this is the growth of culturally-sensitive employee assistance programs (EAPs) in such organizations as BC Hydro, IBM Canada, and Petro-Canada.[18] These EAPs make special efforts to reach employees in their own language and to be sensitive to ethnic differences in such areas as helping employees with personal problems. Allon Bross, president of FGI, an EAP provider, points out that the whole idea of solving problems by talking to someone is not a concept shared by all cultures. "Many ethnic groups rely upon their family system for support. Even in some of these cultures, some problems are just not discussed—inside or outside the family."[19]

Gender diversity will be as important as ethnic diversity in the workforce of tomorrow. As women, born inside or outside Canada, become the majority, HRM practices will have to offer "family-friendly" benefits.[20] A family-friendly organization is one that has flexible work schedules and provides employee benefits such as child care. Even organizations that use part-time and temporary help have found that family-friendly benefits are needed if these groups are to remain productive and committed to the organization.[21] We'll look more closely at family-friendly organizations in Chapter 14.

In addition to the diversity brought about by gender and nationality, HRM must be aware of the age differences that exist in our workforce. Today, there are at least four distinct groupings identified by David K. Foote: the pre-boomers, the baby boomers, the baby busters and the baby boom echo. The pre-boomers are those born prior to 1947. This group of workers—the by-product of the post-Depression era—are security oriented and have a committed work ethic. Although often viewed as the foundation of the workforce, they are regarded by the other age groups as having obsolete skills and being inflexible in their ways. The baby boomers, those born between 1947 and 1966, the largest group in the workforce, are regarded as the career climbers—at the right place, at the right time. Unsurpassed organizational growth during their initial years of employment led to careers advancing rapidly. Yet, many see them as unrealistic in their views and as workaholics. Thirdly, there's the generation Xers, those born between 1967 and 1979. These twentysomething baby busters are bringing a new perspective to the workforce. They are less committed, less rule bound, more interested in themselves and their own gratification, and intolerant of the baby boomers and their attitudes.[22] As a result, they are viewed as being selfish and not willing to play the "corporate game." The final group of employees are the baby boom echos, the children of the baby boomers, born between 1980 and 1995. Because the sheer number of boomers is particularly large in Canada, this fourth group is expected to play an important role in the workplace of the future.

The challenge for HRM is to design integrated work places in which all groups of employees blend well together. Human resources management must train these groups to manage effectively, deal with one another, and respect the diversity of views that each offers.[23] In situations like these, a more active management approach also appears to work better.[24] For example, employers like the Travelers and the Hartford insurance employers go to great lengths to train their younger

Pre-Boomers   Those individuals born before 1947.

Baby Boomers Those individuals born between 1947 and 1966.

Baby Busters Those individuals born between 1967 and 1979.

Baby Boom Echos Those individuals born between 1980 and 1995.

managers how to deal with older employees. Inasmuch as work conflict is natural, these companies have been successful in keeping problems to a minimum.[25]

Changing Skill Requirements

In any discussion of the changing world of work, the issues of skill requirements must be addressed. Remember that as recently as the end of the last century, Canada was primarily an agrarian economy. Our great-grandparents worked the land with sheer brawn, growing food for themselves and those in the community. As the Industrial Revolution continued to introduce machine power, assembly lines, and mass production, people left the farm and moved to cities to work in factories. For a generation or two, these workers helped Canada to become a leading industrialized nation, producing quality goods in our manufacturing industries. But many of these manufacturing jobs have disappeared, replaced by more efficient machines or by lower-cost labour overseas. Today, the North American economy is essentially driven by service, not manufacturing. Eighty per cent of workers are now employed in service, and by the year 2000, that number is expected to increase to 88 per cent.[26] What does all this mean for our workers?

Manufacturing assembly lines like this one, once the engine of Canada's economic development, are giving way to service facilities as Canada moves further into the post-industrial era.

Segments of our workforce are deficient in skills necessary to perform the jobs required in the twenty-first century. This is brought out all too clearly in a Conference Board of Canada study.[27] Despite record investment in machinery and equipment, Canada's productivity record has been disappointing, and its economic performance remains below potential. Unemployment is high, the outlook for youth is discouraging, and the country's relative position in the global economy has fallen. According to the Conference Board of Canada, evidence is beginning to emerge that places part of the responsibility on inadequate employee skills and training. Their survey of forty-one companies found that more highly skilled and literate people are the key to increasing Canadian productivity.[28] New entrants to the workforce are often not adequately prepared. High-school graduates sometimes lack the necessary reading, writing, and mathematics skills needed to perform today's high-tech jobs.[29] Others in the workforce are computer illiterate.

The Implications for HRM

Skill deficiencies The gap between required and available skills.

Skill deficiencies translate into significant losses for the organization in terms of poor-quality work and lower productivity, increases in employee accidents, and customer complaints,[30] all of which cost billions of dollars.[31] This is a major problem that cannot be ignored, but it is one that cannot be tackled by companies alone. For example, the inability of a significant portion of the Canadian population to read and write either official language adequately has been recognized as a serious problem. To attack functional illiteracy will require joint cooperation with human resources of all the relevant parties in the work situation: employers, employees, unions, and governments. Joint employer-union cooperation was a key element in the successful opening of the Molson Personal Learning and Development Centre at the company's Etobicoke, Ontario brewery.[32] According to Lloyd Livingstone, brewing training specialist and coordinator for the learning centre, Molson had relied far too much on the "bums in seats" method of training. But what really made this initiative work was the support received from the union and their desire to have a more educated workforce. "That was a nice fit," said Livingstone. "The benefit has been great; you can't hold them back."

Governments also need to get involved, perhaps particularly in the assessment phases of training. An example of an innovative program is the career skill assessment exercise of the Nova Scotia Department of Education and Culture (NSDEC).[33] This program is part of a broad-based combination of skills assessment and aptitude tests that have been applied in government-business partnerships in companies ranging from Canada Post and the large pulp and paper company Stora Forest Products, to the smaller crafts shop Amos Pewterers. This is a good example of the way in which progressive HRM programs can be applied to both large and small organizations.

Corporate Downsizing

Downsizing An activity in an organization aimed at creating greater efficiency by eliminating certain jobs.

The **downsizing** (sometimes referred to as restructuring, retrenchment, or delayering) of corporate Canada has swept across the country. Canadian companies have worked to become lean and mean organizations. As a result of deregulation in certain industries (such as the airlines), foreign competition, mergers, and takeovers, organizations have been forced to trim the fat, or the inefficiencies, from their ranks. Unfortunately, prior to these changes that occurred during the 1990s, a pattern of haphazard growth in employment typified our industries. Individuals were hired seemingly at random, jobs were frequently ill defined, and a host of mid-level management positions were created. The cost of this was often passed on in terms of "invisible" price increases that consumers took for granted.

Changing world economies, increases in inflation at home, and reduced profit levels led, in part, to the changing corporate Canada that we see today. In fact, by the mid-1990s, almost all major companies had cut staff and trimmed operations. Downsizing has been particularly evident in the sector of the workforce covered by federal legislation in Canada. Between 1994 and 1996, the workforce in the private sector decreased by 1.7 per cent, while in the federal public service, the decline was 7.7 per cent. Significantly, for the sixth year in a row, firings have exceeded hirings in both sectors.[34] And this downsizing did not occur only in Canada or the United States. For example, some of Japan's largest organizations, like Matsushita and Toyota, have had to cut jobs and reassign workers to functions in the organizations that are more productive.[35] There were massive protests in South Korea over similar moves by Hyundai and Samsung. The "job for life" was disappearing from the Asia-Pacific region, just as it had earlier from North America.

The Rationale Behind Downsizing

Whenever an organization attempts to delayer, it is trying to create greater efficiency,[36] which means, in part, getting the same output with fewer inputs. That is the foundation of downsizing. While individuals actually producing goods and services have not been immune to lay-offs, much of the focus of recent downsizing efforts has been on the management ranks. Companies began exploring just what added value they got from management positions and began to consider what would happen if fewer levels of management existed. What is occurring here is a movement towards a greater span of control—the number of employees a manager can direct effectively and efficiently. In the most basic assumption, if a manager can direct the activities of more employees, then that manager is more efficient.

Figures 2-2 and 2-3 identify two managerial spans of control: one prior to retrenchment, and one post downsizing. In Figure 2-2, the span of control is four employees. That means that each manager is directly responsible for four individuals. In this simplified case, there are six layers of management, totalling 1,365 managers. There are also 4,096 employees—individuals who produce the goods and services. Realizing that the ratio of managers to employees is not very efficient, this company decides to double the span of control to eight. What happens? Figure 2-3 shows the results. After the restructuring, there are now only four layers of management, and 585 managers direct the activities of these same 4,096 employees. What are the savings? By increasing the span of control, the company successfully eliminates two layers of management, constituting 780 positions. Using an average salary of $45,000 per year for all the positions eliminated, this action saves the company more than $35 million in direct pay.[37] When collateral savings such as employee benefits, cost of office space, utilities and so on, are included, the savings are significant, especially to a company having financial difficulties.

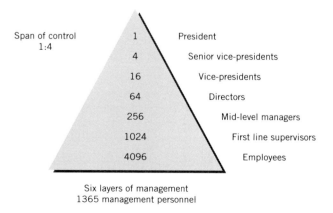

Span of control
1:4

1	President
4	Senior vice-presidents
16	Vice-presidents
64	Directors
256	Mid-level managers
1024	First line supervisors
4096	Employees

Six layers of management
1365 management personnel

Figure 2-2
Span of Control Before
Downsizing

Downsizing raises a number of other issues besides cost savings. First, let's look at the jobs remaining. A job that once required one manager for every four employees has changed overnight. The surviving manager is now doing the work of two or more people.[38] And although our example above focused only on management levels, downsizing in reality is hitting all levels of employees. Accordingly, it is conceivable that a number of today's workers are being expected to produce what three employees once did. Consequently, restructuring for downsizing's sake without proper job redesign or training of employees may be counter-productive.

Too many companies have downsized without regard to the people dimension of the process. What about the people leaving? What dignity were they afforded in being separated from the company? Were they informed ahead of time, or were they herded into a large auditorium, told their jobs had been eliminated, and escorted out of the building? And what about the surviving employees? How has the company prepared to deal with their anger over friends being dismissed? Their fear that they may be next or their job stress from doing the work of several individuals?[39] These effects of corporate restructuring are real issues facing human resources management.

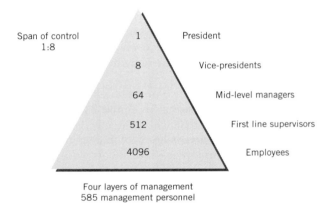

Figure 2-3
Span of Control After
Downsizing

The Implications for HRM

So, what role should human resources management play in the downsizing of corporate Canada? In one sense, if they are linked to the strategic direction of the organization, human resources must have input into the downsizing process. HRM must ensure that proper communications occur during this time. They must minimize the negative effects of rumours and ensure that individuals are kept informed. HRM must also deal with the actual lay-off. They must have outplacement and other programs ready to assist the severed workers. For example, there are the immediate uncertainties that laid off employees face. Will they receive severance pay? How will health insurance be handled? Will they have any benefits from their retirement plan? These and similar questions should be anticipated and responses prepared.

The point here is that human resources management cannot be omitted from the downsizing discussion, nor can it ignore or abdicate its responsibilities to its employees. That can be difficult to do when human resources managers are also affected by the retrenchment. They, as with any employee group, are not immune to this corporate action, but they still must maintain their composure in the process.[40]

Finally, although downsizing has been prevalent over the past few years, this is not true of all areas of the Canadian economy. In certain sectors such as technology and financial services, there has actually been substantial growth. In such situations, the challenge of HRM is to ensure the availability of sufficient trained and motivated people to cope with rapid growth. However, even in those areas of the economy subject to downsizing, there's some indication that the significant number of cuts may be declining. In fact, in a few organizations, the cuts were so deep that after the economy improved, they had to hire some employees back. These new positions are not, however, across the board. Rather, they are in organizations in the service sector, especially skilled, professional-level jobs.[41] We can expect some of the "lost" jobs to return where it is prudent to hire full-time staff to assist in achieving organizational goals, and where that hiring does not negatively affect an organization's efficiency. New positions will only appear if they are productive, leading towards organizational goal attainment. HRM, then, must work with top management to show this linkage and then, attract and retain these people.

Mergers and Acquisitions

Downsizing is sometimes the outcome of mergers or acquisitions in which one organization results from the amalgamation of two or more others. The Canadian work scene is replete with examples of such mergers. The highest profile ones, at the time of writing, are those proposed in the banking industry (Royal Bank with Bank of Montreal and CIBC with TD Bank); the motor industry (Chrysler with Daimler Benz).

Many of the same issues we discussed above in downsizing also apply to organization mergers. HRM has to deal with employees threatened by change, real anxieties about job security, and reassigning workers displaced or redundant in the newly merged operation. In addition, HRM has the major task of integrating employees and HRM policies from often quite different organizations into the new organizational entity. The challenge is to ensure that the new organization benefits from the synergy of its component groups rather than ending up with lower morale and decreased efficiency.

Total Quality Management

If there is one area of change that particularly affects North American organizations it is the search for quality and customer service. This mantra is heard, not just in large private sector corporations, but in government, the non-profit sector, and especially in small business where the quality of their service is often their competitive edge. Total Quality Management (TQM) has become the watchword of Canadian employers.

Total Quality Management takes a long-term view on how an enterprise will operate.[42] It is a continuous improvement process whereby an organization builds a better foundation from which to serve its customers. For TQM, this involves "a company-wide initiative that includes customers and suppliers, supported by top management and implemented in a top-down [manner]."[43] That is, TQM means that a company changes its operations to focus on the customer and to involve workers in matters affecting them.[44] At the heart of the TQM initiative, then, is continuous process improvement.[45]

Total Quality Management (TQM) An organization-wide perspective on quality and broad interventions aimed at its improvement.

TABLE 2-2   Deming's Fourteen Points for Improving Organizational Quality

1. Plan for the long-term future, not for next month or next year.
2. Never be complacent concerning the quality of your product.
3. Establish statistical control over your production processes, and require your suppliers to do so as well.
4. Deal with the fewest number of suppliers—the best ones, of course.
5. Find out whether your problems are confined to particular parts of the production process or stem from the overall process itself.
6. Train workers for the job that you are asking them to perform.
7. Raise the quality of your line supervisors.
8. Drive out fear.
9. Encourage departments to work closely together rather than to concentrate on departmental or divisional distinctions.
10. Do not be sucked into adopting strictly numerical goals, including the widely popular formula of "zero defects."
11. Require your workers to do quality work, not just to be at their stations from 9 to 5.
12. Train your employees to understand statistical methods.
13. Train your employees in new skills as the need arises.
14. Make top managers responsible for implementing these principles.

Source: W. Edwards Deming, "Improvement of Quality and Productivity Through Action by Management," *National Productivity Review* (Winter 1981–82), pp. 12–22. Copyright 1981 by Executive Enterprises Inc., 22 West 21st St., New York, NY 10010–6904. Reprinted by permission of John Wiley & Sons, Inc.

Continuous Process Improvement A Total Quality Management concept whereby workers continue toward 100 per cent effectiveness on the job.

Continuous process improvement is a technique whereby companies make constant efforts to better what they produce. Although perfection is an ultimate goal, reality dictates that we never get there. However, through continuous process improvement, companies strive to improve anything that they do—from hiring quality people, to administrative paper processing, to meeting customer needs. Therein lies the importance of TQM. Quality is not a new phenomenon to businesses. In fact, quality concerns date back some fifty years with the pioneering work of W. Edwards Deming. Deming believed that quality could be measured and achieved through a process of statistical controls, which were intended to reduce variances in products and achieve a level of uniformity in each one made.[46] From Deming's perspective, that meant that the 51,084th computer chip produced on an assembly line should have the same quality properties as the first one. Although Deming's analysis was statistical by nature, he focused on a unique element of quality that was unheard of at the time. His message was that management had more effect on productivity than the actual workers performing their jobs (see Table 2-2). The problems with low productivity, according to Deming, were the fault of management, not the worker.

Deming reinforced this by developing specific requirements for productivity improvements.[47] For reasons unknown, North American businesses ignored Deming's message, so he took his ideas to Japan which was then rebuilding after World War II. Japanese productivity prior to Deming's arrival was often shoddy; in fact, during the 1950s and 1960s, "Made in Japan" often meant the product was junk. But with Deming's help, many Japanese companies turned themselves around. By applying his principles, these organizations were able to grow to be the industrial giants they are today. And quality is still at the root of their success.

It has taken much longer for the management of Canadian organizations to recognize the need for quality. Instead of promoting quality, North American management has concentrated on short-term profits as opposed to long-term development. In the past, they simply removed themselves from the reality of impending global competition.[48] In other words, they failed to scan the external environment. Not until Canadian consumers turned their buying power to quality products—products from abroad that at times might cost even more than local products—did these managers begin to address the problem. To help stave off any further erosion of North America's competitive nature, TQM was born.[49] Since that time, TQM has become fashionable in almost every organization—private and public—and even in institutions of higher education.[50]

TQM Today and the Arrival of ISO 9000 Certification

The focus on continuous process improvements in organizational operations gained momentum in the early 1990s. Unfortunately, TQM is not something that can be easily implemented nor dictated down through the many levels in an organization. Rather, TQM is likened to an organization-wide development process;[51] that is, the process must be accepted and supported by top management and driven by collaborative efforts throughout each segment in the organization.[52] A key element in quality is having clear and documented standards of what constitutes a quality product or service, and this is where the Geneva-based International Standards Organization (ISO) has come in. They have developed a set of global quality standards known as ISO 9000 (and related numbers) aimed at simplifying international trade which have become virtually mandatory for business in the European Union. Enthusiasm for ISO 9000 has been growing in Canada, perhaps at the cost of such earlier initiatives as quality circles and even TQM itself. In the growing trend towards global sourcing ISO certification is emerging as a key element. Government Services Canada and organizations such as Inco, Northern Telecom, Chrysler, Ford, and GM of Canada are slashing the number of their suppliers, while at the same time, requiring companies to become ISO 9000-registered or be dropped from their preferred lists.[53]

> **ISO 9000** Set of global quality standards established by the International Standards Organization in Geneva.

However, it is essential that all these quality improvement initiatives are in congruence with each other and the organization itself if they are to succeed. TQM stresses the employee participation and process improvement aspects of quality, while ISO 9000 certification provides the necessary performance standards to assess the progress made. For this reason, we continue to prefer the term TQM to emphasize the broad and far-reaching nature of quality enhancement. The essence of TQM is that every individual must understand what quality means to them on their job and what effort needs to be exerted to achieve the move towards "perfection." These same organizational members must recognize that failing to do so could lead to unsatisfied customers—customers who may take their purchasing power to competitors who do produce quality products and services.[54]

Unions also understand the need for this cooperative effort to continuously improve. This has resulted in unions believing that by supporting continuous improvement efforts, the company recognized the importance of its employees.[55] That translates into training, job security, and other rewards. The bottom line is that if the organizations don't keep their customers, the employees don't keep their jobs.

HRM Support of TQM

Human resources management plays an important role in the implementation of TQM programs. Whenever an organization embarks on any effort such as TQM, it is introducing change into the organization, and HRM must prepare individuals for that change. This requires clear and extensive communication of why the change will occur, what is to be expected, and the effects it will have on employees. TQM efforts may result in changes in work patterns, in operations, and even in reporting relationships. HRM must be available to help the affected employees overcome resistance to the change and the fear that is often associated with change.

TQM efforts are also going to result in new ways of doing things. Consequently, HRM must be prepared to train employees in these new processes and help them to attain new skill levels that may be associated with the "new, improved" operations.[56] "Quality is not what you do," explained Marnie Ferguson, Monsanto Canada's Mississauga-based vice-president. "It's who you are. It's a state of being. It's a constant reminder of what you stand for."[57]

Re-engineering Work Processes for Improved Productivity

Although TQM is a positive start in many organizations, it focuses on continuous improvement or ongoing incremental change. Such action is intuitively appealing—the constant and permanent search to make things better. Yet, many of our companies function in a dynamic environment facing rapid and constant change. As a result, Total Quality Management techniques may not be in the best interest of the organization.

The problem with continuous process improvement is that it may provide a false sense of security. It may give managers a feeling that they're actively doing something positive, but ongoing incremental change avoids facing up to the possibility that what the organization may really need is radical change. It does little good to have the "best" reorganization of the deckchairs on the *Titanic*. Such drastic change results in the re-engineering of the organization.

Re-engineering Radical, quantum change in an organization.

Re-engineering occurs when more than 70 per cent of the work processes in an organization are evaluated and altered.[58] It requires organizational members to rethink what work should be done, how it is to be done, and how best to implement these decisions. That is, re-engineering in companies such as BC Hydro, and Bell Canada, and in provincial governments across the country focuses on simplifying the operations and making them more efficient and more customer focused. As a result, re-engineering typically includes three main features: a customer focus, an organizational structure that is production "friendly," and a desire to think about organizational work from scratch.

For example, re-engineering efforts at Mutual Life Insurance Company focused attention on making its customer insurance applications process more effective. By implementing a new process allowing a case manager total authority from the time an application is received until the policy is issued, Mutual Benefit has eliminated the work of five separate departments and nineteen different people. Consequently, the length of the application process has decreased from almost one month to as little as four hours.[59] Overall, re-engineering efforts have led to improvements in production quality, speed, innovation, and customer service.[60]

Although re-engineering may prove worthwhile for many organizations, some caution is in order. It is not a one-time procedure and as such, is not a quick fix. It should not be used simply as a ploy to downsize the organization. Instead, it's a continuous review of the organization's structure and its practices—including how managers manage—to increase productivity and meet organizational objectives.[61] And the role of management cannot be ignored. Even James Champy and Michael Hammer, the two individuals credited with introducing re-engineering to corporate North America, have recognized management's part in all of this. In fact, the chief reason cited for the failure of re-engineering efforts is management itself.[62] Re-engineering that is limited to technical change alone without changing leadership styles, changing the attitude of workers, involving workers in those things that affect them and their jobs, and building work teams, will not bring about the desired results. That's why individuals like Glen Quarrington, vice-president of HRM at Eaton's, who recognize their major role in the process, can make the necessary changes that lead to substantial improvements.

HRM and Re-engineering

If we accept the premise that re-engineering will change how we do business, it stands to reason that employees will be directly affected. In which case, generating the gains that re-engineering offers will not occur unless we address the people issues. First of all, re-engineering may have left employees, at least the survivors, confused and angry. Although a preferred method of change would have been to involve employees throughout the process, we need to recognize that re-engineering may have left some of the employees frustrated and unsure of what to expect.[63] Long-time work relationships may have been severed and stress levels magnified. Accordingly, HRM must have mechanisms in place for employees to get appropriate answers and direction of what to expect, as well as assistance in dealing with the conflict that may permeate the organization.

Although the emotional aspect is difficult to resolve, for re-engineering to generate its benefits HRM needs to train its employee population. Whether it's a new process, a technology enhancement, working in teams, having more decision-making authority, or other undertakings, employees are going to need new skills. Consequently, HRM must be in a position to offer the skills training that is necessary in the "new" organization. Even the best process will fail if employees do not have the requisite skills to perform.

Furthermore, as many components of the organization have been redefined, so too will be many of the HRM activities that affect employees. For example, if redesigned work practices have resulted in changes in employee compensation packages (e.g., bonus/incentive pay), such changes need to be communicated to employees. Likewise, performance standards and how employees will be evaluated must also be understood.

The Contingent Workforce

Years ago, employment patterns in organizations were relatively predictable. In good times, when work was plentiful, large numbers of employees were hired. Then, as the economy went into a recession and fewer goods were being purchased, companies simply laid off their "surplus" employee population.[64] When the economic picture improved, a new cycle started. But downsizing, restructuring, and re-engineering have all changed this management practice. Organizations today often do not have the luxury of hiring many individuals when times are good and letting them go when the economy turns down. The costs of hiring employees frequently, coupled with the costs of firing employees

Core Employees Workers who hold full-time jobs in organizations.

Contingent Workforce The part-time, temporary, and contract workers used by organizations to fill peak staffing needs, or perform work unable to be done by core employees.

(such as severance pay and increases in employment insurance premiums) are forcing employers to rethink the old work cycles.

In a number of organizations, this dynamic situation has led organizations to employ two types of workers. The first are core employees—workers who hold full-time jobs at managerial or clerical levels in organizations. These employees usually provide some essential job tasks—for instance, the chief software designer of a high-tech software development company or customer service support—that require commitment and permanence in the organization. Employees who hold these core positions enjoy the full slate of employee benefits that were traditionally provided to full-time employees. Beyond these essential employees are many individuals who "sell" their services to an organization. These workers are referred to collectively as the contingent workforce, and they constitute the third "leaf" of Handy's "shamrock" organization structure in addition to the two types of core employees.[65] Contingent workers include individuals who are hired for short periods of time to perform specific tasks that often require special job skills when an organization hasn't enough core employees to complete the necessary tasks. When the special need is fulfilled, these workers are let go, but they are not laid off in the traditional sense. Contingent workers have no "full-time" rights in the organization. Consequently, when their project is finished, so too is their affiliation with the organization. Because of their status, these workers often do not receive any of the employee benefits that are provided to core workers.

In 1995 in the US, upward to 30 per cent of the workforce was comprised of contingent workers,[66] and given the trends in restructuring and re-engineering, that number is expected to climb to almost 50 per cent by the turn of the century.[67] Canadian figures are very similar. Indeed, the Canadian Chamber of Commerce found that so-called alternative work arrangements—alternative to full-time employment—are becoming the new norm.[68] This is supported by current Canadian census data[69] showing sharp increases in part-time employment and continuing decreases in full-time employment. The census also reports a 28 per cent rise in self-employment in the past five years.

So who makes up the contingency pool? Contingent workers are any individuals who work part-time as temporaries or as contract workers (see Table 2-3), and they may hold such diverse jobs as secretaries, accountants, nurses, assembly line workers, lawyers, dentists, computer programmers, engineers, marketing representatives, and human resources professionals. Contingent workers are not all traditional office support temps; more and more, the new temp is likely to be a manager or technical person who is brought in on a contract. For example, John Riley, a network administrator for Kelly Services (Canada) Ltd., got the experience he needed and the chance to move from sales to information systems through the range of projects he carried out for a variety of companies.[70]

Meet

Michelle Hutchinson
Owner,
Hutchinson Communications

On any given day at Hutchinson Communications, a dozen or so employees may be seen hard at work in the brightly coloured offices, creating manuals, on-line help files, training materials, and other technical documents for a variety of large corporate clients. But if you ask Michelle Hutchinson, president and owner of this ten-year-old firm, how many people she has working for her right now, she answers, "About thirty—and we're still growing."

So where is everybody? Some are visiting clients, but many others work at home, full- or part-time. Hutchinson is one of many dynamic Canadian firms that has realized that the old notion of a worker as someone who comes into the office every day is as out of date as the quill pen.

"About half the people working on my projects are freelancers and half are employees," explains Ms Hutchinson. The quality of the work is what's important, not the details of the arrangement. "I have people working from Cambridge, Woodstock, Newmarket. But we're in touch all the time by e-mail, conference calls, and regular meetings as needed. We hope to get into Internet videoconferencing soon. The technology boom in the last decade, but especially in the past few years, has really made a big difference in how companies can work."

In fact, she points out, plenty of work is done these days by "virtual companies" that have no permanent existence at all. A team of people gets together for a specific project, then disbands when it's done." Others exist as corporate entities but do not have physical central office space anywhere. (Ms Hutchinson finally moved her own rapidly growing company out of her home when her business had grown so much that her son announced one day, "Gee, mom, I'm surprised you don't have a computer set up in the bathroom yet!")

And what will the future mean for the way an entrepreneur like Ms Hutchinson hires staff and how they work together? "As technology continues to make business speed up," she predicts, "it will also bring more fun to the job....Being on the cutting edge gets the adrenalin going. Excitement gets generated. We can do things faster, smarter, better."

TABLE 2-3 The Contingent Workforce

Part-time Employees:	Part-time employees are those who work less than a full workload, typically under about forty hours a week. Generally, part-timers are afforded few, if any, employee benefits. Part-time employees are generally a good source for organizations to staff their peak hours. For example, a bank that expects its heaviest business between 10 A.M. and 2 P.M. may bring in part-time tellers for those four hours. Part-time employees may also be a function of job sharing, where two employees split one full-time job.
Temporary Employees:	Temporary employees, like part-timers, are generally employed during peak production periods and can also act as fill ins when some employees are off work for an extended period of time. For example, a secretarial position may be

•

filled using a temp while the secretary is taking his unpaid leave of absence following the birth of his daughter. Temporary workers are a fixed cost to an employer for labour used during a specified period.

Contract Workers:

Contract workers, subcontractors, consultants, and other freelance individuals are hired by organizations to work on specific projects. These workers, often very skilled, perform certain duties and often have their fees set in a contract and are paid only when the organization receives particular deliverables. Organizations use contract workers because their labour cost is then fixed, and they don't incur any of the costs associated with a full-time employee. Some contract arrangements may exist because the contractor can provide virtually the same good or service in a more efficient manner. In Chapter 10, we link the *portfolio* career model to these employees.

Are Contingent Workers Throwaway Workers?

Over the past ten to fifteen years, we have witnessed significant changes in how organizations are staffed. As the changing world of work affects our businesses, reality has indicated that today's organizations simply cannot compete if they have surplus employees. The strategic nature of both business and HRM requires that they be prepared for "just-in-time" (JIT) employees. What that means is that organizations must find the proper balance between having a ready supply of skilled workers available when the need arises without having a surplus pool of idle workers waiting for something to arise. In order to meet this dual goal, however, organizations must keep staffing levels flexible.[71] Contingent workers conveniently fill that void but at what cost to them?

Are workers freely becoming contingent workers out of their desire to fulfil personal work, family, lifestyle, or financial needs? Or have they been forced into this employment limbo as a result of downsizing and cutbacks? The answer to both is unequivocally yes.[72] There are those individuals who prefer contingent work because it offers them the greatest flexibility in work scheduling, something that workers, especially women, have been requesting from corporate Canada. With the increasing diversity of the workforce, contingent work arrangements permit one to blend family and career goals.[73] Using this logic, contingent positions are, in fact, beneficial to employees.

There is, however, another side to this issue. Many organizations are using contingent work simply to save money. Employing contingent workers saves an organization as much as 40 per cent in labour costs partly because no benefits are provided. Furthermore, hiring contingent workers protects an organization's core employees from work fluctuations.[74] To achieve this, some employees are, in fact, being forced into contingent employee roles. For example, in a major bank, an employee with more than fourteen years' experience was given a choice: reduce work time to nineteen hours a week and receive no benefits, or be severed from the bank permanently.[75] Because of financial responsibilities, this employee took this minimal offer and looked for another part-time job. Unfortunately, individuals in this situation may work forty hours or more each week, but for several organizations, and not have the luxury of the benefits they would have received had they worked full-time for one company. This process has been repeated thousands of times in all the major Canadian banks and other financial institutions. Some companies are simply, "dumping" the majority of their full-time workforce and replacing it with lower-paid temporaries or contractual workers.[76]

The debate over the use of contingent workers will continue. There will always be those who want to be full-time employees but simply cannot find that opportunity. However, the rising trend to be lean and mean, the competitive nature of business, and the more diverse workforce will result in the creation of more temporary jobs (see "What If"). Revenue Canada, of course, is paying close attention this latter activity. Failing to withhold payroll taxes or health and employment insurance premiums for temporary workers who are actually working on the company premises for even short durations has led to investigations, and fines and penalties for those companies that have "misclassified" their workers.[77]

The Implications of Contingent Workers for HRM

In the past, HRM practices have assumed a permanent workforce for whom it makes sense to carry out extensive recruitment, development, and career planning. The shift towards a contingent workforce requires a significant shift in HRM orientation from position focused upon full-time employees, towards portfolio focused upon part-time employees.[78] Portfolio-focused HRM (developed further in Chapter 10) is concerned with contingent employees who bring a portfolio of skills and competencies to specific, shorter-term contracts, as opposed to the permanent slotting of a full-time employee into a traditional job. The employment relationship with contingent workers brings with it numerous HRM challenges. These include being able to have these "virtual" employees available when needed, providing scheduling options that meet their needs, and making decisions about whether or not benefits will be offered to the contingent workforce.

No organization can make the transition to a contingent workforce without sufficient planning, and when these strategic decisions are being made, HRM must be an active partner in the discussions. After all, it is HRM's responsibility to locate and bring into the organization these temporary workers. Just as HRM has played an integral role in recruiting full-time employees, so too must it play a major part in securing needed just-in-time talent.

As temporary workers are brought in, HRM will also have the responsibility of quickly adapting them to the organization. Although not as extensive as the orientation for full-time employees, that for the contingent workforce is still essential. New JIT employees must be made aware of the organization's culture, and some training may be required. Even an experienced systems analyst brought in to work on a specific computer programming problem will need to be brought up to speed rather quickly on the uniqueness of the organization's system.

HRM will also have to consider how to effectively attract quality temporaries, particularly with the increased competition for the "good" talent. Accordingly, HRM will need to re-examine its compensation philosophy. If temporaries are employed solely as a cost-cutting measure, the pay and benefits offered to contingent workers might have to be different than those offered to other workers who are used part-time as a result of restructuring and re-engineering. HRM, then, will need to begin understanding specifically what these employees really want. Is it the flexibility in scheduling, the autonomy, or the control over their career destiny that these jobs offer that attracts them? Or were they just forced into this situation by bad luck? It will be essential to understand the motivation of these workers.[79]

Position-Focused HRM HRM activities organized around specific jobs or positions in an organization.

Portfolio-Focused HRM HRM activities organized around the skill sets or portfolios of employees in an organization.

What If:

HRM in a De-Jobbed Organization

If we were able to turn the clock back a couple of centuries, we would notice something strikingly similar to what is happening today. Our ancestors worked hard on their jobs, but they did so at home. They were farmers and craftspeople, producing goods that society needed to survive. Their days were long and hard; they had no set working hours, no supervisors to tell them what to do, and they had no job description to rely on for hints on what to do at work. With the Industrial Revolution came large, centralized work locations and new formalities of work life. Today, these structured norms are quickly vanishing as workers handle information, not physical goods, and the changing environment in which they work demands rapid responses. As a result, we are witnessing the disappearance of the job as we know it.

Yesterday's jobs were dominated by rigidity—workers performed the same tasks, day in and day out. Every once in a while, those tasks changed, and the job description was rewritten, but once that happened, the routine was reinstated. Today, that luxury doesn't exist. Tasks change too frequently to be accurately reflected in a job description. As this dynamic situation progresses, organizations have to continue to look for new ways of finding the skills necessary to complete the required tasks.

Work, then, will be built around what needs to be done. Individuals will work with others workers for a specified period of time, then move on to another project, which may be in the organization as well as outside it. Workers will perform their duties as members of project teams, not necessarily as representatives of departments within the organization. Workers will be expected to perform whatever tasks the project demands, as opposed to the limited set of jobs that their departmental jobs required. And working with these project teams will be the contingent workers—the part-time, temporary, contract, and consultant individuals.

As a result of these changes plus the infusion of technology—computers, modems, fax machines, and so on—workers will rarely have the routine 9-to-5 job. Rather, work hours will be a function of the work to be done, and hours worked may not equal hours paid. Employees will be paid for project results at a rate that is consistent with the value the project added to the organization. Some workers on these project teams may never be seen by their peers. Instead, through the existing technology, they may work at locations anywhere in the world and be linked to the team via telecommuting technology.

Will tomorrow's work be a throwback to yesteryear before "traditional" jobs? If current trends are any indication, there's a strong possibility that this will occur, but the loss of the job as we know it may not be all that bad. Although workers will no longer have the security and predictability of the traditional jobs, de-jobbing may give individuals the opportunity to have the flexible schedules and autonomy that they have been asking for.

Source: Vignette based on William Bridges, "The End of the Job," *Fortune* (September 19, 1994), pp. 62–74. Also see, for example, Peter F. Drucker, "The Age of Social Transformation," *The Atlantic Monthly* (November 1994), pp. 53–80.

The Canadian census figures quoted earlier also reveal that relatively more women than men are beginning to work part-time. For example, in the 1995, the last year for which census data are available, 12 per cent of paid female workers worked part-time through the year, while only 4 per cent of men did so.[80] One of the reasons for this difference is that some women chose part-time work to ease the crunch of juggling family and work.

Finally, HRM must be prepared to deal with the potential conflict that may arise between core and contingent workers. The core employees may become envious of the higher pay rates and flexible schedules of contingent workers. In the total compensation package, which includes benefits, core employees might earn substantially more money, but these employees may not immediately include the "in-kind" pay (their benefits) when comparing rates of compensation. For example, paying a training consultant $3,000 for a two-day project management training program might result in much envy and some conflict with core HRM trainers. If the consultant is offered twenty-five two-day programs over the year, earning $75,000 in consulting fees, a $40,000-a-year company trainer might take offence although the co-trainer is receiving $16,000 in benefits. Consequently, HRM must ensure its communication programs anticipate some of these potential conflicts and address them before they become detrimental to the organization, or worse, provide an incentive for core employees to leave.

Telework

The following example is based on actual research we have carried out in the public sector in Ontario and the federal government.[81] The names of the individuals and departments concerned have been disguised at the request of the participants.

> Smythe Pelissier of the Citizen Services Department (CSD) was faced with the tough dilemma of maintaining the department's operation with a reduction in resources of almost 25 per cent. Smythe concluded that the best solution was to close five regional offices and much of the head office in Ottawa and ask employees to work at home as an alternative to lay-off. One employee, Sally Servantes, took offence.
>
> It wasn't that Servantes objected to working out of her home. She clearly saw the benefit of being closer to her clients. What she did challenge, however, was the fact that CSD wouldn't compensate her for the costs she would incur by having her office at home. Although the department was setting up the office—furnishings, supplies, and equipment— Servantes knew her monthly electric bill, insurance premiums, and the like would increase. Simply put, she wanted to be reimbursed for added expenses. Furthermore, because the organization was saving money on warehousing by requiring employees to have spare department literature needed by clients stored in their homes, Servantes wanted to be compensated for the lost space in her house. But Pelissier's policy was clear: employees were not going to be paid any additional money for working out of their home. As a result and an inability to reach a satisfactory compromise, Sally Servantes was taken off teleworking and laid off.

Telework   Work performed
at a distance outside of the
organization's central office
environment

What happened to Sally may be an extreme case, but one that will surely come to light as more and more companies move to having employees work at home. This teleworking arrangement in which employees work at a distance from their corporate office has advantages and disadvantages. This will create new issues for HRM.

Work Is Where Your Computer Is

As mentioned in the "What If" box, if you go back 150 years in Canadian history, it was not uncommon for workers to be performing their craft out of their homes. In fact, most workers performed some tasks, produced a finished product, and took it to a market to sell. But the Industrial Revolution changed all that. Large manufacturing companies drew workers away from rural areas and into the cities. Along with this movement came the "traditional" job—one that required employees to show up at the company's facility and spend eight to twelve hours per day there.

But downsizing and re-engineering are changing all of that. Jobs as our parents and grandparents knew them are disappearing. When you factor in the massive technological changes that have occurred in the past decade, *where* we do our jobs is likely to change as well.

Telework, or telecommuting, is not a new idea, and work such as catalogue sales and customer information services has been done via telework for some time. What is new is the advent of relatively inexpensive and sophisticated computer-based systems which have made it possible to set up flexible telework arrangements for a far wider range of jobs and types of employees than ever before.[82]

In this age of increasing energy costs, long commutes to work, expensive central city locations, the requirement to give physically challenged individuals a fair chance at employment, and the increasing popularization of results-oriented management, telework seems to hold real promise for the progressive manager. In addition, it also suggests the basis for new models of human resources management. These offer the potential for supervisors to facilitate human resources development programs for employees spread among several worksites rather than being limited to the traditional common office or factory building.

Computers, modems, fax machines, and telephones are making decentralized worksites attractive for several reasons. Telecommuting capabilities that exist today have made it possible for employees to be located anywhere on the globe. For example, if Aetna Insurance in Saskatchewan finds that it is having problems attracting qualified local applicants for its claims-processing jobs and a pool of qualified workers is available in Winnipeg, Aetna doesn't need to establish a new facility in Manitoba. Instead, by providing these employees with computer equipment and appropriate ancillaries, the work can be done hundreds of kilometres away, and then be transmitted to the home office.

Telecommuting also offers an opportunity for a business in a high-labour-cost area to have its work done in an area of lower wages. Take the publisher in Vancouver who finds manuscript editing costs have skyrocketed. By having that work done by a qualified editor in Sydney, Nova Scotia, the publisher could reduce labour costs. Likewise, not having to provide office space in the city to this editor, given the cost per square foot of real estate in the area, adds to the cost savings.

Decentralized worksites also offer opportunities that may meet the needs of the diversified workforce. Those who have family responsibilities, may prefer to work in their homes rather than travel to the organization's facility.

Telework allows some people to combine work and home life and is particularly attractive to parents with young children.

Telecommuting, then, provides the flexibility in work scheduling that many members of the diversified workforce desire.

Finally, there's some incentive from government agencies for companies to consider these alternative work arrangements. For example, provincial governments, in their effort to address environmental concerns, may offer incentives to any efforts to reduce traffic congestion in heavily populated areas. One means of achieving that goal is for businesses to receive some incentive, such as a tax break, for implementing decentralized worksites. In a similar fashion, provincial departments of labour may also provide an incentive to businesses to relocate to economically depressed areas.

The trend towards teleworking continues at a rapid pace and it is estimated that by the year 2001, there will be one million teleworkers in Canada. In a recent survey of over four hundred firms across Canada, KPMG Canada[83] found that about 30 per cent had teleworkers, and that teleworkers accounted for an average of 6 per cent of the total workforce among these organizations. Teleworking occurred in almost all areas of the organizations and across many job levels, from senior management to clerical and administrative employees. The majority (62 per cent) of the employers reported that teleworking had increased since 1993, and more than 50 per cent of the respondents predicted an increase over the next three years especially for professional, technical, and middle management employees.

Telework is not limited to organization-based jobs, but can also afford doctors, lawyers, accountants, and all types of service people the opportunity to conduct their business directly out of their homes. Telework truly constitutes what Frances Cairncross[84] has so aptly termed "the death of distance." But it does bring with it several issues with which HRM must deal.

Ethical Decisions in HRM:

Health and Accident Insurance

It is deeply ingrained into the minds of human resource managers that they are partly responsible for ensuring that the workplace is free from hazards that may cause health-related problems or injuries. Along those lines, too, it is understood that if an employee is injured in the course of performing his or her duties on the job, that employee will be afforded some sort of income continuation—partly through government workers compensation, but primarily through the employers own insurance policies. For instance, if an employee is required to retrieve supplies from a supply room one flight down and falls down the steps while attempting to replenish her office supplies, workers' compensation and insured benefits apply. But should that same "courtesy" apply to home workers?

For example, decentralized worksites frequently require employees to store supplies in their homes for office use. These supplies, and possibly spare parts, belong to the organization, and were furnished by the organization at no cost to the employee. They are simply being warehoused at the employee's home. Accordingly, if in the course of a day's work, the home worker must go into his or her basement to retrieve supplies, and falls down the basement steps, should the employee be covered by the organization's employee health insurance? What if that same employee decided to take a break from telecommuting and went into the kitchen for a cup of coffee. If, the employee falls and breaks a leg while on the way there, should this employee's income be continued under the organization's employee insurance program?

What responsibility does the organization have for its employees who work at home? Even though a similar situation at the organization's facility might require it to cover the employee injury, should the organization be held responsible for worker injuries that occur at home, when the home (off-site) employee is performing regular duties? What if the employee is injured while using company-furnished equipment for personal business? Should the organization be held responsible? What's your opinion?

HRM and Telework

Despite the potential of telework, it is not without controversy. Telework continues to be an area about which employers and workers have strong feelings—either seeing it as a panacea for all the business and work woes of the present, or as an insidious means of continuing the worker manipulation of the past. While offering employees flexibility, telework does not necessarily increase the power of employees over their own work nor guarantee them trouble-free supervision. Indeed, the manager who does a poor job of face-to-face supervision is likely to have even more difficulties as a telemanager. Telework requires more, not fewer, skills than regula. work, and places more, not less, responsibility on the telemanager and teleworker. In addition, the employee who is an unsatisfactory worker in the central office is likely to continue to perform poorly as a teleworker.

Many of the challenges for HRM revolve around training managers in how to establish appropriate work standards and ensure that the work is done on time. Traditional "face time" is removed in decentralized worksites, and managers' need to control the work will have to change. Instead, there will have to be more employee involvement, allowing workers the discretion to make those decisions that affect them. For instance, although a due date is established for the work assigned to employees, managers must recognize that home workers will work at their own pace. That may mean instead of an individual focusing work efforts over an eight-hour period, the individual may work two hours here, three hours at another time, and another three late at night. The emphasis, then, will be on the final product, not the means by which it is accomplished.

Working at home gives employees more flexibility in sheduling their workday but adds new challenges for HRM.

Work at home may also require HRM to rethink its compensation policy. Will it pay workers by the hour, on a salary basis, or by the job performed? More than likely, because certain jobs such as claims processing can be easily quantified and standards set, pay plans will be in the form of pay for actual work done.

Beyond these issues, HRM must also anticipate potential legal problems that may arise from telecommuting.[85] For example, if an employee works more than forty hours during a work week, are they entitled to overtime pay? If yes, decentralized worksite activities will have to be monitored by HRM to ensure that employees are not abusing overtime privileges and that those workers who rightfully should be paid overtime are compensated.

Because employees in decentralized worksites are full-time employees, it will be the organization's responsibility to ensure the health and safety of the decentralized worksite. For example, the organization is responsible for providing equipment that does not lead to employee injury or illness. Although HRM cannot constantly monitor workers in their homes, it must ensure that these workers understand the proper techniques for using the equipment. Additionally, if accidents or injuries occur, employees must understand the regulations for reporting them. Generally, that means reporting them within forty-eight hours, for instance, at which time HRM must investigate immediately (see "Ethical Decisions in HRM").

Telework also has significant implications on labour relations and unions in Canada. As will be seen in Chapter 17, unions are under some stress in Canada. While keen to make up for a decline in their traditional membership base in the manufacturing industry, unions do not find it easy to organize teleworking employees. Teleworkers frequently are independent, geographically distant, and outside of the head office HRM practices. All this means that some teleworkers may not have the same protections as their unionized on-site colleagues. This places an additional responsibility upon HRM to ensure that all employees, centralized or decentralized, are covered by effective HR policies.

Employee Involvement

Whenever significant changes occur in an organization, subsequent transformations in the way work gets done must also occur. With respect to downsizing, many companies today are demanding that their employees to do more with less. The sheer magnitude of the work alone dictates that it cannot be done without some assistance, but involving employees means different things to different organizations and people. But by and large, for today's workers to be successful, there are a number of employee involvement concepts that appear to be accepted.[86] These include: delegation, participative management, and work teams—the empowering of employees. Let's elaborate on these a bit.

How Organizations Involve Employees

With the increasing complexity of individual tasks and projects, each employee cannot handle every aspect of a job and be expected to complete multiple tasks under today's work arrangements. Accordingly, more employees at all levels will be required to delegate some of these activities and responsibilities to other organizational members. This means that employees are going to have to be given certain amounts of authority to make decisions that directly affect their work. Even though delegation was once perceived as something that managers did with lower levels of management, it will now be required at all levels of the organization.

In addition to being required to take on more responsibilities, employees will be expected to make decisions without the benefit of the tried-and-true decisions of the past. And because all these employees are part of the process today, there is more of a need for them to have a say in the decision-making process. Gone are the days of top-down management where the strong hand ruled. To facilitate customer demands and fulfill corporate expectations, today's employees need to be more involved. Group decision making enables these employees to have input into the processes, enables them to have access to needed information, and makes them part of the strategic management process.[87] Participative management is also consistent with a work environment that requires increased creativity and innovation.

Another method of involving employees is an emphasis on work teams.[88] The bureaucratic structure of yesterday—where clear lines of authority existed and the chain of command was paramount—is not appropriate for most of today's companies. Workers from different specializations are increasingly required to work together to successfully complete complex projects. As a result, traditional work areas have given way to more of a team effort, building and capitalizing on

Employee Involvement Techniques that aim at including employees in decision-making processes.

Delegation A management activity in which activities are assigned to individuals at lower levels in the organization.

Participative Management A management concept giving employees more control over the day-to-day activities on their job.

Work Teams Formal work groups made up of interdependent individuals who are responsible for attainment of a specific goal.

the various skills and backgrounds that each member brings to the team. Consider, for example, what kind of group it takes to put together a symphony. One person could not possibly handle all the varied instruments, especially playing them all at the same time. Accordingly, to blend the music of the orchestra, symphonies have string sections, brass instruments, woodwinds, percussion, and so on. At times, however, a musician may cross over these boundaries, like the trombonist who also plays the piano. The basis of these work teams, then, is driven by the tasks at hand.

Involving employees allows them an opportunity to focus on the job goals. By giving them more freedom, employees are in a better position to develop the means to achieve the desired ends.

The Implications for HRM

Up until now, we have addressed some components of employee involvement, but for an organization, that is not enough. What is needed is communication and training, and that's where human resources management can make a valuable contribution. Employees expected to delegate, to have decisions participatively handled, to work in teams, or to set goals cannot do so unless they know and understand what it is they are to do. The same information technology that supports the growth in telework can also facilitate employee involvement programs. Management can directly transmit company information to all employees and gain the direct input from whole work groups through shared computer networks. In addition to communication, empowering employees requires extensive training in all aspects of the job. Workers may need to understand how new job designs, processes, and other aspects will affect them. They may need training in interpersonal skills to make participative management and work teams function properly. All in all, we can anticipate much more involvement from HRM in all parts of the organization.

But employee involvement comes at a price. The question then, is Is it worth it? From all indications, it appears to be. First of all, better control over one's work activities, coupled with better "tools," have been shown to improve productivity.[89] We are doing more with less but are doing it smarter and more productively. Also, as employees see the commitment the organization and HRM has made to them, there is evidence that their commitment and loyalty to it will increase.[90] The old personnel department will truly have become, in the words of David Ulrich, "human resource champions."[91]

Study Tools and Applications

Summary

This summary relates to the Learning Objectives identified on p. 29.

After having read this chapter, you should know:

1. Globalization is creating a situation where human resources management must begin to search for mobile and skilled employees capable of successfully performing their job duties in a foreign land. This means that these employees must understand the host country's language, culture, and customs.

2. The workforce composition has changed considerably over the past thirty years. Once characterized as having a dominant number of white males, the workforce composition of the late1990s is comprised of a mixture of women, visible minorities, immigrants, and white males.

3. The most significant implications for human resources management regarding the changing workforce composition are language and skill deficiencies of available workers, changing management practices to accommodate a diverse work group, dealing with conflict among employees, and providing family-friendly benefits.

4. Changing skill requirements require human resources management to provide extensive training. This training can be in the form of remedial help for those who have skill deficiencies, or specialized training dealing with technology changes.

5. Corporate downsizing is a phenomenon that has swept through Canadian corporations in an effort towards making them more efficient. In many cases, this has meant eliminating layers of management by increasing the span of control. In downsizing, HRM acts as the employees' advocate, communicating all necessary information to affected employees.

6. Total Quality Management (TQM) refers to a process that promotes continuous improvement in an organization. It seeks to build customer satisfaction through these continuous improvements and employee involvement. ISO 9000 provides the quality assessment standards against which to judge TQM initiatives.

7. Re-engineering refers to the radical change that occurs in the organization when the majority of work processes are evaluated and changed. HRM is instrumental in re-engineering by preparing employees to deal with the change and training them in new techniques.

8. The contingent workforce includes those part-time, temporary, consultants, and contract workers who provide services to organizations on an as-needed basis. The HRM implications of a contingent workforce include attracting and retaining skilled contingent workers, adjusting to their special needs, and managing any conflict that may arise between core and contingent workers.

9. Organizations use teleworking arrangements because they enable them to find qualified employees without having to relocate business facilities. Telework also provides cost savings to the organization, as well as fulfilling some special needs of a diversified workforce. For HRM, teleworking arrangements will require training for managers on managing and controlling work and establishing pay systems to reflect this work arrangement. HRM will also have to monitor the hours home workers spend on the job, as well as ensure the health and safety of workers in the home office.

10. Employee involvement can best be defined as giving each worker more control over his or her job. To do this requires delegation, participative management, work teams, goal setting, and employee training. If handled properly, involving employees should help in developing more productive employees who are more loyal and committed to the organization.

baby boomers
baby boom echos
baby busters
contingent workforce
continuous process improvement
core employees
cultural environments
decentralized worksites
delegation
downsizing
employee involvement

global village
ISO 9000
mature workers
participative management
portfolio-focused HRM
position-focused HRM
pre-boomers
telework
Total Quality Management (TQM)
workforce diversity

EXPERIENTIAL EXERCISE:

Generational Similarities and Differences

The diversity that exists in our workforce today is exceptionally well documented. Workers come from all walks of life, yet while these differences can be celebrated, focusing the varied backgrounds towards common organizational goals can be challenging. Something as simple as age difference can reveal this challenge. For example, there are basically four separate generations that coexist in our workforce today: those born before 1947, those born between 1947 and 1966, those born between 1967 and 1979, and those born in 1980 or after. In this exercise, we'll explore some of these differences.

Step 1:

Your professor will divide the class into four groups: Group 1, those born before 1947 (pre-boomers); Group 2, those born between 1947 and 1966 (baby boomers); Group 3, those born between1967 and 1979 (baby busters); and those born after 1979 (baby boom echos).

Should a particular generation not be represented in the class, the professor will ask some students to form a group addressing the issues and answering the questions from the perspective of their parents or grandparents.

Step 2:

After meeting in your generational group, answer the following questions by generating lists:
a. What do you value in life?
b. What do you want from a job?
c. What do you expect from an organization?
d. What are your three favourite television shows?
e. What are your three favourite musical groups?
f. What is your ideal vacation?
g. How do you view the other three groups? For instance, if you are a baby boomer, how does your view describe the characteristics of the baby busters and the baby boom echos?

Step 3:   Each group will report to the class its responses to Step 2. This information will be recorded by your instructor.

Step 4:   As a large group, now that all views have been presented, what similarities are their between the three groups? What differences exist? What challenges do you believe these differences create for organizational members?

CASE APPLICATION:

Rethinking a Kind and Gentle Past at Dofasco[92]

Dofasco, Inc. of Hamilton, Ontario has always been known as a great place to work, where the well-being of employees comes ahead of mean and nasty bottom-line considerations. The corporate statement trumpets, "Our product is steel, our strength is people." The founding brothers, Clifton and Frank Sherman, saw unions as a social evil and vowed to keep them out by firing organizers in the 1930s, but more particularly, by instituting a program of "welfare capitalism" to win over their employees.

Over the years, this benevolence in HRM became something of a watchword among employees. Not only did employees benefit from profit sharing, a company newspaper, Christmas party, picnics, sports teams, and even, at one point, a choir, but the owners genuinely wanted to keep their workers happy. Most Dofasco employees who worked under Frank Jr. (who took over the company in the early 1960s) remember him as a saintly boss who most of the time sided with the workers over management on personnel issues.

All this made sense in the years of high demand for steel and surplus resources, but things dramatically changed in the late 1980s. In just a decade, almost a third of North America's steel-making capacity was wiped out, and the real problems began with the badly timed decision to purchase Algoma Steel in 1988. Things came to a head in January 1993 when John Mayberry assumed the title of CEO and implemented a textbook corporate turnaround. This included chopping the workforce by a third, wrestling costs to the ground, selling off assets, shuttering ancient facilities, and extensive investing in new technology and training. The good news was that a sufficient economic turnaround occurred to make Dofasco the darling of shareholders and analysts, but the bad news was that this occurred at a high human cost. The problem was that it was very difficult to translate the new economic realities into changed HRM practices in a company that made a legend out of how it treated employees. While Mayberry knew they "had to change the culture," many employees had expectations based on historic ties through the kind and gentle years, now quite out of step with the cutthroat environment of modern steel making.

An illustration of this difficulty is in the case of thirty-four-year-old Mark Sertic, who was dismissed from his position as general labourer when a job-related injury made his tasks difficult to complete. Sertic can show you a 1938 edition of the company newspaper with a picture of his grandfather at work at a Dofasco furnace; his own father worked for the company for thirty-five years. Sertic feels that he fell victim to a new crackdown on the part of Dofasco on injured workers who had been kept on the payroll doing modified duties.

Mayberry recognizes that the changes have made the remaining employees "horribly uncomfortable and nervous," but he considers that the important task he has ahead of him is to get the message to these employees and the public that the worst effects of Dofasco's turnaround moves are over. When asked about the likelihood of a union coming to the company, however, Mayberry comments, "I would take it as a very significant personal failure if we became unionized." In this respect, at least, he still shares the founding values of the company.

Questions

1. How does this case illustrate the impact of globalization on Canadian business, and what are the implications for HRM?
2. Can you think of any other Canadian organizations that face the same culture change difficulties as Dofasco, and are their responses likely to be similar or very different?
3. We are told very little about a specific role for HRM in the changes at Dofasco. Is this because there would be nothing that HRM could contribute to the situation? Discuss your answer.

Testing Your Understanding

How well did you fulfil the learning objectives?

1. Globalization has changed the work of the human resources professional. All of the following statements are globalization issues except
   a. training is often provided through the employing organization.
   b. culture sensitization must be provided, often through the employing organization.
   c. conflict reduction techniques may be needed as workers from different countries are combined into work groups.
   d. management training must include how to deal with workers from many different countries.
   e. in Canadian organizations, HR professionals are responsible for screening future employees to make sure they speak English and share Canadian values.

2. Why has workforce diversity changed the work of the human resources professional?
   a. Most human resources professionals are women and thus, represent a means of correcting past injustices such as pay differences between men and women.
   b. Workers with different backgrounds, values, and expectations have different needs that must be accommodated with different compensation and benefit packages.
   c. Most human resources departments are now also responsible for on-site day care centres.
   d. Laws require quotas for the employment of all minority groups.

   e. Workforce diversity is not an issue for the human resources professional.

3. What employee involvement concepts are accepted in today's organizations?
   a. Delegation is a sign of weakness. Employees need to know that the boss is "in charge" to feel secure.
   b. Participative management gives employees more control over the day-to-day activities of their jobs.
   c. Goals should be set by management and clearly spelled out for each employee.
   d. Don't let employee work teams have responsibility for safety or quality. That action leads to suspicion and mistrust.
   e. Employee involvement can be used to increase productivity, but it stifles creativity and should never be used in a research and development division.

4. Why are human resources departments assuming responsibilities for language training for employees?
   a. Corporate communications may be sent in multiple languages if no single language or group of languages is shared.
   b. The wrong word may cause major ill will if it is interpreted as an insult.
   c. Hiring people with certain skills may necessitate hiring those who don't speak the host company's language.
   d. Global organizations, by definition, require people of different language backgrounds to work together.
   e. Language training is important for all of these reasons.

5. Why are cultural considerations critical to the success of any global business?
   a. Most people want to work with people from other cultures.
   b. Making sure that workers in other countries adhere to Canadian values is an important human resources function.
   c. Managers must be flexible and adaptable to deal with working conditions and social systems throughout the world.
   d. Collective societies stress family values, while individualistic societies stress the work ethic. Therefore, Canadian firms should only do business with organizations in individualistic societies.
   e. It is important to place employees only in positions where they will be most comfortable and familiar.

6. What is the best way to help a multicultural group of individuals work together?
   a. Assign them major projects with other members of their ethnic group.
   b. Pass laws that require them to work together.
   c. Make promotions and raises dependent on working together well.
   d. Engage in cross-cultural team building activities. Provide training on possible tension-causing areas and thus, reduce conflict.
   e. There is no evidence that multicultural work groups have any more conflicts than single-culture work groups.

7. What changes are causing an increased diversity in the Canadian workforce?
   a. Most white males are not going to work in the future.
   b. Baby boomers have glutted the labour market. No one else will be able to get jobs for decades.
   c. Increased globalization and changes in employment laws are bringing more women and racial and ethnic minorities into the labour pool.
   d. Work attitudes change as employees get older.
   e. Anti-gay sentiments are decreasing.

8. Luke, vice-president of human resources for a large, multinational firm headquartered in Canada, is planning major staffing requirements. Today, 80 per cent of the employees in the organization are white males under the age of thirty-five. Which statement is probably true, based on the projected labour pool profiles for the next two decades?
   a. Luke will hire more women in the next decade.
   b. The average age of his employees will decrease in the next decade.
   c. Hiring will probably be restricted to Canadian citizens.
   d. New managers will have to be hired from outside the organization rather than promoted from within.

   e. New managers should be promoted from within.

9. If you were vice-president of a major Canadian corporation and could only do one of the following in the next decade, which action would be most responsive to the future sources of Canadian immigrants?
   a. Offer Spanish language classes. Make sure all company communications are in Spanish, English, and French.
   b. Offer Portuguese language classes. Make sure all company communications are in Portuguese, English, and French.
   c. Offer Russian language classes. Make sure all company communications are in Russian, English, and French.
   d. Offer German language classes. Make sure all company communications are in German, English, and French.
   e. Offer Chinese language classes. Make sure all company communications are in Mandarin, English, and French.

10. Why should the director of human resources for Ford Motor Company consider hiring elementary-school teachers?
    a. Teachers work well with robots on the assembly line.
    b. Teachers work well with the Teamsters on the assembly line.
    c. Teachers who work for the summer go back to their classrooms and make positive comments about the quality of life on the assembly line to elementary-school students, thus reducing the negative image that union workers have with younger people.
    d. Over $200 million a year is currently spent in remedial education by Ford Motor Company. Employees on the payroll with elementary-school teaching credentials would be a good investment.
    e. The mission statement of Ford Motor Company includes a directive to hire significantly from any occupational group that is underemployed.

11. The basis of Deming's pioneering work
    a. was created in Japan.
    b. is about twenty years old.
    c. is that quality can be measured and achieved through a process of statistical controls.
    d. is that workers on the line have more control over the quality of work than the production managers.
    e. all of these.

12. Considering continuous process improvement activities in organizations, should "zero defects" really be a goal?
    a. Yes. Perfection is a reasonable goal.
    b. No. 0.1 per cent errors can be corrected much more efficiently than they can be prevented.

c. Yes. Most industries find this an attainable goal.

d. No. Current levels of 97 per cent accuracy are adequate.

e. Sometimes. For some mistakes, cost benefits cannot be calculated.

13. What's the difference between re-engineering and TQM?

a. Re-engineering involves incremental change focusing on customers, while TQM involves radical change in an effort to redesign the organization.

b. Re-engineering involves radical change, while TQM involves incremental change.

c. Re-engineering is a function of downsizing and restructuring, while TQM focuses on making quantum changes in the organizations' operations.

d. Re-engineering is the application of the tools Deming taught Japanese businesses, while TQM deals with statistical control mechanisms.

e. There is no difference between re-engineering and TQM.

14. Contingent workers offer organizations opportunities to smooth out staffing fluctuations. Which one of the following would not be a reason for an organization to hire contingent workers?

a. Reducing labour costs.

b. Existing skill deficiencies in the workforce.

c. Promoting family-friendly benefits.

d. Replacing core employees who are not productive.

e. Increasing workforce diversity.

15. Teleworking offers several advantages to organizations and to employees. Which one of the following is not considered an advantage of telework?

a. Increased work schedule flexibility.

b. Reduced health and safety regulations.

c. Increased pool of skilled workers.

d. Enhanced job opportunities in depressed areas.

e. All of the above are advantages of telework.

16. Why should an organization be wary of moving towards employee involvement?

a. Involved employees have more self-confidence and are less loyal to the organization.

b. Although involved employees are happier employees, they are less productive employees.

c. Employee involvement can't happen overnight. An organization should schedule time to change and implement this kind of change slowly.

d. Control functions are all but eliminated in an employee-involved organization. Accurate performance data are nearly impossible to collect.

e. All of these statements should be concerns for an organization that is contemplating a move towards empowerment.

Chapter Three

DIVERSITY AND EMPLOYMENT EQUITY

LEARNING OBJECTIVES

AFTER READING THIS CHAPTER, YOU WILL BE ABLE TO:

1. Identify those groups afforded protection under the *Canadian Human Rights Act* of 1985.
2. Discuss the importance of the *Employment Equity Act* of 1996.
3. Describe employment equity or affirmative action plans.
4. Define what is meant by the terms systemic discrimination or adverse impact, adverse treatment, and protected group members.
5. Explain the provisions for maternity leave and job security for women before and after the birth of a child, as well as family and medical leave.
6. Describe how the principle of reasonable accommodation applies to organizations that are reluctant to employ individuals with disabilities (and other individuals protected under human rights legislation).
7. Discuss how a business can protect itself from discrimination charges.
8. Explain the importance to HRM of the *Griggs* v. *Duke Power* case.
9. Define the phenomenon of harassment in general, and sexual harassment in particular, in today's organizations.
10. Discuss what is meant by the terms glass ceiling and glass walls.

What's in a job? For most workers, a job entails specific work activities that are routinely performed. On occasion, because of the dynamic nature of business today, other duties, many too numerous to name, must also be done. These work activities generally take place in the employers' offices where many different people come together to achieve certain goals.

By nature, work environments differ widely. Just as individuals have personalities, each organization and each office has its own culture. Yet there should be one common element to all of them—that is, whatever occurs in the office should be related to organizational efforts. Every once in a while, however, this concept evades an employer, and when it does, it can be a costly lesson. Consider the case of IMP Group International Inc., a privately held limited company located in Halifax which employs approximately three thousand personnel located in seven of the ten Canadian provinces and in the United States, England, and Russia.[1]

In 1987, Michelle Dillman, a seamstress, joined IMP's fabric shop. After six months, she transferred to the sheet metal shop and began training as a technician. Here is where her troubles began. Dillman was the first woman to "invade" this all-male environment, and she quickly fell out with her instructor who waylaid and verbally abused Dillman repeatedly. Of course, that was unacceptable work behaviour, and when she complained to her superiors, management and the union issued a letter warning the supervisor to stop the abuse. A copy of the letter was also placed in the supervisor's personnel file. When she found out that Ken Rowe, the head of IMP, had complied with the supervisor's request to have the letter removed from his personnel file, Dillman filed a complaint with the Nova Scotia Human Rights Commission.

In its ruling, the Nova Scotia Human Rights Commission found that IMP had failed to stop "a pattern of harassment"[2] against Dillman. Far from setting an example, the commission said, IMP had "created a work environment that encouraged such activity."[3] The commission also took strong exception to a decision by IMP not to attend the hearing. It said that IMP's absence showed its "apparent lack of concern over human rights issues in the workplace."[4] IMP was ordered by the commission to undertake a training program in gender sensitivity, to pay Dillman $ 27,040 in damages, and finally, produce a clear and acceptable policy on gender issues.

What does the Dillman case mean for organizations in Canada today? In essence, sexual harassment is a violation of an employee's rights. Employers must post a policy statement concerning sexual harassment in the workplace and ensure that all employees are aware of it. When sexual harassment is alleged, the organization had better investigate it and take appropriate action because failure to do so could leave it legally vulnerable and drastically affect its bottom line.

Introduction

What do VIA Rail, the Canadian Armed Forces, Health Canada, and the Alberta Telephone Company have in common? Each has paid out significant amounts of money for practices that discriminated against women, minorities, and people with disabilities. In Chapter 1, we introduced the concept of federal and provincial legislation as it affects employment practices. In this chapter, we will explore this critical influence to provide an understanding of the legislation. Why? Because it is a fact of doing business. Almost every Canadian organization must abide by the guidelines established in the 1982 *Canadian Charter of Rights and Freedoms*, the 1985 *Canadian Human Rights Act*, the 1996 *Employment Equity Act*, the 1971 *Canada Labour Code*, or the relevant provincial and territorial acts and codes governing employment practices. The importance of such legislation cannot be overstated as the effect of these laws permeates all HRM functions in the organization.

Another frequently cited reason to ensure fair treatment includes the strategic issue of having a diverse workforce. Many organizations realize that managing diversity is the key to future growth.[5] Fair treatment and demonstrating commitment to employment equity may lead to an increase in employee morale, the ability to attract the best-qualified employees (including visible minorities and women), and a good image in the local and national community.

Keep in mind that although our discussion will mostly be limited to federal employment legislation, there are also provincial and municipal laws that go beyond what the federal government requires. Approximately 90 per cent of employees in Canada are covered under provincial and municipal legislation, and 10 per cent under federal legislation. While it is impossible to cover all of these provincial and municipal laws in detail, HR managers must know and understand the additional requirements they face. Ignoring the legal aspects of HRM can result in costly and time-consuming legal struggles, negative attitudes on the part of the Canadian public, and low perceptions of justice that may contribute to lowered morale of employees.

Laws Affecting Discriminatory Practices

Federal and provincial legislation has a common objective: the provision of equal employment opportunities—that is, equal access to a job and fair treatment in a job for all Canadians. Basically, four legal mechanisms affect discriminatory employment practices: the *Canadian Charter of Rights and Freedoms*, the *Canadian Human Rights Act*, the *Employment Equity Act*, and the *Canada Labour Code*.[6] We will discuss these legal mechanisms next. In addition, several legal concepts and principles that have come out of federal, provincial, and municipal legislation will be addressed. A sound understanding of the various laws and legal concepts will help managers to develop and implement non-discriminatory employment policies.

Charter of Rights and Freedoms

Constitution Act Supreme law of Canada enacted in 1982.

The *Canadian Charter of Rights and Freedoms* is part of the *Constitution Act* of 1982, which is the supreme law of Canada. This means that the Constitution has precedence over all other legal mechanisms discussed in this chapter and thus has a tremendous impact on employment practices such as hiring, performance appraisal, compensation, and terms, conditions, or privileges of employment. Any law that is inconsistent with the provisions of the Constitution is, to the extent of the inconsistency, of no force or effect.[7] Under the Constitution, every individual, regardless of race, national or ethnic origin, colour, religion, sex, age, or mental or physical disability, is equal before and under the law and enjoys equal protection and benefit of the law.

Sections 1 to 34 of Part 1 of the *Constitution Act* are known as the *Canadian Charter of Rights and Freedoms (Charter)*. In both spirit and wording, the Charter provides the guidance through which the federal government seeks to ensure the full and equal partnership of all Canadians in the life of the country. The *Charter* states the rights and responsibilities of all citizens. The fundamental freedoms guaranteed by the *Charter* to every Canadian include: (1) freedom of conscience and religion; (2) freedom of thought, belief, opinion, and expression including freedom of the press and other media of communication; (3) freedom of peaceful assembly; and (4) freedom of association.

In addition, the *Charter* identifies several basic rights including: (1) fundamental freedoms; (2) democratic rights; (3) mobility rights; (4) legal rights; (5) equality rights for all individuals; (6) officially recognized languages of Canada; (7) minority language educational rights; and (8) general (e.g., recognition and affirmation of the rights of aboriginal peoples). These rights and freedoms that Canadians enjoy under governments at all levels are not absolute; they are often qualified or limited in order to protect the rights of other individuals. Therefore, the courts often have the delicate task of balancing individual and collective rights. An example is the prohibition of hate propaganda. Hate messages over the telephone are illegal in Canada. In 1993, human rights tribunals and courts ordered the Heritage Front, the Canadian Liberty Net, the Manitoba Knights of the Ku Klux Klan, and the National Knight Network to stop playing recorded hate messages. The messages attacked recent immigrants, Jews, lesbians, and gay men. When some of those responsible refused to comply with a court order, they were sent to jail.[8] Similarly, much to the disappointment of Canadian unions, the rights to bargain collectively and to strike are not fundamental freedoms; rather, these are statutory rights created and regulated by the legislature. Finally, as we will discuss later in more detail, there may be perceived conflicts between the rights guaranteed in the *Charter* and other legislative mechanisms. For example, though the *Charter* gives individuals protection on the basis of age, organizational policies may require police officers and airline pilots to retire at age 60.[9] This is because age may be deemed a justifiable job requirement.

Sections 15(1) and 15(2) of the *Charter* are frequently cited in employment law; these sections lay out the principle of equality rights:

> 15(1) Every individual is equal before and under the law and has the right to the equal protection and equal benefit of the law without discrimination and, in particular, without discrimination based on race, national or ethnic origin, colour, religion, sex, age, or mental or physical disability.
>
> 15(2) Subsection (1) does not preclude any law, program, or activity that has as its object the amelioration of conditions of disadvantaged individuals or groups including those that are disadvantaged because of race, national or ethnic origin, colour, religion, sex, age, or mental or physical disability.

The significance of subsection 15(2) is that it allows for employment equity programs that organizations are encouraged to implement under the *Employment Equity Act*. Thus, the *Charter*'s equality guarantees do not rule out laws and special programs designed to favour individuals (such as aboriginal people, and disabled persons) who may be at a disadvantage in society.

Canadian Human Rights Act

The *Canadian Human Rights Act (CHRA)* gives all Canadians an equal opportunity to work and live without discrimination.[10] All individuals have the right to be treated on the basis of their personal merits without discrimination and to be accorded equality of opportunity. As used in human rights laws, discrimination means making a distinction between certain individuals or groups (including employees and customers) based on a prohibited ground. Under the *CHRA*, it is against the law for any employer and provider of goods or services (e.g., public transportation or restaurants) that falls within federal jurisdiction to make unlawful distinctions based on the following prohibited grounds: (1) race; (2) national or ethnic origin; (3) colour; (4) religion; (5) age; (6) sex (including pregnancy and childbearing); (7) marital status; (8) family status; (9) pardoned criminal conviction; (10) physical or mental disability (including previous or present dependence on alcohol or drugs); and (11) sexual orientation.

On June 5, 1996, the Canadian Parliament passed a bill to ban discrimination against gay men and lesbians in federal agencies and federally regulated companies.[11] Thus, organizations are not allowed to have separate policies for heterosexuals and homosexuals. For example, it is a discriminatory practice to fail to provide employees with same-sex partners with the same employment benefits as those with opposite-sex partners. This constitutes the first federal protection for homosexuals in North America.

The *CHRA* applies to the following employers and service or goods providers: (1) federal departments, agencies, and Crown corporations; (2) television and radio stations including the CBC; (3) Canada Post; (4) the Canadian Armed Forces; (5) chartered banks; (6) national airlines; (7) interprovincial communications and telephone companies; (8) buses and railways that travel between provinces; and (9) other federally regulated industries (e.g., mining operations, or trucking companies providing interprovincial transport).

Note that the ten provinces and two territories have similar human rights acts or codes forbidding discrimination in their areas of jurisdiction. That is, individuals may find protection under provincial or territorial human rights laws in case they are not covered under federal legislation. For example, an organization cannot refuse a female a security employee licence, a necessary condition of her employment, if the administrators are concerned about the possible criminal activities of her husband. If the employee believes that she faced discrimination based on marital status, she can file a complaint with the provincial Human Rights Commission. However, as can be seen in Table 3-1, even though provincial human rights acts or codes in many cases mirror the federal act, there are several differences in the grounds of discrimination prohibited between federal and provincial human rights legislation.

TABLE 3-1 Employment: Prohibited Grounds of Discrimination*

Prohibited Grounds	Federal	British Columbia	Alberta	Saskatchewan	Manitoba	Ontario	Quebec	New Brunswick	Prince Edward Island	Nova Scotia	Newfoundland	Northwest Territories	Yukon
Race or colour	•	•	•	•	•	•	•	•	•	•	•	•	•
Religion or creed	•	•	•	•	•	•	•	•	•	•	•	•	•
Age	•	• (19-65)	• (+18)	• (18-64)	•	• (18-65)	•	•	•	•	• (19-65)	•	•
Sex (incl. pregnancy or childbirth	•	•	•	•	•1	•2	•	•	•3	•	•3	•	•
Marital status	•	•	•	•	•	•	•4	•	•	•	•	•	•
Physical/mental handicap or disability	•	•	•	•	•	•	•	•	•	•	•	•	•
Sexual orientation	•	•		•	•	•	•	•		•	•3		•
National or ethnic origin (incl. Linguistic background	•			•5	•	•6	•	•	•	•	•	•5	•
Family status	•	•	•	•7	•	•	•4			•		•	•
Dependence on alcohol or drugs	•	•3	•3	•3	•3	•3		•3,8	•3	•8			
Ancestry or place of origin		•	•	•	•	•	•					•	•
Political belief		•				•		•		•	•		•
Based on association						•	•	•	•	•			•
Pardoned conviction	•					•	•					•	
Record of criminal conviction		•					•						•
Source of income			•	•9	•					•			
Assignment, attachment or seizure of pay											•		
Social condition/origin							•				•		
Language							•3	•					

Source: Reprinted with permission by the Canadian Human Rights Commission, August 1996.

Harassment on any of the prohibited grounds is considered a form of discrimination.

* Any limitation, exclusion, denial, or preference may be permitted if a bona fide occupational requirement can be demonstrated.
1) Includes gender-determined characteristics.
2) Ontario accepts complaints based on a policy related to female genital mutilation in all social areas on the grounds of sex, place of origin, and/or handicap.
3) Complaints accepted based on policy.
4) Quebec uses the term "civil status".
5) Defined as nationality.
6) Ontario's code includes only "citizenship".
7) Defined as being in a parent-child relationship.
8) Previous dependence only.
9) Defined as "receipt of public assistance".

Threatening, intimidating, or discriminating against someone who has filed a complaint, or hampering a complaint investigation is a violation of provincial human rights codes and at the federal level, is a criminal offence.

69

The following are two examples of discriminatory behaviour under the *CHRA* or provincial human right acts or codes:[12]

1. An employer wants its waitresses to wear skimpy costumes to increase business even though the waitresses complain that the outfits are demeaning and too revealing. The waiters, however, continue to wear regular non-revealing clothing. This use of employees in business promotions constitutes a form of discrimination—exploiting female employees' sexuality while treating male employees differently.
2. A British Columbia human rights tribunal recently found that the British Columbia Ministry of Municipal Affairs discriminated against a female employee because of her sex when it refused to allow her to breastfeed her child in the workplace.

Human rights legislation, however, provides for exceptions (Section 15 of the *CHRA*).[13] Examples of exceptions include bona fide occupational requirements, mandatory requirement, equal pay guidelines, and maternity and childcare.

Bona Fide Occupational Requirement (BFOR) A particular discriminatory practice that is reasonably necessary to assume the efficient safe, and economical performance of the job.

Bona fide occupational requirement (BFOR) It is not a discriminatory practice if any refusal, exclusion, expulsion, suspension, limitation, specification, or preference in relation to any employment is established by an employer to be based on a bona fide occupational requirement. In other words, the employer can show that it has acted in good faith and that a particular discriminatory practice is reasonably necessary to assure the efficient, economical, and safe performance on the job.[14] For example, in 1985, the Supreme Court of Canada held that Canadian National Railway's rule that all coach yard workers wear hard hats constituted a BFOR regardless of the special circumstances of the complainant who was a turbaned Sikh and could not wear other head apparatus in accordance with his religion.[15] Wearing a hard hat is a requirement for all workers in the occupation and not susceptible to individual application. Similarly, a minimum hearing standard policy for RCMP recruits, even though it constitutes discrimination based on the basis of disability, constitutes a BFOR. The lack of such a standard would increase the risk run by the recruits themselves and endanger the safety of constables, their co-workers, and the general public.[16]

We should state here unequivocally that any test used in making employment decisions must measure the knowledge and skills required in a job fairly in order not to discriminate against certain groups.[17] If an employer cannot show that a particular rule or procedure is necessary given the nature of the job, it will be compelled under the law to drop the practice. For example, a company cannot hire a maintenance employee using the requirements of an intelligence test and a high-school diploma unless these criteria can be demonstrated to relate to performance on the job in question. This guideline was adopted in a landmark United States Supreme Court case, namely, *Griggs v. Duke Power Company*,[18] which significantly affected selection procedures in both the United States and Canada.

Griggs v. Duke Power Landmark U.S. Supreme Court decision stating that tests must fairly measure the knowledge or skills required for a job.

Sometimes, individuals are excluded from performing a job where it would be possible to accommodate their particular needs so as to allow them to perform the job without causing undue hardship on the goals of the organization. Under human rights legislation, however, the employer is under a duty to accommodate a potential employee, short of undue hardship (e.g., disruption of collective agreements, problems of morale of other employees, and interchangeability of workforce and facilities).[19] Thus, if the employee is qualified to perform the essential tasks of a job, and if the financial costs of accommodating the employee's disability would not create an undue hardship on the organization, accommodation is required.[20] For example, employers can be ordered by

Undue Hardship The accommodating an employee's disability or needs does not exceed reasonable costs (e.g. financial costs, disruption of collective agreement, or work scheduling).

the courts to accommodate employees with AIDS and those who are HIV positive so that they may continue to work. Possible accommodations include changes in work schedules and job responsibilities, reduced work hours, time off for medical appointments, transfer to a different job to reduce stress, and installation of needed equipment, such as an elevator. Similarly, if special hearing or reading equipment is available and could assist an individual who is legally deaf or blind in doing the job, then the company must provide this equipment if that accommodation does not present an undue financial hardship. In Canada, reasonable accommodation is required for all aspects covered under the federal and some provincial human rights law. Therefore, reasonable accommodation also includes measures such as allowing shifts excluding Saturdays and Sundays for religious reasons, allowing mothers to breastfeed babies, and allowing translators for non-English-speaking applicants.

Reasonable Accommodation Making adjustment to the work or workplace so that individuals with particular needs can effectively perform their job.

Finally, we should mention that once an employment practice has been established as a BFOR, there is typically no need for the employer to accommodate the special circumstances of the individual. For example, an applicant for the position of a special airport constable who wears a hearing aid might be turned down because the type of activity required involves a sufficient risk of loss or breakage that it is reasonable to establish a standard based on uncorrected hearing for purposes of recruitment.[21]

Mandatory Retirement A worker can be retired at the age that is considered "normal" for the kind of work involved. For example, police officers and firefighters are often forced to retire at age sixty. Backers of this policy say older workers are often unfit (e.g., the risk of cardiovascular disease and a decline of aerobic capacity) and injury prone. In contrast, foes say the policy is discriminating because age is not a true indicator of job fitness.[22] Similarly, both the Human Rights Commission and the Human Rights Tribunal have ruled that mandatory retirement at the age of sixty for pilots-in-command on international flights does not constitute age discrimination.[23] Age sixty is a benchmark after which the International Civil Aviation Organization believes that medical research can show that the necessary skills to handle an emergency may be lacking or to significantly decline.[24] Thus, using age sixty as the determining factor, airlines are permitted to remove a pilot-in-command at that age for public safety reasons. However, a sixty-year-old pilot might decide to be a flight engineer, and the individual may apply for the job if an opening exists. Failure on the part of the organization to allow its retiring pilots to do so is in violation of the *CHRA*. Similarly, a teachers' union can lay a discrimination complaint with the provincial Human Rights Commission if cash-strapped school boards prevent older, experienced, and hence costlier, substitute teachers from getting full-time jobs.[25]

Mandatory Retirement The age that is considered "normal" for the kind of work involved.

Mandatory retirement, however, may seem particularly unfair to those individuals who have taken time out of the workforce because of childcare responsibilities and for those who have experienced extensive periods of unemployment.[26] For example, if forced into retirement, these individuals may well have difficulty building up enough pension credits to live comfortably. Recently, the Canadian Human Rights Commission took the position that "compulsory retirement clearly discriminates against those who are capable of working and want to do so. It is high time this form of discrimination ceased to be protected by the *Canadian Human Rights Act*."[27] Only time will tell what happens to mandatory retirement provisions.

Comparable Worth Equal pay for similar jobs, jobs similar in skills, responsiblility, working conditions, and effort.

Equal Pay Guidelines All parts of Canada have some form of equal pay legislation prohibiting employers from paying male and female employees differently if they perform identical, similar, or substantially similar work. Some jurisdictions—namely, the federal government, Manitoba, Nova Scotia, New Brunswick, Ontario, Prince Edward Island, and Quebec—have gone one step further. There, it is discriminatory for employers under federal jurisdiction to pay different wages to men and women performing work of equal value; men and women employed in the same establishment who perform jobs of equal value must be paid the same wages. Equal pay law was introduced because of the large differences between the earnings of men and women. In 1995, women working full-time still made an average of only 75 cents for every dollar earned by men.[28]

Several reasons exist for the discrepancy in pay between men and women.[29] First, one can attribute the wage gap to deliberate policies in the past—wage laws passed in the first decades of this century effectively set women's base salaries about a third lower than men's. Second, society has traditionally undervalued jobs filled predominantly by women. In years past, many jobs were formally viewed as being male- or female-oriented. For example, librarians, nurses, and elementary schoolteachers were considered typical jobs for women. In contrast, police officers, truck drivers, and top management positions were regarded as the domain of men. Historically, this attitude resulted in the traditional female-oriented jobs being paid significantly less than the male-oriented positions. This differentiation eventually led to concerns over gender-based pay systems, commonly referred to as the **comparable worth** issue.[30] For instance, a nurse may be judged to have a job comparable to that of a police officer. Both must be trained, both are licensed to practice, both work under stressful conditions, and both must exhibit high levels of effort, but generally, they are not paid the same. Under comparable worth, estimates of the importance of each job are used in determining and equating pay structures. Thus, comparable worth translates to equal pay of equal value.

The value or worth of a job can be calculated using job evaluations which rate the skill (e.g., intellectual and physical qualifications acquired by education and training), responsibility (e.g., technical, financial, and human resources), physical and intellectual effort required, and working conditions (e.g., health hazards and physical danger).[31] The total point score received by each job represents its value. This process will be described in more detail in Chapter 13: "Rewards and Compensation."

According to the notion of equal pay for work of equal value, pay structures should be based solely on the value of the job. The result is that dissimilar jobs equivalent in terms of responsibility, skills, knowledge, and abilities are paid similarly. Examples of jobs that might be of equal value, and hence should be paid the same, are nursing assistants and electricians or secretaries and maintenance staff.

It should be recognized, however, that a difference in wages between men and women performing work of equal value in an establishment may be justified by different performance ratings, employment experience or seniority, internal labour shortages and surpluses, the external labour market, rehabilitation assignments, and regional wage rates. Thus, differences in wages for jobs of equal or comparable worth do not always, by definition, imply discrimination. However, if gender dominance is the cause of the difference, then the equal pay statutes are being violated.

At the federal level, the enforcement of this section of the *CHRA* is mostly based on a complaint-driven model. In contrast, several jurisdictions, including

Manitoba and the Yukon, have implemented mandatory compliance models. Over the past several years, the Canadian Human Rights Commission has reported some impressive pay equity achievements.[32] In 1991, a human rights tribunal awarded $6 million to three hundred community health workers on First Nations reserves. In 1995, a settlement was offered to 1,700 nurses and others for $12.7 million a year in lost wages. In 1998, the Canadian Human Rights Tribunal ruled that the government had been underpaying its female workers for 13 years; the required settlement was established to cost at least $3 billion.

Maternity and Childcare In the past, the Human Rights Commission and the Human Rights Tribunal have ruled that pregnancy provides a perfectly legitimate health-related reason for not working and hence, should be treated like other health-related causes of inability to work.[33] Not to compensate for pregnancy and raising children would contradict the purpose of human rights laws, which is to remove unfair disadvantages suffered by certain groups. Furthermore, while society in general benefits from procreation, organizations cannot place the major costs of procreation on one group—women. Women should not bear a disproportionate share of the burden involved in raising children.

Under the *CHRA*, companies under federal jurisdiction may not terminate a female employee for being pregnant, refuse to make an employment decision based on one's pregnancy, or deny insurance coverage to the individual. The law also requires organizations to offer the employee a reasonable period of

An employer does not have to pay any wages to a woman on pregnancy leave, which is seventeen or eighteen weeks according to the Canada Labour Code. The employee may, however, be eligible for maternity benefits.

time off work. Under the *Labour Standards of the Canada Labour Code*, a pregnant woman is entitled to pregnancy leave, usually consisting of seventeen to eighteen consecutive weeks.[34] The employer does not have to pay pregnant women any wages when they are on pregnancy leave; however, eligible employees can apply for maternity benefits during their pregnancy leave. Every province has parallel legislation and similar time limits. At the end of this leave, the employee is entitled to return to work without loss of seniority or benefits. If the exact job is unavailable, a similar one must be provided. Also, note that parental leave is a right new parents (mothers, fathers, and adopting parents) have under *Labour Standards*; they can take time off when a child comes into their care. Both parents are entitled to a combined parental leave of up to twenty-four weeks, but major differences exist between provinces. Finally, the employer can grant a female employee special leave or benefits in connection with pregnancy or childbirth or grant employees special leave or benefits to assist them in the care of their children.

Finally, the *Canada Labour Code* provides for family matters such as care for a sick family member, death of an immediate family member (bereavement leave), and one's own illness (sick leave and work-related illnesses and injury). For example, an employer may not dismiss, lay off, demote, or discipline any employee because of an absence due to a family-related absence or a work-related illness. An employee is protected for any absence not exceeding twelve weeks. Generally, employees are guaranteed their current job or an equivalent one upon their return to work.

Employment Equity Act

Employment equity, a phrase coined by Judge Rosalie Abella who chaired the Royal Commission on Employment Opportunities for Groups and Individuals,[35] simply means fairness in the workplace. That is, employment and promotion opportunities should be based solely on the ability to do the job. No one should face employment barriers by virtue of being a woman, an aboriginal, disabled, or a visible minority. The fact is, however, that qualified members of these four groups have traditionally been hired, employed, compensated, and promoted at rates well below their availability in the labour market.[36] For example, the unemployment rate for people with disabilities is somewhere between 60 and 80 per cent, which is unacceptably high.[37] Excluding people with disabilities costs Canada millions of dollars, especially in disability benefits. Reducing employment barriers (and putting an end to discrimination) would mean big savings in the long run, but more importantly, it would enable people with disabilities to become more productive and self-sufficient.

Employment equity legislation benefits society by helping to create a climate of respect for the dignity and worth of all citizens in which all citizens are able to contribute to the development of the community.[38] The University of Manitoba, for example, recognizes that in developing an employment equity workplace, it enhances its ability to attract high-calibre academic and support staff and thereby increases its competitiveness in the academic community. The university has thus agreed to follow the employment equity guidelines established by the federal government.

The aim of the *Employment Equity Act (EEA)* is essentially threefold[39]: (1) to draw attention to some obvious inequalities in an employer's past treatment of designated group members; (2) to convince them of the rightness and the benefits of doing something about it; and (3) to work with them to explore how this can best be done.

Employment Equity Act (EEA) Aimed to remove employment barriers and achieve equality in the workplace so that no qualified individual (woman, aboriginal people, visible minority, or a person with a handicap is denied employment opportunities.

Thus, employers are ultimately required to remove employment barriers and to achieve equality in the workplace so that no qualified person is denied employment opportunities. Federal and some provincial governments (Ontario and Quebec) have passed equity legislation. In 1995, the Ontario Tory government repealed the *EEA* passed by the previous NDP government, replacing it with Equal Opportunity Plan which encourages everyone—employers, employees, and government—to work in partnership to build workplaces where merit is the basis for employment decisions. New Brunswick does not have a formal employment equity act; however, the *Human Rights Act* of New Brunswick allows for employment equity programs.

The *CHRA* and the *EEA* have the same overall goal, but the requirements under the *EEA* are generally more stringent than those of human rights legislation which only require the employer to respond to a specific complaint (e.g., compensate for lost wages and humiliation and job reinstatement). The *EEA* requires proactive, not reactive, steps to reduce inequities in the workplace. As we will discuss later in more detail, employment equity programs often require an extensive overhaul of an organization's HR system.

The new and more vigorous *EEA*, which came into force on October 24, 1996, updates the legislation that had been in effect for over a decade. It is hoped that the new *EEA* will speed up the employment equity progress since the results under the 1986 *EEA* had been uneven and unacceptably slow.[40] While progress was achieved for women, visible minorities remained severely under-represented in the public service. Similarly, the failure to make real inroads in the employment levels of aboriginal peoples and people with disabilities raised questions about the road ahead under the old *EEA*.[41]

The updated *EEA* applies to the federal public service, Crown corporations, and federally regulated private sector employers with on hundred or more employees (e.g., the post office, national airlines, railroads, interprovincial bus and trucking companies, chartered banks, and telephone and broadcasting companies). In addition, the *EEA* applies to contractors who bid for goods and services contracts with the federal government valued at $200,000 or more (the **Federal Contractors Program**). Under the new *EEA*, employers are required to[42]:

- Provide employees with a questionnaire which allows them to indicate whether they belong to one of the four designated groups.
- Identify jobs in which the percentage of designated group members falls below their availability in the labour market (taking into consideration factors such as qualification, location, and industry).
- Communicate information on employment equity to its employees and consult and collaborate with employee representatives.
- Identify possible barriers in existing employment systems which may be limiting employment opportunities of designated group members.
- Develop an employment equity plan aimed at promoting a fully equitable workplace. This plan must include positive policies and practices, measures to remove employment barriers, timetables and goals based on availability of qualified workers in the labour market, and must be sufficient to achieve reasonable progress towards a representative workplace. For example, if the work force resembles the community for all job classifications, then the organization is demonstrating that its equity plan is working.
- Make all reasonable efforts to implement plans.
- Monitor the changing composition of the internal workforce over time, and review and revise plans from time to time.
- Prepare an annual statistical report on employment equity data and activities that is available to the public.

Federal Contractors Program
Companies that bid for goods or services contracts with the federal government (valued at $200,000 or more a year) must comply with the *EEA*.

•

Auditing Process The CHRC inspects whether and ensures that companies covered under the *EEA* comply with this law.

Progress under the old *EEA* was slow, in part because it lacked the proverbial teeth of enforcement. The 1996 *EEA* gives the Canadian Human Rights Commission the authority to ensure compliance through an auditing process.[43] Audits will look at issues such as how employers surveyed their workforce, measures adopted to provide improved opportunities to members of under-represented groups (e.g., offering telephone services and sign language interpretation for people who are deaf or hearing impaired and providing information in large print or Braille), and consultation with employees and unions. If the audit shows that one or more objectives of employment equity has not been met, the commission and the employer will work together to negotiate a solution to this problem. The commission, with the assistance of the Canadian Human Rights Tribunal, may also issue a direction should persuasion and negotiation fail. For example, in *Chander and Joshi v. Department of Health and Welfare*, the Canadian Human Rights Tribunal ordered that 18 per cent of all promotions to senior management positions in Health Canada for the next five years go to visible minorities.[44] This was because the tribunal concluded that the department had discriminated against the complainants because of their race, national or ethnic origin, and colour. Similarly, in what has become a landmark case, the Canadian Human Rights Tribunal ruled that Canadian National Railways (CN) had discriminated against women in the St. Lawrence region who were seeking employment in non-traditional blue-collar jobs.[45] Subsequently, CN was ordered that one out of every four new hires into unskilled blue-collar jobs had to be a woman until women represented 13 per cent, the national percentage for women working in equivalent jobs.

In summary, as it exists today, the *EEA* stipulates that organizations must do more than just discontinue discriminatory practices. Organizations are expected to actively promote the entry and retention of members of the four designated groups to correct past injustices in our employment processes. For example, BC Telephone Company joined with the Native Education Centre and the Vancouver Vocational Institute and Access Ability to offer work experience programs for aboriginals and disabled people.[46] Alternatively, organizations may give preference to minority group members in employment decisions. This action is commonly referred to as affirmative action. By implementing such temporary employment equity programs, many employers are helping to bring about a workplace that truly reflects society or the demographics of the area.

Affirmative action Some individuals would have one believe that the inequities reflected in the employment statistics are somehow self-correcting. However, the Royal Commission on Equity in Employment concluded that[47]:

> It is not that individuals in the designated groups are inherently unable to achieve equality on their own; it is that the obstacles in their way are so formidable and self-perpetuating that they cannot be overcome without intervention. It is both intolerable and insensitive if we simply wait and hope the barriers will disappear with time. Equality in employment will not happen unless we make it happen….

Examples of barriers that the Royal Commission is referring to include higher hiring requirements for individuals in designated groups, lower performance appraisals for the same performance, and less ability to use benefits such as educational reimbursements (e.g., some people cannot afford upfront costs of education).

Employment equity legislation and the resulting affirmative action programs, have been controversial. There are several misperceptions about federal and provincial approaches to the implementation of employment equity programs. Programs to foster the careers of women and minorities have grown immensely, but while this action was needed to correct past abuses, what about the white male?[48] Some white males feel that affirmative action plans work against them. In some situations, this feeling has resulted in less commitment and loyalty to the organization,[49] or to charges of reverse discrimination. As a result of employment equity programs, some people argue, they are now facing discrimination. In particular, individuals may believe that employers promote a member of a protected group over a more qualified individual who is not a member of a protected group. Furthermore, individuals have interpreted quotas as meaning that one is no longer treating people as equals but rather as members of a group,[50] and that, qualifications and merit are therefore secondary. However, discrimination based on any of the prohibited grounds is illegal under human rights legislation. Thus, anyone who believes he or she suffers from discrimination can seek protection under the appropriate legislation. In addition, in order to correct the inequities in the workplace, the *EEA* does not impose arbitrary quotas of under-represented groups.[51] Instead, realistic goals or targets and timetables are set for measuring progress in hiring employees from the four designated groups. The process of setting goals does not mean individuals will lose their jobs to make room for members of the four designated groups. Instead, goals are based on predicted new employment opportunities. In hiring individuals from designated groups, applicants should be considered only if there is a reason to believe that they will perform successfully on the job. In the world of business, tokenism, or putting someone in a job solely because he or she is a member of a designated group, does not make good sense.

Thus, in operating an employment equity program, a few key issues arise. First of all, the company must know what the job requires in terms of skills, knowledge, and abilities (see "What If"). Candidates are then evaluated on how well they meet these criteria, and if they do, they are essentially qualified to successfully perform the job. Nowhere under the *EEA* does the federal government require an organization to hire unqualified workers. They do require organizations to actively search for qualified minorities to be able to show significant improvements in hiring and promoting members of the four designated categories or justify why external factors prohibited them from achieving their employment equity goals.

Throughout much of this discussion, we have addressed practices that are designed to assure equal employment opportunity for all individuals, but how do we know whether equal employment programs are operating properly? The answer to that question may lie in the concept of adverse (disparate) impact.

Adverse (Disparate) Impact Adverse impact, sometimes referred to as systemic discrimination, can be described as anything that results in a greater rejection rate (e.g., in selection, performance appraisal, promotion, training opportunities, and compensation) for a minority group than it does for the majority group in the occupation. Adverse impact is an example of unintentional discrimination. For example, in what has become a landmark case, the Supreme Court of Canada found in 1985 that Theresa O'Malley was discriminated against because of her religion.[52] Her full-time employment was terminated because she refused to work Friday evenings and Saturdays because her religion required strict observance of the sabbath from sundown Friday to sundown Saturday. Accordingly,

Affirmative Action A practice in organizations that goes beyond discontinuance of discriminatory practices, including actively seeking, hiring, and promoting minority group members and women.

Reverse Discrimination People, in particular White males, feel the victim of *EEA* programs and claim that as a result of these programs they are now discriminated against.

Adverse (Disparate) Impact A consequence of an employment practice that results in a greater rejection rate for a minority group than it does for the majority group in the occupation.

Systemic Discrimination A seemingly neutral employment practice discriminates (unintentionally) against one or more protected groups.

●

Adverse (Disparate) Treatment An employment situation where protected group members receive different treatment than other employees in matters like performance evaluations, promotions, etc.

Protected Group Member Any individual who is afforded protection under employment discrimination laws.

using the requirement of working Friday evenings and Saturdays had the effect of reducing the job opportunities for this group of people. The concepts of adverse impact or systemic discrimination, then, result from a seemingly neutral employment practice. There is no intention to discriminate, but specific organizational procedures allow it to happen. In this case, Simpsons-Sears had discriminated against O'Malley on the basis of religion. As mentioned previously, if the employer does not make a reasonable attempt to accommodate the religious practice of its workforce, it can be found guilty of violating the *CHRA*.

Adverse (Disparate) Treatment There is another issue that differs from adverse impact but follows a similar logic. This is called adverse (disparate) treatment. Adverse treatment occurs when members of a protected group (those afforded protection under discrimination laws) receive different treatment than other employees.[53] For example, if protected group members receive fewer organizational rewards, adverse treatment may have occurred. Direct and intentional discrimination often play a role in adverse treatment. For example, a woman (and not a man) may be quizzed about childcare, and depending on her answers, she may not receive a promotion or be given a coveted assignment.

Guarding Against Discrimination Practices

Facing a number of laws and regulations, it is critical for HRM departments to implement practices that are non-discriminatory. Recall from our earlier discussion that discrimination in employment may stem from a decision that is based on factors other than those relevant to the job. Should that occur frequently, the organization may face charges that it discriminates against some members of a protected group. Determining what constitutes discrimination, however, typically requires more than one individual being adversely affected. To determine if discrimination occurred, one of four tests can be used: the four-fifths rule, restricted policies, geographic comparisons, and the McDonnell-Douglas Test.[54]

Determining Discriminatory Practices

The Four-Fifths Rule A rough indicator of discrimination, this rule requires that the number of minority members that a company hires must be at least 80 per cent of the majority members in the population hired.

The Four-fifths Rule One of the first measures of determining potentially discriminatory practices is to use a rule of thumb called the four-fifths rule. This rule is not a definition of discrimination, but a practical device to draw the attention of the enforcement agencies to serious discrepancies in hiring and promotion rates or other employment decisions.[55] To see how the four-fifths rule works, suppose we have two pools of applicants for jobs as sales associates—forty are members of the majority and fifteen, of the minority population.[56] The minority population can be any group including women, visible minorities, aboriginal peoples, and even males. For example, males can be the minority group in occupations such as flight attendants and secretaries. After the testing and interview process, the following number of people are hired: twenty-two majority and eight minority members. Is the organization in compliance? Table 3-2 provides the analysis. In this case, yes, it is, because the ratio of minority to majority members is 80 per cent or greater (the four-fifths rule). So, even though fewer minority members were hired, no apparent discrimination has occurred. Table 3-2 also shows the analysis of an organization not in compliance.

Remember, whenever the four-fifths rule is violated, it only indicates the possibility that discrimination may have occurred. Should the analysis show that the

What If:

HRM in a De-Jobbed Organization

One of the basic premises of human resources management is the requirement that an organization must "hire right." Right, in these cases, means hiring individuals who possess the necessary skills, knowledge, and abilities in order to successfully perform the essential elements of the job. These skills, knowledge, and abilities are identified through a process of analysing jobs, and that information is then translated into a document that describes the job and the requisite skills in detail.

Yet, as we saw in Chapter 2, a fundamental issue of the new de-jobbed organization will be the realization that jobs, if they exist, will be ill defined, if they are defined at all. Accordingly, it will be difficult to pinpoint precisely what specific skills, knowledge, and abilities will be needed to perform the variety of ever-changing tasks. So, what effect will this have on hiring, and more importantly, on equal employment opportunity?

A basic tenet of the employment equity laws is the concern that employment practices do not create an adverse impact. HRM practitioners attempt to meet that requirement by selecting the best qualified applicant who meets the essential requirements of the job. Yet that may be, at best, a toss of the dice if organizations are unable to describe their jobs. Consequently, what will we be looking at in the next decade as a means of ensuring that discriminatory practices do not exist?

Furthermore, we recognize that in a de-jobbed organization, more and more tasks will be performed by contingent workers—the part-time or independent contracting worker. Will employment equity laws have to be changed to reflect this new cadre of the workforce, or will the laws no longer have the effect that they do now in guiding HRM activities? On the one hand, we can point to the fact that employers will hire smarter, hiring those contingent workers who can successfully perform the tasks. Successful performance, then, will be the key. But how will we know if certain groups are being adversely affected in the workplace? Will employers have to extend employment regulations and affirmative action programs to their independent contractors? Will reporting requirements change to reflect this de-jobbed phenomenon? The answer is unknown at this time, but it would seem reasonable to predict that organizations will have to pay particular attention to this concern. If employment practices revert to the blatant discrimination of the pre-1986 era and organizations fail to police themselves, societal pressure to enact some sort of "protective employment" legislation is bound to occur. History has taught us that lesson very well.

Source: The stimulus for this thought piece comes from William Bridges, "The End of the Job," *Fortune* (September 19, 1994), pp. 62-74.

ratio of minority to majority members is less than 80 per cent, then more elaborate statistical testing is needed to confirm or reject that there was an adverse impact. Many factors can enter into the picture. For instance, if Company A finds a way to keep most minority group members from applying in the first place, it will only have to hire a few of them to meet its four-fifths rule, but if Company B actively seeks out minority group applicants, although it hires more than Company A, it still may not meet the four-fifths rule.

TABLE 3-2   Applying the Four-Fifths Rule

In Compliance						
Majority Group (MAJ) = 40 applicants			*Minority Group (MIN) = 15 applicants*			
Item	*Number*	*Per cent*	*Item*	*Number*	*Per cent*	*%Min/%Maj*
Passed Test	30	75%	Passed Test	11	73%	73%/75% = 97%
Passed Interview	22	73%	Passed Interview	8	72%	72%/73% = 98%
Hired	22	100%	Hired	8	100%	100%/100% = 100%
Analysis	22/40 = 55%		Analysis	8/15 = 53%		
Passed Test	30	75%	Passed Test	11	73%	73%/75% = 97%
Passed Interview	26	86%	Passed Interview	4	36%	36%/86% = 41%
Hired	26	100%	Hired	4	100%	100%/100% = 100%
Analysis	26/40 = 65%		Analysis	4/15 = 26%		
Ratio of Minority/Majority 26%/65% = 40%						

Restricted Policy   An HRM policy that results in the exclusion of a class of individuals.

Restricted Policy A restricted policy infraction occurs whenever an enterprise's HRM activities result in the exclusion of a class of individuals. For instance, assume a company is downsizing and laying off primarily individuals who are over age forty and at the same time, is recruiting for selected positions on university campuses only. Because of economic difficulties, this company wants to keep salaries low by hiring people just entering the workforce. Those over the age of forty, who were making higher salaries, are not given the opportunity to even apply for these new jobs. By these actions, a restricted policy has occurred—that is, through its hiring practice (intentional or not), a class of individuals (in this case, those protected by age discrimination legislation) has been excluded from consideration.

Geographical Comparisons A third means of testing discriminatory claims is through the use of a geographic comparison. In this instance, the characteristics of the qualified pool of applicants in an organization's hiring market is compared to the characteristics of its employees. If the organization has a proper mix of individuals at all levels in the organization that reflects its recruiting market, then the company is in compliance. The key factor here is the qualified pool according to varying geographic areas.

Some authors suggest using the appropriate labour pool and the four-fifths rule together such that the percentage of minority employees in a job should be compared with the percentage of minority employees in the relevant labour pool. If minorities in the organization are less than four-fifths of the available representation, then there is an indication of discrimination. For example, suppose that 20 per cent of the available managers are female, but the company has only 10 per cent female managers. Ten per cent is half (.50) of 20 per cent, which is less than four-fifths (.80). Therefore, we can conclude that discrimination may have occurred.

McDonnell-Douglas Test Named for the *McDonnell-Douglas Corp. v. Green* United States Supreme Court case,[57] this test provides a means of establishing a solid case.[58] Four components that must exist include: (1) the individual is a member of a protected group; (2) the individual applied for a job for which he or she was qualified; (3) the individual was rejected; and (4) the enterprise, after rejecting this applicant, continued to seek other applicants with similar qualifications.[59]

If these four conditions are met, an allegation of discrimination is supported, and it is up to the company to refute the evidence by providing a reason for such action. Should that explanation be acceptable to an investigating body, the protected group member must then show that the reason used by the company is inappropriate.

If any of the above four tests are met, the company might find itself having to defend its practices. In the next section, we'll explain how a complaint of discrimination can be filed with the Canadian Human Rights Commission and how an organization can defend its practices.

Providing a Response to a Charge of Discrimination

Whether we like it or not, the equality of opportunity that Canadians believe to be basic to our society is not always available to everyone. Under the *CHRA*, employees could sue for discrimination and also seek punitive and compensating damages.

In some situations, discrimination is relatively easy to observe. For example, if an employer comes right out and says you were not hired for the job because you tested HIV positive or you have AIDS, you know that this is direct and intentional discrimination. HIV/AIDS is considered a disability and thus one of the grounds of discrimination prohibited under the *CHRA*. If challenged, the burden is on the employer to prove to the human rights investigator that the rule

An AIDS ribbon. HIV/AIDS is considered a disability and thus one of the grounds of discrimination prohibited under the CHRA.

of "no HIV/AIDS person can be employed in this job" is valid in application to all individuals with HIV/AIDS. That is, all individuals with HIV/AIDS are unable to do the work.

However, discrimination can be more subtle and hence, harder to stop. For example, an employer may not mention your pardoned criminal conviction or sexual orientation but may say you did not get the job because you would not fit in with the culture of the organization. Such allegations and suspicions are particularly difficult to prove, and complaints of discrimination based on the grounds of disability, national or ethnic origin, and race are therefore frequently dismissed for lack of evidence.

Finally, as discussed earlier, particular employment practices may result in adverse impact. Though the days of purposely excluding certain individuals from jobs are over for the most part, a long-standing rule that appears to be neutral and to apply equally to all employees (e.g., the requirement of a high-school diploma) may unintentionally discriminate against members of protected groups. Thus, discrimination of this type can be disguised in the way the HR system works.

If individuals believe that they are discriminated against, they can do something about it. For example, if a situation such as a sexual harassment joke offends people or makes them feel uncomfortable, they should speak to the people involved and attempt to resolve the problem on the spot. What at first may seem to be discrimination or harassment might just be a misunderstanding. For example, if the manager does not provide a clear rationale for a poor performance appraisal, an individual may erroneously conclude that he or she is the victim of discrimination. Many employers have policies against discrimination or harassment, and there may be a union or company grievance procedure with a specific contact person that employees can follow.

If these two steps do not lead to satisfactory results, individuals may want to contact the Canadian Human Rights Commission (CHRC) or the appropriate provincial body. The CHRC looks into allegations of discrimination and helps create equality of opportunity. Human rights legislation in all jurisdictions provides for the establishment of human rights commissions to enforce that legislation. Individuals must file a complaint within one year of the discriminatory practice.

Enforcing Employment Equity

Federal and provincial human rights commissions are responsible for enforcing employment equity legislation.

Canadian Human Rights Commission (CHRC)

The CHRC administers the *Canadian Human Rights Act (CHRA)*, and ensures that the principles of equal opportunity and non-discrimination are followed in all areas of federal jurisdiction. Specifically, the mandate of the CHRC includes:

1. Receiving, investigating, and conciliating complaints of discrimination in employment and in provision of services based on the ground enumerated in the *CHRA*. Table 3-3 lists the number and type of complaints received by the CHRC between 1994 and 1997. The CHRC may also choose to start an investigation on its own if it feels that there are sufficient grounds for a finding of a discriminatory practice. This is what the Ontario Human Rights Commission did when they accused the Toronto Fire Fighters Association of encouraging unfair hiring practices.[60]

Meet

Monique Lanteigne
Côte St. Luc, Quebec Fire Department

Monique Lanteigne has been battling fires in Côte St. Luc, Quebec since 1986, working with a team of eight other firefighters—all men. In fact, when she was hired, Ms Lanteigne was the only female firefighter in Quebec. "I did not choose this job because I wanted to be the first woman firefighter," insists Ms Lanteigne, "I choose it because it was something I wanted to do." Nevertheless, she is something of a pioneer in one of the most male-dominated professions in Canada where only about 0.01 per cent of firefighters are women.

Employment equity is one of the most important issues facing the human resources profession in Canada today, and nowhere is it more fraught with controversy than in the nation's fire departments.

In Toronto, for example, there was an uproar when in 1997, forty new positions were filled from a pool of 160 applicants by a random draw. This resulted in all but three of the jobs going to white males. Some councillors and human rights groups had argued that the eleven women and minority candidates in the pool should have been hired first. The Ontario Human Rights Commission launched an investigation.

The physical requirements for becoming a firefighter were so stringent that very few women were able to qualify. Some have argued that the tests are more rigorous than they need to be and therefore exclude women unfairly. They point out that once hired, firefighters are not asked to keep to the same physical standards they had to meet on applying.

Meanwhile, the few women who have become part of this courageous profession continue to meet its challenges. "I love my job," said Ms Lanteigne. "I will continue as long as I am physically able to do it."

Sources: Montreal Gazette, June 17, 1996, E3; *Toronto Star*, December 17, 1997, A1.

---

2. Investigating complaints alleging inequities in pay between men and women who are performing work of equal value.

3. Monitoring the annual reports filed by federally regulated employers under the *EEA* and, where appropriate, taking action under the *CHRA*. The commission files its annual report with the minister of justice who tables it before Parliament.

4. Monitoring programs, policies, and legislation affecting designated groups to ensure that their human rights are protected.

5. Developing and conducting information programs to promote public understanding of the *CHRA* and the role and activities of the CHRC. The CHRC consults on a regular basis with community groups, educators, employers, unions, and provincial human rights commissions, and provides human rights information to the general public via the media (e.g., speaking engagements, Internet, and public events). An example of its recent information activities includes the development of a poster called "Stop the Hatred" and an Internet game "Erasing the Hydra of Hate."[61] Both initiatives were aimed at educating young people about racism and hate propaganda. The "Stop the Hatred" poster was developed in collaboration with educators and community organizations in Winnipeg.

Ethical Decisions in HRM:

English-Only Rules

Can an organization require its employees to speak English or French on the job? Several items are at issue here. First, the *Official Languages Act* of 1988 states that the public has the right to request and receive services from offices of federal institutions in English or French, where there is a significant demand for these services or where the nature of the services is such that they should be available in both official languages. For example, employees working for federal departments and agencies who frequently interact with the media and the general public should be proficient in both English and French. Similarly, some employers have identified the need to have a common language spoken at the worksite. Employers must be able to communicate effectively with all employees, especially when safety or productive efficiency matters are at stake. For example, even though Canadian Airlines gives instruction to the passengers in both English and French, management states that to avoid a misunderstanding among the crew, they communicate on safety-related issues in English unless the crew are all French speaking. Thus, if a common language is a valid requirement of the job, the practice of English or French only could be permitted.

A third issue is an employer's desire to have one language because some workers may be harassing and insulting other workers in a language they cannot understand. And with today's ever-increasing concern with protecting employees, especially women, from hostile environments, English- or French-only rules serve as one means of exercising reasonable care. In stores, for example, it would only make sense to speak English or French to customers who speak that language; in this way, the organization can avoid hostility and discomfort on the part of the customer.

A counterpoint to these language rules firmly rests with the workforce diversity issue. Workers in today's organizations come from all nationalities and speak different languages. The recent census indicated that in 1996, no fewer than 4.6 million people (17 per cent of the population, compared to 15 per cent in 1991) cited a language other than English or French as their mother tongue. That was a 15 per cent increase since 1991. What about their desire to speak their language, to communicate effectively with their peers, and to maintain their cultural heritage? To them, English- or French-only rules are discriminatory in terms of national origin. In several discrimination cases, human rights commissions have ruled that there was no evidence that employees would need to speak English to do the job because other employees were available to translate for them. In summary, English- or French-only policies may leave organizations open to complaints of discrimination based on national or ethnic origin.

Should employers be permitted to demand that only English or French be spoken in the workplace even if it is not necessary for successfully performing the task or doesn't create a safety or health hazard? Should the courts of Canada view this as a discriminatory practice, or should they render a decision that would create a single, nationwide standard on English or French only? What's your opinion?

Source: Commerce Clearing House, Human Resources Management, "English-Only Rules Not Necessarily Invalid, Contrary to EEOC Guidelines," *Ideas and Trends* (July 20, 1994), p. 124; Andrew Phillips, "The English-Only Debate," *MacLean's—Toronto Edition* (May 5, 1997), p. 42. Treasury Board of Canada Secretariat, *English and French in the Workplace: What Federal Employees Need to Know.* Ottawa, Ontario.

TABLE 3-3 Number of Complaints Received by Ground of Discrimination, 1994 to 1997.

	1994		1995		1996		1997	
Ground	No.	(%)	No.	(%)	No.	(%)	No.	(%)
Disability	700	31	579	32	602	33	445	29
Age	209	9	130	7	140	8	375	25
Sex	551	25	420	24	405	23	250	16
Race/Colour	257	11	198	11	220	12	143	9
National/Ethnic origin	205	9	157	9	161	9	133	9
Family/Marital status	163	7	119	7	147	8	118	8
Sexual orientation	69	3	76	4	92	5	37	2
Religion	69	3	103	6	31	2	24	2
Pardon	6	–	1	–	1	–	2	–
Total	2,261	100	1,783	100	1,799	100	1,527	100

Source: Canadian Human Rights Commission Annual Report 1997. (Ottawa: Minister of Public Works and Government Services Canada) 1998.

What Happens to Complaints Filed with the CHRC?

The following seven steps are followed when a complaint of discrimination is filed with the CHRC.[62] First (Step 1), the CHRC will decide if it is the right agency to handle the complaint and if so, accepts it for investigation. If not, the complaint is referred to another appropriate agency. For example, if the complaint is not a federal matter, the person will be referred to a provincial agency or other authority. The CHRC may also refuse to accept a complaint if it is thought to be trivial, or if it is filed in bad faith. If the complaint is accepted, an investigation begins in which the human rights investigator researches to see whether there is enough evidence of discrimination to require some corrective action (Step 2). What must be proven is a causal relation between the impugned action and a negative effect on the employment of people based on a prohibited ground. Investigators will ask individuals for evidence of discrimination. Examples of evidence include overt expressions of prejudice, data showing that treatment of individuals from designated groups was different from treatment of individuals from non-designated groups, subjective performance evaluations, and evidence of an employer's failure to explain why someone was not considered for something such as a training course. In order to present their case as clearly and forcefully as possible, it is important to:

1. Be specific. Reporting exact words, gestures, and other details will help in presenting a case.
2. Keep a diary. Memories can be vague; it is best to write down the details about the incident including the date, place, any actions aimed at resolving the situation, and specific words and actions as soon as possible.
3. List all possible witnesses. Writing down the names of possible witnesses will help the human rights investigator gather evidence. A witness can also be a person who experienced the same or a similar act of discrimination.
4. Save all physical evidence. Sexist or racist material such as cartoons is valuable evidence and could help to prove a complaint.[63]

Sometimes, the investigation results in an early settlement to which both parties agree. This will end the investigation and the matter will be considered resolved. If the complaint cannot be settled, the investigator will put the evidence in a report prepared for commission review (Step 3). If there is not enough evidence to suggest that discrimination did indeed happen the Commission may then dismiss the complaint. If there is evidence, it will attempt to resolve the complaint with the help of an appointed conciliator.

If conciliation does not result in a settlement between the two parties, the case is returned to the commission for decision (Step 4). The commission may then decide to refer the complaint to the Human Rights Tribunal. Cases referred to the tribunal generally involve complicated legal issues, new human rights issues, and unexplored areas of discrimination. Since January 1, 1997, the tribunal was separated from the CHRC which had previously funded it. Separating the tribunal from the CHRC was a way of enhancing the tribunal's independence and impartiality in the eyes of the Canadian public and its clientele.[64]

A public hearing takes place at the tribunal (Step 5). Both the complainant and the employer are permitted representation by legal counsel in this hearing. The tribunal will either dismiss the complaint or, if the employer is found to have engaged in a discriminatory practice, impose a penalty. Those responsible for a discriminatory practice may be required to end the discrimination, establish programs to correct unfairness, produce a plan to correct discriminatory practices, compensate for lost wages or hurt feelings, and pay other costs of settling the complaint. Unless appealed, tribunal decisions are binding on the parties.

Tribunal decisions can be appealed to a review tribunal or the courts by the complainant, the employer, or the commission (Step 6). For example, if enough evidence exists, an employer may choose to defend its HRM practices that allegedly resulted in systemic discrimination. Generally, three defences can be used when confronted with an allegation of discrimination. The first of these is job relatedness or **business necessity**; the second is BFOR (bona fide occupational requirements); and the third is systems of seniority.

An organization has the right to operate in a safe and efficient manner and obtain its goals. These are a business necessity. Without it, the survival of the organization could be threatened. A major portion of business necessity involves **job-related criteria** or having the right to expect employees to perform successfully. This means that employees are expected to possess the required skills, knowledge, and abilities needed to perform the essential elements of the job. Job-related criteria are substantiated through the validation process. (We will return to this topic in Chapter 6.)

A second defence against discriminatory charges is a BFOR. As discussed previously, a BFOR is permitted where such requirements are reasonably necessary to meet the normal operation of an organization. For years, airlines have cited BFOR as the reason for hiring solely female flight attendants. The airlines' position was that most of their passengers were male who preferred to see stew-

Business Necessity Certain employment requirements are reasonably necessary to meet the normal and safe operation of an organization.

Job-Related Criteria Criteria that predict on the job performance.

At one time airlines hired only single, attractive females as cabin attendants, but this practice has long been elim-
inated in Canada since gender and age are not BFOR for this position.

ardesses. The courts, however, did not hold the same view. As a result, it is now common to see both sexes today as flight attendants. Using sex as a criterion for a job is difficult to prove.

Finally, the organization's bona fide seniority system can serve as a defence against discrimination charges. So long as employment decisions such as lay-offs are the function of a well-established and consistently applied seniority system, decisions that may adversely affect protected group members may be permissible. However, an organization using seniority as a defence must be able to demonstrate the appropriateness of its system. Although three means are available for organizations to defend themselves, BFOR and seniority defences are often subject to great scrutiny and at times, are limited in their use; the best approach usually revolves around job relatedness.

Finally, review tribunal decisions can be appealed to the Federal Court of Canada or, in some cases, to the Supreme Court of Canada (Step 7).

Generally speaking, the vast majority of discriminatory acts are not malicious. In the majority of cases, problems arise from long-standing employment practices, legitimate concerns of the employer (such as safety concerns), or conflicting interpretations of the statute and precedents (e.g., when dealing with relatively new requirements and different interpretation of adjectives such as "good faith"). Table 3-4 lists complaint outcomes between 1994 and 1997.

The tribunal has a second role. As well as being the Human Rights Tribunal, it is also the Employment Equity Tribunal.[65] In other words, the tribunal also reviews cases that fall under the *Employment Equity Act.*

TABLE 3-4   Complaint Outcomes, 1994 to 1997

	1994	**1995**	**1996**	**1997**
Early resolution	144	96	57	48
Settled during investigation or at conciliation	149	242	268	169
Referred to alternate redress mechanisms	488	410	327	301
Referred to tribunal	48	54	9	24
Not dealt with[1]	26	18	18	28
Dismissed for lack of evidence	273	277	245	221
No further proceedings[2]	397	430	198	147
Discontinued[3]	986	571	989	1,087
Total	2,511	1,998	2,111	2,025

Source: Canadian Human Rights Commission Annual Report 1997. (Ottawa: Minister of Public Works and Government Services Canada) 1998.

[1] Cases which the commission decided not to pursue because they were filed more than one year after the alleged act of discrimination or were technically without purpose.

[2] Cases in which the complainants withdrew or abandoned their complaints, the matters were outside the commisssion's jurisdiction, or the complaints did not warrant referral to a tribunal.

[3] Cases that were closed prior to investigation because the complainants did not wish to pursue them or a link could not be established between the alleged act and a prohibited ground of discrimination.

Right to protection

Individuals should not be afraid of the employer, co-workers, or someone else getting back at them if they file a complaint with the CHRC or are a witness. It is a criminal offence for anyone to threaten, intimidate, or discriminate against an individual who has filed a complaint or to hamper the investigation process.[66] The CHRA provides for fines up to $50,000 for such offences.

Current Issues in Employment Law

Equal employment opportunity legislation today addresses concerns such as discrimination based on religion and sexual orientation, the rights of aboriginal peoples, and discrimination in compensation and benefits. There are, however, two compelling issues: sexual harassment and the glass ceiling. Of course, these are only two of many important issues.

Sexual harassment

Sexual Harassment Anything of a sexual nature that results in a condition of employment, an employment consequence, or creates a hostile or offensive environment.

Sexual harassment is a serious issue. Data indicate that almost all Fortune 500 companies in North America have had complaints lodged by employees, and about a third of them have been sued.[67] Not only were the settlements in these cases at a substantial cost to the companies in terms of litigation, it is estimated that it costs a "typical Fortune 500 company $6.7 million per year in absenteeism, low productivity, and turnover."[68] That amounts to more than $3 billion annually. Moreover, sexual harassment creates an unpleasant work environment for people and undermines their ability to perform their job. The 1996 Annual Report of the Canadian Human Rights Commission reported on several surveys that provide evidence that sexual harassment in the Canadian workplace remains remarkably common.[69] For example, a survey of the Hibernia construction project in Newfoundland indicated that almost half of the female workers involved had been sexually harassed by male co-workers at one time or another. Similarly, almost two-thirds of female RCMP officers had encountered offensive sexist materials in the workplace, and nearly half had experienced unwanted and inappropriate sexual advances from a male co-worker, quite often a higher-ranking member. And the problem is not just a North American phenomenon; it is a worldwide one.[70] Sexual harassment charges have been filed in such countries as Japan, Australia, the Netherlands, Belgium, New Zealand, Sweden, and Ireland.[71] But just what is sexual harassment?

If you feel uncomfortable when a co-worker or supervisor touches you, you should tell that person that you do not like to be touched. On the other hand, an invitation to dinner from a supervisor is not necessarily sexual harassment; invitations can be made, accepted, or rejected innocently. However, sexual harassment does occur when a supervisor implies that an invitation must be accepted or there will be employment consequences (such as being passed over for a promotion).

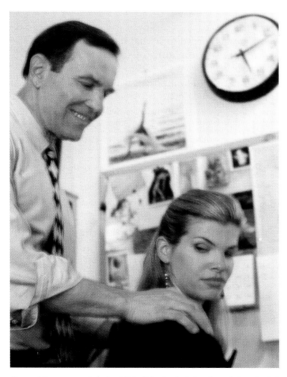

Sexual harassment is prohibited by both federal and provincial human rights legislation.

Although protection from such activities is included under the CHRA (sex discrimination), it has not been until recent years that this problem has gained recognition. In the 1990s, the number of sexual harassment complaints and suits have been rising in Canada.[72] Charges of sexual harassment continue to appear in the headlines on an almost regular basis. For example, in 1997, in what became a highly controversial case, Simon Fraser University fired its swim coach over an alleged sexual harassment episode with a twenty-two year-old female swimmer.[73] In 1996, Al McLean quit as Ontario's Speaker as a controversy raged over sexual harassment charges and his handling of them. The complainant accused McLean of repeatedly sexually harassing a female employee since he hired her; McLean vigorously denied the charges.[74]

Both federal and provincial human rights legislation prohibits sexual harassment since sexual harassment is considered a form of sex discrimination. Furthermore, in Saskatchewan and Quebec, sexual harassment is also handled as an occupational health and safety issue.[75] Division XV.1 of Part III (Labour Standards) of the 1971 *Canada Labour Code* establishes an employee's right to employment free of sexual harassment and requires employers to take positive action to prevent sexual harassment in the workplace.[76]

Under the *Canada Labour Code*, employers are required to make every reasonable effort to ensure that no employee is the victim of sexual harassment. The law is fairly specific in outlining the responsibilities of employers in dealing with workplace sexual harassment. For example, employers under federal jurisdiction must issue a sexual harassment policy containing at least seven items:

1. A definition of sexual harassment that is substantially the same as the one in the *Canada Labour Code*.
2. A statement to the effect that every employee is entitled to employment free of sexual harassment.
3. A statement to the effect that the employer will make every reasonable effort to ensure that no employee is subjected to sexual harassment.
4. A statement explaining how complaints of sexual harassment may be brought to the attention of the employer.
5. A statement to the effect that the employer will take disciplinary measures against any person under his or her direction who subjects any employee to sexual harassment.
6. A statement to the effect that the employer will not disclose the name of the complainant or the circumstances related to the complaint to any person unless disclosure is necessary for the purposes of investigating the complaint or taking disciplinary measures in relation to the complaint.
7. An explanation of the employee's right to make a complaint under the *Canadian Human Rights Act*.

Employers must keep their policy statement concerning sexual harassment in the workplace posted and ensure that all employees are aware of it. To ensure an effective and workable policy, it is essential that all employees have the opportunity to provide input. Employee involvement and commitment to the process of establishing a sexual harassment policy will provide employees with the feeling of ownership of the ultimate policy.[77]

Much of the problem associated with sexual harassment is determining what constitutes this illegal behaviour. People are often not sure of what exactly constitutes sexual harassment. It can exist under one of three conditions (1) where such an activity is a condition of employment; (2) where such action has employment consequences (such as promotion or dismissal); and (3) where the activity creates a hostile environment.[78]

Most would agree that the first two conditions are fairly clear-cut. In fact, these are often referred to as quid pro quo sexual harassment cases, or getting something for giving something. It is the third component that is problematic for organizations. Just what is a hostile environment? How do organizational members determine if something is offensive or humiliating? For instance, does sexually explicit language in the office create a hostile environment? How about off-colour jokes or pictures of naked women? The answer is: It could. It depends on the people in the organization and the environment in which they work. Challenging hostile environment situations gained support from several legal cases. For example, although *Potapczyk v. MacBain* did not involve overt sexual advances by the respondent, the defendant was found to have sexually harassed the complainant by creating a humiliating work environment by making sexual comments to her and by subjecting her and other female staff to unnecessary and offensive physical closeness.[79] In *Clark v. Canada*, the court found that the complainant was sexually harassed by male colleagues and supervisors when she was a member of the RCMP.[80] Clark was subjected to various forms of harassment including verbal taunts and suggestive remarks and the playing of pornographic videos and displaying of centrefolds. The complainant's immediate supervisor was well aware of the sexual harassment and refused to do anything.

In addition to supporting hostile environment claims, what do these two cases tell us? First, in sexual harassment cases, an organization can be held liable for the harassing behaviour of its employees and how they treat sexual harassment charges against personnel (see also *Robichaud v. Brennan*[81]). Ignorance or lack of awareness of the offensive nature of the harassing behaviour is no defence. Second, we all must be sensitive to what makes fellow employees uncomfortable, and if we don't know, then we should ask. Organizational success now and in the future will, in part, reflect how sensitive each employee is towards others in the company. At DuPont, for example, that is exactly what Ed Bardzik is doing with his "A Matter of Respect" program.[82] This program is designed to eliminate sexual harassment through awareness and respect for all individuals. This means understanding one another and, most importantly, respecting others' rights. Similarly, George Gaffney, executive vice-president and general manager of Royal Bank's Metropolitan Toronto district, believes that "companies that treat people with dignity and respect will prosper, and those which don't will have a tough time competing for customers and employees."[83] The Royal Bank is seen by many people as a "best practices" company in terms of promoting and integrating diversity in the workplace. The bank is not just talking about diversity; it is using it as a business advantage and taking its place as a socially responsible business leader.

If sexual harassment carries with it potential costs to the organization, what can a company do to protect itself? In any harassment case, the courts want to know two things: (1) Did the organization know about, or should it have known about, the alleged behaviour? and (2) What did management do to stop it? With the cost in time and money of the awards against organizations today, there is even a greater need for management to educate all employees on sexual harassment matters and have mechanisms available to monitor employees (see "HRM Skills").

In addition to sexual harassment, there are other forms (as specified in the *CHRA* and provincial and territorial human rights acts or codes) which are also illegal. Examples of illegal behaviour are racial and religious harassment.

The Glass Ceiling

The **glass ceiling** refers to the invisible barrier that blocks females and minorities from ascending into upper levels of an organization.[84] It appears that while significant gains have been made by minorities and women in gaining entry to organizations, they still hold a relatively low percentage of senior management positions. This is not to say that women are not moving up the corporate ladder; it is that progress is slow.[85]

Glass Ceiling The invisible barrier that blocks female minorities from ascending into upper levels of an organization.

Protecting the Organization from Sexual (and Other) Harassment Charges

1. **Issue a sexual harassment policy describing what constitutes sexual harassment and what is inappropriate behaviour.** Just stating that sexual harassment is unacceptable at your organization is not enough. In this policy, specific unacceptable behaviours must be identified. The more explicit these are, the less chance there is of misinterpretation later on.

2. **Institute a procedure (or link to an existing one) to investigate sexual harassment charges.** Employees (as well as the courts), need to understand what routes are open for an employee to lay a complaint. This, too, should be clearly stated in the policy and widely disseminated to employees.

3. **Inform all employees of the sexual harassment policy.** Educate these employees about the policy and how it will be enforced. Don't assume that the policy will convey the information simply because it is a policy. It must be effectively communicated to all employees. Some training may be required to help in this understanding.

4. **Train management personnel on how to deal with sexual harassment charges and what responsibility they have to the individual and the organization.** Poor supervisory practices in this area can open the company to a tremendous liability. Managers must be trained on how to recognize signs of sexual harassment and how to get help for the victim. Because of the magnitude of the issue, a manager's performance evaluation should reinforce this competency.

5. **Investigate all sexual harassment charges immediately.** All means all—even those that you suspect are invalid. You must pay attention to each charge of sexual harassment and investigate it by searching for clues, witnesses, and so on. Investigating the charge is also consistent with our societal view of justice.

6. **Take corrective action as necessary.** Discipline those doing the harassing and "make whole" the harassed individual. If you find that the charge can be substantiated, you must take some corrective action, up to and including dismissing the perpetrator. If the punishment does not fit the crime, you may be reinforcing or condoning the behaviou. The harassed individual should also be given whatever was taken away. For example, if the result of sexual behaviour led to an individual's resignation, "making whole" the person would mean reinstatement, with full back pay and benefits.

7. **Continue to follow up on the matter to ensure that no further harassment occurs, nor does retaliation.** One of the concerns that individuals have in coming forward with such charges is that there may be some retaliation against them, especially if the harasser is disciplined. You must continue to observe what is affecting these individuals, including follow-up conversations with them.

8. **Periodically review turnover situations to determine if a potential problem may be arising.** This may include commission audits, exit interviews, and the like. There may be a wealth of information at your disposal that may indicate a problem. For example, if only females are resigning in a particular department, that may point to a serious problem. Pay attention to your regular reports and search for trends that may indicated cause for concern.

9. **Don't forget to recognize privately individuals who bring these matters forward.** Without their courageous effort, the organization might have been faced with tremendous liability. These individuals took a risk in coming forward, so show your appreciation. Besides, if others know that the risk is worthwhile, they may feel more comfortable in coming to you when any type of problem arises.

Sources: Adapted from Anne B. Fisher, "Sexual Harassment: What to Do," *Fortune* (August 23, 1993), pp. 84-88; Clifford M. Koen, Jr., "Sexual Harassment Claims Stem from a Hostile Work Environment," *Personnel Journal* (August 1990), pp. 97-98; Martha E. Eller, "Sexual Harassment: Prevention, Not Protection," *The Cornell H.R.A. Quarterly* (February 1990), p. 87; Maureen P. Woods and Walter J. Flynn, "Heading Off Sexual Harassment," *Personnel* (November 1989), p. 48; and Jacqueline F. Strayer and Sandra E. Rapoport, "Sexual Harassment: Limiting Corporate Liability," *Personnel* (April 1986), pp. 32-33.

A recent International Labour Organization report found that while women have made progress in closing the gender gap in managerial and professional jobs worldwide, most female managers are still barred from the top levels of organizations, whether in the private or public sector or in political life.[86] And even when they manage to rise to the top, female executives nearly always earn less than men even when they consistently exceed performance expectations. The report also indicated that, in Canada, 40 per cent of the managers and 20 per cent of the senior managers are women. In worldwide rankings, Canada came up short behind Australia and the United States but ahead of several European countries.

What factors cause the glass ceiling effect? Interestingly, men and women strongly disagree on the answer.[87] A recent survey indicated that male CEOs believe that until recently, the executive talent pool has simply not included many women with the kind of managerial experience that makes them capable of being promoted to senior positions. They believe that the imbalance will one day right itself. In contrast, many of the women who participated in the study mentioned that their careers had been stymied by negative attitudes and perceptions (that they are distracted by motherhood and are unable to travel or work overtime). Often, women do not have advocates in the organization or do not have access to executive search firms. Finally, old boy networks do their bit too. Many men feel comfortable with other men—they can go out drinking with them, play golf, and talk with no inhibitions. As a result of their exclusion from the old boy networks, women's opportunities are more limited. Women may not know when a job is coming available, finding out about it after it has been filled.

The survey also indicated that 93 per cent of the male CEO participants believe that opportunities for women have somewhat or greatly improved in their companies over the past five years. In contrast, female executives were more pessimistic: 15 per cent reported that no progress had been made towards shattering the glass ceiling, and 24 per cent said the conditions had improved only slightly.

Research has also indicated that women and minorities experience **glass walls**, which involves discrimination in transfers and job assignments that, in turn, limits their access to special, visible, and critical tasks or jobs that are necessary for promotion. They are simply not allowed to get experience essential for promotion because people would like to protect women and minorities from failure on an assignment that is visible. "People" include supervisors, managers, or colleagues. Both women and minorities face glass walls.

As a result of the frustrations associated with the glass ceiling and walls, many women change careers, scale back, opt out, or start their own businesses.[88] High drop-out rates for women have been reported in professional services firms such as law, accounting, and management consulting.[89] If organizations are to remain productive and competitive in an increasingly demanding global market place, they must recruit, develop, promote, and retain, their most talented people, regardless of their sex or race.

Glass Walls Discrimination in the assignment of particular jobs that in effect limit people's (women and visible minorities) access to special and critical jobs that are necessary for promotion.

To begin to correct this invisible barrier, the CHRC is working to expand its audit compliance reviews. For example, in these reviews, the auditors will be looking to see if government contractors do indeed have training and development programs operating to provide career growth to the affected groups. Should these be lacking, the CHRC can plan to take legal action to ensure compliance.

Scholars have identified several strategies to correct the glass ceiling problem.[90] Organizations such as BC Tel, Bank of Montreal, and General Motors of Canada have implemented several of these recommendations. Examples of such best practices include:

1. The CEO must communicate viable and continuing commitment to workforce diversity and enact policies that promote it.
2. Efforts to achieve workforce diversity should be an integral part of corporate strategic business plans, and line managers must be held accountable for progress towards breaking the glass ceiling.
3. Organizations must expand their traditional executive recruitment networks and seek out candidates with non-customary backgrounds and experiences.
4. Formal mentoring and career development programs can help stop minorities and women from being channelled into staff positions that provide little access to the executive suite. Promoting from within and preparing all individuals for top-level positions may eventually shatter the glass ceiling.
5. Work life and family-friendly policies should be adopted (e.g., flexible hours and day care facilities).
6. Enforcement agencies must increase their efforts to carry out existing equal employment opportunity legislation and update regulations and policies to keep up with the changing workplace environment.

Without initiatives such as access to mentors and developmental job assignments, too many qualified minorities and women are stopped short before they fulfil the promise of their abilities. General Motors of Canada is one company that launched a public initiative in the early 1980s to increase the opportunities for women within GM and to integrate them into core operational jobs. With its women's advisory council, women working clerical positions could switch to operational positions. Senior managers and the president attended the council's annual review to evaluate GM's progress at integrating and promoting women. Since Maureen Kempston-Darkes became GM Canada's president in 1995, the company has more than tripled the number of women at senior management levels to more than 30 per cent from 9 per cent.

Study Tools and Applications

Summary

This summary relates to the Learning Objectives identified on p. 64.
After reading this chapter, you should know:

1. The *Canadian Human Rights Act* of 1985 gives individuals protection on the basis of race, national or ethic origin, colour, religion, age, sex, marital status, family status, conviction for an offence for which a pardon has been granted, physical or mental disability, and sexual orientation. In addition, provincial and territorial human rights legislation may supplement this list.

2. The aim of the *Equal Employment Act* of 1995 is to remove employment barriers that have affected women, aboriginal peoples, visible minorities, and people with disabilities. The enforcement arm is the Canadian Human Rights Commission. Employment equity legislation exists at the federal and, to some extent, at the provincial level.

3. Employment equity plans are attempts by organizations to actively recruit and hire protected group members. *The Employment Equity Act* of 1996 requires some employers to develop an employment equity plan aimed at promoting a fully equitable workplace and to monitor its progress.

4. Systemic discrimination (including adverse impact) is any consequence of employment that results in a disparate rate of selection, promotion, termination, and so on of protected group members. Adverse treatment occurs when members of a protected group receive different treatment than other employees. A protected group member is any individual who is afforded protection under the *Employment Equity Act* of 1996.

5. Organizations may not terminate an employee for being pregnant, refuse to make an employment decision based on one's pregnancy, or deny insurance coverage to the individual. The law requires organizations to offer the employee a reasonable period of time off work without loss of seniority or benefits. Parents are entitled to parental leave. The *Canada Labour Code* provides for family matters such as care for a sick family member, death of an immediate family member, and other illness.

6. If an employee is qualified to perform the essential tasks of a job, and if the cost of accommodating the employee's disability does not create an undue hardship on the organization, the employer is under an obligation to accommodate the employee. Note that reasonable accommodation is required for all aspects covered under human rights legislation.

7. A business can protect itself from discrimination charges first by having HRM practices that do not adversely affect protected groups, through supported claims of job relatedness, bona fide occupational qualifications, or through a valid seniority system.

8. *Griggs v. Duke Power* was one of the most important US Supreme Court cases pertaining to employment equity opportunities. Based on this case, items used to screen applicants had to be related to the job. After the Griggs ruling, the burden was on the employer to prove discrimination did not occur. This case has had a considerable impact on both US and Canadian employment legislation.

9. Sexual harassment is a serious problem in today's enterprises. It is defined as any unwelcome sexual advances, requests for sexual favours, or other verbal or physical contact of a sexual nature where the result is a condition of employment, has an employment consequence, or creates a hostile environment. Harassment based on other protected grounds is also illegal.

10. The glass ceiling is an invisible barrier existing in today's organizations that is keeping minorities and women from ascending to higher levels in the workplace. Similarly, glass walls involve discrimination in transfers and assignments; as a result, women and minorities do not have access to special, visible, and critical tasks that are necessary for promotion.

Key Terms

adverse (disparate) impact
adverse (disparate) treatment
affirmative action
auditing process
bona fide occupational requirement (BFOR)
business necessity
comparable worth
Constitution Act
Employment Equity Act (EEA)
Federal Contractors Program
four-fifths rule
glass ceiling

glass wall
Griggs v. Duke Power Company
job-related criteria
mandatory retirement
protected group members
reasonable accommodation
restricted policy
reverse discrimination
sexual harassment
systemic discrimination
undue hardship

EXPERIENTIAL EXERCISE:

Know Your Rights

Just as a company should have a policy and educate its workforce on sexual harassment issues, so too should a university. Do you know your college or university's policy on sexual harassment? Do you know what to do if you are being sexually harassed? If you do, congratulations. Your institution is getting the information out to you. If you don't know, you need to find out. For this exercise, contact the office of student affairs (or whatever it is called on your campus) and ask for the institution's policy on sexual harassment. You'll may find that it is also reprinted in your student handbook. Nevertheless, look at the policy and how it is enforced. In groups, discuss the policy and how well the college or university has established ways for people to seek help. Your professor should then lead a discussion on the policy, what constitutes sexual harassment on the campus, and the complaint procedure available if one has a problem.

CASE APPLICATION:

The Canadian Public Service

Visible minorities are an integral part of Canadian society. Though their proportion of the labour force has significantly increased over the past ten years, their representation in the public service has been unacceptably low. Federal departments have not been very successful in recruiting and hiring visible minorities. Moreover, it is likely that a high number of visible minorities will depart (retirement, resignations, and deaths) the public service because of their age profile, so that future representation of visible minorities could actually *decrease* while their percentage of the labour force rises. In contrast, the federally regulated private sector has had much more success in attracting members of visible minorities in line with their availability in the labour force. For Canada, known to be a racially tolerant country, this low representation of visible minorities in the public service is simply less than acceptable. The federal government exists for all Canadians, and the public service should reflect Canadian diversity in its workforce.

Observers have suggested that top management of the public sector must be more strongly committed to the process of hiring and promoting visible minority employees. In order to do so, there must be a crystal-clear policy on the direction and objectives of the program, including an education and training program for all personnel. Visible minorities, too, believe that there is a lack of vision on the part of administrators who fear change and lack the will to change. Thus, it appears that cultural diversity is still not widely accepted as beneficial to the public service by upper and middle management and that genuine commitment to employment equity interventions is lacking. Perhaps for that reason, the revised *Employment Equity Act* applies to the federally regulated private sector and the public service.

Questions

1. Can you think of specific business advantages (e.g., ability to do the work better and provide for better service) that would result from a workforce (e.g., customs officials and the RCMP) that reflects the population?

2. What factors, other than lack of commitment to employment equity, can account for the striking difference in the representation of members of visible minorities in the federal public service and federally regulated private sector companies (banks, in particular)?

3. What can public service employers learn from the federally regulated private sector when it comes to managing a diverse workforce?

4. Develop an action plan that will increase public service employers' commitment to employment equity programs, and increased participation of visible minorities.

Source: John Samuel and Associates Inc., *Visible Minorities and the Public Service of Canada* (Ottawa): 1997.

Testing Your Understanding

How well did you fulfil the learning objectives?

1. Why was additional employment equity legislation passed in 1996?
   a. Times had changed and new rules were needed.
   b. There was such backlash against the 1996 *Employment Equity Act* that it was repealed.
   c. The original legislation lacked compelling enforcement mechanisms.
   d. Women were not protected under the original legislation.
   e. Age was not protected under the original legislation.

2. Leisure, Inc. is an equal employment opportunity employer with an active affirmative action program. What does that mean?
   a. Leisure, Inc. actively pursues female and minority candidates and makes good-faith efforts to get them into the applicant pool.
   b. Leisure, Inc. hires only females and minorities during a designated five-year period.
   c. Leisure, Inc. systematically retires and fires more White males than any other group of employees.
   d. Leisure, Inc. hires a larger percentage of minorities and females than White males.
   e. Leisure, Inc. has historically employed large percentages of females and minorities.

3. Which one of the statements is accurate regarding adverse impact?
   a. Adverse impact may result from a seemingly neutral employment practice.
   b. Adverse impact is a deliberate discriminatory practice.
   c. Adverse impact is reverse discrimination against White males.
   d. Adverse impact is a public attitude towards an organization that refuses to hire female and minority job applicants.
   e. Adverse impact is a public attitude towards an organization that refuses to hire White males.

4. A thirty-five year-old mother of two has been with her firm for fifteen years. She wants to transfer to the computer room of her organization. She is charging adverse impact for which one of the following conditions found in the posted job description for "computer room assistant"?
   a. Must be able to lift fifty pounds.
   b. High-school diploma required.
   c. Prior military experience preferred.
   d. Must be familiar with organizational communications systems and requirements.
   e. Must be able to file and catalogue tape and disc resources.

5. What is the difference between adverse impact and adverse treatment?
   a. There is no difference; the terms are synonymous.
   b. Adverse impact typically refers to organizational hiring practices, while adverse treatment generally refers to organizational promotion and performance evaluation practices.
   c. Adverse impact is physical abuse. Adverse treatment is mental abuse.
   d. Adverse impact is emotional and subjective. Adverse treatment is objective and impersonal.
   e. Adverse impact is legal. Adverse treatment is illegal.

6. You are a manager in one of the chartered banks. It has just come to your attention that one of your accounting department employees has tested HIV-positive. What workplace protection to this employee is provided under the law?
   a. Under the *Canadian Human Rights Act*, the employee's immediate supervisor and co-workers must be informed within forty-eight hours.
   b. Under the *Canadian Human Rights Act*, all job actions must be based on job performance requirements.
   c. Under the *Canadian Human Rights Act*, the employee must be assigned a job with other HIV-positive workers within six weeks.

d. Under the *Canadian Human Rights Act*, the employee will no longer be allowed to meet with other employees outside of her own area.

e. The *Canadian Human Rights Act* does not have provision for people with AIDS.

7. Barbara has worked for Immigration Canada for five years and is pregnant with her first child. What benefit provision is she allowed under the *Canadian Human Rights Act*?

a. No provision. The *Canadian Human Rights Act* does not apply to Immigration Canada.

b. No provision. The law covers only "vested" employees who have been employed seven years.

c. She can take up to seventeen weeks of paid leave and resume her old job when she returns.

d. She is entitled to her old job or an equivalent position upon returning to work.

e. She is entitled to 85 per cent of her pay during her leave; in addition, she can collect unemployment benefits.

8. Robert is a mortgage loan officer for a large financial institution. He has had a roller-coaster year. He took a six-week leave without pay in March to spend with his newly adopted son. He took a five-week leave without pay in June-July to care for his wife who had surgery. He is now telling you, the benefits coordinator for his section, that he may occasionally need some time off (without pay, of course) from the last week in October through the first of December to care for his father who will be out of the hospital around October but can't be placed in a nursing home until December 1. You need to be sure that he is treated in accordance with the provisions of the *Canadian Human Rights Act* and the *Canada Labour Code*. What action will you take?

a. Fire him.

b. Transfer him to a lower paying, less responsible, job.

c. Tell him he is entitled to only one additional week this year of unpaid leave, and that other arrangements will have to be worked out with his supervisor and the vice-president of benefits.

d. Grant him the leave. Tell him he is not eligible to apply again for additional unpaid leave for twenty-four months.

e. A responsible decision is to grant him the leave. You realize that you can reasonably accommodate Robert's absences.

9. You are accused of discriminatory hiring practices by a Sri Lankan rights group, which states the only minorities your organization hires are Hong Kongers. Which statement is an appropriate application of the four-fifths rule?

a. In the last year, one hundred Hong Kongers applied for positions, while only ten Sri Lankans applied.

b. There are no Sinhalese or Tamil-speaking neighbourhoods in four-fifths of the geographical locations of the organization.

c. During the interview process, all applicants who were approved by four of the five interviewers were hired.

d. Forty out of eighty White applicants were hired. Two out of three Sri Lankan applicants were hired.

e. Eighty per cent of all applicants were not hired.

10. An allegation of discrimination could best be supported under which one of the following geographical comparisons test?

a. Company position advertisements state that travel is required approximately ten to twelve days per month.

b. The Leisure, Inc. company has a policy of promoting from within. They only hire inexperienced, newly graduated applicants, mostly from local universities.

c. A large Vancouver-based financial institution has no Asian people on the payroll.

d. Jon, an HIV-positive postal worker, was passed over for promotion because of his physical condition. He had successfully completed all training requirements and passed the qualifying examination.

e. Company position available announcements are posted in English, Mandarin, and French.

Chapter Four

EMPLOYEE RIGHTS AND ETHICAL ISSUES

LEARNING OBJECTIVES

AFTER READING THIS CHAPTER, YOU WILL BE ABLE TO:

1. Explain how ethical considerations affect Human Resources Management.
2. Describe the intent of the *Access to Information Act* and the *Privacy Act* of 1983 and their effect on HR practices.
3. Discuss the guidelines for alcohol and drug testing in organizations.
4. Discuss the legal protection available for organizational whistle-blowers.
5. Explain how organizations should develop and implement policies regarding employee monitoring that will be accepted by employees.
6. Discuss the concepts of just cause and wrongful dismissal.
7. Discuss the legal protection available for employees who have been wrongfully dismissed.
8. Define discipline and the contingency factors that determine the severity of discipline.
9. Describe the general guidelines for administering discipline.

Martin Entrop was first employed by Imperial Oil Limited in 1977. Entrop had been an alcoholic, but he stopped drinking in 1984. In 1991, Entrop held a safety-sensitive position: a senior control board operator at Imperial's Sarnia, Ontario refinery. In 1991, three years after the Exxon Valdez oil tanker crash, Imperial introduced its revised alcohol and drug policy.[1] The purpose was to minimize the risk of impaired performance due to substance abuse, and it was considered one of the most rigorous programs of its kind developed in Canada, with clear standards and consequences for use and possession of alcohol and drugs. For example, the policy stated that employees with past alcohol or drug problems and who presently hold or apply for safety-sensitive positions are required to disclose their past substance abuse problem.

When Martin Entrop disclosed his past alcohol abuse problem, which he had overcome more than seven years earlier, he was immediately reassigned to a non-safety-sensitive (but comparable) position. His wages were maintained at the same level he had received in the position of senior control board operator. Over a period of a few months, Entrop was assessed to ensure that he posed no safety risk in a safety-sensitive position, and eventually, he was reinstated to his former position. However, a condition of his reinstatement was that he agree, in writing, to undergo additional (and random) alcohol tests under the company policy, yearly medical examinations, quarterly performance assessments, and report any alcohol relapse or alcohol-related charge to management. In January 1992, Entrop filed a complaint with the Ontario Human Rights Commission alleging he had been discriminated against on the basis of handicap and that his employer's drug and alcohol testing policy was an invasion of his privacy.

In September 1996, University of Western Ontario law professor Constance Backhouse, who presided over the hearings, ruled that most of Imperial's drug and alcohol policy was unlawful and that Martin Entrop's human rights had been violated.[2] Backhouse concluded that drug abuse and addiction are handicaps within the meaning of the Ontario Human Rights Code, and it is therefore a discriminatory practice to base employment decisions on such addictions. Furthermore, in response to Imperial's requirement to disclose past substance abuse problems, Backhouse found no justification for such an unlimited and wide-ranging rule of disclosure. For example, it is possible for an individual to be completely rehabilitated from drug dependence. Imperial Oil appealed the ruling, but in February 1998, the Ontario Divisional Court rejected this appeal to maintain a policy that includes random testing and asking employees about any history of past substance abuse.[3]

Introduction

What started out as a routine exercise to implement a drug and alcohol testing program turned into a legal battle—a fight for one's job and to protect one's privacy. But shouldn't doing our jobs and doing them in an appropriate and safe manner be considered? Certainly there is a need for managers to be able to direct the activities of their workers without being questioned or even second-guessed. Employers have the right to ensure that their business operations are conducted safely and a corresponding right to assess whether employees are incapable of performing their essential duties. But does this mean that employers are all-powerful in this arena? That is, can they do whatever it takes to achieve the objective of a safe and efficient work environment? Can an organization implement random and mandatory alcohol and drug testing procedures in order to safeguard their operations? Was Martin Entrop treated fairly? Was his privacy violated? What rights did Entrop have in the workplace? It is answers to questions such as these that we will address in this chapter.

The topic of employee rights has become one of the most important issues for human resources management to deal with in the 1990s—attention to workplace rights is a critical issue facing contemporary management. As we discussed in Chapter 3, "Diversity and Equal Employment Opportunities," individuals are guaranteed certain rights based on the *Canadian Charter of Rights and Freedoms*, the *Canadian Human Rights Act*, and the *Canada Labour Code*. Individuals not protected under federal legislation (approximately 90 per cent of the Canadian workforce) may find protection under provincial or territorial human rights legislation and employment standards legislation. For example, in Chapter 3, we discussed that employees have the right to a work environment free of sexual harassment. Similarly, human rights legislation protects individuals with physical and mental disabilities. And fortunately, Canadian legislation protects employees from wrongful dismissal.

But can an organization subject all its employees to a polygraph (lie-detector) test to find out more about a sudden rise in theft? Can a bank require its employees to take an honesty test in order to maintain a high degree of public trust? Can an organization ask its HR department to develop and implement a selection system that will screen out all new applicants who have pro-union attitudes so that in the near future, the union can be defeated in a de-certification vote? The answers, for the most part, are no. In more and more situations, organizational practices such as random drug and alcohol testing, terminating employees, and maintaining health files on employees for insurance purposes are limited.[4] Various laws and court rulings are establishing guidelines for employers dealing with employee privacy and other matters.

Employee Rights A collective term dealing with varied employee protection practices in an organization.

Dilemmas of HRM and Ethics

Part of any discussion regarding employee rights should also include a discussion on ethics. Human resources management is all about treating people ethically. We can define ethics as those guiding principles that help us decide between what is right and what is wrong and what may and may not be done. Unfortunately, these principles are not specific rules, but rather, they are guidelines that help establish acceptable parameters in which we are to operate. During the past decade, these guidelines have come under renewed fire. Major

Ethics Going beyond the law in employment decisions designed to protect employee rights and dignity.

Canadian and US corporations have been accused of allowing questionable practices because of their focus on bottom line results. For example, as a result of the 1992 Westray Mine disaster, the Nova Scotia Department of Labour filed dozens of charges against several management employees alleging numerous violations of the *Coal Mines Regulation Act* and the *Occupational Health and Safety Act*.[5] But in 1998, the Nova Scotia prosecution service announced that it would not proceed with manslaughter and criminal negligence charges against mine managers.[6] Similarly, stock market investors and business deal makers came to believe that "greed is good," subtly encouraging unethical behaviour and questionable schemes. The legal profession, in particular, has been accused of a sharp decline in professionalism and ethical standards.

What do you tell your employees if the company announces lay-offs amid great profitability? Or think of a research and development team that shreds files and research reports because of potential threats of liability suits. And the list could go on. All managers and employees must consider the ethical dimensions of their decisions, including those in the HRM area.

Ethical Issues in Human Resources Management

When we speak of ethics for HRM practitioners, we are referring to actions that go beyond what is required by the law. As we know, HRM is highly regulated by federal, provincial, and territorial laws, but mere compliance with, say, the *Employment Equity Act* does not always indicate ethical practices. For example, take the four-fifths rule. If HRM practices result in an exact compliance with the required ratio, then the activities are legal, but the intent may be considered suspect. What we are concerned about is creating an environment where decisions go beyond the law to take into account the best interests of all employees. Even though organizations have every right to meet the bare minimum legal requirements, to do so might not be in the best long-term interests of their employees (see "HRM Skills: Ethics Training"). Ethical HRM should be an end in itself rather than just responding to legislation and meeting legal requirements. We will address this issue in more detail later. Now let's first look at some specific ethical issues facing HRM practitioners today.

Examples of Ethical Dilemmas in HRM

No one can claim to have right or wrong answers regarding ethical issues in human resources management beyond the laws. However, we can identify a number of instances that raise ethical awareness. How would you react to the following situations?

Situation 1   Your company has a drug-free policy. For current employees, a drug test is administered only as part of the disciplinary process and at the discretion of the immediate supervisor. If performance problems exist and substance abuse is suspected, the supervisor can require the employee to be tested. If the presence of a substance is found and the test is corroborated with a second sample, the employee is terminated. One of your employees is having performance problems of late, and you've heard rumours that some substance abuse may be involved. But this employee has made a great business contact, and you'd really rather not get into this whole issue of drug testing and its implications. You'd rather handle the situation differently to turn this individual's performance around. Is this ethical?

Ethical Decisions in HRM:

Ethics Training

1. **Have a policy on ethics**. Such a policy describes what the company perceives as ethical behaviour and what it expects employees to do. In setting out these standards of conduct, the company will clarify what are and what are not permissible practices. Things such as not using supplies and equipment for personal business and not compelling subordinates to help you with personal activities might be included. Without this policy as a guideline, ethics is left to an individual, subjective judgement call.

2. **Communicate this policy to employees**. Employees must receive and understand the policy. Employees must have a good understanding of the integral role ethics plays within the organization as well as in their long-term professional career.

3. **Train employees to make ethical decisions**. Ethical decision making is never a cut-and-dried process. As such, the training should focus on situations that permit employees to make decisions. Then, these decisions should be analysed in terms of how ethical they were and compared to other decisions that may have been more appropriate. A number of training games ("simulations") are on the market that assist in this endeavour. Role-playing and case studies can also be used to stimulate and develop ethical reasoning skills. The ethics training and awareness sessions need to be evaluated as described in Chapter 9, "Employee Training and Development."

4. **Reinforce the fact that all decision makers face similar dilemmas**. Everyone needs to know that they are not alone in having to make difficult ethical choices, but that the organization expects them to make ethical decisions. Accordingly, they need to feel the support of top management and peers when unpopular but ethical decisions are made.

5. **Reward ethical decision makers**. Nothing will reinforce the ethics policy more than if decision makers are rewarded for making the appropriate choice. The particular situation should be highlighted in some way to reinforce the fact that there is top management support for such decisions.

Situation 2 Your company has a poor safety record. Although safety inspectors find no violation, it is clear that you meet only the minimum health and safety requirements. Last year, forty-three injuries were reported, three resulting in fatalities. Even though the company was not legally liable, is it ethically liable to do more?

Situation 3 An executive of a big farming company ordered the HR department to contact Immigration Canada and the RCMP anonymously and inform them that illegals were working on the farm lands. The executive believes that the frightened employees would scatter when the immigration officers appear and that most of them would not return to collect their wages. Is this ethical? How would HR managers resolve a conflict between their own values and the executive's order?[7]

Situation 4 Your company has had poor relations with the union representing your employees. During negotiations, you demand a cap on employees' salaries. The union rejects your limitations and threatens to strike. You persist, they strike, and you immediately hire replacement workers ("scabs") to keep the company operating. Is this ethical behaviour?

Situation 5 You are an investment manager, and you privately purchased some shares in an Alberta-based mining company. You know that investment managers can hike the price of any stock by buying shares on behalf of an institution. You acquired stock—at double the price you paid for your personal stock—for some funds you are managing. This behaviour is not unusual nor is it illegal, but is this ethical?

Situation 6. You are in the garment business, and you discover that two of your sewing subcontractors in Bangladesh are using child labour. You also learn that if these children lose their jobs, some of them may be driven into prostitution. What's the "right" thing to do?[8]

Human resources management faces many dilemmas—situations in which HR managers have to balance the rights of management with those of workers as well as the rights of the individual employee with those of his or her colleagues. To guide HR managers in their decision making, professional human resources associations in Canada have written ethical codes and standards to provide guidance on ethical matters to their members.[9] Some of these professional associations include: the Canadian Psychological Association, Human Resources Professionals Association of Ontario, the Society of Management Accountants of Canada, and the Human Resource Management Association of Manitoba. For example, ethical standards specified in the Canadian Code of Ethics for Psychologists cover issues such as confidentiality of test results, informed consent, and the competence of psychologists administering and interpreting test results.

Ethical Codes and Standards Ethical codes or standards guide HR managers in their decision making on ethical matters that they may confront in their job.

Benefits of Establishing a Code of Ethics

Establishing a code of ethics can offer a number of benefits to the organization.[10] First, evidence is mounting that well-constructed ethical and social programs can attract customers, raise employee morale and productivity, and strengthen relationships of trust with other key constituencies. Second, a code of ethics can enhance an organization's reputation, and reputation often has a direct impact on organizational success. Nowadays, society expects organizations to employ their assets and human resources in a socially responsible manner by adhering to ethical principles in their relationships with competitors, suppliers, customers, and employees.[11] Third, better government relations may result if an organization establishes a code of ethics. Today, governments at all levels are doing more than simply checking to see if legal and regulatory standards are met. As we discussed in earlier chapters, the federal and provincial governments are looking at how well organizations are educating their employees in current values and monitoring progress in programs such as employment equity, health and safety initiatives and sexual harassment. Clearly, federal and provincial governments will look favourably on those organizations that go beyond the minimum legal requirements and behave like good corporate citizens.

Best Practices Ethics Program

Best Practices A series of principles or "proven" strategies in implementing an ethics program.

There are several best practices that may help prevent the vast majority of ethics violations if they are systematically applied. These best practices include the following:[12]

1. A *vision statement* gives management and employees a first screening test for decisions. Organizational members should ask themselves "will this decision or action move the organization closer to its vision?" If organizational or departmental goals require one to act in unethical ways, then it should be rejected.

2. A *values statement* defines general principles of required behaviour (e.g., fairness, honesty, and integrity). As such, it's the standard against which organizational decisions and actions should be evaluated to determine if they meet the company's and employees' requirements.

3. An *organizational code of ethics* gives specific definitions of what's expected and required of organizational members; it also defines the consequences of failure to meet standards.

4. An *ethics officer* ensures that the ethics systems are in place and functioning. For example, the officer usually oversees the ethics communication strategy and mechanisms for organizational members to report suspected wrongdoing.

5. The *ethics committee* oversees the company's ethics initiative and supervises the ethics officer. For example, the committee is the final interpreter of the ethics code and the final authority on the need for revising ethics policies.

6. An *ethics communication strategy* ensures that organizational members have the ethics information they need and that the organization is encouraging employee communication regarding the values, standards, and the conduct of the organization and its members.

7. *Ethics training* teaches organizational members what the organization requires, gives them the opportunity to practise applying the values to hypothetical situations and challenges, and prepares them to apply those same standards in the real world.

8. An *ethics help line* should be in place, which allows the reporting of unethical conduct as well as making it easier for employees to contact an expert when the intent of an ethics policy is unclear.

9. If ethical conduct is *assessed* and *rewarded* and if unethical conduct is *identified* and *dissuaded*, organizational members will believe that management is serious when it says the code of ethics is important.

10. Employee behaviour should be *monitored* and *tracked*. However, it is also important to *assess* the extent to which organizational members *accept* and *internalize* the values and ethics code. For example, do employees agree with their importance and appropriateness?

11. *Periodic evaluation* of the effectiveness of the program is critical. For example, is the commitment to the program still there, and are ethics-related goals achieved?

12. Ethics is a *leadership* issue. Organizational leaders set the tone, shape the climate, and define the standards. To the extent that managers are trustworthy and trusted, their motivations are honourable, and their expectations are clear, and if they're paying attention to ethics as an integral part of every business decision, ethics problems will be rare.

Current Issues Regarding Employee Rights

Recently, much emphasis has been placed on curtailing specific employer practices as well as addressing what employees may rightfully expect from their organization. Let's now turn to various aspects of human rights and employment legislation that had better be followed (whether or not management chooses to be ethical). In the next sections, we address some basic issues: employee privacy, drug and alcohol testing, whistle-blowing, employee monitoring and workplace security, dismissal, and discipline.

Privacy Act Requires federal government agencies to make available information in an individual's personnel file.

Employee Privacy

A major concern of employees in today's workplace is the *right of privacy*. There are two laws that regulate distribution of, and access to, personal information by the federal government: the *Access to Information Act* and the *Privacy Act*.[13] The Access to Information Act, enacted on July 1, 1983, gives Canadians the right of access to information contained in federal government records. This act ensures that individuals can ask for and see any information the federal government has, unless it is exempt or excluded on the grounds of national security. The *Privacy Act*, also enacted on July 1, 1983, protects Canadians against unauthorized disclosure of their personal information. These are federal laws, but every province and territory has legislation parallel to the federal *Access to Information Act* and the *Privacy Act*. For example, Manitoba's *Freedom of Information and Protection of Privacy Act*, which came into force May 4, 1998, grants individuals a right of access to information held by the provincial public sector. The act also regulates the confidentiality, collection, disclosure, and use of personal information.

The implications of the federal and parallel provincial legislation are relatively straightforward for organizational practices. For example, when an organization begins the hiring process, it establishes a personnel file for each individual that is maintained throughout the person's employment. Any pertinent information such as the completed application form, university transcripts, letters of recommendation, performance evaluations and any disciplinary warnings, medical records, and copies of materials reflecting professional development are kept in the file. Prior to 1983, access to these files often was limited to managers and members of the HR department. *The Access to Information Act* and the *Privacy Act* (and parallel provincial legislation) sought to change that imbalance of information. For example, the *Access to Information Act* requires that an employee's personnel file be open for inspection. This means that employees are permitted to review their own files periodically to ensure that the information is accurate.

A second implication of this legislation means that job applicants are entitled to receive feedback on their test performance (including reference and background checks) and on any decisions that are based on those tests.[14] This information must be provided in non-technical language that can be easily understood by the applicant. Before providing information, prospective employees must be informed about the reasons they are being tested, that the information which is collected is relevant to the job, how job-related information will be used in employment decisions, and who will have access to it.

The *Access to Information Act* and the *Privacy Act* can also help protect employees from invasive practices such as alcohol and drug testing, electronic monitoring (including inspecting e-mail), and misuse of employee records by the employer. For example, once the employer collects a blood sample from the applicant, it might obtain a profile on the applicant's health including personal aspects which may not be job-related (e.g., HIV-positive or data on DNA structure).[15]

A manager may not arbitrarily convey personal information to others, so that, information provided by the employee in a selection interview must be held in confidence, for example. Similarly, most employees want privacy on issues such as the filing of a sexual harassment complaint and prior criminal convictions. Employees do not have a right to know that their colleague has AIDS. Individuals who obtain such personal information about their colleagues have no right to disclose it to others in the organization and can be disciplined if they do.

There are, however, situations in which organizations (and the courts) have the difficult task of balancing individual and collective rights. This is where the issue of organizational ethics is critical. One can think of situations where the disclosure of HIV infection beyond the affected individual may be warranted and hence support a reason to know. For example, when a job requires certain types of contact with other individuals, say a health care provider performing invasive surgery, then the employer and colleagues ought to know that the person is HIV-infected.[16] Thus, the collective right of the employing organization may be deemed to have a higher priority that the individual's right to privacy, particularly where certain physical standards are a bona fide occupational qualification (BFOQ). Similarly, a HR department may face the daunting task of balancing a worker's privacy against other employees' physical safety. Sometimes, to protect other employees, an employer may have a duty to disclose confidential information about a threatening employee.[17] Such disclosure may include telling employees that a person has a violent background or personal problems.

Although organizations may require employees to take a medical upon being hired, the more appropriate concern is what happens if the organization finds out the employee is HIV-positive. Many companies appear to be grappling with this issue, particularly with regard to safeguarding employee confidentiality (and to reasonably accommodate the employee).[18] Organizations have to develop policies and codes of ethical conduct regarding how managers are to treat this information, specifically emphasizing the need to protect the privacy of the worker. Failure to protect the individual's privacy may result in a lawsuit.[19] Because of such pressures, many organizations have begun to pay greater attention to privacy issues and outline corporate policies on how to address privacy.

Obviously, there are some limitations on the release (or the prohibition) of personal information. For example, the law can require that personal information be released. A case in point is the *Employment Equity Act*. As discussed in Chapter 3, employers covered under that act must submit an annual report indicating progress towards employment equity goals and initiatives undertaken to attain those goals. This report becomes public information. Or suppose that you want to have access to the written reports of your harrassment case. You may be denied access to reports if these contain personal information about other individuals including the complainants, because under the *Freedom of Information Act*, you are not allowed access to personal information about other individuals.[20]

Note that the *Access to Information Act* and the *Privacy Act* (and the parallel provincial legislation) as discussed above apply only to public sector organizations. There are no laws that regulate what private businesses can do with your personal information. Thus, there is nothing to prevent a private company such as insurance companies and pharmacies from distributing your personal information to other businesses. Nevertheless, many of the larger private organizations adhere to a voluntary code so that the privacy of their employees and customers is protected. Such codes are based on the premise that employees' and clients' personal information should not be misused and individuals should have access to their personal information.

Drug and Alcohol Testing

Recently, many Canadian organizations have begun a process of drug testing. Why? Let's look at some facts. It is estimated that approximately 10 per cent of the Canadian workforce can be classified as heavy drinkers.[21] In 1996, 8 per cent of the labour force reported using illicit drugs, and 11 per cent reported that their co-worker had a drug problem.[22] Several studies have indicated that alcohol and other drug use is related to high levels of turnover, workplace accidents, absenteeism, lateness, violence, sick benefits and insurance claims, loss of productivity and human potential, low quality of products and services, and theft at work.[23] These studies show that alcohol and drug abusers have two to four times as many accidents as people who do not use drugs and alcohol, and that they can be linked to 40 per cent of industrial fatalities. Drug and alcohol use may also have a negative impact on morale and corporate image and may increase corporate liability regarding employee and public safety and the environmental impacts associated with accidents.

Drug and alcohol abuse are serious problems in the Canadian workplace, but attempts to test workers can lead to employee alienation and violation of privacy rights.

Nowadays, organizations are concerned about the liabilities associated with not taking appropriate action to prevent accidents that may result from workplace drug and alcohol use.[24] Examples include accidents caused by a drunk train engineer and an operator of a tower crane on a high-rise construction site who used marijuana. And if that weren't enough, it has been estimated that the cost of using illicit alcohol, drugs, and tobacco to Canadian society is well over $18 billion annually.[25] These data have encouraged many Canadian organizations in all industry sectors to develop and implement comprehensive programs to curb substance-related problems in their organization or reviewing and upgrading existing policies. However, in attempting to address the problem of drug abuse in the workplace, employers must balance responsibility for due diligence in dealing with potential safety risks using effective and reliable investigative and preventive tools against the dangers of creating a work atmosphere that alienates employees or violates their privacy rights.

The Martin Entrop case that we discussed at the beginning of the chapter was a precedent-setting human rights case. It was the first ruling by a provincial human rights commission that looked at whether drug testing programs violate provincial laws. Both the Ontario Board of Inquiry and the Ontario Divisional Court ruled that Imperial Oil's policy of pre-employment and random drug testing was unlawful. This decision may have important implications for any company with a workplace alcohol and drug policy that includes testing. However, given that this case is among the first in this area, companies should not conclude that it provides a final position on testing in Canada.

The courts recognized that an employer has the right to ensure that its business operations are conducted safely and to assess whether employees are incapable of performing their essential duties as listed in the job description. The courts further recognized that for safety-sensitive jobs, companies have the right to assess whether their employees are not impaired on the job—whether caused by alcohol or drug abuse or otherwise. However, without dismissing the negative impact that alcohol and drug use may have on individuals and organizations, the Ontario Board of Inquiry and the Ontario Divisional Court found that drug and alcohol testing procedures at Imperial Oil couldn't establish impairment. Let's look at this ruling and its implications in more detail.

The Ontario Board of Inquiry argued that in order to justify its actions, Imperial Oil had to prove two things.[26] First, the company had to establish that Martin Entrop—and other individuals that it disciplines, discharges, or refuses to hire on account of a positive test result—was incapable of fulfilling the essential duties of the safety-sensitive position. Specifically, Imperial Oil had to demonstrate with clear and convincing evidence that drug testing is relevant in determining whether the individual is capable of performing the essential components of the job safely and reliably, and that alcohol and drug tests reduce job accidents. However, no such data could be presented by Imperial Oil. Second, the company had to prove that Martin Entrop could not be accommodated without undue hardship. The board argued that supervisory assessment (e.g., training supervisors to detect alcohol impairment in employees), peer control (e.g., employees monitoring each other's fitness to work), and employee assistance and health promotion programs are acceptable methods of detecting impairment in the workplace. Since these alternative methods are less intrusive than the actions taken by Imperial Oil, the board found that the company had not met its duty to accommodate Entrop.

Other guidelines for alcohol and drug testing in the workplace that were identified during the Imperial Oil ruling and similar court cases include the following:[27]

1. Employers should only test for drug and alcohol use where such use results in recurring unscheduled absences from work or habitual lateness, or adversely affects the safety of the employee, other employees, or the public.
2. With respect to pre-employment testing, testing should only be conducted after the initial screening and selection process is completed and a written offer of employment has been made conditional upon successful completion of a drug test. The test cannot be used to decide whether to make an offer of employment.
3. Testing must meet rigorous standards with respect to equipment, procedure, and the qualifications and care of the technician responsible for it. The test results must be reliable. Steps must also be taken to ensure the confidentiality of all test results.
4. A blood or urine sample taken for testing can only be analysed for the substance for which the sample was taken and cannot be used for any other purpose such as HIV testing or genetic screening.

Meet

Alan Jarvis, CHRP
Director, Human Resources, McCarthy Tetrault

Every employer hopes never to have to deal with a sexual harrassment scandal—or, even worse, a lawsuit—but managers at McCarthy Tetrault, Canada's largest law firm, decided to do more than just hope. They have instituted a proactive policy designed to stop problems involving harrassment of any kind before they even start.

When this policy was first instituted, a consultant was hired, and every single employee—lawyers, administrative staff, managers, everyone—received two hours of training in harrassment issues, explains Alan Jarvis, Director of Human Resources at the firm's Toronto office. "We make it clear that harrassment—not just sexual harrassment, but all forms of workplace harrassment, because they are all unacceptable," stresses Mr Jarvis, "won't be tolerated here, and we educate employees about exactly what they can do if it does happen."

All new employees are given a short but thorough briefing on the matter during orientation. "At first, some people are taken aback to hear such a touchy issue brought up on their first day on the job," explains Mr Jarvis. "But the idea is that by talking about this issue so early on and so honestly, we give employees the idea of how seriously we take it."

If any problems do arise, McCarthy Tetrault's policy is structured to nip them in the bud as much as possible. At the first level, employees are encouraged to communicate directly to their colleagues about any behaviour they find unacceptable. "Nine times out of ten," says Mr Jarvis, "the person will apologize immediately and the behaviour stops."

If this approach doesn't work, or if for any reason employees don't feel able to use it (say, if the offending party is the boss), then they have a second level of defence: a group of harrassment advisors. These are McCarthy Tetrault employees from all areas and levels of the organization who have had extensive training in harrassment issues. Their names, phone numbers, and photographs are all published in the policy manual. They can be approached informally, off the record, to give advice, reassurance, or support as needed.

But if the offence is very serious, or if the first two levels of recourse have not solved the problem, then an employee can make a formal complaint to the harrassment committee, which consists of Mr Jarvis and three very senior partners. Committee members will listen to both sides, take written statements, and take any action warranted by the facts.

"We have very few formal complaints," says Mr Jarvis. "And we sincerely believe that this is because of the proactive, open attention we pay to this issue. We don't start with a policy. We start with the right working environment where employees are educated, feel empowered, and know exactly where they stand. And we back it up with a policy. And it's working."

What happens if the drug or alcohol test is positive? If an employee or potential employee fails a drug or alcohol test, efforts must be made to accommodate the employee. These efforts could include granting the employee leave of absence from work for medical treatment or helping the employee get into a rehabilitation program. If employees don't accept the help offered by the employer or fail several other tests, they may be terminated.[28]

Programs that test substance abuse are controversial. Many employees may recognize the need for drug testing, but they question whether the process is fair. For example, if the organization decides to implement a testing program, employees expect to be treated humanely and want safeguards built in to allow them to challenge false results. And if there is a problem, they want help not punishment. To limit employee resistance to alcohol and drug testing programs, organizations must draft a clear policy on substance abuse. In designing and implementing the policy, the employer may want to encourage employees to provide input. It is important that HR managers explain in depth to every employee the organization's policy. This policy must state what is expected of employees in terms of being substance-free, under what conditions individuals may be tested, the penalties regarding infractions of the policy, and how the process of testing and follow-up will be handled.[29] By making clear what is expected as well as what the organization intends to do, the emotional aspect of this process may be reduced.[30] Where such a policy exists, questions of legality and employee privacy are reduced.[31] Where drug testing is related to preventing accidents and actual job performance, tests have been shown to be viewed more positively by employees.[32]

Whistle-Blowing

Over the past few years, more emphasis has been placed on companies being good corporate citizens. The story of Roger Boisjoly, a Morton-Thiokol engineer, who voiced concerns about the effectiveness of O-rings but was unable to convince a stubborn bureaucracy at NASA to do anything about it, and the accusations of a systematic pattern of sexual abuse in the Canadian Armed Forces have fuelled interest in the area. One aspect of being responsible to the community at large is permitting employees to challenge management's practice without fear of retaliation. This challenge is referred to as whistle-blowing.

Whistle-blowing occurs when an employee reports the organization to an outside agency for what the employee believes is an illegal or unethical practice. In the past, these employees were often subjected to severe punishment for doing what they believed was right. For example, several years ago, an employee working in a factory engaged in the manufacture of tanks used in well water systems experienced serious health problems which he attributed to toxic airborne chemicals.[33] Furthermore, he noticed that allergic reactions, rashes, nosebleeds, and respiratory difficulties were common among his colleagues. The employee reported his concerns to management, but they did not respond. He then decided to file a written report with a local occupational health and safety office. After they conducted their investigation in the factory and management learned the identity of the whistle-blower, a supervisor physically threatened the employee for contacting the health and safety office. His personnel file rapidly became crammed with reports from his supervisors, and a video-camera secretly videotaped his performance. Eventually, the employee was fired under allegations that he had performed his job improperly. Unfortunately, no law protected him then, but this has since changed.

The federal government, as well as every province and territory, has now enacted some kind of legal protection for employees who go over their bosses' or colleagues' heads to raise questions about improper workplace conditions and management practices—in particular health and safety issues—with government authorities.[34] Today, employees are legally recognized as full partners in the pursuit of proper practices and workplace health and safety. The law also protects individuals if their employer tries to punish them in any way (e.g., threatening dismissal or suspension). If the employer is found guilty of "punishing" the employee, it can be forced to pay a hefty fine, reinstate the employee in his or her former position, and repay any lost benefits and wages. Specific

Whistle-Blowing A situation in which an employee notifies authorities of wrongdoing in an organization.

whistle-blowing provisions have been written into Nova Scotia's *Environment Act*, Ontario's *Environmental Protection Act* and *Environmental Bill of Rights*, the Yukon's *Environment Act*, and the federal government's *Canadian Environmental Protection Act*. In provinces that haven't enacted specific protection for whistle-blowing in their environmental statutes, employees may file a health-related complaint under the occupational health and safety right to refuse unsafe work (see Chapter 15, "Health and Safety").

Organizations that are not covered under federal or provincial acts may voluntarily adopt policies to permit employees to identify problem areas. The thrust of these policies is to have an established procedure to allow employees to safely raise concerns regarding organizational practices so that company can take correct action. A suggested whistle-blower policy is presented in Figure 4-1. It is important to have a workable policy in place that has the commitment of both management and employees. In the past, whistle-blowing all too often put an honest employee at loggerheads with management and created tension with colleagues who saw such actions as disloyal to the organization.[35]

Employee Monitoring and Workplace Security

Technology, enhanced in part by improvements in computers, has done some wonderful things in our work environment. It has allowed us to be more productive, to work smarter, not harder, and to bring about efficiencies in organizations that were not possible two decades ago. It has also provided us with a means of employee monitoring—what some would call spying on our employees!

Employee Monitoring An activity whereby the company is able to keep informed of its employees' activities.

Workplace security has become a critical issue for employers. Workplace security can be defined as actions on behalf of an employer to ensure that the employer's interests are protected. That is, workplace security focuses on protecting the employer's property and its trade business.[36] Without a doubt, employers must protect themselves. Employee theft or revealing trade secrets to competition can be extremely damaging to the company. In part because of significant advances in technology, it is possible to change, copy, and corrupt valuable information very quickly and sometimes undetectably. But how far can this protection extend? Can an organization conduct a search of employees' desks? Can an organization monitor employees' business calls and e-mails because it wants to preserve the sensitive nature of the work it does? Do employee monitoring tactics such as these invade an employee's privacy? Don't we need to consider employees' rights too? Obviously, the answer is yes, but how is that balance created?

Consider what happened at Canadian National Railway.[37] CNR was working to negotiate a contract with the Canadian Auto Workers Union of Canada and had submitted an offer to the conciliator. CAW then charged CN with monitoring its e-mail and filed charges of bargaining in bad faith and interfering in union affairs. However, a CN spokesperson said that the electronic system was company property for use in company business and accordingly, the company had the right to see what was going on. Furthermore, he argued that workers were regularly reminded that management could access the electronic system (e.g., employees' files and their e-mail messages) without employees' permission.

Whatever employers deem fair game, they should explain to employees in terms of a company policy.[38] For example, the organization should let its employees know that the e-mail system is not a private medium and that the employee is using company resources. Employees may be disciplined if they use company resources for anything other than company business.[39] The organization may include this policy in the employee handbook and employment applications. It can then be signed by each employee to indicate that the employee

1. Develop the policy in written form. Prepare and distribute a policy regarding appropriate business conduct that addresses issues such as giving and receiving gifts from vendors and customers and compliance with health and safety laws. Just as with an employer's sexual harassment policy, this business conduct policy should explain to the employees how they may lodge complaints and inform them that no retaliation will be taken against an employee for bringing any violation of the policy to the firm's attention.

2. Seek input from top management in developing the policy, and obtain their approval for the finished work.

3. Communicate the policy to employees in a variety of ways. Including it in the employee handbook is not enough. Active communication efforts such as ethics training (e.g., how to handle complaints of illegal activities), departmental meetings, and employee seminars will increase awareness of the policy and highlight the company's commitment to ethical behaviour.

4. Provide a reporting procedure for employees which does not require them to go to their supervisor first. Instead, designate a specific office or individual to hear initial employee complaints. Streamline the process and cut the red tape. Any employee complaints about wrongdoing should be investigated promptly and thoroughly.

5. Make it possible for employees to report anonymously, at least initially.

6. Guarantee that employees who report suspected wrongdoing in good faith will be protected from retaliation from any member of the organization. The policy should prohibit employees from retaliating against, intimidating, or otherwise interfering with other persons making disclosures of suspected wrongdoing. Make this guarantee stick.

7. Develop a formal investigative process and tell employees exactly how their reports will be handled. Use this process to investigate all reported wrongdoing. Avoid dismissing what at first glance appear to be frivolous allegations. Instead, treat all complaints seriously and report the findings of your investigation to the complaining employee.

8. If the investigation reveals that the employee's suspicions are accurate, take prompt action to correct the problem. Employees will quickly lose confidence in the policy if disclosed wrongdoing is allowed to continue. Whatever the outcome of the investigation, communicate it quickly to the whistle-blowing employee.

9. Provide an appeals process for employees dissatisfied with the outcome of the initial investigation. Provide an advocate (probably from the HR department) to assist the employee who wishes to appeal an unfavourable outcome.

10. Finally, a successful whistle-blowing policy requires more than a written procedure. It requires a commitment from the whole organization, from top management down. This commitment must be to create an ethical work environment.

Source: Timothy R. Barrett and Daniel S. Cochran, "Making Room for the Whistleblower," *HR Magazine* (January 1991), p. 59. Reprinted with permission of *HR Magazine,* published by the Society for Human Resource Management, Alexandria, Virginia.

understands and consents to the policy. Some organizations also place the policy on log-in screens to appear each time an employee uses the computer.

Part of the problem with regard to employee monitoring goes back to the balance of security versus privacy. Abuses by some employees—using the company's computer system to work on personal matters, to run their own businesses, to waste time playing computer games, for gambling, spreading of racism, or harrassing co-workers[40]—have resulted in companies taking a stronger policing role. As employee monitoring issues become more noticeable, one should keep a few things in mind. As long as they have a policy regarding how employees are monitored, employers may continue to check on employee behaviour. Specifically targeted for this monitoring are system computers, e-mail, and the telephone. In companies such as Federal Express, Bell Canada, and UPS, employees are continually told that they may be monitored. Some organizations have a policy but don't monitor employee behaviour, while there are organizations that do not have a policy but do monitor their employees. However, it is considered unethical not to inform employees that management will monitor their behaviour (or already does).[41] Undoubtedly, the debate regarding the ethics of employee monitoring will continue (see "Ethical Decisions in HRM"). Nonetheless, only when employees understand what the company expects, the relationship between its security and their privacy, and how it will gather its information will their rights be safeguarded.[42]

Dismissal

Dismissal A disciplinary action that results in the termination of an employee.

Dismissal means any kind of termination by an employer and includes firing, lay-off, suspension, lockout, plant closure, and so on. Employers have a right to terminate employees; no employee is automatically entitled to employment for life. Individuals may be dismissed for reasons such as excessive absenteeism, lateness, theft, fraud, and poor performance. A job, however, may also be terminated for reasons beyond the control of either the employee or the employer. For example, an organization can be forced to reorganize and lay off some of its employees. Similarly, a natural disaster may damage the workplace and the employer may have no other choice but to temporarily terminate the contracts of its employees. Whatever the reason for losing their jobs, and despite the fact that Canadian labour law is fairly employer-friendly, employees do have some basic legal protection.[43] For example, employees can challenge the legality of their dismissal and argue that they were wrongfully discharged. Furthermore, employers can only terminate the contracts of employees without reasonable notice when just cause exists. This section addresses such questions as: "Can my employer fire me?" "How valid are its reasons for firing me?" "Does my employer have to give me notice?" "What actions can I undertake if I believe my dismissal is unfair?" and "What is the significance of 'good faith and fair dealing' in dismissal?"

Reasonable Notice The employer has to let the employee know, and offer a specific and reasonable time frame, that he or she will be dismissed.

Reasonable Notice and Pay in Lieu of Notice Dismissal can take many forms including lay-off, firing, demotion, the sale of the business, and so on. In any of these cases, the employer needs to provide employes with **reasonable notice** in writing to help them in their transition to new employment. Severance payment is still owed by the employer, even if an individual finds other work quickly after his or her dismissal. The length of reasonable notice is determined in several ways. First, it is spelled out in collective agreements. Every province and territory requires that all collective agreements contain a clause providing for arbitration of disputed disciplinary action, principally dismissals.[44] These clauses must address reasonable notice as well as grievance and arbitration procedures.

Second, employment standards legislation contains provisions regarding reasonable notice. Though there are differences between provinces and territories, a typical notice period under provincial employment standards legislation is as follows:

Ethical Decisions in HRM:

Employee Monitoring

If you worked for Canadian National Railway in almost any of their many jobs and used their e-mail system, how would you feel if your supervisor routinely read your computer messages? Or how would you feel if the organization you work for installed a pinhole camera in the ceiling over your desk to keep an electronic eye on you? Used alone or in conjunction with other technology, pinhole cameras can capture a person stealing electronic equipment, loading up on copier paper, sleeping on the job, or spending hours on the Internet. Technology today makes it possible, even easy, for companies to monitor their employees. Electronic surveillance in Canada has grown, in part because equipment is readily available and relatively inexpensive. Many organizations use such equipment in the hopes that it will help both them and their employees become more productive and more quality-oriented. For example, Bell Canada monitors telephone calls to assess quality of customer service work.

Consider that it is almost kids' play to monitor cellular phone conversations or to intercept and copy fax transmissions. Or, take the case of Olivetti, which has employees wearing "smart" identification badges which can track the whereabouts of an employee. That can be helpful in having messages transferred to your location, but it also means that Olivetti managers may know their employees' every move. An important consideration is when such employee snooping becomes unethical.

Just how pervasive is this practice of monitoring employees? Exact numbers are simply not known, but according to a recent study by the American Management Association, almost two-thirds of the firms that responded—including banks, realtors, insurance firms, and brokerages—said they practised some form of electronic monitoring and surveillance (e.g., videotaping theft and sabotage, recording the number and duration of phone calls, and reviewing e-mail messages and computer files). It is believed that a similar percentage of Canadian organizations monitor their employees electronically.

Employers should issue an employee monitoring policy that details what is monitored, when information or behaviour is monitored, and how this information is used. When such steps are taken, employees appear more tolerant of being monitored, but even then, employees appear to exhibit more stress-related symptoms than employees who are not being monitored.

Yes, employee monitoring can help enhance performance and provide valuable feedback to both the employer and the employee, but at what point does the organization's need for that information violate an employee's right to privacy? What's your opinion?

Source: Adapted from Lee Smith, "What the Boss Knows About You," *Fortune* (August 9, 1993), pp. 88-93; Peter Fitzpatrick, "CAW Union Says CN Spies on Workers," *Financial Post*, April 6, 1998, p .10; AMA Survey: *Electronic Monitoring and Surveillance*, (New York: University Publications of America, 1997); Johanna Powell, "Keeping An Eye on The Workplace," *Financial Post*, September 8, 1997, p. 24; "The Games We Play: Monitoring the Computer Habits of Your Employees", *Benefits Canada*, Vol. 21, No. 9, October, 1997, p. 11.

a. one week if an employee worked for at least three consecutive months for the employer;
b. two weeks if an employee worked for twelve months;
c. three weeks for three years of work; and
d. An additional week of notice for each extra year up to a maximum of eight weeks notice.[45]

Length of service obviously is a key factor in the establishment of reasonable notice. However, reasonable notice may also be affected by the number of people dismissed as well as the reason for dismissal. At the federal level, the *Canada Labour Code* contains provisions regarding reasonable notice for employers and employees whose operations fall under federal jurisdiction.

Third, employees may decide to sue the employer for **wrongful dismissal**.[46] Note that in most situations, wrongful dismissals focus on the insufficient length of notice rather than whether the person should or should not have been dismissed. The courts generally stipulate much larger notice periods than the minimum requirements set by employment standards legislation. For example, in a recent Ontario Court of Appeal decisions, a fifty-five-year-old female clerical employee with twenty-nine years of service was awarded a notice period of twenty months,[47] which was later reduced to twelve months' notice on appeal. The courts generally consider a number of criteria for establishing the reasonable notice period.[48] Factors may include:

1. length of service;
2. level of position;
3. age of the employee;
4. ability to find comparable employment;
5. nature of industry the employee works in;
6. industry custom with regard to dismissal and notice;
7. employee's experience, training, and qualifications; and
8. circumstances of hiring (e.g., was the employee lured from another job, perhaps from out of town, and therefore was the spouse forced to leave a good job?).

In calculating damages for breach of the implied employment contract, the courts have observed an informal upper limit of twenty-four months' notice. Basically, the damages—salary and employment benefits—that are awarded are intended to put employees in the position they would have been in if the employer had given them proper notice.

Alternatively, an employer may choose to provide a severance payment instead of notice. That is, the employer gives the employee a cheque for the equivalent of the wages and benefits that would have been earned over the reasonable notice period.[49] This is known as **pay in lieu of notice**.

Under certain conditions, the employer is not required to give the employees reasonable notice or provide pay in lieu of notice. For example, if a company fails and creditors foreclose, no advance notice to employees is required. Similarly, reasonable notice is not required when an employee refuses a reasonable offer of another job with the employer. Furthermore, certain groups of employees are not covered under the dismissal provisions of employment standards legislation (e.g., professionals, domestic servants, people working in the agricultural sector, and individuals who do contract work). However, these individuals can file complaints with the courts to enforce their rights.

The Concept of Just Cause The employer is not required to give advance notice in writing or offer a severance payment when the employee is dismissed for just cause. Dismissal based on just cause arises when individuals are considered to

Wrongful Dismissal The employee has been given an insufficient length of notice.

Pay in Lieu of Notice Rather than giving the employee reasonable notice, the organization offers the employee a lump sum of money that would have been earned over the reasonable notice period.

have broken the employer-employee relationship.[50] One example of just cause is excessive absenteeism and lateness, which can be a very serious issue, in an emergency hospital room, for example. Consequently, an employer can dismiss the employee based on just cause. In other less serious conditions, the employer would be expected to warn the employee formally before proceeding with dismissal. A second example of just cause dismissal is improper conduct. For example, a school board can dismiss a teacher who sexually molested a student. There is, however, no hard and fast rule as to what exactly constitutes just cause.

When individuals believe they were dismissed without just cause, they may seek the assistance of a Labour Standards branch, a Human Resources Development Canada branch, or the courts to address their dismissal. For example, an employer may have no proof that Stan stole the missing computer equipment, but it suspects he did it. If Stan is dismissed under these circumstances, he may file a complaint with the court. Similarly, an employer may consciously try to avoid paying an employee severance pay by claiming that she has been dismissed for just cause. Therefore, individuals should always look carefully at the reasons that are given for dismissal. The fact that the organization may be losing money or that a job has become redundant because of technological changes in the workplace, is not a good enough reason for just cause dismissal, and hence, notice must be given. If challenged, it is up to the employer to prove that the dismissal was for just cause. Unionized employees should consult their collective agreement and find out about clauses providing arbitration in dismissal disputes.

There are a few guidelines derived from labour arbitration of collective bargaining relationships (we'll look at discipline in labour-management relationships in Chapter 18, "Handling a Grievance") under which just cause can be shown:

1. Was there adequate warning of consequences of the worker's behaviour?
2. Are the rules reasonable and related to safe and efficient operations of the business?
3. Before discipline was rendered, did a fair investigation of the violation occur?
4. Did the investigation yield definite proof of worker activity and wrongdoing?
5. Have similar occurrences, before and after this event, been handled the same and without discrimination?
6. Was the penalty in line with the seriousness of the offence and with the worker's past employment record?

If the courts or a human rights tribunal are not convinced that dismissal was based on just cause, it can order the employer to do a number of things. Organizations can be ordered to pay the employee a severance payment, to reinstate the employee in his or her former job, or to compensate the employee for lost wages and benefits. Of course, claims filed by the employee may also be dismissed.

Discrimination laws such as those discussed in Chapter 3 further limit an employer's use of terminations. For example, an employer cannot fire an employee based on his or her age just because that would save the company some money. Human rights legislation protects employees from being dismissed for reasons such as age, race, religion, and physical disability.

Good Faith and Fair Dealing It's crucial that in the process of dismissing employees, the employer treats them with respect and dignity. Recent court cases have indicated that the employer will be held accountable if it treats people with disrespect (e.g., frogmarching the employee out the door under the escort of a security guard).[51] Specifically, where the employee has been dismissed in a way that leads to mental distress (see "Case Application: Heartlessness Has a

●

Good Faith and Fair Dealing
In the process of dismissal,
the employer should treat
the employee with respect
and dignity.

Constructive Dismissal The
employer unilaterally changes
the conditions of employ-
ment to the effect that employees are demoted without
their consent.

Price" at the end of the chapter), or increased difficulty in securing alternative employment (e.g., the employer is not willing to write a reference letter or made false accusations of theft), some courts have awarded damages to the employee well in excess of what normally constitutes reasonable notice. Thus, even if an employee has been caught stealing or showed a complete disregard for the health and safety of colleagues, it is important that the employer treats individuals with respect as opposed to acting in an outrageous fashion. If an employer does not treat its employees with good faith and fair dealing when being dismissed, the courts may decide to impose damages in addition to reasonable notice or pay in lieu of notice.[52] In conclusion, an obligation of good faith and fair dealing in dismissal should, just like reasonable notice, be an implied term of the employment contract.

Employers must also watch what they say after the employee is gone. In the past, poorly considered remarks about the departed employee have resulted in high awards. For example, in 1997, in *Deildal v. Tod Mountain Ltd.*, the British Columbia Court of Appeal ruled that Bruce Deildal, who was employed as general manager, was not only wrongfully dismissed, but that his employer defamed him by saying that he had been fired for gross incompetence and misappropriating $750,000 of the company's funds.[53] The company had no evidence to support the charges, and Deildal was awarded $155,983.

Constructive Dismissal We should note here that dismissal may be much more subtle than firing people. Individuals may have been demoted, had their salary reduced, or their responsibilities limited—for example, a plant superintendent whose duties are confined to those of a yard supervisor. In this case, the employer has unilaterally changed the conditions of employment. This is known as constructive dismissal. Alternatively, an employer may force an employee to resign. For example, the employer can make threats of a demotion and reduce an employee's hours of work. This, too, is a case of constructive dismissal. However, what exactly constitutes constructive dismissal is seldom clear-cut, and cases often need to be examined on an individual basis in which all the unique conditions of the specific situation must be weighed before a judgement can be rendered.[54] For example, even though a change in the location of employment can be grounds for constructive dismissal, it is not where the employee is moved to another location in the same city or if the employee knew that potential relocation was part of the job.

The courts have determined that the unjust dismissal provisions of the *Canada Labour Code* and employment standards legislation apply to instances of constructive dismissals. A landmark case is *Farber v. Royal Trust Co.*[55] In 1984, David Farber, an executive with Royal Trust Co., sued his employer, claiming that he had been constructively dismissed. In 1983, Farber held the position of regional manager for Western Quebec in which he supervised twenty-one Royal Trust branches employing approximately four hundred real estate agents. His total remuneration that year was close to $150,000. In 1984, as part of a major restructuring of its operations, Royal Trust decided to eliminate a number of regional management positions including that of Farber. In replacement of his lost position, Farber was offered the position of branch manager. He had held a similar position eight years earlier, but unlike his previous one, this one did not include a guaranteed salary. Moreover, the office in question was one of the least profitable in the province. Based on the performance of the branch, Farber expected that his income would be cut in half. Farber was not successful in negotiating an alternative, more advantageous agreement, and he eventually sued Royal Trust Co. In 1997, the Supreme Court of Canada found that Royal

Trust Co. made a unilateral and substantial negative change to the fundamental terms of employment.[56] Farber had no longer the same status (regional manager versus branch manager), and the loss of the basic salary was significant. Even though Farber rejected the change and left his job, the Supreme Court ruled that Farber had been constructively dismissed—he did not resign—and hence was entitled to reasonable notice. Farber was awarded $150,000.

This case has significant implications for organizations. It suggests, for example, that employees affected by reorganizations do not necessarily need to accept new positions that the employer offers to them, especially if these are paid less and have less prestige than the previous positions. However, any employer retains the right to unilaterally make changes to the employee's situation as long as these changes are permitted by the employment contract. Thus, smart employers will recognize the ever-increasing importance of having detailed and well-drafted employment contracts.

Discipline

The previous discussion may be leading you to think that it is virtually impossible for employers to terminate employees, or that they are significantly limited in their action, but that is not the case. There are many possible reasons for dismissal. But regardless of the reason, dismissal must follow a specific process. This process, and how its works, is covered in the topic we call discipline.

What Is Discipline? For the most part, employees discipline themselves by conforming to what is considered proper behaviour because they believe it is the right thing to do. Once they are made aware of what is expected of them and assuming they find these standards or rules to be reasonable, they seek to meet those expectations. But not all employees accept the norms of responsible employee behaviour. These employees, then, require some degree of disciplinary action, frequently labeled punishment, which is expected to decrease the probability of the reoccurrence of the unwanted behaviour. Some of the most common problems that warrant disciplinary action include the non-performance of job duties, chronic absenteeism and lateness, disruptive relationships with co-workers and supervisors, and the damaging of company property. It is this need to impose disciplinary action that we will address in the following sections.

Factors to Consider When Disciplining Before we review disciplinary guidelines, we should look at some major factors that need to be considered if we are to have fair and equitable disciplinary practices. The following contingency factors can help us analyse a discipline problem:[57]

1. **Seriousness of the Problem**: How severe is the problem? As noted previously, dishonesty is usually considered a more serious infraction in a bank teller than reporting to work twenty minutes late.
2. **Duration of the Problem**: Have there been other discipline problems in the past and over how long a time span? Violations do not take place in a vacuum. A first occurrence is usually viewed differently than a third or fourth offense.
3. **Frequency and Nature of the Problem**: Is the current problem part of an emerging or continuing pattern of disciplinary infractions? We are concerned with not only the duration, but also the pattern of the problem. Continual infractions may require a different type of discipline than that applied to isolated instances of misconduct. They may also point out a situation that demands far more severe discipline in order to prevent a minor problem from becoming a major one. For example, absenteeism may become chronic and hence, of great concern to the employer.

Punishment Penalizing an employee for undesirable behaviours.

4. **Extenuating Factors**: Are there any extenuating circumstances related to the problem? An employee who snapped at a client because he made a request for sexual favours is likely to have her behaviour assessed more leniently than will one who snapped at a client who was reluctant to sign the mortgage.

5. **Degree of Socialization**: To what extent has management made an earlier effort to educate the person causing the problem about the existing rules and procedures and the consequences of violations? Discipline severity must reflect the degree of knowledge that the violator holds of the organization's standards of acceptable behaviour. In contrast to Point 4, a new employee is less likely to have been socialized to these standards than a five-year veteran. The organization that has formalized, written rules governing employee conduct is more justified in enforcing violations of the rules aggressively than is one whose rules are informal or vague.

6. **History of the Organization's Discipline Practices**: How have similar infractions been dealt with in the past? Has there been consistency in the application of discipline procedures? Equitable treatment of employees must take into account precedents within the unit where the infraction occurs as well as previous disciplinary actions taken in other units within the organization.

7. **Management Backing**: If an employee decides to take his or her case to a higher level in management, will you have reasonable evidence to justify your decision? Should the employee challenge your disciplinary action, it is important that you have the data to back up the necessity and fairness of the action taken and that you feel confident that your superiors will support your action. No disciplinary action will carry much weight if violators believe that they can challenge and override their manager's decision.

How can these seven items help? There are many reasons why an employee might be disciplined, but these may be minor or serious depending on the situation. For example, concealing defective work on a hand tool assembly line may be viewed as minor, whereas the same action in a pharmaceutical manufacturing plant is more serious. A minor offence may result in a lecture, while a serious offence might mean not being allowed to return to one's work for a period of time, depending on the circumstances.

Disciplinary Guidelines All human resources managers should be aware of some disciplinary guidelines. In this section, we will briefly describe them.

Make Disciplinary Action Corrective Rather than Punitive The object of disciplinary action is not to deal out punishment.[58] The purpose of discipline is to improve job-related behaviour and performance. While punishment may be a necessary means to that end, one should never lose sight of the ultimate objective. Punishment has at least two drawbacks.[59] First, it tells the individual to stop doing something but does not tell them what to do instead. Second, punishment can produce anger, outrage, resentment, and retaliatory behaviour against the person administering the punishment. For example, employees may engage in sabotage or display uncooperative behaviour if they feel that a reprimand was unjust. Thus, punishment can be a risky strategy to suppress unwanted behaviour.

Make Disciplinary Action Progressive Although the type of disciplinary action that is appropriate may vary depending on the situation, it is generally desirable for discipline to be progressive.[60] The punishment should fit the crime and should escalate with the seriousness of the infraction. Only for the most serious violations will an employee be dismissed after a first offence. For example, an employer may decide to dismiss an employee who dumped a dozen litres of highly toxic and hazardous materials (see Chapter 15, "Health and Safety") down the drain, straight into the sewer. Progressive discipline tries to resolve a work-related conflict using the least severe action necessary to correct an unwanted behaviour.

Typically, **progressive disciplinary action** begins with a verbal warning or reprimand and proceeds through a written warning, suspension without pay, and, only in the most serious cases, dismissal. Thus, more severe forms of punishment result if the unwanted behaviour continues or if the severity of the infractions increases. In order for progressive discipline to work, both the manager and employee must be aware of the standards of conduct and job performance requirements and of the possible consequences for violating these standards.

Follow the Hot-Stove Rule Administering discipline is like touching a hot stove—both are painful to the recipient. But the analogy goes further. When you touch a hot stove, you get an immediate response; the burn you receive is instantaneous, leaving no question of cause and effect. You have ample warning; you know what happens if you touch a red-hot stove. Furthermore, the result is consistent—every time you touch a hot stove, you get the same response: you get burned. Finally, the result is impersonal—regardless of who you are, if you touch a hot stove, you will get burned. The comparison between touching a hot stove and administering discipline should be apparent, but let us briefly expand on each of the four points in the analogy. [61]

The longer the time between the infraction and the penalty, the less impact a disciplinary action will have. The more quickly the discipline follows the offence, the more likely it is that the employee will associate the discipline with the offence rather than with the manager imposing the discipline. As a result, it is best that the disciplinary process begin as soon as possible after the violation is noticed. This also communicates the seriousness of the infraction both to the employee who violated the policy and others in the organization who may have witnessed the violation. However, before taking any action, it is important to evaluate the situation and gather all the facts. If all the facts are not in, managers may temporarily suspend the employee pending a final decision in the case. The manager has an obligation to give advance warning prior to initiating formal disciplinary action. This means the employee must be aware of the organization's rules and accept its standards of behaviour. Disciplinary action is more likely to be seen as fair by employees when there is clear warning that a given violation will lead to discipline and what that discipline will be.

Fair treatment of employees also demands that disciplinary action be consistent. When rule violations are enforced in an inconsistent manner, the rules will lose their impact and morale will decline. For example, if Tanya and Marie both have a poor attendance record and Tanya is reprimanded while Marie is not, Tanya is likely to question the fairness of the action. The point, then, is that discipline should be consistent. This need not result in treating everyone exactly alike because that ignores the contingency factors we discussed earlier, but it does put the responsibility on management to clearly justify disciplinary actions that may appear inconsistent to employees.

The last guideline that flows from the hot-stove rule is: keep the discipline impersonal. Penalties should be connected with a given violation, not with the personality of the violator. That is, discipline should be directed at what the employee has done, not directly at the employee. As a manager, you should make it clear that you are avoiding personal judgements about the employee's character. You are penalizing the rule violation, not the individual, and all employees committing the violation can expect to be penalized. In addition, the employee will be sensitive to the quality of the interpersonal treatment received during the enactment of organizational procedures.[62] Does the manager display social sensitivity such as when he treats employees with respect and dignity (e.g.,

Progressive Disciplinary Action The discipline process generally follows a sequence from less to more severe punishment or discipline.

listening to an employee's concerns or providing adequate explanations for decisions)? Furthermore, once the penalty has been imposed, you as manager must make every effort to forget the incident; you should attempt to treat the employee in the same manner you did prior to the infraction.

Disciplinary Action Discipline generally follows a typical sequence of four steps: written verbal warning, written warning, suspension, and dismissal[63] (see Figure 4-2). Let's briefly review these four steps.

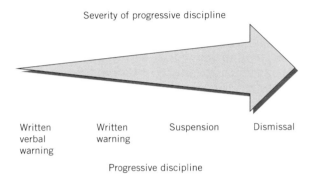

Severity of progressive discipline

Written verbal warning   Written warning   Suspension   Dismissal

Progressive discipline

Figure 4-2
The Progressive Discipline Process

Written Verbal Warning The mildest form of discipline is the written verbal warning. A written verbal warning is a temporary record of a reprimand that is then placed in the manager's file on the employee. This should state the purpose, date, and outcome of the interview with the employee. This, in fact, is what differentiates the written verbal warning from the verbal warning. Because of the need to document this step in the process, the verbal warning must be put into writing. The difference, however, is that this warning remains in the hands of the manager—that is, the warning is not forwarded to the HR department for inclusion in the employee's personnel file.

The written verbal reprimand works best if done in a private and informal environment rather than in front of co-workers to protect the self-worth and dignity of the employee. The manager should begin by clearly informing the employee of the rule that has been violated and the problem that this has caused. For example, if the employee has been late several times, the manager would reiterate the organization's rule that employees are to be at their desks by 8:30 a.m. Then she should proceed to give specific evidence of how violation of this rule has resulted in an increase in workload for others and has lowered departmental morale. After the problem has been made clear, the manager should then allow the employee to respond and encourage her to give her side of the story. The employee must be given an opportunity to answer or explain any complaints or allegations about her behaviour or performance. Is she aware of the problem? Are there any extenuating circumstances that may justify her behaviour? What does she plan to do to correct her behaviour? The manager should ask as many questions as she needs to understand the situation from the employee's perspective.

After the employee has been given the opportunity to make her case, the manager must determine if the employee has proposed an adequate solution to the problem. If not, the manager should direct the discussion towards helping the employee figure out ways to prevent the trouble from reoccurring. Once a solution has been mutually agreed upon, the manager should ensure that the employee understands what, if any, follow-up action will be taken if the problem reoccurs.

If the written verbal warning is effective, further disciplinary action can be avoided. If the employee fails to improve, however, the manager will need to consider more severe action.

Written Warning The written warning is the first formal stage of the disciplinary procedure because the written warning becomes part of the employee's official personnel file. This is achieved by not only giving the warning to the employee, but also by sending a copy to the HR department to be inserted in the employee's permanent record. In all other ways, however, the procedure concerning the writing of the warning is the same as the written verbal warning; that is, the employee is advised in private of the violation, its effects, and potential consequences of future violations. The only difference is that the discussion concludes with the employee being told that a formal written warning will be issued. Then the manager writes up the warning—stating the problem, the rule that has been violated, any acknowledgment by the employee to correct her behaviour, and the consequences from a reoccurrence of the deviant behaviour—and sends it to the HR department.

Some organizations may not agree with the principle of a written warning. Instead they may consider the formal letter of reprimand that is part of the personnel file outdated and hence, will remove it from the file when the immediate supervisor determines that the deficiency giving rise to the reprimand has been overcome.

Suspension A suspension or lay-off would be the next disciplinary step, usually taken only if the prior steps have been tried without success. There are exceptions—where a suspension is given without any prior verbal or written warning—if the infraction is of a serious nature (such as stealing computer equipment or fighting in the workplace) which call for immediate action.

A suspension, often without pay, may be for one day or for several weeks. Some organizations skip this step completely because it can have negative consequences for both the company and the employee. From the organization's perspective, a suspension means the loss of the employee for the lay-off period. If the person has unique skills or is a vital part of a complex process, his or her loss during the suspension period can have a severe impact if a suitable replacement cannot be located. Other costs to the organization may include the recruiting and training of a replacement employee, and damage to the organization's reputation following dismissal. From the employee's standpoint, a suspension can result in the employee returning with a more unpleasant and negative attitude.

Why should management consider suspending employees as a disciplinary measure? The answer is that a short lay-off without pay is potentially a rude awakening to problem employees. It may convince them that management is serious and shock them into accepting responsibility for following the organization's rules. Alternatively, employees may be given time to think about what they are doing and whether they want to continue working for the company.

Dismissal Management's ultimate disciplinary punishment is firing the problem employee, which should be used only for the most serious offences. Yet it may be the only feasible alternative when an employee's behaviour is so bad that it seriously interferes with the organization's operation. For example, mutual fund managers face a potential conflict between their own interests and those of clients when they invest for themselves instead of for the funds they manage. If they break the organizational policy, they may be severely punished, even barred from the industry.[64]

Long and hard consideration should be given before dismissing an employee. For almost all individuals, being fired from a job is an emotional trauma. For employees who have been with the organization for many years and for those over fifty years of age, dismissal can make it difficult to obtain another job without extensive retraining. In addition, management should consider the possibility that a dismissed employee will take legal action to fight the decision. As discussed earlier, the organization can be held responsible for legal and court fees including damage awards if the suspension or dismissal was wrongful.

Positive Discipline: Can It Work? Although discipline is often regarded as negative—punitive action taken out on someone who has done something wrong—positive discipline attempts to remove the punitive nature from the process. Positive discipline treats discipline as a necessary educational process, the aim of which is to correct undesirable and unacceptable behaviour by letting an employee know through concrete experience what is expected.[65] When problems arise, rather than promptly responding with a written verbal warning, positive discipline attempts to get the employee back on track by helping to convince the individual to abide by company performance standards. Positive discipline teaches employees to take perspective and may lead them to develop ways of putting themselves into another person's shoes. Together with the manager, the employee then tries to identify and implement a solution for the problem behaviour (e.g., did the employee greet and offer help to customers soon after they entered the store, and did the employee suggest other products and point out their features). The basis of positive discipline is presented in Table 4-1.

Positive Discipline A form of discipline that tries to eliminate the punitive nature from the discipline process and instead treats discipline as an education process.

TABLE 4-1 Steps in Positive Discipline

Step 1: An Oral Reminder	Notice here that the word warning is removed. The oral reminder serves as the initial formal phase of the process to outline the work problems the employee is having. This reminder is designed to identify what is causing the problem and ways to correct it before it becomes larger.
Step 2: A Written Reminder	If the oral reminder was unsuccessful, a more formalized version is implemented. This written reminder once again reinforces what the problems are and what corrective action is necessary. Specific timetables that the employee must accept and abide by, and the consequences for failing to comply are often included.
Step 3: A Decision-Making Leave	Here, employees are given a decision-making leave—time off from work, often with pay—to think about what they are doing and whether or not they want to continue work for the company. This "deciding day" is designed to allow the employee an opportunity to make a choice to correct the behaviour or face separation from the company.

Study Tools and Applications

Summary

This summary relates to the Learning Objectives provided on p. 99.

After having read this chapter, you should know:

1. Ethical considerations affect human resources management in a number of ways—in selection, laying off employees, in dealing with unions, employee safety, and so forth. To protect employee rights and dignity, ethical consideration means going beyond the law in employment decisions.

2. The intent of the *Access to Information Act* of 1983 was to give Canadians access to information contained in federal records. The *Privacy Act* of 1983 protects individuals against unauthorized disclosure of their personal information. Provinces and territories have legislation that parallels these federal acts. For example, under these acts, employers are required to make available to employees information in their personnel files; alternatively, managers may not arbitrarily reveal personal information to others.

3. The first important guideline of alcohol and drug testing in the workplace is that it must be relevant in determining whether the individual has the capability to perform the essential components of the job safely and reliably, and that alcohol and drug tests reduce job accidents. Second, with regard to privacy, the employer must show that employees cannot be accommodated without undue hardship.

4. The federal government and the provinces and territories have enacted some kind of legal protection for employees who wish to report the organization to an outside agency for what they believe is an illegal or unethical practice. This legislation protects individuals from employers who try to punish them for their acts. Organizations that are not covered under federal or provincial acts or codes often voluntarily adopt policies to permit employees to identify problem areas.

5. Employers need to explain their monitoring systems to employees and make sure that the monitoring is related to the job or business. For example, the employer needs to explain under what conditions employees may be monitored and how the process of violations of the policy will be handled. Organizations can include the monitoring policy in the employee handbook or place the information on log-in screens. In designing and implementing the policy, the employer may want to invite employee input; this may reduce the emotional aspect of the policy.

6. Dismissal based on just cause arises when an employee behaves in such a manner that he or she is considered to have broken the employer–employee relationship or the employment contract. Wrongful dismissals typically focus on the insufficient length of notice given by the employer.

7. Employees who believe they have been wrongfully dismissed can seek the help of the courts (case law) or a labour standards branch (employment standards legislation). Unionized employees may consult the collective agreement that outlines grievance and arbitration procedures.

8. Employees generally conduct themselves in accordance with the organization's rules and standards of acceptable behaviour, but when they do not, discipline is imposed. How severe the chosen action is should be based on things such as the seriousness and duration of the problem, its frequency and nature, the employee's work history, extenuating circumstances, degree of orientation, history of the organization's discipline practices, implications for other employees, and management backing.

9. General guidelines in administering discipline include making disciplinary actions corrective, making them progressive, and following the hot-stove rule—be immediate, provide ample warning, be consistent, and be impersonal.

Key Terms

best practices
constructive dismissal
dismissal
employee rights
employee monitoring
ethical codes and standards
ethics
good faith and fair dealing

pay in lieu of notice
positive discipline
Privacy Act
progressive discipline
punishment
reasonable notice
whistle-blowing
wrongful dismissal

EXPERIENTIAL EXERCISE

Drug testing continues to be one of the more intrusive aspects of our hiring process. Many see the need for drug testing but may object to how it is done. For this exercise, you need to form two groups. One group will develop reasons supporting drug testing of all applicants and employees; the other will develop reasons against such a process. Once you have generated your facts, the two groups should come together and debate the merits of their case. Each side should prepare a ten-minute, uninterrupted presentation. After both sides have presented, allow ten minutes for each group to respond to questions. After points and counterpoints have been addressed, answer the following questions.

1. What were the main issues raised by both groups?
2. What similarities existed between the two? What differences existed? Explain.

CASE APPLICATION:

Heartlessness Has a Price

In 1986, Jack Wallace, a long-time salesman for United Grain Growers Ltd. in Winnipeg, was dismissed without notice or explanation. Fourteen years earlier (1972), he had been lured away from a secure job with promises that if he performed as expected, he would be employed with United Grain Growers Ltd. until retirement. Jack Wallace enjoyed great success in the company. He was at one time the company's top printing division salesperson. A few days before his dismissal, Jack Wallace was complimented by his boss on his performance.

The employer decided to play hardball about a severance payment and claimed that Jack Wallace was fired for just cause. United Grain Growers Ltd. claimed that Jack Wallace had been insubordinate and failed to carry out his duties. However, the company later admitted that he was fired for no good reason. Rumours about the reasons for his firing haunted Jack Wallace, and he was unable to find another job. He became depressed, sought psychiatric help, and eventually filed for personal bankruptcy.

In 1993, the Manitoba Court of Queen's Bench awarded Jack Wallace twenty-four months' salary ($157,718) in lieu of notice. This lengthy period was warranted given his age, his fourteen-year tenure, and his limited prospects for re-employment. Also taken into consideration was the fact that Jack Wallace was earlier induced to leave secure employment. In addition, Jack Wallace collected $15,000 in aggravated damages for his mental distress. This was one of the highest no-notice awards in Canada. However, the Manitoba Appeal Court later reduced the twenty-four months to fifteen months of salary and tossed out the aggravated damages claim. Jack Wallace then appealed to the Supreme Court of Canada which, in 1998, unanimously restored the twenty-four-month pay award, but refused to give him the extra $15,000. The Supreme Court of Canada later commented that bad-faith conduct in the manner of Jack Wallace's dismissal was a factor compensated for by an addition to the notice period.

The implication of this ruling by the Supreme Court is relatively straightforward for employers. Calculating reasonable notice and the financial settlement of dismissal used to be largely a function of the number of months or years an employee had worked for the company. Under the recent Supreme Court ruling, however, employers who terminate staff are obliged to be sensitive to the departing person's feelings and must be reasonable and honest in the way they handle the dismissal. Bad-faith conduct in the manner of dismissal (e.g., subjecting employees to insensitive treatment in their dismissal, humiliation, embarrassment, and showing no regard for their welfare) is another factor that should be compensated for. Stated differently, compensation given to a fired employee can be affected by the way the employee is treated, and employers have an obligation of good faith and fair dealing when dismissing employees.

The Supreme Court argued that since the employee is most vulnerable at the point at which the relationship between employer and employee ruptures (e.g., the employee often lacks bargaining power), he or she is in need of protection. To recognize this need, the Supreme Court of Canada felt that the law ought to encourage conduct that minimizes the economic and personal damage that may result from dismissal.

Questions

1. The ruling by the Supreme Court of Canada has some far-reaching implications for organizations. What possible problems do you see with this ruling?
2. The termination interview is very important and requires skill. The courts have been increasingly critical of employers who conduct terminations in a heartless manner. What is the right way to fire someone, and how would you handle a termination interview?

Source: Laura Ramsay, "Court Decision Lays Down the Law on Firings: Companies Can Expect to Pay Out Extra Compensation if Termination Procedure Ignores Employee's Vulnerability," *Financial Post*, November 8, 1997, p. 41; Michael Fitz James, "Winnipeg Case Advances Law of Wrongful Dismissal," *Financial Post*, November 4, 1997, p. 16; *Wallace v. United Grain Growers Ltd.*, 1997, S.C.J. No. 94.

Testing Your Understanding

How well did you fulfil the learning objectives?

1. Dana is rewriting the section of the policies and procedures manual for her organization regarding employees' access to their employment history files. Which statement is most appropriate?
   a. No employee shall have access to any data in his or her file.
   b. Any employee may have access to any employee file data with supervisor approval.
   c. An employee may have access to his or her file with twenty-four-hour notice to personnel. The file must be reviewed in the human resources department area.
   d. Any employee file may be requested by the employee. File contents will be mailed to the employee's official home address.
   e. Any employee may have access to his or her employee file with signatory approval of the immediate supervisor and one additional level of management.

2. The *Access to Information Act* and the *Privacy Act* contain which provision?
   a. An employer can refuse an employee's request to examine his or her medical records in the personnel file.
   b. Prospective employees must be informed how the information in selection tests will be used and who will have access to these data.
   c. Genetic screening for the purpose of selecting a workforce that is free of potential genetic liabilities such as cancer and diabetes.
   d. Job applicants may refuse to submit letters of recommendation and a credit check. Organizations must hire them anyway if all other relevant selection criteria are met.

e. Once the selection decision has been made, letters of recommendation must be removed from an employee's file within ninety days.

3. A vice-president of human resources for a large farm equipment contractor has developed a drug-free workplace compliance policy that defines expected employee behaviours and states penalties for non-compliance. This policy should also include
   a. providing substance-abuse awareness programs for all employees.
   b. requiring one hundred hours of community service work for all first-time offenders.
   c. sponsoring public service announcements on local television or radio stations about substance abuse.
   d. working with local school systems to prevent substance abuse in the schools.
   e. Supplying an article in the company newsletter that identifies offenders.

4. An applicant was subjected to a drug test when she applied for a job as a management information systems manager for a large provincial electrical utility company. She "failed" the test and was subsequently removed from the applicant pool. What recourse, if any, does the individual have?
   a. If the applicant is a minority candidate, she can appeal the decision.
   b. She can notify the Human Rights Commission, which may start an investigation and ask the human resources department for data that indicates that the test used is both reliable and valid in predicting job performance and reducing workplace accidents. In addition, the commission may investigate whether the applicant's right of privacy has been violated.
   c. She may file criminal action against the human resources manager who administered the test. If guilty, that person could be jailed for up to a year.
   d. She does not have any legal recourse. There are no other methods available that will allow the organization to identify and investigate suspicions and allegations of employee misconduct.
   e. She does not have any legal recourse. The requirement of being "clean" is reasonable in this position.

5. An accounts payable manager for a sixty-five-employee graphic arts manufacturer has been on the job for twenty-seven months. On Monday morning, she is told that this would be her last week of work for the company. Through some investigations, she finds out that the company is facing business problems and is slashing payroll to stay afloat. What protection is given to this accounts payable manager under current Canadian legislation?
   a. Under employment standards legislation, she is entitled to an amount equal to pay and benefits for up to sixty days.

b. No protection. Employees working for a company that has less than a hundred employees are not covered under employment standards legislation.
   c. No protection. Losing a job because of business problems is a fact of life that employees need to accept.
   d. Her old firm must pay agency fees to have her placed with another organization. She is entitled to a job of equal value.
   e. She turn to common law and sue the company.

6. The use of medical tests in employment decisions
   a. is not legal in Canada.
   b. allows the employer to test for a several diseases identified by the Canadian Human Rights Commission as "highly contagious."
   c. is permissible only after the employer has made a written offer of employment.
   d. is mandatory in Canada. The employer must submit the results of the tests to insurance companies.
   e. allows the organization to reduce complaints of discrimination.

7. Greg worked for three consecutive years in a large retail organization. He lost his job soon after his new manager took her position. Greg was not given notice. Which of the following statements regarding wrongful dismissal is false?
   a. Canadian law provides individuals protection regarding wrongful dismissal.
   b. Greg suspects that wrongful dismissal has occurred and decides to challenge the legality of his termination. The employer must then provide evidence that Greg's dismissal was for just cause.
   c. Reasonable notice is required even if Greg is dismissed for just cause.
   d. If the court decides that Greg was wrongfully dismissed, it may rule that the organization should reinstate Greg with back pay.
   e. An organization may offer a severance payment (pay in lieu of notice) as an alternative for reasonable notice.

8. The concept of just cause means that
   a. if employers can fire whenever they want, employees should be able to quit whenever they want.
   b. an employer may choose to provide a severance payment instead of providing reasonable notice.
   c. just because architects are not covered under provisions of employment standards legislation, they cannot file a complaint of wrongful dismissal with the courts.
   d. individuals behave in such a poor manner that they are considered to have broken the employer-employee relationship.
   e. an employer does not have to provide a reason for dismissal.

9. A manager of a fast food franchise has learned that one of his employees, the night manager, has been stealing supplies. He called corporate headquarters to check with the human resources representative before beginning disciplinary procedures. What contingency factor is he considering?

   a. Nature and extent of the problem.
   b. Extenuating circumstances.
   c. History of the organization's disciplinary procedures.
   d. Severity of the problem.
   e. Degree of socialization.

10. A long-time worker in a steel manufacturing plant no longer wears steel-toed shoes, an insulated work suit, and safety glasses on the work floor even though safety standards require such protective clothing. When his boss confronts him on the matter, he says that he has not had an accident in twenty years on the job and, therefore, has no need for such hot and heavy gear. What would be the next best step the manager should follow?

    a. Let the matter drop. The employee is successfully performing the duties of his job.
    b. Put a written warning of insubordination in the employee's file. Permit him to review the file twenty-four hours after the document has been received by the HR department.
    c. Arrange an "accident" close enough to the employee to scare him into compliance.
    d. Explain to the employee the legal requirements and the importance of his influence on less-experienced workers, and tell him to conform to safety standards. Explain that further infractions will result in written documentation and could lead to his dismissal.
    e. Hold a special safety training session for all steel workers, explaining the legal safety requirements and the penalties for non-compliance.

11. John gambles at work. He runs a lucrative football pool for the accountants. Steve, his supervisor, has talked to him about the rules of the organization that prohibit gambling and the consequences for such behaviour ultimately lead to dismissal. Steve filed a written warning with human resources after John resumed his activities for last year's Grey Cup. Now, at the start of a new football season, it is obvious that John is at it again. What should Steve do to administer progressive discipline?

    a. Send John home for two days without pay to think about the seriousness of the gambling offence.
    b. Fire John. Enough is enough.
    c. Give up. Let John run the pool as long as no one complains.
    d. Talk to John and remind him of the consequences of gambling on the job.
    e. Transfer John to an area of the company that is not likely to support his gambling activities.

12. If a manager follows the hot-stove rule of administering discipline, she will

    a. refer the case to a manager she knows has a hot temper, who will then take care of the matter.
    b. administer discipline that is immediate, forewarned, consistent, and impersonal.
    c. administer discipline that is swift, painful, and deliberate.
    d. administer discipline in hot anger and with large, visible consequences.
    e. administer discipline in a folksy, supportive, parental, and coaching sort of way.

13. In their job, HR managers face many dilemmas—situations in which the rights of individuals and groups have to be balanced. Which of the following statements is true? To guide HR managers in their day-to-day decision making,

    a. organizations need to educate their HR managers that bending organizational rules and procedures once in a while is inevitable and a fact of doing business.
    b. the federal and provincial governments need to implement more legislation that clearly identifies what is "right" and what is "wrong."
    c. organizations need to select one or two stakeholders to which they commit.
    d. those in leadership positions need to set an example in ethical decision making—they should serve as the conscience of the organization.
    e. organizations should select individuals who have similar values and act alike.

14. Vicki suspects that one of her colleagues, Jamie, has falsified research data. She decides to share her suspicions with the department head. What should the department head do?

    a. Vicki should be disciplined; her acting as a whistle-blower will only lead to a decrease in trust and morale in the department. Besides, such allegations may give the department bad publicity for which Vicki is in part responsible.
    b. Share Vicki's suspicions with the entire department; falsification of data is a despicable practice and every researcher should be aware that such practices will not be tolerated.
    c. Since Vicki has not had much success as a researcher over the past two years, the department head believes that envy may play a role in the accusations. The department head should thus dismiss such frivolous allegations of wrongdoing and focus on more important issues.
    d. Even if the accusations are proven true, Jamie should be given the right to appeal the outcome of the decision.
    e. The department head should contact the Human Rights Commission, which will contact the local police who will conduct a formal investigation.

Chapter Five

STRATEGIC HUMAN RESOURCES PLANNING

LEARNING OBJECTIVES

AFTER READING THIS CHAPTER, YOU WILL BE ABLE TO:

1. Describe the importance of strategic human resources planning.
2. Define the steps involved in the strategic human resources planning process.
3. Explain what human resources management systems (HRMSs) are used for.
4. Define the term job analysis.
5. Identify the six general techniques for obtaining job information.
6. Discuss specific techniques such as Functional Job Analysis and the Position Analysis Questionnaire.
7. Explain the difference between job descriptions, job specifications, and job evaluations.
8. Describe the difference between downsizing and rightsizing.
9. List various methods of achieving staff reduction goals.
10. Explain what is meant by outplacement services.

In November 1992, Michael O'Brien took over as executive vice-president of Sunoco, Inc., a wholly owned subsidiary of Calgary's Suncor Inc. Toronto-based Sunoco was in trouble. Earnings were sinking and staff was demoralized after a series of reorganizations and cuts that were carried out with little participation from the workers and even less communication from top management.[1]

The company buys and sells crude oil from Suncor's oil sands plant near Fort McMurray, Alberta. The oil is piped to Sunoco's refinery in Sarnia, Ontario, where it is processed and the products moved to gas stations (in 1997, Sunoco had over five hundred gas stations in Ontario) and other customers.

The first thing O'Brien did was to carry out a strategic review. His job, he told everyone, was to decide whether Sunoco was to stay in business or not. The key challenge, however, was to get the employees on side in a process that saw Sunoco's service network cut by 30 per cent and its staff reduced by one-quarter. O'Brien said, "we set up some principles up front ... [to] really and truly involve people, let them know the good news and the bad ... and be open and communicative all the way through."

The news was not good. In the process of making Sunoco smaller, more focused, and more productive, more than one hundred employees would be working themselves out of their jobs over the next three years. "The bottom line is that when people understood the way things were going to roll out, they were able to handle that very well, as opposed to being in a state of fear," O'Brien recalled.

Sunoco set some measurable HR strategy goals. The performance management process was redone with "cascading goals." Employees had individual plans which were linked to their supervisors' plan and so on up to O'Brien. "People jokingly said, 'If you can't connect it with the vision, then you shouldn't be doing it'," said Patricia Anderson, Sunoco's director of HR and public affairs. The compensation system was also modified so that it was linked with six core "value drivers," which include manufacturing costs and safety; a bonus program allowed all employees to be rewarded when targets were met or exceeded.

When Sunoco proposed cutting the Sarnia refinery staff by 10 per cent, the employee association suggested reducing the work week from forty-two to forty hours. O'Brien feared that this would produce a "whole pile of disgruntled employees," something the company didn't want. But 92 per cent of the employees agreed to the work week reduction.

Sunoco's earnings went from $9 million in 1992 to $32 million in 1996, and market share grew from 12 per cent in 1992 to about 20 per cent in early 1997. The company was moving from survival to growth, and Anderson said that HR was now able to look at long-term development planning and filling gaps through recruitment and training. Training and development focused on leadership development.

"We've got a responsibility to ensure that we're helping people build their own competencies so they can move as the organization moves," said O'Brien. "It's a very different role than it has been in the past ... and we're looking for the HR department to lead us through that."

Introduction

Michael O'Brien realized that changes do occur in organizations, but adapting to them requires all organizational members to understand where the organization is going and to support what the enterprise is about to do. Individuals such as Michael O'Brien understand that before you can depart on a journey, you have to know your destination. Just think about the last time you took a vacation. For example, if you live in Edmonton and decide to go to a California beach for spring break, you need to decide specifically what beach—such as Newport or Laguna—you want to go to and the best route to take. In an elementary form, this is what planning is all about—knowing where you are going and how you are going to get there.

The same holds true for human resources management. Whenever an organization is in the process of determining its human resources needs, it is engaged in a process we call **strategic human resources planning (SHRP)**. SHRP is one of the most important elements in a successful human resources management program[2] because it is a process by which an organization ensures that it has the right number and kinds of people, at the right place, at the right time, capable of effectively and efficiently completing those tasks that will help the organization achieve its overall objectives. Strategic human resources planning, then, translates the organization's overall plans and objectives into the number and types of workers needed to meet those objectives. Without clearcut planning, estimating of an organization's human resources needs is reduced to mere guesswork.

Strategic human resources planning cannot exist in isolation. It must be linked to the organization's overall strategy.[3] Twenty years ago, in a typical firm, few employees, outside of the firm's top executives, really knew the company's long-range objectives. In fact, in many cases, even top management didn't really know where the organization was heading. Their strategic efforts were often no more than an educated guess in determining the organization's direction. But things are different today, as the Sunoco example shows. Aggressive domestic and global competition, for instance, has made strategic planning virtually mandatory. Although it's not our intention to go into every detail of the strategic planning process in this chapter, senior HRM officials need to understand the process because they're playing a more vital role in the strategic process. It is HRM's responsibility to lead the entire management team in "showing the best way to take charge of the new workplace."[4] Let's look at a fundamental strategic planning process in an organization.

Strategic Human Resource Planning (SHRP) The process of linking human resources planning efforts to the company's strategic direction.

An Organizational Framework

The strategic planning process in an organization is both long and continuous.[5] At the beginning of the process, the organization's main emphasis is to determine what business it is in. This is commonly referred to as developing the **mission statement**. Without knowing this information, the organization will, at best, flounder. Why is the mission statement important? Take, for instance, a part of Bombardier's mission statement—to be the "leader in all the markets in which it operates … in the fields of transportation equipment, aerospace, motorized consumer products, financial services, and services related to its products and core competencies."[6]

Mission Statement A declaration of the reason an organization is in business.

What that statement does is clarify for all organizational members what exactly the company is about. Accordingly, the company specifies clearly why it exists and sets the course for company operations. A sound mission statement facilitates the decision-making process. For example, if Bombardier's managers wanted to make and sell small airplanes, such a decision to enter that market would be within the boundaries set by the mission; however, these same managers would know that any effort to expand the company's product lines to include selling washers and dryers would be time ill spent. Of course, that is not to say that mission statements are written in stone; they can be changed at any time, after careful study and deliberation. For example, the March of Dimes was originally created to facilitate the cure of infantile paralysis (polio). When that disease was essentially eradicated in the 1950s, the organization redefined its mission as seeking cures for children's diseases. Nonetheless, the need to specifically define an organization's line of business is critical to its survival.

After reaching agreement on what business the company is in and who its consumers are, senior management then begins to set **strategic goals**.[7] During this phase, these managers define objectives for the company for the next five to twenty years. These objectives are broad statements that establish targets the organization will achieve. For example, Bombardier establishes broad areas of emphasis: transportation, aerospace, and motorized consumer products, and the financial and other services that support these areas.

Strategic Goals Organization-wide goals setting direction for the next five to twenty years.

After these goals are set, the next step in the strategic planning process begins—the corporate assessment. During this phase, a company begins to analyse its goals, its current strategies, its external environment, its strengths and weaknesses, and its opportunities and threats in terms of whether or not they can be achieved with the current organizational resources. Commonly referred to as a gap or SWOT (strengths, weaknesses, opportunities, and threats) analysis, the company begins to look at what skills, knowledge, and abilities are available internally and where shortages, in terms of people skills or equipment, may exist. For Sunoco, this meant looking at what people skills were needed in order to be successful in the new market place. Their analysis resulted in their changing the company's HRM activities in an attempt to develop people with the specific leadership skills they wanted.[8] This phase of the strategic planning process cannot be overstated. It serves as the link between the organization's goals and ensuring that the company can meet its objectives—that is, it establishes the direction of the company through strategic planning.

The company must determine what jobs need to be done and how many and what types of workers will be required. In management terminology, we call this *organizing*. Thus, establishing the structure of the organization assists in determining the skills, knowledge, and abilities required of job holders.

It is only at this point that we begin to look at people to meet these criteria, and that's where human resources management comes in. To determine what skills are needed, HRM conducts a job analysis. Figure 5-1 is a graphic representation of this process. The key message in Figure 5-1 is that all jobs in the organization ultimately must be tied to the company's strategic direction. Recall in Chapter 2 our discussion of effectiveness and efficiency in terms of corporate downsizing. Unless jobs can be linked to the organization's goals and objectives, achieving these goals becomes a moving target. It's no wonder, then, that strategic human resources management has become more critical in organizations. Let's look at how human resources planning operates within the strategic planning process.

Mission	Determining what business the organization will be in
Objectives and goals	Setting goals and objectives
Strategy	Determining how goals and objectives will be attained
Structure	Determining what jobs need to be done and by whom
People	Matching skills, knowledge, and abilities to required jobs

Figure 5-1
The Strategic Direction—
Human Resources Linkage

Linking Organizational Strategy to Human Resources Planning

To ensure that people are available to meet the requirements set during the strategic planning process, human resources managers engage in strategic human resources planning. The purpose of strategic human resources planning is to determine what HRM requirements exist for current and future supply and demand for workers. For example, if a company has set as one of its goals to double the number of operations over the next five years, such action will require that individuals be available to handle the jobs in the new ventures. After this assessment, strategic human resources planning matches the supply and demand for labour, supporting the people component.

Assessing Current Human Resources

Assessing current human resources begins by developing a profile of the organization's current employees. This is an internal analysis that includes an inventory of the workers and the skills they currently possess. In an era of complex computer systems, it is not too difficult for most organizations to generate a human resources inventory report. The input to this report would be derived from forms completed by employees and then checked by supervisors. Such reports would include a complete list of all employees by name, education, training, prior employment, current position, performance ratings, salary level, languages spoken, capabilities, and specialized skills.[9]

From a strategic human resources planning viewpoint, this input is valuable in determining what skills are currently available in the organization. They serve as a guide for supporting new organizational pursuits or in altering the organization's strategies. This report also has value in other HRM activities, such as selecting individuals for training and development, promotion, and transfers.

The completed profile of the human resources inventory can provide crucial information for identifying current or future threats to the organization's ability to perform. For example, the organization can use the information from the inventory to identify specific variables that may have a particular relationship to training needs, productivity improvements, and succession planning. A characteristic such as technical obsolescence, or workers who are not trained to function with new computer requirements, can, if it begins to permeate the entire organization, adversely affect the organization's performance.

Human Resources Management Systems   To assist in the HR inventory, organizations have implemented a **human resources management system (HRMS)**. An HRMS is designed to quickly fulfil the human resources management informational needs of the organization. The HRMS is a database system that keeps important information about employees in a central and accessible location. When such information is required, the data can be retrieved and used to facilitate human resources planning decisions. Its technical potential permits the organization to track most information about employees and jobs and to retrieve that information when needed. An HRMS may also be used to help keep track of employment equity data.[10] Figure 5-2 is a listing of typical information tracked on an HRMS.

Figure 5-2
Information Categories of Human Resources Management Systems

Group 1 Basic Non-Confidential Information
Employee name
Organization name
Work location
Work phone number

Group 2 General Non-Confidential Information
Information in the previous category, plus:
Social Insurance Number
Other organization information (code, effective date)
Positionrelated information (code, title, effective date)

Group 3 General Information with Salary
Information in the previous categories, plus:
Current salary, effective date, amount of last change, type of last change, and reason for last change)

Group 4 Confidential Information with Salary
Information in the previous categories, plus:
Other position information (position ranking);
Gender or minority status if needed for tracking employment equity programs
Education data

Group 5 Extended Confidential Information with Salary
Information in the previous categories, plus:
Bonus information
Projected salary increase information
Performance evaluation information

Source: Adapted from Joan E. Goodman, "Does Your HRIS Speak English?" *Personnel Journal* (March 1990), p. 81. Used with permission.

HRMSs have grown significantly in popularity in the past decade. This is essentially due to the recognition that management needs timely information on its employees and that new technological breakthroughs have cut the cost of these systems.[11] Additionally, HRMSs are now more user-friendly and provide quick and responsive reports,[12] especially when linked to the organization's management information system.

Human Resources Management System   A computerized system that assists in the processing of HRM information.

At a time when quick analysis of an organization's human resources is critical, the HRMS is filling a void in the strategic planning process. With information readily available, companies are in a better position to quickly move forward in achieving their organizational goals.[13] Additionally, the HRMS is useful in other aspects of human resources management, providing data support for compensation and benefits programs as well as providing a necessary link to corporate payroll.[14]

Replacement Charts In addition to the computerized HRM system, some organizations also generate a separate senior management inventory report. This report, called a replacement chart, typically covers individuals in middle-to-upper-level management positions. In an effort to facilitate succession planning—ensuring that another individual is ready to move into a position of higher responsibility—the replacement chart highlights those positions that may become vacant in the near future due to retirements, promotions, transfers, resignations, or deaths of the incumbents. But not all companies use replacement charts, and this can create confusion, or even worse. When Disney sought a replacement for their ailing CEO Michael Eisner,[15] lack of action, in part, resulted in the resignation of the heir apparent.[16] Of course, replacement charts cannot foresee everything. When Chrysler Canada president Yves Landry died suddenly in March 1998, there was much speculation regarding his succession since he was expected to stay on the job until his retirement five years or so later. But the team of five vice-presidents was able to operate smoothly during the difficult transition period.[17] Chrysler Canada's succession planning would be even more stressed when Landry's successor, William Glaub, died of a heart attack while on his honeymoon in the Caribbean on November 26, 1998.

Against this list of positions is placed the individual manager's skills inventory to determine if there is sufficient managerial talent to cover potential future vacancies. This "readiness" chart then gives management an indication of time frames for succession as well as helping to spot skill shortages that may exist. Should skill shortages exist, human resources management can either recruit new employees or intensify employee development efforts (see Chapter 9).

Replacement charts look very similar to organizational charts. With the incumbents listed in their positions, those individuals targeted for replacement are listed beneath with the expected time in which they will be prepared to take

Replacement Charts HRM organizational charts indicating positions that may become vacant in the near future and the individuals who may fill the vacancy.

Succession Planning Ensuring that there are individuals ready to move into positions of higher responsibility.

Replacement charts are an important tool in succession planning. They help to keep track of positions that may become vacant in the near future.

on the needed responsibility. We have provided a sample replacement chart in Figure 5-3.

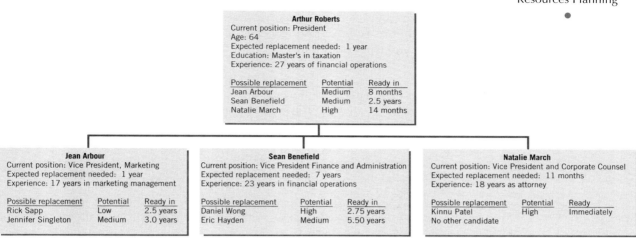

Figure 5-3
A Sample Replacement Chart

The Demand for Labour

Once an assessment of the organization's current human resources situation has been made and the future direction of the organization has been considered, a projection of future human resources needs can be developed.

It will be necessary to perform a year-by-year analysis for every significant job level and type. In effect, the result is a human resources inventory covering specified years into the future. These pro forma inventories obviously must be comprehensive and therefore, complex. Organizations usually require a heterogeneous mix of people, but people are not perfectly substitutable for each other within an organization. For example, a shortage in engineering cannot be offset by transferring employees from the purchasing area where there is an oversupply. If accurate estimates are to be made of future demands in both qualitative and quantitative terms, more information is needed than just to determine that, for example, in sixteen months we will have to hire another 110 people. It is necessary to know what types of people are required in terms of skills, knowledge, and abilities. Accordingly, our forecasting methods must allow for the recognition of specific job needs as well as the total number of vacancies.

Human Resources Inventory
A roster that describes the skills that are available within the organization.

Implementation of Future Supply

Estimating changes in internal supply requires the organization to look at those factors that can either increase or decrease its human resources. As previously noted in the discussion on estimating demand, forecasting of supply must also concern itself with the micro, or unit, level. For example, if one individual in Department X is transferred to a position in Department Y and an individual in Department Y is transferred to a position in Department X, the net effect on the organization is zero. However, if only one individual is initially involved— say, promoted and sent to another location in the company—it is only through effective strategic human resources planning that a competent replacement will be available to fill the position vacated by the departing employee.

An increase in the supply of any unit's human resources can come from a combination of four sources: new hires, contingent (temporary) workers, transfers-in, or individuals returning from leaves. The task of predicting these new inputs can range from simple to complex.

New hires and contingent workers are easy to predict since they are self-initiated. A unit recruits to meet its needs, and hence, at least in the short term, the number and types of new hires or contingent workers that will be added can be determined with high accuracy.

It is more difficult, however, to predict transfers-in to a unit since they often depend on concurrent action in other units. While the net effect on the total organization by a lateral transfer, demotion, or promotion may be zero, there are clear effects on individual departments and the mix within departments. If, for example, Ms X is to be promoted from Department A to Department B, the effect on the employees in Department B must be known.

Finally, the net effect on internal supply by people returning from leaves must be considered. Examples of this include absences due to international assignments, military service, maternity, disability, or sabbatical leaves. Such increases, however, are generally easy to estimate since they usually last for some fixed duration—twelve weeks, six months, two years, and so forth.

Decreases in the internal supply can come about through retirements, dismissals, transfers-out of the unit, lay-offs, voluntary quits, sabbaticals, prolonged illnesses, or deaths. Some of these occurrences are easier to predict than others. The easiest to forecast are retirements, assuming that employees retire after a certain length of service and the fact that most organizations require some advance notice of one's intent to retire. Given a history of the organization, HRM can predict with some accuracy how many retirements will occur over a given time period.

At the other extreme, voluntary quits, prolonged illnesses, and deaths are difficult to predict. Deaths of employees are the most difficult to forecast because they are usually unexpected. Although large corporations such as IBM or Chrysler can use statistics to estimate the number of deaths that will occur, such techniques are useless for forecasting in small organizations or for estimating the exact positions that will be affected in large ones. Voluntary quits can also be predicted by utilizing probabilities when the population size is large. In a company like Northern Telecom, managers can estimate the approximate number of voluntary departures for the entire company during any given year. In a department consisting of two or three workers, however, probability estimation is essentially meaningless. Weak predictive ability in small units is unfortunate, too, because voluntary quits typically have the greatest impact on such units.

In between these extremes, transfers, lay-offs, sabbaticals, and dismissals can be forecast within reasonable limits of accuracy. Since all four of these types of action are controllable by management—that is, they are either initiated by management or are within management's veto prerogative—each type can be reasonably predicted. Of the four, transfers out of a unit—such as lateral moves, demotions, or promotions—are the most difficult to predict because they depend on openings in other units. Lay-offs are more controllable and forecastable by management, especially in the short run. Sabbaticals, too, are reasonably easy to forecast since most organizations' sabbatical policies require a reasonable lead time between request and initiation of the leave. For example, at the McDonald's corporation,[18] employees with ten years of continuous service are eligible for an eight-week sabbatical. The sabbatical can be taken during any eight continuous weeks, but with advanced approval of management. This gives the corporation ample time to find a replacement, if needed.

Meet

David Foot
Demographer

Since the publication of his book, *Boom, Bust, and Echo*, in 1996, Australian-born academic David Foot has become a reluctant guru of the Canadian economy. Dr. Foot specializes in demographics, the study of human populations. He argues that the overall shape of the population, and the predictable ways that this shape changes over time, is the most important factor in economic and social trends. Because these trends include the job market and corporate structures, Dr. Foot's theories offer important lessons for the strategic human resource planning process.

The generation known as the baby boomers, born between 1947 and 1966, is the largest demographic group in North American history, Dr. Foot explains. In fact, the boomer group is larger, relative to the total population, in Canada than anywhere else in the world. Thirty-three per cent of Canadians fall into this group—all of them entering the workforce in the late 1960s and 1970s. Most of Canada's corporations at this point, especially large ones, had a pyramid structure: one or a very few decision-makers at the top, and a growing number of subordinates in each level of the hierarchy below. Throughout most of the first half of this century, Canada had more young employees than older ones, and this structure was a successful one.

But by the mid-1980s, the oldest of the boomers had the experience and seniority to be considered for senior management positions. Unfortunately, there were simply too many of them, and not enough high-level jobs to promote this "rectangle" of workers up through the "triangle" of the corporate pyramid. Thousands of hard-working, deserving workers found themselves "plateaued," increasingly overqualified and unsatisfied with their current jobs but with little hope for advancement. Meanwhile, corporations were having trouble hiring enough qualified entry-level employees.

Smart companies responded to this inevitable phenomenon by flattening their corporate structures. (IBM is a prime example; it went from about ten levels of hierarchy to about four.) For the next few decades, a more flattened structure will be the most sensible for most companies to adopt.

Flatter corporate structures require some changes to traditional thinking about human resources. Employees should be encouraged to make horizontal moves as well as vertical ones; a good human resources plan will make counselling, education, and on-the-job training opportunities available. A less triangular company also compensates workers differently, taking into account factors other than a worker's place on the corporate "ladder." And a company structured for the new millennium will be prepared for the seller's market in labour that will hit when the small demographic group born from 1995 to 2005—the children of the "baby busters," enters the workforce in the early part of the twenty-first century.

Dr. Foot makes it clear that these demographic changes are inevitable; children born in 1985 will turn twenty in 2005, no matter what. The successful human resource planner, therefore, won't be taken by surprise by these developments, but will take advantage of them.

Source: David K. Foot with Daniel Stoffman, *Boom, Bust, & Echo: How to Profit from the Coming Demographic Shift* (Toronto: McFarlane Walter & Ross, 1996).

Dismissals based on inadequate job performance can usually be forecast in the same way as voluntary quits, using probabilities where large numbers of employees are involved. As well, performance evaluation reports are a reliable source for isolating the number of individuals whose employment might have to be terminated at a particular point in time due to unsatisfactory work performance.

In small organizations, as in the smaller individual units of large corporations, it is not possible to use statistical models for the prediction of demand for labour. It is not that the cost of generating the information outweighs its usefulness, but that statistical and probability models require large numbers for their predictions to have any validity at all. In these situations, managers are well advised to have good relationships with sources of labour (such as colleges and universities, for example) so that they can fill vacancies rapidly when the need arises. Perhaps more important is that the individual managers or supervisors must have a good feel for the likely behaviour of their subordinates. If one knows that Joe is likely to take early retirement, that Caroline is thinking of going back to school to get a Master's degree, or that one of Manuel's ambitions is to take a year off to backpack through India and Nepal, one is better prepared to plan for such events.

Estimated Changes in External Supply

The previous discussion on supply considered internal factors. We will now review those factors outside the organization that influence the supply of available workers. Recent graduates from schools, colleges and universities expand the supply of available human resources. This market is vast and includes everyone from high-school graduates to individuals who have received highly specialized training at the graduate level. Entrants to the workforce from sources other than schools include homemakers—both male and female—seeking full-time or part-time work to supplement the family income, individuals returning to work on a full-time basis in the capacity of primary breadwinner, students seeking parttime work, job seekers who have been recently laid off, and so on. Migration into a community, increases in the number of unemployed, and employed individuals who are seeking other employment opportunities also represent sources for the organization to consider as potential additions to its labour supply.

It should be noted that consideration of only the supply sources just identified tends to understate the potential labour supply because many people can be retrained through formal or on-the-job training. Therefore, the potential supply can differ from what one might conclude by looking only at the obvious sources of supply. For example, with some training, a journalist can become qualified to perform the tasks of a book editor; thus, an organization that is having difficulty securing individuals with skills and experience in book editing should consider those candidates who have had recent journalism or similar experience and are interested in being editors. In similar fashion, the potential supply for many other jobs can be expanded.

The Labour Market

The labour market is the pool of persons from which employers can choose their employees. Labour markets are generally defined by geographical area and occupational type. For example, the labour market for jobs such as assembly line workers or retail salespersons is usually local, within commuting distance of the employer's location. On the other hand, the market for engineers is at least regional, if not national. Thus, Northern Telecom will recruit at faculties of engineering at all Canadian universities. And anyone who follows the sports pages knows that the market for professional athletes is international: just look at the team roster of last year's Stanley Cup winners.

The geographic extent of the labour market is not fixed. When certain types of trained workers are very scarce at the local level, companies have to roam farther afield. Canadian employers may be allowed to recruit internationally for scarce skills such as information technology specialists, or tool and die makers. Such international searches are not limited to large companies. Small tool and die firms that supply the automotive industry from Windsor, Ontario, have had to recruit skilled workers and technicians in Europe.

Employers should monitor the state of their relevant labour markets so they are not caught at a disadvantage. Employers who are aware that there is likely to be a shortage of a certain type of labour that they will need in the next few years can take steps to be prepared: by developing their own internal training programs, by funding special programs at local community colleges or universities, and by devising means to retain their own highly skilled workers, because under such circumstances, it is not unusual for a company to "poach" employees from their competitors by offering tempting salaries or working conditions.

Employers have a number of resources available to gather this information. Human Resources Development Canada (HRDC) provides labour market information through provincial regional offices and Canada Employment Centres in towns and cities across Canada. (The centres also serve as local clearing houses for job vacancies). Other useful resources are the Canadian Career Information Association, an association of professionals in career information resources, and the Conference Board of Canada, a private applied research institution.[19] Industry associations perform an invaluable service for small firms by collecting and analysing this type of information.

Demand and Supply

The objective of strategic human resources planning is to bring together the forecasts of future demand for workers and the supply for human resources, both current and future. The result is to pinpoint shortages both in number and in kind; to highlight areas where overstaffing may exist (now or in the near future); and to keep abreast of the opportunities existing in the labour market to hire good people, either to satisfy current needs or to stockpile for the future.

Attention must be paid to identifying potential shortages. Should an organization find that the demand for human resources will be increasing in the future, it will have to hire additional staff or transfer people within the organization, or both, to balance the numbers, skills, mix, and quality of its human resources. An often overlooked action, but one that may be necessary because of inadequate availability of human resources, is to change the organization's objectives. Just as inadequate financial resources can restrict the growth and opportunities available to an organization, the unavailability of the right types of people can also act as such a constraint, even leading to changing the organization's objectives.

As organizations such General Motors, Noranda, and Inco reorganize and re-engineer, another outcome is likely: oversupply. When this happens, human resources management must undertake some difficult steps to sever these people from the organization—a process sometimes referred to as "decruitment." We'll return to this issue under the discussion of corporate downsizing later in the chapter.

Corporate strategic planning and strategic human resources planning are two critically linked processes; one cannot survive without the other. Accordingly, to perform both properly requires a blending of activities, which are portrayed in Figure 5-4.

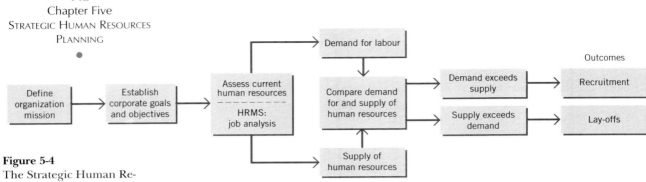

Figure 5-4
The Strategic Human Resources Planning Process

Determining Required Skills, Knowledge, and Abilities

Educational Training and Development Systems (ETDS), a corporate training and development firm, has experienced a 20 per cent turnover of trainers over the past eighteen months. An analysis of the trainer resignations indicated that the average length of stay has been only six months. Perplexed by this dilemma and the resulting loss to productivity and revenue, senior managers at ETDS insisted on an investigation to find out why such a high turnover exists.

The investigation involved contacting most of the individuals who resigned to ask them why they quit. The responses were that what they were hired to do and what they were required to do were different things. The latter required different skills and aptitudes. Feeling frustrated and bored and not wanting to jeopardize their career records, they quit. At the same time, the company's training costs had run approximately 300 per cent over budget in the past three years. When one of the senior managers asked what it was about the job that made it so difficult to properly match the job requirements with people skills, no one had an answer. It appeared that no one had conducted job analyses; in other words, no one had taken the time to find out what the jobs were all about.

What Is Job Analysis?

Job Analysis Provides information about jobs currently being done and the knowledge, skills, and abilities that individuals need to perform the jobs adequately.

A job analysis is a systematic exploration of the activities within a job. It is a technical procedure used to define the duties, responsibilities, and accountabilities of a job. This analysis "involves the identification and description of what is happening on the job ... accurately and precisely identifying the required tasks, the knowledge, and the skills necessary for performing them, and the conditions under which they must be performed."[20] Let's explore how this can be achieved (see "HRM Skills: Conducting the Job Analysis").

Job Analysis Methods

The methods that managers can use to determine job elements and the essential knowledge, skills, and abilities for successful performance include the following:

Observation Method Watching employees at work (directly or on film) to determine what their jobs entail.

Observation Method. Using the observation method, a job analyst watches employees directly or reviews films of workers on the job. Although the observation method provides first-hand information, workers often do not function

Conducting the Job Analysis

1. **Understand the purpose of conducting the job analysis.** Before embarking on a job analysis, one must understand the nature and purpose of conducting it. Recognize that job analyses serve a vital purpose in such HRM activities as recruiting, training, setting performance standards, evaluating performance, and compensation.
2. **Understand the role of the jobs in the organization.** Every job in the organization should have a purpose. Before conducting the job analysis, one must understand the linkage that the job has to the strategic direction of the organization. In essence, one must answer why the job is needed.
3. **Benchmark positions.** In a large organization, it would be impossible to evaluate every job at one time. Accordingly, one should select jobs based on how well they represent other, similar jobs in the organization. This information, then, will be used as a starting point in later analysis of the other positions.
4. **Determine how you want to collect the job analysis information.** Proper planning at this stage permits one to collect the data desired in the most effective and efficient manner. This means developing a game plan on how the data are to be obtained. Several methods or combinations can be used. Select the ones that best meet your job analyses goals and timetables.
5. **Seek clarification wherever necessary.** Some of the information collected may not be totally understandable to the job analyst. Accordingly, when this occurs, one must seek clarification from those who possess the critical information. This may include the employee and the supervisor. Failure to understand and comprehend the information will make Step 6 (writing the job description), more difficult.
6. **Develop the first draft of the job description.** Although there is no specific format that all job descriptions follow, most include certain elements. These include the job title, a summary sentence of the job's main activities, the level of authority and accountability of the position, performance requirements, and working conditions. The last paragraph of the job description typically includes the job specifications or those personal characteristics the job holder should possess to be successful on the job.
7. **Review draft with job supervisor.** Ultimately, the supervisor of the position being analysed should approve the job description. Review comments from the supervisor can help in determining a final job description document. When the description is an accurate reflection, the supervisor should sign off or approve the document.

---

most efficiently when they are being watched, and distortions in the job analysis can occur. This method also requires that the entire range of activities be observable. This is possible with some jobs but not for many—most managerial jobs, for example.

Individual Interview Method.   Using the individual interview method, job incumbents are selected and interviewed extensively. The results of these interviews are combined into a single job analysis. This method is effective for assessing what a job entails, but it is very timeconsuming. Caution is warranted because individuals may inflate the importance or the number of the tasks required for their job.

Individual Interview Method
Meeting with an employee to determine what his or her job entails.

Group Interview Method
Meeting with a number of employees to collectively determine what their jobs entail.

Structured Questionnaire Method
A specifically designed questionnaire on which employees rate tasks they perform on their jobs.

Technical Conference Method
A job analysis technique that involves extensive input from the employee's supervisor.

Diary Method A job anaysis method requiring job incumbents to record their daily activities.

Functional Job Analysis (FJA) A job analysis process developed on the basis of the US Department of Labor's methodology.

Dictionary of Occupational Titles A US government publication that lists more than 30,000 jobs.

Standard Occupational Classification Based on the National Occupational Classification, it provides a structure that allows analysts to categorize jobs.

National Occupational Classification Published by Human Resources Development Canada, it includes over 10,000 job descriptions.

Position Analysis Questionnaire (PAQ) A job analysis method that allows analysts to quantitatively group interrelated job elements into dimensions.

Group Interview Method.   The group interview method is similar to the individual interview method except that a number of job incumbents are interviewed simultaneously. Accuracy in assessing jobs is increased, but group dynamics may hinder effectiveness.

Structured Questionnaire Method.   Under the structured questionnaire method, workers are sent a specifically designed questionnaire on which they check or rate things they do on their job from a long list of possible task items. This technique is excellent for gathering information about jobs. However, exceptions to a job may be overlooked, and special mechanisms must be set up to ask follow-up questions or to clarify the information received.

Technical Conference Method.   The technical conference method utilizes supervisors with extensive knowledge of the job. Here, specific job characteristics are obtained from the "experts." Although a good data gathering method, it often overlooks the incumbent workers' perceptions about what they do on their job.

Diary Method.   The diary method requires job incumbents to record their daily activities. It provides much information but is seldom applicable to job activities. The diary method is the most intrusive of the job analysis methods, requiring much work and therefore much time on the part of the incumbent. To capture the entire range of work activities, this method may have to extend over long periods of time—all adding to its cost.

These six methods are not mutually exclusive, and no one method is universally superior. Even obtaining job information from the incumbents can create a problem, especially if these individuals describe what they *think* they should be doing rather than what they actually do. The best results, then, are usually achieved with some combination of methods, with information provided by individual employees, their immediate supervisors, a professional analyst, or an unobtrusive source such as filmed observations.

There are a number of standardized forms of some of these methods: for example, the functional job analysis and the Position Analysis Questionnaire. Functional Job Analysis (FJA) was developed by Sidney Fine[21] on the basis of the US Department of Labor's job analysis process. The FJA helps the job analyst, who gathers data through observation and interview, by classifying tasks into three "work function" scales related to data, people, and things. There is a behavioural hierarchy within each scale. For example, the lowest level in the People scale is taking instructions, which is the simplest interaction that can be performed with other people; the highest level, and the most complex interaction, is mentoring (see Figure 5-5).

The US Department of Labor's process resulted in the Dictionary of Occupational Titles, which includes more than thirty thousand jobs and is available in many libraries; it is a useful tool to assist in the job analysis process. Similarly, Statistics Canada's 1991 Standard Occupational Classification, based on Human Resources Development Canada's National Occupational Classification, provides a structure that allows analysts to categorize the range of occupational activity in Canada.

The Position Analysis Questionnaire (PAQ) was developed by researchers at Purdue University. It generates job requirement information that is designed to be applicable to all types of jobs. This standardized questionnaire presents a

Figure 5-5
Fine's Functional Job Analysis (FJA) Scale

Data	People	Things
1 Comparing	1a. Taking instruction	1a. Handling
	1b. Serving	1b. Feeding/off-bearing
		1c. Tending
2. Copying	2. Exchanging information	2a. Manipulating
		2b. Operating/controlling
		2c. Driving/controlling
3a. Computing	3a. Coaching	3a. Precision work
3b. Compiling	3b. Persuading	3b. Setting
	3c. Diverting	
4. Analysing	4a. Consulting	
	4b. Instructing	
	4c. Treating	
5a. Innovating	5. Supervising	
5b. Coordinating		
6. Synthesizing	6. Negotiating	
	7. Mentoring	

Source: Sidney Fine, *Functional Job Analysis Scales: A Desk Aid* (Kalamazoo, MI: W.E. Upjohn Institute for Employment Research, 1973). Used with permission

more quantitative and finely tuned description of jobs than the FJA. The PAQ involves "194 elements that are grouped within six major divisions and 28 sections"[22] (see Figure 5-6).

The PAQ allows management to group interrelated job elements into job dimensions in a scientific and quantitative manner. This, in turn, should allow jobs to be compared with each other. However, research on the usefulness of the PAQ suggests that it is more applicable to lower-level, blue-collar jobs.[23]

Figure 5-6
Categories of the PAQ and Their Number of Job Elements

Category	Number of Job Elements
1. *Information input* Where and how does the worker get the information he or she uses on the job?	35
2. *Mental processes* What reasoning, decision making, planning, etc., are involved in the job?	14
3. *Work output* What physical activities does the worker perform and what tools or devices are used?	49
4. *Relationships with other people* What relationships with other people are required in the job?	36
5. *Job context* In what physical and social contexts is the work performed?	19
6. *Other job characteristics* What special attributes exist on this job (e.g., schedule, responsibilities, pay)?	41

Source: Reprinted with permission from the Position Analysis Questionnaire, Copyright 1969, Purdue Research Foundation.

Other Job Analysis Techniques In addition to these methodologies, other specific job analysis techniques are summarized in Table 5-1.

TABLE 5-1 Other Job Analysis Techniques and Their Uses

Device	*Used For*
Management Position Description Questionnaire (MPDQ)	Analyse managerial job activities in terms of responsibilities, restrictions, demands, and activities
Occupational Analysis Inventory (OAI)	Vocational guidance and occupational exploration.
Job Element Inventory (JEI)	An adaptation of the PAQ, but presented at a much lower reading level.
Critical Incident Method	Focuses on behaviour that attributes to job success.

Source: Adapted from Wayne Cascio, *Applied Psychology in Personnel Management,* 4th ed. (Englewood Cliffs, N.J., Prentice-Hall, 1991), pp. 207, 208, 211. Used with permission.

Although a variety of techniques are available, some preparatory work is necessary before implementing any one of them. Job analysis is not difficult per se, but it is detailed. To conduct the job analysis, you should gather as much background information as possible about the job to be analysed. This information is readily available through old job descriptions and other literature such as the organization chart. Once you have this information, you need to identify those particular jobs to be reviewed. Remember, all jobs need to be analysed, but not all at the same time. In identifying the job, you also identify those individuals with specific or expert relevant job information. Working with these people, you now employ one of the techniques described. Once this has been done, your data gathering endeavour is over, but you are not finished. You must now analyse the information and produce the end results—the job description and the job specification.

Purpose of Job Analysis

No matter what the method used to gather data, the information gathered and written down from the job analysis process generates three outcomes: job descriptions, job specifications, and job evaluation. It is important to note that these are the tangible products, not the job analysis, which is the conceptual, analytical process or action from which we develop these outcomes. Let's look at them more closely.

Job Descriptions

Job Description A written statement of what the job holder does, how it is done, and why it is done.

A **job description** is a written statement of what the job holder does, how, under what conditions, and why it is done. It should accurately portray job content, environment, and conditions of employment. A common format for a job description includes the job title, duties to be performed, distinguishing characteristics of the job, environmental conditions, and the authority and responsibilities of the job holder.

An example of a job description is shown in Figure 5-7. You will notice that the emphasis is on the tasks the engineer is expected to perform. Job descriptions for management positions tend to emphasize the position's responsibilities and accountabilities rather than the duties the individual is expected to perform. Thus, the job description for the manager this component engineer reports to would emphasize the activities the *unit* carries out and for which the manager is responsible. In one large multinational corporation, managers' job descriptions are actually called *Statements of Responsibilities*.

Figure 5-7
Job Description of an Engineer

Job Description

Position Title: Component Engineer

Position Purpose: To hand off new product projects to production with a reliable and qualified supply base. Provide component/materials engineering support for wireless products (both new and in production).

Responsibilities:
- Conduct quality audits of existing and prospective suppliers with a focus on supply risk.
- Evaluate potential risks of components identified during new product design and introduction.
- Prepare and execute risk mitigation plans.
- Formulate and execute component/supplier qualification plans.
- Work in close collaboration with designers and buyers on supplier and technology selection.
- Perform detailed assessments and root cause analysis on various types of components.
- Realize significant cost improvements through the management of key technologies and by partnering with world class suppliers. Recommend and implement alternate technology/alternate supplier solutions.
- Generate Nortel Procurement Specifications (NPS) to define and protect design requirements for specific components.

Job Specifications

Minimum Competencies Required: Experience in Component Engineering or a related field (such as manufacturing engineering or design); experience in RF technology an asset.

Skills: ability to learn and apply new technology on an extremely aggressive ramp to work independently with no supervision, and a desire and ability to share lessons learned and improve the skills of other. Project management skills and the ability to prioritize tasks and meet critical deadlines under pressure. Excellent interpersonal and communication skills.

Education: Must have a degree in engineering from a recognized university (Electrical or Eng. Physics preferred). A CQA (Certified Quality Auditor) designation and/or business education or experience would be an asset.

Source: Northern Telecom job posting, June 1998 (http://jobs.careermosaic.com)

When we discuss employee recruitment, selection, and performance appraisal, we will find that the job description acts as important resource for: (1) describing the job (either verbally by recruiters and interviewers or in written advertisements) to potential candidates; (2) guiding newly hired employees in what they are specifically expected to do; and (3) providing a point of comparison in appraising whether the actual activities of a job incumbent align with the stated duties. Furthermore, under employment equity legislation, job descriptions have taken on an added emphasis in identifying essential job functions.

Job Specification

Job Specification Statements indicating the minimal acceptable qualifications incumbents must possess to successfully perform the essential elements of their jobs.

The **job specification** states the minimum acceptable qualifications that the incumbent must possess to perform the job successfully. Based on the information acquired through job analysis, the job specification identifies the knowledge, skills, education, experience, certification, and abilities needed to do the job effectively. Individuals possessing the personal characteristics identified in the job specification should perform the job more effectively than those lacking these personal characteristics. The job specification, therefore, is an important tool in the selection process, because it keeps the selector's attention on the list of qualifications necessary for an incumbent to perform the job and assists in determining whether candidates are essentially qualified.

Job Evaluation

Job Evaluation The process of determining the value of each job in relation to the other jobs in the organization.

In addition to providing data for job descriptions and specifications, job analysis is also valuable in providing the information that makes comparison of jobs possible. If an organization is to have an equitable compensation program, jobs that have similar demands in terms of skills, knowledge, and abilities should be placed in common compensation groups. **Job evaluation** contributes that end by specifying the relative value of each job in the organization. Therefore, job evaluation is an important part of compensation administration, as will be discussed in detail in Chapter 13. In the meantime, you should keep in mind that job evaluation is made possible by the data generated from job analysis.

The Pervasiveness of Job Analysis

One of the overriding questions about job analysis is: If it is done at all, is it being done properly? The answer to this question varies from organization to organization. Most do conduct some type of job analysis, and that is generally more extensive than required for meeting the minimum legislated employment equity requirements. Almost everything that HRM does is directly related to the job analysis process (see Figure 5-8). Recruiting, selection, compensation, and performance-appraising activities are most frequently cited as being directly effected by the job analysis, but there are other areas, too. Employee training and career development are assisted by the job analysis process in identifying necessary skills, knowledge, and abilities. Where deficiencies exist, training and development efforts can be used. Job analysis can also help in determining health and safety requirements, and is also required in unionized companies as part of the labour relations process. Accordingly, the often lengthy and complex job analysis process cannot be overlooked.

We cannot overemphasize the importance of job analysis as it permeates most of the organization's activities. If an organization does not do its job analysis well, it probably does not do many of its other human resources activities well either. If individuals in the organization have a good grasp of human resources activities, they should understand the fundamental importance of job analysis.

The job analysis, then, is the starting point of sound human resources management. Without knowing what the job entails, the material covered in the following chapters may merely be an effort in futility (see "What If: HRM in a DeJobbed Organization").

Figure 5-10
The Pervasivenesss of the Job
Analysis Process

What If:

HRM in a De-Jobbed Organization

Much of the discussion in this chapter revolves around the importance of having the right people in the right place at the right time for the organization to attain its strategic goals and objectives. This means that the organization has to identify the goals to be met and put in place a structure that leads to goal attainment. A critical component of that structure is the people who possess the necessary skills, knowledge, and abilities (SKAs). Throughout the discussion identifying those SKAs, one element is common: job analysis.

The job analysis, as an activity in HRM, is designed to properly assess what skills, knowledge, and abilities are needed for a job holder to perform on the job successfully. Furthermore, the results of this analysis permeate almost every activity conducted in HRM. Yet, a basic premise of job analysis is that through a systematic exploration of the jobs and their tasks, we can identify what workers ought to do and what personal characteristics they must possess. But what if that basic premise is wrong?

In a de-jobbed organization, the duties and responsibilities of a job change frequently—at times, almost constantly. Thus, it will become almost impossible to accurately evaluate jobs, because a description of what is done now might not apply a short time later. In addition, in situations where employees perform activities according to the job description, critical task activities for a current project may be lost. We've seen some of that already: many job descriptions include an ending catchall phrase like "and other duties as assigned." What if, however, all the work is, in fact, "other duties as assigned"? Will this significantly decrease or eliminate the need for the job analysis process? Will HRM activities that revolve around the job description—activities like recruiting, selection, performance appraisals, safety or health, or labour relations—simply become non-existent? Or will something else replace the job analysis so that some "order" can be restored? In a de-jobbed organization, even that something else may become a moot point.

Source: William Bridges, "The End of the Job," *Fortune* (September 19, 1994), p. 64.

●

Downsizing An activity in an organization aimed at creating greater efficiency by eliminating certain jobs.

Rightsizing Bringing the number of employees in line with the organization's strategy and needs.

Current Issues in SHRP

Earlier in this chapter, we identified a situation in the strategic planning process in which the supply of workers exceeds demand. In this case, organizations must take measures to reduce the number of workers, which is known as **downsizing**. (The process of moving workers out of the organization has been called "decruitment," a euphemism for "firing" or "laying off.") Recall from Chapter 2 the necessity for such action. The guiding theme was to make the organization more "lean and mean"—in other words, more efficient. But cutting for efficiency's sake may not be appropriate. Rather, companies today are looking at the need to correctly staff the organization with the needed skills, knowledge, and abilities. We call this **rightsizing**. Let's look at the downsizing/rightsizing issue facing companies.

Downsizing: Past and Present

Over the past few decades, we have witnessed the continued shrinkage of the once-strong smokestack industries—steel, auto, and rubber.[24] Competition in the high-tech industries has also soared during this time, giving rise to massive lay-offs at such companies as Apple, DEC, IBM, and Wang. Conglomerates, too, began shedding less-profitable business units or closing down altogether. And the continual increase in foreign competition created additional problems for Canadian organizations.

Strategic human resources planning tended to ignore issues in managing declining organizations such as those in the industries described above. Going bankrupt (Wang), divesting holdings (GM), or eliminating unprofitable product lines (Chrysler) are activities that are not prevalent in a growing enterprise. These activities, however, have a major impact on the employee population. Human resources planning, as we described earlier, had to change to a more strategic focus.[25] As we move into the twenty-first century, even how we downsize may be changing.

Previously, under downsizing, certain topics associated with traditional human resources planning, such as recruitment and selection, became somewhat irrelevant. It was believed that in order to cut costs and turn around ailing companies, body counts had to be high. So many organizations embarked on a process of downsizing. By 1994, almost all major North American corporations had reduced their workforces, in many cases massively: General Motors had eliminated almost 75,000 jobs and IBM, 20,000.[26] The practice became quite commonplace: *The Globe and Mail* alone reported 180 announcements of lay-offs by ninety companies in Canada in the period between January 1989 and August 1992.[27] Many other such announcements were reported only in the local press and seldom made front-page news. And they were not limited to the private sector; governments, too, in an effort to cut costs, downsized their operations. In 1995, the federal government announced that 45,000 civil service jobs were to be eliminated over three years, which was all the more shocking because the civil service traditionally provided job security.[28] Provincial governments have launched similar downsizing efforts.

Cutting employees didn't produce the results that organizations were looking for. In many cases, operating costs didn't decrease. What did happen was that fewer people were left to do the work that needed to be done, and productivity fell. For example, Marjorie Armstrong-Stassen found that in a federal department implementing the elimination of 9,000 jobs over three years, downsizing

The impact of downsizing is felt by more than just the person laid off. Spouses, children, and even co-workers are also affected.

had a perceived negative effect on its TQM program, its teamwork, and on client service and performance.[29] Many companies simply did not look at the long-term effects of downsizing.[30]

This is changing today and is manifested in a way that appears bizarre at first sight: companies that are laying off employees are also hiring. American Airlines, for instance, cut 5,000 jobs in 1993 and 1994, but hired almost 2,500 people in the same period.[31] Bell Canada reduced its staff by 15,200 between the summer of 1995 and July 1997, while making 2,000 new hires.[32] Isn't this contradictory? How can this be explained? The answer lies in strategic human resources planning. Companies are refocusing their efforts on those things that meet their strategic direction. Those activities and jobs that lead to achieving the strategic goals and add value to the organization are getting the necessary resources—and that includes people. The result can be increased effectiveness. American Airlines claims that their remaining managers are 26 per cent more productive than before.[33]

Don't be lulled into a false sense of security by believing that the downsizing trend is over. It isn't: Bell Canada announced plans to let 2,200 people go in July 1997, for instance.[34] The point of this discussion is that companies are (or should be) continually linking their employee needs to the organization's strategy. Those jobs that are not directly linked to the strategy are being cut, while those essential to the strategy are retained and even expanded. Rather than downsizing, companies are rightsizing. That's just the point made in Figure 5-4. But what does this mean for the employees, especially for those who survived the cuts?

What About the Survivors?

There is no doubt that workers' lives have changed.[35] Downsizing, mergers, acquisitions, and the like have thrown employment relationships into a quandary. The job security that employees enjoyed a generation ago is gone. At best, it appears that organizations will have a core group of employees, who will be assisted by a contingent workforce. Good work and loyalty to the organization may not be enough. Promotions and career advancement may be serverely limited, if they exist at all. Employees won't have the luxury of knowing precisely what their jobs entail for they will frequently change—with the direction the company is currently pursuing and the projects it undertakes. And just because employees successfully made it through the merger or the latest cuts, doesn't mean their jobs are guaranteed. Even management may not be able to predict future needs as the direction of the organization and the requisite skills, knowledge, and abilities go through continuous adaptation. But it must prepare its workforce for the inevitable changes that will occur. This means ample training to ensure that core employees will be prepared to meet the demands of tomorrow, having flexible management practices, and communicating openly and honestly to employees about what is taking place.[36] Even so, as one writer has put it, "The old [game] has changed: Now, in good times, companies will fire. In bad times, they'll fire even more."[37] Employees, then, must recognize these facts and do those things that keep them desirable to employers. This means showing an interest in doing the work the organization needs, continuously developing and refining skills to do those jobs, and accepting the reality that their tenure with a company may not last beyond the current project.[38]

Methods of Achieving Reduced Staffing Levels

The discussion of rightsizing dealt primarily with situations where organizations changed the numbers and assignments of employees on a relatively permanent basis to meet their strategic focus. There are times, however, when more temporary solutions are required. This may be due to the seasonal nature of some businesses or even economic downturns. Under such circumstances, when jobs must be cut and staffing levels temporarily reduced, there are a number of ways to achieve that goal. These include not only the traditional lay-offs, but also leaves of absence without pay, loaning, work sharing, reduced work hours, early retirement, and attrition.[39] Let's take a closer look at these staff reducing efforts.

Lay-Off Temporary or permanent dismissal of workers from their jobs.

Lay-offs   Lay-offs can take many forms and can be temporary or permanent. Temporary lay offs usually occur during slack periods when workloads do not warrant such a large workforce. As soon as work resumes its normal level, workers are recalled. Although this is a cost-cutting measure, it can result in turning workers into cyclical employees and could also increase a company's employment insurance premiums if the federal government tied EI premiums to unemployment rates, as has been proposed and is the practice in several US states.

Proper strategic human resources planning and the levelling out of the workforce at the proper staffing level can help reduce this yo-yo effect. For example, by knowing when peak times as well as valleys exist, proper staffing can be achieved. However, proper staffing can mean a permanent lay-off for other employees whose skills, knowledge, and abilities no longer comply with the strategic direction of the company.

Leaves of Absence Without Pay   One means of cutting labour costs temporarily is to give workers the opportunity to take leaves of absence without pay. This may provide time for an employee who is financially able to leave the organization to pursue personal interests. These could range from attending college or university (to increase the employee's marketability and mobility) to engaging in other endeavours such as starting a business. Individuals offered this leave are usually those whose jobs may be eliminated in the future. Thus, this concept serves as a way to help employees prepare for coming changes.

Loaning   The loaning of valuable human resources to other organizations is a means of keeping "loaned" employees on the organization's payroll and bringing them back after a crisis has subsided. Usually higher-level managers are loaned for special projects with government or quasi-governmental agencies such as school boards, charitable organizations, or civic associations. The organization pays these managers a reduced salary, and the difference is made up by the agency. While an organization may ultimately lose some of these managers, many do return.

Work Sharing   This usually involves two people sharing the responsibilities of one job. This arrangement is attractive to those who want to strike a balance between work and family or study. The cost to the employer is more or less the same as one full-time job. A recent study by Statistics Canada reported that some 171,000 persons shared jobs in Canada in 1995 or about 8 per cent of all part-time workers. This is still a small proportion of the total Canadian workforce—under 2 per cent of all workers.[40]

The approach gained much popularity in the early 1980s when some Japanese and North American firms turned to it to offset some of the problems brought about by economic downturns. Employees tended to appreciate the commitment demonstrated by management, and this had a positive impact on their morale.[41]

Leaves of absence Permission to be absent from one's job.

Loaning Permitting employees to work for not-for-profit organizations, where the employee pays a portion of the employee's salary.

Work Sharing A work concept whereby two or more individuals share one full-time job with the remaining time spent on individual pursuits.

Family-friendly organizations are those that have policies and practices that allow the employee to structure the job around their own needs.

Interest in work sharing is now motivated not only by the desire to cut employee costs. Faced with more diversity in the workplace, and a workforce that is about half female, employers find that a substantial number of people, primarily women, wish to blend their careers with their personal lives; 50 per cent of Canadian job-sharers had children under twenty-five at home, compared to 35 per cent of regular part-time workers.[42] Some companies are offering work-sharing arrangements as part of what is being called a family-friendly organization.[43]

A **family-friendly organization** is one that has policies and practices such as flextime, work sharing, or off-site work that structures the job around employee needs. Although there is some debate over the merits of the family-friendly organization,[44] such work arrangements have generally shown positive results. Because the crux of the family-friendly organization lies in employee benefits, we'll return to this topic in Chapter 14 in our discussion of current issues in benefits administration.

Family-Friendly Organization An organization that has flexible policies and practices that are supportive of caring for a family.

Reduced Work Hours Reducing staffing levels through **reduced work hours** is based on the concept that an organization has only so much money to spend on its payroll. How it is spent may be up to the workers. For simplicity's sake, let us assume that we have $600,000 a year for labour costs. We originally had twenty workers with annual incomes of $30,000. Now, as the company is experiencing economic hardships, only $480,000 a year is available to pay the workers. With no change in the hours worked, four employees would have to be laid off. To eliminate this dilemma, each worker agrees to work fewer hours and receive less pay so that the four jobs are saved. In this simplified case, instead of a forty-hour work week, each employee is paid for only thirty-two hours of work. All twenty employees will continue to be employed, but each will earn $6,000 less per year.

Reduced Work Hours A staff reduction concept whereby employees work fewer than forty hours and are paid accordingly.

While the example is exaggerated, it does reveal an effort on behalf of employees to forgo some of their salaries and benefits in order to keep all workers employed. The rationale is that receiving less is better than receiving nothing at all. However, it takes a strong personal conviction to accept that philosophy unless you are one of the one about to be laid off. For instance, during the early 1990s, many provincial and municipal organizations in Ontario faced severe budget shortages. In some cases, rather than laying off a number of workers, these agencies opted for leaves without pay, adding up to the savings that would have been realized if lay-offs had occurred. These forced leaves were not popular—they were dubbed "Rae Days" in a sarcastic reference to the province's premier at the time—and contributed to the government losing the next election. A number of companies with unionized employees took similar steps; for example, Canadian Airlines received wage concessions from its pilots in an effort to preserve the financial viability of the company and to save fellow workers' jobs. In Saguenay, Quebec, Alcan developed a voluntary program called "40/38": employees work forty hours a week, but are paid for thirty-eight; the two hours are taken as vacations. Seventy-three per cent of employees participate in the program, and as a result, 112 employees have kept their jobs.[45]

Early Retirement Another method of staff reduction is **early retirement**. Many of the industry giants have resorted to using early retirement inducements to reduce the number of workers, especially higher-level management personnel. Regardless of the specifics of these offers, the purpose is clear: Buy out some of the highest-paid individuals in the organization and delegate their responsibilities to other employees making less money.

Early Retirement A downsizing effort that gives employees close to retirement some incentive to leave the company earlier than expected.

Usually, the prime candidate for early retirement is an individual who is just a few years away from retiring. The company may offer this person a reduced retirement benefit until he or she reaches the agreed retirement age or years of service.

Another option is for the company to "buy" the years of service remaining until normal retirement for a sum of money equal to the amount that would have been contributed to the individual's pension. In either case, the result is the same: a reduction in the cost of paying very high salaries to those individuals. Although this is an effective cost-saving plan, an organization may lose some key executives.

An interesting approach combines work sharing with early retirement in Montreal's Sucre Lantic plant: employees over fifty-five years of age can form pairs with each partner working six months a year.[46]

Attrition The process of attrition occurs when incumbents leave their jobs for any reason (retirement, resignation, transfers, etc.), and those jobs are not filled. Usually, this process is accompanied by a hiring freeze which dictates that no hiring will take place for jobs that are vacated.

Attrition and hiring freezes can be implemented organization-wide (used to reduce overall employment numbers) or can be directed towards particular departments or jobs that may no longer be needed. The bottom-line result is that attrition with a hiring freeze is a short-term means of addressing a surplus of employees.

Whenever companies use methods such as those previously described, a philosophical issue arises. Especially in the case of trimming layers of management personnel from the company, what should a company do to help these displaced workers? Does a company have any responsibility, legally or ethically, to these individuals? The answer to such questions lies in the concept of outplacement.

Outplacement Services

Recall that in our discussion in Chapter 1 of the goals of human resources management, we stated that the objective of the maintenance function was to be such that commitment and loyalty to the organization were maintained. Under growth circumstances, such a goal is possible. However, in downsizing or other staff reduction activities, the emphasis of that goal changes. The company must demonstrate its support for the past commitment and loyalty of the severed employee. Outplacement delivers that support. By definition, outplacement is a process of assisting existing employees in their search for another job.[47]

This process includes providing career guidance, retraining those employees who can be productively placed elsewhere in the organization, and assisting those who can't with résumé writing, training in interviewing techniques, career and personal counselling, and job-search methods. Companies need to recognize that many of these long-term loyal employees have no idea how to go about getting a job outside the company. The crucial period for this employee appears to be the first three to six months[48] in which a number of key factors come into play. First of all is the psychological aspect of looking for a job. A lack of success for more than six months leads to negative self-image that can only hurt in interviewing situations and tends to cause an individual to feel that he or she will never get a job. Second is the money issue. After six months, money—even severance pay—may be running out, which only adds to the other psychological problems. That is why outplacement is so crucial—to help these individuals deal

Attrition A process in which the jobs of incumbents who leave for any reason are not filled.

Outplacement The process of assisting company employees to search for jobs outside the organization.

with these tough times. Through proper counselling, networking, and other assistance, outplacement can help.[49] It does not come cheap—the costs range into the thousands of dollars per individual—but most employers offering outplacement services indicate that it is money well spent.[50]

Study Tools and Applications

Summary

This summary relates to the Learning Objectives provided on p. 130.
After having read this chapter, you should know:

1. Strategic human resources planning is the process by which an organization ensures that it has the right number and kinds of people capable of effectively and efficiently completing those tasks that are in direct support of the company's mission.
2. The steps in the strategic human resources planning process include mission formulating, establishing corporate goals and objectives, assessing current human resources, estimating the supplies and demand for labour, and matching demand with current supplies. The two outcomes of this process are recruitment and decruitment.
3. A human resources information system is useful for quickly fulfilling human resources management information needs by tracking employee information and having that information readily available when needed.
4. Job analysis is a systematic exploration of the activities surrounding and within a job. It defines the job's duties, responsibilities, and accountabilities.
5. The six general techniques for obtaining job information are observation, individual interview, group interview, structured interview, technical conference, and diary.
6. Functional Job Analysis is a procedure that describes what a workers does in terms of three "worker function" scales of data, people, and things. The Position Analysis Questionnaire quantifies the job analysis process by means of 194 job elements, organized into six major job divisions.
7. Job descriptions are written statements of what the job holder does (duties and responsibilities); job specifications identify the personal characteristics required to perform successfully on the job; and job evaluation is the process of using job analysis information in establishing a compensation system.
8. Downsizing refers to the process of restructuring the organization that results in the organization reducing its number of employees. Rightsizing may involve downsizing, but more appropriately, focuses on having the right people available to work on activities directly related to the strategic direction of the company.
9. Various methods of achieving staff reductions include lay-offs, leaves of absence, loaning, work sharing, reduced work hours, early retirements, and attrition.
10. Outplacement services are programs offered by an employer to assist employees about to be severed from the organization in obtaining employment. These services include training, résumé writing, interviewing techniques, office and clerical assistance, and career counselling.

Key Terms

attrition	loaning
diary method	mission statement
Dictionary of Occupational Titles	National Occupational Classification
downsizing	observation method
early retirement	outplacement

family-friendly organization
Functional Job Analysis (FJA)
group interview method
human resources inventory
human resources management system
 (HRMS)
individual interview method
job analysis
job description
job evaluation
job specification
lay-offs
leave of absence

Position Analysis Questionnaire (PAQ)
reduced work hours
replacement chart
rightsizing
Standard Occupational Classification

strategic goals
strategic human resources planning (SHRP)
structured questionnaire method
succession planning
technical conference method
work sharing

EXPERIENTIAL EXERCISE:

Downsizing Staff

One of the more difficult tasks any manager faces is deciding who to lay off. Following is a list of possible candidates. Company records indicate that two full-time positions must be eliminated. Data for your use are provided as follows. All workers are market analysts.

Sarah Baker — White female, age thirty-four, seven years with the company in current job. Outstanding performance rating past two years. B.Comm. Sarah is a single mother and is currently in week four of a twelve-week leave of absence. Although her performance has been good the past two years, some decline was noted earlier this year. In fact, a written verbal warning about her performance was given six months ago. Some improvement has been noted, but her performance has not reached its previous level. You believe she is upset because she did not get the promotion to product development manager she applied for six months ago.

Raj Biswas — Asian male, age thirty-nine, six months in marketing, three and one-half years with company. Average performance ratings the past three years. Has an MBA, with a B.Sc. in Computer Science. Raj is the highest paid analyst. He saved the company $200,000 last year through his implementation of an automated sales monitoring program. He is about the only one who knows the program and can keep it running.

Tom Kelly — White male, age sixty-three, forty-one years in marketing. Started as a clerk and moved up to his current position. Tom has a high-school diploma and has taken some university courses in marketing. His performance ratings over the past three years were outstanding, average, and above average.

Claude Ouellette — White male, age forty-four. Four years with company, all in marketing. Claude was a freelance consultant specializing in consumer product development. Claude's excellent consulting work with your organization led to a job offer being made. Claude's performance the past two

	years, however, has slipped, going from average to below average. You suspect that he is not happy with the job any more now that the corporation is putting fewer resources into consumer products.
Judy Myers	African-Canadian female, age twenty-four. Recent college graduate with an A average in advertising. Just completed her probationary period with the organization. Judy was permanently disabled in an auto accident four years ago and is about to settle with the insurer of the driver who caused the accident. Rumours cite a settlement in the $4-million range.
Yu Chen	Asian male, age twenty-seven. B.Comm. concentrating in finance. Yu was transferred from accounting and finance to bring into line your marketing costs. To date, he has revamped your sales promotion program, resulting in a 45 per cent decrease in sales promotion costs for the organization. You accidently saw a copy of the employment section of a regional financial association journal on his desk, lying next to what appeared to be an updated résumé.

Based on these five descriptions, decide how you will downsize the unit by the two positions. Then, in your group, reach consensus on how the group would approach the problem. Are there similarities? Differences? On what basis did you make your decision? Could you support it if it were challenged in court? How?

CASE APPLICATION:

Family and Succession at Bentall Corp.

Charles Bentall, a British immigrant, bought Vancouver-based Dominion Construction in 1919, eight years after being hired by the company. Over the years, Dominion grew and became a unit of Bentall Corp., one of the premier real estate companies in Western Canada. Charles gave shares in the company to his sons Clark, Howard, and Bob, and shares were given to later generations of Bentalls.[51]

While the companies were successful, problems typical of family businesses began to arise—from the lack of board meetings to making decisions as to whether or not to sell parts of the company. The most important argument came over the next generation. Clark Bentall wanted his son David to be the next CEO, but Clark's younger brother Bob, then the CEO, did not think David was suitable.

In 1986, an industrial psychologist and consultant, Linda Wagner, spoke to the Canadian Association of Family Enterprises and later to a Bentall family meeting on the issue of succession planning. They worked together on the problem, and in 1988, David developed a plan, but it had no place in it for Clark's son David. Bob believed that neither he nor any other family member was competent to run a business as large as Bentall Corp. The solution was to sell Dominion Construction, a Bentall subsidiary, to Clark Bentall. Eventually David became Dominion's CEO.

In 1992 the family sold 23 per cent of Bentall to Prudential Insurance Co. of America and a British Columbia government pension fund. In 1994, the company hired its first non-family CEO, Mark Shuparski; he took over from Bob Bentall, who remained as chairman. In 1996, 57 per cent of Bentall Corp. was sold to the Caisse de dépôt et placement du Québec for $70 million. While holdings are not made public, Clark Bentall's family has sold off its 10 per cent stake in the company, and it is estimated that the Bentall family holds about a third of the shares (Prudential and the BC government pension fund also reduced their holdings).

Bob Bentall is not sad about selling a business that had been in his family's hands for almost eighty years. "I've always wanted what's best for the company," he said in an interview. The process was painful—Bob and Clark no longer speak to each other—but at least it was resolved outside the courts, unlike other much-publicized Canadian succession wars like the McCains' and the Steinbergs'.

Questions

1. If you were an HRM consultant, what advice would you have given Bob and Clark Bentall regarding succession planning?
2. What advice would you give Mark Shuparski and Bentall Corp.'s new board of directors on the importance of developing a succession plan?

Testing Your Understanding

How well did you fulfil the learning objectives?

1. Diane is vice-president of human resources of a large manufacturing firm. When should she become involved in strategic planning for her organization?
   a. She should do all of it as part of her job.
   b. She should never be involved in it. That function belongs in financial management and marketing.
   c. Her real contribution comes after organizational assessment is completed.
   d. She should be included in mission development.
   e. She should be included in the maintenance phase.

2. Supply and demand forecasts, combined, provide all of the following for human resources managers except
   a. highlighting areas where overstaffing might currently exist.
   b. highlighting areas where overstaffing might exist in the future.
   c. pinpointing anticipated shortages in engineering areas.
   d. pinpointing anticipated budget changes in recruiting and maintenance.
   e. keeping abreast of opportunities to stockpile good people for anticipated needs.

3. The vice-president of human resources in a large manufacturing firm has just received a gap analysis report. It indicated staffing needs over the next five years for one hundred additional shipping clerks, one hundred fewer shop technicians, one hundred additional sales representatives, and one hundred fewer research specialists. What should the vice-president do?
   a. Internal transfers can take care of all these needs.
   b. Corporate outplacement services need to be secured for four hundred employees over the next five years.
   c. Recruiting efforts for research areas need to be increased immediately.
   d. Examine current human resources inventories to determine retirement, internal transfers, and probable dismissals over the next five years.
   e. No additional shipping clerk candidates should be interviewed for five years.

4. Human resources management systems usage has grown significantly in recent years for all of these reasons except
   a. skill demands have become less complex for most of the workforce.
   b. technology costs have come down.
   c. managers are often overwhelmed with information.
   d. systems are more user-friendly.
   e. staffing decisions need to be made more quickly.

5. During a job analysis, all of these tasks are performed except
   a. duties and responsibilities of a job are defined.
   b. a description of what happens on a job is provided.
   c. skills and abilities necessary to perform a job are precisely identified.
   d. basic pay ranges for a job are set.
   e. conditions under which a job should be performed are described.

6. Job analysis can be performed in all of these ways except
   a. observing hourly workers.
   b. reviewing exit interviews conducted with departing employees.
   c. studying diaries or daily journals that managers kept over a threemonth period.
   d. listening to fifteen assembly line workers in a group discussion.
   e. giving workers checklists to indicate which tasks on the list are performed during job execution.

7. Monique, the director of job analysis, must write job descriptions for two hundred new jobs in a new plant for her large manufacturing firm. The new robotics line will make this location different from the company's other five sites. Ten new supervisors have been recruited from outside the organization because of their experience with robotics production technology. Ten current supervisors have been sent to robotics production training. In addition, 150 workers have been targeted to work on the line, but none of them has any robotics experience. Which job analysis method should she use?
   a. Observation.
   b. Structured questionnaire.
   c. Technical conference.
   d. Diary.
   e. Gap analysis.

8. The Purdue University Position Analysis Questionnaire (PAQ) and Fine's Functional Job Analysis (FJA) are best compared by which statement?
   a. The PAQ is the same as the FJA.
   b. The PAQ is used to develop the FJA.
   c. The PAQ produces a more quantitative and finely tuned job description than the FJA.
   d. The PAQ works more effectively for white-collar, managerial jobs, while the FJA is more effective for blue-collar, unskilled jobs.
   e. The FJA is used only in the public sector. The PAQ is used only in the private sector.

9. Which statement best compares job specifications and job descriptions?
   a. Job description focuses on qualifications for job holders. Job specification focuses on what the job holder does.
   b. Job specification focuses on qualifications for job holders. Job description focuses on what the job holder does.
   c. Job specification occurs before job analysis. Job description occurs after job analysis.
   d. Job description is the same as job specification.
   e. Job specification occurs after job analysis. Job description occurs before job analysis.

10. Which statement accurately reflects the current state of job analysis in most organizations today?
    a. Job analysis is not done.
    b. Job analysis is performed by senior human resources professionals.
    c. The primary purpose of job analysis is to assist in the recruiting and selection activities.
    d. Job analysis affects most HRM activities.
    e. Job analysis is developed from the human resources skills inventory.

11. Stan is vice-president of human resources in a medium-size manufacturing firm. He is being sued for not hiring Mildred, who is confined to a wheelchair, to work in the plant. Which document will he use in his defence?
    a. Job description.
    b. Job analysis.
    c. Job evaluation.
    d. Job qualification.
    e. Job specification.

12. Jordan is the vice-president of human resources for a large manufacturing organization. His company is in a temporary slump. He has to cut 40 per cent of the costs for the current year but will need all the competent employees he has currently plus 18 per cent more at the start of next year when eight major contracts will begin. All of these options should be pursued except
    a. leaves of absence.
    b. loans.
    c. lay-offs.
    d. early retirements.
    e. reduced work hours.

13. The vice-president of human resources of a major manufacturing organization has convinced the executive committee of the organization to become a more family-friendly organization. Which one of the following statements best reflects what the organization will do?
    a. The organization will issue a policy indicating that the company will establish a day care centre and allow maternity and paternity leaves.
    b. The organization will extend the Christmas vacation period from December 23 through January 3 and give a holiday bonus to employees with more than five years' seniority.
    c. The organization will implement flexible work arrangements that meet employee needs.
    d. The organization will hire more single parents and pay them a higher salary so they can better afford day care.
    e. The organization will provide employer paid family health insurance coverage for a period not to exceed four years for all employees who are permanently laid off.

14. If outplacement costs can range into thousands of dollars per employee, why do downsizing organizations have outplacement centres?
    a. They do not. Downsizing organizations use outplacement firms.
    b. They do not. Outplacement is only performed by organizations in growth mode.
    c. The costs are overstated. Outplacement is usually around $100 per employee.
    d. Outplacement is a refocused goal in the downsizing organization to reward loyalty and commitment in employees.
    e. Outplacement centres are required under the *Employment Standards Act.*

15. HRMS usage has grown significantly in recent years for all of these reasons except
    a. skill demands have become less complex for most of the workforce.
    b. technology costs have come down.
    c. managers are often overwhelmed with information.
    d. systems are more user-friendly.
    e. staffing decisions need to be made more quickly.

16. During a job analysis, all of these tasks are performed except
    a. duties and responsibilities of a job are defined.
    b. a description of what happens on a job is provided.
    c. skills and abilities necessary to perform a job are precisely identified.
    d. basic pay ranges for a job are set.
    e. conditions under which a job should be performed are described.

17. Which job analysis method would be avoided by a job analyst because it may miss important parts of a job?
    a. Observation.
    b. Individual interview.
    c. Group interview.
    d. Diary.
    e. Gap analysis.

18. An adaptation of the Position Analysis Questionnaire presented at a much lower reading level is the
    a. Management Position Description Questionnaire.
    b. Job Element Inventory.
    c. Occupational Analysis Inventory.
    d. Critical Incident Method.
    e. Dictionary of Occupational Titles.

Chapter Six

RECRUITMENT AND THE FOUNDATIONS OF SELECTION

Successful strategic human resource planning is designed to identify an organization's human resource needs. Once these are known, an organization will want to do something about meeting them. Assuming that demand for certain skills, knowledge, and abilities is greater than the current supply, the next step in the staffing function is recruitment. This activity makes it possible for a company to acquire the people necessary to ensure the effective operation of the organization. Recruiting is the process of discovering potential candidates and attracting them for actual or anticipated organizational vacancies. From another perspective, it is the linking activity of bringing together those with jobs to fill and those seeking jobs, and that frequently requires creativity and ingenuity. Anyone can place an advertisement in a newspaper and get a response, but will it achieve the kind of response expected? In early 1998, it was reported that the Canadian army was budgeting $1.5 million for an advertising campaign to attract physically fit, outdoors-oriented, young women to combat careers.[1] In response to criticisms from a human rights tribunal, the army started integrating women into combat roles in 1989 but found it difficult to retain those it recruited. The attrition rate has averaged about 42 per cent per year compared to 10 per cent for men. Only 1 per cent of the army's 13,000 combat positions were held by women.

The Canadian Army began integrating women into combat roles a decade ago but has found it difficult to retain those it recruited.

Traditionally, military women have served in nursing, administrative, clerical, logistical, and maintenance positions. Few have achieved senior leadership ranks because the army rewards field experience in combat positions. No female officer has commanded a brigade, the largest combat formation in the Canadian army.

Captain Maureen Wellwood, who commanded a platoon of thirty crack combat soldiers on peacekeeping operations in Bosnia in 1996, believes that female combat soldiers will break through this glass ceiling. About a possible promotion to general, she says, "If I deserve it, I would like to get there one day."

The army must recruit more women to combat positions if it is to appoint women to top ranks. Unlike the navy and air force, which are implementing budget cuts and cutting Cold War-based operations, the army continues to need combat soldiers because of the increase in the number of peacekeeping missions.

The advertising message is that combat careers are open to women. However, the army must address the negative attitudes of many women towards military careers. A poll conducted by the Environics Research group revealed that women do not believe that they have equal career opportunities in the military and are much less interested than men in joining the Canadian Forces.

The army's 1998 recruiting drive is intended to create a "critical mass" of women who could support each other in basic training and in the later advanced infantry training. This is expected to help reduce the attrition rates. There will be no "easier" criteria for women in recruitment or training: all recruits, men and women, will have to meet the same demanding performance standards. For example, all infantry soldiers must be able to carry rucksacks that weigh twenty-five kilograms. But the army is redesigning the standard rucksack, which many women found ill-fitting and uncomfortable.

Goals of Recruiting

The Canadian Forces' attempts to attract women recruits are hampered by the fact that apparently few women are interested in military careers. Hence, the army tries a number of strategies to make military careers appear attractive to potential recruits. These include recruiting shows where soldiers can display their skills and an advertising campaign based on marketing research.[2]

For the recruiting process to work effectively, there must be a large enough pool of candidates to choose from, and that may not be easy, especially in a tight labour market. The first goal of recruiting, then, is to communicate the position in such a way that job seekers respond because the more applications received, the better the recruiter's chances for finding an individual who is best suited to the job requirements. Simultaneously, however, the recruiter must provide enough information about the job that unqualified applicants will not apply.

The army's television advertisements show people in outdoor and combat activities so that those who dislike strenuous physical activity or are repelled by the idea of combat will not apply because they would know that they would not feel comfortable in the organization.

Why is it important to human resources management to discourage unqualified applicants? There are a number of reasons. For example, the company acknowledges the receipt of applications, and that costs time and money. Then there are the application reviews and a second letter rejecting the unsuccessful applications. This again, incurs costs and because of that organizations only acknowledge those applications that are selected for further processing. In such cases, it is common that the advertisement include a phase like "only those applicants contacted for an interview will be acknowledged." For these reasons, a good recruiting program should attract the most qualified people but not attract unqualified people; this will minimize the cost of processing unqualified candidates.

Factors that Affect Recruiting Efforts

Although all organizations will, at one time or another, engage in recruiting activities, some do so to a much larger extent than others. Obviously, size is one factor; an organization with 100,000 employees will find itself recruiting continually. So, too, will fast food firms, smaller service organizations, and companies that pay lower wages. Certain other variables will also influence the extent of recruiting. The level of unemployment in the community where the organization is located will influence how much recruiting takes place. Working conditions and salary and benefit packages will influence turnover and, therefore, the need for future recruiting. Organizations that are not growing or that are actually declining will find little need to recruit. On the other hand, those that are expanding rapidly, like the new casinos in Windsor and Niagara Falls, will find recruitment a major human resources activity.

Recruitment, even in these growing companies, is no easy task. Recall in Chapter 2 the discussion of skill deficiencies. Quality workers are becoming harder to locate. Therefore, HRM will have to develop new strategies to locate and hire those individuals possessing the skills the company needs.[3]

Mountain Equipment Co-operative, with stores in Vancouver, Calgary, Edmonton, Toronto, and Ottawa, has sales staff that is very well regarded in the retail industry because of their product knowledge and positive attitude. MEC is able to attract such employees partly because of its reputation for treating its people better than most other retailers and partly because it uses effective recruiting methods to attract and hire people who are active and outdoors-oriented. According to one former employee, "working at MEC is a means to sustain their interest in the outdoors."[4]

Constraints on Recruiting Efforts

While the ideal recruitment effort will bring in a large number of qualified applicants who will take the job if it is offered, the realities cannot be ignored. For example, the pool of qualified applicants may not include the "best" candidates; or the "best" candidate may not want to be employed by the organization. These and other constraints on recruiting limit managers' freedom to recruit and select a candidate of their choice. However, we can narrow our focus by suggesting five specific constraints: image of the organization, attractiveness of the job, internal organizational policies, government influence, and recruiting costs.

Constraints on Recruiting Factors that can affect or limit the effectiveness of external recruiting.

Image of the Organization We noted that the prospective candidate may not be interested in working for the particular organization. The image of the organization, therefore, should be considered a potential constraint. If that image is perceived to be low, the likelihood of attracting a large number of qualified applicants is reduced.[5]

Business students in universities and colleges know, for example, that the people in the top positions at Canada's major banks earn excellent salaries, receive superior benefits, and are well respected in their own communities and nationally. The banks are also well known for their training programs. Thus, among most business graduates, the banks have a positive image. The hope of eventually having a shot at one of the top jobs, being in a favourable spotlight, and having a position of power, means that the banks have little trouble in attracting business graduates to entry-level positions. But not all large organizations have a positive image in the eyes of graduates. In fact, some have a decidedly negative image. Many firms have a reputation for being in a declining industry, engaging in practices that result in polluting the environment, producing poor-quality products, having unsafe working conditions, or being indifferent to employees' needs. Such a reputation can and does reduce an organization's abilitiy to attract the best personnel available.

Attractiveness of the Job If the position to be filled is unattractive, recruiting a large pool of qualified applicants will be difficult. In recent years, for instance, many employers have been complaining about the difficulty of finding suitably qualified individuals for secretarial positions. These jobs traditionally appealed to females, but today, women have more job opportunities and higher aspirations, resulting in a severe shortage of qualified secretaries. Given the status,

•

pay, and career potential of most secretarial jobs, many individuals who previously would have sought such positions now consider them unattractive. Any job that is viewed as boring, hazardous, anxiety-creating, low-paying, or lacking in promotion potential seldom will attract a qualified pool of applicants. Even during economic slumps, people have refused to take these jobs.[6]

Internal Organizational Policies Internal organizational policies, such as "promote from within wherever possible," give priority to individuals inside the organization. This will usually ensure that all positions, other than the lowest entry-level positions, will be filled from within the ranks. Although this is attractive to employees, it will reduce the number of applications from outsiders if they believe they have little chance of getting the job advertised.

Government Influence The government's influence in the recruiting process should not be overlooked. An employer can no longer seek out preferred individuals based on non-job-related factors such as physical appearance, sex, or religious background. An airline wishing to have only attractive female flight attendants for example, will find itself in violation of the law if comparably qualified male candidates are rejected on the basis of gender. The airline would have to demonstrate that being female is a bona fide occupational requirement (BFOR), also called a bona fide occupational qualification (BFOQ), which would be virtually impossible. That is why a Canadian airline will have male and female cabin attendants. Government regulations on what constitutes a BFOR will, of course, vary from one jurisdiction to another: Singapore Airlines' cabin attendants are all female, for example.

Recruiting Costs The last but not least constraint is one that centres on recruiting costs. Recruiting is expensive. Sometimes continuing a search for long periods is not possible because of budget restrictions. Accordingly, when an organization considers various recruiting sources, it does so with some sense of effectiveness in mind. That is, recruiting expenditures are made where the best return on the investment can be realized. Unfortunately, because of limited resources, these expenditures must be prioritized. Those lower in priority do not get the same resources, and this can ultimately limit a recruiter's attempts to attract the best person for the job.

Bona Fide Occupational Qualifications (BFOQ) Bona Fide Occupational Requirements (BFOR) A justified reason for discrimination based on business necessity (i.e., needed for the safe and efficient operation of the organization). Also, a requirement that can be shown to be essential to the tasks the employee is expected to perform.

Recruiting from an International Perspective

When beginning to recruit for overseas positions, the first step, as always, is to define the relevant labour market, and for international positions that is the whole world. As mentioned in Chapter 2, we first must decide if we want to send a Canadian overseas, recruit in the host country where the position is, or ignore nationality and do a global search for the best person available. Thus, our possibilities are to select someone from Canada, the host country, or a third country.

To some extent, this basic decision depends on the type of occupation and its requirements as well as the stage of national and cultural development of the overseas operations. Although production, office, and clerical occupations are rarely filled outside a local labour market, executive and sometimes scientific, engineering, or professional managerial candidates may be sought in national or international markets. If the organization is searching for someone with extensive company experience to launch a very technical product in a country where it has never sold before, it will probably want a **parent-country national**. This approach is often used when a new foreign subsidiary is being established and headquarters wants to control all strategic decisions, but technical expertise and experience are needed. It is also appropriate where there is a lack of qualified host-country nationals in the workforce.

In other situations, it might be more advantageous to hire a **host-country national (HCN)**. For an uncomplicated consumer product, it may be a wise corporate strategic decision to have each foreign subsidiary acquire its own distinct national identity. For example, clothing has different styles of merchandising, and an HCN may have a better feel for the best way to market the sweaters or jeans of an international manufacturer.

Sometimes the choice may not be entirely left to the corporation. In some countries, most African nations for example, local laws control how many **expatriates** a corporation can send. There may be established ratios, such as twenty host-country nationals must be employed for every foreigner granted working papers. Also, using HCNs eliminates language problems, as well as the high cost of training and relocating an expatriate with a family. It also minimizes one of the chief reasons international assignments fail—the family's inability to adjust to their new surroundings. Even when premiums are paid to lure the best local applicants away from other companies, the costs of maintaining the employee are significantly lower than with sending a Canadian overseas. In some countries, where there are tense political environments, an HCN is less visible and can somewhat insulate the foreign corporation from hostilities and possible terrorism.

The third option is to ignore nationality when recruiting. This develops an international executive cadre with a truly global perspective and may reduce national identification of managers with particular organizational units. For example, a large Canadian manufacturing firm could rotate its managers between assignments in its plants in Canada, the United States, Mexico, and Austria. A company that does this will have to develop uniform policies for the treatment of employees sent on international assignments. Just imagine the problems that could arise if the company were starting a plant in Brazil, say, and had managers from Canada, the US, Mexico, and Austria working together with Brazilians—each of them treated differently regarding salary, vacations, expense allowances, and so on.

Parent-Country National (PCN) A citizen or permanent resident of the country where a multinational firm has its headquarters, assigned to work for the company as an expatriate in another country.

Host-Country National (HCN) A citizen or permanent resident of a given country, hired by a multinational firm to work in that country.

Expatriates Individuals who work in a country in which they are not citizens or permanent residents.

Recruiting Sources

Recruitment is more likely to achieve its objectives if recruiting sources reflect the type of position to be filled. For example, an ad in the business employment section of *The Globe and Mail* is more likely to be read by a manager seeking an executive position in the $125,000-to-$175,000-a-year bracket than by an automobile assembly line worker looking for a new job. Similarly, a recruiter who is trying to fill a management training position and visits a community college in search of a recent university graduate with an undergraduate degree in engineering and a master's degree in business administration is looking for the right person in the wrong place.

Obviously, some recruiting sources are more effective than others for filling certain types of jobs. In the following sections, the strengths and weaknesses of each source for different levels of personnel will be emphasized.

The Internal Search

Internal Search Seeking to fill a position with current employees of the organization.

Many large organizations will attempt to develop their own employees for positions beyond the lowest level. This can occur through an internal search of current employees who have either applied for the job, been identified through the organization's human resources management system, or been referred by a fellow employee. The advantages of such searches—a "promote from within wherever possible" policy—are:

1. It is good public relations.
2. It builds morale.
3. It helps retain productive and motivated employees.
4. It improves the probability of a good selection since information on the individual's performance is readily available.
5. It is less costly than going outside to recruit.
6. Those chosen internally already know the organization.
7. When carefully planned, promoting from within can also act as a training device for developing middle- and top-level managers.

There can also be distinct disadvantages to using internal sources. It can be counter-productive for an organization to use inferior internal sources just because they are there when better qualified candidates are available outside. However, an individual from the outside may appear more attractive simply because the recruiter is unaware of the outsider's faults. Internal searches may also generate infighting among the rival candidates for promotion as well as lower morale among those not selected.

It is important that the organization avoid excessive inbreeding. It may be necessary to bring in some new blood occasionally to broaden the current ideas, knowledge, and enthusiasm and to question the "we've-always-done-it-that-way" mentality. As noted in the discussion of human resources inventories in Chapter 5, the organization's HRM files should provide information as to which employees might be considered for vacancies. Most organizations can utilize their computer information system to generate a list of those who have the potential to fill the vacant position.

In many organizations, it is standard procedure to post any new job openings and to allow any current employee to "bid" for the position. This approach complies with the requirements of employment equity legislation at the federal and provincial levels. The posting notification can be communicated on a central "open positions" bulletin board in the plants or offices, in the organization's newsletter, or, in some cases, in a specially prepared posting sheet from human resources outlining those available positions. Even if current employees are not interested in the position, they can use these notices to recommend friends or associates. The employee referral is an important source of candidates.

Employee Referrals/Recommendations

One of the best sources for individuals who will perform effectively on the job is a recommendation from an employee because, they will rarely recommend someone unless they believe that the individual can perform adequately. Such a recommendation reflects on the recommender, and when someone's reputation is at stake, we can expect the recommendation to be based on considered judgement. With employee referrals, the recommender often gives the applicant more realistic information about the job than could be available through an employment agency or newspaper ad. This reduces unrealistic expectations and increases the length of time the employee will stay on the job. As a result of these pre-selection factors, employee referrals tend to be more acceptable applicants, to be more likely to accept a job offer, and, once employed, to have a higher job survival rate. Additionally, employee referrals are an excellent means of locating potential employees in those hard-to-fill positions. For example, because of the difficulty in finding computer programmers, engineers, or nurses with specific skills, some organizations have turned to their employees for assistance. In one, a reward is paid to the employee if their candidate is hired for specifically identified hard-to-fill positions. Thus, both the organization and the employee benefit; the employee receives a monetary reward, and the organization obtains a qualified candidate without the major expense of an extensive recruiting search.

There are, of course, some potentially negative features of employee referral. For one thing, recommenders may confuse friendship with job performance competence. Individuals often like to have their friends with them for social and even economic reasons; it may be as simple as being able to share rides to and from work. As a result, an employee may recommend a friend for a position without giving an unbiased consideration to that person's competence. Employee referrals may also lead to nepotism—that is, hiring individuals who are related to persons already employed by the organization. The hiring of relatives is particularly widespread in family-owned organizations. Although such actions may not necessarily fulfil the objective of hiring the most qualified applicant, interest in the organization and loyalty to it may be long-term advantages.

Employee referrals can also lead to an adverse impact. If a predominantly White male workforce recommends other White male acquaintances for jobs, and if they are hired, this could be excluding visible minorities or females. Employee referrals do, however, appear to be used everywhere. Lower-level and managerial-level positions can, and often are, filled by the recommendation of a current employee. In higher-level positions, however, it is more likely that the referral will be a professional acquaintance rather than a friend with whom the recommender has close social contact. In jobs where specialized expertise is important and where employees participate in professional organizations that foster the development of this expertise, it can be expected that employees will be acquainted with, or know about, individuals they think would make a contribution to the organization.

Employee Referral A recommendation from a current employee regarding a job applicant.

External Searches

In addition to looking internally for candidates, it is customary for organizations to open up recruiting to the external community. These efforts include advertisements, employment agencies, schools, colleges, and universities, professional organizations, and unsolicited applicants.

Advertisements The sign outside the construction location reads: "Now Hiring—Bricklayers." The newspaper advertisement reads:

> Sales Management Trainee. We are looking for someone who wants to assume responsibility and wishes to learn the winter outerwear business. Minimum of two years' sales experience required. University degree or

One method of recruiting external candidates is the printed advertisement which can be placed in a daily newspaper or a specialty trade journal.

equivalent desired. Salary to $40,000. For appointment, call Ms Davies at 555-0075.

Most of us have seen both types of advertisements. When an organization wishes to communicate to the public that it has a vacancy, advertisements are one of the most popular methods used. However, where the ad is placed is often determined by the type of job. Although it is not uncommon to see blue-collar jobs listed on placards outside the plant gates, we would be surprised to find a vice-presidency so listed. The higher the position in the organization, the more specialized the skills, or the shorter the supply of that resource in the labour force, the more widely broadcast the advertisement is likely to be. The search for a top executive might include advertisements in a national publication such as *The Globe and Mail* or *The National Post.* On the other hand, ads of lower-level jobs are usually confined to the local daily newspaper or regional trade journal.

A number of factors influence the response rate to advertisements. There are three important variables: identification of the organization, labour market conditions, and the degree to which specific requirements are included in the advertisement. Some organizations place what is referred to as a blind-box ad where there is no specific identification of the organization. Respondents are asked to reply to a post office box number or to an employment firm that is acting as an agent between the applicant and the organization. Large organizations with a national reputation seldom use blind-box advertisements to fill lower-level positions; however, when the organization does not wish to publicize the fact that it is seeking to fill an internal position or when it seeks to recruit for a position where there is a soon-to-be-moved incumbent, a blind-box advertisement may be appropriate. This is especially true when a very large number of applicants is expected. Using the blind-box ad relieves the organization from having to respond to every individual who applies. The organization notifies only those it wishes to see.

Although blind-box ads can assist HRM in finding qualified applicants, many individuals are reluctant to answer them. Obviously there is the fear, usually unjustified, that the ad may have been placed by their own employer, which could be embarassing or worse. Also, the organization itself is frequently a key deter-

Advertisement Materials informing to the general public that a position in a company is open.

Blind-Box Ad An advertisement in which there is no identification of the advertising organization.

minant of whether the individual is interested in a position. Also, these blind-box ads have a bad reputation because organizations have placed ads when no position existed in order to test the supply of workers in the community, to build a list of potential applicants, to identify those current employees who are interested in finding a new position, or to "satisfy" employment equity requirements when the final decision, for the greater part, has already been made.

The job analysis process is the basic source for the information placed in the ad. A decision must be made as to whether the ad will focus on descriptive elements of the job (job description) or on the applicant (job specification). The choice made will often affect the number of replies received. If, for example, you are willing to sift through a thousand or more responses, you might place a national ad in *The Globe and Mail, The National Post*, or a regional newspaper's employment section.

Let us compare two advertisements published in the same issue of *The Toronto Star*. They appeared on a Saturday, a day on which many employment ads are published. Since people know this, those looking for a job tend to read the Saturday newspaper which, in turn, encourages prospective employers to place advertisements on Saturdays.

The ad in Figure 6-1 will probably attract a lot of applicants. It uses primarily applicant-centred criteria to describe the successful applicant. Most people would probably claim to be energetic, to like working with people, and to be dynamic, creative, and a team player. The company can probably look forward to seeing a large number of people applying in person on the following Sunday and Monday. On the other hand, Figure 6-2 describes a job requiring precise abilities, qualifications, and experience. The requirements of a degree in engineering and at least five years' experience in a very specific manufacturing process will certainly reduce the respondent pool.

Why would one want a large number of applicants? Simply because, other things being equal, one is more likely to be able to find one good prospect in a pool of ten applicants than from just two. But the likelihood of making a good decision is also greater the more the pool of applicants matches the company's needs. So Mr Draper at Bonar will probably be choosing from among a small group of experienced and skilled applicants, while Silver City's recruiters will be faced with a large number of bright, dynamic, and enthusiastic team players. But then, Silver City's jobs seems to require little in the way of specific training or experience, and they clearly have a good number of positions to fill.

Employment Agencies There are three types of employment agencies: public or government agencies, private employment agencies, and executive search firms. The major difference between these three is the type of clientele served. The federal government provides a **public employment service** through Human Resources Development Canada's Canada Employment Centres (CECs). The main function of this agency is closely tied to unemployment benefits, which are conditional on registering and actively seeking employment. Accordingly, the CECs will tend to attract and list individuals who are unskilled or have had minimum training. This, of course, does not reflect on the agency's competence but, rather, on the image of the agency.

Canada Employment Centres are perceived by prospective applicants as having few high-skilled jobs, and employers tend to see them as having few high-skilled applicants. Therefore, they will tend to attract and place predominantly low-skilled workers. The agency's image, as perceived by both applicants and employers, thus tends to result in a self-fulfilling prophecy: that is, few high-skilled indi-

Public Employment Service Government-funded agencies, such as Canada Employment Centres, that assist employers to find workers and individuals to find jobs.

Figure 6-1
Advertisement with a High
Response Rate Likelihood

Casting Call.

8725 Yonge Street (Yonge & HWY 7)

Are you a movie buff? Energetic? And love working with people? Then you could be part of our talented team at Famous Players. We are auditioning for bright, dynamic and enthusiastic team players for days, evenings, late nights and weekends to join us on a part-time basis.

But wait there's more

We're looking for dynamic and creative team players, so why not come dressed up as your favourite movie star — The Creature from the Black Lagoon, Woody Allen, whoever?

We are also looking for people with the above qualifications for our food service areas within the complex. Experience in fast food would be an asset.

Smiling faces a necessity!!

Please apply in person to:
8725 Yonge Street (Yonge & HWY 7)
March 28 and 29 from 10:00 a.m. to 5:00 p.m.

Another Great New Location!

Source: *The Toronto Star* (March 21, 1998), p. D16

Figure 6-2
Advertisement with a Low
Response Rate Likelihood

FLEXOGRAPHIC PRINTING SUPERVISOR

Bonar Inc., a leading manufacturer of flexible packaging in North America, requires a responsible, experienced person to take charge of the printing department in our Guelph Small Bags Division.

The ideal candidate will have a technical degree/diploma from a recognized college or university, preferably in Industrial Engineering, and will have 5 to 10 years experience in flexographic process printing.

To qualify for this position, you must exhibit strong interpersonal and leadership skills. You should be knowledgeable in Health and Safety Legislation and most comfortable on the shop floor where you will utilize your knowledge and skills in a unionized environment.

Responsibilities will include supervision of operating personnel, establishment of machinery and product standards, scheduling, quality control, approvals of make ready, and prepress.

If your qualifications meet these requirements and you are looking for a challenging career opportunity with a competitive salary and benefits package, send your resume to:

Bonar Inc.
Paul Draper
Human Resources
2360 McDowall Rd.,
Burlington, Ont. L7R 4A1

Bonar Inc.
A Low & Bonar company

Source: *The Toronto Star* (March 21, 1998), p. H12

Meet

Janet Wright
Owner, Janet Wright & Associates, Inc.

When Sheridan College in Oakville, Ontario needed a new president in 1996, it did just what most Canadian post-secondary institutions would have done. First, it formed a search committee which included board members, faculty, staff, administrators, and students. Next, the committee called Dr Janet Wright.

Head of Janet Wright & Associates, a Toronto executive search firm, Dr Wright is an expert in hiring top-level academic administrators. It has been common for a long time for businesses to hire headhunters to help fill top positions, and colleges and universities find the expert advice just as helpful.

"The feeling is," says Dr Wright, "that for a very senior position, you want to do the most comprehensive job possible—it's too important not to leave any stone unturned."

An expert consultant, she explains, starts by working with the search committee to pin down the qualifications needed for the position. Some of these may be quite general, such as leadership or management experience, but others may be specific to the school's situation. Sheridan's requirements, for example, included experience in creating partnerships between business and academic institutions.

A search consultant can also help get the word out to qualified candidates. "A major academic position is usually advertised nationally," she explains, "but that's primarily to let the community know about it. The bulk of candidates are recruited directly or nominated through suggestions from people in the field."

At the interview stage, the search consultant might speak to eight or ten candidates, then select a short list of three to five to interview. The committee makes the final decision, of course, but busy committee members' time is saved and many errors of inexperience avoided if it's a decision informed by the professionalism and expertise of someone like Dr Wright, who has helped fill literally hundreds of top positions in Canadian educational institutions. After all, she says, "it's the search consultant's day job."

viduals place their names with the agency, and, similarly, few employers seeking individuals with high skills list their vacancies or inquire about applicants at Canada Employment Centres. Yet this is not always the case. CECs can serve to coordinate the search for specific, highly qualified personnel, and university and college students are familiar with their role in matching students to employers for summer jobs that do, indeed, require well-trained workers.

How does a private employment agency, which has to charge for its services, compete with a government agency that gives its service away? They must do something different from what the public agencies do, or at least give that impression.[7] The major difference between public and private employment agencies is their image—that is, private agencies are believed to offer positions and applicants of a higher calibre. Private agencies may also provide a more complete line of services. They may advertise the position, screen applicants against the criteria specified by the employer, and provide a guarantee covering six months or a year as protection to the employer should the applicant not perform satisfactorily. The private employment agency's fee can be totally absorbed by either the employer or the employee, or it can be split. The alternative chosen usually depends on the demand-supply situation in the community involved.

Private Employment Agency A private firm specializing in recruiting workers.

●

Executive Search Firm Private employment agency specializing in middle and top management as well as hard-to-fill positions.

The third agency source consists of the management consulting, **executive search**, or "headhunter" firms. These private employment agencies specialize in middle- to and top-level executive placement,[8] as well as hard-to-fill positions such as computer programmers. In addition to the level at which they recruit, the features that distinguish executive search agencies from most private employment agencies are their fees, their nationwide contacts, and the thoroughness of their investigations. For example, in searching for a vice-president whose compensation package may far exceed $200,000 a year, the potential employer may be willing to pay a very high fee (as much as 30 per cent of the executive's first-year salary) to locate exactly the right individual to fill the vacancy.[9]

Executive search firms canvass their contacts and do preliminary screening. They seek out highly effective executives who have the skills to do the job, can effectively adjust to the organization, and most importantly, are willing to consider new challenges and opportunities. Such individuals are possibly frustrated by their inability to move up rapidly enough in their current organization, or they may have recently been bypassed for a major promotion. The executive search firm can act as a buffer for screening candidates and, at the same time, keep the prospective employer anonymous. In the final stages, senior executives in the prospective firm can move into the negotiations and determine the degree of mutual interest.

Schools, Colleges, and Universities Educational institutions at all levels offer opportunities for recruiting recent graduates. Most educational institutions operate placement services where prospective employers can review credentials and interview graduates. Whether the educational level required for the job involves a high-school diploma, specific vocational training, or a university background with a bachelor's, master's, or doctoral degree, educational institutions are an excellent source of potential employees, especially for entry-level positions in organizations.[10]

High schools or vocational-technical schools can provide applicants for lower-level positions; business or secretarial schools can provide administrative staff personnel; and community colleges and universities can often provide managerial-level personnel. While educational institutions are usually viewed as sources for young, inexperienced entrants to the workforce, it is not uncommon to find individuals with considerable work experience using an educational institution's placement service. They may be workers who have recently returned to school to upgrade their skills or former graduates interested in pursuing other opportunities.

College and University Placements An external search process focussing recruiting efforts on college and university campuses.

College and University Placements A good source of applicants can be costly in terms of the recruiter's expenses in travel, lodging, and the like if the school is not in the organization's area. An organization must weigh the benefits of this recruiting source with its costs—in many cases, over $2,000 per school. This appears to be one of the reasons why interviews on campuses severely decline during economic downturns.

Professional Organizations Organizations whose members share a common profession or occupation, such as labour unions, engineering societies, and the like. These organizations frequently provide placement services for their members.

Professional Organizations Many **professional organizations**, including labour unions, operate placement services for the benefit of their members. The professional organizations include such varied occupations as industrial engineering, psychology, and many academic specializations. These organizations publish rosters of job vacancies and distribute these lists to members. It is also common practice to provide placement facilities at regional and national meetings where individuals looking for employment and organizations looking for employees can find each other.

Professional organizations, however, can also control the labour supply in their discipline. In those professional organizations where the organization placement service is the focal point for locating prospective employers and where certain qualifications are necessary to become a member (such as special educational attainment or professional certification or licence), the professional organization can significantly influence and control the supply of prospective applicants. If, for example, the Law Society makes it more difficult for LLBs to be called to the Bar, or the Association of Professional Engineers makes it more difficult to achieve the P.Eng. designation, then the supply of lawyers, or engineers will be smaller.

Unsolicited Applicants Walk-ins, whether they reach the employer by letter, telephone, or in person, constitute a source of prospective applicants. Although the number of unsolicited applicants depends on economic conditions, the organization's image, and the job seeker's perception of the types of jobs that might be available, this source does provide an excellent supply of applicants to be stockpiled—the application can be kept on file for later needs.

Walk-Ins Unsolicited applicants for employment may be a prospective source for recruitment depending on their particular circumstances.

Unsolicited applications made by unemployed individuals, however, generally have a short life. Those who have adequate skills and who would be prime candidates for a position in the organization if one were available usually find other employment quickly. However, in times of economic stagnation, excellent prospects are often unable to locate the type of job they desire and may remain in the job market, actively looking for many months. On the other hand, applications from individuals who are already employed can be referred to many months later and can provide applicants who are interested in considering other employment opportunities and regard the organization as a possible employer.

Recruiting on the Internet Interested applicants can search the World Wide Web for corporate Web pages to find a wealth of information on what a company does, where it does it, and so on, and decide if this is a company he or she might want to work for. Since the Web site usually includes information on how to contact the company, the Web surfer can then send a letter or e-mail message.

This, of course, can generate a good number of unsolicited applications from individuals with the initiative and skill to do a Web search, but it is not very efficient. So a growing number of companies are posting information on their career opportunities. For example, in August 1998, Northern Telecom's "menu of job opportunities" allowed individuals to search for job vacancies by type of job and preferred location.[11] For each job, the description and specification are included, and applications may be made on-line or by "snail mail." Contraste Canada, a provider of consulting services in computer networking, listed positions in Montreal, Eastern Canada, Belgium, and Luxembourg.[12]

In a way, these are modern, high-tech versions of the "help wanted" sign on the factory door or shop window. Potential applicants have to find the factory and read the sign, and while it is easier and cheaper to sit at a computer terminal to do a job opportunities search, the prospective applicant must still know where to go. Thus, tools for reaching a larger audience were needed and were developed. A search for the words "job application" in Canada revealed corporate sites as well as CareerMosaic Canada,[13] where a growing number of employers can post their job openings (for a fee) and search the résumés posted by job searchers (the service is free for applicants). Potential applicants find it easier to find jobs they may be interested in: they can specify types of jobs, locations, and so on. This makes the Web site more attractive to job seekers and thus, more effective for companies.

The World Wide Web is evolving so rapidly that more sophisticated and effective tools will certainly be operational by the time you are reading this. From both employees' and employers' points of view their attractiveness is in being a low-cost, effective method for matching a pool of qualified candidates with appropriate job openings.

Recruitment Alternatives

Much of the previous discussion on recruiting sources implies that these efforts are designed to bring into the organization full-time, permanent employees. However, economic realities, coupled with management trends such as rightsizing, have resulted in a slightly different focus. Companies today are looking at hiring temporary help (including retirees), leasing employees, and using the services of independent contractors.[14]

Temporary Employees Employees hired for a limited time to perform a specific job.

Temporary Help Services Organizations such as Kelly Temporary Services, Accountemps, and Temp-Force Inc. can be sources of employees when individuals are needed on a temporary basis (see "Ethical Decisions in HRM: Hiring Contingent Workers"). Temporary employees are particularly valuable in meeting short-term fluctuations in HRM needs.[15] While traditionally developed in the office administration area, the temporary staffing service has expanded its coverage to include a broad range of skills. It is now possible, for example, to hire temporary nurses, computer programmers, accountants, librarians, and drafters or drafting technicians as well as temporary secretaries.[16] Some companies are even contracting HRM professionals as temporary employees. For example, Mississauga's PPL Marketing Services has a senior HRM professional come in up to two days a week to handle critical issues.[17]

In addition to specific temporary help services, another quality source of temporary workers is older workers who have already retired or have been displaced by rightsizing in many companies.[18] An ageing workforce and individuals who have retired earlier has created skill deficiencies in some disciplines. Older workers bring those skills back to the job. In fact, at multinational chemical firm Monsanto, the company has capitalized on this rich skill base by establishing its own temporary, in-house employment agency, the Retiree Resource Corps (RRC).[19] Then, when there is a need for temporary help somewhere in the organization, the RRC provides the needed talent pool. For Monsanto, such a temporary workforce is saving the company almost $2 million a year.

While the reasons many of these older workers wish to continue to work vary,[20] they bring with them several advantages such as, "flexibility in scheduling, low absenteeism, high motivation, and mentoring abilities for younger workers."[21] Unfortunately, despite these attributes, many older workers find that not all employers are as enlightened. Age bias is a serious problem for many Canadians, as a survey commissioned by the public interest group One Voice revealed in 1997.[22]

Employee Leasing The hiring of personnel through a leasing firm for long periods of time.

Employee Leasing Employee leasing is a term used to reflect the hiring of personnel for long periods of time. Whereas temporary employees come into an organization for a specific short-term project, leased employees typically remain

Ethical Decisions in HRM:

Hiring Contingent Workers

Hiring temporary or contingent workers provides an organization with great flexibility. It enables it to deal with variable performance times without having to add permanent staff to its payroll (or lay them off). For many workers, especially older ones and individuals who wish to spend more time on personal matters, like child rearing, this part-time work serves a fundamental need. It permits them to explore those things they prefer to do, without being hampered by the requirements of a full-time position. But not every contingent worker sees part-time work in the same light. It is suggested that several million workers would prefer to work full-time but can't find anything but part-time employment. As such, the organizational emphasis on a contingent workforce is adversely affecting today's workers.

Part-time workers often don't receive the benefits that full-time employees get. They often receive no health insurance benefits nor enjoy an opportunity to participate in a company-sponsored retirement plan. They have little, if any, opportunity for career advancement, and their tenure with an organization is only as long as the project they are working on.

Organizations, however, appear to gain in this scenario. Hiring contingent workers is a cost-effective means of staffing because they rarely need to provide them with the full array of benefits that they provide their permanent employees. In addition, part-time employees may sometimes be exempt from certain employment equity regulations. Are these organizations exploiting contingent workers? Are they acting responsibly towards a society that keeps them in business? Or are we headed down that proverbial historical path so that one day, legislation will be passed to protect the contingent worker?

Modern technology is also making it easier for people to work from their homes, connected to their bosses, co-workers, and customers through telephones, fax machines, and on-line computers. These workers may not only receive fewer benefits than permanent employees, but they also may have to provide their own insurance for work-related accidents, pay their own hydro and heating bills, and even buy their own equipment. Legislation for this type of worker is lagging behind technological change. Are organizations exploiting contingent workers? What do you think?

with an organization for longer periods. Under a leasing arrangement, individuals work for the leasing firm.[23] When an organization has a need for specific employee skills, it contracts with the leasing firm to provide a certain number of trained employees. Alberta-based Resource Professionals hires out workers on contract to the energy industry. Contracts may be short or long: Resource Professionals placed Bruce Mills on a short-term contract to do joint ventures for Elan Energy Inc. Six years later, he was still there.[24]

One reason for leasing's popularity is cost.[25] The acquiring organization pays a flat fee for the employees. The company is not responsible for benefits (vacation pay, workers' compensation, employment insurance, and Canada/Quebec Pension Plan payments) or other costs it would incur for a full-time employee. This is because leased employees are, in fact, employees of the leasing firm. Furthermore, when the project is over, employees are returned to the leasing company, thus eliminating any cost associated with lay-offs or discharge.

Leased employees are also well-trained individuals. (Resource Professionals, for example, claims that the people they place are often better qualified than the client companies' permanent employees.[26]) They are screened by the leasing firm, trained appropriately, and often go to organizations with an unconditional guarantee. Thus, if one of these individuals doesn't work out, the company can get a new employee or make arrangements to have its fee returned. There are also benefits from the employee's point of view. Today's workers frequently prefer more flexibility in their lives. Working with a leasing company and being sent out at various times allows individuals to work when and as long as they want.

Independent Contractors Another means of recruiting is the use of **independent contractors**. Often referred to as consultants, independent contractors are taking on new meaning in the 1990s. Companies may hire independent contractors to do very specific work at a location on or off the company's premises. For instance, claims-processing or word-processing activities can easily be done at one's home and forwarded to the employer on a routine basis. With the growing use of personal computers connected to the Internet via modems, fax machines, and voice mail, employers can ensure that home work is being done in a timely fashion.

Independent contractor arrangements benefit both the organization and the individual. Because the company does not have to regard this individual as an employee, it saves costs such as employment insurance and workers' compensation premiums associated with full- or part-time personnel. As well, such an arrangement is also a means of keeping good individuals associated with your company. Suppose an employee wants to work but also be at home when the kids are home. This cannot be done through typical work arrangements, but allowing the individual to work at home can generate a win-win solution to the problem.

We have identified a number of sources of potential candidates. If we've achieved our goal and located a number of qualified applicants, it's time to begin to filter through the stack. This filtering process is called selection.

Independent Contractors
Temporary employees offering specialized services to an organization.

Goals of the Selection Process

A recent HRM graduate went on his first interview.[27] Not knowing what to expect, he prepared as best he could. He was dressed exquisitely in a new navy pinstriped suit and was carrying his new black leather attaché case. As he entered the human resources management office, he encountered two doors. The first door read, "Human Resources Management Majors." On the second was, "All Other Majors." He entered Door One which opened up to two more doors. On Door One was, "B+ or better average"; Door Two, "All Other Averages." Having an A– average, he once again entered Door One and found himself facing yet two more choices. Door One stated, "Took Conflict Resolution Techniques Course," and Door Two, "Didn't Take Conflict Resolution." Because this course was not required in his program, he went through Door Two. Upon opening the door, he found a box with pre-printed letters saying, "Your qualifications did not meet the expectations of the job. Thanks for considering our organization. Please exit to the right."

Although fictional, this story illustrates the **selection process**. All selection activities exist for the purpose of making effective selection decisions. Each activity is a step in the process that results in a prediction—managerial decision makers seeking to predict which job applicants will be successful if hired. "Successful," in this case, means performing well on the criteria the organization uses to evaluate its employees. For a sales position, for example, the criteria should be able to indicate to the assessors which applicants will generate a high volume of sales; for a teaching position such as a university professor, they should predict which applicants will get high student evaluations or generate many high-quality publications or both.

Selection Process The process of selecting the best candidate for the job.

The Selection Process

Selection activities typically follow a standard pattern beginning with an initial screening interview and concluding with the final employment decision. The selection process may consist of seven steps: initial screening, completing the application form, employment tests, comprehensive interview, background investigation, medical or physical examination, and the final job offer. Each of these steps represents a decision point requiring some affirmative feedback for the process to continue. Each step in the process seeks to expand the organization's knowledge about the applicant's background, abilities, and motivation, and it increases the information from which decision makers will make their predictions and final choice. However, some steps may be omitted if they do not yield data that will aid in predicting success or if the cost of the step is not warranted. Applicants should also be advised what specific screening such as credit checks, reference checking, or drug tests, will be done. The flow of these activities is depicted in Figure 6-3. (Note that for ease of presentation, the activities are presented in sequence as hurdles or screens to be overcome by the applicants. As we will discuss later, this is only one way of organizing the process). Let us take a closer look at each step in the selection process.

Initial Screening

As a culmination of our recruiting efforts, we should be prepared to initiate a preliminary review of potentially acceptable candidates. This **initial screening** is, in effect, a two-step procedure: (1) the screening of inquiries and (2) the provision of screening interviews. If our recruiting effort has been successful, we will be faced with a number of potential applicants, some of whom can be eliminated based on the job description and job specification. Factors that might lead to a negative decision at this point include inadequate or inappropriate experience or education.

The screening interview is also an excellent opportunity for the company recruiter to describe the job in enough detail so that the candidates can consider whether they are really serious about it. Sharing job description information with the individual frequently encourages the unqualified or marginally qualified to voluntarily withdraw from candidacy with a minimum of cost to the applicant or the organization. Another important point during the initial

Initial Screening The first step in the selection process whereby inquiries about a job are screened.

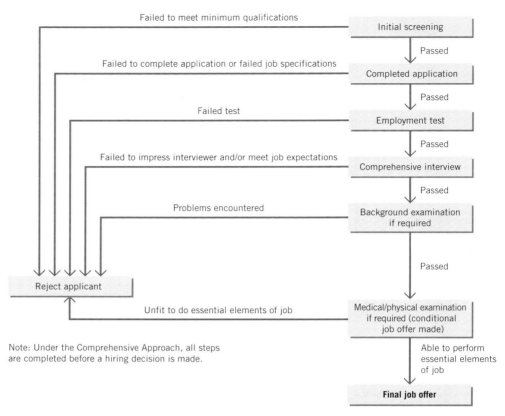

Figure 6-3 Decision Points in a Selection Process: The Hurdle Concept

Note: Under the Comprehensive Approach, all steps are completed before a hiring decision is made.

screening phase is to identify a salary range. Most workers are concerned about their salaries, and while a job opening may sound exciting, a low salary may preclude an organization from obtaining excellent talent. During this phase, if HRM has been properly conducted, there should be no need to mask salary data.

Completing the Application Form

Application Form Company-specific employment forms used to generate specific information the company wants.

Once the initial screening has been completed, applicants are asked to complete the organization's **application form**. The information required may be only the applicant's name, address, and telephone number. On the other hand, some organizations may request the completion of a more comprehensive employment profile. In general terms, the application form gives a job-performance-related synopsis of what applicants have been doing during their adult life, their skills, and their accomplishments. It can also be used as legal authorization to verify references and acknowledgement of the terms and conditions of employment. Applications are also useful in that they gather information the company wants. Also, completing the application serves as another hurdle; that is, if the job, for example, requires one to follow directions and the individual fails to do so on the application, that is a job-related reason for rejection. Lastly, applications require a signature attesting to the truthfulness of the information given and to give permission for check references. If at a later point the company finds out the information is false, it can result in the immediate dismissal of the individual.

Some organizations have developed statistical analyses of the relationship between responses to questions on the application form and measures of job performance such as absenteeism and turnover. These result in what are known as a **weighted application blank (WAB)**, which can be very effective screening devices, but only about 4 per cent of Canadian companies report using them.[28]

Employment Tests

Organizations historically relied to a considerable extent on intelligence, aptitude, ability, and interest tests to provide major input to the selection process. Even handwriting analysis (graphology) and honesty tests have been used in the attempt to learn more about the candidate—information that supposedly led to a more effective selection.

In the 1970s and early 1980s, reliance on traditional written tests for selection purposes decreased significantly. This was attributed directly to legal rulings requiring employers to justify any test used as job-related.[29] Given the historical difficulty and costs in substantiating this relationship, some organizations merely eliminated employment testing as a selection device.

Since the mid-1980s, however, that trend has reversed. It is estimated that more than 60 per cent of all organizations use some type of employment test today.[30] A 1992 survey by James Thacker and Julian Cattaneo of the University of Windsor revealed that half of responding Canadian companies used some form of aptitude test, while personality tests were used by 32 per cent, and a variety of other tests were also employed in the selection process.[31] For these organizations, there is recognition that scrapping employment tests was equivalent to "throwing out the baby with the bathwater." They have come to recognize that some tests are quite helpful in predicting who will be successful on the job. The key in employment testing, then, is to use a test that accurately predicts job performance, which will be discussed later in the chapter.

Comprehensive Interview

Those applicants who pass the initial screening, application form, and required tests are generally given a **comprehensive interview** next. The applicant may be interviewed by HRM interviewers, senior managers within the organization, a potential supervisor, potential colleagues, or some or all of these. In their 1992 survey, Thacker and Cattaneo found that 99 per cent of Canadian companies reported using interviews during the selection process,[32] while all respondents in a later study used some form of interview.[33]

The comprehensive interview is designed to probe areas that cannot be addressed easily by the application form or tests, such as assessing one's motivation, ability to work under pressure, and ability to fit in with the organization. However, this information must be job-related. The questions asked and the topics covered should reflect the job description and job specification information obtained in the job analysis. Questions must also be used consistently for all applicants. We'll take a much more in-depth look at interviews in the next chapter.

Background Investigation

The next step in the process is to undertake a **background investigation** of those applicants who appear to offer potential as employees. This can include contacting former employers to confirm the candidate's work record and to ob-

Weighted Application Blank (WAB) An application form wherein several elements have been statistically related to job outcomes.

Comprehensive Interview A selection device in which in-depth information about a candidate can be obtained.

Background Investigation The process of verifying information job candidates provide.

tain their appraisal of his or her performance, contacting other job-related and personal references, verifying the educational credentials shown on the application,[34] checking credit references and criminal records, and even using third-party investigators to do the background check.[35]

Common sense dictates that HRM find out as much as possible about its applicants before the final hiring decision is made. Failure to do so can have a detrimental effect on the organization, both in terms of cost and morale. But getting the needed information may be difficult, especially when there may be a question about invading someone's privacy. In the past, many organizational policies stated that any request for information about a past employee be sent to the HRM department, which generally only supplied information on employment dates and positions held. This was because companies wanted to avoid being sued by a previous employee and so, simply verified "the facts." But that has changed.

Based on a concept of *qualified privilege*, the courts have ruled that employers must be able to talk to one another about employees. And those discussions are legal and do not invade privacy rights so long as the discussion is a legitimate concern for the business. For example, had one McDonald's restaurant learned that one of its applicants had a history of child sexual assault, it might have been able to avert both the sexual assault of a three-year-old in its restaurant, the embarrassment, and the $210,000 judgement against it.[36]

Medical or Physical Examination

The last step in this process may consist of having the applicant take a **medical or physical examination**, but only after a **conditional job offer** has been made. Remember, however, that in doing so, a company must show that the reasoning behind this requirement is job-related. Physical exams can only be used as a selection device to screen out those individuals who are unable to physically comply with the requirements of a job. For example, firefighters are required to perform a variety of activities that require a certain physical condition. Whether it is climbing a ladder, lugging a ten-centimetre water-filled hose, or carrying an injured victim, these individuals must demonstrate that they are fit for the job.

Aside from its use as a screening tool, there is another purpose for the physical exam: to show that minimum standards of health exist to enrol in company health and life insurance programs. A company may also use this exam to provide base data in case of an employee's future claim of injury on the job. This occurs, however, after one has been hired. In both cases, the exam is paid for by the employer.

One last event fits appropriately under medical examination: the drug test. As we mentioned in Chapter 4, increasingly more companies require applicants to submit to a drug test. Where in this process that test occurs is somewhat immaterial; the fact remains that failing an employment drug test may result in failing to get the job.

It is worth remembering that companies cannot require drug testing indiscriminately: they must show that the requirement is job-related. Canadian Pacific Railways, for instance, requires pre-employment drug testing for safety-sensitive positions (and under certain conditions may test employees if the company has reason to believe the employee is impaired on the job). But the Toronto Dominion Bank's policy to test all new employees for drug use was struck down by the Federal Court of Appeal.[37] Opposition to drug testing is based primarily on the need to protect individuals against invasions of privacy or discrimination

Medical or Physical examination An examination to determine whether an applicant is medically or physically fit to perform the job.

Conditional Job Offer An offer of employment that is firm except for the requirement that the applicant must pass a medical or physical examination.

(drug dependency is considered a disability under human rights legislation). In July 1998, the board of the Toronto Transit Commission rejected a proposal to test prospective drivers and mechanics (the TTC hires up to six hundred workers a year). Ironically, under the proposal, casual drug users would have been rejected outright, but drug-dependent individuals would have the right to reapply within eighteen months under provincial human rights legislation.[38]

Final Job Offer

Those individuals who perform successfully in the preceding steps are now considered to be eligible to receive an offer of employment. Who makes that offer? The answer is, it depends. For administrative purposes (processing salary forms, maintaining employment equity statistics, etc.), the formal offer is often made by the human resources management department, but their role should be only administrative. The actual hiring decision should be made by the manager of the department where the vacancy exists. There are two reasons for this. First, the applicant will eventually work for this manager, and therefore a good fit between boss and employee is necessary. Second, if the final decision made is not correct, the hiring manager must assume the responsibility.

If the organization's selection process has been effective in differentiating between those individuals who will make successful employees and those who will not, the selection decision is now in the hands of the applicant. Is there anything management can do at this stage to increase the probability that the individual to whom an offer is made will accept? Assuming that the organization has not lost sight of the process of selection's dual objective—evaluation and a good fit—we can expect that the potential employee has a solid understanding of the job being offered and what it would be like to work for the organization. Yet it might be of interest at this point to review what we know about how people choose a job. This subject—job choice—represents selection from the potential employee's perspective rather than that of the organization.

Research indicates that people gravitate towards jobs that are compatible with their personal orientation.[39] In other words, individuals appear to move towards matching their work with their personality. Social individuals lean towards jobs in clinical psychology, foreign service, social work, and the like. Investigative individuals are compatible with jobs in biology, mathematics, and oceanography. Careers in management, law, and public relations appeal to enterprising individuals. This approach to the matching of people and jobs suggests that management can expect a greater proportion of success if it has properly matched the candidate's personality to the job and to the organization, thereby making the good fit.[40]

Not surprisingly, most job choice studies indicate that an individual's perception of the attractiveness of a company is important.[41] People want to work somewhere they have positive expectations about and where they believe their goals can be achieved. This, coupled with conclusions from previous research, should encourage management to ensure that those to whom offers are made can see that the job is compatible with their personality and goals.[42]

Before we leave this last step in the selection process—the final job offer—we should ask: What about those applicants who did not receive an offer?[43] We believe that those involved in the selection process should carefully consider how rejected candidates are treated. What is communicated and how will have a central bearing on the image that the rejected candidates will have of the organization, and that impression may last a lifetime. The young graduate rejected for a posi-

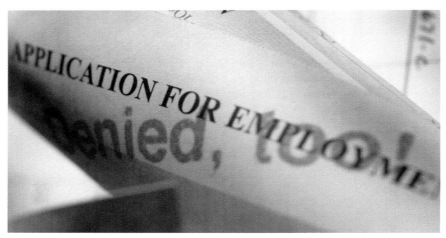

It is essential that rejected candidates be handled with tact and sensitivity, if only because that person may come to have dealings with the organizations in the future, and first impressions can be lasting.

tion by a major computer manufacturer may be the influential decision maker for his or her current employer's computer purchases a decade later, and the image formed earlier may play a key part in the decision.

The Comprehensive Approach

We have presented the general selection process as being comprised of multiple hurdles, beginning with a screening interview and culminating with a final selection decision. This discrete selection process is designed so that stumbling over any hurdle puts one out of the race. This approach, however, may not be the most effective selection procedure for every job. If, for example, the application form shows that the candidate has only two years of relevant experience but the job specification requires five, the candidate is rejected without going any further in the process. Yet, in many jobs, negative factors can be counterbalanced by positive ones. Poor performance on a written test, for example, may be offset by several years of relevant job experience. This suggests that sometimes it may be advantageous to do comprehensive rather than discrete selection. In comprehensive selection, all applicants are put through every step of the selection process, and the final decision is based on a comprehensive evaluation of the results from *all* stages.

Comprehensive Selection Applying all steps in the selection process before rendering a decision about a job candidate.

The comprehensive approach overcomes the major disadvantage of the discrete method (eliminating potentially good employees simply because they received an acceptable, but low evaluation at one selection step). The comprehensive method is more realistic. It recognizes that most applicants have weaknesses as well as strengths. It is, however, also more costly since all applicants must go through all the screening hurdles, and it consumes more of management's time and can demoralize many applicants by building up hope. Yet, in those instances where many qualities are needed for success in the job and where finding candidates who are strong in every quality is unlikely, the comprehensive approach is probably preferable to the usual discrete method.

No matter which approach is used or which steps are involved, one critical aspect must be present: The devices used must measure job-related factors. In other words, these tools must be able to indicate how one would perform on the job.

Selection from an International Perspective

The selection criteria for international assignments are broader in scope than those for domestic selection. To illustrate the point, in addition to such factors as technical expertise and leadership ability, an international assignment requires greater attention to personality and especially to flexibility. The individual must have an interest in working overseas and a talent for relating well to all kinds of people. The ability to interact with different cultures and environments, a sensitivity to different management styles, and a supportive family are often selection requirements.

Not surprisingly, many corporations consider personal factors such as maturity and age and the "family situation factor" far more important in their international assignments than in domestic placements. Although not all expatriates are married, many human resources managers believe that marital stability reduces a person's likelihood of returning home early, and in many countries, it enhances the individual's social acceptability.

Canadian women have been successful in the business world and it is unacceptable in our culture to discriminate on the basis of gender in employment, but organizations know that some Middle Eastern countries will not grant working papers to foreign women executives. On the other hand, in Asia, where common wisdom has held that women executives are less effective, the opposite has proven true. Although few Asian women are at or above middle-management levels, North American women are often highly respected because they have risen to be experts in their fields. Thus, past reluctance to assign women to overseas positions where culture rather than law once made them rare is vanishing, and North American women executives are more common in Asia and Latin America. In foreign postings, not only may the candidate's gender be considered, but also the social acceptability of single parents, unmarried partners, and blended families.

In addition, such personal factors as health, ethnic, family, social background, and education may be considered in international placements. In fact, the ideal candidate for many corporations is an older couple in good health, with no young children at home and a long and stable marital history. These are all factors that would play no role in domestic assignments. You will have noticed that in this brief discussion of selection for international assignments, we have introduced criteria such as age, gender, and marital status, which are not part of selection decisions in Canada under employment equity legislation. But you should also have noticed that such criteria may be bona fide occupational requirements for international assignments in that a smooth adaptation to the foreign environment may be absolutely critical to the success in the assignment. If the Bank of Nova Scotia, for example, sends a high-potential manager to Taiwan for a three-year assignment, both the bank and the employee will lose if the manager has to return home after six months because her husband simply couldn't adapt to Taiwan.

When younger candidates are appropriate, many Canadian corporations will seek foreign students on Canadian university campuses who want to return to their home countries. These students provide a well-educated labour pool with experience in both their home and Canadian cultures. Multinationals based in other countries (like Britain or the US) will often follow this approach.

Canadian multinational companies recruiting locally (for example, if Magna International is recruiting Mexican employees for a plant in Saltillo) will, of course, be governed by local regulations and customs. Does this mean that if it is common practice in Santiago, to hire, say, only attractive young women as secretaries and only young men as engineers, that the management of the local subsidiary can completely ignore Canadian laws banning discrimination on the basis of age or gender? Probably not. What will the company's shareholders say when they find out? For example, North American companies whose subsidiaries obeyed the South African government's apartheid legislation in the 1980s, arguing that it was "the law of the land," were often subjected to boycotts by North American consumers who found that racist legislation abhorrent).

Key Elements for Successful Predictors

We are concerned with selection activities that can help us predict which applicants will perform satisfactorily on the job. In this section, we want to explore the concepts of reliability, validity, and cut scores. For illustration purposes, we will emphasize these elements as they relate to employment tests, but they are relevant to any selection device.

Reliability

Reliability A selection device's consistency of measurement.

For any predictor to be useful, the scores it generates must possess an acceptable level of **reliability** or consistency of measurement. This means that the applicant's performance on any given selection tool should produce consistent scores each time the device is used. For example, if your height were measured every day with a wooden yardstick, you would get highly reliable results, but if you were measured daily by an elastic tape measure, there would probably be considerable disparity between your height measurements from one day to the next. Your height does not change from day to day—the variability is due to the unreliability of the measuring device.

Similarly, if an organization uses tests to provide input to the selection decision, they must give consistent results. If the test is reliable, any single individual's scores should remain fairly stable over time, assuming that the characteristic it is measuring is also stable. An individual's intelligence, for example, is generally a stable characteristic, and if we give applicants an IQ test, we should expect that someone who scores 110 in March would score close to that if tested again in July. If, in July, the same applicant scored 85, the reliability of the test would be highly questionable. On the other hand, if we were measuring something like an attitude or a mood, we would expect different scores on the measure because attitudes and moods change.

Validity

Validity The proven relationship of a selection device to some relevant criterion.

High reliability may mean little if the selection device has low **validity**—that is, if the measures obtained are not related to some relevant criterion, such as job performance. Just because a test score is consistent is no indication that it is measuring important characteristics related to job behaviour. It must also differentiate between satisfactory and unsatisfactory performance on the job. We should be aware of three specific types of validity: content, construct, and criterion-related.

Content Validity Content validity is the degree to which the contents of the test or questions about job tasks, as a sample, represent the situations on the job. All candidates for a particular job are given the same test or questions so that applicants can be properly compared. A simple example of a content-valid test is a typing test for a word-processing position. Such a test can approximate the work to be done on the job; the applicant can be given a typical sample of typing, and his or her performance can be evaluated based on that sample. Assuming that the tasks on the test or the questions about tasks constitute an accurate sample of the tasks on the job (ordinarily a dubious assumption at best), the test is content valid.[44]

Construct Validity Construct validity is the degree to which a test measures a particular trait related to successful performance on the job. These traits are usually abstract in nature, such as the measure of intelligence,[45] and are called constructs. Construct validity is complex and difficult. It takes the effort of a trained industrial psychologist—whom you would typically hire as a consultant should it become necessary—to ascertain construct validity. In fact, it is the most difficult type of validity to prove because you are dealing with constructs or abstract measures.

Criterion-Related Validity Criterion-related validity is the degree to which a particular selection device accurately predicts the level of performance or important elements of work behaviour. This validation strategy shows the relationship between some predictor (test score, for example) and a criterion of job performance (e.g., production output or managerial effectiveness). To establish criterion-related validity, either of two approaches can be used: **predictive validity** or **concurrent validity**.

To validate a test predictively, an organization would give the test it wishes to validate to all prospective applicants. The test scores would not be used at this time; rather, applicants would be hired as a result of successfully completing the rest of the selection process. At some prescribed date, usually at least a year after the applicants are hired, the employees' job performance would be evaluated by their supervisors. The ratings of the evaluations would then be compared with the initial test scores, which have been stored in a file over the period. At that time, an analysis would be conducted to see if there was any relationship between test scores (the predictors) and performance evaluation (the measure of success on the job or the criterion). If no clear relationship exists, the test may have to be revised. However, if the organization can statistically show that the employees who scored below a given score (called a **cut score**, determined by the analysis) were unsuccessful performers, then management could appropriately state that any future applicants scoring below the cut score would be ineligible for employment. Unsuccessful performers are handled like any other employee who has received poor evaluations: training, transfer, discipline, or discharge.

The concurrent validity method validates tests using current employees as the subjects. These employees are asked to take a proposed selection test experimentally. Their scores are immediately analysed, revealing a relationship between their test scores and existing performance appraisal data. Again, if there is a relationship between test scores and performance, then a valid test has been found.

Predictive validity is preferred. Its advantage over concurrent validity is that it is demonstrated by using actual job applicants, whereas concurrent validity

Content Validity The degree to which the content of the test is representative of the phenomenon that it is intended to measure.

Construct Validity The degree to which a given test successfully measures an abstract trait of property (the construct).

Criterion-Related Validity The degree to which a particular selection device accurately predicts the important elements of work behaviour (e.g., the relationship between a test score and job performance).

Predictive Validity Validating tests by using prospective applicants as the study group.

Concurrent Validity Validating tests by using current employees as the study group.

Cut Score A point on the scoring of a test at which: applicants scoring below are rejected.

focuses on current employees. Both validation strategies are similar, with the exception of the people who are tested and the time that elapses between gathering of predictor and criterion information (see Figure 6-4).

While the costs associated with each method are drastically different, predictive validation strategies should be used if possible. Concurrent validity, although better than no validity at all, leaves many questions to be answered.[46] Its usefulness has been challenged on the premise that current employees know the jobs already and that a learning process takes place. Thus, there may be little similarity between the current employee and the applicant.

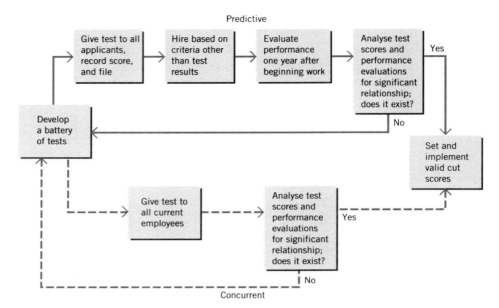

Figure 6-4
Predictive versus Concurrent Validation

The Validity Analysis

Correlation Coefficients   A statistical   function   that shows the strength of the relationship between two variables (in this case, between the score on a test and job performance).

Correlation coefficients used to demonstrate the statistical relationships existing between an individual's test score and his or her job performance are called validity coefficients. The correlation analysis procedure can result in a coefficient ranging from -1 to +1 in magnitude. The closer the validity coefficient is to the extreme (-1 or +1), the more accurate the test[47]—that is, the test is a good predictor of job performance. For example, Figure 6-5 contains two diagrams. In each diagram, we are trying to determine if a positive relationship exists between test scores and successful job performance.

In diagram A, there is no relationship. Statistically speaking, the score on the test bears no relationship between test score and performance. In this case, our test is not valid. It does not help us distinguish between the successful and unsuccessful job performers. Diagram B reveals that there is a positive relationship between test scores and job performance. Those individuals scoring higher on the test have a greater probability of being successful in their jobs than those scoring lower. Based on this relationship, this test appears to be valid. When we have a valid test as determined by our correlation analysis, we are then able to identify the test score that distinguishes between successful and unsuccessful performers (the cut score). (See the "Experiential Exercise" at the end of the chapter).

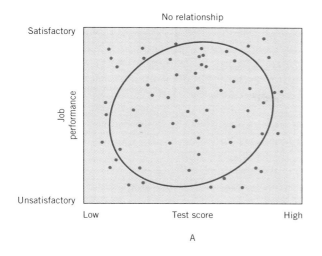

No relationship

A

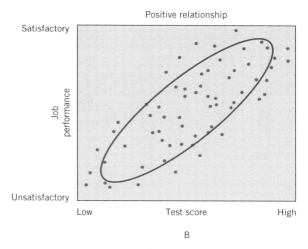

Positive relationship

B

Figure 6-5
Validity Correlation Analysis

Cut Scores and Their Impact on Hiring

In this discussion, we have been referring to test scores and their ability to predict successful job performance. By using our statistical analyses, we are able to generate a point at which applicants scoring below that point are rejected—the cut score.[48] However, existing conditions (e.g., availability of applicants) may cause an organization to change the cut score. If so, what impact will this have on hiring applicants who will be successful on the job? Let us review again the positive relationship we found in our validity correlation analysis. We have reproduced the main elements in the graph in Figure 6-6.

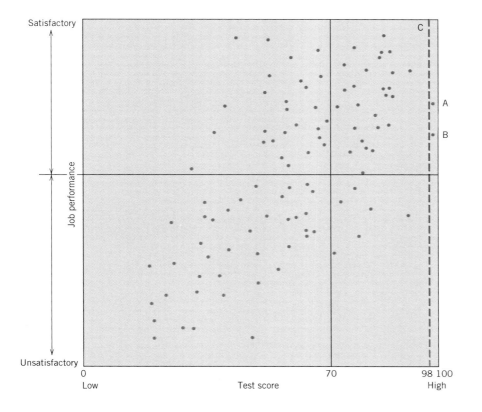

Figure 6-6
Validity Correlation Analysis after Cut Score is Raised

189

Let us assume that after our analysis, we determined that our cut score should be 70. At this cut score, we have shown that the majority of the applicants who scored above 70 have a greater probability of being successful performers on the job, and the majority scoring below that, unsuccessful performers. If we change our cut score, however, we alter the number of applicants in these categories. For example, suppose the organization faces a "buyer's market," and because of the many potential applicants, it can afford to be very selective. In a situation such as this, the organization may choose to hire only those applicants who meet the most extreme criteria. To achieve this goal, the organization increases its cut score to 98. By so doing, the organization has rejected all but two candidates (A and B in Figure 6-6). However, many potentially successful job performers also would be rejected (individuals shown in area C). What has happened here is that the organization has become more selective and has put more faith in the test than is reasonable. If there were 100 applicants and only two were hired, we could say that the selection ratio (the ratio of number hired to the number of applicants) is 2 per cent. That selection ratio would mean that the organization is very particular about who is hired.

Lowering the cut score also has an effect. Using the same diagram, let us lower our cut score to 50 and see what results. We have graphically portrayed this in Figure 6-7. By lowering the cut score from 70 to 50, we have increased our number of eligible hires who have a greater probability of being successful on the job (area D). At the same time, however, we have also made eligible more applicants who could be unsuccessful on the job (area E). Although using a hiring process where we know that more unsuccessful applicants may be hired seems not to make sense, conditions may necessitate the action. Labour market conditions may be such that there is a low supply of potential applicants who possess particular skills. For example, in some cities, finding a good computer

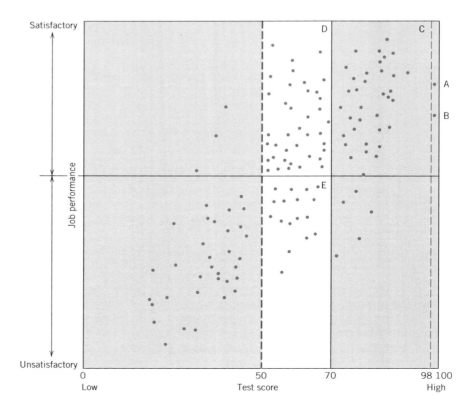

Figure 6-7
Validity Correlation Analysis
after Cut Score is Lowered

modeller may be difficult. Because the supply is low coupled with many openings, companies may hire individuals on the spot (more commonly referred to as an open-house recruiting effort). In this approach, the organization hires almost all the applicants who appear to have the skills needed (as reflected in a score of 50), puts them on the job, and filters out the unsuccessful employees at a later date. While this may not appear to be effective, the organization is banking on the addition of individuals in area D of Figure 6-7.

Validity Generalization

In the late 1970s, two researchers published a model that was able to support a phenomenon called **validity generalization**.[49] Validity generalization refers to a situation where a test may be valid for screening applicants for a variety of jobs and performance factors across many occupations.[50] In general, a validity study conducted for one job can be generalized to another if both are similar—even if one job is in Canada and the other in the United States.[51] What distinguishes validity generalization is its use of a statistical technique called meta-analysis. Through meta-analysis, researchers can determine correlations that may exist among numerous variables and correct or adjust for any variances that may exist in predictor–criterion relationships.

Validity Generalization The extent to which the validity of a test can be statistically extended across several different situations.

Study Tools and Applications

Summary

This summary relates to the Learning Objectives provided on p. 162.
After having read this chapter, you should know:
1. Recruitment is the discovering and attracting of potential applicants for actual or anticipated organizational vacancies.
2. The two goals of recruiting are to generate a large pool of qualified applicants from which to choose while simultaneously providing enough information for individuals to eliminate themselves from the process.
3. Influences that constrain HRM in determining recruiting sources include image of the organization, attractiveness and nature of the job, internal policies, government requirements, and the recruiting budget.
4. The principal sources for recruiting employees include internal search, employee referral/recommendations, advertisements, employment agencies, schools, colleges, and universities, professional organizations, and casual or unsolicited applicants. As we move through the 1990s, temporary employees, employee leasing, and independent contractors are also providing a source of workers.
5. Proper selection can minimize the costs of replacement and training, reduce legal challenges, and result in a more productive workforce.
6. The primary purpose of selection activities is to predict which job applicant will be successful if hired. During the selection process, candidates are also informed about the job and organization.
7. The discrete selection process would include the following: initial screening, completing the application form, employment tests, comprehensive interview, background investigation, medical or physical examination, and final job offer.
8. There are three validation strategies: content, construct, and criterion-related validity.

9. Validity is determined either by discovering the extent to which a test represents actual job content or through statistical analyses that show the test used relates to an important job-related trait or to performance on the job.
10. Validity generalization refers to a process whereby tests are validated for numerous occupations through the use of meta-analysis.

Key Terms

advertisements
application form
background investigation
blind-box ad
bona fide occupational qualification (BFOQ)
bona fide occupational requirement (BFOR)
college and university placements
comprehensive interview
comprehensive selection
concurrent validity
conditional job offer
constraints on recruiting
construct validity
content validity
correlation coefficients
criterion-related validity
cut score
employee leasing
employee referral

executive search firm
expatriates
host-country national (HCN)
independent contractors
initial screening
internal search
medical or physical examination
parent-country national (PCN)
predictive validity
private employment agency
professional organizations
public employment service
reliability
selection process
temporary employees
validity
validity generalization
walk-ins
weighted application blank (WAB)

EXPERIENTIAL EXERCISE

Validating a Test

Determining validity is one of the most critical components in any selection process. To provide you with some idea of how it is done (and to give you an opportunity to apply an HRM Skill), below are presented test scores and performance ratings for forty individuals.[52] Conduct a correlation analysis using the statistical formulas that follow. Determine how strong a relationship exists between test and performance scores, and if a strong relationship exists, calculate the cut score. (Hint: You may wish to review correlation analysis in a statistics textbook. The basis for conducting the analysis is to perform the necessary calculations required in the formula—that is, you'll need to calculate the (ΣX); (ΣY); (ΣXY); $(\Sigma X)^2$; $(\Sigma Y)^2$; (ΣX^2); (ΣY^2); and N, which in this case is 40. From the data below, test scores = the X variables; Performance Scores = the Y variables.)

Applicant Number	Test Scores	Performance Score
1	170	75
2	150	52
3	164	50
4	158	60
5	156	75
6	155	70

7	172	80
8	164	75
9	183	85
10	188	82
11	192	90
12	187	80
13	120	50
14	116	50
15	128	60
16	138	40
17	144	70
18	110	55
19	156	60
20	161	70
21	165	77
22	145	52
23	167	54
24	159	65
25	166	77
26	145	70
27	175	86
28	162	73
29	187	88
30	190	84
31	191	89
32	177	80
33	130	53
34	126	50
35	138	64
36	131	44
37	154	72
38	109	51
39	166	62
40	160	75

The formula for correlation coefficient is:

$$r = \frac{N\Sigma XY) = (\Sigma X)(\Sigma Y)}{\sqrt{(N\Sigma X^2 - (N\Sigma X)^2)(N\Sigma Y)^2 - (N\Sigma Y)^2}}$$

To determine a cut score, you need to find the slope of the line (b) and the intercept (a).

To find a: $a = Y - bX$ 　　　　To find b: $b = \dfrac{N\Sigma XY - (\Sigma X)(\Sigma Y)}{N\Sigma X^2 - (\Sigma X)^2}$

After finding a and b, calculate the cut score as follows:
$$Y = a + bX$$

where $Y = 70$ = satisfactory performance; solve for X, the cut score.

CASE APPLICATION:

Recruiting Internationally

In January 1997, Castrol (Thailand) Limited, a joint British-Thai venture in the petroleum industry, was expanding rapidly and needed to hire a number of employees for a variety of jobs—from technical service engineers to personnel officers. The manager of recruitment and employee relations developed an advertisement that was published in Bangkok's English-language newspaper, *The Nation*. The ad is presented in Figure 6-8.

Suppose you are a HRM consultant hired by Castrol Ltd., the British parent company, to advise on their recruitment policies and practices. Analyse the ad and respond to the following questions:

Figure 6-8
Advertising for employees in Thailand.

Source: The Nation (Bangkok). (January 20, 1997), p.4.

Questions:

1. What features of the ad are likely to result in an adequate pool of qualified applicants for Castrol (Thailand) Ltd.?
2. What aspects of Castrol (Thailand)'s recruiting process appear to be similar to what would be done in Canada? What aspects are different? Why do you think they are different?
3. Do these differences work to Castrol (Thailand)'s advantage or disadvantage? Why?

Testing Your Understanding

How well did you fulfil the learning objectives?

1. Recruiting efforts are usually lighter in organizations
   a. that are large rather than small.
   b. that are growing rather than declining.
   c. that have poor, rather than good, compensation packages.
   d. that have good, rather than poor, working conditions.
   e. that are service, rather than public, sector.

2. Which of the following indicates effectiveness for a director of recruiting for a large corporation?
   a. Recruiting costs have increased 8 per cent during the past two years.
   b. The applicant pool is increasing in size.
   c. The director of recruiting's secretary spends three times as much time acknowledging ad responses from underqualified applicants as she did a year ago.
   d. The director of recruiting's secretary spends less than one-third of the time acknowledging ad responses from underqualified applicants as she did a year ago.
   e. The applicant pool is becoming global.

3. The director of recruiting at a medium-size manufacturer in an Atlantic province is unable to hire the best people for her company because of a new restriction that no longer pays airfare for university recruiters. Therefore, her staff is limited to going to university job fairs within a 240-kilometre radius of the company. Which one of the following recruiting constraints is most affecting her organization?
   a. Organizational image.
   b. Job unattractiveness.
   c. Internal organizational politics.
   d. Government influence.
   e. Costs.

4. Bob needs to hire two managers for a Hamilton paint manufacturing plant by the end of the year. His organization is under pressure to have females and visible minorities better represented at top levels of the organization. Currently, all executives are White and male. What recruiting technique should he use?
   a. Employee referrals.
   b. Public employment agencies.
   c. Headhunters.
   d. University and college placement centres.
   e. Walk-ins.

5. A manager of human resources of a small accounting firm needs 2,000 extra person hours of work during the first two weeks of every April for data entry and word processing. What is the manager's best recruiting alternative?
   a. Independent contractors.
   b. Professional organizations.
   c. Executive search firms.
   d. University or college placement centres.
   e. Temporary help.

6. Which of the following is the most successful selection outcome for the XYZ organization?
   a. Ann was hired by XYZ, but she was unable to perform the job.
   b. Amy was hired by XYZ, but she was bored and left after three weeks.
   c. Andrea was hired by XYZ, and she quit the firm two months later for a better offer.
   d. Angela was not hired by XYZ, but she got an equivalent job with another firm where she has done very well.
   e. Arnie was not hired by XYZ and could not get an equivalent job anywhere else in town.

7. A director of recruiting for a large Canadian-based global corporation is looking for a country manager for a newly acquired South American affiliate. Her best choice, to minimize language, culture, and family problems is a
   a. home-country national.
   b. host-country national.
   c. local expatriate.
   d. third-country national.
   e. new foreign subsidiary.

8. Don, director of international staffing for a large Canadian-based manufacturing firm, needs to hire a production manager for an Asian country. He should make all of the following considerations except
   a. an Asian female being regarded as less effective, would not be a likely candidate.
   b. a married employee will be less acceptable than a single one.
   c. health requirements for this assignment are more important than for a domestic assignment.
   d. prior experience in Hong Kong and other Pacific Rim countries would be a plus.
   e. a Canadian female would be highly respected and regarded as an expert in her field.

9. Julie, vice-president of human resources for a large manufacturing firm, is concerned that 40 per cent of the clerical workers hired last year lacked basic reading, writing, and filing skills. She thinks these workers should have been eliminated from the applicant pool, as early as the _____ step of the selection process.
   a. application form
   b. physical examination
   c. comprehensive interview
   d. employment tests
   e. background investigation

10. Jan runs an employment agency that provides experienced secretarial help. She gives keyboarding tests to job candidates to make sure they can type as part of the selection process. This is an example of a test having
    a. content validity.
    b. reliability.
    c. construct validity.
    d. differential validity.
    e. predictive validity.

11. Ruth runs an employment agency that provides experienced secretarial help. She gives typing tests to applicants during the selection process, but she does not hire based on these scores. She compares these test scores to their performance evaluations six months after employment. What is Ruth doing?
    a. Establishing reliability.
    b. Establishing content validity.
    c. Using cut scores.
    d. Establishing predictive validity.
    e. Decontextualizing construct validity.

12. Mariah is selection manager for a large manufacturing organization. The machinists' test has a validity coefficient of .75. Scores typically run evenly from 0 to 100, with 50 as the average. Mariah expects 1,000 applicants in this year's pool to fill seventy-five openings. What cut score is appropriate?
    a. 750.
    b. 90.
    c. 100.
    d. 50.
    e. She should interview all the applicants.

13. In the recruiting process, positive self-removal happens when
    a. human resources gets out of the hiring loop. Working divisions advertise for and interview their own job candidates.
    b. there is a streamlined human resources office arrangement. Candidates can escort themselves out, thus reducing the need for receptionists and security personnel.
    c. all applicants are encouraged to apply for jobs.
    d. unqualified applicants do not apply for jobs.
    e. women and minority applicants are discouraged and do not apply for jobs.

14. How does the selection process differ when hiring for international versus domestic positions?
    a. There is no difference.
    b. Married employees are preferred for domestic employment. Single employees are preferred for international assignments.
    c. Personality is more important for international assignments. Technical expertise is more important for domestic employment.
    d. Gender discrimination is not allowed in domestic or international situations.
    e. Age discrimination is not allowed in domestic or international situations.

15. Standard selection activities follow which pattern?
    a. Screen, physical exam, comprehensive interview, tests, decision.
    b. Physical exam, screen, tests, interview, decision.
    c. Background investigation, screen, physical examination, decision.
    d. Physical examination, background investigation, forms completion, decision.
    e. Forms completion, comprehensive interview, background investigation, decision.

16. Predictive validity is preferred to concurrent validity because
    a. it is easier to establish.
    b. it is quicker to establish.
    c. it is cheaper to establish.
    d. it focuses on current employees.
    e. it focuses on current job applicants.

17. Criterion-related validity may be established by
    a. predictive or concurrent validity.
    b. cut scores or construct validity.
    c. content or construct validity.
    d. reliability or cut scores.
    e. concurrent or contaminant validity.

Chapter Seven

SELECTION DEVICES

LEARNING OBJECTIVES

AFTER READING THIS CHAPTER, YOU WILL BE ABLE TO:

1. Identify the purpose of selection devices.
2. Discuss why organizations use application forms.
3. Explain the usefulness of weighted application blanks.
4. Discuss the purposes of performance simulation tests.
5. Describe assessment centres and how they are conducted.
6. Describe the use of graphology, polygraphy, and other tests.
7. Discuss the problems associated with job interviews and means of correcting them.
8. Identify the organizational benefits derived from realistic job previews.
9. Explain the purpose of background investigations.
10. Describe when medical or physical examinations are appropriate in the selection process.

After years of budget cuts and downsizing in the federal government, the unemployment rate was still high, and job prospects for former or aspiring civil servants were not bright. But this was not the picture in the high-tech sector. In April 1998 in the Ottawa region there were more than 800 high-tech companies with a total revenue in excess of $8 billion, employing approximately 47,000 people in high-tech jobs and another 95,000 in related positions. There were 2,000 high-tech jobs vacant, and the companies were expected to add more than 16,000 new positions by the year 2001.[1]

Companies are always concerned with recruiting, selecting, and retaining high-quality employees, but in the extremely competitive high-tech job market where companies are poaching each others' employees, these issues are doubly critical. First, potential employees must be reached. There is a broad range of approaches: Northern Telecom's career fairs, Cadence Design System's television ads during Ottawa Senators hockey games, and companies that use e-mail, the Internet, and voice mail to reach people with personal messages. Competition for employees goes to the extreme: Cisco Systems even put up a billboard outside Northern Telecom's main Ottawa offices, showing a group of young engineers with the caption "we know where your friends are."

Several of the companies collaborate in national recruiting efforts through the Ottawa Centre for Research and Innovation. Recruiting pamphlets emphasize the attractions of Ottawa, and larger companies emphasize career prospects: Northern Telecom points out that it has 250 locations around the world, for instance. Smaller companies, like 110-employee Semiconductor Insights, tell prospective candidates that they will be working with the latest and greatest technology.

A second part of the issue is to select the best and brightest from the pool of candidates and to ensure that there is a good fit between the employee and the organization. In some cases, this has meant providing the workforce with things they value—from good salaries through flexible working hours to gyms and health foods (Northern Telecom's 11,500 Ottawa employees have access to the city's second-largest gym).

Highly competent employees are cru-

Fitness facilities are one method used to attract and retain high-quality employees. For example Northern Telecom boasts the second-largest gym in Ottawa.

cial. Randall Freeborn, human resources director of Semiconductor Insights, says, "The more qualified people you have, the better the business growth." Software and hardware engineers and micro-chip designers must have appropriate technical training as well as experience. And if the employee and company are properly matched, it will be less likely that the employee will be lured away. According to Shirley-Ann George of the Canadian Advanced Technology Association, in Silicon Valley North, most experienced engineers are "courted" several times a month.

Introduction

Selection is always an important human resources management activity, but it is in circumstances like those just described, when there are far more jobs to be filled than competent candidates available, that the recruiting and selection process becomes absolutely critical. In Chapter 6, we noted that the selection process is composed of a number of steps, each of which provides managers with information that will help them predict whether or not an applicant will prove to be a successful job performer. One way to conceptualize this is to think of each step as a higher hurdle in a race. The applicant able to clear all the hurdles wins the race, victory being the receipt of a job offer.

The selection steps presented in Chapter 6 attempt to make predictions based on either evaluating the past or sampling the present. The application form, background investigation, and comprehensive interview attempt to find out what the applicant has done in the past and then to project these experiences and accomplishments into the future. You should be aware that this method of prediction implies certain assumptions concerning the relationship of the past to the future. Specifically, it assumes that a candidate's past behaviour can be a guide for predicting future behaviour, and that the candidate will remain the same person in the future as he or she was in the past. While these assumptions may be accurate and this approach satisfactory, it appears that tools such as job-related tests, where relevant, may also be good predictors because they sample present behaviour in order to predict future behaviour.

It is logical that selection devices that simulate actual work behaviour and are as current as possible should stand the best chance of being good predictors, but is this true in practice? In the following pages, we will review the devices discussed in Chapter 6. Since each of these is a potential tool in the selector's tool kit, and using several in combination is often best, we want to look carefully at each in the context of how good a tool it is and under what conditions it should be used.

The Application Form

In all Canadian jurisdictions, laws and subsequent court rulings prohibit discrimination on the grounds of sex, race, ancestry, place of origin, religion, citizenship, age, or marital status, as discussed in Chapter 3. Sexual orientation is also prohibited grounds for discrimination in most jurisdictions, and in 1998, the Supreme Court of Canada found that Alberta's failure to ban discrimination on the grounds of sexual orientation was in violation of the Constitution. It

Meet

Pat Murray
Administrator, Rabbittown Community Development Centre

Everyone knows that when you apply for a job, you generally need to fill out an application form, go through an interview, and supply references. But these days, you may well have to go through a similar process even to volunteer your services for free. Pat Murray, who runs the Rabbittown Community Development Centre in St John's, Newfoundland, recruits a lot of volunteers. "Like anyone, we try to get the most capable people available," he explains.

Funding for permanent staff, he explains, is scarce: "There's basically me. We have some temporary positions funded by grants, so right now there are four of us." With a large community to serve, and a full range of programs from employment counselling to day care to a literacy centre, a lot of important work needs to be done by volunteers. Rabbittown can't afford to let them do a bad job.

So each would-be volunteer is given an application form not unlike an employment application. It asks for previous experience (which might cover anything from babysitting to working for a Lion's Club) as well as education (Rabbittown is a short walk from Memorial University, so many volunteers are students in the social work program there). It also asks for the applicant's strengths and areas of interest—is he or she sport-oriented? Good with children? A computer whiz?

Murray then interviews the applicants, again, much as if he were hiring an employee. "I look for how they answer questions and how they present themselves generally," he explains. "And I ask some scenario questions such as, 'If you were playing ping-pong with a small child and she swore at you, how would you react?'"

He also checks their references even though these volunteers are often teachers or coaches from the community and are already known to Mr Murray. An agency that serves children has to be especially careful to check the background of volunteers these days in the wake of several widely publicized sexual-abuse incidents involving hockey coaches, he explains.

Finally, a new volunteer is accepted on a probationary basis, again, not unlike at a "real" job, to see how he or she does on the job. "In this field, many people think that anyone can do the work," says Mr Murray. "But my good volunteers deserve a little more respect than that."

is also important to point out that in most Canadian jurisdictions, discrimination on the basis of age is prohibited for purposes of employment as long as the individual is between eighteen and sixty-five years old.[2]

The only exceptions to these prohibitions are cases where it can be shown that these criteria are bona fide occupational requirements (BFOR). For example, one job where it would make sense to use religion as a criterion of eligibility is that of chaplain in the Canadian Forces, and since the Catholic church does not yet ordain women as priests, this is one of only two jobs—the other is that of submarine crew—not open to women.[3]

Many of the items that traditionally appeared on the application form—religion, age, marital status, occupation of spouse, number and ages of children, hobbies—may have been interesting to know, but often could not be shown to be job-related. Given this reality, it is not surprising to find different application forms are

Application Form Company-specific employment forms used to generate specific information the company wants.

used today; these forms must conform to the guidelines of the appropriate human rights legislation. Figure 7-1 shows the Employer's Guide to Application Forms and Interviews issued by The Saskatchewan Human Rights Commission; the guidelines issued in other jurisdictions are similar in content. Since the onus is on management to demonstrate that information requested of applicants be job-related, anything that cannot be so demonstrated should be omitted.

In addition to restrictions about what can be asked on an application form, one important thing has been added. Note the statement at the bottom of Figure 7-2. Such statements serve a vital purpose—the right of an employer to dismiss an employee for falsifying information. Furthermore, the applicant is giving the company permission to obtain previous work history and to release previous employers from legal liability. Of course, an applicant has the right not

SASKATCHEWAN

HUMAN RIGHTS COMMISSION

Employer's Guide to Application Forms and Interviews

Inquiries Before Hiring	Okay	Don't Ask
1. Address	Okay to ask about current and previous addresses in Canada and how long applicant stayed there.	Don't ask about foreign addresses which would indicate national origin.
2. Birthplace, nationality, ancestry, place of origin.	**After hiring**, may ask for birth certificate.	Don't make any inquiry about place of birth or national origin. That includes asking about the national origin of relatives or asking for a birth certificate or baptismal certificate.
3. Photographs	**After hiring**, okay to ask for photos if needed.	**Before hiring**, don't ask for photo.
4. Religion	**After hiring**, may ask about religion to determine when leave-of-absence may be required for the observance of religious holidays.	**Before hiring**, don't ask anything that would identify religious affiliation. That includes asking for a pastor's recommendation or reference.
5. Citizenship	May ask if applicant is legally entitled to work in Canada.	Don't ask about applicant's citizenship status—it could reveal applicant's nationality, ancestry or place of origin. That includes questions about proof of citizenship or the date citizenship was received.
6. Education	Okay to ask about schools where education was obtained and about foreign language skills.	Don't ask about the religious or racial affiliation of educational institutions.
7. Relatives	**After hiring**, may ask for a contact name in case of emergency.	**Before hiring**, don't ask questions that would require someone to reveal their marital or family status.
8. Organization	Okay to ask about clubs and organizations that would reveal a person's affiliation based on race, disability, sexual orientation, etc. **as long as** applicants are told: "You may decline to list organizations which would indicate your religion, race, etc.	
9. Work Schedule	May ask applicants whether they are able to work the required schedule. If applicants are not able to work the required schedule because of religious practices or family needs, the employer must determine if accommodation is possible.	

Figure 7-1
Pre-employment Questions and Employment Equity Guidelines

10. Sex		On the application form, don't ask about the sex of the applicant.
11. Age	Okay to ask if the applicant is younger than the minimum age or older than the maximum age required by employment law.	**Before hiring**, don't ask for any record (like a birth certificate) or other information that would reveal the applicant's age.
12. Marital Status	Although you can't ask about an applicant's marital status, if the job requires it you **can ask** if the applicant is willing to travel or be transferred.	Don't ask whether an applicant is single, married, remarried, engaged, divorced, separated, widowed, living common-law. Don't ask a woman for her birth name.
13. Family Status	May ask if applicant is able to work the required schedule. If she can't because of family needs, the employer must try to accommodate her.	Don't ask about the number of children or other dependents. Don't ask about child-care arrangements. Don't ask applicant whether she is pregnant, breastfeeding, using birth control, or plans to have children.
14. Disability	The following questions should be asked: (i) do you have a disability which will affect your ability to perform any of the functions of the job for which you have applied? If the answer to the above is yes, then ask: (ii) what functions can you not perform and what accommodations could be made which would allow you to do the work adequately?	Don't ask about disabilities or health problems except as set out in the adjacent column. Don't ask if applicant has ever had previous work injuries or made a claim for Workers' Compensation.
15. Drug Testing	**After hiring**, may ask employees to take a drug test. If an employee has a drug-related disability, employers may be required to accommodate.	**Before hiring**, may not conduct drug tests.
16. Height and Weight		Don't ask unless it can be shown they are essential to the performance of the job.
17. Sexual Orientation		Don't ask about applicant's sexual orientation.
18. Receipt of Public Assistance		Don't ask if applicant is receiving assistance under *The Saskatchewan Assistance Act* (welfare) or *The Saskatchewan Income Plan Act*.

Figure 7-1 Continued

Source: Used with permission of the Saskatechewan Human Rights Commission, *Application Forms and Interviewer Guide.* http://www.gov.sk.ca/shrc/appforms.htm

to sign the application. In that event, however, the application is removed from consideration.

The fact that application forms have had to be revised and limited in the questions they may ask does not mean that the application form is not an effective predictor. In fact, evidence indicates that hard and relevant biographical data on the application that can be verified—for example, rank in high-school graduating class—may be a more valid measure of potential job performance than many of the intelligence, aptitude, interest, and personality items that traditionally have been in the selection decision.[4] When application form items have been appropriately weighted to reflect job relatedness, we find that the application can successfully predict performance criteria for such diverse groups as sales clerks, engineers, factory workers, district managers, clerical employees, draftspersons, and army officers.[5] A review of studies using biographical data acquired from the application form found a number of items that successfully predicted differences between short- and long-tenure employees.[6] Let's look at how these are used.

The Weighted Application Blank

The weighted application blank appears to offer excellent potential in helping recruiters to differentiate between potentially successful and unsuccessful job performers. To create such an instrument, individual form items—such as number of years of schooling, number of years or months on last job, and salary data for all previous jobs—are validated against performance and turnover measures and given appropriate weights. Let's assume, for example, that management is interested in developing a weighted form that would predict which applicants for the job of accountant would stay with the company. They would select from their files the application forms from each of two groups of previously hired accountants—one, a group that had short tenure with the organization (accountants who stayed, say, less than a year), and the other, a group with long tenure

Weighted Application Blank (WAB) An application form in which several elements have been statistically related to job outcomes.

JOHN WILEY & SONS CANADA LIMITED
APPLICATION FOR EMPLOYMENT

WILEY

JOB REQUIREMENTS

Position Desired: _____ Salary Desired: _____

Date Available to Begin Work _____

Type of Employment Desired ☐ Full Time ☐ Part Time ☐ Temporary ☐ Summer ☐ Co-op Term

Are you legally entitled to work in Canada? ☐ Yes ☐ No
Are you willing to relocate?   ☐ Yes ☐ No Preferred Location: _____
Have you ever been convicted of an offense for which a pardon has not been granted? ☐ Yes ☐ No

PERSONAL

Name: _____
            Family   First   Middle

Present Address: _____
                 Street, P.O. Box   Apt   City   Province   Postal Code

Telephone Number: _____ Business/Alternate Number: _____
                  Area Code   Number   Area Code   Number

EDUCATION

Name Of School	Major Subject/ Program	Last Year Or Grade Completed	Diploma Or Degree Received Or Expected
Secondary			
College/University			
Other			

Figure 7-2
Employment Application Form

EMPLOYMENT

Name of present/last employer Address	Present/last job title	
	Period of Employment From To	Present/Last Salary
Telephone	Name of Supervisor	May we contact? ☐ Yes ☐ No
Type of Business	Reason for leaving	
Duties/Responsibilities		
Name of previous employer Address	Present/last job title	
	Period of Employment From To	Present/Last Salary
Telephone	Name of Supervisor	May we contact? ☐ Yes ☐ No
Type of Business	Reason for leaving	
Duties/Responsibilities		
Name of previous employer Address	Present/last job title	
	Period of Employment From To	Present/Last Salary
Telephone	Name of Supervisor	May we contact? ☐ Yes ☐ No
Type of Business	Reason for leaving	
Duties/Responsibilities		

REFERENCES

Please list three persons to whom John Wiley & Sons Canada, Ltd. may refer:

1. ______________________
Name Telephone # Relationship

2. ______________________
Name Telephone # Relationship

3. ______________________
Name Telephone # Relationship

I certify that the above information is full, complete, and true to the best of my knowledge. I understand that, if employed, falsified statements of any nature whatsoever made on this application may disqualify me from consideration for employment, or shall be sufficient cause for my immediate dismissal. I authorize John Wiley & Sons Canada, Ltd. to investigate the accuracy and completeness of this information. I also release from liability or damage those individuals or corporations who provide information relating to my prior employment or character.

Signature of Applicant Date

Figure 7-2 Continued

(say, five years or more). These old application forms would be screened item by item to determine how employees in each group responded. In this way, management would discover items that differentiate the groups. These items would then be weighted relative to how well they differentiate applicants.

If, for example, 80 per cent of the long-tenure group had a university degree, while only 30 per cent of the short-tenure group did, then possession of a university degree might be given a weight of, say, 4. But if 30 per cent of the long-tenure group had prior experience in a major accounting firm while 20 per cent of the short-tenure did, this item might be given a weight of only 1. Note, of course, that this procedure would have to be done for every job in the organization and balanced against the factors of those that do not fall into the majority category. In other words, while 80 per cent of the long-tenure individuals had a university degree, we would need to factor into our weighing scheme those who had a university degree and were successful on the job but only had short tenure with the company.

Items that predict long tenure for an accountant might be totally different from items that predict it for an engineer or even a financial analyst. However, with the continued improvement in sophisticated computer software, the task of developing the weighted application blank for each job may be more manageable.

A Successful Application

As noted earlier, the application form has had wide success in selection for a number of diverse jobs. For instance, in various positions in the hotel industry, analysis shows that the application form has been valuable. In one study, it was found that seven items on the application were highly predictive of successful performance as measured by job tenure.[7]

Evidence that the application form provides relevant information for predicting job success is well supported across a broad range of jobs, but care must be taken to ensure that application items are validated for each job. Also, since the predictive ability of items may change over time, they must be continuously reviewed and updated. Finally, management should be aware of the possibility that the information given on the application is erroneous. A background investigation can verify most of the data.

Employment Tests

In this section, we want to look at employment tests—the better-known written tests that attempt to assess intelligence, abilities, and personality traits as well as the lesser-known performance simulation tests including work sampling and the tests administered at assessment centres. In addition, we will look at and evaluate the validity of polygraph tests and handwriting analysis (graphology) as selection devices and will see how the use of tests may be different in a global environment.

Employment Test Any selection examination that is designed to determine if an applicant is qualified for the job.

Written Tests

We noted in Chapter 6 that historically, written tests have served as significant input into the selection decision. And although there was a hiatus after the *Griggs v. Duke Power* decision in the mid-1970s (which, while directly affecting organizations in the US, created concerns regarding the validity of employment standards in many jurisdictions), a number of companies recognized that testing served a vital purpose. There has been renewed interest in written tests since those that have been validated can aid significantly in the acquisition of efficient and effective workers. However, remember that the company has the sole responsibility for demonstrating that tests used for hiring or promotion are related to job performance (see "The Bell Curve Controversy").

There are literally hundreds of tests that can be used by organizations as selection tools.[8] One can use tests that measure intellect, spatial ability, perception skills, mechanical comprehension, motor ability, and personality traits. Written aptitude tests are used in the selection process by as many as half of all Canadian companies.[9] Personality tests are somewhat less common, with around 30 per cent of Canadian companies reporting using them in the selection process.[10] A recent addition to the vast array of tests is the Emotional

Written Test An organizational selection tool designed to indicate whether an applicant will be successful on the job if hired.

Quotient Inventory (EQ-I) which measures "emotional intelligence," a series of traits purported to have more impact on life success than intelligence alone. The first commercially available EQ-I test was developed by Israeli psychologist Reuven Bar-On and includes 152 statements such as, "I like everyone I meet" and "I do very weird things,"[11] with respondents indicating their agreement on a five-point scale. In Canada, the test was presented for the first time in Toronto in the summer of 1996 and was adopted by several consultants.[12] Among the companies using the EQ concept is Enterprise Rent-a-car. On its Web site, you can find a brief explanation of the concept together with the statement, "now wouldn't you like to work for a company that values your emotional intelligence instead of your GPA?" You could then take the company's EQ test which consists of just fifteen multiple-choice questions, check which of the company's Canadian locations have job openings, and send in your job application.[13]

This is a necessarily short overview of written selection tests. For more detail on the tests themselves, you could consult a textbook on industrial psychology.[14] It is also important to remember that all tests should be validated: they should measure what they claim to measure, and that should be job-related.

The Bell Curve Controversy:

The Case for IQ Tests in Employee Selection

It was undoubtedly the most controversial social science book published during the first half of the 1990s. *The Bell Curve*, by Richard Herrnstein and Charles Murray, presents evidence that IQ, not education or opportunity, is the key factor determining where a person ends up on the American social scale. The book was controversial because the authors claimed that economic inequalities between racial groups are related to differences in average IQ levels between races. Like the work of the University of Western Ontario's J. Phillipe Rushton, this position is strongly assailed by many scientists, journalists, and politicians who see it as providing a justification for the dismantling of social programs. Let us look, however, at their position on the relationship between IQ and job performance.

Herrnstein and Murray began by making six statements that they categorize as "beyond significant technical dispute":

1. There is such a thing as a general factor of cognitive ability on which human beings differ.

2. All standardized tests of academic aptitude or achievement measure this general factor to some degree, but IQ tests expressly designed for that purpose measure it most accurately.

3. IQ scores closely match whatever it is that people mean when they use the word "intelligent" or "smart" in ordinary language.

4. IQ scores are stable, although not perfectly so, over much of a person's life.

5. Properly administered IQ tests are not demonstrably biased against social, economic, ethnic, or racial groups.

(continued)

6. A substantial portion of cognitive ability (no less than 40 per cent and no more than 80 per cent) is genetically inherited.

Using these six points as a foundation, the authors argue forcibly that IQ is a powerful predictor of job performance, or to use their terms, "a smarter employee is, on average, a more proficient employee."

According to Herrnstein and Murray, all jobs require cognitive ability. This is relatively self-evident in professional occupations such as accountants, engineers, scientists, architects, and physicians, but it is also true for semi-skilled blue-collar jobs and even for unskilled manual jobs. For instance, they point out that there are better and worse busboys in restaurants. The really good busboy uses his intelligence to solve job-related problems, and the higher his intelligence, the more quickly he comes up with solutions and can call on them when appropriate. As jobs become more complex, IQ becomes more important in determining performance, and this advantage holds over time. Work experience doesn't significantly close the gap. "The cost of hiring less intelligent workers may last as long as they stay on the job."

The authors demonstrate that an IQ score is a better predictor of job performance than any other single criterion—better than a job interview, reference check, or college or university transcript. They claim that "an employer that is free to pick among applicants can realize large economic gains from hiring those with the highest IQs."

Current legislation in Canada limits the use of intelligence tests for selection purposes; employers must demonstrate that any test they use is job-related. In addition, there are real difficulties regarding the definition and measurement of intelligence. There are those who question whether intelligence can be measured at all. Others, like Earl Hunt, argue that while "intelligence" exists and can be measured, it is not a simple variable but a three-fold one, and that intelligence is actually the interaction between brainpower, knowing how to use it, and access to appropriate data. Nevertheless, Herrnstein and Murray state that biographical data, reference checks, college or university transcripts are "valid predictors of job performance in part because they imperfectly reflect something about the applicant's intelligence. Employers who are forbidden to obtain test scores nonetheless strive to obtain the best possible workforce, and it happens that the way to get the best possible workforce, other things equal, is to hire the smartest people they can find."

Source: Richard J. Herrnstein and Charles Murray, *The Bell Curve: Intelligence and Class Structure in American Life* (New York: The Free Press, 1994). Also see Martin Lexin, "Warning: Bell Curve Ahead," *The Globe and Mail* (August 17, 1995), p. A18, and Earl Hunt, "The Role of Intelligence in Modern Society," *American Scientist* (July–August 1995).

Performance Simulation Tests

To avoid criticism and potential liability that may result from the use of psychological, aptitude, and other types of written tests, there has been increasing interest in the use of performance simulation tests. The single identifying characteristic of these tests is that they require the applicant to engage in specific behaviours necessary for doing the job successfully. In contrast to the types of tests discussed above, performance simulation tests should more easily meet the

Performance Simulation Tests Tests that require the applicant to perform tasks that are part of the job, as in work sampling tests and assessment centres.

Work Sampling A selection device requiring the job applicant to actually perform a small segment of the job.

requirement of job relatedness because they are made up of actual job behaviours rather than surrogates.

Work Sampling Work sampling is an effort to create a miniature replica of a job, in which applicants demonstrate that they have the necessary talents by actually performing the tasks. By carefully devising work samples based on job analysis data, it is possible to determine the knowledge, skills, and abilities needed for each job. Then, each work sample element is matched with a corresponding job performance element. For example, a work sample for a bank teller at the National Bank of Canada involving computation on a calculator would require the applicant to make similar computations. Ever wonder how a checkout clerk at Home Depot is screened for a job to scan the prices of your purchases quickly and accurately? Most go through a similar work sampling session where supervisors demonstrate how to scan accurately, ensuring that the product did indeed ring up. Then the candidate is given an opportunity to show that he or she can handle the job. Work sampling, then, reflects actual hands-on experience. Of course, the new employee's basic ability is later enhanced by appropriate training (Home Depot calls it "cashier school"[15]) as will be discussed in further depth in Chapter 9.

The advantages of work sampling over traditional pencil and paper tests are obvious. Because content is essentially identical to job content, work sampling should be a better predictor of short-term performance and should minimize discrimination.[16] Also, because of the nature of their content and the methods used to determine content, well-constructed work sample tests should easily meet employment equity legislation content validity requirements.[17] The main disadvantage is the difficulty in developing good work samples for each job. Furthermore, work sampling is not applicable to all levels of the organization. It is often difficult to use for managerial jobs because it is hard to create a work sample test that can address the full range of managerial activities. In the following section, we will look at a type of performance simulation test that is more directly related to mid-level managerial positions.

Assessment centres employ exercises that are designed to stimulate the work that managers actually do. They have been very successful in predicting later job performance in professional and managerial positions.

Assessment Centres Facilities where performance simulation tests are administered. These are made up of a series of exercises and are used for selection, development, and performance appraisals.

Assessment Centres A more elaborate set of performance simulation tests specifically designed to evaluate a candidate's managerial potential is administered in assessment centres. Assessment centres use procedures that incorporate group and individual exercises. Applicants go through a series of these exercises and are appraised by line executives, practising supervisors, and/or trained psychologists as to how well they perform. As with work sampling, because these exercises are designed to simulate the work that managers actually do, they tend to be accurate predictors of later job performance. In some cases, the assessment centre also includes traditional personality and aptitude tests.

How does an assessment centre work? Essentially, the procedure goes something like this:[18]

1. A small group of applicants comes to the assessment centre.

2. The assessment centre has approximately six to eight individuals who have been trained as assessors. Some of them are trained psychologists, while others are managers who are at least two levels above the individual being assessed.

3. For about two to four days, the assessees are asked to participate in exercises such as:
   a. Interviews
   b. "In basket" exercises where applicants solve day-to-day problems that managers managers might find in their in baskets
   c. Case exercises
   d. Leaderless group discussions
   e. Business games
   f. Personality tests
   g. General ability tests

4. Assessors, usually in pairs, observe and record the behaviour of applicants in group and individual situational problems. A clinical psychologist summarizes the personality tests.

5. Each assessee is rated on twenty to twenty-five characteristics (such as organization and planning, decision making, creativity, resistance to stress, and oral communication skills).

6. A judgement is made about the assessee's potential for meeting the job requirements.

Assessment centres normally operate as described in Figure 7-3. Evidence supporting the effectiveness of assessment centres is impressive. They have consistently demonstrated results that predict later job performance in professional positions like sales as well as lower- to mid-level management positions.[19] Even when the costs of conducting assessment centre evaluations are taken into account—training of assessors, consultant fees, time away from the job, purchase of tests and exercises, and so on—the pay-offs in terms of more effective selection are usually more than justified.[20] For instance, AT&T has assessed thousands of employees in its management development centre and has found the centre to be very effective in indicating which individuals would be successful on jobs that provide greater responsibility and accountability.[21]

One note of caution has been offered concerning the impressive and consistent results from assessment centre selection. It has been proposed that the measures of job performance may be contaminated.[22] Assessment centre results may not be valid because they generally use the success measures of promotions and salary increases as determinants of "job performance." Given that promotions and salary increases may not be based solely on performance, assessment evaluators will come up with effective results if they know what factors senior management actually uses to make decisions about raises and promotions. Accordingly, assessors may not be evaluating true performance but such non-performance-related factors as the candidate's social skills, likeability, "proper" background, appearance, or attitude. For instance, assessors who correctly realize that upper-level managers like and tend to promote "yes types" and conformists may unintentionally assess candidates for these traits. Whenever assessment centre ratings and success measures contain a common component unrelated to job performance, the results will be contaminated and the validity of the procedure questionable.

Figure 7-3
An Example of an Assessment Agenda

Day 1
Orientation Meeting
Management Game: "Conglomerate" Forming different types of conglomerates is the goal, with four-person teams bartering companies to achieve their planned result. Teams set their own acquisition objectives and must plan and organize to meet them.

Background Interview A ninety minute interview conducted by an assessor.

Group Discussion: "Management Problems" Short cases calling for various forms of management judgement are presented to groups of four. In one hour, the group, acting as consultants, must resolve the cases and submit its recommendation in writing.

Individual Fact-Finding and Decision-Making Exercises: "The Research Budget" The participants are told that they have just taken over as division manager. They are given a brief description of an incident in which their predecessor had recently turned down a request for funds to continue a research project. The research director is appealing for a reversal of the decision. The participants are given fifteen minutes to ask questions to dig out the facts in the case. Following this fact-finding period, they must present their decisions orally with supporting reasoning and defend it under challenge.

Day 2
In Basket Exercise: "Section Manager's In Basket" The contents of a section manager's in basket are simulated. The participants are instructed to go through the contents, solving problems, answering questions, delegating, organizing, scheduling, and planning, just as they might do if they were promoted suddenly to the position. An assessor reviews the contents of the completed in basket and conducts a one-hour interview with each participant to gain further information.

Assigned Role Leaderless Group Discussion: "Compensation Committee" The Compensation Committee is meeting to allocate $8,000 in discretionary salary increases among six supervisory and managerial employees. Each member of the committee (participant) represents a department of the company and is instructed to "do the best they can" for the employee from their department.

Analysis, Presentation, and Group Discussion: "The Pretzel Factory" This financial analysis problem has the participant role-play a consultant called in to advise Carl Flowers of the C.F. Pretzel Company on two problems: what to do about a division of the company that has continually lost money and whether the corporation should expand. Participants are given data on the company and are asked to recommend appropriate courses of action. They make their recommendation in a seven-minute presentation after which they are formed into a group to come up with a single set of recommendations.

Days 3 and 4
Assessors meet to share their observations on each participant and to arrive at summary evaluations relative to each dimension sought and overall potential.

Source: Reprinted from the *Training and Developmental Journal.* Copyright December 1971, the American Society for Training and Development. Reprinted with permission. All rights reserved.

Other Tests

Two other tests—graphology (handwriting analysis) and polygraph (lie detector) and honesty tests—receive a disproportionate amount of media attention. Because of this attention and the controversy surrounding their validity, we will conclude our discussion of tests with a brief review of these devices and look at testing issues in a global arena.

Graphology It has been said that an individual's handwriting can suggest the degree of energy, inhibitions, and spontaneity to be found in the writer, disclosing idiosyncrasies and elements of balance and control from which many personality characteristics can be inferred.[23] **Graphology** is not used by many Canadian companies (only 1 per cent of respondents to the Thacker & Cattaneo 1992 survey reported using such tests[24]), and most Canadian specialists are extremely sceptical of the technique. Linda Pitney, a Toronto-based graphologist, has less than twenty customers. "I wish I spoke French," she says. "Then I could get out of Toronto and go to Paris." It is estimated that 80 per cent of companies in France, Switzerland, and Germany use graphologists as part of the selection process.[25] In Latin America, it is not uncommon for employment advertisements to require a handwritten letter from the applicant. Graphology is supposed to diagnose personality characteristics, which is why it is used as an employment test. The argument is made that a large percentage of occupational failures are due to personality defects, not lack of education or ability. Given the inadequacies of many standardized methods for assessing personality characteristics, handwriting analysis, if it really does tell us something about applicants' personality, might have validity, but only if the job analysis had identified these personality characteristics as relevant to the job (See Figure 7-4).

Despite the popularity of graphology among companies in France, Germany, Switzerland, and Latin America, there is little substantial evidence to support the method as a valid selection device; one must bear in mind that legal requirements for demonstrating the validity of employment tests are less stringent in those countries than in North America.

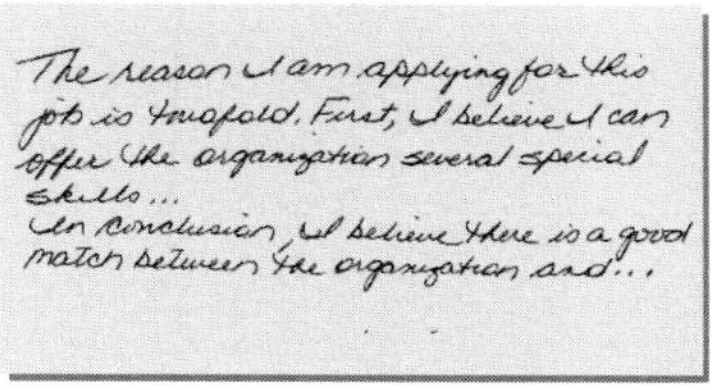

Graphology Handwriting analysis which purports to disclose personality characteristics.

In graphology an analyst would evaluate the writing sample provided by the applicant. That evaluation would present a psychological profile.

Figure 7-4
A Handwriting Sample of Graphology

Polygraph and Honesty Tests You will recall from Chapter 4 that because of concerns with the validity of lie detectors (polygraphs) as well as with their intrusiveness, their use has fallen into disfavour, and in many jurisdictions, such as Ontario, the use of polygraphs in the selection process is prohibited. Only one of over 500 Canadian companies responding to a national survey reported using the polygraph in the selection process.[26] Problems with the use of the polygraph led to the development of pencil and paper honesty tests.

As we mentioned in the discussion of employee rights, companies sought to do something to combat the estimated $40 billion lost to employee theft each year.[27] One means of beginning the attack (without using the polygraph) is the honesty test which is designed to assess an individual's integrity and to predict those who are more likely to steal from an employer[28] or otherwise act in a manner unacceptable to the organization.

Although the questions asked may appear to be relatively innocent, those taking the test do not know how they will be interpreted. For example, the response to "Have you ever cheated on a test in your life?" may not have a correct response on its face value. If you say yes, you admit that you've cheated; a no response might indicate that you are lying. Nonetheless, the question patterns are such that even those who try to outsmart the test often fail. These tests often contain questions that repeat themselves in some fashion, and the examiner then looks for consistency in responses.

Since polygraphs are all but unusable for the typical firm, honesty testing has become more widespread. By the early 1990s, it was estimated that nearly 17 per cent of all American Management Association affiliated firms used honesty tests.[29] In fact, their use has become so extensive, that it has grown into a $50-million-a-year business for these honesty-psychological testing firms.[30]

While honesty testing is a growing business, particularly in the United States, it has not really caught on for selection purposes in Canada. Part of the problem, of course, is that companies must demonstrate that such tests are job-related; this is quite difficult to do for most jobs.

Testing in a Global Arena Many of the standard selection techniques described in this text are not easily transferable to international situations. Where the decision has been made to recruit and employ host-country nationals, typical North American testing will be acceptable in some countries but not in others. As mentioned earlier, although handwriting tests are seldom used in Canada, they are frequently used in France. In Great Britain, most tests such as graphology, polygraph, and honesty tests are rarely used in employment. In some countries, gender can be used as a selection criterion (remember the *Bangkok Times* advertisement at the end of Chapter 6?).

Another consideration is that tests used by Canadian companies in Canada may not transfer easily to a foreign country. It is not enough to translate the test from English into Portuguese, say, for using it in Brazil: what assumptions does the test make regarding the education received by the candidates and the environment in which they live? Certainly a test based on a case about junior hockey coaches will be meaningless to Brazilians who have never even seen the game, just as references to Brazilian soccer star Romario would be mystifying to most Canadians. Accordingly, whenever Canadian corporations prepare to do business abroad, their practices must be adapted to the cultures and regulations of the country in which they will operate.

Interviews

Interview A selection method that involves a face-to-face meeting with the candidate.

Whether we're discussing initial screening interviews or comprehensive ones, a common question arises: Are interviews effective for gathering accurate information from which selection decisions can be made? The interview has proven to be an almost universal selection tool, but it can take a number of forms. It can be a one-on-one encounter between the interviewer and the applicant (the traditional interview) or involve several individuals (a panel interview). Interviews can follow some predetermined pattern wherein both the questions and the expected responses are identified (a form of structured interview). Interviews can also be designed to create a difficult environment in which the applicant is put to the test to assess his or her confidence levels. These are often referred to as the stress interview (see "Ethical Decisions in HRM" on page 213).

Stress Interview An interview designed to see how the applicants handle themselves under pressure.

Irrespective of how the interview is conducted, it is understood that few people get jobs without one or more interviews. This is extremely interesting given that the validity of the interview as a selection tool has been the subject of considerable debate. Let's look at the research findings regarding interviews.

Ethical Decisions in HRM:

The Stress Interview

Your interview day has finally arrived. You are all dressed up to make that lasting, first impression. You finally meet Mr Henderson, and he shakes your hand and invites you to be seated. Your interview has begun! This is the moment you've waited for.

The first few moments appear mundane enough. The questions to this point, in fact, seem easy. Your confidence is growing. That little voice in your head keeps telling you that you are doing fine, to just keep on going. Suddenly, the questions get tougher. Mr Henderson leans back and asks about why you want to leave your current job—the one you've been in for only twenty-four months. As you begin to explain that you wish to leave for personal reasons, he begins to probe more. His smile is gone. His body language is different. All right, you think, be honest. So you tell Mr Henderson that you want to leave because you think your supervisor's incompetent and only got the position because he is related to someone in senior management. This has led to a number of confrontations, and you're tired of dealing with the situation. Mr Henderson looks at you and replies: "If you ask me, that's a childish reason for wanting to leave. Are you sure you're mature enough and have what it takes to make it in this company?" How dare he talk to you that way! Who does he think he is? So you respond with an angry tone in your voice. And guess what? You've just fallen victim to one of the tricks of the interviewing business—the stress interview.

So-called stress interviews are becoming more commonplace in today's business environment. Every job produces stress, and at some point, every worker has a horrendous day. So these types of interviews become predictors of how you may react at work under less than favourable conditions. Interviewers want to observe how you'll react when you are put under pressure. Those who demonstrate the resolve and strength to handle the stress indicate a level of professionalism and confidence. It's those characteristics that are being assessed. Individuals who react to the pressure interview in a more positive manner indicate that they should be more able to handle the day-to-day irritations that exist at work. Those who don't, well....

On the other hand, they are staged events. Interviewers deliberately lead applicants into a false sense of security—the comfortable interaction. Then suddenly and drastically, they change. They go on the attack. And it's usually a personal affront that picks on a weakness they've uncovered about the applicant. Possibly, it's humiliating; at the very least, it's demeaning.

So, should stress interviews be used? Should interviewers be permitted to assess professionalism and confidence and how one reacts to the everyday nuisances of work by putting applicants into a confrontational scenario? Does getting angry in an interview when pressured indicate one's propensity towards violence should things not always go smoothly at work? Should HRM advocate the use of an activity that could possibly get out of control? What's your opinion?

Source: Based on Stephen M. Pollan and Mark Levine, "How to Ace a Tough Interview," *Working Woman* (July 1994) p. 49.

The Effectiveness of Interviews

Wouldn't it be nice if all interviews were as clear-cut as the following:[31]

After several minutes in an interview, the job applicant interrupted the recruiter and asked what the IBM in the company name stood for.

Another applicant, when asked why he wanted to work for the major bank to which he was applying, responded that he didn't know because he would really prefer to work for the bank's competitor which was much closer to his home.

A third applicant, in response to a question why he was applying for a job in a trust company, simply stated that it was because the job was available.

Unfortunately for recruiters, situations aren't always this cut and dried. Rather, many other factors enter into the deliberation in determining if a candidate is a good fit for the organization.[32] Although interviews are part of every job search process, summaries of research on interviewing have concluded that the reliability and validity of interviews are generally low.[33] Despite their popularity (as mentioned in Chapter 6, practically all Canadian companies use interviews as part of the selection process[34]), interviews are expensive, inefficient, and usually not job-related.[35]

More specifically, a review of the research has generated the following conclusions:[36]

1. Prior knowledge about the applicant can bias the interviewer's evaluation.
2. The interviewer often holds a stereotype of what represents a "good" applicant.
3. The interviewer often tends to favour applicants who share his or her own attitudes.
4. The order in which applicants are interviewed often influences evaluations.
5. The order in which information is elicited influences evaluations.
6. Negative information is given unduly high weight.
7. The interviewer may make a decision as to the applicant's suitability in the first few minutes of the interview.
8. The interviewer may forget much of the interview's content within minutes after its conclusion.
9. Structured and well-organized interviews are more reliable.
10. The interview is most valid in determining an applicant's organizational fit, level of motivation, and interpersonal skills.

These conclusions, generated over the past few decades, still hold true today. Let's elaborate on a few of them.

When an interviewer has already seen the candidate's résumé, application form, test scores, or appraisals of other interviewers, bias may be introduced, and the interviewer no longer relies on the data gained in the interview alone. Based on the data received prior to the interview, an image of the applicant is created. Much of the early part of the interview, then, becomes an exercise wherein the interviewer compares the actual applicant with the image formed earlier.

For example, a classic study of interviewer stereotyping focused on the Canadian Army.[37] In this study, it was concluded that army interviewers developed a stereotype of what a good job applicant was. This was not an individual bias but one that was shared by all interviewers who had a reasonable amount of experience and who operated in a similar environment. This stereotype changed very little during the interview, and, in fact, most interviewer decisions changed very little during the interview. Based on this research, which appears to be still valid today, a "good applicant" is probably characterized more by the absence of unfavourable characteristics than by the presence of favourable ones.[38] Thus, negative information in an interview has a greater impact on assessment of evaluations than does positive information. This is of some concern today when the Canadian Forces have embarked on a serious process of modifying the gender balance of the officer corps. Interviewers must be trained so that they do not see a female officer's gender as negative because it is different from "the way things used to be."

In addition to interviewer bias is something that is directly related to the applicant's actions. This is referred to as impression management which, quite simply, is the interviewee's attempt to project an image that will result in receiving a favourable outcome.[39] Thus, if an applicant can say or do something that is viewed favourably by the interviewer, then that person may be viewed more favourably for the position. For example, suppose you find out that the interviewer values workers who can work seven days a week, twelve-plus hours a day, if needed. Understandably, few, if any, workers can sustain this work schedule over a long period of time, but that's the interviewer's view nonetheless. Accordingly, making statements of being a workaholic, which conforms to this interviewer's values, may result in creating a positive impression.

Interviewers have a remarkably short and inaccurate memory. For example, in one study of an interview simulation, a twenty-minute videotape of a selection interview was played for a group of forty managers following which the managers were given a twenty-question test. Although all the questions were straightforward and factual, the average number of wrong answers was ten. The researchers' conclusion was that even in a short interview, the average manager remembers only half of the information.[40] Taking notes during an interview has been shown to reduce memory loss.[41] Note taking is also useful—albeit possibly disconcerting for the interviewee—for getting more accurate information and for developing a clearer understanding of the applicant's fit by allowing follow-up questions to be asked. An alternative approach is to tape-record each interview.[42] Recruiters have found that by taping the interview, better, more thorough responses are elicited. Furthermore, taping the interview serves as one means of showing that all candidates were given equal treatment. Of course, a recruiter cannot record the interview without the permission of the applicant.

Evidence lends strong support to the view that structured interviews are more reliable and valid than unstructured ones.[43] When two interviewers are allowed to use their own idiosyncratic pattern for questions and evaluation, they will frequently arrive at two different decisions. This happens, in part, because a different set of questions will elicit different information from the same applicant. Unstructured interviews thus make for very low inter-interviewer reliability. It is encouraging to report that a survey of Canadian organizations in 1997 revealed that 94 per cent of companies with more than 500 employees used structured interviews. Unfortunately, smaller companies are more likely to use unstructured interviews, particularly if they have no human resources professional on staff.[44]

Another research finding points out that the interview offers the greatest value as a selection device in determining an applicant's organizational fit, level of motivation, and interpersonal skills.[45] This is particularly true of senior management positions. Accordingly, it is not unlikely for candidates for these positions to go through many extensive interviews with executive recruiters, company executives, and even board members before a final decision is made. Similarly, where teams have the responsibility to hire their own members, it is commonplace for each team member to interview the applicant.

One final issue about interviews revolves around when the interviewer actually makes the decision. Early studies, like the Canadian army example, indicated that interviewers made their choice to hire or not to hire a candidate

Impression Management Influencing the interview by portraying an image that is desired by the interviewer.

Structured Interview An interview in which there are fixed questions that are presented to every applicant.

Interviewing Job Candidates

1. **Obtain detailed information about the job for which applicants are being interviewed.** When you are provided with a substantial amount of information about the job, you rely primarily on job-relevant factors in making selection decisions. When such information is unavailable, you may tend to rely more on factors less relevant to the job, allowing bias to enter into the assessment. Therefore, at a minimum, you should have a copy of a recent position description as an information source. You are now ready to structure the interview.

2. **Structure the interview so that it follows a set procedure**. Reliability is increased when the interview is designed around a constant structure. A fixed set of questions should be presented to every applicant. In the trade-off between structure and consistency versus non-structure and flexibility, structure and consistency have proved to be of greater value for selection purposes. The structured interview also aids you in comparing all candidates' answers to like questions.

3. **Review the candidate's application form and/or résumé**. This step helps you to create a more complete picture of the applicant in terms of the information on the résumé/application and what the job requires (from Step 1). This will help you to identify specific areas that need to be explored in the interview. For example, areas not clearly defined on the résumé but essential for job success become a focal point for interview discussion.

4. **Put the applicant at ease**. Assume the applicant will be nervous. Putting the interviewee at ease is essential if you are to obtain the kind of information you will need. Introduce yourself, and open with some small talk about the weather, the traffic, etc. But be careful: Don't venture into illegal areas with small talk about the applicant's family. Keep it impersonal!

5. **Ask your questions**. The questions you are asking should be designed to make applicants provide detailed descriptions of their actual job behaviours. You want to elicit concrete examples of how the applicant demonstrates certain behaviours that are necessary for successful performance on the job for which the interview is being held. If you are unsatisfied with the applicant's response, probe deeper to seek elaboration. The key here is to let the applicant talk. A big mistake is to do most of the talking yourself. During this part of the interview, take notes, because people tend to forget what was actually said. This will lead to increased accuracy in evaluation.

6. **Conclude the interview**. Let the applicant know that all of your questioning is finished. Summarize what you have heard from the applicant, and give him or her an opportunity to correct anything that is unclear or discuss anything that you may have not addressed in the interview. Inform the applicant what will happen next in the process and when he or she can expect to hear from you.

7. **Complete a post-interview evaluation form**. Along with a structured format should go a standardized evaluation form. You should complete this form item by item shortly after the interview while the information is still fresh in your mind. The information on this evaluation can then be summarized into an overall rating or impression for the candidate. This approach increases the likelihood that the same frame of reference will be applied to each applicant.

within the first few minutes of the interview. While that belief was widely held, subsequent research does not support these findings.[46] In fact, this research identified that initial impressions may have little effect unless that is the only information available for an interviewer to use.

The behaviour-based interview is based on the development of a competency profile based on the behaviours necessary to be successful at the job that is being filled and training the people involved in the selection process in the appropriate techniques. One Canadian company that applied this technique in their campus interviewing for engineers reported a saving of $500,000 in three years, resulting from lower turnover, lower training costs, and a better fit of their new engineers with the company.[47] This type of interview is used increasingly in Canada with 58 per cent of companies with over 500 employees claiming to use it.[48]

Two types of behaviour-based interviews worth mentioning are the situational interview and the behavioural interview. In the situational interview, the applicant is presented with a hypothetical situation and asked how she or he would deal with it. In the behavioural description interview (BDI), the focus is on real work incidents: the applicant is asked what she or he actually did. For example, a candidate for a management position could be asked "what did you do to implement budget cuts in your unit?" In both types of interview, it is important that the situations, whether hypothetical or real, be relevant for the position under consideration. This is best achieved through job analysis. And it should also be clear that these are structured interviews—all applicants would be queried about the same situations.

So what sense can we make of these issues raised about interviews and where might interviews be most appropriate? If interviews continue to have a place in the selection decision, they probably will be more appropriate for the high-turnover jobs and the less routine ones like middle- and upper-level managerial positions. In jobs where these characteristics are important in determining success, the interview can be a valuable selection input. In non-routine activities, especially senior managerial positions, failure (as measured by voluntary terminations) is more frequently caused by a poor fit between the individual and the organization than by lack of competence on the part of the individual.[49] Interviewing can be useful, therefore, when it emphasizes the candidate's ability to fit into the organization rather than specific technical skills.

Interviewing: An Interviewer's Perspective

The differences we have described may seem to cast a dark cloud over the interview, but the interview is far from worthless. It can help us to better assess the candidate as well as be a valuable vehicle for relaying information to prospective employees.

For anyone who interviews prospective job candidates, whether as a recruiter in HRM or in any other capacity, there are several suggestions we can offer for improving the effectiveness of interviews (see "HRM Skills: Interviewing Job Candidates" on page 216).

Interviewing: A Candidate's Perspective—The Realistic Job Preview

Clara Stevens was a recent graduate of Saint Mary's University's MBA program. During the recruiting process with one company, the aspiring marketing manager was guaranteed that she would be closely involved in the company's annual sales meeting, working with several key decision makers in the market-

Behaviour-Based Interview A type of structured interview that is based on inquiring about actual behaviours needed on the job.

Situational Interview Structured interview designed to see how the applicants handle themselves under pressure.

Behavioural Description Interview (BDI) A type of structured interview in which the interviewee is asked questions about what he or she actually did in specific work-related situations.

Realistic Job Preview (RJP) A selection device that allows job candidates to learn negative as well as positive information about the job and organization.

ing division. Impressed by the thought of having an active part in the meeting, the job offer seemed very appealing. She accepted the job and within weeks was actively involved in the sales meetings. She saw to it that coffee was available for both morning and afternoon breaks and made several trips a day to local businesses to pick up audio-visual equipment. This, she was told, was the involvement she had been promised. Clara quit in frustration.

The primary purpose of selection devices is to identify individuals who will be effective performers, but it is not in management's best interest to find good prospects, hire them, and then have them leave the organization. Therefore, part of selection should be concerned with reducing voluntary turnover and its associated costs.[50] One device to achieve that goal is the **realistic job preview (RJP)** which may include brochures, films, plant tours, work sampling, or merely a short script made up of realistic statements that portray the job accurately. The key element in RJP is that negative as well as positive information about the job is shared. While the RJP is not normally treated as a selection device, it does take place during the interview, and it has demonstrated effectiveness as a method for increasing job survival among new employees. That is why it was included here.

During the selection process, every applicant acquires a set of expectations about the organization and about the specific job the applicant is hoping to be offered. It is not unusual for these expectations to be excessively inflated as a result of receiving almost uniformly positive information about the organization and job during recruitment and selection activities.[51] Evidence suggests, however, that managers may be erring by giving applicants only favourable information. More specifically, research leads us to conclude that applicants who have been given a realistic job preview (as well as a realistic preview of the organization) hold lower and more realistic expectations about the job they will be doing and are better prepared for coping with the job and its frustrating elements.

Realistic job previews also appear to work best for those jobs that are more attractive to the individual, resulting in lower turnover rates. Most studies demonstrate that giving candidates a realistic job preview before offering them the job reduces turnover without lowering the acceptance rates.[52] Of course, it is not unreasonable to suggest that exposing an applicant to RJP may also result in the hiring of a more committed individual.

Background Investigation

Background investigations are intended to verify that the information on the application form is correct and accurate. And while the chief means of verifying that data is reference checks, HRM has witnessed significant changes in this area. For instance, by the late 1980s, organizations began questioning how much information should be given to another employer. These questions arose over the fear of being sued for giving information that had a negative effect on an individual's employment prospects elsewhere. The result was that as employee privacy rights issues began to hit the courts, employers all but stopped giving any references, positive or negative.

Since then, and as a result of companies being held liable for the actions of their employees,[53] courts have changed their judgements about background investigations and related employee privacy issues. Companies are more concerned than they used to be about the possible behaviours of prospective employees. There is evidence to support the premise that an individual's past be-haviour is a good predictor of his or her future behaviour,[54] as well as data that suggests that as many as one-third of all applicants exaggerate their background or experience.[55] Accordingly, companies must assess the liability that potential employees create, and delve into their backgrounds in as much depth as is nec-essary to limit the risk.[56] For example, local school boards must go to great lengths to ensure that potential teachers do not pose a risk to children. Similarly, hospitals need to feel confident that the staff they hire is drug-free. Should an unfortunate event occur, the courts will come down hard on an orga-nization that did not exercise due care in the selection process.

In conducting a background investigation, two methods can be used: the in-ternal and the external investigation. In the internal investigation, HRM ques-tions former employers and personal references, and possibly examines credit sources. This viable option is commonly used, but the investigation must be thorough or little useful information will be found. On the other hand, the ex-ternal investigation generally involves using a reference checking firm[57] which costs more, but such firms have a better track record of gathering pertinent in-formation and are better informed on privacy rights issues.[58] However it is done, documentation is essential.[59] Should an employer be called upon to jus-tify what has or has not been found, supporting documentation is invaluable.

As an example of external investigation, in 1997, the Protestant School Board of Greater Montreal (Since dissolved as Quebec's school boards were reorga-nized along linguistic rather than—religious lines.) started requiring all new personnel, including teachers, to be screened by the Montreal Urban Community Police (MUCP). The school board wished to maintain the confi-dentiality of such information, so rather than conduct the investigation or store the reports itself, the board required prospective employees to sign a consent form allowing the MUCP to search data banks including its own and those of the RCMP, the Sûreté de Québec, the Quebec Automobile Insurance Board, and the Montreal courthouse. The MUCP kept the information confidential, sending the board a letter stating simply that the candidate is "recommended" or "not recommended."[60] If necessary, the supporting documentation would be available from the MUCP.

Sources	Recommended actions
Education	Verify dates of enrolment, diplomas, or degrees obtained.
Former employers	Verify dates stated on application or résumé. Verify whether former employers are prepared to rehire the person.
References	Verify relationship to applicant (personal relationships do not make good references: they tend to see only positive aspects; former supervisors are preferable). Probe, especially if the reference is lukewarm or appears to be ducking questions. Ask the reference to compare the applicant with other people he or she has known in similar situations. Check with other references, particularly if there are negative comments or conflicting viewpoints.
Credit, criminal records, etc.	Only if relevant—best handled by specialized agencies. Note that human rights legislation limits this type of probe.

Figure 7-5
The Background Check

The need for background checks was dramatically highlighted in June 1998 when it was revealed that a man who had not graduated from medical school had used forged transcripts to obtain a Michigan medical licence and surgical residences in Ohio, Michigan, and London, Ontario. He was caught because a background check of his application to membership in a Michigan surgical practice revealed that his claims to have graduated from Rush University Medical College and Loyola University (both in Chicago) were false.[61] While extreme, this case points to a problem that is not all that unusual. In a survey of 400 résumés, Mississauga-based reference checking firm InfoCheck found that 23.5 per cent of the candidates had lied about either their educational attainments, professional affiliations, or job performance.[62] Figure 7-5 lists some questions that should be asked when doing the background check.

Medical/Physical Examinations

A medical exam can only be demanded for jobs that require certain physical characteristics which includes a very small proportion of jobs today. Should a medical clearance be required to indicate that the applicant is physically fit for the essential job elements, a company must be able to show that it is a job-related requirement. Failure to do so may result in the physical examination creating an adverse impact. Also, the company must keep in mind that it may not discriminate against the disabled. Thus, even a valid physical examination may only be required after a conditional job offer. Having a physical disability may not be enough to exclude an individual from the job. As we mentioned in Chapter 3, companies must make reasonable accommodations for these individuals.

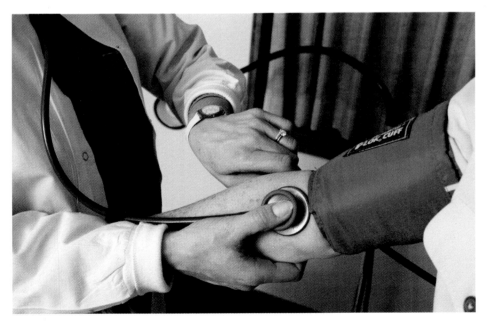

Medical exams cannot be demanded for the vast majority of jobs today. To require such an exam, the company must be able to demonstrate clearly that physical fitness, for example, is a job-related requirement.

Selection for Self-Managed Teams

Much of the discussion about selection devices throughout the past two chapters has assumed one fact: that somewhere in HRM lies the responsibility for the selection process. Today, however, that may not always be the case. Many companies are implementing team approaches in all or part of their operations, as in the Ford Motor Company of Canada's Windsor Engine Plant. Such organizations empower their employees to take responsibility for the day-to-day functions in their areas. Accordingly, these employees may now work without direct supervision and take on some or all of the management responsibilities that were once the province of first-line supervisors'.[63] One aspect of this change has been a more active role in the hiring of co-workers.[64] In the case of Ford Canada, this has required some interesting adjustments, since the position of supervisor (a non-union position) has been abolished and in its place the team has a team leader who is a union member like the rest of the team.[65] The selection of workers is now no longer a management prerogative but a decision made entirely by union members.

Do you remember a time when you took a course that required a group project? How was your team formed? Did the professor assign you to a group, or were you permitted to form the group yourself? Assuming your professor permitted you to select your own group, what did you look for in a potential group member? Was it students who shared your values in getting the work done, on time, and of a high quality? Or was it those who you knew would pull their own weight and not let one or two in the group do all of the work? Well, that's the same premise behind the selection by self-managed work teams. In any organization, a critical link to success is how well employees perform their jobs. It is also understood that when those jobs require the interaction of several individuals, it takes time for the team to come together as a unified unit.[66] How long that takes depends on how the team views its goals and priorities and how open and trusting group members are. What better way to begin this team building than to have the people involved actually make the hiring decision?

When workers are empowered to hire their co-workers, they bring varied experiences and backgrounds to the selection process. This enables them to "better assess applicants' skills in their field of expertise."[67] Just like you in your class project, they, also want to hire someone they can count on, who will perform his or her duties, and not let the others down. This means that they will focus their attention on the duties of the job due and on those special skills and qualifications needed to be successful. From our previous discussion of validation (Chapter 6), we have seen that that's precisely the focus of the selection process. In this case, a more objective evaluation may be obtained.

That is not to say that self-managed work teams choosing new employees are not without problems. If these workers are unfamiliar with proper interviewing techniques or the legal ramifications of their hiring decisions, they, too, could experience many of the difficulties often associated with interviews and with the selection process as a whole.

Study Tools and Applications

Summary

This summary relates to the Learning Objectives provided on p. 197.
After reading this chapter, you should know:

1. Selection devices provide managers with information that will help them predict whether an applicant will prove to be a successful job performer.
2. The application form is an effective way of getting hard biographical data that can ultimately be verified.
3. Weighted applications blanks are useful in that through statistical techniques, the links between certain relevant information and job success can be determined and the information used in selection decisions.
4. Performance simulation tests require the applicant to engage in specific behaviours that have been demonstrated to be job-related. Work sampling and the assessment centre, which are performance simulations, receive high marks for their predictive capability.
5. Assessment centres are a type of performance simulation test. They are carried out over a period of a few days with a number of observers studying how the individuals handle or react to various business situations.
6. There are several techniques that are popular in certain sectors but whose validity is questioned: graphology (handwriting analysis), polygraph testing (the lie detector) and paper-and-pencil honesty testing.
7. Interviews consistently achieve low marks for reliability and validity, but this has more to do with interviewer problems than with the interview itself. Interviewing validity can be enhanced by using a structured process.
8. Realistic job previews reduce turnover by giving the applicant both positive and negative information about the job.
9. Background investigations are valuable when they verify hard data from the application, but they tend to have little practical value as a predictive selection device.
10. Medical/physical examinations are valid when certain physical characteristics are essential to be able to perform a job. Such examinations are usually given after a conditional job offer is made.

Key Terms

application form
assessment centres
behavioural description interview
behaviour-based interview
employment test
graphology
impression management
interview

performance simulation tests
realistic job preview (RJP)
situational interview
stress interview
structured interview
weighted application blank (WAB)
work sampling
written test

EXPERIENTIAL EXERCISE:

The Awful Interview[68]

Purpose

1. To practise interviewing skills especially in dealing with difficult interview questions frequently asked by interviewers.
2. To sharpen your awareness of your strengths and weaknesses in interviewing for a job.

Advanced Preparation

Read the Introduction below, and think about some good questions that might be included in the list in Step 1. If you can't think of good, mind-boggling questions, ask friends who have some experience in job interviews.

Group Size:	*Trios or quartets.*
Time Required:	*1-1/4 hours (trios), 1-1/2 hours (quartets).*
Special Physical Requirements:	*Small meeting rooms or an area suitable for holding conversations relatively free of distractions.*

Introduction

Employment interviews are frequently traumatic experiences; interviewers know what they are looking for, and you don't. They are prepared, and you are not. They are relaxed, and you are tense. It seems that the cards are all stacked in the interviewer's favour. Interviewers are also notorious for asking disconcerting questions: "Tell me about your goals in life." "Why do you want to work for International Widgets?" If you answered such questions candidly but right off the top of your head, you might never get a job. ("My only goal is to get a job so I can begin to find out whether I really like it," or "I want to work for International Widgets because I don't have any other good prospects right now.")

If you have been confronted with questions such as these, you will understand why we have titled this exercise "The Awful Interview." You don't have to let interviewers catch you by surprise. This exercise is based on the assumption that practice can help you prepare for interview situations. We will also assume that honesty really is the best policy. The job hunter who concentrates on giving a prospective employer the impression that she or he is just the person wanted is employing a defensive strategy. You may become so preoccupied with projecting an "image" that you will have little energy left for the real problem of showing the interviewer what careful thought you have given to planning your career.

Procedure

Step 1: 15 minutes

The entire group will develop and list the ten most awful questions one can be asked in a job interview. An "awful" question is one that you would find threatening or difficult to answer honestly in a job interview. List only serious questions that have actually been asked in job interviews you or somebody else has experienced.

Step 2: 5 minutes

The group leader will specify whether the total group should break into smaller groups of threes or fours. Choose people with whom you will be comfortable—people who can be most helpful in providing useful feedback on your interviewing style. When the groups are formed, the group leader will tell you where you are to hold your small group meetings.

Step 3: 45 to 60 minutes

Meet with your trio or quartet. Proceed as follows: One member volunteers to answer the first question while another is chosen to ask the question. Choosing a question from the list of the ten, the interrogator asks the first question, and the interviewee must try to answer it as truthfully and honestly as he or she can. After the answer, other members of the group provide feedback to the interviewee about the answer just given. Upon completion of the feedback, the interviewee becomes the interrogator, chooses a question and a new interviewee, and a new round begins. Continue taking turns until each person has answered at least three questions, or until you are instructed by the group leader to stop.

Step 4: 10 minutes

Take ten minutes and write a brief note to yourself covering the following (this note is for you alone—nobody else will see it): What questions did I handle well? What were my strengths? What questions did I handle poorly? What questions asked of others would give me problems? What can I do to deal more effectively with the questions that give me problems?

Step 5:

Reconvene with the entire group for discussion of the exercise.

Discussion Questions

1. What did you learn during the exercise about how to answer interviewer's questions more effectively?
2. Do you think the interviewers got valid data in the interview? Why?
3. If you were an interviewer, what kinds of questions would you ask?

CASE APPLICATION:

Applied Computer Technology

Cindy Koehler is a true entrepreneur.[69] She had a vision of building a successful company. She wanted to pursue her own interests and fulfil a special dream she had, so she took some bold steps, accepted the risk, and ventured into business, starting a computer manufacturing company—Applied Computer Technology.

Early in the start-up, Cindy made it a practice to hire family and friends. Her selection criterion was that these people wanted to help and she needed some workers, so on the payroll they went. But before too long, problems erupted. When certain activities were needed, sometimes in a rush, some of her employees couldn't get the work done. It appeared that sometimes they just weren't at work—they had left early or worse, just decided to take the day off without any notice. Compounding the problem was the realization that Koehler didn't feel comfortable expressing her displeasure to her employees; after all, she had a personal relationship with them. She didn't want to hurt anyone's feelings, but the problems got so far out of control that they were threatening her vision of building a successful company. Consequently, Cindy cracked down on her less-than-committed workforce. As a result, several friends quit, and the relationship between Cindy and some of her family and friends was, at best, strained.

Although Cindy Koehler has learned a hard lesson, she knows now what went wrong. Simply stated, she mixed business and friendship. Those two are often in conflict, especially in the selection process.
How well did you fulfil the learning objectives?

Questions:

1. In terms of the selection process, where did Cindy Koehler go wrong? What would you recommend she do to correct the problems she experienced?
2. In a small business, it is not uncommon for family and friends to be employees, but no organization can afford to experience what Koehler did. Assuming that family and

friends are going to be hired, what would you recommend an entrepreneur do to prevent another Applied Computer Technology hiring fiasco?

3. How could a realistic job preview have been used to the benefit of both Cindy and her family and friends? Explain.

Testing Your Understanding

How well did you fulfil the learning objectives?

1. A director of selection at a large manufacturing firm is reviewing the selection techniques used by three engineering specialist interviewers. One relies solely on the interview but does not thoroughly read the application form and never does a background check. The second does not trust the reliability of interviews and conducts extensive background checks on each applicant. The third looks for related work experiences on the application form and asks each applicant to bring a portfolio of current work samples (diagrams, designs, etc.) to the interview. The director concludes:
   a. Interviewers one and two are better than interviewer three because they rely on one selection device.
   b. Interviewer three does not assess past or current work-related behaviours.
   c. The three interviewers all perform roughly equivalent processes.
   d. Each interviewee should be seen by all three interviewers to improve the quality of the interview process.
   e. A selection test should be written and added to the devices used.

2. A director of selection for a large manufacturing organization wants to weight application forms for employees in the new robotics plant. That plant, scheduled to open in eighteen months, will utilize new technology that will create substantially different job requirements than any existing organizational jobs. How should the director proceed?
   a. Delay the opening of the plant until a weighted application blank is developed for current jobs in the robotics plant.
   b. Wait until the plant has been opened a year, then examine the application forms for good and poor workers to identify patterns of differences.
   c. Hire a consultant to conduct the analysis and submit a report on the reliability of weighted application forms.
   d. Examine work records from good and poor performers over the past five years. Identify differences in application form items.
   e. A weighted application form is inappropriate for a robotics plant. They work only in the sales and financial areas of a company where hard biographical data are more readily available.

3. University professors interviewing for jobs at a large university in the Atlantic provinces are asked to prepare and deliver a "class" for selected students. Given this information, which one of the following statements is most correct?
   a. This is an example of an in-basket simulation. It is unique to hiring faculty in universities.
   b. The class session is a type of work sampling at least for the teaching part of the job.
   c. The "class" is representative of an assessment centre for new faculty to determine the new member's rank.
   d. The "class" is part of the interviewing process used to determine attainment of technical degree.
   e. The "class" is an a typical feedback test.

4. As part of the selection process, a day care centre in Winnipeg has each applicant come to work for a day before final hiring decisions are made. Why?
   a. The management has a chance to evaluate the hands-on capabilities of each applicant.
   b. The organization is understaffed. This system provides free help.
   c. The *Manitoba Employment Standards Act* requires this for all childcare providers.
   d. This process takes less time than a real interview.
   e. Workdays have replaced background checking in most childcare organizations.

5. How do employment tests differ from performance simulation tests?
   a. Employment tests are conducted before hiring decisions are made. Performance simulation tests are conducted after hiring decisions are made.
   b. Employment tests are conducted after hiring decisions are made. Performance simulation tests are conducted before hiring decisions are made.
   c. Performance simulation tests are pencil and paper exercises. Employment tests are measured by manager observation.
   d. Performance simulation tests have high content validity. Employment tests may also have construct validity.
   e. Employment tests are more expensive than performance simulation tests.

6. What is the difference between work sampling and assessment centres?
   a. Work sampling is another term used to describe the assessment centre.

b. Work sampling is a type of employment test. Assessment centres are a performance evaluation technique.

c. Work sampling procedures usually have fewer evaluators than assessment centres.

d. Assessment centres usually take less time to conduct than work sampling procedures.

e. Assessment centres are usually done for blue-collar work. Work sampling procedures are conducted for managerial job candidates.

7. Jason interviews candidates for technical consultant positions in a large aerospace manufacturing firm. He was trained to do this last year because of his extensive technical background and job knowledge. At the end of a typical day, he will have interviewed eight to ten people, asking them all the same questions, in the same order. At 4:00 p.m., he fills out standard forms for each person and forwards his recommendations to corporate headquarters. He complains that he makes mistakes and can't really remember facts and details about his candidates while completing the evaluation forms. What should be done to make Jason's interviews more effective?

a. Nothing can be done. Interviews are not effective predictors of successful job performance.

b. Jason should ask a different set of questions with each applicant.

c. Jason should conduct no more than four interviews per day.

d. Jason should learn some memory-enhancing techniques.

e. Jason should complete the forms after each interview.

8. What could have been done differently in the case of Clara Stevens, the Saint Mary's graduate who quit her job because she had to get coffee and run errands during her first annual sales meeting?

a. The interviewer should have offered Clara coffee during the interview process to model appropriate behaviour.

b. The company should have offered Clara more money to help ease the burden of performing routine tasks.

c. The interviewer should have told Clara that the early part of her assignment would include menial tasks.

d. The interviewer should have been honest with Clara and told her that the firm did not have a job suitable for someone with her credentials.

e. The company should have reviewed all of its job descriptions.

9. Realistic job previews are fine, but what do you do when you have a job that no one wants? Tom had been interviewing for more than a year for the position of manager in his south-eastern furniture manu-

facturing plant. The hours would be long. The workers were underskilled and unwilling to work. The plant was old, with inefficient and unsafe machinery. Tom spoke frankly to the 120 prospective managers he interviewed. No one accepted the job.

a. Tom should consider job redesign or plant relocation. The problem in this case is not with interviewing techniques.

b. Tom should hire a consultant to teach him how to present a realistic job preview in more favourable terms.

c. Tom should keep interviewing. The right person who is dedicated and seeking a challenge will turn up.

d. Tom should raise the salary offered.

e. Tom should let someone else do the interviewing.

10. A vice-president of human resources for a large manufacturing organization wants to start a background investigation process on all new employees in her company who have access to financial information or funding, such as accountants. How should she proceed?

a. Begin a policy of credit checking for new employees.

b. Call former employers of potential employees.

c. Be suspicious of any employee who has held more than two jobs in any five-year period. Hire a professional to follow such an individual for a period of time before hiring.

d. Give candidates polygraph tests.

e. Hire an external investigator for a more thorough job than could be done internally.

11. Don is interviewing Sandy, who is confined to a wheelchair, for a secretarial position in his company. She has passed the usual selection criteria—the employment test, the background check, and all interviews. What should Don do?

a. Have Sandy take a physical examination before hiring her.

b. Recommend that Sandy be hired if she can supply a desk/chair arrangement that would be suitable.

c. Recommend that Sandy be hired.

d. Conduct more interviews with Sandy.

e. Interview employees who would have to work with Sandy.

12. A vice-president of human resources wants to exclude physical examinations from the selection process because in the past year, his firm has been sued four times because of them. However, most jobs in the machine shop require moving heavy, sensitive machines. What else can the organization do to protect its equipment investment?

a. Perform a thorough background check.

b. Add weighted items to the application form about health club memberships.

c. Close the production facility.

d. Initiate a work sampling procedure for the jobs in question.

e. Ask applicants about their physical abilities during the intensive interview.

13. Biographical data on job application forms
    a. is illegal under human rights legislation.
    b. is often a good predictor of future job success.
    c. is seldom a good predictor of future job success.
    d. is useful only to identify mental lapses indicated by large time periods between jobs.
    e. is standardized across all Canadian organizations.

14. How do organizations use application forms since equity legislation was introduced and conditioned their contents?
    a. They have no real use. In fact, most companies are eliminating application forms.
    b. They are used to avoid adverse impact.
    c. Validated information, such as class standing, can be a good predictor of job success.
    d. They are used to document compliance with equal rights legislation.
    e. They are used to validate compliance with employment equity legislation.

15. All of these statements are true about assessment centres except
    a. personality tests may be included in the assessment.
    b. groups of applicants are evaluated together.
    c. applicants may be asked to solve day-to-day problems that managers find in their in baskets.
    d. the most important element is the leaderless group discussion.
    e. evaluation is done by groups of assessors.

16. According to the text, graphology is
    a. not recommended for use. There is little evidence to support its use as a selection technique.
    b. recommended for checking educational level.
    c. recommended for validating job skills.
    d. recommended for identifying personality defects.
    e. recommended for job analysis.

17. Art runs a chain of convenience stores on the Prairies. He could have used all of the following to try to find honest employees for his night clerk jobs except
    a. reference checking.
    b. intelligence testing.
    c. honesty tests.
    d. credit and references checking.
    e. background investigation.

18. Why do realistic job previews result in lower turnover rates?
    a. When unfavourable information is disclosed, most candidates are no longer interested, so fewer job offers are made.
    b. They do not result in lower turnover rates.
    c. Providing unfavourable as well as favourable information about a job helps people brace themselves for the realities of work. When new employees find out the job is not all bad, they are less inclined to voluntarily resign.
    d. Training that provides new employees with coping skills helps to reduce turnover.
    e. More committed employees are hired.

Chapter Eight

EMPLOYEE ORIENTATION

LEARNING OBJECTIVES

AFTER READING THIS CHAPTER, YOU WILL BE ABLE TO:

1. Define socialization.
2. Identify the three stages of employee socialization.
3. Describe what is meant by the outsider–insider passage.
4. Explain the purpose of orientation programs.
5. Discuss how organizational socialization conveys the organization's culture.
6. Identify the critical theme of socializing new employees.
7. Explain the role of the CEO in orientation.
8. Describe HRM's role in orientation.
9. Discuss the supervisors' role in the socialization process.
10. Describe a sample orientation program.

Can you remember your first day of work at a new company? If so, what are your predominant feelings about those experiences? We would confidently predict two things about your answer to these questions. First, that for many of you, your first day of work is still quite a sharp memory, however long ago it took place and second, that your feelings about that day depend on the way you were introduced into your new position. If you had a good experience of being invited to be a valued part of your new organization, the positive effects of that treatment stayed with you for a long time. On the other hand, a bad initial experience may have coloured your perceptions for your entire time at the organization. The following illustrates one of our own experiences:[1]

> On my first day of work, I pulled into the parking area I had used a number of times while interviewing for my new job. I was just locking the car when a security guard came up and, after discovering that I was a new junior employee, summarily kicked me out of the "management" parking area. Feeling about a centimetre tall, I slunk out of the lot, noticing a group of employees all lined up together at the windows, laughing at my predicament. I later discovered that checking on the arrival of rookies was the entertainment for the month among the front-office employees, but the effects of my humiliation affected my relationships with the company and my colleagues right up to the point when I left the organization two years later.

Such incidents seem relatively minor, but they can have devastating effects on employees, affecting both the likelihood of their staying with an organization (most turnovers occur in the first few months of a new appointment) and their likely success in a new position. The effects are felt particularly among younger or more vulnerable employees who do not have a track record of success upon which to base a healthy sense of self-esteem. Thus, it is critical for HRM to have professional orientation programs in which employees are smoothly inducted into new organizations and new positions. To emphasize the importance of orientation, we often refer to it as *managing the joining-up process.*

Note that orientation flows directly out of employee selection discussed in the previous chapter. In fact, the orientation process actually begins during the selection process. Executive recruiters know this is particularly important in the successful placement of senior-level employees. Gerlinde Hermann, president of the Hermann Group, stresses that successful orientation begins even before the right candidate is chosen. "We spend a large amount of time with the client first to get an idea of what the company is like, what the style is like, and what kind of individual would have the probability of being successful."[2] The close link between selection and orientation was noted in our discussion of the realistic job preview (RJP) in the previous chapter. The power of the RJP is that it puts employees into the situation of someone actually doing a new job even before they start. The use of RJPs can greatly increase the effectiveness of orientation programs.

Orientation programs are designed to help employees fully understand what working in the organization is all about. Their intent is to help employees successfully learn the ropes of their new jobs. From the company's point of view, this is important because it means that people know and accept the behaviour that the organization views as desirable. And if you don't think that is important, consider this: It is estimated that the average costs of recruiting and selecting for an entry-level position average is $6,000,[3] and that quickly escalates to tens of thousands for more senior employees. Furthermore, more than half of all those hired will resign within the first seven months.[4] Consequently, HRM must ensure that the goals of both recruitment and selection are met and then help these new employees learn what is important in the organization. In this chapter, we will show how employees are socialized into their job environments and the ways that HRM can influence the socialization process.

Much of the discussion in this chapter will refer to larger organizations which can afford formal orientation programs. But orientation is just as important to smaller companies, particularly since it is often the responsibility of the senior manager or owner. In all companies, effective orientation programs increase significantly the likelihood of employees offering their best to the organization.

The Outsider–Insider Passage

Socialization A process of adaption that takes place as individuals attempt to learn the values and norms of work roles.

Socialization is a process of adaptation. In the context of organizations, the term refers to all passages undergone by employees. For instance, when you begin a new job, accept a lateral transfer, or get a promotion, you are required to make adjustments. You must adapt to a new environment—different work activities, a new boss, a different, and most likely diverse group of co-workers, and probably a different, set of standards for what constitutes good performance.[5] Although, as we noted in opening this chapter, we recognize that this socialization will go on throughout our careers—within as well as between organizations—the most profound adjustment occurs when we make the first move into an organization: the move from being an outsider to being an insider. We now turn to a discussion of the outsider-insider passage or what is more appropriately labelled organization-entry socialization.

Your first day on the job makes a lasting impression which is why it is critical for HRM to have professional orientation programs.

Socialization

Do you remember your first day in university, college, or perhaps even high school? What feelings did you experience? Anxiety over new expectations? Uncertainty over what was to come? Excitement at being on your own and experiencing new things? Fear based on all those things friends said about how tough the courses were? Stress over what classes to take and what teachers you'll get? Well, you probably experienced many of these things. As the chapter's opening example demonstrates, entry into a job is no different. For organizations to assist in the adjustment process, a few things must be understood. We'll call these the assumptions of employee socialization.[6]

The Assumptions of Employee Socialization

Several assumptions underlie the process of socialization. The first is that socialization strongly influences employee performance and organizational stability. Second, organizational stability is increased through socialization. Also, new members suffer from anxiety; socialization does not occur in a vacuum; and the way in which individuals adjust to new situations is remarkably similar. Let's look a little closer at each of these assumptions.

Socialization strongly influences employee performance and organizational stability Your work performance depends to a considerable degree on knowing what you should or should not do. Understanding the right way to do a job indicates proper socialization. Furthermore, the appraisal of your performance includes how well you fit into the organization. Do you get along with your co-workers? Do you have acceptable work habits? Do you demonstrate the right attitude? These qualities differ among jobs and organizations. For instance, on some jobs, you will be evaluated higher if you are aggressive and outwardly indicate that you are ambitious. On another job or on the same job in another organization, such an approach might be evaluated negatively. As a result, proper socialization becomes a significant factor in influencing both your actual job performance and how it is perceived by others.[7]

Organizational stability is increased through socialization[8] When jobs are filled and vacated with a minimum of disruption over many years, the organization will be more stable. Its objectives will be more smoothly transferred between generations, and loyalty and commitment to the organization should be easier to maintain because its philosophy and objectives will appear consistent over time. Given that most managers value high employee performance and organizational stability, the proper socialization of employees is important.

New members suffer from anxiety The outsider–insider passage produces anxiety. Stress is high because the new member feels a lack of identification—if not with the work itself, certainly with a new superior, new co-workers, a new work location, and a new set of rules and regulations. Loneliness and a feeling of isolation are not unusual. This has at least two implications. First, new employees need special attention to put them at ease. This usually means providing an adequate amount of information to reduce uncertainty and ambiguity. Second, the existence of tension can be positive in that it often acts to motivate individuals to learn the values and norms of their newly assumed role as quickly as possible.[9] We can conclude, therefore, that the new member is anxious about the new role but is motivated to learn the ropes and rapidly become an accepted member of the organization.

Socialization does not occur in a vacuum The learning associated with socialization goes beyond the formal job description and the expectations of people in human resources or the new member's manager. Socialization is influenced by statements and behaviours of colleagues, management, employees, clients, and other people with whom new members come in contact.

The way in which individuals adjust to new situations is remarkably similar This holds true even though the content and type of adjustments may vary. For instance, as pointed out previously, anxiety is high at entry, and the new member usually wants to reduce that anxiety quickly. The information obtained during the recruitment and selection stages is always incomplete and usually distorted. New employees, therefore, must alter their understanding of their role to better fit the complete information they get once they are on the job. The point is that there is no instant adjustment—every new member goes through a settling-in period that tends to follow a relatively standard pattern.

The Socialization Process

Socialization can be seen as a process made up of three stages: pre-arrival, encounter, and metamorphosis.[10] The first stage includes the learning the new employee has gained before joining the organization. In the second stage, the new employee gets an understanding of what the organization is really like and deals with the realization that the expectations and reality may differ. In the third stage, lasting change occurs. Here, new employees become fully trained in their jobs, perform successfully, and fit in with the values and norms of co-workers.[11] These three stages ultimately affect new employees' productivity on the job, their commitment to the organization's goals, and their decision to remain with the organization.[12] Figure 8-1 is a graphic representation of the socialization process. Let's take a closer look at each of these three stages.

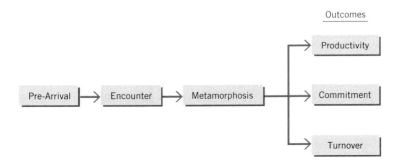

Figure 8-1
A Socialization Model

Pre-Arrival Stage The socialization process stage that recognizes individuals arrive in an organization with a set of organizational values, attitudes, and expectations.

Pre-Arrival Stage The pre-arrival stage explicitly recognizes that each individual arrives with a set of organizational values, attitudes, and expectations. These may cover both the work to be done and the organization. For instance, in many jobs particularly high-skilled and managerial ones, new members will have undergone a considerable degree of prior socialization in training and in school.[13] Part of teaching business students is to socialize them to what business is like, what to expect in a business career, and what kind of attitudes will lead to successful assimilation in an organization. Pre-arrival socialization, however, goes beyond the specific job. Generally the selection process is used to inform prospective employees about the organization as a whole. In addition, interviews also act to ensure that the candidate chosen is of the "right type" who will fit in.[14] "Indeed, the ability of individuals to present the appropriate face during the selection process determines their ability to move into the organization in the first place. Thus, success depends on the degree to which aspiring members have correctly anticipated the expectations and desires of those in the organization in charge of selection."[15]

The Bank of Montreal has established an $8-million Possibilities Foundation aimed at helping minority, disabled, and aboriginal students prepare for the world of work through post-secondary education.[16] They realize that this pre-arrival socialization can't take place too early for disadvantaged groups who may have low expectations of success in a banking career. As an initial part of the program, the bank has ten Grade 12 students working for a day per week for the bank during the school year and offers summer employment and scholarship opportunities for promising participants. In addition, bank employees act as mentors to help students learn, develop skills, and succeed in the workplace.

Encounter Stage   On entering the organization, new members enter the **encounter stage**. Here the individuals confront the possible contradiction between their expectations—about their jobs, co-workers, supervisors, and the organization in general—and reality. If expectations prove to have been more or less accurate, the encounter stage merely reaffirms the perceptions generated earlier. However, this is often not the case. Where expectations and reality differ, new employees must undergo socialization that will replace their previous assumptions with the organization's pivotal standards.[17] For example, Chantale Detillieux discovered the hard way that what she had thought was the "cool" Starbucks chain did not go for her tongue stud.[18] "The people training [me] from the Toronto store said they didn't see it as a problem, so I thought it wasn't a problem." However, her boss in the downtown Ottawa Starbucks outlet did not agree and asked her to remove her oral jewelry; when she resisted, she was fired from her part-time position. If Chantale had gone through an orientation process that had clarified what her new boss required, she would at least have known, ahead of time, what to expect at Starbucks.

Socialization, however, cannot solve all the problems due to the gap between expectation and reality. At the extreme, some new members may become totally disillusioned with the realities of their jobs and resign, but proper selection, including the realistic job preview, should significantly reduce this.

Metamorphosis Stage   Finally, the new employee must work out any problems discovered during the encounter stage, which may mean going through changes. That is why we call this third stage the **metamorphosis stage**. But what is a desirable metamorphosis? Metamorphosis is complete—as is the socialization process—when new members have become comfortable with the organization and their work teams. In this situation, they will have internalized the norms of the organization and their co-workers and understand and accept these norms.[19] New employees will feel accepted by their peers as trusted and valued individuals and will be confident that they can complete their jobs successfully. They will have acquired an understanding of the organizational system not only of their own tasks, but the rules, procedures, and informally accepted practices as well. Finally, they will know how they are going to be evaluated. In other words, they've gained an understanding of what criteria will be used to measure and appraise their work. They'll know what is expected of them and what constitutes a good job.

Encounter Stage The socialization stage in which individuals confront the possible contradiction between their organizational expectations and reality.

Metamorphosis Stage The socialization stage in which the new employee must work out any inconsistencies discovered during the encounter stage.

Wendie van der Woerd
Mountain Co-op Equipment

Knowledgeable staff has always been one of the great assets of the Mountain Equipment Co-op. That's why new employees at the outdoor equipment retailer's stores across Canada undergo an intensive orientation program. The first day of this program is dedicated to providing background information about the co-op.

This day-long crash course in MEC, however, had some problems. "For one thing, it didn't sufficiently explain the term co-op," explains Wendie van der Woerd of MEC's human resources department. "For another thing, it was really kind of dry."

So Ms van der Woerd and a team at the co-op's Vancouver head office set out to redesign this part of the orientation program. They made it much more interactive, introducing discussion groups, worksheets, and even a *Jeopardy*-style trivia game. The aim was to "minimize the amount of presentation and maximize the amount of participation."

Another new component to the program was a video that, as Ms van der Woerd explains, "had all the information we needed, but also really reflected our culture—young, fun, outdoorsy, and very dynamic. We showed staff members telling their stories and using our products—skiing and so on. And all the music was provided by bands our employees are in."

The video was a hit among MEC staff. Now all new employees watch it on their first day of orientation. They also receive much more information about the history of MEC and about co-ops in general.

In fact, all MEC employees went through this information section of orientation and found that even those who had been working there for years learned something. Ms van der Woerd thinks the new knowledge also helped increase staff members' pride in the organization.

The Importance of Orientation

Effective employee orientation is important to all organizations—large or small, public or private. As Figure 8-1 shows, successful socialization will have a positive effect on new employees' productivity and their commitment to the organization and will reduce the likelihood that they will leave any time soon.[20] Thus, if HRM recognizes that certain assumptions hold for new employees entering an organization and that they typically follow a three-stage socialization process, they can develop a program to help these newcomers adapt to the company. The onset of that HRM program lies in the orientation process. Let's turn our attention to this aspect of organizational life: socializing new employees through the orientation process.

New Employee Orientation Topics

Orientation The process of adapting new employees to the organization.

New employee orientation covers the activities involved in introducing a new employee to the organization and to his or her work unit. It expands on the information received during the recruitment and selection stages and helps to reduce the initial anxiety we all feel when beginning a new job. A typical orientation program will cover at least the following five major topic areas.

- The *organization* and its top management, including history, objectives, and policies.
- The key *HRM policies*, including both company regulations and compensation. Included in the latter are items such as work hours, pay procedures, overtime requirements, and company benefits.
- The *work situation* in which the employee will actually function—physical location, including safety regulations and rest or food centres.
- The *job* the employee will be doing in terms of specific duties and responsibilities.
- The *people*, both supervisors and co-workers, with whom the employee will work.

Figure 8-2 illustrates a generic new employee orientation agenda used in one organization. Notice that orientation includes both tangible items, such as pay and work hours, as well as less tangible items such as norms, values, and expectations. The tangible items are often given prominence in orientation programs since these are easier to specify formally. Imagine a new recruit sitting across an "orientation" table, from the organization's manager. Think of the tangible orientation items as being laid out on top of the orientation table. The intangible items are often left unsaid under the table even though they may actually play a bigger role in job success. Both types of items should be placed on top of the table. In Figure 8-2, you will see that both tangible and intangible items are laid out on top of the table during the supervisory orientation on Day 2.

Figure 8-2
A Sample New Employee Orientation Schedule

NEW EMPLOYEE:	Ryan Bradshaw (Recent B. Comm. from University of Manitoba)
JOB TITLE:	Accountant I
DEPARTMENT:	Accounting and Finance
Prior to Orientation:	Review company information on Web page and information package supplied by mail.

DAY 1:

8:00 a.m.	Report to Human Resources Receive formal orientation package, including brochures on company and management not already supplied.
8:30	Welcome by company president, Mr Goyeau. Meet available senior management.
9:00	Meet with employment supervisor, Ms Burke. Review employment policies and practices and available training.
10:00	Meet with compensation supervisor, Mr Carroll. Ensure all tax forms completed and arrangements made for receiving pay.
10:30	Break
11:00	Overview and enrolment in benefit programs.
12:00	Lunch with supervisor, Mr Fournier, and key colleagues.
1:00	Tour of work area. Take time to study sample of accounting reports and procedures manuals.

DAY 2:

8:30 a.m.	Meet with information services manager, Ms Kritovsky. Review available software and data information services.

8:30	Set up new computer with computer consultant, Ms Jerome.
8:30	Detailed tour of accounting department. Review of overall structure and organization, official department rules and procedures. Introduction to all coleagues.
11:00	Meet with supervisor, Mr Fournier. Discuss job expectations and objectives.
12:00	Luch with colleagues.
2:00	Join new colleagues in department meeting. Discuss office procedures with work goup after the meeting.
DAY 3:	
9:00	Introduction to some key customers by Mr Fournier (two meetings of an hour each).
11:00	Employee begins regular duties.

Who is responsible for orienting the new employee? This can be done by either the new employee's supervisor, the people in HRM, or some combination of the two. In many medium-sized and most large organizations, HRM takes charge of explaining such matters as overall organizational policies and employee benefits. But in most small firms and some medium-sized ones, new employees will receive their entire orientation from their supervisor. Figure 8-2 demonstrates a situation where the process takes place over three days and is shared between the HRM staff and the new member's supervisor and co-workers.

Of course, the new employee's orientation may not be formal at all. For instance, many small organizations use the sink or swim method in which orientation consists of the new member reporting to her supervisor, who then assigns her to another employee, who will introduce her to those persons with whom she will be working closely. This may then be followed by a quick tour to show her where the washroom, cafeteria, and coffee machine are. Then the new employee is shown to her desk and left to fend for herself. New employee orientation requires much more than this. In today's organizations, it is imperative that new employees understand what the organization is about—that is, the organization's culture. [21]

Understanding the Organization's Culture

Culture The rules, jargon, customs, and other traditions that clarify acceptable and unacceptable behaviour in an organization.

Every organization has its own unique culture that includes long-standing and often unwritten rules and regulations: a special language that facilitates communication among members; shared standards of relevance about the critical aspects of the work that is to be done; matter-of-fact prejudices; standards for social etiquette and demeanour; established customs for how members should relate to peers, subordinates, superiors, and outsiders; and other traditions that clarify what is appropriate and "smart" behaviour within the organization and what is not.[22] An employee who has been properly socialized into the organization's culture, then, has learned how things are done, what matters, and which work-related behaviours and perspectives are acceptable and desirable and which are not.

Norms Tell group members what they ought or ought not do in certain circumstances.

To better understand the concept of unique organizational cultures, we should look at the concepts of roles, values, and norms. Every job requires the incumbent to behave in certain specified ways, which is more or less expected of people who are identified with certain jobs. We call the set of such behaviours **roles**. Your instructor acts a certain way in the classroom, but that is not the way this individual behaves at sporting events. Why? Because your instructor is not "playing teacher" at the game.

Roles, values, and norms interrelate. What a person does on the job depends on the standards that the organization and his or her work group convey as appropriate. The parameters of the role—whether one is an accountant, lawyer, teacher, librarian, or sales clerk—change in response to the values and norms in the environment where one performs that role. This explains, for instance, why many employees in customer relations at Scotiabank generally come to work dressed in their business attire, while their counterparts in software development at Corel Canada wear casual clothes.

Roles Sets of behaviours that job incumbents are expected to display.

New employees must absorb the organization's long-standing and unwritten rules that define such things as what is appropriate behaviour and what is not.

You may be wondering how these concepts relate to the socialization process. The answer is that individuals, in their work roles, may accept all, some, or none of the organization's standards.[23] Those who readily accept all of them may become conformists, the "yes-persons." At the other extreme, those who rejects all the organization's standards are rebels or "misfits." Rebels rarely last long, being expelled from the organization for their inability to adapt to "the way we do things around here." In between, we get people who accept some standards but not others. It is important that individuals accept at least the pivotal or key values of the organization. Pivotal values are those deemed essential by the organization. For example, refraining from bad-mouthing the company in public is often considered a pivotal value. Relevant values, by contrast, are deemed desirable but not absolutely essential for success in the organization. Reading financial periodicals, for example, may be a relevant value for employees at a financial institution such as ScotiaBank but not at a software developer like Corel. People who are able to distinguish between key and relevant standards are often innovative and creative and perform the role of the healthy questioner. They have accepted those standards necessary to maintain member-ship in the organization. They are comfortable in their jobs and demonstrate commitment to the organization.

It may not be management's wish to get every employee to accept all of the or-ganization's standards. To do so could create a conforming and apathetic organi-zational environment, but the pivotal values must be conveyed and accepted. Without this acceptance, new employees will lack commitment and loyalty to the interests of the organization and will pose a threat to management and experi-enced members. Furthermore, they will never be accepted as full-fledged mem-bers of the organization. Successful socialization will mean having employees who fit in by knowing the dos and don'ts of being a "good employee."

A Few Examples

Tenure is a familiar concept to academics at Canadian universities. Teachers and professors who are granted tenure, in effect, are given permanent, lifetime employment, and as a result, it is highly prized. To achieve tenure, a prospect must endure the watchful eye of those who are already tenured for a trial pe-riod normally lasting five to seven years. Prospects who "measure up" will get tenure. Measuring up means that the individual has been well socialized to the values of the tenured group. Prospects who accept and demonstrate by their be-haviour that they fit in with the tenured members are granted permanent em-ployment. Those who fail may be expelled from the organization.

For those who think this practice is an oddity confined to educational institu-tions, consider the process in large accounting and law firms. New employees start out as associates, most with the goal of some day becoming partners. But partnership (which means owning a piece of the firm and enjoying permanent employment) is withheld for some extended period—usually five to fifteen years—while the associates prove to the current partners that they are "worthy." This means that the potential partners must demonstrate through what they say and do that they know the rules and can be trusted.

The CEO's Role in Orientation

Traditionally, new employee orientation operated, if at all, without any input from the company's executive management. That began to change in the 1980s due in part to consultants and authors such as Tom Peters who strongly advo-cated that senior management "manage by walking around."[24] What Peters and others advocated was that senior managers become highly visible in the organi-zation, meeting and greeting employees and listening to employee concerns. At the same time, these individuals were given the opportunity to talk about the company—where it is going and how it is going to get there. In management terminology, this was called *visioning*.

As more and more successful companies began to be cited in business litera-ture for their leaders' ability to be involved in the workforce, one question arose. If it appeared to work well for existing employees, what would it do for new ones just joining the organization? The answer appeared to be a lot.[25] Let's look at this more closely.

One of the most important tasks of orientation is to deal with employees' anxieties. One of the more stressful aspects of starting a new job is the thought

Orientation is the best chance HRM has to inform new employees what it can do for them in the future.

of entering the unknown. Although a previous organization may have done something undesirable—like paying considerably lower wages than what the market valued your job—at least you knew what you had. The values and priorities of your previous CEO were well known and you had adjusted to them. However, the values of the CEO in the new organization might be quite different. Consider the widely different cultures being brought together in the major bank mergers under review, even more dramatically, the merger of two national cultures in the new DaimlerChrysler.

Starting any new job is frightening. Did you do the right thing, make the right choice? Having the CEO address you on day one helps to allay some of those fears. The CEO's first responsibility is to welcome new employees aboard and reinforce the fact that they made a good job choice. In fact, this segment of new employee orientation can be likened to a cheerleading pep rally. The CEO is in a position to "turn on" these new employees by talking about what it is like to work for the organization and discuss what really matters in the company—an indoctrination into the organization's culture.[26] The CEO's presence is sending the message that the company cares about its employees. And even when scheduling conflicts arise, companies can be prepared: Levi Strauss uses videotaped messages that carry the same message.[27]

As the CEO concludes his or her presentation, a final question-and-answer period can prove worthwhile. During this stage, new employees can get answers from the top about any concerns they may have, once again reinforcing the message: "Communications are important." Seeing the CEO matches the name to a face and establishes an atmosphere from which to build organizational commitment.

In smaller companies, most of the orientation is the shared responsibility of the CEO and HRM manager. In larger organizations, much of the process is broken down into parts that are handled by various specialists within HRM. To illustrate this, let's look at HRM's role in the orientation process.

HRM's Role in Orientation

The orientation function can be performed by HRM, line management, or a combination of the two. Although our example in Figure 8-2 indicates a preference for a combination strategy, it remains true that HRM plays a major role in new employee orientation: the role of *coordination* which ensures that the appropriate components are in place. In addition, HRM also serves as a participant in the program. Consequently, it is important to recognize what HRM must do. For example, in our discussion of making the job offer (Chapter 6), we emphasized that the offer should come from human resources. This was necessary to coordinate the administrative activities surrounding a new hire. The same holds true for new employee orientation. Depending on how the recruiting takes place, there should be a systematic schedule of when new employees join a company.

As job offers are made and accepted, HRM tells the new employee when to report to work, and before the employee formally arrives, HRM must be prepared to handle some of the more routine needs of these individuals; for example, new employees usually have a long list of questions about benefits. More proactive organizations such as Ford Motor Company of Canada and Bell Canada prepare a package for new employees much of which is accessible on the Internet. This package generally focuses on the important decisions that a new employee must make—the choice of health insurance, institutions for direct deposit of pay cheques, and tax withholding information. By providing this information a few weeks before an individual starts work, the HRM unit gives new hires ample time to make a proper choice, one that, quite possibly, must be made in conjunction with a working spouse's options. Furthermore, forms often require information that most employees do not carry with them, such as social insurance numbers of family members and medical histories. Accordingly, having that information before the orientation session saves time.[28]

HRM's second concern revolves around its role as a participant in the process. Most new employees first get to know the organization via HRM, but after the hiring process is over, HRM quickly fades from the picture unless there is a problem. Therefore, HRM must spend some time in orientation addressing what it can do for employees in the future. This point cannot be overemphasized. HRM provides an array of services such as career guidance and training to individual employees and departments of the organization. It is essential to let these new employees know what HR can do for them.

Let's go through an orientation program that reflects the responsibilities of the four areas of HRM identified in Chapter 1—employment, training and development, compensation and benefits, and employee relations.

Employment's Role

Recall from Chapter 1 that employment is the recruiting arm of HRM and the area which has had more contact with applicants and new hires than any other. That is why employment specialists should serve as the coordinating body for the orientation process, notifying the new employee of the start date, sending out the pre-employment package, and answering any questions relating to it. And because of the relationship that has been built through the selection process, the HR employment representative should serve as an orientation host, making sure that new employees are met and escorted to the orientation area. In companies like IBM Canada, much of employee commitment to the organization is often linked to the feeling established on the first day on the job.[29]

After those preliminaries, employment specialists must then switch hats and become presenters in the process. During this segment, the representative should provide an overview of the HR function, describing what it does. Although this will be primarily recruiting, which is now complete for this group of new employees, there will be further dealings with the employment area as these individuals are permitted to "bid" for other positions after a period of time.

When these new employees get into that stage of career development, they will be required to follow certain HRM policies, and will want to know how internal promotions or job transfers work. It is important to disseminate these policies when the employee joins the organization so that the employees can make plans for their future and know what to expect. For instance, if jobs are posted in a particular way such as on a bulletin board in the lunch room, these new employees need to know that. Furthermore, they also need to know if HRM looks at applications from both internal and external sources and whether current employees will receive preferential treatment. For example, employment specialists are bound to review résumés and applications in search of information indicating that the applicant has the requisite skills to do the job. If current employees do not have an updated résumé or believe that the employment representative will know what skills they possess, they may be making a mistake. Enlightening new employees to this possibility serves an important role.

The employment area of HRM can also serve as a "decruitment" branch. Should downsizing or retrenchment occur, the employment division is generally responsible (in conjunction with other HRM units) for laying off employees. If policies exist that offer certain rights to employees, those must be explained. For example, if lay-offs are based solely on seniority, can one employee bump another with less seniority? If so, this should be conveyed. Likewise, if no guarantees are offered, that too has to be communicated.

After the HR employment function has been explained, it is time to move on to the training and development function.

Training and Development's Role

Many organizations offer a wide range of training programs which, generally speaking, focus on two elements—job training and personal development (we will discuss this further in Chapter 9). Depending on the structure of the organization, HR training and development group may or may not be involved in the actual job training process. If not, they will have only limited exposure to new employees. But if they do provide job-specific training, then more than likely they will be spending a great deal of time with the new employees over the first few weeks.

For orientation purposes, however, training and development should focus on communicating just what development means to employees and what programs and training sessions are available both right away and long term. The role of training and development in the career development process should be emphasized. Services that are available should be outlined in addition to how new employees can take advantage of such programs as tuition assistance, computerized career assessments, or any psychological assessments the development specialists are trained to administer.

We should also find training and development personnel spending some time during this presentation discussing corporate culture issues.[30] Generally charged with facilitating the change and maintaining the organization's culture, the training and development presenter should use this opportunity to reinforce what the CEO stated in the opening remarks. Once again, hearing the same thing from different people in the orientation only emphasizes the importance of the message. An indication of the successful performance of the training and development role in orientation is the seamless introduction of the new employee into the work situation. Don Manuel of TTG Systems Inc. of Edmonton, Alberta puts it this way: "If you were to watch somebody, you wouldn't know if they were a beginner or a long-time qualified worker because they're using the same tools." Manuel was describing his company's performance-support systems enabling new employees to be easily introduced into companies as different as Alberta Pacific Forest Industries Inc. in the far north of Alberta, and Bayer Inc.'s petrochemical plant in Sarnia, Ontario.[31]

Compensation and Benefits' Role

There is no doubt that new employee orientation programs help to eliminate many problems in the compensation and benefits area. There are so many forms to be completed when one is hired that having these employees at a convenient location at a specified time facilitates the process. For example, imagine you are the benefits administrator and you need to get new employees enrolled for tax

Figure 8-3
Forms Often Completed at Orientation for New Employees

Health Insurance Enrolment Form	• may involve multiple forms if there are choices available between alternative health insurance providers
Dependent Coverage Forms	• provides health insurance coverage to employee's dependents
Vision and Dental Enrolment Forms	
TD1 Income Tax Form	• supplies necessary dependents and other information to Revenue Canada
Direct Deposit Form	• instructs payroll where— i.e., to which financial institution—to deposit your net pay
Credit Union Enrolment Form	
Life Insurance Enrolment Form	
Dependent Life Insurance Form	• extends life insurance coverage to dependents
Personal History Form	• captures information not permitted to be obtained on application form— (e.g., SIN, next of kin, emergency contact)
Accidental Death and Dismemberment Enrolment Form	
Retirement Account Enrolment Form	• required when employees may choose how their retirement funds are to be invested

deductions and for their health insurance coverage. Suppose that thirty new employees started on the same day, all at different locations. To get the forms completed, you would have to go to each location and deal with each employee individually, spending, say, an hour processing the forms, and repeat this thirty times. What a nightmare! New employee orientation eliminates this ordeal. All new employees are brought together so the compensation and benefits department has a captive audience for a period of time. Questions can be answered in a group forum. It is not unusual for this enrolment phase to take up to half of the total time spent on new employee orientation (although this can be shortened considerably by the use of on-line, electronic registration systems). Some of the forms that may be required are listed in Figure 8-3.

Aside from completing the forms, there is other information that new employees need to know. First of all is the question of salary. Although new hires will know their starting salary, they will also want to know how salaries are set in the company. Compensation specialists should discuss how the company establishes its salary grades and ranges. Not every detail need be explained, but sufficient information should be conveyed so these new employees know that their salary is based on an analysis of the relevant data, not on some whim. Furthermore, compensation must address how performance is evaluated and how pay increases operate. Are raises tied to performance? Are they based on seniority? Just how does the company make its determination? What role does a union play? This presentation must describe the process in enough detail so that the new employees understand.

Included in this discussion should be something that must never be taken for granted—pay dates. Does the company hold back the first pay cheque, and, if so, when can these new employees expect to receive their first payment? Nothing upsets employees more than being surprised by the fact that they must wait a month for their first cheque. This should be spelled out explicitly during the hiring process and reiterated in orientation.

New employees need to be informed about the benefits they are to receive.[32] Some benefits such as sick leave and vacations may not kick in until employees have been on board for six months or so. Employees also need to know about observed holidays, whether the company offers personal leave days, and how and when they can be used. Finally, retirement questions should be reviewed. Employees need to know just how much, if any, will be deducted from their pay to contribute towards their pension and insurance programs, and whether the company matches those amounts. In Chapter 14, we will discuss the choices most companies offer in their pension and insurance programs, and who contributes what.

Employee Relations' Role

As the generalist's function in HRM, employee relations could address many points of interest for new employees. Three programs, in particular, are critical: the company's communications, employee assistance, and its employee recognition programs.

Employee relations (ER) must explain to new employees what the various communication programs are about. For example, the complaint procedure must be carefully reviewed so that employees know what to do if they face a problem in their unit that they cannot get rectified. Remember the discussion of sexual harassment in Chapter 3? One of the necessary components, to protect an organization from being liable for its supervisors' behaviours, is that it has an avenue to raise the sexual harassment concerns. That is exactly what ER must tell new employees—that a process exists and can be used to their benefit. But not all communication programs are complaint-based. There may be a monthly "town meeting" to discuss the issues or concerns of employees in the organization. New employees should be informed about these meetings, their purposes, and how they can benefit from them.

ER is also frequently responsible for the health and safety of employees. During new employee orientation, ER should address what the company does to ensure employee welfare and explain once again what employees should do if they encounter a problem. If that problem is personal, employees may want to use some sort of employee assistance program. For example, a movement spreading rapidly across Canada is the creation of the smoke-free workspace. When companies implement such policies, they have to consider the effect it may have on employees. Furthermore, to help foster the smoke-free environment, companies may offer stop-smoking programs to their employees. (We'll take a closer look at employee assistance programs in Chapters 14 and 15.) Despite their particular focus, employee assistance programs are designed to help employees with personal problems before they become so overwhelming that they affect their work. ER should mention how the program works and how confidentiality is guaranteed.

Finally, employee relations frequently will have various programs recognizing employees for their accomplishments. Whether they are rewards for money-saving suggestions, service awards, or the company-sponsored softball or bowling team, ER should make sure that new employees understand what is available to them.

At the end of the presentations about the four areas of HRM, the formal orientation program ends, but the process does not stop there. The orientation process continues with the new managers and co-workers in the new employees' respective job areas.

Supervisor's Role in Orientation

Just as HRM plays an integral role in orienting new employees, immediate supervisors also have a responsibility to assist in the adaptation process. When you consider that new employees will be spending almost all their time in their new job location, it's obviously imperative that managers get involved. Indeed, in smaller organizations, most of the orientation process is handled in partnership with the supervisor. But what should the supervisor's involvement be? It usually involves the initial indoctrination into the unit.

In the first stage of indoctrination, management must do whatever it can to make the new employee feel welcome. For example, knowing that people are nervous about their new jobs and the people they will work with, the manager should take new employees around and introduce them to their colleagues. This simple gesture goes a long way in making new employees feel part of the group. There are also other things the manager can do to facilitate this process; one is to take the new employee and new co-workers out for lunch on the first day. In fact, considering that HRM may have the employee for the first half day, meeting the new employee when HRM's program is completed and taking the employee to lunch can once again reinforce the organization's commitment to its people. By including colleagues, the astute manager is laying the groundwork for the new employee's peers to become actively involved in the adaptation process. In fact, studies suggest that new employees not only welcome this

Management must do whatever it can to make the new employee feel welcome.

peer orientation, but often prefer it[33] and rely on it as a source of information. One of the most successful examples of peer orientation is the Labatt Safety Day when the entire metro brewery plant in Etobicoke, Ontario shuts down for safety training which is largely developed and led by Labatt employees. As Keith Postill, the brewery's resource manager and Safety Day coordinator puts it, "when we have our people developing it and delivering it, they own it."[34]

Lastly, organizations must recognize the importance of these initial few days for building employee loyalty. In order to minimize the turnover that accompanies poor socialization processes, organizations must be willing to invest in training managers on just what is required to help new employees adapt. This training involves learning how to establish performance standards, how to coach and counsel new employees, and how to be an effective mentor. Even though much of orientation appears to verge on the "touchy-feely" side of HRM, we cannot forget the main reason we hired the new employee—to do a job. Accordingly, managers must be capable of defining job requirements, furnishing the necessary tools to enable the employee to do the job, and providing ample feedback.

Peer Orientation Co-workers assist in orienting new employees.

New Technology and Orientation

The basic processes and objectives of effective orientation programs have been in place for a number of years, but the technologies available have changed dramatically. The Internet enables both employees and organizations to gain a range of information about each other from the comfort of the desktop computer screen. Interactive video and information processing systems allow employees to learn about almost any aspect of their new work situation at their own pace.

For example, working with Edmonton, Alberta-based TTG Systems Inc., Alberta Pacific Forest Industries Inc. prepared a comprehensive training and orientation program for employees covering safety requirements, troubleshooting, equipment-specific maintenance training and equipment overviews. The package of material for new employees included overviews, cognitive knowledge, demonstrated procedures, and field checklists. Each module contained text and graphics (some with audio), graphical animations and full-motion videos featuring the company's staff and equipment.[35]

This new technology is exciting, but there are two caveats to be noted:

First, technology, however dramatic, does not eliminate the critical importance of face-to-face socialization as part of orientation. In fact, it could be argued that the growth of alternative working arrangements such as telework actually increases the importance of establishing good social networks from the beginning of a new position. Consider, for example, how much easier it is to take part in a conference call or video-based interview once you have met all participants face to face.

Secondly, newer technology-based orientation programs may entail some considerable investment which some organizations may be reluctant to undertake in times of restructuring and restraint. We would argue, however, that investments in employee orientation are more than justified by improved performance and morale on the part of employees.

Study Tools and Applications

Summary

This summary relates to the Learning Objectives provided on p. 228.
After having read this chapter, you should know:

1. Socialization is a process of adaptation. Organization-entry socialization refers to the adaptation that takes place when an individual passes from outside the organization to the role of an inside member.
2. The three stages of employee socialization are the pre-arrival, the encounter, and the metamorphosis.
3. The outsider-insider passage refers to the adaptation to a new work environment resulting in different work activities, a new boss, or a different group of co-workers.
4. Orientation is part of socialization and covers the activities involved in introducing a new employee to the organization and to his or her work unit.
5. Organizational socialization attempts to adapt the new employee to the organization's culture by conveying how things are done and what matters.
6. The critical theme of socializing employees is that new employees accept the organization's pivotal standards.
7. The CEO's role in orientation is to welcome the new employees, reaffirm their choice of joining the company, and discuss the organization's goals and objectives while conveying information about the organization's culture.
8. Each function in HRM has a specific role in orientation. For instance, employment discusses how the promotion from within process works; training and development covers development programs offered; compensation and benefits has forms completed and discusses salary and benefits; and employee relations discusses the company's health, safety, communications, and complaint procedures.
9. Supervisors serve a role of continuing orientation after HRM's formal program is over. This may include activities ranging from taking the employee to lunch to introducing him or her to colleagues.
10. A sample orientation program involves many areas. Coordinated through HRM, such a program would include a welcome by the senior management member and presentations on all functions of HRM. Employees' managers would then pick up where HRM leaves off.

Key Terms

culture	peer orientation
encounter stage	pre-arrival stage
metamorphosis stage	roles
norms	socialization
orientation	

EXPERIENTIAL EXERCISE

College and University Orientation

In today's companies, we spend time thinking about planning and implementing orientation programs, and universities have followed suit. In many colleges and universities, new students are invited to spend a day with institutional representatives who go over various aspects of campus life that are important to the new student. Among these are campus tours, housing and dining information, major announcements, campus services, and course registration. Inasmuch as this process assists new students, it is often general in nature; specific information for each program or major may be limited.

Therefore, as business students, your exercise is to develop an orientation program to be used in your school. As a group of three to five students, develop an orientation plan that could be given to the dean of the faculty for immediate implementation. Make sure you address the time frame for the process and decide who should conduct the orientation. Also, consider any modifications to your program to reflect unique needs of women and minority students.

CASE APPLICATION:

Anne Wallace: The Homesick Expatriate[36]

Anne Wallace had been excited to be offered a position as a product management trainee at Universal Telesystems. Universal is a Canadian-based company that develops, manufactures, and services communications equipment around the world through its many international operations. A position as a management trainee would enable Anne to gain a great deal of valuable experience. She would be able to apply the knowledge she had gained while completing her degree in marketing at the University of Saskatchewan. Anne had also recently completed a one-year French immersion program in Quebec City, and if she performed well during her initial training, there was a possibility that she would be given a special foreign assignment, she hoped at Universal's plant in Montereau, France. As she began her training at Universal Telesystem's head office in Milton, Ontario, Anne looked forward to the exciting new experiences that lay before her.

The first six months of training at head office proved to be a challenging and rewarding experience. Anne's supervisor said that her performance had been impressive and that she had been highly recommended for a special assignment abroad. Soon Anne was informed that she would be going to Ireland for three months to train at the Universal operations near Dublin. After that, she would be moving to Montereau for a two-year assignment. Anne was a little nervous but extremely excited to be travelling and working abroad.

Dublin was beautiful, but Anne was a little lonely. Her co-workers were kind enough, but being so far away from home did have an effect on her. She kept herself very busy with work and visited various tourist attractions on the weekends. The scenery of Ireland reminded Anne of her childhood trips to visit her grandparents in Prince Edward Island. These memories left Anne feeling lonelier still, but she knew that she would only be in Ireland for a few months. She anticipated that she would adjust with time and that she would feel more at home in France. She hoped she would be able to make more lasting friendships in Montereau and that the glamour and excitement of living in France would keep her from missing her homeland.

After her three months in Ireland, Anne moved on to France. Within a month, she had settled into a cosy apartment in Montereau, a beautiful little town on the Yonne River, about fifty kilometres south-east of Paris. Her new responsibilities at work were challenging, as she was now finding it necessary to apply all the theory she had learned from books to actual real-life problems. The reality of being a manager and no longer a trainee was beginning to sink in, and at times would cause Anne a great deal of stress. The first few weeks in France were exciting, but she soon realized that two years was going to be a very long time. Adding to her difficulties was the fact that many of the technical communication terms that Anne had learned during her training in English were useless at the plant where only French terms were used.

Communication was more difficult than she had anticipated. People spoke much more quickly than she could understand and used words she had not heard in Quebec. Anne also found that people wondered about her strange accent and often thought she must be from some remote part of the world. A group of co-workers did try to help her feel more at home by taking her to Paris for an evening of entertainment at a comedy club. Anne did appreciate their efforts but had difficulty understanding the comedian and his French humour. She felt her co-workers were laughing at her confusion more than at the comedian. She ended up feeling more homesick than ever.

As time went on, Anne's situation did not improve. Her difficulty in fulfilling work responsibilities continued to be stressful for her. She gave up trying to make close friends and began to feel quite sorry she had ever accepted this special assignment. Anne could not understand how she could end up feeling so depressed and disappointed when she had thought this job would be the most exciting experience of her life. The more she thought about her situation, the more she was sure that she could not continue in her position in France. Her difficulties in adjusting to a new country had taken their toll on her emotional stability, her physical health, and her performance at work. She knew that it was unfair for her to continue in her position when she could not perform the way Universal Telesystems needed her to. Both for herself and for the company, she reluctantly decided to resign.

Questions

1. What are some of the difficulties Canadians such as Anne encounter when working overseas?
2. At what points in the socialization model presented in Figure 8-1 did these difficulties occur?
3. What assistance might Universal Telesystems have been able to provide in their orientation programs for Anne?
4. As her superior in Montereau, what help would you have given Anne in the orientation program?
5. What orientation program would you offer for a person from another country to help them adjust to life in Canada?

Testing Your Understanding

How well did you fulfil the learning objectives?

1. Proper socialization is indicated by
   a. cheerfully accepting every assignment you are given.
   b. questioning few assignments you are given.
   c. understanding the right way to do a job.
   d. completing assigned tasks ahead of schedule.
   e. completing assigned tasks without errors.

2. Outsider-insider work passages may be triggered by all of the following changes except
   a. a new boss.
   b. a new occurrence of a disability.
   c. new co-workers.
   d. new performance evaluation standards.
   e. new job activities.

3. The metamorphosis stage of socialization is best associated with
   a. permanent change.
   b. reinforcement.
   c. stability and commitment.
   d. none of the above.

4. What is the difference between roles and values?
   a. Values are behaviours that employees display in organizations. Roles are attitudes that employees hold.
   b. Values have no place in organizations. Roles are what is required in organizations.
   c. Roles are expected behaviours. Values are convictions about what is right and wrong, important and unimportant.
   d. Roles and values are different terms for the same thing.
   e. Roles determine organization culture. Values are determined by organizational culture.

5. Ray teaches international human resources management at a prestigious university in Atlantic Canada. He travels every summer to collect data and writes and publishes a short book of comparative human resources practices when he returns. Ray usually wears souvenirs to school throughout the month of September. For instance, last year he went to Barbados and came back wearing flowered shirts. The year before, he went to Argentina and wore gaucho pants, and be-

fore that, it was Australian Aboriginal art. The school is known for its conservative, business like approach. Suits, ties, and briefcases are the uniform of the day. This year, Ray got promoted to full professor and was awarded outstanding scholar status. Which statement is accurate about the organization's culture?

a. Ray's values are different from most members of the organization.

b. No norms apply to Ray. Tenured university professors can do whatever they want.

c. Roles in the business school are different from other parts of the university. Norms cannot be identified in such an institution.

d. Norms and roles about scholarship are more important in this university than norms and roles about appearance.

e. Values, roles, and norms in this university are clearly defined and consistent.

6. Military boot camp, the academic tenure system, and becoming a partner in a law firm are all examples of

a. archaic institutions with rigid cultures that direct most employees' behaviours according to specified rules and regulations.

b. formal, deliberate processes to teach newcomers the dos and don't's of organizational life.

c. acceptable organizational cultures.

d. unacceptable organizational cultures.

e. no such examples were given.

7. The vice-president of human resources wants to include the CEO in the orientation process. What would be the best way to do this?

a. Have the CEO explain the company benefits packages.

b. Have the CEO dress up like a clown and sing or do a stunt. That will help employees realize she is just one of the team members.

c. Have the CEO moderate the film about the first hundred years of company history.

d. Have the CEO share the vision of the organization, what she hopes to accomplish and to welcome the new employees to that vision.

e. Have the CEO go to lunch with each new employee.

8. Some companies send a packet of benefits information to the employee's home by mail or the Internet a week or so before the new employee starts work. All of these reasons were given for this arrangement except

a. time is not used during formal orientations to have an employee fill out forms.

b. decisions about insurance coverage often have to be made in conjunction with coverage already provided by a working spouse.

c. often, employees change their mind about working for a firm when they see the benefits options in writing. Sending the information home reduces embarrassing scenes in the human resources office.

d. some of the forms require information that a person would not routinely carry to work.

e. this process expedites handling routine needs.

9. Managers typically perform all of these functions during the indoctrination process except

a. taking the new employee to management briefings or helping the new employee to begin networking with other managers.

b. welcoming the new employee and providing a "welcoming" gift in his or her office.

c. introducing the new employee to colleagues.

d. taking the new employee out to lunch.

e. allowing colleagues to chat informally with the new employee.

10. When a new employee was hired by a large manufacturing organization, his supervisor gave him a few hours to just "get acquainted" with his peers. How was that part of his indoctrination process?

a. It was not a part of indoctrination.

b. It gave the boss a chance to observe the new employee in a group setting.

c. It made the new employee self-reliant and thus more confident.

d. It gave the new employee's colleagues a chance to decide whether or not they wanted to work with him.

e. None of the above.

11. Firms with high organizational stability

a. are slow to respond to external pressures.

b. have philosophy and objectives that appear consistent over time.

c. have higher turnover rates than other firms.

d. focus on stable production processes.

e. do not need to spend much time in employee socialization.

12. All of the following are examples of organizational dos or don'ts for this human resources class except

a. do arrive to class on time.

b. don't cut the class more times than the instructor allows.

c. don't cheat on exams.

d. do turn in papers on time.

e. do avoid certain local bars on weekends.

13. Your text describes CEO involvement in orientation programs in all of these ways, except

a. they welcomed new employees aboard and told them they made a good job choice, like leading a pep rally.

b. they indoctrinated new employees into the organization's culture by sharing the philosophy and mission of the organization.

c. they advocated company goals.

d. they conducted company tours.

e. they emphasized the importance of communications by having an open question-and-answer period.

Chapter Nine

EMPLOYEE TRAINING AND DEVELOPMENT

LEARNING OBJECTIVES

AFTER READING THIS CHAPTER, YOU WILL BE ABLE TO:

1. Explain why employee training is important.
2. Define training.
3. Discuss the relationship between effective training programs and various learning principles.
4. Describe how training needs evolve.
5. Identify the two types of formal training methods.
6. Define employee development.
7. Explain organizational development and the role of the change agent.
8. Discuss on-the-job and off-the-job employee development techniques.
9. Explain what is meant by the mentoring/coaching process.
10. Identify how employee counselling can be used as a development tool.
11. Describe the methods and criteria involved in evaluating training programs.
12. Explain issues critical to international training and development.

An investment in employee training and development has paid off for Stentor Communications—beyond their wildest dreams![1] Where many organizations are content to follow the lead of other benchmarked competitors, Stentor Resource Centre Inc., a subsidiary of Stentor Communications, the alliance of Canada's largest telecommunications companies, set out to lead the pack in its learning organizational model. The Resource Centre marketed national products and services for the member companies and offered training and development services to them. Investment in this learning laboratory resulted in a revenue stream for the company of $72 million.

Connie Simington, Stentor's strategic partner, learning and development, argues that the key to success was in the realism, practical application, and assessment procedures included in the learning program. "I kept a learning and results measurement index on actual projects that we took on in the company, so we were able to keep track of the results." The earned revenues certainly got the attention of executives. Simington notes with pride, "By the end of the year, we had the company president and four senior leaders sitting down asking us, 'When are you going to coach our teams?'"

Practices taught at the learning lab include collaborative consulting, coaching skills, marketing skills for the future, creativity, and innovation. The training is done in real time on real projects tailored to what is needed for each client. One of the most important characteristics of the lab is that Stentor brought in actual clients to work with the students in the program. So far, about 100 students have graduated to spread their knowledge to the 154,000 other employees in the Stentor organization. "We now have a waiting list to get into the program. Once someone gets on the team, they will not leave," Simington observes. "Our relationships with our client companies are much stronger than they have ever been." As the Stentor alliance scaled down in the wake of deregulation of the telecommunications of Stentor Resources Centre were expected to be allocated between the member companies.[2]

Employee training focuses on enhancing the specific skills and abilities of individuals to allow them to perform their jobs immediately, whereas employee development is more concerned with future roles in the organization.

Introduction

Every organization needs to have well-trained and experienced people to perform the activities that must be done. Larger organizations may be able to afford quite sophisticated programs like the one at Stentor Communications, but the need is no less true for smaller organizations. Indeed, it could even be argued that training is more important to smaller organizations because of their greater dependence on each person employed. Naturally, in smaller organizations, training may be carried out in partnership with other organizations or even totally subcontracted to training consultants. But the fact remains that since jobs in today's dynamic organizations have become more complex, the importance of employee education has increased. When jobs were simple, easy to learn, and were influenced to only a small degree by technological changes, there was little need for employees to upgrade or alter their skills. But that situation rarely exists today. Instead, rapid job changes are occurring, requiring employee skills to be transformed and frequently updated.[3] In organizations, this takes place through what we call employee training and development.

Training and Development

Employee Training Present-oriented training, focusing on individual's current jobs.

Employee Development Future-oriented training, focusing on the personal growth of the employee.

Training is a learning experience that seeks to bring about a relatively permanent change that will improve individuals' ability to perform on the job. We typically say training can involve the changing of skills, knowledge, attitudes, or behaviour.[4] It may mean changing what employees know, how they work, their attitudes towards their work, or their interaction with their co-workers or supervisor.

For our purposes, we will differentiate between **employee training** and **employee development**. Although both are similar in the methods used to affect learning, their time frames differ. Training is more oriented to the present, focusing on individuals' current jobs and enhancing those specific skills and abilities to perform their jobs immediately. For example, suppose, after graduating, you get a job as an HRM recruiter. Although you have a business administration degree with a major in human resources management, when you are hired, some training is needed. Among other things, you'll need to learn the company's HRM policies and practices and other pertinent recruiting methods. This, by definition, is job-specific training or training that is designed to make you more effective in your current job.

Employee development, on the other hand, generally focuses on future roles in the organization.[5] As your job and career progress, new skills and abilities will be required. For example, if you become a director of HRM, the skills needed to perform that job are quite different than those required as a recruiter. Now you will be required to supervise a number of HRM professionals, requiring a broad-based knowledge of HRM and very specific management competencies like communication skills, evaluating employee performance, and disciplining problem individuals. As you are groomed for positions of greater responsibility, employee development efforts will help prepare you for that day.

Whether we are involved in employee training or employee development, the same outcome is required—learning. As Kjersti Powell, manager of training and development for Syncrude Canada, based in Fort McMurray, Alberta, puts it: "I need to be able to develop the human and organizational capacity to learn because training and learning are directly connected to business performance."[6] If she is right and learning is critical for making employees more effective and so contributing to the success of an organization, we need to take a closer look at what is meant by learning.

Learning

We have previously described training and development as a learning process. Of course, much of an employee's learning about a job takes place outside of specific training activities, as was demonstrated in Chapter 8 on orientation. But if we are to understand what training techniques can do to improve an employee's job performance, we should begin by explaining how people learn. We will go into some detail on this topic because we believe that a knowledge of how people learn is fundamental to designing and evaluating effective training and development programs. As you go through this section, consider how these learning theory principles apply to your own experience. You will probably find that the learning principles summarized in Table 9-1 go a long way towards explaining the effort you put into learning to drive a car, for example.

Theories of Learning

Learning is the process of bringing about relatively permanent change through experience. This can be done through direct experience by doing or indirectly through observation. Regardless of the means by which learning takes place, we cannot measure learning per se; we can only measure the changes in attitudes and behaviour that occur as a result of learning. For our discussion, we will emphasize *how* we learn rather that *what* we learn. Two ways of learning have dominated learning research over the years: operant conditioning and social learning theory.

TABLE 9-1 Principles of Learning

Learning Is Enhanced When the Learner Is Motivated.	An individual must want to learn. When that desire exists, the learner will exert a high level of effort. There appears to be valid evidence to support the adage, "You can lead a horse to water, but you can't make him drink."
Learning Requires Feedback.	Feedback, or knowledge of results, is necessary so that learners can correct their mistakes. Feedback is best when it is immediate rather than delayed; the sooner individuals have some knowledge of how well they are performing, the easier it is for them to compare performance to goals and correct their erroneous actions.
Reinforcement Increases the Likelihood that a Learned Behaviour Will Be Repeated.	The principle of reinforcement tells us that behaviours that are positively reinforced (rewarded) are encouraged and sustained. When the behaviour is punished, it is temporarily suppressed but is unlikely to be extinguished. What is desired is to convey feedback to the learners when they are doing what is right to encourage them to keep doing it.
Practice Increases a Learner's Performance.	When learners actually practise what they have read or seen, they gain confidence and are less likely to make errors or to forget what they have learned.
Learning Begins Rapidly, then Plateaus.	Learning rates can be expressed as a curve that usually begins with a sharp rise, then increases at a decreasing rate until a plateau is reached. Learning is very fast at the beginning but then plateaus as opportunities for improvement are reduced.
Learning Must Be Transferable to the Job.	It doesn't make much sense to perfect a skill in the classroom and then find that you can't successfully transfer it to the job. Therefore, training should be designed for transferability.

Operant Conditioning Operant conditioning views learning as a change in behaviour which is the result of certain consequences. In other words, people learn to act in a particular way to achieve something they want or to avoid something they don't want. The tendency for an individual to repeat such behaviour, then, is influenced by the reinforcement (or lack thereof) stemming from the consequences of behaviour. Reinforcement, therefore, strengthens actions and increases the likelihood that an individual will repeat the behaviours.

As originally proposed by B. F. Skinner, operant conditioning (sometimes referred to as behaviour modification) focuses on learning from external sources[7] as opposed to learning that takes place from within. Skinner and his followers have argued that by creating consequences to follow certain behaviours, the frequency of that behaviour will be altered. That is, individuals will most likely engage in appropriate behaviours if they are reinforced for doing so. For example, suppose you're unsure about spending the time to answer the "Testing Your Understanding" questions at the end of each chapter. For the first exam, you do, and you score very well. For the next exam, however, you didn't have the time, slacked off, and didn't answer the questions at all. Your second grade was

Operant Conditioning A type of conditioning in which behaviour leads to a reward or prevents punishment.

significantly lower. Operant conditioning, then, would suggest that you'll be studying the questions again (the modified behaviour) because there was a positive reward (reinforcement) in doing so. This same analogy applies to your work. If, by learning, as demonstrated by some proficiency level, you'll be taken off probation, then that reward will foster a learning endeavour.

In operant conditioning, there are four ways in which behaviour can be shaped. These are positive reinforcement, negative reinforcement, punishment, and extinction (see "HRM Skills"). **Positive reinforcement** occurs when a response makes a behaviour more likely to be repeated. A raise, a promotion, or even praise for a job well done could encourage a behaviour to continue. **Negative reinforcement** occurs when removal of a stimulus makes a behaviour more likely to continue. Consider an employee who comes to work on time to avoid hearing the boss's reprimand: the employee has learned that by being in the office on time, the unpleasant nagging stops. On the other hand, **punishment** involves applying an unpleasant response to an undesired behaviour. Suspending an employee for coming to work drunk, or flunking a student who is caught cheating on an assignment, are examples of punishment. Finally, if we withhold reinforcement, we elicit **extinction** of the behaviour. If management never responds to employees' suggestions, the employees will stop making any more suggestions. All of these approaches affect learning, but positive reinforcement appears to have the greatest influence on permanent behavioural change.[8]

Social Learning **Social learning theory** sees learning as a continuous interaction between individuals and their environments.[9] Social learning theory acknowledges that we can learn by observing what happens to other people, by being told about something, or through direct experience. In other words, much of what we learn comes from watching others—family members, teachers, co-workers, the media, and the like. Since much of employee training is observational in nature, this theory appears to have considerable application potential.

Social learning theory can be viewed as an extension of behaviour modification because it, too, recognizes the importance of results on behaviour. But social learning theory also includes what individuals observe and the importance of their perceptions in the learning process. That is, individuals respond to situations with regard to how they perceive consequences affecting them, not necessarily the consequences themselves. For instance, if you observe that employees who agree with the supervisors' opinions are rewarded—even if you have never experienced that yourselves—you will act on the belief that agreement gets rewarded.

The influence of others, and things we'll call models, are central to the social learning viewpoint. Four processes have been found to determine the influence a model will have on an individual: 1. Attentional Processes; 2. Retention Processes; 3. Motor Reproduction Processes; and 4. Reinforcement Processes.

1. *Attentional Processes* People only learn from models when they recognize and pay attention to their critical features. We tend to be most influenced by models that are attractive, repeatedly available, that we think are important, or that we see as similar to us.
2. *Retention Processes* A model's influence will depend on how well the individual remembers the model's action even after the model is no longer readily available.
3. *Motor Reproduction Processes* After a person has seen a new behaviour by observing the model, the watching must be converted to doing. This process then demonstrates that the individual can perform the modelled activities.
4. *Reinforcement Processes* Individuals will be motivated to exhibit the modelled behaviour if positive incentives or rewards are provided. Behaviours that are reinforced will be given more attention, learned better, and performed more often.

Positive Reinforcement Providing a response to a behaviour that makes it more likely to be repeated.

Negative Reinforcement Removing a response to a behaviour so that the behaviour is more likely to be repeated.

Punishment Providing an unpleasant consequence to an undesirable behaviour.

Extinction Removing reinforcement to a behaviour so that individual's eventually cease doing it.

Social Learning Theory Theory of learning that views learning as occurring through observation and direct experience.

Social learning theory offers us insights into what a training exercise should include. Specifically, it tells us training should provide a model,[10] grab the trainee's attention, provide motivational properties, help the trainee file away what he or she has learned for later use, and, if the training has taken place off the job, allow the trainee some opportunity to transfer what has been learned to the job (see Table 9-1 on page 259).

The Learning Curve

Learning begins rapidly, then it plateaus. As such, learning rates can be expressed as a curve that usually begins with a sharp rise, then increases at a diminishing rate until a plateau is reached. The learning curve principle can be illustrated by observing individuals in training to run the kilometre. At first, their time improves rapidly as they get into shape. Then, as their conditioning develops, their improvement plateaus. Obviously, knocking one minute off a ten-minute kilometre is a lot easier than knocking one minute off a five-minute kilometre. If you have ever learned to type on a keyboard, you may have had an experience that somewhat follows the pattern shown in Figure 9-1. The specific criterion is words typed per minute, and the time element is in weeks. Note the shape of the curve in Figure 9-1. During the first three weeks, the rate of increase is slow as the subject learns the typing technique and becomes familiar with the keyboard. During the next three weeks, learning accelerates as the subject works on developing speed. After six weeks, learning slows as progress evolves into refinement of technique.

Learning Curve Depicts the rate of learning.

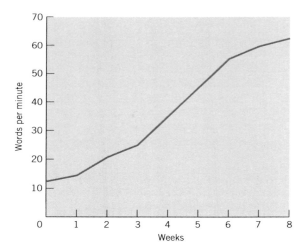

Figure 9-1
Learning Curve on a
Computer Keyboard

Employment Equity

Employment equity is most prevalent in the hiring process, but it is also important in training. Remember that discrimination may exist whenever any HRM activity adversely affects designated group members in hiring, firing, and promoting. So what impact does employment equity have on training programs? Let's briefly take a look.

Training programs may be required for promotions, job bidding (especially in unionized workplaces), or for salary increases. In each of these cases, it is the responsibility of the organization to ensure that training selection criteria are related to the job, and that equal training opportunities exist for all employees. If members of minority groups more frequently fail to pass a training program than majority group members, this may indicate a problem and the need to modify the training that is offered. Once again, organizations should monitor these activities and perform periodic audits to ensure compliance with employment equity regulations. They should also make a conscious effort to make training as accessible to employees as possible. This is very much the philosophy that underlies the Royal Bank of Canada's Royal Learning Network (RLN).[11] Gay Mitchell, executive vice-president at the Royal Bank, notes that Royal's development of its human capital differs in some fundamental ways from the strategies other firms have followed. "One major difference is that we have widened the access to learning. We are opening up access to knowledge, skill building, and competency development to a much larger number of people than ever before."

Employee Training

Now that we have a better understanding of what training is and how individuals learn, we can turn to a more detailed analysis of the training and development process. The definitions given earlier distinguish between training as present-oriented and job-related, and development as future-oriented and growth-related. Both training and development, however, follow a similar process consisting of three major elements: needs assessment, implementation, and evaluation, and generally they happen in the order we have given them. The need for training has to be determined, then programs are implemented through various methods of training and development, and finally, completed programs are evaluated for their effectiveness. In the balance of this chapter we examine these major elements in the training and development process.

Determining Training Needs

Now that we have a better understanding of what training is and how individuals learn, we can look at a more fundamental question for organizations: How does an organization assess whether there is a need for training? We propose that management can determine this following a process depicted in Figure 9-2.

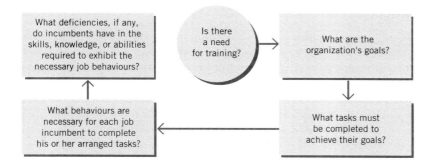

Figure 9-2
Determining Training Needs

Recall from Chapter 5 that these questions demonstrate the close link between strategic human resources planning and the determination of training needs. Based on our knowledge of the organization's needs, the type of work to be done, and the type of skills necessary to complete this work, our training program should follow naturally. Once we can identify where deficiencies lie, we have a grasp of the extent and nature of our training needs.

What kinds of signals can warn a manager that employee training may be necessary? The more obvious ones relate directly to productivity: inadequate job performance or a drop in productivity. The former is likely to occur in the early months on a new job. When a manager sees evidence of inadequate job performance, assuming the individual is making a satisfactory effort, attention should be given to raising the worker's skill level. When a manager is confronted with a drop in productivity, it may suggest that skills need to be fine-tuned.

In addition to productivity measures, quality problems such as keyboarding errors or high product rejection rates, may indicate a need for employee training. A rise in the number of accidents reported also suggests that some type of retraining is necessary. There is also the question of future changes that are being imposed on the worker as a result of a job redesign or a technological advance. These types of job changes require training that is a part of planned change rather than a reaction to immediately unsatisfactory conditions.

If deficiencies in performance are uncovered, it doesn't necessarily follow that the manager should take corrective action. It is important to put training into perspective. It has costs, which are often high, ranging from a few hundred dollars to several thousand per employee trained, and training should not be viewed as a panacea. Rather, training should be judged by its contribution to performance where performance is a function of skills, abilities, motivation, and the opportunity to perform. Managers must compare the value received from the increased performance due to training with its costs.

Once it has been determined that training is necessary, goals must be established. Management must state explicitly what results it wants for each employee. It is not enough merely to say that change in employee knowledge, skills, attitudes, or behaviour is "desirable"; we must clarify what is to change and by how much. These goals have to be tangible, verifiable, and measurable, and they should be clear to both management and employees. For instance, a firefighter might be expected to jump from a moving fire truck travelling at twenty-five kilometres per hour, successfully hook up a ten-centimetre hose to a hydrant, and turn on the hydrant—all in less than forty seconds. Such explicit goals ensure that both management and the employee know what is expected from the training effort.

Training Methods

The most popular training and development methods used by organizations can be classified as either on-the-job or off-the-job training. In the following pages, we will briefly introduce the better-known techniques of each category.

On-the-Job Training The most widely used training methods take place on the job. They are popular because they are relatively simple and appear to be less costly to operate than off-the-job methods. On-the-job training places the employees in actual work situations and makes them appear to be productive immediately. It is learning by doing. For jobs that either are difficult to simulate or can be learned quickly by watching and doing, on-the-job training makes sense.

One of the drawbacks of on-the-job training can be low productivity while the employees develop their skills. Another drawback can be the errors made by the trainees while they learn. However, when the damage the trainees can do is minimal, where outside training facilities and personnel are limited or costly, and where it is desirable for the workers to learn the job under normal working conditions, the benefits of on-the-job training frequently offset the drawbacks. Let's look at two types of on-the-job training: apprenticeship programs and job instruction training (JIT).

People seeking to enter skilled trades—to become, for example, plumbers, or electronic technicians—are often required to undergo **apprenticeship training** before they are elevated to master status. Apprenticeship programs put the trainee under the guidance of a master worker, the argument being that the required knowledge and skills are so complex that nothing less than a period of time understudying with a skilled master will work.[12] As the technology requirements of jobs increase, apprenticeship is becoming an increasingly attractive option for skills training, and it is estimated that each year, Canadians register for an estimated 1.2 million spaces in courses, including, among other areas, technology and pre-apprentice trades.[13] In total, there are close to 170 recognized apprenticeship programs in Canada, which still do not fully meet industry's needs.

Apprenticeship Training Putting the trainee under the guidance of a master worker; common in the skilled trades.

During the Second World War, a systematic approach to on-the-job training was developed to prepare supervisors to train employees. Known as **job instruction training (JIT)**, it proved highly effective and became extremely popular. Job instruction training consists of four basic steps:

1. Preparing the trainees by telling them about the job and overcoming their uncertainties.
2. Presenting the instruction and giving essential information in a clear manner.
3. Having the trainees try out the job to demonstrate their understanding.
4. Placing the workers into the job on their own, with a designated resource person to call upon should they need assistance.[14]

Job Instruction Training (JIT) A systematic approach to on-the-job training consisting of four basic steps.

Use of job instruction training can achieve impressive results.[15] By following these steps, studies indicate that employee turnover can be reduced, employee morale increased, and employee accidents decreased.[16]

Off-the-Job Training Off-the-job training covers a number of techniques—classroom lectures, films, demonstrations, case studies and other simulation exercises, and programmed instruction. The facilities needed for each of these techniques vary from a small, makeshift classroom to an elaborate development centre with large lecture halls supplemented by small conference rooms with sophisticated instructional technology equipment. We have summarized the majority of these methods in Table 9-2. Because of its importance in today's technology-oriented organizations, however, programmed and on-line instruction especially warrants a closer look.

TABLE 9-2 Off-the-job Training Methods

Classroom Lectures	Lectures designed to communicate specific interpersonal, technical, or problem-solving skills.
Videos and Films	Using various media productions to demonstrate specialized skills that are not easily presented by other training methods.
Simulation Exercises	Training by actually performing the work. This may include case analysis, experiential exercises, role-playing, or group decision making.

Computer-Based Training	Simulating the work environment by programming a computer to imitate some of the realities of the job.
Vestibule Training	Training on actual equipment used on the job but conducted away from the actual work setting—a simulated work station.
Programmed Instruction	Condensing training materials into highly organized, logical sequences. May include computer tutorials, interactive video disks, or virtual reality simulations.
Internet	Information-based learning from relevant Web sites.

Programmed Instruction Material is learned in a highly organized, logical sequence, that requires the individual to respond.

Programmed instruction can take the form of programmed tests, manuals, or video displays, while in some organizations, teaching machines are utilized. All programmed instruction approaches have a common characteristic: They condense the material to be learned into highly organized, logical sequences that require the trainee to respond. The ideal format provides for nearly instantaneous feedback that informs the trainee if his or her response is correct. In short, they are interactive.

Meet

Barbara Syer
Director and academic dean,
University of Sun Life

Most major Canadian corporations offer some kind of training to their employees, but Sun Life, one of Canada's oldest and largest insurance firms, has taken the concept of training and development one step further by establishing its own in-house "university".

One of the earliest proponents of this idea was Barbara Syer, who is now head of USL. After hearing about a number of US corporate "universities", she explained, she and a colleague sought and got a mandate to research the idea of founding one at Sun Life. A conference sponsored by the US group Corporate University Xchange, at which concepts pioneered by American corporate "universities" (such as General Electric, Motorola, and Disney) were presented, influenced the final model chosen by Sun Life.

"I sold it to our management team, and they were highly enthusiastic," recalls Ms Syer.

Why a "university"? "USL allows us to better align training across the whole corporation," answers Ms Syer. "We used to have five independent training departments—one for core skills, one for executive training, etc. If an employee needed help with a skill—say, to learn a software package—she or he would have to start by tracking down the right department.

"Now the departments still exist but 'behind the scenes.' The employees' access to training is now transparent," Ms Syer explains. So the employee needing software training can just look up the software in the USL course catalogue on-line.

Centralizing training at USL is also cost-effective, offering economies of scale with outside vendors. But the main advantage of USL is that Sun Life can better ensure that training is aligned with its corporate goals. "And because each school or college at USL is headed by a dean who is part of a Sun Life business unit," Ms Syer emphasizes, "it is the stakeholders in the business who are responsible for identifying the business needs. They work with curriculum managers to determine how these can best be driven by training."

USL classes and resources are currently available at both the Montreal and Toronto offices of Sun Life, but future plans are to take them across the country, creating a "virtual university" and offering training via Internet, intranet, and videoconferencing.

So what's it like to be a corporate academic dean? "It's really exciting," Ms Syer concludes. "We feel so lucky to be a part of it!"

As technology continues to evolve, we can expect programmed instruction to become more prominent. Two versions—interactive video disks (IVD) and virtual reality—are gaining momentum in corporate training. **Interactive video disks** allow users to interact with a personal computer usually via a CD-ROM-based system while simultaneously being exposed to video pictures. This multimedia technology enables the trainee to experience the effect of his or her decision in real time.[17] Many Canadian companies now use such technology as a matter of course in their training programs. For example, the centre of the workplace learning experience in the Royal Bank's learning centre, mentioned earlier, is the computer-based Personal Learning Network. Its CD-ROM technology uses video, graphics, and sound to create learning that is both interesting and interactive.[18]

Interactive Video Disks (IVD) Videos that permit the user to make changes/selections and see the effects of their decisions in real time.

Virtual reality is a newer concept in corporate training.[19] Virtual reality systems simulate actual work activities, giving the individual a chance to perfect his or her skills without disrupting the actual workplace. One type of virtual reality requires an individual to wear a helmet and visor, inside which are sensors that display both visual and audio simulations of an event. For instance, skiers can be taught to ski with virtual reality. Under the system, an individual standing on dry land can be made to feel like he or she is actually landing a plane with simulated speed, obstacles, and weather. This sophisticated simulation allows individuals to interact with their environment as if they were really there. Although such systems are promising, their expense at this time precludes their use except for extremely large organizations and very complex jobs.

Virtual Reality A process which simulates actual activities allowing the individual to refine his or her skills.

The Internet The **Internet** is a source of vast information resources that can be used to great advantage for training if carefully structured. Because of its ubiquitous character, it is a training method that can be used both on and off the job. In some ways, the Internet is like a huge reference library sitting on the desks of everyone with a computer and Internet link. It is important to use the Internet efficiently since we all know, only too well, what a magnificent time-waster it can be! Therefore, it is important to direct trainees to specific sites and provide clear objectives for searches undertaken and a clear requirement to account for time spent.

Internet The international network of computers that allows communication via electronic mail and the World Wide Web.

While training delivery via Internet still has several problems—slow transmission of video clips, for example—intranets (multimedia systems internal to the organization) are a more promising immediate alternative. Since they can be easily updated, their development can be much more cost-effective than CD-ROMS and videotapes. A number of Canadian companies such as Xerox Canada, IBM Canada, and Royal Bank of Canada are actively pursuing virtual training through the Internet and intranet.[20]

The World Wide Web provides exciting possibilities for the delivery of training programs.

Employee Development

Employee development, by design, is more future-oriented and more concerned with education than employee training. By education, we mean that employee development activities attempt to instil sound reasoning processes—to enhance one's ability to understand and interpret knowledge—rather than just to impart a body of facts or teach a specific set of motor skills. Development, therefore, focuses more on the employee's longer-term personal growth.

Successful employees prepared for positions of greater responsibility have analytical, human, conceptual, and specialized skills. They are able to think, analyse, and understand. Training, per se, cannot overcome an individual's inability to understand cause-and-effect relationships, to synthesize from experience, to visualize relationships, or to think logically. As a result, employee development should be predominantly an education process rather than simply a training one.

It is important to remember one critical component of employee development: All employees at all levels can be developed, although historically, this was reserved for potential management personnel. Although it is critical for individuals to be trained in specific skills related to managing—planning, organizing, leading, controlling, and decision making—time has taught us that these skills are also needed by non-management personnel. The use of work teams, reductions in supervisory roles, allowing workers to participate in setting the goals of their jobs, and a greater emphasis on quality and customer satisfaction have changed the way employee development is viewed. Organizations now require new skills, knowledge, and abilities of all employees, and the methods used to develop managerial personnel are the same as those used to develop employees in general.

Employee Development Methods

Development of an individual's abilities can take place on or off the job. We will review three popular on-the-job techniques—job rotation, assistant positions, and committee assignments—and three off-the-job methods—lecture courses and seminars, simulation exercises, and outdoor training.

On the Job

Job Rotation Job rotation involves moving employees to various positions in the organization in an effort to expand their skills, knowledge, and abilities. Job rotation can be either horizontal or vertical. Vertical rotation is essentially a promotion, while horizontal job rotation is better understood as a short-term lateral transfer.

> **Job Rotation** Moving employees horizontally or vertically to expand their skills, knowledge, or abilities.

Job rotation represents an excellent method for broadening individuals' knowledge of company operations and for turning specialists into generalists. In addition to increasing individuals' experience and allowing them to absorb new information, it can reduce boredom and stimulate the development of new ideas. It can also provide opportunities for a more comprehensive and reliable evaluation of employees by their supervisors.

Assistant Positions Employees with demonstrated potential are given the opportunity to work under a seasoned and successful manager often in different areas of the organization. Working as staff assistants or, in some cases, serving on "junior boards," these individuals perform many duties under the watchful eye of a supportive coach. In doing so, these employees get exposure to a wide variety of management activities and are prepared to assume the duties of the next higher level.

Committee Assignment Committee assignments can provide an opportunity for the employee to share in decision making, learn by watching others, and investigate specific organizational problems. When committees are of an ad hoc or temporary nature, they often take on task force activities designed to delve into a particular problem, ascertain alternative solutions, and make a recommendation for implementing a solution. These temporary assignments can be both interesting and rewarding to an employee's growth. Appointment to permanent committees increases the employee's exposure to other members of the organization, broadens his or her understanding, and provides an opportunity to grow and make recommendations under the scrutiny of other committee members.

Off the Job

Lecture Courses and Seminars Traditional forms of instruction revolved around formal lecture courses and seminars. These offered an opportunity for individuals to acquire knowledge and develop their conceptual and analytical abilities. For many organizations, they were offered in-house by the organization itself, through outside vendors, or both. Today, technology has brought significant improvements to the training field. A growing trend at companies such as Pacific Bell and BC Telecom[21] is to provide lecture courses and seminars revolving around what we call distance learning.[22] Through the use of digitized computer technology, a facilitator can give a lecture which is transmitted simultaneously to several other locations over fibre optic cables, in real time. For example, British Airways uses distance learning to train its employees for supervisory positions.[23] Workers, located in ten different countries, receive training from five different organizations, saving both time and money.[24]

Distance learning has always been important, but the recent advances in information technology such as the Internet have truly brought this teaching method to the forefront. The future opportunities seem almost limitless. For example, at the time of writing, one of the text's authors will shortly participate in a virtual conference on telework which will bring participants together from all over the world.[25] Each author will make an electronic presentation, discussion will take place in a formal "virtual classroom," and then everyone will get together informally in a "chat room."

Simulation Exercises Training techniques which try to recreate an envisionment which closely mirrors actual managerial problems.

Simulation Exercises Simulation Exercises were first introduced as a training technique, but they are probably even more popular for employee development. The more widely used simulation exercises include case studies, decision games, and role-playing.

The case study approach to employee development was popularized at the Harvard Graduate School of Business. Taken from the actual experiences of organizations, these cases represent attempts to describe as accurately as possible real problems that managers have faced. Trainees study the cases to determine problems, analyse causes, develop alternative solutions, select what they believe to be the best solution, and implement it. Case studies can provide stimulating discussions among participants as well as excellent opportunities for individuals to defend their analytical and judgemental abilities. It appears to be a rather effective method for improving decision-making abilities within the constraints of limited information.

Simulated decision games and role-playing exercises have individuals act out managerial problems. Games, which are frequently played on a specially programmed computer, provide opportunities for individuals to make decisions and to consider the implications of a decision on other segments of the organization. Role-playing allows the participants to act out problems and to deal with real people. Participants are assigned roles and are asked to react to one another as they would have to do in their managerial jobs.

The advantages to simulation exercises are the opportunities to attempt to create an environment similar to real situations managers face without paying the high costs involved should the actions prove undesirable. Of course, the disadvantages are that it is difficult to duplicate the pressures and realities of actual decision making on the job, and individuals often act differently in real-life situations than they do in a simulated exercise.

Outdoor Training Specialized training that occurs outdoors focuses on building self-confidence and teamwork.

Outdoor Training A recent trend to employee development has been the use of **outdoor** (sometimes referred to as wilderness or survival) **training**. The primary focus of such training is to teach trainees the importance of working together, gelling as a team. This training generally involves some major emotional and physical challenge, such as whitewater rafting, mountain climbing, or surviving a week in the jungle. The purpose of such training is to see how employees react to the challenges that nature presents to them. Do they face these dangers alone? Do they panic? Or are they controlled and successful in achieving their goal? The reality of today's business environment does not permit loner employees and has reinforced working closely with one another, building trusting relationships, and succeeding as a member of a group.[26]

One of the most exciting examples emanates from the peaceful Niagara-on-the-Lake "squadron headquarters" of Air Combat Canada (ACC).[27] ACC operates two aerobatic aeroplanes that take up individuals into the all-too-realistic simulation of taking part in an actual aerial dogfight. The "pilots" experience a full 400-degree roll in one second and shoot laser guns at the "enemy". The experience is designed for corporations looking for a unique team-building adventure for employees who discover their own limitations and their impact on colleagues in the exercise. This unusual program can handle up to twelve people in an all-day exercise, costing about $1,000 per person. This is no cheap show—the cost of setting up ACC was about $1 million.

"Outward bound" training programs purport to build team work and develop management skills by subjecting employees to dangerous situations in a setting that bears no relationship whatever to the workplace.

Two Special Cases of Development: Mentoring and Counselling

Two special cases of development continue to attract a great deal of attention. These are the mentoring /coaching process and employee counselling.

Mentoring/Coaching It has become increasingly clear over the years that employees who aspire to management need the assistance and advocacy of someone higher up in the organization.[28] These career progressions often require having the favour of the dominant "in group" which sets corporate goals, priorities, and standards.[29] Paul Woolner, principal of Toronto's Woolner and Associates, argues that HRM professionals play a critical role in the process as their function changes from "traditional teacher to developmental coach."[30]

When a senior employee takes an active hand in guiding another individual, we refer to this activity as mentoring or coaching. Just as sports coaches observe, analyse, and attempt to improve the performance of their athletes, coaches on the job can do the same. The effective coach, whether on the playing field or in the corporate hierarchy, gives guidance through direction, advice, criticism, and suggestion in an attempt to aid the employee's growth.[31] These individuals offer to assist certain junior employees in terms of providing a support system. The senior employee shares his or her experiences with the protégé, providing guidance on how to make it in the organization. Coaching of employees can occur at any level and can be most effective when the two individuals do not have any type of reporting relationship with each other.

Accordingly, in organizations that promote from within, those who aspire to succeed must have the corporate support system[32] in their favour. This support system, guided by a mentor, vouches for the candidate, answers for the candidate in the highest circles within the organization, makes appropriate introductions, and advises and guides the candidate on how to move through the system effectively. In one study, such support generated significant outcomes.[33] For example, these researchers found that where a significant mentoring relationship existed, those protégés had better and more frequent promotions and were paid significantly more than those who were not mentored.[34] They also had a greater level of commitment to the organization and greater career success.[35] But there was a caution in this study; the benefits from mentoring generally went to white male employees. Why? Because women and minorities are more recent arrivals on the corporate scene, and fewer of them are in senior positions where they can function as mentors.[36] (see "Ethical Decisions in HRM").

Mentoring or Coaching The actively guidance of a junior employee by a more senior one.

Ethical Decisions in HRM:

Special Mentoring Programs for Women and Minorities

We have been witnessing many discussions lately regarding how more women and minorities can break through the glass ceiling. There is no doubt that these groups are under-represented at the top echelons of organizations. Several reasons have been well documented detailing why this occurred. One of those reasons centres around the issue of mentoring.

Finding a mentor to support you is rarely easy. In fact, more often than not, a mentor approaches you to begin the relationship. In the past, many of these individuals were white males, and historically, women and minorities found it difficult to gain the favour of these mentors simply because mentors preferred someone more like themselves.

With the changing workforce composition, employment legislation, and changing societal views of women and minorities in the workplace, mentoring relationships for this group are occurring more frequently. But it is not, as yet, fully ingrained in the minds and hearts of some managers. Consequently, a number of organizations have developed special mentoring programs for women and minorities—formalizing a practice that typically evolved naturally. In some respects, at this time, this may be the best way to help further advance these two groups. Leaving it up to nature just doesn't work well. The prevalence of the glass ceiling dilemma attests to that. On the other hand, can a mentoring relationship be forced and regulated? The crux of these relationships is for an individual to become very close to his or her protégé in an effort to further his or her career. Won't forcing these people together—two individuals who have not come together naturally—lead to a constrained relationship? Given the degree of conflict that may arise between the two, it's possible more harm than good may result for the protégé's career.

Should women and minorities be given special treatment in the mentoring relationship by having organizational policies dictating who will mentor and how it will be handled? Should there be special guidelines to ensure that mentoring for women and minorities occurs? And what about the white male? Is he being left out? What do you think?

Mentor A senior employee who supports the career development of a junior employee.

One of the main reasons for the existence of the glass ceiling[37] is that women do not have many role models sitting high in the organization who can help them through the system.[38] There may be some explanation. **Mentors** sometimes select their protégés on the basis of seeing themselves, in their younger years, in the employee. Since men rarely can identify with younger women, many are unwilling to play the part of their mentor.[39] Of course, as women have battled their way into the inner circle of organizational power, some success is being witnessed.[40] Organizations are beginning to explore ways of advocating cross-gender mentoring. This revolves around identifying the problems associated with such an arrangement,[41] deciding how they can be handled effectively, and providing organizational support.[42]

The technique of senior employees coaching individuals has the advantages that go with learning by doing and high interaction and rapid feedback on performance. Unfortunately, its two biggest disadvantages are its tendencies to perpetuate the current styles and practices in the organization and its heavy reliance on the coach's ability to be a good teacher. In the same way that we recognize that all excellent athletes do not make good coaches, excellent employees are not all effective coaches. An individual can become an excellent performer without necessarily having the knack of passing those skills on. This technique is only as effective as its coach.

Mentoring usually occurs between junior and senior employees, but it can also exist between peers. A number of Canadian organizations such as Vancouver City Credit Union, Custom Leather of Waterloo, Ontario, and Bellewood Health Services of Scarborough, Ontario are successfully implementing peer mentoring programs.[43] Janice Hambley, vice-president of Bellewood Health Services, says, "I've found peer training to be an effective approach for the development of both management skills and new procedures."

One of the fastest growing trends in Canada, is the use of consultants hired as external coaches, (i.e, outside the organization). This is a reflection of both a growth in teleworkers (outside of a central location) and an environment of downsized HR departments. One such coach is Simon Reilly, based in Vancouver and offering regular coaching sessions for around $500 a month.[44] Reilly aims to increase his clients' success by helping them set goals, better plan their business lives, and work more efficiently. Since it was founded in 1992, the International Coach Federation has attracted more than 1,000 members, over a hundred of them in Canada. Of particular interest to women is the role coaches play in the difficult exercise of balancing work and family, focusing values, and clarifying life goals.

Employee Counselling In an attempt to assist employees in performing their assigned jobs, it sometimes may be necessary for the manager to counsel them. In terms of employee counselling, however, a distinction needs to be made. In the discussion above, we've referred to coaching and mentoring techniques as ways of helping to develop employees and to assist in their career growth. Although employee counselling takes a similar approach, there is one major difference from coaching. Employee counselling is typically used when a performance problem arises. Thus, the focus of this discussion is more appropriately aligned with the discipline process.

Whenever an employee exhibits work behaviours that are inconsistent with the work environment (i.e., stealing, chronic absenteeism, inability to get along with co-workers, and so forth) or is unable to perform his or her job satisfactorily, a manager must intervene. But before any intervention can begin, it is imperative for the manager to identify the source of the problem. If the performance problem is related to a lack of ability, training and development can help.[45] This type of intervention is then more closely aligned to coaching. However, when the problem is one related to attitude, whether voluntary or involuntary, employee counselling is the next logical approach.[46]

Although **employee counselling** processes differ, some fundamental steps should be followed when counselling an employee (see "HRM Skills"). As a prerequisite, a manager must have good listening skills.[47] The purpose of employee counselling is to uncover the reason for the poor performance, which must be elicited from the employee. A manager who dominates the meeting by talking may undermine the potential benefits of an effective counselling session.

Employee Counselling A process whereby employees are guided in overcoming performance problems.

In employee counselling, the manager must deal with the inappropriate behaviour, not the person. For instance, telling employees they are poor workers is only asking for trouble, whereas stating that they have been late four times in the past month, which has caused a backlog of accounts payables, can be understood and dealt with. By dealing with performance-related behaviour, the manager and the employee are in a better position to solve the problem as adults.

The manager must discuss the unacceptable behaviour with the employee to determine its cause. It is important to note that the manager is not attempting to be a psychologist; he or she is only interested in the behaviours that affect performance. If the problem is a personal one, under no circumstances should the manager attempt to "fix" it. Rather, the well-informed manager, recognizing a personal problem, will refer the employee to an appropriate source of assistance (like the company's employee assistance program). No matter where the problem lies, the manager must get the employee to understand and accept the problem and then, to find ways to correct it. At this point, the manager may offer whatever assistance he or she can, but the employee must understand that it is his or her sole responsibility to make the change. Failure to do so will only result in disciplinary procedures.

Counselling Employees

1. **Document all problem performance behaviours.** Document specific job behaviours, such as absenteeism, lateness, and poor quality work, noting dates, times, and what happened. This provides you with objective data.
2. **Deal with the employee objectively, fairly, and equitably.** Treat each employee similarly. That means that one should not be sent to counselling while another gets away scot-free. Issues discussed should focus on performance behaviours.
3. **Confront job performance issues only.** Your main focus should be on those things that affect performance. Even though it may be a personal problem, you should not try to psychoanalyse the individual. Leave that to the trained specialists. You can, however, address how these behaviors are affecting the employee's job performance.
4. **Offer assistance to help the employee.** Just pointing the finger at an employee serves no useful purpose. Chances are, if the employee could have "fixed" the problem alone, he or she probably would have. Help might be needed—yours and the organizations, so offer this assistance where possible.
5. **Expect the employee to resist the feedback and become defensive.** It is human nature to dislike constructive, but negative feedback. The individual will be uncomfortable with the discussion, but make every effort to keep the meeting calm so that the message can get across. Documentation, fairness, focusing on job behaviors, and offering assistance helps to reduce this defensiveness.
6. **Get the employee to own up to the problem.** After all, its his or her problem and not yours. The employee needs to take responsibility for his or her behaviour, and begin to look for ways to correct the problems.
7. **Develop an action plan to correct performance.** Once the employee has taken responsibility for the problem, develop a plan of action designed to correct the problem. Be specific as to what the employee must do (e.g., what is expected and when it is expected) and what resources you are willing to commit to assist.

8. **Identify outcomes for failing to correct problems.** You need to inform the employee what the consequences will be if he or she does not follow the action plan. You're there to help, not carry a poor performer forever.
9. **Monitor and control progress.** Evaluate the progress the employee is making. Provide frequent feedback on what you're observing. Reinforce positive efforts.

Source: Adapted from Commerce Clearing House, "The Do's and Don'ts of Confronting a Troubled Employee," *Topical Law Reports* (Chicago: Commerce Clearing House, Inc., October 1990), pp. 4359–60; Gerald D. Cook, "Employee Counseling Session," *Supervision* (August 1989), p. 3; and Andrew E. Schuartz, "Counseling the Marginal Performer," *Management Solutions* (March 1988), p. 30.

Organizational Development

Although our discussion so far has been related to the people side of business, it is important to recognize that organizations change from time to time. With the changes experienced with respect to downsizing, rightsizing, Total Quality Management, diversity, and re-engineering, it is necessary to move the organization forward through a process we call organizational development (OD). The basis of organizational development is to help people adapt to change. Although there are different perspectives on how that change should occur, one of the best descriptions of the process is illustrated by Kurt Lewin.[48]

According to Lewin, change occurs over three stages. These include the unfreezing of the status quo, the change to the new state, and refreezing to ensure that the change becomes permanent. We have graphically portrayed this process in Figure 9-3. What Lewin identified was the movement in the organization away from the status quo. Portraying the status quo in Figure 9-3 as circles, the change effort helps the organization move in the direction of the squares or new state. Through OD efforts, the intervention can take place, with the change effort supported by continual reinforcement to make it permanent.

Organizational Development (OD) A process in the organization that helps employees adapt to change.

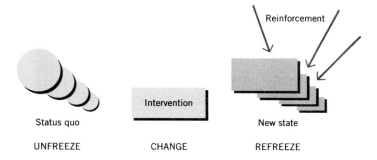

Figure 9-3
Lewin's Change Process

Organizational Development and Its Methods

Development efforts in human resources management go beyond the individual. There are instances like changing an organization's culture where system-wide change and development are required. Organizational development techniques have been created to change the values and attitudes of people and the structure of organizations in order to make them more adaptive. Among the more popular OD techniques are three that rely heavily on group interactions, participation, and collaboration. These are survey feedback, team building, and third-party intervention.[49]

Attitude Survey Data gathering questionnaires used to elicit responses or interviews from employees regarding how they feel about their jobs, work groups, supervisors, and the organization.

Survey Feedback One tool for assessing attitudes held by organizational members, identifying discrepancies among perceptions, and resolving these differences is the attitude survey. Organization members may be asked to respond to a set of specific questions or may be interviewed to determine what issues are relevant. A questionnaire (see Figure 9-4) will ask members for their perceptions and attitudes on a broad range of topics such as: decision-making practices; leadership; communication effectiveness; coordination between units; and satisfaction with the organization, job, co-workers, and immediate supervisor.

The data from this questionnaire are tabulated and then become the springboard for identifying problems and clarifying issues that may be creating difficulties for people. It is hoped that addressing these questions will result in the group agreeing on commitments to various actions that will remedy the problems that have been identified.

Figure 9-4
A Sample Attitude Survey

Rate each of the following statements using the following scale:

> 1 = strongly agree
> 2 = agree
> 3 = undecided
> 4 = disagree
> 5 = strongly disagree

1. The environment in this organization is conducive to productive work.	5	4	3	2	1
2. Getting ahead in this organization is strictly a function of one's performance.	5	4	3	2	1
3. My salary is fair and competitive.	5	4	3	2	1
4. Employee benefits are appropriate and meet my personal needs.	5	4	3	2	1
5. I have the opportunity to make decisions about my job for those things that affect it.	5	4	3	2	1
6. I have an open and trusting relationship with my boss.	5	4	3	2	1
7. Clear work expectations exist for my job.	5	4	3	2	1
8. My job challenges me to use my skills, knowledge, and abilities.	5	4	3	2	1
9. The organization encourages a team environment.	5	4	3	2	1
10. Managers of this organization have a clear direction for the next ten years.	5	4	3	2	1

Team Building Organizations are composed of people working together to achieve some common end. Since people are frequently required to work in groups, considerable attention has been focused on OD for team building.

Team building can be applied within groups or between them where activities are interdependent, but for our discussion, we will emphasize the intragroup level. The activities included in team building usually include goal setting, development of interpersonal relations among team members, role analysis to clarify each member's role and responsibilities, and team process analysis. Of course, team building may emphasize or exclude certain activities depending on the purpose of the development effort and the specific problems with which the team is confronted. Basically, however, team building attempts to increase involvement among group members to build trust and openness.

Third-party Intervention Third-party intervention seeks to change the attitudes, stereotypes, and perceptions groups have of each other. For example, in one company, the marketing representatives saw HRM as being a bunch of smiley-types who sit around and plan company picnics. Such stereotypes have an obvious negative impact on the coordinating efforts between departments, and can lead to conflict.

Although there are a number of approaches for third-party intervention, conflict resolution strategies are often dominant.[50] In conflict resolution, the OD professional attempts to get both parties to see the similarities and differences existing between them and focus on how the differences can be overcome. Achieving some movement towards reducing these differences is often gained through consensus building—finding a solution that is acceptable to both parties.

OD in the Re-Engineered Organization

Today, organizational development has taken on a renewed importance. Brought about by continuous improvement goals, many organizations have changed drastically the way they do business. For example, companies such as Stentor, Royal Bank, Syncrude, and Labatts' are making significant changes in their development programs and business processes to achieve results. Attaining these goals, however, directly affects the organization's operations and its people.

Whenever change occurs, four areas are usually affected: the organization's systems, its technology, its processes, and its people. No matter what the change is or how minor it may appear, understanding its effect is paramount for the change to be supported and lasting. That is where OD comes into play.

OD efforts are designed to support the strategic direction of the business. For instance, if work processes change, people will need to learn new production methods, procedures, and even skills. OD becomes instrumental in bringing about the change because whenever change occurs, its effect becomes an organizational culture issue. Accordingly, OD must ensure that all organizational members support the new culture and provide whatever assistance is needed to bring the new culture to fruition.

The Role of Change Agents

No matter what role OD takes in an organization, it requires facilitation by an individual well versed in organization dynamics. In HRM terms, we call this person a change agent.[51] Change agents are responsible for fostering the environment in which change can be made and working with the affected employees to help them adapt to the change that is taking place. To achieve this goal, change agents must possess two critical skills: the ability to take risks and outstanding communication skills.[52]

Marc Gagnon, vice-president of human resources for Cirque du Soleil, the Montreal-based circus, argues that as change agents, he and his staff of twenty-

Change Agent Individuals responsible for fostering the change effort and assisting employees in adapting to the changes.

four have to do as much juggling as the performers do under the big top.[53] "We try to manage like we build our shows—we try to be innovative and creative. But to be a creator, you also have to have a little bit of anarchy. If you have too many systems, if you overmanage, you're going to get a lousy show." Gagnon points out that his company employs four people as change agents and spends about $1 million a year on internal communications.

Change agents may be either internal employees (often associated with the training and development function of HRM) or external consultants. Successful applications of the change agent role have been witnessed in many organizations, particularly around the introduction of major new systems. For example, in a study carried out by Templer and Solomon[54] of the way new information technology was introduced into a major professional organization in Canada, they found that success was brought about through the concerted efforts of one individual who championed the process—the change agent.

Evaluating Training and Development Effectiveness

Any training or development effort must be cost-effective. That is, the benefits gained by training must outweigh its costs, and only by analysing such programs can effectiveness be determined. In Chapter 7, we discussed the effectiveness of selection devices. We were concerned, for example, with whether employment tests actually differentiated between satisfactory and unsatisfactory job performers. This same concern for effectiveness arises when we discuss training or development activities (referred to collectively in this discussion as training). We cannot merely assume that any training an organization offers is effective; we must develop substantive data to determine whether the program is achieving its goals—is it correcting the deficiencies in skills, knowledge, or attitudes that were assessed as needing attention? Finally, training and development programs are expensive, averaging about $850 per employee in Canada according to a survey of 219 Canadian companies,[55] which works out to a mind-boggling $4 billion per annum in Canada[56] and more than $40 billion in the US.[57] These costs alone justify evaluating the effectiveness of all training programs.

It would be nice if all companies could boast returns on investments in training as do Motorola executives, who claim they receive $30 in increased productivity for every dollar spent on training.[58] But such a claim cannot be made without properly evaluating training. This is a problem in Canada since, as a recent survey found, fewer than one-third of the organizations surveyed could put a precise figure on their training costs.[59] Perhaps as a reaction to this problem, an increasing number of Canadian companies are turning to outsourcing some of their training activities.[60] This frees them from worrying about training inputs and allows them to focus on learning outcomes.

In Canada, training programs are typically evaluated by asking for the reactions of those who took a course. For instance, several managers, representatives from HRM, and a group of workers who have recently completed a training program are asked for their opinions. If the comments are generally positive, the program will probably get a favourable evaluation, and the organization will continue it until someone decides, for whatever reason, it should be eliminated or replaced. Evaluating reactions remains by far the most widely used evaluation method in Canada.[61]

The reactions of participants or managers, while easy to get, are the least valid. This is because their opinions are heavily influenced by factors that have little to do with the training's effectiveness—things like difficulty, entertainment value, or personality characteristics of the instructor. Therefore, let us direct our attention to three approaches, each of which offers more than subjective opinions.

Performance-Based Evaluation Measures

Post-Training Performance Method The first approach is referred to as the post-training performance method. Participants' performance is measured after attending a training program to determine if behavioural changes have been made. For example, after a week-long seminar for HRM recruiters on structured interviewing techniques, we follow up one month later with each participant to see if, in fact, the techniques addressed in the program were used and how. Any changes that occurred are attributed to the training, but caution is in order. We cannot positively state that the change in behaviour was directly related to the training. Other factors, like reading a current HRM journal, may have also influenced the change. Accordingly, the post-training performance method may overstate the benefits of training.

Post-Training Performance Method Evaluating training programs based on how well employees can perform their jobs after they have received the training.

Pre-Post-Training Performance Method In the pre-post training performance method, each participant is evaluated prior to training and rated on actual job performance. After instruction—of which the evaluator has been kept unaware—is completed, the individual is re-evaluated. As with the post-training performance method, the increase is assumed to be attributed to the instruction. However, in contrast to post-training performance method, the pre-post-performance method deals directly with job behaviour.

Pre-Post Training Performance Method Evaluating training programs based on the difference in performance before and after employees receive training.

Pre-Post-Training Performance with Control Group Method The most sophisticated evaluative approach is the pre-post-performance with control group method. With this evaluation method, two groups are established and evaluated on actual job performance. Members of the control group work on the job but do not undergo instruction while the experimental group does. The two groups are re-evaluated after the training is complete. If the training is really effective, the experimental group's performance will have improved, and its performance will be substantially better than that of the control group. This approach attempts to correct for factors other than the instruction program that influence job performance.

Pre-Post Training Performance with Control Group Method Evaluating training by comparing pre- and post-training results with individuals who did not receive the training.

Although a number of methods for evaluating training and development programs may exist, these three appear to be the most widely recognized. Furthermore, the latter two methods are preferred because they provide a stronger measure of behavioural change directly attributable to the training effort.

International Training and Development Issues

Important components of international human resources management include both cross-cultural training and a clear understanding of the overseas assignment as part of a manager's development.

Training

Cross-cultural training is necessary for expatriate managers and their families before, during, and after foreign assignments. It is crucial to remember that when the expatriates arrive, they are the foreigners, not the host population. Before the employee and family are relocated to the overseas post, it is necessary to provide much cultural and practical background.[62] Language training is essential for everyone in the family.

Although English is the dominant business language worldwide, relying on it read trade journals and newspapers that contain useful business information and will be reliant on translators. This will slow down discussions and even worse, can distort the meaning in the process. Even if an expatriate manager is not fluent, a willingness to try communicating in the local language makes a good impression on the local business community, and the insistence that all conversation be in English appears arrogant.

Foreign language proficiency is also vital for family members to establish a social network and accomplish the everyday tasks of maintaining a household. Canadians may be able to go to the market and, like tourists, point to what they recognize on display, but if the shop has unfamiliar meats or vegetables, it helps to be able to ask what each item is and to understand the answers.

Fluency is important, but cross-cultural training is much more than just language training. It should provide an appreciation of the new culture including details of its history and folklore, economy, politics (both internal and its relations with Canada), religion, social climate, business practices, and any other specific practices and beliefs to avoid inadvertently insulting business associates or social contacts.

Cross-cultural training for expatriate managers and their families begins with language instruction but must also include sensitizing them to local social and cultural nuances.

All this training can be carried out in a variety of ways. Language skills are often provided through classes and audio tapes, while cultural training utilizes many different tools. Lectures, reading materials, videotapes, and movies are useful for background information, while cultural sensitivity is more often taught through role-playing, simulations, and meetings with others who have previously been stationed there[63] as well as natives of the foreign countries now living in Canada.

While all this training in advance of the overseas relocation is important, an enormous amount of cultural learning takes place during the assignment as well. One North American corporation provides some of the following suggestions for adapting to a foreign environment: Forget the word *foreign*. Learn how things get done at work, at home, at school, at social gatherings. Watch television, even if you don't understand it yet. Read as many newspapers as possible. Visit parks, museums, and zoos. Make friends with local people and learn from them. Plan vacations and day trips in the new country.[64]

After the overseas assignment has ended and the employee has returned home, more training is required. All family members must reacclimatize themselves to life in Canada. The family must face changes in the extended family, friends, and local events that have occurred in their absence. Teenagers find re-entry particularly difficult since they are ignorant of the most recent jargon and the latest trends, even though they are often more sophisticated and mature than their local friends. Perhaps some students reading this can identify with the difficulty of readjusting to Canada even after something as relatively unchallenging as a sojourn to sunny California.

The employee must also adjust to organizational changes, including the inevitable promotions, transfers, and resignations that have taken place during his or her absence. Returnees are anxious to know what they missed, where they fit in, or if they have been gone for so long that they no longer are on a career path.

Management Development

In the current global business environment, the overseas assignment should be a vital component in the development of top-level executives. This is more common in Europe and Japan than it is in Canada, but many Canadian managers return richer for their experiences, having been relatively independent of headquarters. Mid-level managers in particular, were able to take on greater responsibilities than others at their level at home and acquire greater sensitivity and flexibility to alternative ways of doing things. Unfortunately they are often ignored and untapped after their return.

One survey showed that although 70 per cent of international assignments were presented as career opportunities, only 30 per cent of the sample's respondents were told anything about their career prospects after returning. Only 54 per cent reported there was a specific job waiting for them; 23 per cent reported being promoted upon their return, while 18 per cent reported being demoted.[65]

It is vital for the organization to make the overseas assignment part of a career development program. In the absence of such a program, two negative consequences often occur. First, the recently returned manager who is largely ignored or underutilized becomes frustrated and quits. This is extremely costly because the investment in developing this individual is lost and the talent the individual has will likely be recruited by a competitor, either at home or overseas. Second, when overseas returnees are regularly underused or leave out of frustration, other potential expatriates become reluctant to accept overseas posts, inhibiting the organization's staffing ability.

When the overseas assignment is completed, the organization has four basic options. First, the expatriate may be assigned to a domestic position, beginning the repatriation process, with the hope that this new assignment will build on some of the newly acquired skills and perspectives. Second, the return may be temporary, with the goal of preparing for another overseas assignment. This might be the case when a manager has successfully opened a new sales territory and is being asked to repeat that success in another region. Third, the expatriate may retire, either at home in Canada or in the country where she or he spent the past few years. Finally, employment may be terminated either because the organization has no suitable openings or because the individual has found opportunities elsewhere.

All of these options involve substantial costs in both human and financial investment. A well-thought-out and organized program of management development is necessary to make overseas assignments a part of the comprehensive international human resources management program.

Study Tools and Applications

Summary

This summary relates to the Learning Objectives provided on p. 250.
After having read this chapter, you should know:
1. Employee training has become increasingly important as jobs have become more sophisticated and influenced by technological and corporate changes.
2. Training is a learning experience that seeks a relatively permanent change in individuals that will improve their ability to perform on the job.
3. An effective training program should be consistent with the following learning principles: learning is enhanced when the learner is motivated; learning requires feedback; reinforcement increases the likelihood that a learned behaviour will be repeated; practice increases a learner's performance; learning begins rapidly, slows, then plateaus; and learning must be transferable to the job.
4. An organization's training needs will evolve from seeking answers to these questions: (a) What are the organization's goals? (b) What tasks must be completed to achieve these goals? (c) What behaviours are necessary for each job incumbent to complete his or her assigned tasks? and (d) What deficiencies, if any, do incumbents have in the skills, knowledge, or attitudes required to perform the necessary tasks?
5. Formal training methods can be classified as on-the-job training (including apprenticeships and job instruction training) and off-the-job training (including seminars, conferences, films, simulation exercises, and programmed instruction).
6. In contrast to employee training, employee development is more future-oriented and concerned with education and jobs that require greater skills, knowledge, and abilities.
7. Organization development is the process of affecting change in the organization. This change is facilitated through the efforts of a change agent.
8. On-the-job development techniques include job rotation, assistant positions, and committee assignments. Off-the-job development techniques involve lecture courses and seminars, simulation exercises, and outdoor training.
9. Mentoring/coaching is the process whereby senior employees take junior employees under their tutelage and assist them in fostering their career development.
10. Employee counselling is a development effort that attempts to have the employee make behavioural changes affecting performance before discipline becomes required. Employee counselling, then, is a special intermediary step to stave off continued poor performance.

11. Training programs can be evaluated by the methods of post-training performance, the pre-post-training performance, or the pre-post-training performance with control group. In the evaluation, focus is placed on trainee reactions, what learning took place, and how appropriate the training was to the job.
12. International issues in training and development include cross-cultural training, language training, and economic issues training.

Key Terms

apprenticeship training	mentoring
attitude survey	negative reinforcement
change agent	operant conditioning
coaching	organizational development (OD)
cost-benefit analysis	outdoor training
employee counselling	positive reinforcement
employee development	post-training performance method
employee training	pre-post-training performance method
extinction	pre-post-training performance with control group method
Internet	programmed instruction
interactive video disks	punishment
job rotation	simulation
job instruction training (JIT)	social learning theory
learning curve	virtual reality
mentor	

EXPERIENTIAL EXERCISE:
Evaluating an Orientation Program

In the last chapter, you developed an orientation program for students in the school of business. Suppose your program was accepted by the dean and has been running for two semesters. The dean now sends you the following memo:

Dear Students:

Thank you so much for developing an orientation program for us in the school of business. I know much work went into the process, and your efforts appear to be paying off. Yet, like any other program we offer, I must justify its continuance. Would you design an evaluation system that I can use to show the administration that we are funding a good program? I look forward to seeing your work.

Based on your orientation program design, put together an evaluation system. How will you evaluate this program? What criteria will you use? How will the evaluation be administered?

CASE APPLICATION:
Peer Mentoring at VanCity[66]

Training is taken seriously at Vancouver City Savings Credit Union (VanCity), so seriously that it is left up to the employees to train each other. Over the past four years, VanCity, an organization employing 1,000 people, has used a system of peer mentoring developed by Charney & Associates, Inc. of Toronto. The system provides for the establishment of learning teams of peers across the organization who learn together without the use of an external trainer.

In the past, they have struggled with the problem that conventional "show-and-tell" classroom training was seen as little more than entertainment, with 90 per cent of it forgotten a short while afterwards. In contrast, peer mentoring teams receive a one-day orientation during which, among other things, they prioritize and choose the skills they need to learn, decide who will teach each skill, and when they will do it. Team members take responsibility for putting the theory into practice soon after their training session. Judy White, a loans manager at VanCity, raves about the benefits of peer mentoring. "We become mentors to one another as we toss ideas around of how we have dealt with similar issues, successfully or otherwise."

Steve Andrews, a branch manager and member of the initial pilot team, claims that mentoring "provided a great opportunity for people to develop leadership skills. Preparing for and conducting a training session builds self-confidence and the ability to communicate clearly and convincingly, key skills to enhance one's career." Why does peer mentoring work so much better than traditional external expert-based teaching? The answer is illustrated in the following comment from Jay Tuason, another branch manager. "The power of this approach is the ownership we all feel for what we learn." When peers themselves are given the opportunity to pick the skill to be learned, they make sure sessions are effective by drawing on their own actual work experience to demonstrate the skill being covered. As Jay Tuason puts it, "We also feel some pressure to use the skill so that you can come to the next meeting and tell one another how well things worked out in practice."

Questions:

1. What principles of effective learning are demonstrated in VanCity's peer mentoring?
2. Is peer mentoring suitable for all forms of employee training and development in an organization? Discuss.
3. How would you evaluate the training effectiveness of VanCity's mentoring program? What would you evaluate? Given the information provided in the case, how effective would you estimate VanCity's mentoring program to be?

Testing Your Understanding

How well did you fulfil the learning objectives?

1. In which of these organizations is employee training least important?
   a. An organization that is switching to a robotics manufacturing facility.
   b. An organization that can easily recruit employees with the skills and experience necessary to perform jobs.
   c. An organization that has been in existence for more than a hundred years.
   d. An organization that is developing major new products.
   e. An organization that is entering the global arena for marketing.

2. Dana, with a recent B. Comm. in human resources management, was hired as a compensation analyst by a major organization. What training is she likely to get before she starts work?

   a. No training. She should be able to function from day one.
   b. Formal training in compensation plans and alternative financial systems. She could be sent to a local university for some course work.
   c. The company will send her for an MBA before they will let her go to work.
   d. She may need job-specific training such as on a new computer package or how to interpret internally developed pay graphs and charts.
   e. She should spend several weeks designing her career plans and alternatives for the next ten to fifteen years.

3. Chris, Grade 11 goalie for her high-school hockey team in Lethbridge, Alberta, admired Felix Potvin, the goalie for the Toronto Maple Leafs. She watched on television every game Potvin played and attended every game the Leafs played in Calgary. Chris could

mimic, in vivid detail, almost every part of Potvin's style, from his stance to the type of equipment he wore. Yet, at the end of every season, Chris's save percentage decreased even though she paid close attention to Potvin and herself had been nicknamed "The Cat." According to social learning theory, which statement is true?

a. Attentional processes were ineffective.

b. Motor reproduction processes were ineffective.

c. Retention processes were ineffective.

d. Reinforcement processes were ineffective.

e. Cognitive social processes were ineffective.

4. Charles, a newcomer to high school, played soccer for eight years in elementary school. Bored with the sport, he approached the high-school basketball coach and asked for a spot on the team, mentioning his all-star soccer status. The coach had a reputation for letting "stars" skip the try-outs. According to social learning theory, why did the coach make him try out anyway?

a. Socially, the team would not have accepted Charles without try-outs.

b. Socially, try-outs are part of the bonding experience.

c. Charles needed to learn the right way to gain access to desired goals.

d. The coach questioned the positive transfer potential of soccer to basketball.

e. The coach held a social desirability bias against soccer.

5. A director of training for a medium-sized computer software manufacturer has just been asked by a systems software development manager to develop a training program to help fifty programmers "remember" to log off the system when they have completed on-line debugging procedures. The system automatically logs off after twenty seconds of keyboard idle time. The training director estimates it will cost $10,000 to develop and deliver such a training exercise. The computer time is valued at $.01 for each ten seconds logged on. He finds out that none of the other five software development managers has a similar log-off problem. What should he do?

a. Develop the program. The cost of the $10,000 training program is clearly justified by an estimated savings of at least $1 each day.

b. Develop the program. Training exists to meet the needs of users. Questioning or challenging the systems software development manager would only alienate him.

c. Do not develop the program. There is no real performance problem identified.

d. Do not develop the program. The problem is not a training problem.

e. Develop the program. It could be marketed later to other computer software firms.

6. Jean just qualified for military flight school. She is learning to fly wearing a helmet that has sensors to project a horizon and the control panel of her plane. She wears a special glove that interfaces with the helmet projection. What kind of training did Jean receive?

a. Simulation.

b. Vestibule training.

c. Virtual reality.

d. Experiential exercise.

e. Programmed instruction.

7. The training manager for a small bank wants to improve the organizational culture for its twenty-three officers. The bank needs to become more open, proactive, and innovative. They are each completing a managerial skills inventory to identify their own (and each other's) perceptions of managerial skill levels in that organization. What OD strategy is the training manager using?

a. Attitude survey.

b. Team building.

c. Transactional analysis.

d. Third-party intervention.

e. Employee inventory.

8. Last week, Sarah spent the morning watching Stefan work, then she took him to lunch to talk to him about how to improve his job performance. They have been friends for years, and Sarah is head teller of the "A" branch, and Stefan is a teller trainee at the "B" branch of the same bank. What is going on?

a. Sarah and Stefan are part of a job rotation program.

b. Sarah is coaching Stefan.

c. Stefan is an assistant to Sarah.

d. Stefan and Sarah are part of a short-term lateral transfer.

e. None of the above

9. How does mentoring compare to socialization?

a. Mentoring is done when an employee is being prepared for jobs of greater responsibility. Indoctrination is done when an employee first joins an organization.

b. Mentoring is done by the supervisor. Indoctrination is conducted by peers.

c. Mentoring is a required process. Indoctrination is optional.

d. Mentoring is generally regarded as a negative experience by the employee. Indoctrination is generally regarded as a positive experience by the employee.

e. Mentoring and indoctrination are the same thing.

10. When is employee counselling an appropriate approach for dealing with performance problems?

a. When training is too costly.

b. When the performance problem is ability related.

c. When the manager cannot identify the problem.

d. When the performance problem is related to employee willingness to perform the job.

e. When the performance problem occurs often.

11. Mike, director of training for a large manufacturing organization, has developed a program on sexual harassment in the workplace. All employees are given a questionnaire describing various workplace behaviours and asked to decide whether or not sexual harassment is occurring. They will complete a similar questionnaire at the end of the training program. What training evaluation method will Mike use with these questionnaires?
    a. Supervisor and incumbent opinion.
    b. Test-retest method.
    c. Pre-post-performance method.
    d. Experimental control group method.
    e. Employee inventory.

12. Don, an MBA from a prestigious school who speaks fluent German, Japanese, and English, was hired by a Canadian-based global organization for international marketing. He was sent to Japan as director of marketing for a year, returned to Canada for six months, and then was sent to Germany for a year as director of marketing. He was expecting a promotion to vice-president of international marketing when he returned to corporate headquarters. Instead, he was assigned as regional manager for British Columbia. Why do you think he received this assignment?
    a. People with prestigious MBAs often have higher opinions of their abilities than do the organizations who employ them.
    b. Don must have made some really big mistakes in his overseas assignments to be demoted like that.
    c. Most foreign assignments result in demotions. The experience is viewed as a vacation and not to be rewarded.

d. This assignment is not surprising. A recent survey showed that 18 per cent of all returning expatriates were demoted upon return.
    e. This assignment only seems like a demotion. The position of regional manager will give him a lot more autonomy than he had as a country-level manager.

13. Training needs may be assessed by answering the questions that are listed here except:
    a. Historically, what has worked well in this organization?
    b. What are the organization's goals?
    c. What behaviours are necessary to complete assigned tasks?
    d. What tasks are needed to achieve the organization's goals?
    e. What skill deficiencies do job incumbents have related to tasks needed to achieve organizational goals?

14. Why are industry training programs evaluated?
    a. They cannot be evaluated.
    b. With downsizing, everything in industry is being evaluated.
    c. Evaluation is a necessary component of establishing training effectiveness.
    d. Evaluation is required by government regulations.
    e. Employees have the right to comment on the training they receive.

Chapter Ten

DEVELOPING CAREERS

LEARNING OBJECTIVES

AFTER READING THIS CHAPTER, YOU WILL BE ABLE TO:

1. Describe what is meant by the term "career."
2. Discuss the focus of careers for both the organization and for individuals.
3. Describe how career development and employee development are different.
4. Explain why career development is valuable to organizations.
5. Identify the five stages involved in a career.
6. List the Holland vocational preferences.
7. Discuss problem-solving styles and career choice.
8. Discuss how dual-career couples affect career development.
9. Identify how organizational career development can be made more effective.

To those born in the late sixties and the seventies–generation Xers—it often seems that the group ahead of them—the baby boomers—were everywhere. They had all the best jobs and successful careers. Well, there are some new kids on the block, and they're after the boomers' jobs. These are the baby busters, the generation Xers, and they are making headway on the job scene. For example, consider the story of Chris Burdge, a thirty-four-year-old native of Windsor, Ontario, who has succeeded beyond his wildest dreams in the tough world of high tech in Tokyo, Japan.[1]

With no university degree, no gold-plated résumé, and occupying a fairly humble position as a railway mechanic, Burdge, seemed to have few career prospects, and especially not in today's high-tech world. What he did have was the driving ambition to better himself, the willingness to take risks when opportunities presented themselves, particularly in the volatile Asian market, and the good fortune to have been in the right place at the right time.

In 1985, Burdge walked away from the frustrations of his dead-end job and passed through a couple of sales jobs in Canada before setting out on a year-long odyssey, sailing round the world. In 1991, he decided to move to Japan, taught himself Japanese, and began selling space in the English-language *Japan International Journal*. In 1994, he decided to gamble on the rapidly growing popularity of the Internet and joined at the start-up of a company, selling Internet space and Web pages to the corporate world. From that point on, he hasn't looked back and is now the part owner of his company (renamed Internet Access Center KK), with annual sales of about $2.5 million.

Chris Burdge is quite proud of his unusual career progress. He says, "When I go back to Canada, I realize that I'm not doing something usual compared with what everyone else does. That's when I feel special." He admits that he could not have predicted his career path. "To be honest, when I set out to do all this, where I am now was not in my grand scheme of things."

Burdge's career is still the exception in Canada, but it is likely to become less and less so as the nature of work and organizational relationships continues to change. The very essence of work is changing, and careers will increasingly take directions that would previously have been seen as unorthodox. There is no longer a "natural" career progression as there was in the past. Instead, people will stay on a job only for short periods. They'll accept the challenge, work through it, then look for the next exciting thing to do. Come to think of it, isn't that the type of employee a dynamic organization needs to meet future unexpected challenges ahead? Maybe generation Xers like Chris Burdge have just the temperament and skills needed to manage their careers and lead companies well into the next millennium. Chris may not survive in the tough Japanese market of today, but he is an inspiration to us all.

What Is a Career?

Career development is important to us all. Nevertheless, we know that people sometimes have difficulties achieving their career goals. At the same time, managers must now confront new and unexpected complexities in their efforts to mobilize and manage their human resources. The traditional belief that every employee would jump at the chance for a promotion, that competent people would somehow emerge within the organization to fill vacancies, and that a valuable employee would always be a valuable employee are no longer true. Lifestyles are changing, as are the different needs and aspirations of employees. New technology is creating a whole medley of careers unknown to earlier generations. Just look at the computer industry for numerous examples. If managers are to be assured that they will have competent and motivated people to fill the organizations' future needs, they must become concerned with matching the career needs of employees with the requirements of the organizations.

Definition

The term **career** has a number of connotations. In popular usage, it can mean advancement ("He's moving up in his career"), a profession ("She has chosen a career in medicine"), or progressive accomplishment over time ("He's just reached the rank of major in the Forces.")[2] For our purposes, we will define career as "the pattern of work-related experiences that span the course of a person's life."[3] Using this definition, it is apparent that we all have (or will have) careers. A job and a career are not the same thing. An individual will often have a succession of different jobs during a career, and a particular job experience does not, on its own, constitute a career.

Therefore, any work, paid or unpaid, pursued over an extended period of time, can constitute a career. In addition to formal job work, careers can include school work, home-making, or volunteer work. Furthermore, career success is defined not only objectively in terms of promotion, but also subjectively in terms of satisfaction. In previous generations, career success also implied an orderly progression from lower to higher levels in an organization or profession—the so-called career ladder. This is no longer the case, and the sequence of positions that individuals hold during their lives may more accurately resemble a spiral, a roller coaster, or even a jungle gym.

To illustrate the involved sequencing of today's corkscrew careers, take the example of one of our former students, now a successful HRM manager for an auto manufacturer. After graduating with a diploma from a local college, she began her career in nursing. She then began to teach nursing at the community college and needed a master's degree to gain a permanent position there. At that time, our university did not offer a master's in nursing, and so she enrolled part-time in an MBA program. After completing her degree, she used her health care contacts to find her first job as a health-fraud investigator for an insurance company. Discovering an interest in HRM, she then moved on to become HRM manager for a national provider of nursing services and then, HRM manager for an auto parts manufacturer in the same city. Her colleagues are surprised to hear that they have an HRM manager who was initially a nurse, but her type of career path is likely to become increasingly commonplace.

Career The sequence of positions that a person holds over his or her life.

Individual Versus Organizational Perspective

The study of careers takes on a very different orientation depending on whether it is viewed from the perspective of the organization or of the individual. A key question in career development, then, is, "With whose interests are we concerned?" From an organizational or managerial standpoint, career development involves tracking career paths and developing career systems. HR professionals play an important role in developing career systems and in ensuring that both individual and organizational perspectives are considered. The objective of HRM is to provide the information management needs to direct and monitor the progress of various groups of employees and to ensure that capable managerial and technical talent will be available to meet the organization's needs. Career development from the organization's perspective is also called organizational career planning.

In contrast, individual career development or career planning focuses on assisting individuals to identify their major goals and to determine what they need to do to achieve these goals. Note that in the latter case, the focus is entirely on the individual and includes his or her life outside as well as inside the organization. So, while organizational career development looks at individuals filling the needs of the organization, individual career development addresses each individual's personal work career and other lifestyle issues.[4] For instance, an excellent employee, assisted to better understand his or her needs and aspirations through career guidance—counselling or completing career interest inventories, and the like—could decide to leave the organization if it becomes apparent that his or her career aspirations can be best achieved elsewhere.

This chapter blends the interests of both the individual and the organization itself, but since the primary focus of human resources management is on the importance of the careers to the organization, we will emphasize this area.

Career Development Versus Employee Development

Career Development A process designed to assist workers in managing their careers.

Given our discussions in Chapter 9 on employee training and development, you may be wondering what, if any, differences there are between career development and employee development. These topics have a common element, but there are two distinct differences: the time frame and the degree of shared responsibility.

Career development looks at the long-term career effectiveness and success of organizational personnel. By contrast, the kinds of development discussed in Chapter 9 focused on work effectiveness or performance in the immediate or intermediate time frames. These two concepts are closely linked; employee training and development should be compatible with an individual's career development in the organization even though some training may not necessarily be linked to long-term aspirations. But a successful career program, in attempting to match individual abilities and aspirations with the needs of the organization, should develop people for the long-term needs of the organization and address the dynamic changes that will take place over time.

The second major difference between career development and employee development is in the degree of shared responsibility for development between the individual and the organization. We noted in Chapters 8 and 9 that individual participation in training and development is critical to its success, but the primary responsibility for employee development rests with management in the employing organization. In contrast, career development is a *joint* responsibility between the organization and the individual. While we argue, throughout this chapter, that organizations and management play a key role in career development and are responsible for setting its overall direction and policies, it is the individual who is ultimately responsible for his or her own career development. Remember, in the final analysis, no one is as interested in *your* career as *you* are.

Career Development: Value for the Organization

Assuming that an organization already provides extensive employee development programs, why should it need to consider a career development program as well? A long-term career focus should increase the organization's effectiveness in managing its human resources. Research[5] suggests that the average employee continues to exhibit a high degree of company loyalty despite the restructuring that has largely eliminated the notion of a secure, well-paid job. Thus, anything the organization can do to accommodate this commitment through longer-term career planning for its employees still pays handsome dividends. More specifically, we can identify several positive results that can accrue from a well-designed career development program.

Ensures Needed Talent Will Be Available Career development efforts are consistent with, and are a natural extension of, strategic human resources planning. Changing staff requirements over the intermediate and long term should be identified when the company sets long-term goals and objectives. Working with individual employees to help them align their needs and aspirations with those of the organization will increase the probability that the right people will be available to meet the organization's changing staffing requirements.

Improves the Organization's Ability to Attract and Retain High-Talent Employees Outstanding employees will always be scarce, and there is usually considerable competition to secure their services. Such individuals may give preference to employers who demonstrate a concern for their employees' future. If employed by an organization that offers career advice, these people may exhibit greater loyalty and commitment to their employer. Career development appears to be a natural response to the rising concern by employees for the quality of work life and personal life planning. As more and more people seek jobs that offer challenge, responsibility, and opportunities for advancement, realistic career planning becomes essential. As well, social values have changed so that fewer and fewer members of the workforce look at their work in isolation. Their work must be compatible with their personal and family interests and commitments. Again, career development should result in a better individual-organization match for employees and thus lead to less turnover.

Ensures that Minorities and Women Get Opportunities for Growth and Development As discussed in previous chapters, equal employment opportunity legislation has demanded that minority groups and women get opportunities for growth and development that will prepare them for greater responsibilities within the organization. A major problem that remains is the career segregation of men and women in Canada. The latest census figures show that while many more women are entering the paid workforce, they tend to remain in jobs historically considered "women's work."[6] The most popular male job remains the truck driver, while the most popular female jobs are retail sales clerk and office secretary. This job segregation is at odds with the reality that more women than men in their twenties now hold university degrees (51 per cent of women; 41

A major problem in Canada is career segregation of men and women. Few women are entering non-traditional jobs.

per cent of men).[7] Clearly, there is still a lot to be done in targeting career development programs at women and minorities to ensure equal access to all opportunities in Canadian organizations. Career development is also very important to an organization from the point of view of human rights and equity legislation. Not surprisingly, courts frequently look at an organization's career development efforts with these groups when ruling on discrimination suits.

Reduces Employee Frustration Although the educational level of the workforce has risen, so, too, have their occupational aspirations. However, economic stagnation and increased concern by organizations to reduce costs have also reduced opportunities. This has increased frustration in employees who see a significant disparity between their aspirations and actual opportunities. When organizations cut costs by downsizing, career plans often collapse.[8] Career counselling can result in more realistic, rather than raised, employee expectations.

Enhances Cultural Diversity Canada has proudly distinguished itself on the basis of a national "cultural mosaic" policy which encourages the development and celebration of cultural diversity. In this context, all employers in Canada are expected to allow for more varied combination of culture, gender, and race, in their organizations. Effective organizational career development provides access to all levels of the organization for more varied types of employees. Extended career opportunities make cultural diversity, and the appreciation of it, an organizational reality.

Promotes Organizational Goodwill If employees think their employing organizations are concerned about their long-term well-being, they respond in kind by projecting positive images of the organization into other areas of their lives (e.g., volunteer work in the community). For instance, Joe works for a biscuit company. He also coaches junior hockey with other parents. When he talks about what a good employer the company is, his friends might be more inclined to buy the company's cookies.

Career Development: Value for the Individual

Effective career development is also important for the individual. In fact, it is more important today than ever before. Because the definitions of careers and what constitutes success have changed, the value of individual career development programs has expanded. Career success is no longer measured merely by an employee's income or hierarchical level in a large company. Indeed, many Canadians choose to remain in smaller organizations in smaller centres where they enjoy a level of community support and a breadth of position much more difficult to obtain in a large, urban company.

Career success now includes using one's full potential, facing expanded challenges, and having greater responsibilities and increased autonomy. Intrinsic career development, or "psychic income," is desired by contemporary workers who are seeking more than salary and security from their jobs.[9] Contemporary workers seek interesting and meaningful work which is often derived from a sense of being the architect of one's own career.[10] Designing one's own career may also include the flexibility to change one's work patterns to accommodate other interests such as a parallel career outside the organization. For example, Claude Castonguay, vice-chairman of the board of Laurentian Bank of Canada, and John Andras, vice-president of Research Capital Corporation, are both accomplished artists as well as senior executives. As Castonguay puts it, "I've arranged my life in such a way that I can paint on a regular basis."[11]

Careers are both external and internal. The external career involves properties or qualities of an occupation or an organization.[12] For example, a career in business might be thought of as a sequence of jobs or positions held during the life of the individual: undergraduate degree in business; store manager for a small retail chain; graduate training in business; management trainee in a large firm; manager; CEO of a small firm; retirement. External careers may also be characterized by such things as career ladders within a particular organization: junior assistant control clerk; assistant control clerk; control clerk; senior control clerk; control supervisor.

The internal career encompasses a variety of individual aspects or themes: accumulation of external symbols of success or advancement (bigger office with each promotion);[13] threshold definition of occupational types (i.e., physicians have careers, janitors have jobs);[14] long-term commitment to a particular occupational field (i.e., career soldier);[15] a series of work-related positions;[16] and work-related attitudes and behaviours.[17] With careers being the pattern of work-related experiences that span the course of a person's life, we must understand that both personal relationships and family concerns are also intrinsically valued by employees. Subjective and objective elements, then, are necessary components of a theoretical perspective which captures the complexity of career.[18] Success can then be defined in external terms. For example, if after five years at the same company you get a promotion, and Dave, a colleague who was hired the same day you were for the same type of job, has not yet been promoted, then you are more successful than Dave. The external definition also states that a chartered accountant is more successful than a janitor. However, if you consider the subjective, internal valuation of success, the story may be different. A school janitor who defines his job as protecting children from hazards in their classrooms, who goes home at night proud because he has successfully dealt with an electric emergency that day, is successful in his career. Compare that to a CA who works only to buy a new yacht so she can escape from the drudgery of her day-to-day office life of dealing with clients, accounting forms, and automated systems. Is she more or less successful than the janitor?

This differentiation of internal from external is important to the manager who wants to motivate employees (see Table 10-1). Different employees may respond to different motivational tools. For instance, Brad is working as your secretary only to earn enough money to purchase a new couch for his living room; he may quit as soon as he has the $3,000. Diane, your other secretary, joined the company with the expectation that within fifteen years, she will have completed her bachelor's degree and be a management trainee. Would they respond equally to the opportunity to be trained in interpersonal skills? Would both of them be as likely to accept (or reject) a transfer to another city? Probably not, because both have different drives. Thus, we can say that internal and external career events may be parallel, but they result in different outcomes. We have displayed these events in Table 10-1 and discussed them in the context of career stages.

External and Internal Careers
Career value and success as defined externally and internally to the individual.

TABLE 10-1   An Integration of Internal and External Event Perspectives and Career Life Stages

Stage	External Event	Internal Event
Exploration	Advice and examples of relatives, teachers, friends, and coaches	Development of self-image of what one "might" be, what sort of work would be fun
	Actual successes and failures in school, sports and hobbies	Self-assessment of own talents and limitations
	Actual choice of educational path — vocational school, college, university, major, professional school	Development of ambitions, goals, motives, dreams
		Tentative choices and commitments, changes
Establishment	Explicit search for a job	Shock of entering the "real world"
	Acceptance of a job	Insecurity around new tasks of interviewing, applying, being tested, facing being turned down
	Induction and orientation	
	Assignment to further training or first job	Making "real" choices; to take a job or not; which job; first commitment
	Acquiring visible job and organizational membership trappings (ID card, parking sticker, uniform, organizational manual)	Fear of being tested for the first time under "real" conditions, and found to be a wanting
	First job assignment, meeting the boss and co-workers	Reality shock—what the work is really like; doing the "dirty work"
	Learning period, indoctrination	Forming a career strategy on how "to make it"—working hard, finding mentors, conforming to an organization, making a contribution
	Period of full performance—"doing the job"	This is "real"; what I'm doing matters
		Feeling of success or failure—going uphill, either challenging or exhausting
		Decision to leave organization if things do not look positive
		Feeling of being accepted fully by the organization, "having made it"—satisfaction of seeing "my project" succeed
Mid-Career	Levelling off, transfer, and/or promotion	Period of settling in or new ambitions based on self-assessment
	Entering a period of maximum productivity	More feeling of security, relaxation, but danger of levelling off and stagnation
	Becoming more of a teacher/mentor than a learner	Threat from younger, better trained, more energetic, and ambitious persons—"Am I too old for my job?"
	Explicit signs from boss and co-workers that one's progress has plateaued	Possible thoughts of "new pastures" and new challenges—"What do I really want to do?"
		Working through mid-life crisis towards greater acceptance of oneself and others—"Is it time to give up on my dreams? Should I settle for what I have?"
Late Career	Job assignments drawing primarily on maturity of judgement	Psychological preparation for retirement
		Deceleration in momentum
	More jobs involving teaching others	Finding new sources of self-improvement off the job, and new sources of job sat-isfaction through teaching others
Decline	Formal preparation for retirement	Learning to accept a reduced role and less responsibility
	Retirement rituals	Learning to live a less structured life
		New accommodations to family and community

Source: Adapted from John Van Maanen and Edgar H. Schein, "Career Development," in *Improving Life at Work*, (ed.) J. Richard Hackman and J. Lloyd Suttle (Santa Monica, CA: Goodyear, 1977), pp. 55–57.

Career Stages

One way to analyse and discuss careers is to consider them in stages or steps.[19] Progression from a beginning point through phases of growth and decline to a termination point is a natural occurrence that happens to all employees. Most of us begin to form our careers during our elementary and secondary school years, and they begin to wind down as we reach retirement age. We can identify five career stages that are generalizable for most adults, regardless of occupation: exploration, establishment, mid-career, late career, and decline. These stages are depicted in Figure 10-1. These stages are a general guideline to aid your understanding of careers, not necessarily an inevitable framework through which all will pass. Before we look at the stages, you should note that there has been some criticism of the idea of careers passing though a set of identifiable stages, especially in today's vastly different jobs market place.[20]

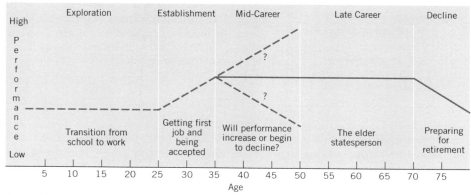

Figure 10-1
Stages in Career Development

The age ranges for each stage in Figure 10-1 are general rules of thumb, and for some individuals in certain careers, this model will be too simplistic. The key is to give your primary attention to the stages rather than the ages. For instance, someone who makes a dramatic career shift to begin a completely different line of work at age forty-five will have many of the same establishment-stage concerns as someone at age twenty-five. The forty-five-year-old university student who starts her program once the children are grown has more in common with the twenty-two-year-old sitting next to her than she does with the thirty-year-old assistant professor who is teaching the class or her career-path contemporaries. However, for the majority of us, the age generalizations in Figure 10-1 are fairly accurate.

Exploration

Many of the critical choices individuals make about their careers are made prior to entering the paid workforce. What we hear from our relatives, teachers, and friends, what we see on television or on the street corner, and what sports we play begin to narrow our career choices and lead us in certain directions. Certainly, the careers of our parents, their interests, their aspirations for us, and their financial resources will be heavy factors in determining our perceptions of what schools, colleges, or universities we might consider and what careers are available. Figure 10-2 summarizes information resources.

Career Stage Steps in the development of an individual's career.

Exploration Stage A career stage that usually ends in one's mid-twenties as one makes the transition from school to work.

Establishment Stage A career stage in which one begins to search for work. It includes getting one's first job.

Mid-Career Stage A career stage marked by a continuous improvement in performance, levelling off in performance, or the beginning of deterioration of performance.

Late-Career Stage A career stage in which individuals are no longer learning about their jobs, nor is it expected that they should be trying to outdo levels of performance from previous years.

Decline Stage The final stage in one's career, usually marked by retirement.

Figure 10-2
Information Resources for Career Exploration

Published Sources:
Human Resources Development
Canada's *Career Handbook*
Periodicals *(Canadian Business, The Globe &*
  Mail's Report on Business Magazine, Fortune)
Newspapers
Corporate annual reports
Trade publications and directories

On the Internet
Human Resources Development Canada
  site
CareerBridge and similar sites

Organizations
Placement offices in universities
  and colleges
Career services and libraries
Canada Employment Centres
Professional societies

People with professional experience
Members of trade associations
Members of professional societies
Visiting speakers at your institution

People with contacts
Doctors and dentists
Lawyers
Bankers, investment analysts, and
  insurance agents

Family and Friends
Who work in a profession, industry or
  company of interest to you
Who know people in a profession,
  industry or company of interest to you
Who know people with contacts
  in a profession, industry or company
  of interest to you

The exploration period ends for most of us in our mid-twenties as we make the transition from school to work. From an organizational standpoint, this stage has the least relevance since it occurs prior to employment. It is, of course, not irrelevant. The exploration period is a time when a number of expectations about one's career are developed, many of which are unrealistic. Such expectations may lie dormant for years and then pop up later to frustrate both employee and employer.

Successful career exploration strategies involve trying a variety of potential fields to see what you like or don't like. College internships and cooperative education programs are excellent exploration tools, giving you the opportunity to see your future co-workers first-hand and to do a "real" job day in and day out. Some successful internships lead to job offers. From a career-stage perspective, an internship that helps you realize that you're bored to death with a particular type of work is also a successful one—it helps you eliminate certain careers as possibilities. In the exploration stage, we form our attitudes towards work (doing homework, meeting deadlines, taking or avoiding shortcuts, attendance), and we also form our dominant social relationship patterns (easygoing, domineering, indifferent, likeable, obnoxious). Therefore, exploration is preparation for work.

Establishment

The establishment stage begins with the search for work and includes getting your first job, being accepted by your peers, learning the job, and gaining the first tangible evidence of success or failure in the real world. It begins with uncertainties and anxieties and is, indeed, dominated by two problems: "finding a niche" and "making your mark."

"Finding a niche" and the right job takes time for many of us. In fact, you may know a forty-year-old who has held a series of seemingly unrelated jobs (for example, after high school, fast food worker, three years; clerk in a sporting goods store, three years; construction worker, two years; TV repair, three years; department store clerk, five years; fishing boat operator, now). This person has looked for a niche—or attempted to establish one—for over fifteen years!

A more typical pattern is to change less frequently than the individual above, but, on the other hand, your first "real" job probably won't be with the company from which you retire. Thorough career exploration helps make this part of the establishment stage an easier.

The second problem of this stage, "making your mark," is characterized by making mistakes, learning from those mistakes, and moving on to increased responsibilities. Individuals in this stage have yet to reach their peak productivity and are rarely given work assignments that carry great power or status. A career takes a lot of time and energy. As shown in Figure 10-2, this stage feels like "going uphill." There is often a sense of growth, of expectation, or anticipation, such as a hiker feels when approaching a crest, waiting to see what lies on the other side. And, just as a hiker "takes" a hill when she stands at the crest, the establishment stage ends when you have "arrived" (made your mark). An example of becoming successfully established in a career is when the individual has achieved *individual contributor* status. This means, among other things, that you know you are becoming established when you become responsible for your own mistakes. (For instance, a motor mechanic or engineer who now sign off for their own completed work).

Mid-Career

Many people do not face their first severe career dilemmas until they reach the mid-career stage[21] This is a time when individuals may continue to improve their performance, level off, or begin to deteriorate. Therefore, although the challenge of remaining productive at work after you are no longer a "learner" is a major challenge of this career stage, the pattern ceases to be as clear as it was for exploration and establishment. Some employees reach their early goals and go on to even greater heights. A worker who wants to be the vice-president of HRM by the time she is thirty-five to forty years old might want to be CEO by the time she's fifty-five or sixty after she has achieved the first goal. Continued growth and high performance are not the only successful results at this stage. Maintenance or holding onto what you have is another possibility of the mid-career stage. These employees are **plateauing**, not failed. Plateaued mid-career employees can still be very productive.[22] They are technically competent and no longer as ambitious as the climbers. They may be satisfied to contribute a sufficient amount of time and energy to the organization to meet production commitments, and they also may be easier to manage than someone who wants more. These employees are not dead wood, but good, reliable employees and "solid citizens." An example would be the same HRM vice-president who decides at forty not to go for the next promotion but to enjoy life more, pursuing her hobbies while still performing well on the job.

The third possibility for mid-career are employees whose performance begins to deteriorate. This stage for this kind of employee is characterized by loss of both interest and productivity at work. Organizations are often limited to shunting such individuals to less conspicuous jobs, reprimanding them, demoting them, or firing them. The same HRM vice-president could become less productive if, by forty-two, she realizes that she will never be CEO and tries to wait it out for thirteen years until she can take early retirement. This option is not likely to be acceptable in the competitive environment of today and such an individual is likely

Plateauing A condition of stagnating in one's current job.

to be let go well before reaching early retirement. Fortunately, some affected individuals can be re-energized by moving them to another position in the organization. This can work to boost their morale and their productivity.[23]

Late Career

For those who continue to grow through the mid-career stage, the late career can be a pleasant time when one is allowed the luxury to relax a bit and enjoy playing the part of the elder statesperson. It is a time when one can rest on one's laurels and bask in the respect of younger employees. The freedom to be an elder statesperson, however, is less and less available to employees in today's competitive world for both cost and control reasons. It is probably only those who largely control their own employment relationship who can afford to settle back and bask in past glories. Even apparent career control may be short lived if the small business you own is bought out by a competitor or the organization you head up finds itself merged into some type of mega-institution. Thus, the reality is that today, in all career stages, individuals must continue to learn and may well be expected to outdo their levels of performance from previous years.

The value of the successful late-career employee to the organization lies largely in their judgement and the range of networks built up over many years and through varied experiences. They can teach others based on the knowledge they have gained.

For those who have stagnated or deteriorated during the previous stage and for those facing downsizing or restructuring, this can be a difficult time. The late career brings home to individuals the reality that they will not have the impact or change on the world as they once had. Employees who declined in late career may fear for their jobs. It is a time when individuals recognize that they have decreased work mobility and may be locked into their current job. One begins to look forward to retirement and the opportunities of doing something different. Mere plateauing is no more negative here than it was during mid-career. In fact, it is expected at late career. The marketing vice-president who didn't make it to CEO might begin delegating more to her next in line. The CEO would begin to think seriously about succession planning. Life off the job is likely to carry far greater importance than it did in earlier years as time and energy, once directed to work, is now redirected to family, friends, and hobbies.

Decline

The final stage in one's career is difficult for everyone but, ironically, is probably hardest on those who have had continued successes in the earlier stages. After decades of continued achievement and high levels of performance, the time has come for retirement. These individuals are forced to step out of the limelight and to relinquish a major component of their identity. However, for those who have seen their performance deteriorate over the years, it may be a pleasant time; the frustrations that have been associated with work are left behind. For the plateaued, it is probably an easy transition to other life activities.

Adjustments, of course, will have to be made regardless of whether one is leaving a illustrious career or a dismal job. Work responsibilities will be fewer, and the structure and regimentation that work provided will no longer be there. As a result, it is a challenging stage for anyone to confront.

However, as we live longer, healthier lives, coupled with laws removing age-related retirement requirements, sixty-two or sixty-five ceases to be as meaningful as it once was. For example, the last thing The Bay expected was that their "retiring" president, sixty-three-year old George Kosich, would take up a position with their arch-rival Eaton's (and Kosich certainly did not expect to quit Eaton's eighteen months later).[24] Employment lawyer Brian Grosman of Grosman, Grosman and Gale comments that The Bay mistakenly assumed that Kosich "was at a certain age and the likelihood was that he would go into full retirement. Companies shouldn't make these assumptions. People, as they get older, accumulate knowledge and expertise. They can become increasingly valuable."

Career Choices and Preferences

The best career choice is the one that offers the best match between what you want and what you need. Good career choice results for any of us should lead to a series of positions that give us an opportunity for good performance, make us want to maintain our commitment to the field, and give us greater work satisfaction. A good career match, then, is one in which we are able to develop a positive self-concept and to do work that we think is important.[25] As we have noted earlier, this positive self-concept is the result of a wide range of job outcomes—pay, benefits, work situation, the work group, and how these match with one's motivations and interests.

Holland Vocational Preferences

One of the most widely used approaches to guide career choices is the Holland vocational preferences model.[26] It consists of three major components. First, Holland found that people have varying occupational preferences; we do not all like to do the same things. Second, his research demonstrates that if you have a job where you can do what you think is important, you will be a more productive employee. Personality of workers may be matched to typical work environments where that can occur. Third, you will have more in common with people who have similar interest patterns and less in common with those who don't. For instance, assume Brian hates his job. He thinks it is boring and a waste of his time packing and unpacking trucks on the shipping dock of a manufacturing firm, and he would rather be working with people in the recruiting area. Pat, on the other hand, enjoys the routine of her work; she likes the daily rhythm of loading and unloading, and does not want to be troubled by human interaction. Do Pat and Brian get the same satisfaction from their jobs? Probably not. Why? Their interests, expressed as occupational interests, are not compatible.

The Holland vocational preferences model identifies six vocational themes (realistic, investigative, artistic, social, enterprising, and conventional) presented in Figure 10-3. An individual's occupational personality is expressed as some combination of high and low scores on these six themes. High scores indicate that you enjoy those kinds of activities. Although it is possible to score high or low on all six scales, most people are identified by three dominant scales. The six themes are arranged in the hexagonal structure shown in Figure 10-4. This scale model represents the fact that some of the themes are opposing while others have mutually reinforcing characteristics.

For instance, realistic and social are opposite each other in the diagram. A person with a realistic preference wants to work with things, not people. A person with a social preference wants to work with people, no matter what else they

Holland Vocational Preferences Model A model that relates personality characteristics to preferred occupational choices.

Career choices can be confusing, but individuals can get some help from guides such as the Holland vocational preferences.

Figure 10-3
Holland's General Occupational Themes

Realistic Rugged, robust, practical, prefer to deal with things rather than people, mechanical interests. Best matches with jobs that are Agriculture, Nature, Adventure, Military, Mechanical.

Investigative Scientific, task-oriented, prefer abstract problems, prefer to think through problems rather than to act on them, not highly person-oriented, enjoy ambiguity. Corresponding jobs are Science, Mathematics, Medical Science, Medical Service.

Artistic Enjoy creative self-expression, dislike highly-structured situations, sensitive, emotional, independent, original. Corresponding jobs are Music/Dramatics, Art, Writing.

Social Concerned with the welfare of others, enjoy developing and teaching others, good in group settings, extroverted, cheerful, popular. Corresponding jobs are Teaching, Social Service, Athletics, Domestic Arts, Religious Activities.

Enterprising Good facility with words, prefer selling or leading, energetic, extroverted, adventurous, enjoy persuasion. Corresponding jobs are Public Speaking, Law/Politics, Merchandising, Sales, Business Management.

Conventional Prefer ordered, numerical work, enjoy large organizations, stable, dependable. Corresponding job is Office Practices.

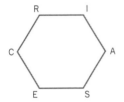

Letters connected by the line indicate reinforcing themes; letters not connected represent opposing themes

Figure 10-4
Hexagonal Relationships of Holland's Themes

do. Therefore, they have opposing preferences about working alone or with others. Investigative and enterprising are opposing themes. Can you identify the scale? (action? decision making?) Artistic and conventional preferences also oppose each other. Can you identify that dimension also? (routine? autonomy?)?

An example of mutually reinforcing themes is the social-enterprising-conventional (SEC) vocational preference structure. André, for example, likes working with people, being successful, and following ordered rules. That combination is perfect for someone willing to climb the ladder in a large bureaucracy. What about Beth? She is realistic-investigative-artistic, preferring solitary work to large groups, asking questions to answering them, and making her own rules instead of following someone else's. How does Beth fit into a large bureaucracy? (As a troublemaker.) Where would she fit better? (In a research lab.) Both the preference of the scientist and the environment of the research lab are characterized by a lack of human interruptions and a concentration on factual material. Of course, vocational preferences can also be expressed off the job in the match between job and hobby or even between on- and off-the-job careers. Think back to the senior executives who are also artists to whom we referred earlier.[27] According to one of them—John Andras, vice-president of Research Capital Corp.—"The business and artistic drives are similar, both involving challenge, risk, and sacrifices."

The Schein Anchors

Edgar Schein has identified *anchors* or personal value clusters that may be satisfied or frustrated by work. When a particular combination of these personal value clusters (technical-functional competence, managerial competence, security-stability, creativity, and autonomy-independence) is held by the worker and characteristically offered by the organization, that person is "anchored" in that job, organization, or industry. Most people have two or three value clusters that are important to them. If an organization satisfies two out of three, that is considered a stable match. For instance, Jean is recent university graduate and wants to use his human resources degree. His father was laid off when his organization downsized last year, and Jean never wants to have to deal with that type of uncertainty. Jean's anchors are technical competence and security-stability. His current job choices are marketing for a new credit card company on a commission basis, or university recruiting for an established manufacturing firm. Which job should he take?

Problem-Solving Style

One of the most useful personality traits to consider in making career choices is **problem-solving style**—the way in which a person goes about gathering and evaluating information in solving problems and making decisions. In this process, information gathering and evaluation are separate activities. Information gathering involves getting and organizing data for use, and the styles of information gathering vary from sensation to intuition. Individuals tending towards sensation prefer routine and order and emphasize well-defined details in gathering information. They would rather work with known facts than look for possibilities. People showing intuition in gathering information prefer the big picture, enjoy solving new problems, dislike routine, and would rather look for possibilities than work with facts.

Evaluation involves making judgements about how to deal with information once it has been collected. Styles of information evaluation vary from an emphasis on feeling to an emphasis on thinking. Feeling-type individuals are oriented towards conformity and try to accommodate themselves to other people. They try to avoid problems that might result in disagreements. Thinking-type people use reason and intellect to deal with problems, and they downplay the emotional aspects of a problem.

One instrument that is frequently used for determining problem-solving styles is the Myers-Briggs Type Indicator. This is a proprietary instrument and so we can only give a brief overview of its dimensions here. The Myers-Briggs measures preferences on four scales: Extraversion-Introversion; Sensing-Intuition; Thinking-Feeling; and Judging-Perceiving. This instrument is used by a variety of organizations in Canada for both employee development and career planning. Table 10-2 sets out some descriptions of a more generic set of four basic problem-solving styles. For each style, we have indicated some possible occupational match-ups. You can see from this table how useful identifying problem-solving styles is to making the right career choice.

Problem-Solving Style The way in which a person goes about gathering and evaluating information in solving problems and making decisions.

Making Personal Career Decisions

Considering career stages and individual job-matching questions all at the same time is a larger bite than most of us can chew. Although each of these theoretical perspectives is important, they're influenced and moderated by each other, and the responsibility for making career decisions is shared between the individual and the employing organization. New technology such as virtual training and the Internet can make the task a little easier, as Ann Miller, director of learning and development at Xerox Canada, has discovered. Xerox's virtual systems have given employees greater control over their own career paths.

TABLE 10-2   Four problem-solving styles and their occupational match-ups

SENSATION-THINKING	*SENSATION-FEELING*	*INTUITIVE-THINKING*	*INTUITIVE-FEELING*
Decisive, dependable, applied thinker, sensitive to details	**Pragmatic, analytical methodical, conscientious**	**Creative, progressive perceptive thinker, helpful**	**Charismatic, participative, people-oriented, with many ideas**
Accounting	Direct supervision	Systems design	Public relations
Production	Counselling	Systems analysis	Advertising
Computer programming	Negotiating	Law	Human Resources
Market research	Selling	Middle/top management	Politics
Engineering	Interviewing	Teaching business, Economics	Customer services

Source: Developed in part from Don Hellriegel, John W. Slocum, Jr., and Richard W. Woodman. *Organizational Behaviour,* 5th ed. (St. Paul, MN: West Publishing Co., 1989), Ch. 4.

"If one of our service people wanted to move into sales, he or she can look at the competencies required, do a self-assessment, find out gaps they might have, and even take a look at the courses they might have to take. All this occurs on-line. And when they finally meet with a manager, they can lay out a realistic training plan to make their career switch possible."[28] For the manager who has employees at various life and career stages with different anchors and preferences, there is no one best answer about how to develop subordinates' careers. Again, career management provides for more satisfied employees.[29] How can the manager provide good career management opportunities for the employees? Several actions may contribute to this process. We offer some suggestions in Table 10-3.

TABLE 10-3   Suggestions for Helping Employees Make Career Decisions

1. **Be aware of an employee's skills's abilities, and preferences.** Understanding who your employees are and what they like is critical to their career success.

2. **Provide opportunities to assess whether employee preferences lie in technical or managerial areas.** Especially during the exploration phase, giving employees an opportunity to work in a number of different types of jobs assists them in determining which they like best and what they excel at.

3. **Take into account the life stage of the worker.** A twenty-five-year-old who wants to "climb" in the organization should not be managed the same as a fifty-year-old who has plateaued.

4. **Encourage exploration and opportunity.** Create positive environments for employees to explore their career options and seek change. Make full use of the Internet as part of this step.

5. **Be aware of and honestly present opportunities for growth and advancement inside and outside your organization.** In today's organizations, job growth may be significantly limited. Be open with employees about their potential future with the organization. Be receptive to the realization that job growth for a good employee just might be in another organization.

The Self-Employment Alternative

It is no easy matter to make the right career choice, but the good news in times of change is that career choice is ongoing so that there is no such thing as a final and irrevocable wrong choice. In addition, the alternative of self-employment is more possible than ever before. Some individuals who value independence and setting their own rules choose to work for themselves, and, indeed, in the competitive and dynamic environment of today, this may be the most sensible career choice for many to make. Self-employment works best when the individual has a marketable skill or idea and the entrepreneurial skills to actually get something going. A number of Canadian companies such as IBM Canada, Ontario Hydro, Bell Canada, and 3M Canada have all helped set up downsized, skilled employees as independent consultants to their former employer.

The self-employment option, however, is not for everyone. While challenging, it is also risky and can be quite lonely—the isolation suffered by some teleworkers (see Chapter 2) can also affect self-employed individuals. On the other hand, if such individuals take on partners or hire employees, then the last thing they are likely to feel is lonely—unless it's the loneliness of being at the top!

Contemporary Issues in Career Development

Several current trends are affecting career development for both organizations and individuals. The more popular issues are dual-career couples, downsizing and careers, and individual responsibility for careers. Let's take a closer look at each of these.

Dual-Career Couples

One of the societal changes that has a significant impact on the workforce is the increase in dual-career couples. When your grandparents were getting out of school and starting their families, it was expected that dad would work and mom would take care of the house and the children. A job change that required moving out of town might be traumatic, but the major issue was usually dad's work. If mom worked, it was probably part-time and merely to supplement dad's primary income; she could find that kind of job anywhere. Today, almost half the workforce is female. Some couples avoid the pressures and complications of dual careers by having one spouse stay at home, but they are increasingly becoming a rarity. When both partners in a household have careers, life may be more complicated. Who takes off a day when a child is ill? Do both partners have the option of considering out-of-town moves to advance their careers? Can employers expect equal commitment from both spouses? Are working women automatically "mommy tracked"—that is, a woman on a career track with a commitment to an organization who, when she leaves the workplace to have children, is assumed to no longer have interest in her career?

Although each **dual-career couple** is unique, they do share several stress areas. Stress can be caused because work and family roles may be incompatible. The work role may require a tough, impersonal attitude, while the homemaker role is usually one of personal support and encouragement. The conflict of roles can lead to stress.[30] Competition and jealousy may cloud the relationship of dual-career couples if success is defined in overlapping areas. Juggling career priorities (e.g., who takes the children to the dentist) and adjusting individual

Dual-career Couple A situation in which both partners have distinct careers outside the home.

career expectations (e.g., "I can't move to Calgary for my next promotion if my spouse can't find a suitable position there") are additional problems.

Dual-career couples are at least as happy with their marriages as are traditional families,[31] but often that is because they have developed special coping strategies that are more characteristic of the team rather than the individual orientation: structural role redefinition, personal role reorientation, and more deliberate time management. Structural role redefinition, the one with the greatest organizational implications, may involve working with management to change the individual's expectations about the job. This includes such activities as developing a flextime schedule and limiting out-of-town travel. Personal role redefinition involves rethinking traditional roles with flexibility and practicality in mind, such as a husband changing diapers or buying groceries or a wife hiring a house-cleaning service. More deliberate time management may mean scheduling a weekend away from the kids rather than counting on spontaneous romantic sparks.

These strategies are characterized by active compromise rather than by just conflict suppression, and by mutual goals rather than self-interest. Planned organizational support for such dual-career strategies is important, and formal programs have been in Canadian workplaces for about a decade. For example, Apple Canada offers a program of permanent part-time work which is mostly filled by women seeking more family time. Lynne Jarjour, HR consultant at Apple, comments: "It's great for me and the kids. My husband travels a lot. My life is no longer in constant chaos. And I don't have to feel guilty when I go to work."

Downsizing and Careers

Many companies and industries go through periodic downsizing. For instance, the construction industry can be said to downsize after each building season, and the parks department does the same at the end of the summer. But the word "downsizing" conjures up the activities that began during the depressed economic times of the early 1990s when companies "restructured." Many organizations and whole industries experienced that phenomenon, reducing jobs and employees by the score. Although generally regarded as negative—society tends to associate growth with health and vitality, while decline suggests decay—downsizing can offer unique career opportunities for both organizations and employees.[32] For example, though it has eliminated over 10,000 jobs, Bell Canada has been able to help its employees cope with change and find new career opportunities after leaving.[33] They have set up a number of career action centres that, among other things, offer career workshops throughout Quebec and Ontario. These help employees discover their transferable skills (career decisions) and learn effective job search techniques (career transitions).

Organizations engage in downsizing activities for various reasons. There are the savings reductions in labour costs and the organizational restructuring for either business line viability or unit operations. Resource allocation changes, due to internal unit suppliers or managerial layer reductions, may also result in organizational downsizing.[34] Organizational problems that occur after downsizing may also present career management opportunities. Survivors may feel guilty. Workers may have less confidence in management and motivation to work and lower levels of organizational participation and commitment.; they may fear and mistrust other employees. Higher absenteeism rates, greater incidence of conflict, and scapegoating may also be observed in workers.

Organizations may counter these problems by developing new career directions. Jobs are redesigned to ensure that work done by those laid off is picked up by other workers. Recall in Chapter 2 the discussion of employee involvement. The effect that involving employees has in making work more challenging for them is applicable to career development. Jobs may be enlarged as some workers pick up additional skills and responsibilities. Others may be deepened as a manager picks up details that were handled by subordinates. If career paths are updated to acknowledge these changes, workers are less likely to feel cut adrift, and morale and commitment may be strengthened.

Organizational definitions and clarification, expressed through explicit mapping of career paths, provides stability and a sense of continuity for survivors. Cross-training and job sharing provide opportunities for growth and a sense of security and continuity. Some firms suggest giving raises to survivors because of their increased workload, while others have given them pay cuts, which leads to fewer lay-offs and less survivor guilt. Bureaucracies tend to increase rules and regulations to protect remaining territories, further reducing organizational effectiveness and efficiency. Good career paths can cut through some of this maze.

Individual Responsibility for Careers

Throughout this discussion, we have addressed what the organization can do to assist in career development. Although these actions are necessary for a fully functioning HRM operation, it is unwise to assume all companies actually carry them out. Indeed, we can expect the continued growth of small entrepreneurial firms and in the proportion of employees hired on a contingent basis. For instance, the majority of respondents in a recent survey of 539 Canadian organizations reported that they do not feel an obligation to provide job security to employees.[35] With a relative decline in the number of Canadians employed full-time in large organizations comes an increase in the individual responsibility for careers. Employers just do not have the resources to take full responsibility for career development initiatives.

We can no longer expect to have our careers "managed" for us. The responsibility for career development is shifting from the organization to the individual. One positive in all this is that computer-based virtual training programs such as the one at Xerox and the Internet are making this easier for the individual. Indeed, new businesses such as CareerBridge[36] are thriving as individuals take more responsibility for their own development.[37] What this all goes to show, as we stressed earlier, is that you—the employee—are responsible for your own career.

Towards More Effective Organizational Career Development

Let's consider the methods or tools that managers can use to better match the career needs of their employees with the requirements of their organization. While these suggestions are not all-encompassing, they are a solid representation of contemporary career development methods.

Challenging Initial Job Assignments

An increasing body of evidence indicates that employees who receive especially challenging job assignments early in their careers do better in later jobs.[38] More specifically, the degree of stimulation and challenge in a person's initial job assignment tends to be significantly related to later career success and retention in the organization.[39] Apparently, initial challenges, particularly if they are successfully met, stimulate a person to perform well in subsequent years.

As we noted in earlier chapters in this book regarding strategic human resources planning, job analysis, recruitment, and selection, there are definite benefits for managers who correctly fill positions with individuals who have the appropriate abilities and interests to satisfy the job's demands. Therefore, managers should be even more concerned with matching new employees to their jobs. Successful placement at this stage can provide significant advantages to both the organization and the individual.

Career Counselling

Career Counselling Assisting employees in setting directions and identifying areas of professional growth.

Although often neglected in the early 1990s, career counselling is beginning to return to corporate Canada as more employees face the stress of restructuring and downsizing. As part of employees' performance review, career counselling assists employees in setting directions and identifying areas of professional growth. What should take place in this encounter? It has been proposed that the dialogue contain the following four elements:[40]

1. the employee's goals, aspirations, and expectations with regard to his or her own career for the next five years or longer;
2. the manager's view of the opportunities available and the degree to which the employee's aspirations are realistic and match up with the opportunities available;
3. identification of what the employee would have to do in the way of further self-development to qualify for new opportunities; and
4. identification of the actual next steps in the form of plans for new development activities or new job assignments that would prepare the employee for further career growth.

This career counselling process may not be easy for the manager. If the employee expresses unrealistic aspirations, the manager should be prepared to give a frank appraisal of where or how the individual falls short, an activity that is rarely enjoyable. The resulting dialogue may suggest that the employee needs further assessment and counselling, which should be offered by the organization. However, the final outcome should be a mutual understanding between employee and manager about realistic career expectations within the organization. The result, to the organization, will be employees with fewer false hopes and expectations about career opportunities. The key, again, is honesty and the conveyance of realistic data. If we err, it should be on the side of communicating too much information, even if the possibility exists of "turning off" an employee who has his or her unrealistic goals deflated. More employee "turnover, underutilization, and frustrated career development has assuredly resulted from too little realistic information, not too much of it."[41]

Career Development Workshops

Management should consider the value of group workshops to facilitate career development (see "HRM Skills"). By bringing together groups of employees with their managers, problems and misperceptions can be identified and, it is hoped, resolved. In practice, these workshops combine research carried out by the individual, using the Internet and other sources of information as well as advice and assistance provided by management.

Entry workshops are a natural extension of realistic job previews and the orientation and socialization activities discussed earlier. Companies also offer psychological assessments to help in this process. In doing so, they provide the opportunity for groups of new employees and their supervisors to share their separate expectations. Discussion can then focus on those areas where mismatches are identified. Where incongruities are significant and not easily resolved, these entry workshops can be extended to work out procedures for reducing the differences by changing the employee's expectations, organizational practices, or both.

Mid-career workshops can be offered to help individuals with similar background and length of tenure in the organization to assess their career development. These workshops frequently include self-diagnostic activities for employees, diagnosis of the organization, and alignment of the separate diagnoses to identify potential mismatches. Where significant differences are found that may create obstacles or frustrations for employees, solutions may take the form of emphasizing the need for individuals to alter their career aspirations, altering the organization's career development practices, or some combination thereof. Another possible outcome is that the employee will find better career opportunities with another organization.

Finally, the organization may provide late-career workshops. These are particularly useful for employees preparing for retirement, but they can also be used to deal with frustrations over unfulfilled career goals, the responsibilities and role expectations of mentors/coaches, developing new life interests, or coping with young and ambitious co-workers.

Continuing Education and Training

Career development can be linked to particular career stages (as mentioned above), but it must also occur as a continuing process throughout careers. Innovative organizations such as Maritime Life are not only aware of the role they have to play in managing careers, but they even offer employees a continuing budget to make this happen.[42] The CDA (career development account) is a sum of 2.5 per cent of gross annual pay given to each employee to be used towards books, subscriptions, courses, and anything else the employee and company agree is beneficial to career development.

The training and educational development activities presented in Chapter 9 reduce the possibilities that employees will find themselves with obsolete skills. Furthermore, they are consistent with employees taking more responsibility for their development. Additionally, when these development activities are carefully aligned with an individual's aspirations and anticipated future organizational needs, they become an essential element in an employee's career growth.

The education and training in an effective career development program could include on-the-job training, educational or skill courses offered by personnel within the organization, or outside courses provided by universities, colleges, or specialized consultants.

Competency-based training approaches are best for career development.[43] An underlying premise of competency-based training is that a person who already possesses a skill does not need to be taught it, thereby saving time and money.[44] Because employees need to acknowledge their needs for training (work or career management skills), they should be actively involved in the decision-making process of what courses to take and where.

Career Assessment

Individual career development requires people to become knowledgeable about their own needs, values, and personal goals. This can be achieved through a three-step, self-assessment process:

1. **Identify and organize your skills, interests, work-related needs, and values.** The best place to begin is by drawing up a profile of your educational record. List each school attended from high school on. What courses do you remember liking most and least? In what courses did you score highest and lowest? In what extra curricular activities did you participate? Are there any specific skills that you acquired? Are there other skills in which you have gained proficiency?

   Next, begin to assess your occupational experience. List each job you have held, the organization you worked for, your overall level of satisfaction, what you liked most and least about the job, and why you left. It's important to be honest in covering each of these points.

2. **Convert these inventories into general career fields and specific job goals.** By completing Step 1, you should now have some insights into your interests and abilities. What you need to do now is look at how these can be matched to an organizational setting or field of endeavor. Then you can become specific and identify distinct job goals. This is where time spent on the Internet will pay off hansomely.

   What fields are available? In business? In government? In non profit organizations? Your answer can be further delineated into areas such as manufacturing, banking, education, social services, or health services. Identifying areas of interest is usually far easier than pinpointing specific occupations. When you are able to identify a limited set of occupations that you are interested in, you can start to align these with your abilities and skills. Do you have the educational requirements necessary for the job? If not, what additional schooling will be needed? What type of people will be your coworkers? Does the job offer the status and earning potential that you aspire to? What is the long-term outlook for jobs in this area? Will certain jobs require you to move? If so, would this be compatible with your geographic preferences? Does the career suffer from cyclical employment? Since no job is without its drawbacks, have you seriously considered all the negative aspects? When you have fully answered questions such as these, you should have a relatively short list of special job goals.

3. **Test these possibilities against the realities of the organization or the job market.** The final step in this self-assessment process is testing your selection against the realities of the market place. This can be done by following up on your Internet searches and by going out and talking with HRM specialists and other knowledgeable people in the fields, organizations, or jobs you desire. These informational interviews should provide reliable feedback as to the accuracy of your self-assessment and the opportunities in the fields and jobs that interest you.

Source: Irving R. Schwartz, "Self-Assessment and Career Planning: Matching Individuals and Organizational Goals," *Personnel* (January-February 1979), p. 48.

Meet

Tony Marranca
VP of Human Resources and
Administrative Services, 3M Canada

Tony Marranca began his career at 3M Canada in London, Ontario as a technologist. Today, he's the vice-president of human resources and administrative services. Along the road to his current post, he worked at several different jobs in manufacturing and logistics.

An unusual career path? Not at 3M. A global Fortune 500 company with operations in over 60 countries (the Canadian subsidiary is almost 50 years old), 3M prides itself on its commitment to innovation. One way this manifests itself is through diversity of product line. Perhaps best known as a maker of tape and the now-ubiquitous Post-It Note, the company sells over 65,000 products worldwide. But diversifying the skills experience of its employees is also important.

"We seek out people who are interested in improving themselves," says Mr. Marranca. "We invest significantly in our people, and we expect them to be willing to invest in themselves—to try new things."

"In the last five years, we've hired one manager from outside and promoted about 150 from within," Mr. Marranca continues. "In the day-to-day impatience to get things done, many companies give in to the temptation to fire people in one area and re-hire in another when they make a change." At 3M, the alternative is a long-term view that gives current employees an opportunity to develop whatever skills the company is seeking to hire.

Mr. Marranca explains, "An employee's development is about 20% from formal education, 20% from networks, and 60% on-the-job training." His job, as he sees it, is to be sure his employees get support in all three areas.

Not every firm has the size and breadth to provide for this degree of career development, of course. But many of those that do simply don't have the corporate will. "Our kind of long-term committment to our people isn't unique, but it's rare," says Mr. Marranca; he can think of only two or three other large companies that work the same way.

You often hear it said that in the current climate, most people are likely to have at least three different careers in their lifetimes. "Well, at 3M", says Mr. Marranca, "you can have those three careers within the one company".

"Moving people through different job opportunities gives them a chance to gain a wide range of experience," he explains. It also gives the company the benefit of fresh eyes on old problems—the committment to innovation again—and of recouping the costs of training. Furthermore, when employees have this diversity of experience, they learn flexibility which makes them better equipped for today's fast-changing business world.

For example, a materials procurement specialist used to placing orders from factories may find herself negotiating with plantation owners in South America for shipments of specialized rubber—to be delivered ten years from now.

"We can't anticipate what problems we'll face, so we need diverse thinking," concludes Mr. Marranca. Helping employees develop their careers at 3M promotes this kind of thinking, while at the same time providing employees with a rare combination of change and stability.

Periodic Job Changes

In addition to encouraging employees to continue their education and training to prevent obsolescence and to stimulate career growth, managers should be aware that periodic job changes within the organization can achieve similar ends.[45] Job changes can take the form of vertical promotions, lateral transfers, job restructuring and sharing, or assignments organized around new tasks such as being made part of a special committee or temporary task force.

The important element in a job change that offers career development opportunities is the diverse and expanded range of experiences that new job tasks can provide. Varied experiences present to the individual new challenges which, if successfully surmounted, build confidence and provide positive feedback. This process encourages the undertaking of further new challenges and greater responsibilities. Of course, periodic job changes also provide management with more varied information on the employee's potential to move higher in the organization. When four supervisors rate an employee as having high potential for promotion, management can be better assured it is receiving a reliable evaluation than when such appraisal comes from only one supervisor.

Multiple Career Tracks

In this section, we use the term "ladder" to describe career structures for convenience and because it still fits in with the general idea of progression over time in career achievements. Do not forget that in many organizations, the shape of actual individual career experiences may be more like a spiral or jungle gym than a ladder. It is true, however, that in some organizations, the only way to get ahead is to be promoted within the managerial track—that is to say, to move up in some kind of management hierarchy. The rewards in this system are for managerial competence. When we examined job-personality fit earlier in this chapter, several other anchors and preferences were identified.

Multiple career ladders in an organization recognize these multiple career motivators. Dual-ladder promotion systems may allow good technical contributors to remain in a technical job and to receive the status and financial recognition given those who become managers. For example, IBM promotes managers from project to branch to division to corporate levels of the organization. The company also promotes systems specialists from analysts to senior analysts to fellows, allowing a good technical expert to remain in a technical job and still be successful. As we mentioned earlier, IBM also assists employees to set up as independent consultants after leaving the organization. Although dual-career ladders provide good career options for the employee, they frequently necessitate structural change in the organization and modifications of policies and procedures. There are mixed reports of success when dual ladders are put into practice.

Failures appear to be due to one of three reasons:

1. offering technical promotions only when managerial promotion has failed;
2. having unequal compensatory practices; and
3. displaying unequal management support for both ladders.[46]

It's tempting to use the alternative ladder as an escape system for the managerial promotion ladder. When a good technician becomes a bad manager and is transferred back to the technical ladder, that action may be perceived by employees as a clear signal that the managerial ladder is preferable, and the technical ladder is devalued. Establishing separate but not equal ladders causes problems in several areas: compensation, evaluation, resource allocations, and responsibility. If the managerial and technical tracks are not compensated in similar fashion, promotion on the technical ladder is quickly regarded as a change in title only, good enough for the plateaued employee but not for a good performer.

Both tracks need to be perceived as supported by senior executives. If X per cent of those on the managerial track receive a promotion every year, then X per cent of employees on the technical track should also. If the system works only to create a diversion from the managerial stream, that fact will surface in a very few years. If the expectation had been created for equal recognition of technical contribution to the organization, that organization risks substantial loss of technical credibility. Providing dual tracks can reduce the perceived incidence of the plateaued employee by providing lateral growth opportunities in addition to the traditional vertical promotion paths.

Professional Associations

Organizations should encourage their professional employees to get involved in their relevant professional associations. For instance, the Canadian Council of Human Resources Associations is the umbrella body coordinating the provincial human resources associations which provide the base for the interaction and development of human resources professionals. Chapters in metropolitan areas often meet monthly to network and to sponsor guest speakers on current topics. These events help professionals keep abreast of current career demands and expectations and provide opportunities for senior staff members to contribute in new ways and perhaps to meet new people.

Mentor-Protégé Relationships

Mentor-protege relationships are significant as career development tools.[47] For the protege, certainly, the relationship has positive career impact, especially for women.[48] For the mentor, the relationship may revitalize the last years of what might have been a stale career. Organizations can encourage these relationships through networking, building mentor expectations into managerial job descriptions, and otherwise recognizing and rewarding successful mentoring efforts.[49]

Supportive Environment

An organization that provides a supportive environment for career development is characterized by a concern for employee well-being and a tolerance of the mistakes that can occur during the exploration efforts and growth experiences of those employees. If an employee wants to try the managerial promotion ladder and fails, a mechanism to make a graceful return to a technical track is provided by an organization with a supportive environment. An organization that brands such an employee a failure is not supportive and may well lose that worker. The existence of career development programs and deliberate career paths, with the expectation that most employees will be long-term employees and that they will grow, is further indication of a supportive environment (see "What If: HRM in a De-Jobbed Organization").

What If:

HRM in a De-Jobbed Organization

Have you ever pondered the express train career ride of the baby boom generation that occurred from the 1960s through the 1980s? Did you ever wonder what existed that promoted some of those meteoric career rises in such a quick period? Were the baby boomers smarter than the generation Xers or just luckier? A precise answer is difficult to pinpoint, but clearly luck played a major role. During the 1960s, organizations in Canada experienced unprecedented growth, and new markets opened up, creating many new jobs. Undoubtedly, many of the baby boomers were in the right place at the right time. But don't chalk it up solely to luck. The baby boomers were better educated than the generation preceding them, and they brought an aggressive trait to the workforce that was rarely witnessed before. Accepting most any challenging assignment, being willing to relocate, and having the support of mentors all added to the career boom. Unfortunately, this prosperity didn't last. In fact, many of those baby boomers who skyrocketed to the top in their first ten to fifteen years on the job were the ones hardest hit by the downsizing that began in the late 1980s. For them and those that follow, fast-tracked career advancement is a thing of the past. Our organizations can no longer afford to promote workers in droves as they once did. And many of the jobs that served as stepping stones to careers may be lost forever. What, then, can those under thirty do to keep careers alive in today's dynamic organizations? For some, the answer lies in the acronym DATA: Desire, Ability, Temperament, Assets.

The D stands for *Desire*. Although experience was once perceived as the best preparation for the future, today, past experience may actually be a hinderance because it can promote a status quo mentality—one that is ill fitted to a dynamic environment. Instead, workers' desire will be a key factor in career growth. Those individuals who desire to be the best, who continually strive to excel, and who perform under a variety of difficult situations will have an advantage over those who don't possess this trait.

Second, workers must have the *Ability* to perform the required work. This means that tomorrow's workers can never sit back on their laurels and bask in their glory. Rather, they must continually upgrade their skills, knowledge, and abilities to ensure that they are the best at their jobs. This also means looking closely inside themselves and identifying their strengths and weaknesses, capitalizing on the strengths, and working to develop the weaknesses.

Tomorrow's employees must also have an appropriate *Temperament*. The security of yesterday's jobs is gone, and you are on your own in many circumstances. And when the job is done, so, too, might be your association with the organization. As such, workers must have a disposition that easily adjusts to an ever-changing work situation. Rigidity and the desire for security may be the ultimate killers of one's career.

Finally, employees must possess a variety of *Assets*. This means that you must be able to provide whatever resources the job requires. This may be

(continued)

(continued)

networking contacts, equipment, or even time commitments—all resources that contribute to a successful performer.

Succeeding in tomorrow's organizations needn't be a hopeless cause, but we must recognize that the career paths of yesterday won't exist. With proper preparation and a positive mindset, the doors to career growth may once again appear open. This time, however, it will be solely our responsibility. The organization may be in no position, and may not have the desire, to offer this kind of assistance.

Source: William Bridges, "The End of the Job," *Fortune* (September 19, 1994), p. 72; see also, Patricia Sellers, "Don't Call Me Slacker!" *Fortune* (December 12, 1994), pp. 181–82.

Study Tools and Applications

Summary

This summary relates to the Learning Objectives provided on p. 281.
After having read this chapter you should know:

1. A career is a sequence of positions occupied by a person during a course of a lifetime.

2. Career development from an organizational standpoint involves tracking career paths and developing career ladders. From an individual perspective, career development focuses on assisting individuals in identifying their major career goals and determining what they need to do to achieve these goals.

3. The main distinction between career development and employee development lies in their time frames. Career development focuses on the long-range career effectiveness and success of organizational personnel. Employee development focuses more on the immediate and intermediate time frames. In addition, there is more clearly a joint responsibility for career development on the part of the individual and the organization than is true for employee development.

4. Career development is valuable to an organization because it (1) ensures needed talent will be available; (2) improves the organization's ability to attract and retain high-talent employees; (3) ensures that minorities and women get opportunities for growth and development; (4) reduces employee frustration; (5) enhances cultural diversity; (6) assists in implementing quality; and (7) promotes organizational goodwill.

5. The five stages in a career consist of exploration, establishment, mid-career, late career, and decline.

6. The Holland vocational preferences are realistic, investigative, artistic, social, enterprising, and conventional.

7. Problem-solving styles, a number of different focuses on personality dimensions of individuals that can be matched to work environments. These include: sensation-thinking; sensation-feeling; intuitive-thinking; and intuitive-feeling.

8. Dual-career couples affect career development in that one of the individual's jobs must become the priority in terms of advancement and relocation. As such, dual-career couples place added strain on an organization's career development process.

9. Organizational career development can be more effective through (1) challenging initial jobs; (2) career counselling; (3) career development workshops; (4) continuing education and training; (5) periodic job changes; (6) multiple career ladders; (7) professional associations; (8) mentor-protégé relationships; and (9) a supportive environment.

Key Terms

career

career counselling

career development

career stage

decline stage

dual-career couple

establishment stage

exploration stage

external and internal careers

Holland vocational preferences model

late-career stage

mid-career stage

plateauing

problem-solving style

EXPERIENTIAL EXERCISE:

Career Planning

Purpose:

1. To diagnose your occupational strengths and weaknesses.
2. To develop a career plan based on your strengths and weaknesses.
3. To introduce you to commonly used career planning techniques.

Advanced Preparation:

This exercise may require substantial advance preparation. Steps 1 to 5 should be completed before the group meets. Participants may need to read or review one of the exercises or readings discussed in the introduction and body of the exercise. Some participants may need to make trips to the library or arrange discussions with persons in the type of work they are thinking about (see Step 3).

Group Size:

The total group may be of any size, but subgroups should be from two to six.

Time Required:

In-class time depends on size of subgroups: ten minutes per group member plus set-up and discussion time (i.e., for subgroups of five, sixty-five to eight-five minutes.)

Special Physical Requirements:

Room or an area large enough to seat small groups comfortably and permit discussions with minimal distraction from others. (Moveable chairs will be helpful.) Separate meeting areas for subgroups are desirable but not essential.

Introduction:

Obviously, different occupations and professions require different strengths (skills, abilities, talents, etc.) of the people who are effective in their work. The skills and abilities required for a particular line of work reflect the activities that are involved in the job which, in turn, are largely dictated by the "raw materials" involved in the work. Broadly speaking, all jobs require dealing with one or more of four types of raw materials: things, data, ideas, and people. These suggest some of the elemental job activities required for each of these raw materials.

Things	Some activities involving **things**: move, manipulate, machine (saw, drill, finish, etc.), adjust, assemble, design, operate, handle, construct, arrange, inspect, clean, deliver, store, drive.
Data	Some job activities involving **data**: compare, collect, copy, analyse, check, compile, organize, summarize, type, collate, store and retrieve, classify, schedule, observe, diagnose.
People	Some job activities involving **people**: counsel, assist, coach, teach, manage, persuade, interview, consult, advise, criticize, lead, communicate, request, encourage, sell, recruit, manage, arbitrate or mediate conflict, negotiate, speak in public, supervise, listen, help others to express themselves.
Ideas	Some job activities involving **ideas**: create, compare, critique, publish, think about, argue, comprehend, decide, plan, interpret, define, establish goals, imagine, invent, synthesize.

Some jobs seem to require the ability to deal with primarily one type of material: bookkeepers work mostly with data, carpenters with things, philosophers with ideas, and sales clerks with people. Most jobs require the ability to deal with at least two types of materials. For example, all managers deal with people, but the controller also works with data, the vice-president of engineering is heavily involved with data and things, and the vice-president of marketing with ideas and data.

Effective planning of your career requires that you identify your personal strengths and find a line of work that will let you use those skills that you enjoy exercising the most. Once you have identified a particular vocational area that capitalizes on your strengths, it is also important that you identify any remediable deficiencies or weaknesses that may hinder you from achieving your full potential in your field. You will need to develop specific plans for moving into your chosen line of work (if you are not already in it) and for overcoming your weaknesses.

Step 1:

1. Take four blank sheets of lined, 8 1/2 x 11-inch notebook paper. Put a heading on each sheet, one sheet for each of the four basic areas of: things, data, ideas, and people.

2. On the first line of each sheet, write "Satisfying Skills." Beginning with *things*, think of and list all of the things you can do really well with physical materials and objects. Think, in particular, of skills that provide you with a deep sense of satisfaction when you exercise them. When you have listed as many skills and abilities as you can think of for *things*, move on to the sheets labelled *data*, *ideas* and *people*. Repeat the process until you feel you have listed all of your really important skills and abilities in each area.

Step 2:

From your lists of satisfying skills, which are the most important to you? On a fresh sheet of paper, make a list of your five most satisfying skills and abilities— those that you enjoy the most (be careful to retain the "things," "data," etc, labels).

Step 3: Do a Or b.

a. For people who are not certain about their career interests: What types of careers tend to require the exercise of your most important skills and abilities? Identify as many possibilities as you can before you select the alternative that seems to fit you best. If you are not sure about some of the possibilities, there are several ways to get more information. Most universities and colleges have placement and counselling centres that will be glad to discuss your interests with you. If you think certain vocations might be a good fit for you, talk to some people in these jobs—don't be afraid to call someone you don't even know. You might be surprised at how willing most people are to help. If you are really at a loss to think of anything, look up some jobs in *Human Resources Development Canada's Career Handbook* in the nearest library.

Once you have identified some likely possibilities, check the library database for anything about these jobs. As you begin to develop some specific feasible alternatives, pick up any information you can about how people get into this line of work. What are the educational, training, and experience requirements you are going to have to fulfil? Is there a practical way for you to meet these requirements? How? Prepare notes on your findings and conclusions. You will need them in Step 5. You are now ready to establish a tentative career objective. When you have stated your career objective, go on to Step 4.

b. For people who are satisfied with career choices already made: Where do you want to go in your occupation or profession? What does it mean to you to "advance" in your field? Don't restrict yourself to thinking only in terms of traditional measures such as salary and organizational level. For the purposes of this activity, define advancement as moving into a new position or redesigning your current job so that it requires you to use even more of your most important and satisfying skills and abilities. Prepare a statement of your career objectives.

Step 4:

Take the original four sheets (things, data, ideas, and people). Turn them over and head up each sheet respectively: weaknesses/deficiencies—things, weaknesses/deficiencies—data, and so on.[50] Respond to the following: things I do poorly, things I would like to stop doing, and things I would like to learn to do well. Which of these deficiencies are most important right now? Which must you do something about first in order to begin moving towards the objective you set for yourself in Step 3? Select and rank the three most important on the piece of paper where you listed your five most satisfying skills and abilities.

Step 5:

Prepare a brief, written plan showing how you plan to move towards your career objective (from Step 3), and include your plans for dealing with the weaknesses that stand between you and your objective.

Step 6: (Optional)

Share your most important strengths and weaknesses, your statement of your objective, and your plan for achieving your objective with the other(s) in your group. As each person explains his or her inventory and plans, the other members of the group should provide feedback, and offer any suggestions that seem warranted for improving the career plan.

Source: Developed by Donald D. Bowen, in Roy J. Lewicki, Donald D. Bowen, Douglas T. Hall, and Francine S. Hall, *Experiences in Management and Organization Behavior*, 3d ed. (New York: John Wiley, 1988), pp. 261-66. Used with permission.

CASE APPLICATION:

The Winding Path to Career Success as a Super Grocer[51]

Pierre Lessard, CEO of the Quebec grocery giant Metro-Richelieu, has achieved remarkable success. Metro's achievement in Quebec is based on careful management and the ability to acquire valuable assets from other grocery chains such as the best store sites from the old Steinberg chain. Under Lessard's leadership, Metro now has a cash reserve of $300 million, offering ample resources for future expansion. Lessard has quietly emerged as one of the country's savviest retail merchants.

At the beginning, however, Lessard's own career was not a sure success story by any means, and his work history illustrates the complex interaction of personality, preferences and opportunities that go into the making of a career in Canada today. He was the son of a deputy industry minister in the Quebec government, went to a Jesuit high school, and took a Bachelor of Arts degree at Laval University. But what distinguished him from the start was his fascination with numbers and fine attention to detail. To ensure a firm educational foundation, he completed a master's in accounting science at Laval, his CA, and then in 1967, an MBA from Harvard. His attention to detail was demonstrated in his choice of an obscure food wholesaler in Sherbrooke with ambitious acquisition plans, rather than accepting more prestigious offers from Bay Street and rue St-Jacques.

Lessard was a quiet and rather nervous man rather than the confident salesperson you might have expected who would become a successful CEO, but he made sure to develop contacts in his chosen field and to build on his strengths. He ran into a number of roadblocks in his career that required all the skills and contacts he could muster to overcome them.

After university, he joined the small wholesaler Denault Ltée as comptroller because it was headed by an ambitious president, Antoine Turmel, who later became CEO of the giant Provigo. In 1976, Lessard became COO of Provigo and seemed set to succeed Turmel when he retired as CEO in 1985. This was not to be, however, and Lessard lost out to much more flamboyant Pierre Lortie. Lessard resigned and left the grocery business for a while to become vice-chairman of Pathonic Communications Inc., a TV network in which he had a major holding. Then he moved on to become president of Aetna-Life Insurance Company.

Though he was out of it, Lessard was set to return to the grocery business as CEO at Metro.

Although he may appear distant at receptions, Lessard has a congenial personality that makes him popular with his close associates and friends. He works extremely hard. For example, he always eats lunch at his desk, never lets meetings end until problems are solved, and has yet to take a two-week holiday. Lessard is best known for his meticulous attention to detail. As a colleague puts it: "If you told him that a store's margin is 18.34 per cent, don't tell him 18.5 per cent three months later. He will ask you where the improvement came from."

Questions

1. Trace Pierre Lessard's career in terms of career stages.
2. Who was primarily responsible for Lessard's career development?
3. How can a demotion or a change in top management impede one's career plans?
4. What lessons can organizations learn about facilitating the career development of their senior executives?

How well did you fulfil the learning objectives?

1. Joan is a wife and mother. She has raised four children but feels stifled in that role. She spends most of her time in volunteer activities—save the whales, quilting, great books clubs, church work. What could she change to have a successful career?
   a. Get paid for the work she does.
   b. Stick to only one volunteer activity for a period of more than fifteen years.
   c. Joan does have a successful career.
   d. Joan should have more children.
   e. If Joan felt satisfied as wife, mother, and volunteer worker, her career could be regarded as successful.

2. A vice-president of human resources for a large, high-technology firm strives to attract and retain highly skilled workers. She is hiring a new manager of training and development, and she wants a progressive person in tune with the needs of the workers and aware of emerging trends in career management. What comment would be a danger signal on an interview with a prospective candidate?
   a. A major focus of the job is developing career ladders and tracking career paths.
   b. Monitoring the progress of special groups, such as minorities and managers, is an important part of the job.
   c. The needs of dual-career couples should be handled in the same ways as single employees to avoid favouritism.
   d. Lifestyle issues and individual analysis should be part of the career planning services offered to employees.
   e. Employee needs and goals should be assessed. Today's worker has different expectations than those of a generation ago.

3. John has worked for the same manufacturing firm for twenty years, but last week, after a training session, he decided to quit, return to school, and open a florist shop. What kind of session did John attend?
   a. Individual career development.
   b. Organizational career management.
   c. Employee development.
   d. Employee training.
   e. Employee inventory.

4. Robyn, vice-president of human resources, has just cut the career development program in response to a 35 per cent directive to cut the budget by. What is likely to happen?
   a. Good employees will not be affected.
   b. All employee training functions will become more effective and efficient because of this move.
   c. In the short term, employees will work harder.
   d. In the long term, employees will be less committed and satisfied with the organization.
   e. The other training functions can easily replace these programs.

5. A large federal agency conducts career management workshops for its employees. More than 30 per cent of workshop attendees leave for employment elsewhere within a year. The program is considered to be a great success in career management because it
   a. keeps those employees out of other training sessions.
   b. increases cultural diversity.
   c. reduces employee frustration.
   d. reduces organizational goodwill.
   e. promotes organizational globalization.

6. Sean is a twenty-seven-year-old university student. He will graduate in the spring with an MBA in accounting and return to full-time work as a senior accountant for the firm that paid his way through school. Identify Mike's career stage.
   a. Decline.
   b. Maintenance.
   c. Exploration.
   d. Establishment.
   e. Mid-Career.

7. Jane is an accounting major who refinishes furniture in her spare time. She is well organized and uses a very impressive time-management calendar. She seems friendly enough and belongs to several campus groups but is not an officer in any of them. What is Jane's "Holland" type?
   a. Realistic-investigative-artistic.
   b. Social-enterprising-xonventional.
   c. Social-conventional-realistic.
   d. Investigative-enterprising-artistic.
   e. Realistic-conventional-artistic.

8. Gloria works for a large bank as a teller manager. She likes the steady hours, the predictable schedule, the pleasant co-workers, the good working relationships with her subordinates, and her status in the bank. What Schein anchors are important to Gloria?
   a. Security, managerial competence.
   b. Security, creativity.
   c. Technical competence, security.
   d. Creativity, autonomy, technical competence.
   e. Creativity, autonomy, security.

9. Jo has an intuitive-feeling problem-solving style. What job would be best for her?
   a. A shoe clerk. She could meet lots of people, measure feet, sell the shoes, and move on to the next customer.

b. A waitress. She could meet lots of people, anticipate their dining needs, make sure everyone in the dining party was happy, and look forward to repeat business.

c. A rocket scientist. She could work in her lab, away from people, and carry out whatever experiments she wanted whenever she wanted.

d. A veterinarian. She could work with animals, not people, make diagnoses in her treatments, and move on to the next dog.

e. A elementary-school teacher. She could work with children, help them be creative, socialize them, and know that, for years to come, she influenced their lives.

10. Sid and Nancy, a dual-career couple, work in Vancouver. Nancy works for a bank. Sid works for a tool and die manufacturer. Nancy is involved in an individual career assessment activity at her bank. In which of these exercises will the dual-career couple pressure appear?
a. Problem-solving style.
b. Schein's anchors.
c. Holland vocational preference profiles.
d. Role-play exercise about real-life priorities.
e. Employee inventory.

11. Matt quit school when he was sixteen to work full-time at the local fast-food chain to pay for his car and video games. Now, at thirty-six, he wants to try something else. What should Matt do?

a. Finish high school.
b. Get into the management training program at the fast-food chain.
c. Spend some time sorting and identifying his skills, interests, needs, and values.
d. Just say no.
e. Check the want ads and interview for other jobs.

12. Individual career management today is different than it was a generation ago for all of these reasons except
a. sex-role stereotypes are crumbling.
b. employee expectations are different.
c. the impact of other life roles and responsibilities on work life has been recognized.
d. choices are more important. There is little opportunity today to change a career once it has been launched.
e. lifestyles are more varied.

13. Which statement best reflects the relationship between career development and employee development?
a. Employee development should replace organizational career management programs.
b. The goals of employee development should be compatible with the goals of career development.
c. The goals of employee development should be considered independently of career development.
d. The relationship is an adversarial one.
e. Employee development should be done before individual career development and after organizational career development.

Chapter Eleven

MOTIVATION AND JOB DESIGN

LEARNING OBJECTIVES

AFTER READING THIS CHAPTER, YOU WILL BE ABLE TO:

1. Define motivation.
2. Identify the three critical components of motivation in an organizational setting.
3. Discuss the process of motivation.
4. Describe how unsatisfied needs create tension.
5. Explain the difference between functional and dysfunctional tension.
6. Discuss the effort–performance relationship, the individual performance–organizational goal relationship, and the organizational goal–individual goal relationships.
7. Identify the five core characteristics of the job characteristics model.
8. Describe the motivational effects of job enrichment and work at home.
9. List several suggestions that can be used to motivate employees.
10. Describe how you might motivate low-tech and high-tech employees.

"People are our most important resource," says Raman Agarwal, president of Ottawa-based Akran Systems Ltd. which supplies high-tech turnkey operations to clients that include hospitals, schools, and government agencies.[1] In Agarwal's view, the business depends on high-quality and excellent consumer service. To deliver, Agarwal needs productive employees. "I have to create an environment that people are happy to work in."

To achieve this, Akran provides employees with profit sharing, bonuses, and salaries that are approximately 5 per cent higher than the industry average. But it also means offering training: Akran invests 10 per cent of sales, an exceptionally large figure, on in-house and outside training programs. This training is vital to remaining competitive in the rapidly changing high-tech field, and it is valued by employees who also appreciate being able to read industry magazines in the company's resource centre.

Excellent salaries, profit sharing, and training are not all. Just as important, says Agarwal, are the little things that let staff know that he values their efforts: casual Fridays, ordering in pizza to celebrate awards or contracts, and days off on employees' birthdays. And it goes beyond that to helping them through difficult times, whether personal or work-related. For example, Agarwal found out that one of the company's employees was troubled. It wasn't that his performance had deteriorated, but "you could tell by his face something was wrong." Gentle probing by Agarwal revealed that the employee had financial difficulties. Agarwal arranged for a company loan, to be repaid through payroll deductions. Problem solved.

The result of this caring is a highly motivated and loyal workforce. And it seems to work very well indeed—Akran's sales increased from $2.1 million to $29.5 million in five years.

Introduction

In any organization, success is contingent on how well its employees perform. Up to this point in our look at HRM, we have focused our attention on obtaining productive employees by using means such as job analysis, proper recruitment and selection techniques, and the adaptation and training of employees. Although these HRM activities are critical, they will not by themselves give us these highly productive employees. We can hire individuals with extraordinary competencies, adapt them to the organization, and further develop their abilities, but this alone will not assure satisfactory performance. The reason is that two distinct factors affect workers' performance on the job: their ability to do the job and their willingness to do it. Recruitment, selection, and training typically focus only on the ability side. Until now, we have not really dealt with employees' willingness. The process of activating this willingness in employees is commonly called motivation. For example, even the most mundane topics in a college or university course can be made interesting by a professor who knows how to excite his or her students. By doing those things necessary to keep students involved and their interest piqued, the professor is activating the learning energies of these individuals—motivating them to learn.

In whatever forum—a university, a company, or a one-on-one relationship—the issue at hand is finding ways to motivate people. This can appear to be a complicated issue, but it boils down to treating people as if they mattered. Raman Agarwal provides things employees value, whether it be training or recognition for a job well done. He noticed when one of his employees was in financial difficulties and did something to help. Let's take a closer look at motivation and how it manifests itself in our organizations.

Characteristics of Motivation

The Motivation Process

One approach to defining motivation is in terms of some observable behaviour. We could say that people who exert a greater effort to perform some task are motivated, and those who exert a lesser effort are not. However, this statement is relative and tells us little. It is more useful to define motivation as the willingness to do something, where this something satisfies some need for the individual.[2] For instance, consider the amount of effort (willingness) you put into a class you take on a pass/fail basis. Most people will exert only enough effort to meet the minimum requirements necessary to pass, which is usually less than if you attempted to get an A. So, an individual's level of effort should be considerably higher when the need is to earn an A rather than merely passing. An individual who is very interested in the subject matter may also put in a good deal of effort. In this case, the need may be "to know more."

This definition is useful in broad terms, but we must modify it when we apply it to organizations. The effort put forth by employees can be misguided—they may be working hard at the wrong things. For organizational success, employees' efforts must be focused towards some organizational goal. It is often assumed that this is the case, but it is our contention that the matter is too important to be left as an assumption. Employees could, perhaps, be working hard to sell a product that is priced below cost. Or consider your own situation. If your goal is to pass the HRM class you are currently enrolled in, you wouldn't put your energies into

Motivation The willingness to do something, conditioned by the action's ability to satisfy some need.

Organizational Goal An objective that the organization seeks to achieve.

When we see people working hard at some activity, we can conclude that they are driven by a desire to achieve some goal that they perceive as having value to them.

studying for a chemistry test to prepare for your HRM mid-term examination. Studying hard is not enough; you must study the right things. Thus, the focus on goals becomes crucial in channelling the effort in the right areas.

There is another reason why the definition we gave needs to be modified. It is important to satisfy both organizational and individual needs. As employers, we must ensure that employee needs are met as well as the organization's goals. Thus, we will base our attempt to meet employees' needs on some tangible evidence that we are also meeting the organization's goals. That evidence is productive work—effort that assists the organization in meeting its goals and objectives. Consequently, employee motivation can now be defined as an individual's willingness to exert effort to achieve the organization's goals, conditioned by this effort's ability to satisfy individual needs. Inherent in this definition, then, are three components: effort, organizational goals, and individual needs. We have portrayed these three components graphically in Figure 11-1. Although we have a general understanding of effort and organizational goals, let's focus for a moment on **individual needs**.

Individual Needs A basic want or desire.

Employee effort exerted → Organizational goals achieved → Individual needs satisfied

Figure 11-1
Components of Motivation

An individual need, in our terminology, means some internal state that makes certain outcomes appear attractive. Regarding Figure 11-1, note that although individual needs can be satisfied without the achievement of organizational goals (by, for example, winning $2 million in Lotto 6/49), our purpose here is to focus only on those needs that are satisfied through work effort in an organization. Needs, and how they relate to our behaviour, are depicted in Figure 11-2.

Unsatisfied need → Increased tension → Effort → Satisfied need → Decreased tension

Deprivation | Functional vs. dysfunctional tension | Outward behaviour | Goal attainment | Calm state

Figure 11-2
The Process of Motivation

•

Deprivation A state of having an unfulfilled need.

Our process of motivation begins with an unsatisfied need, which is anything that we want and do not have. For instance, what if you would just love to purchase a new car? The fact that you don't have one creates an unsatisfied need. Until you do get the automobile, you are deprived of it.

Whenever we are in a state of deprivation—having unsatisfied needs—this results in tension. In common usage, the word "tension" has a negative connotation. But some tension is absolutely necessary. Rather than group all forms of tension under one term, let's recognize both the positive and negative forms—functional and dysfunctional tension.

Functional Tension Positive tension that creates the energy for an individual to act.

Let's first take a look at functional tension. For motivation to occur, we must have functional tension. This is what gives us the energy to perform. Think about what athletes do before a sporting event: They get themselves "pumped up," which is functional tension. As a result of this tension, individuals are able to perform at peak levels.

Effort Outward action of individuals directed towards some goal.

Given that individuals are experiencing some unsatisfied needs and have the desire to change that, the functional tension they have will cause them to exhibit a particular behaviour, called effort, in our model. Effort is the outward action of individuals that focuses on a particular goal. These actions are performed so that the required goals can be achieved. If our efforts are successful in achieving our goal, then we expect our needs to be satisfied. Satisfied needs then reduce or eliminate the deprivation we initially experienced. If we work hard and save for that car, when we finally make our purchase, we will have satisfied that need. Furthermore, when this need is satisfied, our tension is reduced for that particular need, resulting in a temporary calming effect until the next need (like purchasing a house) becomes unsatisfied.

Therefore, we can say that motivated employees are in a state of tension, and to relieve it, they engage in organizational activities. The greater the tension, the greater the drive to bring about relief. Accordingly, when we see people working hard at some activity, we can conclude that they are driven by a desire to achieve some goal that they perceive as having value to them. The problem, however, is that this is a fragile process, one that requires the blending of many pieces of the puzzle. If any of these linkages are missing, the willingness to exert energy will decrease.

Barriers to the Process

Because we are dealing with people—individuals who view things in their own idiosyncratic way—a number of barriers may exist to prevent motivation. These can lie either in the individual or in the organization. While the actual reasons for reduced motivation vary from one situation to another, we can identify some common problems. Let's look again at our diagram of the process of motivation (Figure 11-2).

Dysfunctional Tension Tension that leads to negative stress.

Apathy Significant dysfunction tension resulting in no effort being made.

Problems begin to become apparent in the tension phase during which two major obstacles can exist: dysfunctional tension and apathy. As we mentioned, some tension is crucial to effort, but when that tension becomes dysfunctional, we witness a change in individuals. For instance, suppose that initially an individual is putting forth the effort but is not obtaining the outcome that would satisfy his or her need. Maybe a second attempt is made with the same result. At some point, the tension takes a turn for the worse—creating stress and leading to dysfunctional tension. For example, suppose we have two employees working in an admissions office at a local community college. Yearly performance evaluations conducted on employees result in a pay raise. In this college, three evaluations are possible—outstanding, satisfactory, and needs improvement. The pay increases for each are 6 per cent, 3 per cent, and 0 per cent, respectively. Furthermore, assume the college has a means of quantifying this evaluation based on student applications processed and their quality. To be rated "outstanding," one needs a quantitative score of 85 per cent with less than a 1 per cent error rate; for "satisfactory," 65 per cent with less than a 5 per cent error rate; and "needs improvement" is anything under 65 per cent or an error rate above 5 per cent. During the first evaluation, employee A has a score of 80.3 per cent with no recorded errors; employee B, 69 per cent with a 4 per cent error rate. What pay raise do they get? They both get 3 per cent! For employee A, this is disturbing; a 6 per cent pay raise is what she wants (unsatisfied need). So for period two, she tries even harder to get to 85 per cent. Employee B, on the other hand, is satisfied with the 3 per cent raise. At the end of period two, the evaluations indicate: employee A, 82.1 per cent, no errors; employee B, 67.3 per cent, 3 per cent errors. Their pay raises? Three per cent. By now, employee A is frustrated. She has done all she can to try to satisfy her needs, but apparently she is unable to do so. So how does dysfunctional tension come into play? This employee knows that she can get a 68 per cent rating by working hard until Wednesday afternoon and then taking it easy. So she slows down, thus losing her drive. In the end, she gives the college what she believes is a fair effort consistent with a 3 per cent pay raise.

Apathy also can play a role in this process. By apathy, we mean a condition of little or no drive or just not caring. Employees encounter situations that can feel quite negative such as being disciplined for lateness. But when managers' actions seriously undermine the energy and enthusiasm of their employees (in extreme situations, when they break the employees' spirit), employees become apathetic and simply don't care. Consider what happened at London, Ontario-based Cuddy International Corp., the largest poultry company in Canada.[3] Founder Mac Cuddy first brought in his sons to help him run the company, but in 1993, he began hiring highly qualified outsiders to help him transform the company. Disputes developed between Mac and his sons as well as between the sons themselves. Three of the sons refused to cooperate with the outside managers. These conflicts lowered morale, and several of the managers left in frustration at not being able to do their jobs. Certainly the company could not get much productivity from these employees before they left; as a matter of fact, Cuddy lost $18 million in 1996.

For motivation to exist, it is imperative that certain conditions exist. For HRM, these parameters are the effort–performance relationship, the individual performance–organizational goal relationship, and the organizational goal–individual goal relationship.[4] At this point, a few words are in order about our view of motivation. Whenever discussions of motivation occur, there is a tendency to spend considerable time discussing the theories of Abraham Maslow,[5] Douglas McGregor,[6] Frederick Herzberg,[7] David McClelland,[8] J. Stacey Adams,[9] and Victor Vroom.[10] Since you have undoubtedly reviewed these theorists' contributions in earlier courses, we assume you're already familiar with their theories. Nonetheless, we've summarized them briefly in Table 11-1.

A Model of Motivation

The motivation process is complex. Because individuals and organizations are multifaceted, there must exist an appropriate blend of factors that promote

TABLE 11-1 Recap of Classic Motivational Theories

Theory	Individual	Summary
Hierarchy of Needs	Abraham Maslow	Five needs ranked in an hierarchical order from lowest to highest: physiological, safety, belonging, esteem, and self-actualization. An individual moves up the hierarchy and, when a need is substantially realized, moves up to the next need.
Theory X-Theory Y	Douglas McGregor	Proposes two alternative sets of assumptions that managers hold about human beings' motivation—one, basically negative, labelled Theory X; and the other, basically positive, labelled Theory Y. McGregor argues that Theory Y assumptions are more valid than Theory X and that employee motivation would be maximized by giving workers greater job involvement and autonomy.
Motivation-Hygiene	Frederick Herzberg	Argues that intrinsic job factors motivate, whereas extrinsic factors only placate employees.
Achievement, Affiliation, and Power Motives	David McClelland	Proposes that there are three major needs in workplace situations: achievement, affiliation, and power. A high need to achieve has been positively related to higher work performance when jobs provide responsibility, feedback, and moderate challenge.
Equity Theory	J. Stacey Adams	An individual compares his or her input/outcome ratio to that of relevant others. If there is a perceived inequity, the individual will change his or her behaviour or compare themselves with someone else.
Expectancy Theory	Victor Vroom	Proposes that motivation is a function of valence (value) of the effort-performance and the performance–reward relationships.

Source: For a more detailed discussion, see John R. Schermerhorn, Jr., Andrew J. Templer, R. Julian Cattaneo, James G. Hunt, and Richard N. Osborn, *Managing Organizational Behaviour*, First Canadian Edition (Toronto: Wiley, 1992), Chapter 5: Motivation Theories, pp. 136-67.

need satisfaction. Furthermore, the factors that must exist (what we referred to as the "many pieces of the puzzle") may also change frequently; what one has as an unfulfilled need today may not be important tomorrow. Research has shown us that people do change over time and that at various stages in their careers, certain goals are more important than others. And different people find different things motivating or rewarding. Maple Homes Canada Ltd. of Richmond, BC takes employees on a weekend fishing trip once a year.[11] This is great for employees who like fishing trips but not for those who don't. Such people might even leave the company entirely, and while that would leave behind a company full of fishing trip lovers, it may not be in the company's best interest.

This highlights an important message: To be sure that specific needs are satisfied, you might have to ask employees what those needs are.[12] Even the best motivational device is useless if it misses its intended target. For that direct hit to occur, HRM must ensure that all the potential traps that can sap an individual's motivation are removed. To begin, HRM must ensure that employees clearly see a strong relationship between effort and performance.[13]

The Effort–Performance Relationship

Whenever we hire an employee, there is an implied understanding that we have hired the individual who best fits the job requirements. Accordingly, one of the initial components of the effort–performance relationship focuses on a person's ability to exert the appropriate effort. We said earlier that effort is an inward reaction that is witnessed as outward behaviour. But what should that effort be? For motivation to occur, we must be able to specify what effort is needed. For HRM, this means that jobs must be analysed properly (and updated frequently) to ensure that the job is defined in terms of the tasks, duties,

Effort–performance Relationship The likelihood that putting forth the effort will lead to successful performance on the job.

and responsibilities (Chapter 5). Furthermore, HRM must identify what the job incumbent must possess to be successful. Once these two concepts are in place, HRM must make sure that it has selected the appropriate person for the job (Chapters 6 and 7), adapted them to the organization (Chapter 8), and trained them in doing the job the company way (Chapter 9). In fact, the effort component is indeed the first two legs of our HRM model—staffing, and training and development. By defining the job properly and selecting the appropriate person, we have those competent, adapted individuals with up-to-date skills, knowledge, and abilities. For job performance purposes, staffing and training and development functions serve to address the ability component.

In addition to having ability, employees' jobs must be well designed. Although we'll look at job design in greater detail later in this chapter, here we want to make sure the organization facilitates productive performance. In doing so, a company must assure that employees have the best equipment available to do the job. Even the best ability on a handwritten, paper-based spreadsheet will not provide the same productivity and quality as a computerized version. Consequently, for effort to be exerted, the right tools must be present.

In addition to existing somewhere, the necessary resources must also be readily available. Consider an individual who must spend a considerable part of each day using specific tools. If these are located a distance from the job site, this individual will be less productive than if the tools were readily accessible. Available resources also include knowledgeable people. Famed automobile manufacturer BMW designed its engineering centre so that the engineers working on a given part of the car (say, the engine) have their desks on the same floor as, and only a few steps away from, the engineers who work on the corresponding manufacturing process. Having colleagues nearby increases communication and results in better design solutions and lower costs.

Inasmuch as ability and job design are critical to effort, so, too, is the performance dimension. All the effort in the world will be lost if it is not directed towards some end, and from the HRM viewpoint, that end is performance. An individual will make the effort as long as there is a good likelihood that he or she will be a successful performer. But what is successful performance? At this stage of the motivation model, performance must be defined. Managers must be trained in establishing work standards and communicating those expectations to their employees. These same managers must be able to coach their employees and assist them in achieving their performance levels. And for managers to be proficient at this, they must be trained (by HRM staff or consultants) in performance appraisal processes. Only by showing employees that their effort is required for specified performance and that if such effort exists, they will be successful on the job, will the effort–performance link be completed. Once that milestone is achieved, it's time to tie this performance to organizational goals.

The Individual Performance–Organizational Goal Relationship

Whenever employees perform their duties, their effort should be guided towards some end. As we discussed in Chapter 5, that end is meeting organizational goals. If we have determined the strategic nature of our jobs and linked them accordingly to company objectives, then we can best facilitate their attainment by promoting the appropriate performance. Employees must also be aware of this critical linkage if we expect their behaviour to contribute to organizational goals.

The **individual performance–organizational goal relationship** is designed to provide something of value to the organization. Just as individuals have unsatis-

Individual Performance–Organizational Goal Relationship The expectation that achieving organizational goals will lead to the attainment of individual goals.

fied needs, so, too, do organizations. But the organization's unsatisfied needs (unfulfilled goals) cannot be satisfied without the effort of its people. If employees' performance is not adequate to meet company objectives, the company will be less able to reward its people.

For example, consider Lincoln Electric Company. Known for decades as an organization with some of the highest paid blue-collar workers in the world, Lincoln Electric's methodology is one in which employees share in company profits. Each year, management and employees determine what goals are to be met. If those are achieved, then employees receive a specified amount, and if they are surpassed, as they have been for years, then the employees receive a bonus. How much is directly related to the level of worker performance? Accordingly, through a profit-sharing process, the more the employee performance exceeds organizational goals, the greater their share of the profits. In fact, in situations like this, an individual performance–organizational goal relationship creates a win-win situation for all involved. Bear in mind that such a linkage does not occur automatically. It requires the active involvement of many parts of the organization and the appropriate application, among other things, of several HRM techniques such as an effective performance appraisal system.

For the individual performance–organizational goal relationship to function effectively, the organization must set a clear direction. That is, the organization must set its plans for given time periods and communicate those plans downward in the organization, and employees must have control over the performance measures. At each successive level, then, the plans take on more detail such that at employee levels, each individual knows why his or her job exists and what role it plays in achieving the organization's objectives. At these levels, then, jobs must be clearly focused. Just as in our first relationship, effort–performance, employees must know what is expected of them. Furthermore, they must know what goal performance is and how it will be determined.

In most of our organizations, the linkage to successful performance is measured through some performance evaluation instrument. But, too often, what we measure or how we go about the process may be inappropriate. For example, consider a university professor. One objective of universities is to transmit learning, and one measurement of how this has been achieved is how much students learn. In one simple way, we might assess this information through student evaluations. Are these evaluations an accurate reflection of the individual performance–organizational goal relationship?

The answer is: it depends. Obviously, student reaction is one piece of information. As we mentioned in Chapter 9 on evaluating training effectiveness, participants' reactions are important. Yet they are only part of the story. What about student testing and other assignments the faculty members evaluate? Aren't they better predictors of what was learned? If learning is the outcome measured by a quantifiable student evaluation score, can we be certain that a high score is a valid prediction of high learning or that a low score indicates the opposite? Suppose one faculty member is viewed as being easy, a high grader who entertains the class with a variety of stories. If this individual is rated highly by students, does it mean that the university's goal was met? Quite possibly no. Conversely, another professor who is rigid in grading, not overly charismatic in the classroom, and demands quite a bit of work from students may be rated lower but has helped students learn more.

Whatever the case may be, HRM must ensure that performance evaluations operate properly. Doing so requires significant time and effort by both HRM and the managers who evaluate employees. Because of the intricacies involved, we'll reserve further comments on performance evaluation until the next chapter.

If all is going as planned, we are getting into a better position to motivate our employees. We have defined our jobs, linked them to the strategic nature of the business, communicated to the employees what they must do to be successful, and then measured that effort properly. It is now time to complete the cycle. We have shown employees what they can do for the company, and it is now time to show what the organization will do for them. This part is called the organizational goal–individual goal relationship.

The Organizational Goal–Individual Goal Relationship

Barrick Gold Corporation, the third-largest gold mining company in the world, is a firm believer in financial incentives.[14] Employees in the field get a gold-production bonus, and the company's stock-option program, started in 1984, extends to all 5,000 employees. The company has done phenomenally well over the years, and its shares appreciated 3,600 per cent between 1983 and 1996. The stock-option program has been instrumental in attracting and retaining talented employees. And that's not all: the company has a scholarship fund for the children of Barrick employees. It covers tuition and other expenses at accredited universities, community colleges, and trade schools; the fund has handed out over $4 million.

This example shows that being creative with rewards motivates employees and encourages them to stay on. In the past, however, companies generally did not look for unique and creative ways to "turn on" employees; rather, managers became complacent about what people really wanted out of their jobs. For years, companies believed that rewarding employees meant giving pay raises, some recognition here and there, and providing for an occasional guest motivational speaker. Unfortunately, while their efforts were commendable, what they were trying to achieve actually backfired. If each of us has specific unsatisfied needs that cause us to behave in a particular manner, how can we be expected to meet all those different needs with one reward system? Generally, we can't. Rather, we must tailor our rewards to meet those individual needs if for no other reason than that such a diverse workforce exists, one that indicates that various needs must be met. That is the thrust of this last linkage. The organization requires specific activities to be met to accomplish its goals, so why should employees be any different? Hence, if we truly want to enhance motivation, we must make sure individual goals are met.

How can this be done? Through careful assessment of employee needs and a reward system that reflects individual preferences. If you were to poll all students in a class, you might find that each has a different reason for being there. Some attend because they want to learn more about the subject; some go because it is required or they fear that missing classes will result in poorer test scores and a lower grade; some may even be there out of habit—they go to class because that's what they think they're supposed to do (this latter group often believes that learning will occur just by showing up!) Whatever the reason, each student has a compelling drive that brings him or her to class. Therefore, to satisfy each class member, the instructor must address these diverse needs. But professors will not know what these needs are unless they ask. Ever wonder why some professors begin classes by asking students for their expectations of the course? The instructor is gathering information on students' specific needs so that throughout the semester, they can be met. In cases where a student's expectations go outside the intended class syllabus, the instructor knows that additional materials or reading lists may be needed to fulfil that student's expectations. Unfortunately, many businesses have not yet reached this point. In some companies like MacMillan

Bloedel, some rewards are tailored to meet individual needs. This is done through a process called "flexible compensation." Let's look at how this works.

In organizations, there is a tendency to provide uniform benefits. Everyone, for instance, may get medical coverage and reimbursement for night courses taken at the local college or university. But flexible compensation programs allow people to choose the mix that best fits their needs. Suppose, for example, an individual values more time off from work rather than a bonus or other benefits. Where this freedom to choose does exist, individual choices can be handled. In such companies, employees are presented with a pool of money that reflects increases due to achieving organizational goals through successful performance. Each employee is also presented with a menu of what options are available for the next year and how much each will cost. Employees can choose the benefits they want until they've spent their budgeted amount. Someone wanting more health or life insurance coverage might choose that over more pension contribution, more time off, or extended day care, and the employer can purchase those items that are best suited to his or her individual needs. MacMillan Bloedel employees are issued "flex dollars" that they can use to buy a variety of benefits: an employee can choose an extra ten days of vacation, join the dental plan, or even cash in unused "flex dollars."[15]

Flexible compensation, then, gives choices and allows employees to tailor benefits to their unique needs. Although flexible compensation systems are expensive to implement and administer, where they exist, the benefits have outweighed the costs.[16] We'll revisit this topic in Chapter 14.

Companies are beginning to realize that different people require different incentives and are rewarding employees in many innovative ways.

In addition to formulating compensation programs, companies also need to review how their reward and recognition programs operate. For example, suppose the Swiss Chalet food chain puts the "associate of the month's" name on a sign beside the counter. Not everyone places a high value on such recognition. Doing something that some employees do not value does not have the desired effect on motivation. Consequently, the company may wish to recognize superior performance by giving employees a choice and letting them select the reward they most value. For example, maybe an employee would like $100 in cash, tickets for two to the local symphony, dinner for herself and her spouse, or a night at a downtown luxury hotel. Or maybe an employee wants to pick out a gift from a catalogue. The point is that the money spent on a plaque might be better spent on letting employees select their own rewards.

HRM, then, must ensure that processes are in place that result in employees getting something they want. Yet, above all, these rewards must be seen as being the direct result of their performance. Only by creating and supporting the performance–reward link will the employee be motivated and rewarded and the organization be more productive and moving towards meeting its goals.

Putting the Pieces Together

There are a number of implications to the model we have presented. For one, it shows the need for sound inception and development efforts on the part of HRM, and it reveals that pay for performance can be beneficial to both employees and the company. For pay for performance to work, it is necessary that the organization actually reward performance and that employees clearly understand that. If this is not done, employees will deliver what they think they are being rewarded for, which may be very different from what the organization wants.

In summing up the motivation process, consider Figure 11-3. It shows that the motivation process can be adapted to reflect corporate values of what is important for both the organization and the employee.

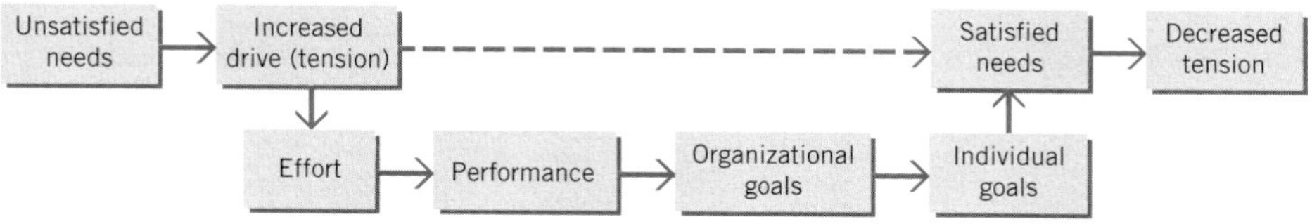

Pay for Performance Rewarding employees based on their performance.

Figure 11-3
Movitation Process for a Work Environment

Implications of the Model for Motivating Employees

Organizations today are recognizing the importance of having a highly energized workforce. To bring this about, they're using more self-managed work teams, allowing for more worker participation, and empowering their employees. But it is still a long way from being ingrained into the everyday life of most companies. For example, it has been suggested that managers, for whatever reasons, are not providing accurate feedback to individuals about their performance. Managers find that identifying group task goals and linking them to the responsibilities of individual members is a time-consuming operation. Some managers avoid mutual

Meet

Guillaume LeBlanc
Finance and Human Resources Manager
Universal Systems Ltd.

It's important to Guillaume LeBlanc that all software and computer equipment at Universal Systems in Fredericton, New Brunswick, is state of the art. To do his job well, he needs access to powerful systems, latest versions of software, and new, high-speed peripherals. But Mr LeBlanc is not a programmer, engineer, or systems expert. He's the finance and human resources manager at Universal, and top-notch equipment is one of the major factors that allows him to attract, keep, and motivate quality employees for the firm.

Universal Systems is the largest software developer in Atlantic Canada and has a sister company in Europe. Developer and marketer of the CARIS software system, used worldwide for geography and mapping applications, Universal hires a lot of high-tech workers. "People in this industry, especially those with good skills, want to work at the leading edge," explains Mr LeBlanc. "It's important to them. So we are constantly upgrading."

In this sector of the labour market, where unemployment is low and pay high, factors such as equipment can sometimes be even more important than financial rewards for motivating employees. Although, Mr LeBlanc points out, "Money does talk" to a certain extent; "you wouldn't be in this business for long if your pay wasn't comparable to other firms'."

The corporate culture at Universal also contributes to motivating its highly skilled employees to do their best. There is a friendly "family" atmosphere, and employees are encouraged to express their ideas to managers. "We have the most innovative supervision in the industry," says Mr LeBlanc. "Employees are given as much opportunity to explore and learn as they need.

"We also don't hand out segments of work or ask people to do the same kind of thing all the time. Our employees work in teams, and they see a project through from beginning to end. If you ask any programming student, they'll tell you how important that is to job satisfaction. People want to see something *finished*."

Universal also takes special care to provide co-op students with a positive experience. "We hold some activities so they can get to know one another and encourage them to support each other on the job," Mr LeBlanc explains. "And we have a recognition night for them." But above all, "we don't treat them any differently from other employees. We throw them right into a project." A student who finds his or her co-op experience interesting and satisfying is more likely not only to do a good job, but to consider coming back eventually as a full-time employee.

When it comes to motivating people, however, Mr LeBlanc is careful to point out that one size doesn't fit all. "You have to know your people and manage them accordingly," he says. "Some people like to work to deadlines; others need to be left alone to do their best work."

Employees also have input into the kind of work they do. At their yearly reviews, they help set their own goals and challenges and let management know what kind of opportunities they want. Right from the start—at hiring interviews—managers try to find out where (and if) an employee will fit in at Universal because ultimately, a motivated employee is one who is doing something he or she wants to be doing.

goal setting (the sharing of the goal-setting activity with the employee) because they believe this is an infringement of management prerogatives. In some cases, task goals are identified, performance is evaluated, and the results are conveyed to the employee, yet the employee remains unsure of management's view of his or her accomplishments in terms of pre-established goals. It therefore appears that many managers fail to recognize the importance of establishing goals and performance feedback as would be suggested by the model.

Furthermore, the model suggests that managers should ensure that high productivity and good work performance lead to the achievement of personal goals. Again, a review of actual organizational practices reveals many exceptions. Unfortunately, organizations too often fail to allocate rewards in such a way as to optimize motivation. While individual performances tend to be widely divergent—a few outstanding, a few very poor, and the majority surrounding the average—rewards tend to be allocated more uniformly. The result is the over-rewarding of incompetence and the under-rewarding of superior performance. Employees perceive that hard work does not necessarily pay off; they place a low probability on its leading to organizational rewards and eventually the attainment of personal goals. As such, they do just enough to get by (see Figure 11-4).[17]

Internal politics is also a vital determinant of who and what will be rewarded. For example, group acceptance may be a personal goal, and high productivity may get in the way of accomplishing this goal. In other words, if the work team one has joined works at a slower pace, leaves exactly at the end of their shift, and takes their breaks precisely on schedule (irrespective of the work that may need to get done at that moment), an employee must follow suit to become "part of the gang." Although, at times, these are the realities of work behaviour, our motivational theories tend to overemphasize the decision-making, goal-oriented rationality of human beings. For example, when unemployment is high, there may be a tendency for work groups to work faster to keep their jobs.

While the above discussion recognizes the difficulties in motivating employees, some suggestions to facilitate the process are summarized in Table 11-2. These suggestions focus on getting tomorrow's managers to understand their employees as individuals rather than trying to judge them based on their own (the managers') value system. Again, with a diverse work group, it is unlikely that a manager's employees will share all of his or her values.

Figure 11-4
A Motivation Device

TABLE 11-2 Suggestions for Motivating Employees

1. **Address individual differences**. Recognize that employees are not homogeneous. Rather, each individual processes a unique set of needs. Accordingly, to effectively motivate any individual, you must understand what those needs are that make them provide the effort.

2. **Properly place employees**. Employees should be properly matched to the job. The best intentions will do little for productive behaviour if the employee lacks the ability to get the job done. Proper recruiting and selection techniques should assist in creating this match.

3. **Set achievable goals**. Employees often work best when challenging but achievable goals are mutually set. These hard and specific goals provide the direction employees may need. Continuous feedback on how well employees are performing helps to reinforce their effort.

4. **Individualize rewards**. Realizing that employees have different needs should indicate that rewards, too, may need to be different. What works for one individual may not motivate another. As such, one should use their understanding of employee differences and tailor rewards to meet these various needs.

5. **Reward performance**. Rewarding individuals for anything other than performance only reinforces that performance may not matter most. Each individual reward must be shown to be the result of achieving organizational goals.

6. **Use an equitable system**. The rewards individuals receive should be viewed as proportional to the effort they have expended. Although perceptions may vary in what is equitable, effort must be made to ensure the reward system used is fair, consistent, and objective.

7. **Don't forget money**. It's easy to get caught up in identifying needs, tailoring rewards, and the like. But don't forget the primary reason most individuals work—money. While it cannot be the sole motivator, failure to use money as a motivator will significantly decrease employee productivity.

Job Designs to Increase Motivation

The Job Characteristics Model

If the type of work a person does is important, can we identify those specific job characteristics that affect productivity, motivation, and satisfaction? J. Richard Hackman and Greg R. Oldham have developed the job characteristics model[18] that identifies five such job factors and their interrelationship. The research with this model indicates that it can be a useful guide in redesigning the jobs of individuals.[19]

Job Characteristics Model A framework for analysing and designing jobs. JCM identifies five primary job characteristics and their interrelationship.

The model specifies five core characteristics or dimensions:

1. *Skill variety*—the degree to which a job requires a variety of different activities so one can use a number of different skills and talents.

2. *Task identity*—the degree to which the job requires completion of a whole and identifiable piece of work.

3. *Task significance*—the degree to which the job has a substantial impact on the lives or work of other people.

4. *Autonomy*—the degree to which the job provides substantial freedom, independence, and discretion to the individual in scheduling the work and in determining the procedures to be used in carrying it out.

5. *Feedback*—the degree to which carrying out the work activities required by the job results in the individual obtaining direct and clear information about the effectiveness of his or her performance.

Figure 11-5 shows the model. Notice how the first three dimensions—skill variety, task identity, and task significance—combine to create meaningful work. In other words, if these three characteristics exist in a job, we can predict that the incumbents will view their jobs as being important, valuable, and worthwhile. Notice, too, that jobs that possess autonomy give the job holders a feeling of personal responsibility for the results, and that if a job provides feedback, the employees will know how effectively they are performing. From a motivational standpoint, the model says that internal rewards are obtained by individuals when they learn (knowledge of results) that they personally (experienced responsibility) have performed well on a task that they care about (experienced meaningfulness).[20] The more that these three conditions are present, the greater will be the employees' motivation, performance, and satisfaction and the lower will be their absenteeism and turnover. As the model shows, the links between the job dimensions and the outcomes are moderated, or adjusted for, by the strength of the individual's growth need—that is, the employee's desire for self-esteem and self-actualization.[21] This means that individuals with a high growth need are more likely to experience the critical psychological states when their jobs are enriched and to respond more positively to the psychological states when they are present.

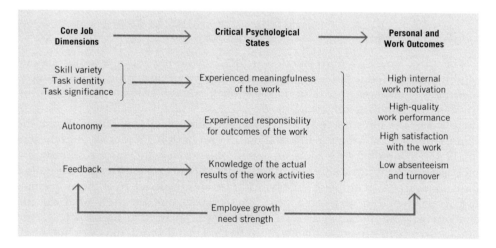

Figure 11-5
The Job Characteristics Model of Work Motivation

At Ford's Windsor engine plant, production workers are organized into teams that are responsible for many of the tasks formerly reserved for supervisors; employees perform all of the jobs required from the team as necessary rather than being constrained to a specific job. This approach increases task variety, task identity, and task significance as well as autonomy, and the teams also receive feedback on how they are performing.[22]

The core job dimensions can be analysed and combined into a single index called the motivating potential score (MPS) as shown in Figure 11-6. Jobs that are high on motivating potential—as derived by answers to specific questions for each dimension—must be high on at least one of the three factors that lead to experiencing meaningfulness, and they must be high on both autonomy and feedback. If jobs score high on motivating potential, the model predicts that motivation, performance, and satisfaction will be positively affected, while the likelihood of absence and turnover is lessened.

Motivating Potential Score (MPS) A predictive index suggesting the motivation potential of a job.

Research findings on the job characteristics model have been generally supportive.[23] These studies have shown:

1. People who work on jobs which are high on the core job dimensions are more motivated, satisfied, and productive than those who do not.

2. People with strong growth needs respond more positively to jobs that are high in motivating potential than do those with weak growth dimensions.

3. Job dimensions operate through the psychological states in influencing personal and work outcome variables rather than influencing them directly.[24]

Figure 11-6
Computing the Motivating Potential Score

$$\text{Motivating potential score} = \frac{\text{Skill variety} + \text{Task identity} + \text{Task significance}}{3} \times \text{Autonomy} \times \text{Job feedback}$$

These findings indicate that the structure of work is an important influence on an employee's motivation level. Certainly the decision about how a job is to be structured reflects other considerations (such as technology, the environment, plant and equipment, and skill levels) besides its motivational potential. But the design of a job and the way work is scheduled are variables that management can readily influence and that affect an employee's motivation. There are several methods that increase employees' motivational potential. They include: job enrichment, job rotation, work at home, and flexible hours.

Job Enrichment

Job Enrichment The process of expanding the depth of the job by allowing employees to plan and control their work more.

The most popularly advocated structural technique for increasing an employee's motivational potential is **job enrichment**. In enriching a job, management allows the worker to assume some of the duties of his or her supervisor. Enrichment requires that workers do increased planning and controlling of their work, usually with less supervision and more self-evaluation. From the standpoint of increasing the internal motivation of doing a job, job enrichment offers great potential,[25] but it is successful only when it increases responsibility, increases the employee's freedom and independence, organizes tasks to allow individuals to do a complete activity, and provides feedback to allow individuals to correct their own performance.[26] These aspects are precisely what the job characteristics model advocates. In addition, we can say that these factors lead, in part, to a better quality of work life (QWL). Furthermore, job enrichment efforts will only be successful if the individuals in the enriched jobs find that their needs are met by the enrichment. If these individuals do not want increased responsibility, for example, then job enrichment will not have the desired effect. Successful job enrichment, then, is contingent on worker input.

A successful job enrichment program should ideally increase employee satisfaction and commitment. But since the primary purpose of an organization is not to create employee satisfaction, job enrichment must benefit the organization directly. There is evidence that job enrichment and QWL programs reduce absenteeism and turnover costs[27] and increase employee commitment,[28] but on the critical issue of productivity, the evidence is inconclusive. In some situations, job enrichment has increased productivity, but in others, it has decreased. However, even when productivity decreases, there does appear to be a consistently conscientious use of resources and a higher quality of product or service. In other words, in terms of efficiency, for the same input, a higher quality of output results; a more complex measure of productivity (which includes quality, for instance) might even show an increase.

Job Rotation

In Chapter 9, we identified job rotation as an on-the-job employee development technique. Job rotation also offers a potential for dealing with the problem of general worker dissatisfaction caused by overstructuring or career plateauing. It allows employees to diversify their activities and overcome boredom.

Note that job rotation does not expand the individual's duties and responsibilities as does job enrichment since no tasks are necessarily transferred from higher-level jobs. The key is doing something different.

Horizontal job transfers can break up the monotony inherent in almost any job after the employee's skills have been refined and the newness has worn off. In some cases, this may be after only a few weeks, while in other cases, it may be years.

Opportunities for diversity, to learn new skills, change supervisors, relocate, or make new job acquaintances can deter or slow the onset of boredom in jobs that have become habitual. Job rotation, therefore, can renew enthusiasm for learning and can motivate workers to performance better.[29]

Work at Home

As we noted in Chapter 2, new technology is creating dramatic new job opportunities in the new millenium. With the advent of home computers, fax machines, modems, networked communication lines, and the World Wide Web, certain types of jobs can be completed in the comfort of one's own home. Many in the workforce—especially women—find that work at home affords them the opportunity to combine both their careers and family responsibility. Furthermore, permitting work to be done at a worker's home also gives the organization an opportunity to save money. By introducing teleworking, having decentralized worksites, and supporting them through telecommunication technology (see Chapter 2), organizations are able to reduce the workspace they must either purchase or lease, thus cutting some overhead costs.

Most of the findings about working at home appear promising. Although home work requires different management techniques—like planning and controlling the productive work flow—the flexibility it offers clearly has a positive motivational effect on employees.[30]

Flexible Hours

Another way to increase workers' freedom and motivation is **flextime**, which is a system that allows employees to contract to work a specific number of hours a week but are free to vary those hours within certain limits. A typical arrangement is for each day to consist of a common core, usually six hours, with flexibility surrounding it. For example, the core may be 10 a.m. to 4 p.m., with the workplace actually opening at 7:30 a.m. and closing at 6 p.m. All employees are required to be at their jobs during the common core period, but they can work the other two hours before or after the core time. Some flextime programs allow extra hours to be accumulated and turned into a free day off each month.

Under flextime, employees assume responsibility for completing a specific job, and that increases their feeling of self-worth. It is consistent with the view

Flextime A scheduling system in which employees are required to work a number of hours per week but are free, within limits, to vary the hours of work.

that people are paid for producing work, not for being at their job stations for a set period of hours—hence, its motivational aspects.

Flextime has been implemented in a number of organizations such as American Express, IBM, Levi Strauss, and PepsiCo.[31] In the United States, it is estimated that such scheduling exists in almost 40 per cent of all companies.[32] Statistics Canada's Survey of Work Arrangements revealed that the proportion of Canadian employees on a flexible work schedule increased from 17 per cent in 1991 to 24 per cent in 1995.[33] And for many of these organizations, there has been some good news. Flextime appears to contribute to reduced lateness and absenteeism, less job fatigue, increased organizational loyalty, and improved recruitment. In fact, when you recall the discussion of the composition of our workforce, a more positive light is shed on flexible arrangements. For example, flextime enables dual-career couples a better opportunity to balance work and family responsibilities.[34] And with more and more single parents coming into the workforce, flexible work arrangements can only better serve both the employer and employee.[35]

Flextime is attractive to enough people that some companies such as Sun Life of Canada's British subsidiary feature it in company advertisements seeking applications for positions in its insurance and actuarial divisions.[36] A number of related work arrangements will be discussed in more detail in Chapter 14: reduced hours (where employees work less than the standard hours per week at a prorated salary), job sharing (where two people share the responsibilities, salary, and hours of work of one job), and the modified work week (where, for example, the employee will work the full weekly hours in four days instead of the usual five). The Royal Bank Financial Group estimates that 25 per cent of its Canadian employees use some form of flexible work arrangement.[37] As a matter of fact, Brenda Lipsett and Mark Reesor of Human Resources Development Canada estimate that only 33 per cent of Canadian workers held a "typical" job in 1995 (where a "typical" job is a full-time, permanent, Monday-to-Friday, nine-to-five day job carried out outside of the home for a single employer).[38]

Another flexible idea is phased-in retirement which allows older employees to gradually reduce their working schedules to four and then three or two days a week. Employers could then phase in new employees through some form of apprenticeship or job-sharing. This arrangement is still curtailed by Canadian pension laws that do not allow employees to collect a pension unless they are fully retired. Still, some Canadian companies such as Nova, Noranda, and Manulife do have policies allowing for this type of work arrangement.[39]

Although the benefits of flexible scheduling appear plentiful, there is still one major drawback. It produces problems for managers in directing employees outside core time periods, or it may cause difficulty in evaluating the performance of an employee who may not be seen eight hours a day.[40] But part of the problem is inherent in that statement. Rather than evaluating employees on how much they've been seen—often called "face-time" in organizations—managers should concern themselves with "results and productivity."[41] As we described in our motivation model, that should be the only thing that matters. Thus, if a scheduling arrangement permits better performance, there is no logical reason for not implementing one.

Unique Motivation Challenges for HRM

Chapter 2 examined the changing workforce and the possibility that we are witnessing a division in the workforce—a split between those who work in the low-tech jobs and those who hold the more prestigious, high-tech positions. Let's explore some of the issues facing managers both in meeting the needs of these two groups as well as in getting the diversified workforce to exert high levels of effort.

Low-Tech Employees

Imagine that you are the first-line supervisor at a local fast food outlet. Working in your restaurant are nineteen employees aged sixteen to eighteen and three who are over seventy. You know the teenagers are full-time students and many will leave within the next year. In fact, your turnover averages 50 per cent a year. You pay $8.25 to $9.00 per hour, depending on the shifts employees work and their responsibilities. How do you motivate these employees? Too often, you consider yourself lucky if they just show up. When they do, you want them to work, not spend time talking to their visiting friends or giving food away. You could give them a pay raise to increase their motivation, but would it do much good? Any significant increase will add to your costs, raise your prices, and likely cut customer demand.

Motivating employees in low-paying, low-skill jobs such as fast food restaurants is a real challenge for HR managers.

Low-paying dead-end jobs such as those in fast food restaurants create challenges for employers. Sadly, there doesn't appear to be a readily available solution. A lot of the linkage, discussed earlier, does not apply because these workers do not have "career" needs and probably just want to earn a few dollars so they can enjoy their leisure time, pay for automobile insurance, or purchase clothing. Still, the low-wage companies of this world must go on, and they need energized people. So what can managers do? Let's look at three possibilities: respect, non-financial rewards, and autonomy.[42]

Respect   One of the first concerns in motivating these workers is to assess how you feel about them. If your attitude is that these are low-level employees lucky to work for you, you may be sending the wrong message. If your employees are made to feel inferior, they won't respond to what is needed to work effectively. Thus, common sense dictates that respect is required here. We all have a need to be respected for what we do, and we want to be treated with kindness even if we aren't the superstar employee. Giving these employees the respect and dignity they deserve can change their perception of you and the job. A little caring, kindness, and concern can go a long way in getting these individuals to perform more productively for the company.

At metal fabricating firm Precision Metalcraft, Inc. in Winnipeg, the message of respect and equality was very tangible: the managers' desks were moved to the shop floor next to the workers and machines, while the executive offices were turned into storage.[43]

Non-Financial Rewards   Furthermore, employees are capable of realizing that employers cannot continue to raise salaries. But just because money isn't available doesn't mean that you can overlook these employees. Rather, you need to look at a variety of non-financial rewards. This may be something as simple as a pat on the back, a smile, or more responsibility on the job. Letting them know you trust them and are willing to help them learn can create a positive work environment. You may also search for some appropriate award like permitting your employee of the month to have a friend over for a meal on the premises and extend the employee's dinner break for the special occasion.

Autonomy   Finally comes the issue of autonomy. Low-paying jobs are not necessarily correlated to activities that must be closely monitored. If you know the employees are well trained, giving them the responsibility to complete the tasks without a watchful eye on them allows them the opportunity to take responsibility. By giving them the freedom to make limited choices, you are sending a message that you trust them and that they are important to your operation.

On a final note, let's not forget about fun.[44] A little enjoyment on the job can go far to create a positive atmosphere. The old saying, "All work and no play makes Jack a dull boy," may have special meaning in our workplaces. When people laugh, they are happy. If we allow happiness to become contagious, people will feel better about their jobs, their bosses, and themselves. Perhaps the popularity of the comic strip *Dilbert* lies in people's need to laugh at work.

High-Tech Employees

You would think that higher-paid employees create fewer motivational problems for organizations because their motivation, by and large, would seemingly be built into the job itself. But organizations today cannot leave it up to individuals to seek their own satisfaction. Instead, they must put into place a variety of mechanisms to retain this worker elite.

Many of the issues discussed in Chapter 2 with respect to employee involvement help to create an environment that is conducive to motivating high-tech employees.[45] These include delegation, participative management, job enrichment, challenging work, and recognition. Charles Loewen, president of the Winnipeg technology consulting firm Online Business Systems, believes that money is not the prime motivator for his company's staff.[46] He feels that while

employees are paid competitively (after all, there is a shortage of such workers, so the best are always receiving job offers), they appreciate such gestures as being treated to dinner for a job well done. The company shares season tickets to sports events, supplies Internet accounts for all seventy employees, and provides an ideal working environment for its employees. Online looked at twenty buildings before selecting its new location. The building, a ninety-year-old warehouse downtown, was renovated to the company's specifications because, Loewen believes, the staff should have a "wonderful environment" to work in.

Hi-tech employees have skills that are in high demand in the market place. Because they are highly marketable, they will move to another organization if it meets their needs better. Delegation gives these individuals the opportunity to make decisions about the various parts of their job, and participative management allows them to control their day-to-day activities.

High-tech employees also need to be given the opportunity to continuously grow and excel. Job enrichment gives them the means to undertake a variety of tasks, thus circumventing boredom. Challenging work lets them stretch their abilities, thus accentuating organizational and personal goals, but the greatest motivation is recognition.[47] Because these workers are generally well paid, money does not become a prominent issue. Rather, their thirst for success dominates, and they need to know that others appreciate and recognize the efforts that they make.

The Diversified Workforce

As we continue to experience the influx of different groups of people into our workforce, it will become increasingly more critical to recognize individual differences and individual needs and to individualize rewards. We know from experience that North American managers have not done this well, even when the workforce was relatively homogeneous. Now that there is increasing diversity, the time has never been better to recognize differences and act on them.

We know that different cultures place value on different things. In Japan, for example, leisure time is not highly prized, although it is in Canada. Similarly, the Japanese place much higher importance on respect and conforming to group norms than Canadians. Managers should probably reflect on the success of such ventures as Toronto's Citytv in Canada's most culturally diverse city.

Canada's workforce is becoming younger and more diverse; what worked in the fifties may not work today. Employees with young children frequently place a higher value on day care and flexible work hours than other employees. This suggests that hours worked, scheduling, recognition, group membership, day care, and similar variables should be considered when trying to optimize the motivation of a diversified workforce.

Study Tools and Applications

Summary

This summary relates to the Learning Objectives provided on p. 314.

After having read this chapter, you should know:

1. Motivation is the willingness to do something to achieve organizational goals and, at the same time, to satisfy individual needs.
2. The three major components for motivation in an organization setting are effort, organizational goals, and individual needs.
3. The process of motivation begins with an unsatisfied need that creates an increase in tension. This tension causes one to behave in a manner (effort) such that the needs can be satisfied and the tension ultimately reduced.
4. An unsatisfied need is a state of deprivation, and because these needs are something you desire, they cause tension.
5. Tension can be viewed in two forms—functional and dysfunctional. Functional tension is positive and causes an individual to act towards goal attainment. Dysfunctional tension is negative and may lead to problems in performance or attitudes.
6. The effort–performance relationship focuses on the energy exerted by employees and its outcome in terms of performance. The premise of this relationship is that if appropriate effort is exerted, an employee will give a successful performance.
7. The job characteristics model consists of skill variety, task identity, task significance, autonomy, and feedback.
8. Job enrichment refers to a situation where workers assume increased responsibility for planning and self-evaluation of their work. This provides an opportunity to fulfil intrinsic and autonomous needs. Working at home enables employees to meet organizational job requirements while simultaneously fulfilling personal needs. Work at home provides the diverse workforce with opportunities to combine both work and family.
9. A number of suggestions can be made regarding how to motivate employees. Among them are: addressing individual differences, properly placing employees, setting achievable goals, individualizing rewards, and rewarding performance.
10. Although no one means of motivating low-tech employees is universally accepted, some action can be taken. In addition to addressing individual differences, properly placing employees, setting achievable goals, individualizing rewards and rewarding performance, these individuals can be given more responsibility. Furthermore, a kind, caring, concerned manager can help to create an environment in which workers are willing to exert higher energy levels. Hi-tech employees, on the other hand, appear to respond to delegating, participative management, job enrichment, challenging work, and recognition.

Key Terms

apathy
deprivation
dysfunctional tension
effort
effort–performance relationship
flextime
functional tension
individual needs

individual performance–organizational goal relationship
Job Characteristics Model
job enrichment
motivation
motivating potential score
organizational goal
organizational goal–individual goal relationship
pay for performance

I:AM Assessment

Motivation processes are based, in part, on needs satisfaction. Although we all have changing needs, there are often certain one that remain dominant over a period of time for us. This assessment is designed to identify those needs. Follow the instructions for the assessment (see Table 11-3) and then answer the following questions:

1. Do these needs seem accurate to you? How do you know?
2. How do these needs affect you (a) in the classroom and (b) on a job?
3. What does this assessment tell you about what it may take to motivate you?

Instrument: I:AM

I:AM is a simple questionnaire for examining one's own motivations and interests. It should be used before getting into any detailed discussion of motivational theories to avoid self-consciousness on the part of individuals. The result can be used as part of an overview presentation on theories of motivation.

Interpretation

The four need scores correspond to the four "higher order" categories of needs (or motives) identified by Abraham Maslow. The "lowest level" need category, physiological needs (food, shelter, water, etc.) is not included since most who will read this and use this instrument have little personal concern for these needs. However, one must remember that most of the world's population is most concerned with this need category.

CASE APPLICATION:

Motivation Explains Behaviour

When employees face turbulent times and their managers pay little attention to their needs, employees tend to get even.[48] This was the finding of a study of three plants of a large manufacturing organization that was dealing with many of the difficulties facing North American companies towards the end of the twentieth century: lower productivity and increased competition. The company had implemented a pay cut to attempt to keep the organization afloat. The major issue was to know how all this was affecting employee morale. How did the employees react? Surprisingly, worse than anticipated!

One of the basic tenets of motivation is that individuals need to feel that they are getting something from the organization—like pay or benefits—that is consistent with their level of effort, education, experience, and anything else they bring to the job. This something that the company provides, then, must equate to the amount of work each performs. For example, if employees feel the organization is not paying them a fair wage, they are more likely to make certain adjustments in their work habits. They might work more slowly, reduce quality, or even quit. Accordingly, any personnel action by the organization will ultimately result in employees comparing what the company has done to them to the amount of effort they give the employer.

Once told of the pending pay cuts, employees in the three plants studied decided to change their behaviour to compensate for less income. What did they do? Steal! In two of the plants, employee theft skyrocketed. These employees

TABLE 11-3 I:AM Instrument

I:AM   An Inventory for Assessing One's Primary Interests
Instructions: Place a check mark under the response that best describes your own feelings about the statement. There are no right or wrong answers; the purpose of this questionnaire is simply to organize your own thoughts about your personal preferences.

	Strongly Agree	Agree	Neither Agree nor Disagree	Disagree	Strongly Disagree
1. My friends mean more to me than almost anything else.	——	——	——	——	——
2. I don't believe in "blowing my own horn" just to be heard.	——	——	——	——	——
3. Searching for and finding what makes me feel happy is the most important thing in life.	——	——	——	——	——
4. I prefer to be by myself a lot of the time.	——	——	——	——	——
5. A secure job and a good salary are number one for me.	——	——	——	——	——
6. Chasing dreams is a waste of one's time and energy.	——	——	——	——	——
7. I get furious when someone else tries to take credit for what I know I did.	——	——	——	——	——
8. I really don't worry about a particular job or what I get for doing it, as long as it's fair.	——	——	——	——	——

Scoring Form

Item	SA	A	?	D	SD		Score	Need Scale
5	5	4	3	2	1	⟶ + =	☐	Safety/security
8	1	2	3	4	5			
1	5	4	3	2	1	⟶ + =	☐	Belongingness/social
4	1	2	3	4	5			
2	1	2	3	4	5	⟶ + =	☐	Self-esteem
7	5	4	3	2	1			
3	5	4	3	2	1	⟶ + =	☐	Self-actualization
6	1	2	3	4	5			

Scores range from 2 to 10 on each of the four need scales.

Source: Marshall Sashkin and William C. Morris, *Experiencing Management* (Reading, MA: Addison-Wesley Publishing Co., 1987), p. 110. Used with permission.

stole an amount from the company that they considered was approximately equivalent to the amount of their pay cut. That was not what the firm had in mind when it implemented pay cuts!

Questions

1. Discuss this case in terms of the behavioural process and equity theory. Was the behaviour of these employees rational? Explain.

2. What suggestions would you make to an organization that faced difficult times and had to cut employee costs by implementing drastic HRM practices? How would these suggestions affect employee motivation? Discuss.

Testing Your Understanding

How well did you fulfil the learning objectives?

1. Employee performance is a function of the employee's ability to do a job and
   a. the employee's willingness to do the job.
   b. the manager's ability to monitor performance.
   c. effective communication throughout the organization.
   d. the employee's salary.
   e. The organization's culture plus a good work environment.

2. A vice-president of human resources for a large manufacturing firm conducted an employee survey to improve employee benefits and working conditions. The survey showed 97 per cent of employees wanted a thirty-hour (or less) work week. Why didn't the vice-president recommend that change to the benefits manager, according to organizational motivation theory?
   a. The vice-president's ability to exert effort was ineffective.
   b. Organizational goals were not defined.
   c. Employees' individual needs changed.
   d. Employees' individual needs would not be satisfied.
   e. Organizational goals would not be met.

3. According to motivation theory, why are some beer commercials set in the desert?
   a. The contrast makes beer look drinkable.
   b. An individual's sense of deprivation is heightened by the parched surroundings.
   c. It's easier to attain a calm state in the desert.
   d. Dysfunctional tension is reduced when distractions are removed.
   e. Most human drives are intensified by heat.

4. How can a teacher produce dysfunctional tension in a straight-A student?
   a. Give boring lectures.
   b. Give difficult tests.
   c. Grade term papers on a curve.
   d. Require oral presentations as part of the class.
   e. Assign grades in a random manner, ranging from A to C, for all written work.

5. Roberta, Ernie's secretary, likes her job and her boss, but she types forty words per minute and has a 5 per cent error rate. Standard performance in the company is eighty words per minute and a 3 per cent error rate. According to motivation theory, should Ernie send Roberta to secretarial school?

   a. No. It would embarrass Roberta.
   b. Yes. It would strengthen the effort–performance link.
   c. No. It would weaken the effort–performance link.
   d. Yes. It would strengthen the individual performance–organizational goal relationship.
   e. No. It would weaken the individual performance–organizational goal relationship.

6. If the goal of an undergraduate business school program is to produce qualified graduates who obtain suitable entry-level positions upon graduation, which question best measures the individual performance–organizational goal linkage?
   a. How many articles does the faculty publish each year compared to faculties at other similar institutions?
   b. How high are the average marks of graduates compared to non-business majors in the university?
   c. What percentage of the graduates get jobs they want compared to graduates from other programs during the same year?
   d. What positions do graduates hold in organizations seven years after graduation compared to other graduates from the same year?
   e. What percentage of graduates go on for MBA degrees within ten years compared to graduates of other undergraduate business programs?

7. A vice-president of human resources for a large service organization has instituted a program that allows employees to choose up to $1,500 worth of goods or services from a range of annual options such as more time off, a cash bonus, tuition reimbursement, or new office furniture. What is the vice-president doing?
   a. Instituting a flexible compensation program to satisfy individual needs.
   b. Saving the company money during a downsizing cycle.
   c. Simplifying the accounting mechanisms for the entire human resources function.
   d. Reducing the number of complaints from workers about their immediate supervisors.
   e. Changing the organization to comply with employment equity legislation.

8. Jobs that score high on the core dimensions are associated with all of these work outcomes in employees with high growth needs except
   a. high work satisfaction.
   b. experienced responsibility for outcomes.
   c. high-quality work performance.

d. high internal work motivation.

e. lower absenteeism.

9. Job enrichment is successful when all of the following are present except

a. responsibility is increased for the employee.

b. pay for performance is increased.

c. the employee's freedom and independence is increased.

d. tasks are reorganized so that an individual performs a complete activity.

e. feedback is provided so that the employee may correct his or her own performance.

10. Don pays minimum wage to the thirty workers who help him run the local food bank. How can he motivate them?

a. Make sure he tells them they are appreciated.

b. Make work fun.

c. Let them have as much autonomy as possible.

d. Involve them in day-to-day decisions about the work to be done.

e. All of these.

11. Motivation is all of the following except

a. the process of activating a willingness to work in employees.

b. evident in "energized" students who want to learn.

c. found in workers who are involved and interested in their work.

d. a necessary component of good job performance.

e. usually measured during the recruitment and selection process.

12. What is the difference between functional tension and dysfunctional tension?

a. There is no difference.

b. Functional tension leads to action that will achieve the desired organizational goal. Dysfunctional tension leads to action that thwarts the desired organizational goal.

c. Functional tension leads to action. Dysfunctional tension leads to inaction.

d. Functional tension satisfies needs. Dysfunctional tension does not satisfy needs.

e. Functional tension is more intense than dysfunctional tension.

13. Managers can do all of the following to strengthen the effort–performance link for their employees except

a. coach employees.

b. assist employees in achieving their performance levels.

c. give raises.

d. establish work standards.

e. communicate performance expectations to employees.

14. Marty won a $10-million lottery on Saturday. Why, according to motivation theory, did he quit his job on Monday?

a. Marty's ability to exert effort had changed.

b. Organizational goals changed.

c. Marty's individual needs changed.

d. Marty's individual interests changed.

e. Organizational needs were realigned.

15. In the motivation theory presented, how is tension created?

a. Pressure is exerted from outside sources.

b. An individual becomes aware of an unsatisfied need.

c. Pleasure is anticipated.

d. Force for action is triggered.

e. Needs are balanced with equity.

Chapter Twelve

EVALUATING EMPLOYEE PERFORMANCE

Every year, most employees experience an evaluation of their past performance. This may be a five-minute, informal discussion between employees and their supervisors or a more elaborate process involving many specific steps over several weeks. Irrespective of their formality, however, employees generally see these evaluations as having some direct effect on their work lives. They may result in pay increases, a promotion, or employee training for personal development. As a result, any evaluation of employees' work can be emotionally charged events. Consider this example which happened at Clarke & Bezaire, a large surveying company.[1]

The company policy is that each employee is evaluated on the anniversary of his or her hiring date, and the supervisor makes pay increase recommendations based on the evaluation. Joe Zanulko, the supervisor, has asked Adam Welsh to come to his office at 11:00 a.m. today. Although Adam is almost certain that it is time for his performance evaluation, he is not totally sure. Nonetheless, he leaves his surveying crew around 10:15 and heads for the office. As he arrives, he notices Joe in his office working on a standardized form used for evaluation. Adam sits impatiently until Joe finishes. With the final touches complete, Joe begins his meeting. Let's eavesdrop on that conversation.

Joe: Adam, glad you were able to make it here today. As you know, this is the anniversary of your hire date, and I am required to fill out an evaluation on you. Sorry I didn't have it done before you got here; it's just been one of those mornings. Well, let me see…

Adam (interrupts): Joe, I've been through this five times before, so just give it to me. What's my raise? I'd really like to get back to my work crew. We're trying to finish up on that Pillette job—the builders want to start the excavation early next week.

Joe: Adam, there's more than just the pay increase. I want to talk about your performance. I believe, overall, you've done some good work, but you have some problem areas, too.

Adam: What do you mean problem areas? I've done my job better than most on my work crew. In fact, you've been using me to train our new surveyors.

Joe: Well, Adam, that's your opinion. Yes, you're helping to train new surveyors, but I have had some complaints from them over the past few months. I think that needs to be addressed.

Adam: So get to the bottom line, Joe. What's my raise? Let's stop the charade.

Joe: Okay, Adam, I am recommending an 80 cents an hour raise. I'd like for you to look over this evaluation and sign it.

Adam: Just give me a pen, let me sign the paper, and I'll get out of here.

Effective performance evaluation? Absolutely not! But maybe not unlike many that are performed each day. What's missing is that neither Joe nor Adam really understand what the appraisal process is about. Adam, in particular, sees little value in the exercise. That's too bad because in order to compete effectively and meet employee and organizational goals either in Canada or abroad, companies need to assess how well employees are performing.

Introduction

Anyone who works in an organization, will likely have his or her performance evaluated, and if you are a manager or supervisor, you will be called upon to evaluate the performance of your subordinates. Performance evaluation or appraisal is not a simple process, and today it is more critical than ever that it focus on key activities of the job. For example, what should Adam have been evaluated on? His ability to perform surveying tasks in a timely and accurate manner? How well he interacts with customers and builders who depend on his work? How about how well he serves as a mentor to new employees? Such questions cannot be overlooked.

At Husky Injection Molding Systems, a high-tech manufacturer of injection moulding systems based in Bolton, Ontario, the issue of performance appraisal was raised at a meeting of employees with the company's founder and president Robert Schad.[2] It seems that supervisors did not complete evaluations on time, and they were inconsistent. New systems analyst Anne Cool was insistent: were the supervisors trained to do the appraisals? Schad was so impressed by Cool that the next day he appointed her the company's new director of human resources, charging her with solving the performance appraisal problem as one of her first priorities. A new performance appraisal system was developed and implemented successfully. This is part of the company's advanced approach to human resources management which has contributed to its success (the company exports 90 per cent of its machinery, with sales growing from US$72 million in 1985 to US$568 million in 1996).

If we want to know how well our employees are doing, we've got to measure their performance—not necessarily an easy task. Many factors go into the performance evaluation process, and questions need to be asked such as: why do we do them, who should benefit from the evaluation, what type of evaluation should be used, and what problems might we encounter. This chapter seeks answers to these and other important factors in the **performance appraisal process**. By developing a valid performance management system, we can maximize the relationship in our motivational model that focuses on the effort-performance linkage. Let's review that linkage for a moment.

Performance Appraisal Process A formal process in an organization whereby each employee is evaluated to determine how he or she is performing.

The Linkage to Motivation

As we discovered in the last chapter, just because employees have the ability to do the job does not mean that they will perform satisfactorily. They also have to be willing to exert high energy levels—they must be motivated. Theoretically, as managers, we should be more interested in ends than in the means; that is, getting the job done.[3] As one football coach remarked in appraising his ungraceful but effective field goal kicker: "It ain't pictures, it's numbers." Similarly, managers should be concerned with quality results.[4] It's performance that counts. It may be difficult for some managers to accept, but they should not be appraising employees on how they look, but rather on whether they can score. We propose, therefore, that organizations exist to "score" rather than to provide an environment for individuals to "look like players." Just like the football coach, managers must be concerned with evaluating their personnel on "numbers" and not on "pictures." However, beware of oversimplification. In certain jobs such as assembly line work, it is relatively easy to count production numbers, but evaluating how a worker does the task may

Managers, like coaches, should be more concerned with quality results. It's performance that counts.

nevertheless help that employee's development. And how well a lawyer deals with clients is as important as how many clients she sees in a day.

Performance is a vital component in the motivation model.[5] Specifically, we must be concerned with the link between effort and performance and between performance and rewards (see Figure 12-1). Employees have to know what is expected of them and how their performance will be measured. Furthermore, employees must feel confident that if they exert an effort, it will result in a better performance as defined by the criteria by which they are being measured. Finally, they must feel confident that if they perform as they are being asked, they will achieve the rewards they value.[6] Do people see effort leading to performance, and performance to the rewards that they value?

Figure 12-1
Performance Appraisals and the Motivation Process

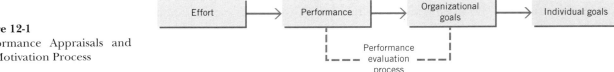

In summary, performance appraisals and their outcomes play a vital part in the model of motivation. If the objectives of individual employees are unclear, if the criteria for measuring those objectives are vague, and if employees lack confidence that their efforts will lead to a satisfactory performance appraisal or that there will be an unsatisfactory pay-off for that performance, we can expect individuals to work considerably below their potential. If we have done our job to hire capable people and develop their basic abilities to do the job, we must also make sure that they know what behaviours are required of them, understand how they are going to be appraised, believe that the appraisal will be conducted in a fair and equitable manner, and that they can expect their performance to be recognized by proper rewards.[7]

Performance Management Systems

The Purposes

The initial purpose of performance evaluation or performance appraisal was, as the name indicates, to evaluate the performance of the employee—determine how well the individual was doing his or her job. The result of the appraisal would help to decide such things as whether the employee was to be given a raise or not, the size of that raise, or even if the employee should be fired. But it became clear very soon that this process could also help managers determine what could be done to *improve* an employee's performance—that is, address developmental concerns. Finally, the requirements of human rights and employment equity legislation have made the issue of documentation important.

Performance appraisals must convey to employees how well they have performed on clearly understood set goals and measures. As our motivation model suggested, without proper two-way feedback about the employee's effort and its effect on performance, we run the risk of decreasing his or her drive. However, just as important to feedback is the issue of development.[8] By development, we are referring to those areas in which an employee is weak or could be better if some effort was expended to enhance performance. For example, suppose a professor demonstrates extensive knowledge in his or her field and conveys this knowledge to students adequately. Although the professor's performance may be considered good, there may also be room for improvement. In this case, development may include exposure to different teaching methods such as more experiential exercises, computer applications, or case analyses in the classroom.

Finally comes the issue of **documentation**. A performance evaluation system must concern itself with the legal aspects of employee performance. In Chapter 3, we discussed employment equity legislation and the need for job-related measures. Those job-related measures must be supported by performance when an HRM decision affects current employees. For instance, suppose a manager has decided to terminate an employee because of poor performance appraisals but the employee was evaluated as satisfactory on recent performance appraisals. In that case, the company's own personnel records do not support the manager's decision unless the employee's performance has worsened substantially since the last performance review, the HRM department or the manager's own supervisor would advise the manager not to fire the employee.

Performance appraisals play a key role in legal challenges. In our discussion of sexual harassment in Chapter 3, we recommended that employees should keep copies of past performance appraisals. If an employee was fired in retaliation for refusing a manager's advances, for example, this documentation could show that the termination was inconsistent with the employee's past performance and therefore inappropriate.

Because lawsuits and similar challenges are common in today's organizations, efforts must be made to ensure that the evaluation system used supports the legal requirements of the organization. However, even though the performance appraisal process is geared to serve the organization, we should also recognize two other important players in the process: employees and their appraisers. We can better serve employees' needs through timely and accurate feedback and development. In doing so, we may also be in a better position to show the effort-performance linkage (see "HRM Skills").

Next, we should keep in mind the needs of the appraiser. If feedback, development, and documentation are to work effectively, appraisers must have a performance appraisal system that is appropriate for their needs—a system that facilitates giving feedback and development information to their employees and one that allows for employee input. For example, if appraisers are required to evaluate their employees using inappropriate performance measures or answer questions about employees that have little bearing on the job, then the system will not provide the benefits needed to be effective.

Documentation The record of the performance appraisal process outcomes.

HRM *Skills*

Conducting the Performance Appraisal

1. **Prepare for, and schedule, the appraisal in advance.** Before meeting with employees, some preliminary activities should be carried out. At a minimum, review employee job descriptions, goals that may have been set, and performance data you may have on employees. Furthermore, you should schedule the appraisal well in advance to give employees the opportunity to prepare their data, for the meeting as well.

2. **Create a supportive environment to put employees at ease.** Performance appraisals conjure up several emotions. Every effort should be made to make employees comfortable during the meeting so that they are receptive to constructive feedback.

3. **Describe the purpose of the appraisal to employees.** Make sure they know precisely what the appraisal is to be used for. Will it have implications for pay increases or other personnel decisions? If so, make sure employees understand exactly how the appraisal process works and its consequences.

4. **Involve the employee in the appraisal discussion, including a self-evaluation.** Performance appraisals should not be one-way communication. Although, as supervisor, you may believe that you have to talk more in the meeting, that needn't be the case. Instead, employees should be given even opportunity to discuss their performance, raise questions about the facts you raise, and add their own data or perceptions about their work. One means of ensuring that two-way communication occurs is to have employees conduct a self-evaluation. You should listen actively to their assessment. This involvement helps to create an environment of participation.

5. **Focus discussion on work behaviour, not on the employees themselves.** Attacking the employee creates emotional difficulties. You should focus your discussion on the behaviour you've observed.

6. **Support your evaluation with specific examples.** Specific performance behaviour will help to clarify to employees the issues you raise. Rather than saying something wasn't "good," which is a subjective evaluation, you should be as specific as possible in your explanations, pointing out problems such as lateness or absenteeism, for instance.

7. **Give both positive and negative feedback.** Performance appraisals shouldn't be all negative. Although there is a perception that this process focuses on the negative, it should also be used to compliment and recognize good work. Positive as well as negative feedback helps employees to gain a better understanding of their performance.

8. **Make sure that employees understand what was discussed in the appraisal.** At the end of the appraisal, especially where some improvement is warranted, you should ask employees to summarize what had been discussed in the meeting. This will help to ensure that you have got your information through to employees.

9. **Generate a development plan.** Most of the performance appraisal revolves around feedback and documentation. But another component is needed. Where specific improvements are needed, a plan should be developed to describe what is to be done, by when, and what you, the supervisor, will commit to aid in the improvement or enhancement effort.

Difficulties in Performance Management Systems

To create the performance management system we desire, we must recognize the difficulties that may exist and look for ways to either overcome them or to deal with them more effectively. When you consider that three constituencies coexist in this process—employees, appraisers, and organizations—coordinating the needs of each may cause problems. By focusing on the difficulties, we can begin to address them and reduce their overall impact on the process. In terms of difficulties, two categories can be considered—the focus on the individual and the focus on the process.

Focus on the Individual Do you remember the last time you received a grade from a professor and felt that something was marked incorrect that wasn't wrong or that your answer was too harshly penalized? How did you feel about that? Did you accept the score and leave it at that, or did you question the instructor? Whenever performance evaluations are administered (and tests are one form of performance evaluation), we run into the issue of having people seeing eye to eye on the evaluation. Appraising individuals is probably one of the more difficult aspects of a manager's job, and because emotions are involved, managers sometimes just don't like to do appraisals.[9] Furthermore, we may all think we are performing in an outstanding fashion, but that may be only *our* perception. And although our work is good, a boss may recognize it but not see it as outstanding. Accordingly, in evaluating performance, emotions may arise. And if these emotions are not dealt with properly (we'll look at ways to enhance performance evaluations later in this chapter), they can lead to greater conflict. In fact, consider the aforementioned test example. If you decide to appeal your marks to your instructor, you should do so quite carefully. If you argue in a confrontational manner, the instructor may become defensive and what should be an open discussion may turn into an altercation, with ill feelings on both sides.

The same can happen during performance appraisal in the workplace when the parties differ in their view of the performance outcomes. When that occurs, it may lead to a situation in which emotions overcome both parties. This is not the way for evaluations to be handled. Accordingly, our first concern in the process is to remove the emotionality from the process. When emotions do not run high in performance appraisal meetings, employee satisfaction with the process increases.[10] And this satisfaction carries over into future job activities where both the employee and supervisor have opportunities to receive ongoing feedback in an effort to fulfil job expectations.[11] For Joe and Adam in the scenario at the beginning of the chapter, clearly this feedback did not occur.

Focus on the Process Wherever performance evaluations are conducted, there is a structure that must be followed. This structure exists to facilitate the documentation process that often allows for a quantifiable evaluation. Additionally, policies often exist that dictate performance outcomes. For example, if a company ties pay increases to performance evaluations consider the following potential difficulty. A manager's budget for salary increases has been set at 4 per cent of the department's payroll. The expectation is that poor performers getting smaller (or no) raises while exceptional performers get larger ones. Now, this manager has six subordinates, five of whom are good performers while the sixth is outstanding. To reward the outstanding performer adequately, the manager would like to give her a 7 or 8 per cent increase. However, this would leave him with only enough money to give his other subordinates increases of only three per cent, which is less than they expect and think they should receive. An alternative is to give everyone a 4 per cent raise, which would make the outstanding performer unhappy. And the manager is likely to feel uncomfortable with either solution. As this example illustrates, company policies and procedures may present barriers to a properly functioning appraisal process.

Furthermore, to get these numbers to balance means that rather than accentuating the positive work behaviour of some employees, an appraiser often focuses on the negative.[12] This can lead to a tendency to search for problems in order to justify a lower rating, which can ultimately lead to an emotional encounter. We may also find from the appraiser's perspective some uncertainty about how and what to measure or how to deal with the employee in the evaluation process.[13] Frequently, appraisers are poorly trained (if at all) in how to evaluate an employee's performance. Because of this, appraisers may make errors in judgement or permit biases to enter into the process. We'll discuss these problems later in greater detail.

Because difficulties can arise, we should begin to develop our performance appraisal process so that we can achieve maximum benefit from it. This benefit can be translated into employee satisfaction with the process. Such satisfaction is achieved by creating an understanding of the evaluation criteria used, permitting employee participation in the process and allowing for development needs to be addressed.[14] To begin doing so requires us to understand the appraisal process.

Performance Appraisals and Employment Equity

Performance evaluations are an integral part of most organizations and can help them achieve their goals by developing productive employees. Although there are many types of performance evaluation systems, each with its own advantages and disadvantages, we must be aware of the legal implications that may arise.

Employment equity legislation requires organizations to have HRM practices that are bias-free. For HRM, this means that performance evaluations must be objective and job-related. In other words, they must be reliable and valid. Furthermore, performance appraisals must also be able to measure "reasonable" performance success. To assist in these matters, two considerations arise: (1) The performance appraisal must be conducted according to some established intervals; and (2) appraisers must be trained in the process.[15] The reasons for this become crystal clear when you consider that any action affecting employees, from a promotion to a termination, must be based on valid data derived from the performance evaluation document[16] (see "Ethical Decisions in HRM"). These objective data often support the legitimacy of such actions.

The Appraisal Process

The appraisal process consists of six steps, as shown in Figure 12-2.

Establish Performance Standards with Employees. The appraisal process begins with the establishment of performance standards in accordance with the organization's strategic goals. These should have evolved out of the company's strategic direction and, more specifically, the job analysis and job description discussed in Chapter 5. These performance standards should also be clear and objective enough to be understood and measured. Too often, these standards are articulated in ambiguous phrases that tell us little, such as "a full day's work" or "a good job." What is a "full day's work," or a "good job"? The expectations managers have of the work performance of their employees must be clear enough in their mind so that they will be able to, at some later date, communicate these

Ethical Decisions in HRM:

The Inaccurate Performance Appraisal

Most individuals recognize the importance of effective performance management systems in an organization. Not only are they necessary for providing feedback to employees and for identifying personal development plans, they serve a vital legal purpose. Furthermore, organizations that fail to manage employee performance accurately often find themselves facing difficult times in meeting their organizational goals.

Most individuals would also agree that performance appraisals must meet employment equity requirements—that is, they must administered in such a way that they result in a fair and equitable treatment for the diversity that exists in the workplace. Undeniably, this is an absolute necessity, but what about those grey areas—instances where an evaluation meets legal requirements but verges on a questionable practice? For example, what if a manager deliberately evaluates a favoured employee higher than one he likes less even though the latter is a better promotional candidate? Likewise, what if the supervisor avoids identifying areas for employee development for individuals, knowing that the likelihood of career advancement for these employees is stalemated without the better skills?

Supporters of properly functioning performance appraisals point to two vital criteria that managers must bring to the process: sincerity and honesty. Yet, there are no legislative regulations such as employment equity laws that enforce such ethical standards. Thus, they may be, and frequently are, missing from the evaluation process. Can an organization have an effective performance-appraisal process without sincerity and honesty dominating the system? Can organizations develop an evaluation process that is ethical? Should we expect companies to spend training dollars to achieve this goal? What do you think?

Source: Larry L. Axline, "Ethical Considerations of Performance Appraisals," *Management Review* (March 1994), p. 62.

expectations to their employees, mutually agree to specific job performance measures, and appraise their performance against these established standards.

Mutually Set Measurable Goals. It is important that the goals are set mutually. Once performance standards are established, it is necessary to communicate these expectations; it should not be part of the employees' job to guess what is expected of them. Too many jobs have vague performance standards, and the problem is compounded when these standards are set in isolation and do not involve the employee. It is important to note that communication is a two-way street. Mere transference of information from the manager to the employee regarding expectations is not communication.

Measure Actual Performance. The third step in the appraisal process is the measurement of performance. To determine what actual performance is, it is necessary to acquire information about it. We should be concerned with how we measure and what we measure.

```
┌─────────────────────────────────────────────────┐
│ 1. Establish performance standards with employees. │
└─────────────────────────────────────────────────┘
                        ↓
┌─────────────────────────────────────────────────┐
│ 2. Mutually set measurable goals.                │
└─────────────────────────────────────────────────┘
                        ↓
┌─────────────────────────────────────────────────┐
│ 3. Measure actual performance.                   │
└─────────────────────────────────────────────────┘
                        ↓
┌─────────────────────────────────────────────────┐
│ 4. Compare actual performance with standards.    │
└─────────────────────────────────────────────────┘
                        ↓
┌─────────────────────────────────────────────────┐
│ 5. Discuss the appraisal with the employee.      │
└─────────────────────────────────────────────────┘
                        ↓
┌─────────────────────────────────────────────────┐
│ 6. If necessary, initiate corrective action.     │
└─────────────────────────────────────────────────┘
```

Figure 12-2
The Appraisal Process

Four common sources of information are frequently used by managers for measuring actual performance: personal observation, statistical reports, oral reports, and written reports. Each has its strengths and weaknesses, and a combination of them increases both the number of input sources and the probability of receiving reliable information. What we measure is probably more critical to the evaluation process than how we measure since the selection of the wrong criteria can result in serious, dysfunctional consequences. And what we measure determines, to a great extent, what people in the organization will attempt to excel at. The criteria we measure must represent performance as it was mutually set in the first two steps of the appraisal process.

Compare Actual Performance with Standards. The fourth step in the appraisal process is the comparison of actual performance with standards. The point of this step is to note deviations between standard performance and actual performance so that we can proceed to the fifth step in the process.

Discuss the Appraisal with the Employee. As we mentioned earlier, one of the most challenging tasks facing managers is to present an accurate appraisal to the employee. Appraising performance may touch on one of the most emotionally charged activities—the assessment of another individual's contribution and ability. The impression that employees receive about their assessment has a strong impact on their self-esteem and, very importantly, on their subsequent performance. Of course, conveying good news is considerably less difficult for both the manager and the employee than conveying the bad news that their performance has been below expectations. It should be clear then, in this context, the discussion of the appraisal can have negative as well as positive motivational consequences.

If Necessary, Initiate Corrective Action. The final step in the appraisal is the initiation of corrective action where necessary. Corrective action can be of two types: one is immediate and deals predominantly with symptoms, and the other is basic and delves into causes. Immediate corrective action is often described as "putting out fires," whereas basic corrective action gets to the source of the problem and to seeks correct it permanently. Immediate action corrects something right now and gets things back on track. Basic corrective action asks how and why performance deviated. In some instances, managers may rationalize that they do not have the time to take basic corrective action and therefore must be content to perpetually put out fires. Good managers recognize that taking a little time to analyse the problem today may save more time tomorrow when the problem may get bigger.

Appraisal Methods

The previous section described the appraisal process in general terms. In this section, we will look at specific ways in which management can establish performance standards and devise instruments that can be used to measure and appraise an employee's performance. Three different approaches exist for doing appraisals. Employees can be appraised against (1) absolute standards, (2) relative standards, or (3) objectives. No one approach is always best; each has its strengths and weaknesses.

Absolute Standards

Our first group of appraisal methods uses **absolute standards**. This means that subjects are measured against some sort of set benchmark and not compared with any other person. Included in this group are the following methods: the essay appraisal, the critical incident appraisal, the checklist appraisal, the adjective rating scale appraisal, forced-choice appraisal, and behaviourally anchored rating scales.

The Essay Appraisal. Probably the simplest method of appraisal is to have the appraiser write a narrative describing an employee's strengths, weaknesses, past performance, potential, and suggestions for improvement. The strength of the essay appraisal lies in its simplicity. It requires no complex forms or extensive training to complete, but its weaknesses are many. Because the essays are unstructured, they are likely to vary widely in terms of length and content. This makes it difficult to compare individuals across the organization, and, of course, some raters are better writers than others. So a "good" or "bad" evaluation may be determined as much by the appraiser's writing skill as by the employee's actual level of performance. However, the essay appraisal can provide considerable information, much of which can be easily fed back and assimilated by the employee. But this method provides only qualitative data, and HRM decisions improve when useful quantitative data, which can be compared and ranked more objectively, are generated. However, the essay appraisal is a good start and is beneficial if used in conjunction with other appraisal methods.

The Critical Incident Appraisal. Critical incident appraisal focuses the rater's attention on critical or key behaviours that make the difference between doing a job effectively and doing it ineffectively. The appraiser writes down anecdotes describing what the employee did that was especially effective or ineffective. A dean of business administration might write the following critical incident about one of her faculty members: "Coached the student team that participated in the National Case Competition." Note that with this approach to appraisal, specific behaviours are cited, not vaguely defined personality traits. A behaviour-based appraisal such as this should be more valid than trait-based appraisals because it is clearly more job-related. It is one thing to say that an employee is "aggressive," "imaginative," or "relaxed," but that does not tell us

Absolute Standards Measuring an employee's performance against some benchmark.

Essay Appraisal A performance appraisal method in which an appraiser writes a narrative about the employee.

Critical Incident Appraisal A performance appraisal method that focuses on the key behaviours that make the difference between doing a job effectively or ineffectively.

anything about how well the job is being done. Critical incidents, with their focus on behaviour, judge performance rather than personalities.

The strength of the critical incident method is that it looks at behaviours. Also, a list of critical incidents on a given employee provides a rich set of examples from which employees can be shown which behaviour is desirable and which calls for improvement. Its drawbacks are basically that: (1) Appraisers are required to regularly write these incidents down, and doing this on a daily or weekly basis for all subordinates is time-consuming and burdensome for managers; and (2) critical incidents suffer from the same comparison problem found in essays—they do not lend themselves to quantification, and, therefore, the comparison and ranking of subordinates is difficult.

Checklist Appraisal A performance appraisal approach in which a rater checks off those attributes of an employee that apply.

The Checklist Appraisal. In the checklist appraisal, the evaluator uses a list of behavioural descriptions and checks off those behaviours that apply to the employee. As Figure 12-3 illustrates, the evaluator merely goes down the list and checks off "yes" or "no" to each question. Once the checklist is complete, it is usually evaluated by the HRM staff, not the manager who completed the checklist. Therefore, the rater does not actually evaluate the employee's performance but merely records it. An analyst in HRM then scores the checklist, often weighing the factors in relationship to their importance. The final evaluation can then be returned to the rating manager for discussion with the subordinate, or someone from HRM can provide the feedback to the employee.

FIGURE 12-3 Sample Checklist Items for Appraising Customer Service Representative

	Yes	No
1. Are supervisor's orders usually followed?	⎯⎯	⎯⎯
2. Does the individual approach customers promptly?	⎯⎯	⎯⎯
3. Does the individual suggest additional merchandise to customers?	⎯⎯	⎯⎯
4. Does the individual keep busy when not servicing a customer?	⎯⎯	⎯⎯
5. Does the individual lose his or her temper in public?	⎯⎯	⎯⎯
6. Does the individual volunteer to help other employees?	⎯⎯	⎯⎯

The checklist reduces some bias since the rater and the scorer are different, but the evaluator usually can pick up the positive and negative implications in each item so bias can still be introduced. From a cost standpoint, this appraisal method may be inefficient if there are a number of job categories because a checklist of items must be prepared for each category.

Adjective Rating Scale A performance appraisal method that lists a number of traits and a range of performance for each. Also known as graphic rating scale.

The Adjective Rating Scale Appraisal. One of the oldest and most popular methods of appraisal is the adjective rating scale also known as graphic rating scale.[17] An example of some rating scale items is shown in Figure 12-4. Rating scales can be used to assess factors such as quantity and quality of work, job knowledge, cooperation, loyalty, dependability, attendance, honesty, integrity, attitudes, and initiative. However, this method is most valid when abstract traits like loyalty or integrity are avoided unless they can be defined in more specific behavioural terms.[18] The assessor goes down the list of factors and notes the point along a scale or continuum (typically five to ten points) that best describes the employee. In the design of the graphic scale, the challenge is to ensure that both the factors evaluated and the scale points are clearly understood and are unambiguous to the rater. Ambiguity breeds bias.

Rating scales are popular because, although they do not provide the depth of information that essays or critical incidents do,[19] they are less time-consuming to develop and administer, they provide a quantitative analysis and comparison, and, in contrast to the checklist, there is more generalization of items allowing a comparison with other individuals in diverse job categories.[20] Small organizations that lack a sophisticated HRM department also tend to prefer such simple techniques.

FIGURE 12-4
Sample of Adjective Rating Scale Items and Format

Performance Factor	Performance Rating				
Quality of work is the accuracy, skill, and completeness of work.	❑ Consistently unsatisfactory	❑ Occasionally unsatisfactory	❑ Consistently satisfactory	❑ Sometimes superior	❑ Consistently superior
Quantity of work is the volume of work done in a normal workday.	❑ Consistently unsatisfactory	❑ Occasionally unsatisfactory	❑ Consistently satisfactory	❑ Sometimes superior	❑ Consistently superior
Job knowledge is the information pertinent to the job that an individual should have for satisfactory job performance.	❑ Poorly informed about work duties	❑ Occasionally unsatisfactory	❑ Can answer most questions about the job	❑ Understands all phases of the job	❑ Has complete mastery of the job
Dependability is following directions and company policies with a minimum of supervision.	❑ Requires constant supervision	❑ Requires occasional follow-up	❑ Usually can be counted on	❑ Requires very little supervision	❑ Requires absolute without supervision

The Forced-Choice Appraisal. When you were in elementary or secondary school, did you ever complete one of those tests that presumably gives you insights into what kind of career you should pursue? (Questions might be, for example, "Would you rather go to a football game with a group of friends or stay home and read *The English Patient* in your room?") If so, then you are familiar with the forced-choice format. The forced-choice appraisal is a special type of checklist, but the rater must choose between two or more statements, all of which may be favourable or unfavourable. The appraiser's job is to identify which statement is most (or in some cases least) descriptive of the individual being evaluated. For instance, students evaluating their instructor might have to choose between: "(a) is patient with slow learners; (b) lectures with confidence; (c) keeps interest and attention of class; or (d) acquaints classes in advance with objectives for each class." All the preceding statements are favourable, but on another list, the choices could all be unfavourable. As with the checklist method, to reduce bias, the right answers are not known to the rater; someone in HRM scores the answers based on the key, which should be validated so management is in a position to say that individuals with higher scores are better-performing employees.

The major advantage of the forced-choice method is that because the appraiser does not know the "right" answers, it reduces bias and distortion.[21] For example, the appraiser may like a certain employee and intentionally want to give her a favourable evaluation, but this becomes difficult if one is not sure

Forced-Choice Appraisal A type of performance appraisal in which the rater must choose between two specific statements about an employee's work behaviour.

which response is most preferred. On the negative side, appraisers tend to dislike this method; many dislike being forced to make distinctions between similar-sounding statements. Raters also may become frustrated with a system in which they do not know what represents a "good" or "bad" answer; hence they may try to second-guess the scoring key in order to get the formal appraisal to align with their intuitive appraisal.

Behaviourally Anchored Rating Scales. An approach that has received considerable attention by academics in past years involves behaviourally anchored rating scales (BARS). These scales combine major elements from the critical incident and adjective rating scale approaches. The appraiser rates the employees based on items along a continuum, but the points are examples of actual behaviours on the given job rather than general descriptions or traits. The enthusiasm surrounding BARS grew from the belief that the use of specific behaviours derived for each job should produce relatively error-free and reliable ratings. Although this promise has not been fulfiled,[22] it has been argued that this may be due partly to departures from careful methodology in the development of the specific scales themselves rather than to inadequacies in the concept;[23] they also may be just too time-consuming. In a survey conducted in Canada in 1992, only 3.1 per cent of responding companies reported using BARS,[24] although in a more recent study, that had risen to 21 per cent.[25]

Behaviourally anchored rating scales specify definite, observable, and measurable job behaviour. Examples of job-related behaviour and performance dimensions are generated by asking participants to give specific illustrations of effective and ineffective behaviour regarding each performance dimension; these behavioural examples are then translated into appropriate performance dimensions. Those that are sorted into the dimension for which they were generated are retained. The final group of behaviour incidents are then numerically scaled to a level of performance that each is perceived to represent. The incidents that are retranslated and have high rater agreement on performance effectiveness are retained for use as anchors on the performance dimension. The results of these processes are behavioural descriptions such as *anticipates, plans, executes, solves immediate problems, carries out orders,* and *handles emergency situations.* Figure 12-5 is an example of a BARS for an employee relations specialist's scale.

The research on BARS indicates that while it is far from perfect, it does tend to reduce rating errors. Possibly its major advantage stems from the dimensions generated rather than from any particular superiority of behaviour over trait anchors.[26] The process of developing the behavioural scales is valuable in and of itself for clarifying to both the employee and the rater which types of behaviour connote good or bad performance. Unfortunately, it suffers from the distortions inherent in most rating methods.[27] These distortions will be discussed later in this chapter.

Relative Standards

In the second general category of appraisal methods, individuals are compared against other individuals. These methods are relative standards rather than absolute measuring devices. The most popular of the relative methods are: group order ranking, individual ranking, and paired comparison.

Group Order Ranking. Group order ranking requires the evaluator to place employees into a particular classification such as "top one-fifth" or "second one-fifth."

Behaviourally Anchored Rating Scales (BARS) A performance appraisal technique that generates critical incidents and develops behavioural dimensions of performance. The evaluator appraises behaviours rather than traits.

Relative Standards Measuring an employee's performance by comparing it to other employees' performance.

Group Order Ranking A relative standard of performance characterized as placing employees into a particular classification such as the "top one-fifth."

Performance dimension scale development under BARS for the dimension "Ability to absorb and interpret policies for an employee relations specialist."

This employee relations specialist

	9	Could be expected to serve as an information source concerning new and changed policies for others in the organization.
Could be expected to be aware quickly of program changes and explain these to employees.	8	
	7	Could be expected to reconcile conflicting policies and procedures correctly to meet HRM goals.
Could be expected to recognize the need for additional information to gain a better understanding of policy changes.	6	
	5	Could be expected to complete various HRM forms correctly after receiving instruction on them.
Could be expected to require some help and practice in mastering new policies and procedures.	4	
	3	Could be expected to know that there is always a problem, but go down many blind alleys before realizing they are wrong.
Could be expected to incorrectly interpret guidelines, creating problems for line managers.	2	
	1	Could be expected to be unable to learn new procedures even after repeated explanations.

Source: Reprinted from *Business Horizons* (August 1976), Copyright 1976 by the Foundation for the School of Business at Indiana University. Used with permission.

This method is often used in recommending students to graduate schools. Evaluators are asked to rank the student in the top 5 per cent, the next 5 per cent, the next 15 per cent, and so forth.

The advantage to this group ordering is that it prevents raters from inflating their evaluations so everyone looks good or from homogenizing the evaluations so everyone is rated near the average—results that are not unused with the graphic rating scale. The predominant disadvantages surface when the number of employees being compared is small. If a rater has twenty subordinates, only four can be in the top fifth and four must be in the bottom fifth. But if the evaluator is looking at only four employees, it is quite possible that all may be excellent, yet the evaluator may be forced to rank them into top, second, third, and bottom quarter. Theoretically, as the sample size increases, the validity of relative scores as an accurate measure increases; but occasionally, the technique is implemented with a small group, utilizing assumptions that apply to large groups.

Another disadvantage which plagues all relative measures is the "zero-sum game" consideration. This means that any change must add up to zero. For example, if there are twelve employees in a department performing at different levels of effectiveness, by definition, three are in the top quarter, three are in the second quarter, and so forth. The sixth-best employee, for instance, would be in the second quartile. Ironically, if two of the workers in the third or fourth quartiles leave the department and are not replaced, then our sixth-best employee now falls into the third quarter. Because comparisons are relative, an employee who is mediocre may score high only because he or she is the "best of the worst." In contrast, an excellent performer who is matched against stiff competition may be evaluated poorly, when in absolute terms, his or her performance is outstanding.

Individual Ranking Listing employees' performance in order from highest to lowest.

Individual Ranking. The individual ranking method requires the evaluator merely to list the employees in order from highest to lowest, and only one can be "best." If the evaluator is required to appraise thirty individuals, this method assumes that the difference between the first and second employee is the same as that between the twenty-first and the twenty-second. Even though some of these employees may be closely grouped, this method allows for no ties. In terms of advantages and disadvantages, the individual ranking method carries the same pluses and minuses as group order ranking.

Paired Comparison Ranking individuals' performance in relation to all others on a one-on-one basis, and counting the number of times any one individual is the preferred member.

Paired Comparison. The paired comparison method is calculated by taking the total of $[n(n-1)]/2$ comparisons. It ranks each individual in relationship to all others on a one-on-one basis. If ten people are being evaluated, the first person is compared, one by one, with each of the other nine, and the number of times this person is preferred in any of the nine pairs is tabulated. Each of the remaining nine persons, in turn, is compared in the same way, and a ranking is formed by the greatest number of preferred "victories." A score is obtained for each employee by simply counting the number of pairs in which the individual is the preferred member. This method ensures that each employee is compared against every other, but it can become unwieldy when large numbers of employees are being compared.

Objectives

The third approach to appraisal makes use of objectives. Employees are evaluated by how well they accomplish a specific set of objectives that have been determined to be critical in the successful completion of their job. Frequently referred to as management by objectives (MBO),[28] it is a process that converts organizational objectives into individual objectives. It consists of four steps: goal setting, action planning, self-control, and periodic reviews.

Management by Objectives (MBO) A performance appraisal method that includes mutual objective setting and evaluation based on the attainment of the specific objectives.

Goal Setting. In goal setting, the organization's overall objectives are used as guidelines from which departmental and individual objectives are set. At the individual level, the manager and subordinate jointly identify those goals that are critical to fulfil the requirements of the job as determined by job analysis. These goals are agreed upon and then become the standards by which the employee's results will be evaluated.

What will these objectives look like? It is important that they be tangible, verifiable, and measurable. This means that, wherever possible, we should avoid qualitative objectives and substitute quantifiable statements. For example, a quantitative objective might be "to cut each day 3,500 metres of cable to standard two-metre lengths, with a maximum scrap of 40 metres," or "to prepare, process, and transfer to the treasurer's office, all accounts payable vouchers within three working days from the receipt of the invoice."

Action Planning. In action planning, the means are determined for achieving the ends established in goal setting; that is, realistic plans are developed to attain the objectives. This step includes identifying the activities necessary to accomplish the objective, establishing the critical relationships between these activities, estimating the time requirements for each activity, and determining the resources required to complete each activity.

Self-Control. Self-control refers to the systematic monitoring and measuring of performance, ideally, by having the individual review his or her own performance. Inherent in allowing individuals to control their own performance is a positive image of human nature. The MBO philosophy is built on the assumption that individuals can be responsible, can exercise self-direction, and do not require external controls and threats of punishment to motivate them to work towards their objectives. This, from a motivational point of view, would be representative of Douglas McGregor's Theory Y.

Periodic Review. Finally, with periodic progress reviews, corrective action is initiated when behaviour deviates from the standards established in the goal-setting phase. Again, consistent with the MBO philosophy, these manager-subordinate reviews are conducted in a constructive rather than punitive manner. Reviews are not meant to degrade the individual but to aid in future performance and should take place at least two or three times a year.

MBO's advantages lie in its results-oriented emphasis. It assists the planning and control functions and provides motivation. It is a good approach to performance appraisal because employees know exactly what is expected of them and how they will be evaluated, and that their evaluation will be based on their success in achieving their objectives. Employees should also have a greater commitment to objectives they have participated in developing than to those unilaterally set by their boss. This may explain why MBO is the most popular performance appraisal method in Canada: 49 per cent of all companies reported using MBO, especially for management and professional-level positions.[29]

The major disadvantage of MBO is that it is unlikely to be effective in an environment where management has little trust in its employees, where management makes decisions autocratically and relies heavily on external controls. The amount of time needed to implement and maintain an MBO process may also cause problems. Many activities must occur to set it up such as meetings between managers and subordinates to set and monitor objectives which take an inordinate amount of the manager's time. Additionally, it may be difficult to measure whether the MBO activities are being carried out properly. The difficulty involved in properly appraising the managers' efforts and performance as they carry out their MBO activities may cause it to fail.

Factors that Can Distort Appraisals

The performance appraisal process and techniques that we have suggested present an objective system in which the evaluator is free from personal biases, prejudices, and idiosyncrasies. This is defended on the basis that objectivity minimizes the potential capricious and dysfunctional behaviour of the evaluator which may be detrimental to the achievement of the organizational goals. Thus, our goal should be to utilize direct performance criteria where possible.

Meet

Brian Reid
Manager, Human Resources, Enbridge Pipelines, Inc.

Enbridge Pipelines has been transporting oil from Western Canada since shortly after an oil well near Leduc, just south of Edmonton, sparked off an oil boom in the area about fifty years ago. The company (formerly known as Interprovincial Pipe Line Inc.) has been growing ever since.

Brian Reid, manager of human resources at Enbridge in Edmonton, is convinced that the key to this kind of success in today's unforgiving, competitive environment is ensuring that the organization has a culture of performance.

"The old idea of performance evaluation as a stand-alone activity just doesn't cut it," explains Mr. Reid. "We can't just discipline employees when they're bad and pat them on the head when they're good. Instead, we need to set up the organization so that we can learn from everything we do. We've got to consider the larger context of performance management, which consists of three key components: performance planning; the performance itself; and performance evaluation and feedback."

The planning phase involves setting individual performance objectives that align with business objectives. In turn, the business objectives should be aligned with the organization's long-range strategic plan. For example, a salesperson might aim to reach a certain sales figure; by meeting this objective, she will help the business unit reach its sales target for the quarter; and the business unit's success contributes towards the overall company revenue objectives. The planning phase also involves setting individual performance objectives that develop an individual's competencies, such as job knowledge, communication skills, or workplace safety.

The performance phase is primarily in the hands of the employee and his or her manager: the employee as doer, the manager as coach and facilitator. For this there needs to be regular and ongoing communication, a way of monitoring performance and regular feedback about that performance.

The evaluation phase doesn't take place in isolation. "Any time an employee's performance is not what it should be," says Mr. Reid, "we should ask: what are the obstacles? Are the skills not there? If they are not, what can we do to develop them? Is there some inhibitor? If so, how can we manage around it?"

These three phases can happen simultaneously. "Performance management should be dynamic and ongoing," says Mr. Reid. "It's not something you can think about once a year. Good performance management is based on regular interaction."

With the right culture in place, an organization needs only the simplest of tools for effective performance management. Currently, Enbridge's main tool is a LotusNotes database known as TARGET. Essentially, it is a central place where information relating to all three phases of performance management is stored. There are fields for departmental and individual objectives, as well as for employees' and supervisors' comments. A logbook section allows the individual to record private notes that they can refer to themselves later. The database information, while it is used as the basis for regular formal reports, can be accessed at any time.

"Many organizations get hung up on the tools," says Mr. Reid. "But it's not the form you use, or even whether you fill it out or not, that matters. What's important is that real feedback—and, therefore, growth, development, and learning takes place."

It would be naive to assume, however, that all practising managers impartially interpret and standardize the criteria upon which their subordinates will be appraised. This is particularly true of those jobs that are not easily programmable and for which developing hard performance standards is most difficult, if not impossible. These would include, but are certainly not limited to, such jobs as researcher, teacher, engineer, and consultant. In the place of such standards, we can expect managers to utilize non-performance or subjective criteria against which to evaluate individuals. Consider for a moment the issue of evaluating the performance of a university or college instructor. What criteria should be used? The instructor's showmanship during lectures? The quality of the instructor's overhead slides and handouts? The marks that the students earn in the course? The amount of learning that takes place (and how would you measure that?)

A completely error-free performance appraisal is only an ideal we can aim for,[30] with all actual appraisals falling. However, we can isolate a number of factors that significantly impede objective evaluation.[31] In this section, we will briefly review the more significant of these factors which include the following: leniency/ harshness error, halo error, similarity error, low appraiser motivation, central tendency, inflationary pressures, inappropriate substitutes for performance, and attribution theory.

Leniency/Harshness Error

Every evaluator has his or her own value system that acts as a standard against which appraisals are made. Relative to the true or actual performance an individual exhibits, some evaluators mark high and others low. The former is referred to as positive leniency error, and the latter as harshness error (also called severity or negative leniency error). Evaluators who are positively lenient in their appraisal overstate an individual's performance and rate it higher than it actually should be. Similarly, a harshness error understates performance, giving the individual a lower appraisal than merited.

If all individuals in an organization were appraised by the same person, this would not be a problem because although there would be an error factor, it would be applied equally to everyone. The difficulty arises when we have different raters with different leniency or harshness errors making judgements. For example, assume a situation where both Jones and Simard are performing the same job, with absolutely identical job performance, but for different supervisors. If Jones's supervisor tends to err towards positive leniency while Simard's errs towards negative leniency, we would be confronted with two dramatically different evaluations.

Leniency Error Rating performance higher than it should be.

Harshness Error Rating performance lower than it should be.

Evaluating the performance of a university or college instructor is no simple task, and results will vary depending on the criteria used.

Halo Error

The **halo error** or effect is a "tendency to rate high or low on all factors due to the impression of a high or low rating on some specific factor."[32] For example, if an employee tends to be conscientious and dependable, we might become biased towards that individual to the extent that we will rate him or her positively on many desirable attributes.

The halo effect is often seen on teaching appraisal forms that university and college students fill out in evaluating the effectiveness of their instructors. Students tend to rate a faculty member as outstanding on all criteria when they are particularly appreciative of a few things he or she does in the classroom. Similarly, a few bad habits—showing up late for lectures, being slow in returning papers or assigning an extremely demanding reading list—might result in students evaluating the instructor poorly across the board. One method frequently used to deal with the halo error is reverse-wording the evaluation questions so that a favourable answer for one question might be 5 on a scale of 1 through 5, while a favourable answer for another question might be 1. Structuring the questions in this manner seeks to reduce the halo error by requiring the evaluator to consider each question independently. Another method, which can be used when there is more than one person to be evaluated, is to have the evaluator appraise all ratees on each dimension before going on to the next dimension.

Halo Error The tendency to let our assessment of an individual on one trait influence our evaluation of that person on other specific traits.

Similarity Error

When evaluators rate other people in the same way that the evaluators perceive themselves, they are making a **similarity error**. Evaluators project the perceptions they have of themselves onto others. For example, the evaluator who perceives himself or herself as aggressive may evaluate others by looking for aggressiveness. Those who demonstrate this characteristic tend to benefit, while others are penalized.

Similarity Error Evaluating employees based on the way evaluators perceive themselves.

Low Appraiser Motivation

What are the consequences of an appraisal? If the evaluator knows that a poor appraisal could significantly hurt the employee's future—particularly opportunities for promotion or a salary increase—the evaluator may be reluctant to give a realistic appraisal. There is evidence that it is more difficult to obtain accurate appraisals when important rewards depend on the results.[33]

Central Tendency

It is possible that regardless of who the appraiser evaluates and what traits are used, the pattern of evaluation remains the same. It is also possible that the evaluator's ability to appraise objectively and accurately has been impeded by a failure to use the extremes of the scale—**central tendency**. Central tendency is "the reluctance to make extreme ratings (in either direction); the inability to distinguish between and among ratees; a form of range restriction."[34] Raters who are prone to the central tendency error are those who continually rate all employees as average. For example, if a manager rates all subordinates as 3, on a scale of 1 to 5, then no differentiation among the subordinates exists. Failure to rate subordinates as 5 for those who deserve that rating and as 1 if the case warrants it will only create problems, especially if this information is used for pay increases.

Central Tendency The tendency of a rater to give average ratings to everyone, good and bad alike.

One of your authors once worked in a company where both central tendency and leniency/harshness errors appeared to be operating simultaneously. The company's performance appraisal system had five levels: unsatisfactory (U), satisfactory (S), satisfactory plus (SP), excellent (E), and outstanding (O). Hardly anyone was ever rated unsatisfactory because that meant that the supervisor who was doing the appraisal had to take immediate corrective action. And out of 2,000 or so employees, only one or two were ever rated outstanding in any year. But in the manufacturing area, over 90 per cent of employees were rated either S or SP, while in the finance and accounting areas, over 90 per cent of employees were rated either SP or E. So while there were five possible ratings, only two were really used. This restriction of range is central tendency error. The "centre" varied, however, from one area to the other. It is possible that all the finance and accounting employees were marvellously competent people, but rater bias is a more likely explanation. Either the managers in manufacturing tended to be excessively harsh, or those in finance and accounting were particularly lenient. The only way to solve this problem is by training the appraisers so that uniform standards apply.

Inflationary Pressures

A middle manager in a large company could not understand why he had been passed over for promotion. He had seen his file and knew that his average rating by his supervisor was 86. Given his knowledge that the appraisal system defined "outstanding performance" at 90 or above, "good" as 80 or above, "average" as 70 or above, and "inadequate performance" as anything below 70, he was at a loss to understand why he had not been promoted with his near-outstanding performance appraisal. The manager's confusion was somewhat resolved when he found out that the actual average rating of middle managers in his organization was 92. This example demonstrates a major potential problem in appraisals—inflationary pressures. This, in effect, is a specific case of low differentiation within the upper range of the rating choices.

Inflationary pressures have always existed but appear to have increased as a problem over the past three decades. As equality values have grown in importance in our society, as well as fear of retribution from disgruntled employees who fail to achieve excellent appraisals, there has been a tendency for evaluation to be less rigorous and for negative repercussions from the evaluation to be reduced by generally inflating or upgrading appraisals. Perhaps that was what was happening to the finance and accounting managers mentioned above.

Inappropriate Substitutes for Performance

It is unusual for the definition of job performance to be absolutely clear and for direct measures to be available for appraising the incumbent. In many jobs it is difficult to get consensus on what is a "good job," and it is even more difficult to get agreement on what criteria will determine performance. For a salesperson, the criteria are affected by factors such as economic conditions and actions of competitors—factors outside the salesperson's control. As a result, the evaluation is frequently made by using substitutes for performance—criteria that, it is believed, closely approximate performance and act in its place. Many of these substitutes are well chosen and give a good approximation of actual performance, but others do not. It is not unusual, for example, to find organizations using criteria such as effort, enthusiasm, neatness, positive attitudes, conscientiousness, promptness, and congeniality as substitutes for performance. In some jobs, one or more of these criteria are part of performance. Obviously, enthusiasm does enhance the effectiveness of a teacher. You are more likely to listen to and be motivated by a teacher who is enthusiastic than by one who is not, and increased attentiveness and motivation typically lead to increased learning. But enthusiasm is not necessarily relevant to effective performance for many accountants, watch repairers, or copy editors. So what may be an appropriate substitute for performance in one job may be totally inappropriate in another.

Attribution Theory

Attribution Theory A theory of performance evaluation which differentiates between what the employee can and cannot control.

There is a theory in management literature called **attribution theory** which states that employee evaluations are directly affected by "managers' perceptions of who is believed to be in control of the employee's performance—the employee or the manager."[35] Attribution theory attempts to differentiate between those things that the employee controls (internal) versus those that the employee cannot control (external). For example, if an employee fails to complete a project that he has had six months to do, a manager may view this negatively if he or she believes that the employee did not manage either the project or his time well (internal control). Conversely, if the project is delayed because top management requested that something else be given a higher priority, a manager may see the incomplete project in less negative terms (external control).

Research has found support for two key generalizations regarding attribution:[36]

1. When managers attribute an employee's poor performance to internal control, the judgement is harsher than when the same poor performance is attributed to external factors.

2. When an employee is performing satisfactorily, managers will evaluate the employee more favourably if the performance is attributed to the employee's own efforts than if the performance is attributed to outside forces.

Impression Management Influencing performance evaluations by portraying an image that is desired by the appraiser.

While attribution theory is interesting and sheds new light on rater effect on performance evaluations, much more study of the topic is needed. Yet it does provide much insight on why unbiased performance evaluations are important. An extension of attribution theory relates to what is called **impression management** which was discussed in Chapter 7 in connection with the selection interview. Impression management takes into account how the employee influences the relationship with his or her supervisor. In one study, impression management was seen to have an effect on performance ratings. When the employee positively impressed his or her supervisor, the outcome was a higher performance rating.[37] In other words, it is possible for employees to get a better performance appraisal by means other than good performance. One could say that these employees triggered leniency and halo errors in their raters.

Creating More Effective Performance Management Systems

The fact that managers frequently encounter problems with performance appraisals should not lead us to throw up our hands and give up on the concept. There are things that can be done to make performance appraisals more effective. In this section, we offer some suggestions that can be considered individually or in combination. They include: behaviour-based measures, combined absolute and relative standards, ongoing feedback, multiple raters, selective rating, trained appraisers, and rewards for accurate appraisers.

Behaviour-Based Measures

As we have pointed out, the evidence favours behaviour-based measures over those developed around traits. Many traits often considered to be related to good performance may, in fact, have little or no relation to performance. Traits like loyalty, initiative, courage, reliability, and self-expression are intuitively appealing as desirable characteristics in employees, but the relevant question is: are individuals who are evaluated as high on those traits higher performers than those who rate low? We cannot answer this question. We know that there are employees who rate high on these characteristics and are poor performers. We can find others who are excellent performers but do not score well on traits such as these. Our conclusion is that traits like loyalty and initiative may be prized by managers, but there is no evidence that they are measures of performance in a large cross-section of jobs.

A second weakness in traits is the judgement itself. What is "loyalty"? When is an employee "reliable"? What you consider "loyalty," I may not. So traits suffer from weak inter-rater agreement. Behaviour-based measures can deal with both of these objections. Because they deal with specific examples of performance—both good and bad—we avoid the problem of using inappropriate substitutes. Also, because we are evaluating specific behaviours, we increase the likelihood that two or more evaluators will see the same thing. You might consider a given employee as "friendly" while I rate her "stand-offish," but when asked to rate her in terms of specific behaviours, we might both agree that she "frequently says 'good morning' to customers," "rarely gives advice or assistance to co-workers," and "almost always avoids idle chatter with co-workers."

Combined Absolute and Relative Standards

A major drawback to individual or absolute standards is that they tend to be biased by positive leniency; that is, evaluators lean towards packing their subjects into the high part of the rankings. On the other hand, relative standards suffer when there is little actual variability among the subjects. The obvious solution is to consider using appraisal methods that combine both absolute and relative standards. For example, you might want to use the adjective rating scale and the individual ranking method. This dual method of appraisal, incidentally, has been instituted at some universities to deal with the problem of grade inflation. Students get an absolute grade—A, B, C, D, or F—and next to it is a relative mark showing how this student ranked in the class. A prospective employer or graduate-school admissions committee can look at two students who each got a B in their cost accounting course and draw considerably different conclusions about each when next to one grade, it says "ranked 4th out of 26," while the other says "ranked 17th out of 30." Obviously, the latter instructor gave a lot more high grades. But is the instructor guilty of leniency error? What if the students in that section really did better?

Ongoing Feedback

A few years back, an international hotel chain advertised, "The best surprise is no surprise." This phrase clearly applies to performance appraisals. Employees like to know how they are doing. The annual review, where the manager shares the employees' evaluations with them, can become a problem especially if the managers put off doing the reviews. This is particularly likely if the appraisal is negative. But the annual review is also troublesome if the manager "saves up" performance-related information and unloads it during the appraisal review. This makes for an extremely trying experience for both the evaluator and employee. In such instances, it is not surprising that the manager may at-

FIGURE 12-6

Performance Appraisal Procedure at Simon Fraser University

1. SUBJECT: PERFORMANCE APPRAISAL

   (Applies to administrative and professional staff only.)

2. GENERAL POLICY STATEMENT

   The Simon Fraser University Performance Appraisal Program has been established to enable employees to receive feedback on their job performance, to assist them to become more effective in their jobs and to inform supervisors of the employee's career aspirations.

3. DEFINITIONS

   Appraisal Date—the month and day of the month that the employee was first appointed to her/his current position or the month and day of the month that the employee's position was last reclassified, whichever occurred most recently.

4. RESPONSIBILITY

   Supervisors are responsible for ensuring that Performance Appraisals are conducted as close as possible to the employee's appraisal date.

5. PROCEDURE

   5.01 The Personnel Department will provide departments with lists of employees to be appraised at least two (2) months in advance of the appraisal date. If requested, Personnel will also furnish copies of current job descriptions.

   5.02 The supervisor and the employee being appraised will both draft responses to each section of the Employee Appraisal form. They will then meet in an appraisal interview and review each section of the form in detail.

   5.03 After the appraisal interview, the evaluator will complete the report. The employee being appraised will review the document, add any comments he or she may wish to make, and sign the form. The evaluator will also sign the form.

   5.04 The Appraisal form will be forwarded to the next higher administrative level for review, comment and signature and then sent to the Dean or Director for review. If the next more senior level is a Dean or Director, the document will be forwarded to the appropriate Vice-President.

   5.05 Completed forms will then be sent to Personnel with copies being routed to the employee and departmental files. The copies sent to Personnel will be kept for three (3) years, then destroyed.

Source: http://www.sfu.ca/policies/admin/ad9-16.htm

tempt to avoid facing uncomfortable issues that, even if confronted, may only be denied or rationalized by the employee.[38]

The solution lies in having the manager and the employee share both expectations and disappointments continually on a day-to-day basis, if possible. By providing the employee with frequent opportunities to discuss performance before reward or punishment enter the picture, there will be no surprises at the time of the annual formal review. In fact, where ongoing feedback has been provided, the formal sit-down step should not be particularly traumatic for either party. And, in an effective MBO system ongoing feedback is the critical element.

Having an established procedure for the timing and conduct of the appraisal interview is also important. Figure 12-6 presents Simon Fraser University's procedure. You will notice that it requires both the appraiser and the appraisee to complete parts of the appraisal form before the appraisal interview. This certainly reinforces the idea that the appraisal interview is a two-way communication, as pointed out in the "HRM Skills" box on conducting the performance appraisal. Take a moment to think of what recommendations you would give the employee who is preparing for the interview.

Multiple Raters

As the number of raters increases, so does the probability of obtaining more accurate information. If rater error tends to follow a normal curve, an increase in the number of raters will tend to find the majority congregating about the middle. If a person has had ten supervisors, nine of whom rated him or her excellent and one poor, then we must investigate what happened with that one. Maybe this rater was the one who identified an area of weakness where training is needed or an area to be avoided in future job assignments. Therefore, by moving employees about within the organization to gain a number of evaluations, we increase the probability of achieving more valid and reliable evaluations (see "What If: HRM in a De-Jobbed Organization").[39]

The assumption has been made that these raters have specific performance knowledge of the employee. Otherwise, more information may not be more accurate information. For example, if the raters are from various levels in the organization's hierarchy, these individuals may not have an accurate picture of the employee's performance; thus, quality of information actually may decrease, and more raters will not produce better appraisals.

Two multiple-rater approaches that have increased in popularity in recent years are worth discussion in some detail: peer evaluations and the 360-degree appraisal.

Peer Evaluations   Have you ever wondered why a professor asks you to evaluate the contributions of each other's work when a group assignment is used in a classroom? The reasoning behind this is that the professor cannot tell what every member did on the project but only what the overall product quality is. At times, it may not be fair to give everyone in the group the same mark, especially if some of the members left most of the work up to the others.

Similarly, managers find it difficult to evaluate their employees' performance because they are not working with them every day. Unfortunately, unless they have this information, they may not be making an accurate assessment. And if the goal of the performance evaluation is to identify deficient areas and

What If:

HRM in a De-Jobbed Organization

The foundation of the performance appraisal process is the concept that standards are clearly identified. This fundamental fact implies that for workers to perform effectively, they must know and understand what is expected of them. This applies only where clear job descriptions exist and where variations to the job are minimal. In other words, conventional performance appraisals were designed to fit the needs of the traditional organization. But what happens to them when the organization is de-jobbed? Let's look at some possibilities.

First, setting goals between a supervisor and an employee may be a thing of the past. Tomorrow's workers are likely to go from project to project, facing rapidly changing demands and requirements. No formalized performance appraisal system will be able to capture the intricacies of the jobs being done. Second, employees, either part of the core group or of the contingent workforce, will have several bosses, not just one individual who directs the work. Just who will have the responsibility for the performance appraisal? It is more likely to be the team members themselves—setting their own goals and evaluating each other's performance. One can even speculate that this will take the format of an ongoing informal process rather than some formal "ritual" held every twelve months or so.

The traditional outcomes of performance evaluations are likely to change also. Because many of tomorrow's workers will not be permanent employees of the organization, the linkage between reward and motivation may be non-existent in terms of how we currently view rewards. Instead, how individuals work on a project and how they perform their duties as team players will probably give rise to continued use of their services or at the least serve as a reference for other organizations.

All in all, while there will be drastic changes in the performance appraisal process, this does not mean that organizations will become less concerned with evaluating employee performance. On the contrary, individual performance will matter most, and employee performance information is likely to be collected from a number of sources—from anyone who's familiar with the employee's work. As such, it's just the formalized measurement systems existing today that will rarely apply in the de-jobbed organization.

Source: William Bridges, "The End of the Job," *Fortune* (September 19, 1994), p. 64.

Peer Evaluations A performance evaluation approach in which co-workers provide input into the employee's performance.

provide constructive feedback to their employees, they have been providing a disservice to these workers by not having all the information. Yet how do they get this information? One of the better means is through peer evaluations. Peer evaluations are conducted by employees' co-workers, people explicitly familiar with the behaviours involved in jobs mainly because they are doing the same thing.[40] This is done because co-workers are the ones most aware of each others' day-to-day work behaviour and should be given the opportunity to provide the management with some feedback.[41]

The main advantage to peer evaluation is that (1) there is a tendency for co-workers to offer more constructive insight to each other so that as members of a unit, each will improve; and (2) their recommendations tend to be more specific regarding job behaviours. Unless this type of detail exists, constructive measures are hard to determine.[42] But caution is in order because these systems, if not handled properly, could lead to increases in halo effects, leniency errors,[43] and fear among employees.[44] Thus, along with training our managers to appraise employee performance, so too must we train peers to evaluate one another.

A slight deviation from peer assessments is a process called the upward appraisal or the reverse review.[45] Used in such companies as Pratt and Whitney and AT&T, upward appraisals permits employees to offer frank and constructive feedback to their managers on such areas as leadership and communication skills.[46]

360-Degree Appraisals The 360-degree appraisal or 360-degree feedback is gaining in popularity.[47] It seeks performance feedback from such sources as oneself, bosses, peers, team members, customers, suppliers, and the like and is being used in large companies such as DuPont, General Electric, Motorola, Procter & Gamble, and UPS.[48] A large number of consulting firms help large and small enterprises to implement the system in North America, the United Kingdom, Australia, and Argentina.[49] In today's dynamic organizations, traditional performance evaluations systems are archaic. Delayering has resulted in supervisors having greater work responsibility and more employees reporting directly to them. In some instances, it is almost impossible for supervisors to have extensive job knowledge of each of their employees. Furthermore, the growth of project teams and employee involvement in today's companies places the responsibility of evaluation where people are better able to make an accurate assessment.

The 360-degree feedback process also has some positive benefits concerning development. Many managers simply do not know how their employees truly view them and their work. For example, Jerry Wallace, GM's Saturn plant's head of personnel, saw himself as being up to date on all the latest management techniques,[50] open to change, and flexible to new ideas, but feedback from his employees indicated that they felt Jerry was a "control freak." After some soul-searching plus an assessment from an external leadership group, Jerry realized his employees were right. He finally understood why nobody wanted to be on a team with him and why he felt that he had to do everything himself.[51] In this case, the 360-degree feedback eliminated a strong barrier to Jerry's career progression.

While 360-degree appraisal is a relatively recent phenomenon, early research studies are reporting positive results where such a system operates. These stem from more accurate feedback, empowering employees, the reduction of subjective factors in the evaluation process, and the development of a competitive advantage in leadership compared to other organizations.[52] However, one must bear in mind that this approach generally requires professional assistance in the development of the data gathering instruments and computer support for scoring them.[53]

Selective Rating

It has been suggested that appraisers should make evaluations only in those areas in which they have significant job knowledge. In this way, we can increase the inter-rater agreement and make the evaluation a more valid process. It has

Upward Appraisal An employee appraisal process whereby employees evaluate their supervisors.

360-Degree Appraisal
360-Degree Feedback
Performance appraisal process in which supervisors, peers, employees, customers, and the like evaluate the individual.

been noted that individuals at different levels in the organization see different behaviours: for example, the manager of a Zeller's store sees a warehouse employee doing different things than the employee's co-workers see. And people at different levels also have different values and expectations regarding workplace behaviours. In general, therefore, we recommend that, in terms of organizational levels, appraisers should be as close as possible to the individual being evaluated. Conversely, the more levels separating the evaluator and evaluatee, the less opportunity the rater has to observe the individual's behaviour and the greater the possibility for inaccuracies.

The specific application of these concepts results in having immediate supervisors or co-workers as the major input into the appraisal and having them evaluate those factors that they are best qualified to judge. For example, it has been suggested that when professors are evaluating secretaries within a university, they use such criteria as judgement, technical competence, and conscientiousness, whereas peers (other secretaries) use job knowledge, organization, cooperation with co-workers, and responsibility.[54] Such an approach appears both logical and more reliable since people are appraising only those areas in which they are experienced and therefore in a position to make judgements.

In addition to taking into account where the rater is in the organization or what he or she is allowed to evaluate, selective rating should also consider the characteristics of the evaluator. If certain appraisers' traits are correlated with accurate appraisals while others are correlated with inaccurate appraisals, then it seems logical to attempt to identify the traits of effective raters. Those identified as especially effective could be given sole responsibility for doing appraisals, or greater weight could be given to their observations.

Trained Appraisers

If you cannot find good raters, the alternative is to make good raters. Evidence indicates that training can make individuals more accurate raters.[55] Common errors such as halo and leniency can be minimized or eliminated in workshops where managers can practise observing and rating behaviour. Why should we bother to train these individuals? Because a poor appraisal is worse than none at all.[56] These negative effects can manifest themselves in demoralized employees, decreased productivity, and making the company liable for wrongful dismissal damages.[57]

Rewards for Accurate Appraisers

Our final suggestion is obvious, but it is frequently overlooked when organizations establish a performance appraisal system. The managers doing the evaluation must understand that it is in their personal and career interest to conduct accurate appraisals. We noted earlier in this chapter that in most organizations, appraisers who assign accurate performance ratings to poor performers face negative consequences. This must be overcome by encouraging and rewarding accurate appraisers.

International Performance Appraisal

In evaluating employee performance in international environments, other factors come into play. For instance, the cultural differences between the parent country and the host country must be considered. The cultural differences between Canada and England are not as great as those between Canada and China, for example. Thus, hostility or friendliness of the cultural environment in which one manages should be considered when appraising employee performance.

International performance appraisals can be difficult because cultural differences play such a large role. For example, participating style management is quite acceptable in Canada but not Asia.

Who Performs the Evaluation?

There are also special issues to consider regarding who will be responsible for the evaluation of expatriate personnel: the host-country management or the parent-country management? Although local management would generally be considered a more accurate gauge, it typically evaluates expatriates from its own cultural perspectives and expectations, which may not reflect those of the parent country. For example, in Canada, a participatory style of management is quite acceptable, while in some Asian countries hierarchical values make it a disgrace to ask subordinates for ideas. This could vastly alter a manager's performance appraisal.[58]

Confusion may arise from the use of parent-country evaluation forms if they are misunderstood either because the form has been improperly translated (or not at all) or because the evaluator is uncertain what a particular question means. The home-office management, on the other hand, is often so remote that it may not be fully informed on what is going on in an overseas office. Because they lack access and because one organization may have numerous foreign operations to evaluate, home-office managements often measure performance by quantitative indices such as profits, market shares, or gross sales.[59] However, "simple" numbers are often quite complex in their calculations, and data are not always comparable. For example, if a company has many operations in South America, it must be aware of the accounting practices in each country. Peru, for instance, counts sales on consignment as firm sales, while Brazil does not. Local import tariffs can also distort pricing schedules which alter gross sales figures, another often-compared statistic. Even when the measurements are comparable, the countries being compared will have an effect. For instance, factory productivity levels in Mexico are well below those of similar plants in Canada and the United States, but US-owned plant productivity in Mexico is far above that of similar Mexican-owned plants. Depending on what the manager's results are compared with, different appraisals may occur. One cannot assume that numerical criteria or indices can be readily or easily interpreted.

Which Evaluation Format Will Be Used?

Other issues surround the question of selecting the best format to use in performance appraisals. If we have an overseas operation that includes both parent-country nationals (PCNs) and host-country nationals (HCNs), we must decide whether we will use the same forms for all employees. While most Western countries accept the concept of performance evaluation, some cultures interpret it as a sign of distrust or even as an insult to an employee. This complicates a decision to use one instrument like a graphic rating scale for all employees. On the other hand, using different formats for PCNs and HCNs may create a dual track in the subsidiary, creating other problems.

The evaluation form presents its own problems. If there is a universal form for the entire corporation, an organization must make sure that it is translated accurately into the native language of each country. Canadian firms have an advantage in this regard since in most cases, they are used to the need to develop and validate forms in both official languages, but still, English forms may not be readily understood by local supervisors. For example, clerical and office jobs do not always have identical requirements in all cultures. As a result, some multinationals may be hesitant about evaluating HCNs and TCNs (third-country nationals). In some countries, such as the former communist countries, individual performance was not assessed. Instead, all workers were treated as part of a group and rewarded only when the group performed: punishment or discipline were rare. Without the ability to reward good individual performance or to punish a poor one, there was little motivation to carry out any individual evaluation at all.[60] This is expected to change as the countries of Eastern Europe and the former USSR become more comfortable with capitalism, but the new format has yet to unfold. However, the collective-oriented system still exists in the People's Republic of China and Cuba where Canada is involved in numerous joint ventures.

Although the subject of international performance appraisal continues to receive research attention, two general recommendations have been suggested as follows:

1. Modify the normal performance criteria of the evaluation sheet for a particular position to fit the overseas position and site characteristics. Expatriates who have returned from a particular site or country can provide useful input into revising criteria to reflect the realities of a given location.[61]

Third-Country National (TCN)
An employee of a multinational company who is not a permanent resident of the country where the corporation has its headquarters, and who is assigned to work as an expatriate in a country different from that of his or her permanent residence.

2. Include a current expatriate's insights as part of the evaluation. This means that non-standardized criteria which are difficult to measure will be included, perhaps on a different basis for each country. This creates some administrative difficulties at headquarters but in the long run will be a more equitable system.[62]

Study Tools and Applications

Summary

This summary relates to the Learning Objectives provided on p. 341.
After having read this chapter, you should know:

1. Performance management systems serve in the process of linking effort and performance. Only through making this linkage apparent can an organization develop its rewards based on performance.

2. The three purposes of performance management systems are feedback, development, and documentation. They are designed to support the employees, the appraisers, and the organization.

3. The six-step appraisal process is to: (1) establish performance standards with employees; (2) mutually set measurable goals; (3) measure actual performance; (4) compare actual performance with standards; (5) discuss the appraisal with the employee; and (6) if necessary, initiate corrective action.

4. Absolute standards refer to a method in performance management systems whereby employees are measured against company-set performance requirements. Absolute standard evaluation methods include the essay appraisal, the critical incident appraisal, the checklist appraisal, the adjective rating scale appraisal, the forced-choice appraisal, and the behaviourally anchored rating scale (BARS).

5. Relative standards refer to a method in performance management systems whereby employees' performance is compared to other employees. Relative standard evaluation methods include group order ranking, individual ranking, and paired comparison.

6. MBO is used as an appraisal method by establishing a specific set of objectives for an employee to achieve and reviewing performance based on how well those objectives have been met.

7. Performance appraisal might be distorted for a number of reasons, including: leniency/harshness error, halo error, similarity error, low appraiser motivation, central tendency, inflationary pressures, and inappropriate substitutes for performance.

8. More effective appraisals can be achieved with behaviour-based measures, combined absolute and relative ratings, ongoing feedback, multiple raters, selective rating, trained appraisers, and rewards for accurate appraisers.

9. In 360-degree performance appraisals evaluations are made by oneself, bosses, peers, team members, customers, suppliers, and the like. In doing so, a complete picture of one's performance can be assessed.

10. Performance management systems may differ in the international arena in terms of who performs the evaluation and the format used. Cultural differences may dictate that changes in the Canadian performance management system are needed.

Key Terms

absolute standards	impression management
adjective rating scale	individual ranking
attribution theory	leniency error
behaviourally anchored rating scale (BARS)	management by objectives (MBO)

central tendency
checklist appraisal
critical incident appraisal
documentation
essay appraisal
forced-choice appraisal
graphic rating scale
group order ranking
halo error
harshness error

paired comparison
peer evaluation
performance appraisal process
relative standards
similarity error
Third Country National (TCN)
upward appraisal
360-degree appraisal
360-degree feedback

EXPERIENTIAL EXERCISE:

The Performance Appraisal

Purpose

1. To practise skills in performance appraisal and supervising employees.
2. To develop skills in communications and problem solving in the performance appraisal process.

Introduction

Any kind of system—whether it be a person, organization, or a spacecraft—needs feedback from its environment to tell how close it is to being on target in achieving its objectives. One of the most important and useful sources of feedback to an employee is his or her supervisor. However, in the day-to-day course of events, we usually get little direct feedback on our performance from our supervisors, and in turn, we give very little to our own employees.

One of the most common mechanisms for feedback between employees and employers is the performance appraisal process. In many organizations, this is a formal process in which the supervisor fills out a standard form describing the employee's work, they discuss it, and the employee signs it. Then it is sent to higher-level managers and is finally placed in the employee's personnel file.

Senior managers in most organizations will describe their performance appraisal system in detail, stressing the requirements (such as the employee's signature) that will ensure that the appraisal will, in fact, be conducted. However, when employees are asked about their performance appraisals, the response is often a blank stare. Many employees do not even know what a performance appraisal is. Others report that it is conducted in a cursory manner; many seem to be conducted during brief encounters in the hallway or by the water-cooler. Thus, there is a mysterious process whereby the performance appraisal is there when one talks to senior managers but gone when one talks to employees. One reason for this is that supervisors feel uncomfortable giving feedback in a one-to-one encounter. This occurs, in part, because they have rarely been trained to do so.

Procedure

1. Working in groups of three, one member will play the role of J.J. Stein and another, the role of T.T. Burns. (Your instructor will provide you with the roles.) The third member (and others, if necessary) will act as observer. (Guidelines for observer's role will also be given to you.)
2. The supervisor conducts the appraisal interview with the employee (20 minutes). The observer is silent and takes notes on the process of the interviewer, using the "general

instructions" as a guide. At the conclusion of the evaluation meeting, the observer gives feedback to the two participants.

3. After all groups have completed their appraisals, the large group will discuss the following: supervisors—what evaluation method did you use? How effective was it? Employee—how did you react to the appraisal method? What did you like? Dislike? Observers—What strengths did you witness in the evaluation? What weaknesses?

Source: Roy J. Lewicki, Donald D. Bowen, Douglas T. Hall, and Francine S. Hall, *Experiences in Management and Organizational Behavior,* 3d ed. (New York: John Wiley, 1988), pp. 41–43. Used with permission.

CASE APPLICATION:

Jeannie Rice

How open will individuals be to receiving feedback from anyone who has contact with them? That depends on many factors. Is the organization supportive of a multifaceted feedback process? Has the organization adopted the 360-degree appraisal into its value system? Do employees feel comfortable saying what they really think? For Jeannie Rice, the picture is a bit clearer.[63]

Jeannie Rice is the manager of buildings and property at a medium-sized university. Jeannie felt she was doing her job to the best of her abilities and that she was successful. She set department goals that supported the mission of the university and, with the help of her staff, achieved them. There didn't appear to be anything unusual operating here nor any underlying dissension among her staff. Oh sure, there were trying times for Jeannie as there are for any manager, right? But her staff saw things differently. Most viewed Jeannie as being too demanding. She was creating a stressful work environment that was not only affecting herself, but many of those who had daily dealings with her.

As part of Jeannie's personal development plan, she was sent to the Centre for Creative Leadership, a private centre where she was provided with numerous assessments and feedback instruments from her colleagues and employees. As a result of this feedback, a program was established for Jeannie to correct her behaviour. One aspect was to return to her job and meet individually with the staff. There she shared the comments that were provided to her and sought some clarification and elaboration. In many cases, however, staff members began with statements such as "I didn't say that about you," or "You used to be that way." Fortunately, Jeannie was able to overcome her staff's initial defensiveness by showing that she was, indeed, interested in and thankful for their feedback. It was possible then to discuss the issues in more depth. As a result, Jeannie has changed the way she does business and has created a more positive work climate for her staff. And Jeannie, too, is now a bit more relaxed.

Questions

1. Describe how a 360-degree appraisal aids in developing an evaluation process that effectively supports the employee and the organization.
2. What role do organizational values play in having an effective 360-degree appraisal? Describe some problems that may arise if these values are not present.
3. Could a 360-degree appraisal work in a college or university classroom? Explain your position.

How well did you fulfil the learning objectives?

1. Performance management systems lead to employee motivation in all of these ways except
   a. work objectives are clarified.
   b. criteria for measuring work objectives are specified.
   c. employees have confidence that their efforts will lead to satisfactory job performance.
   d. employees have confidence that satisfactory job performance will lead to an acceptable reward.
   e. individual value systems are identified.

2. A director of computing services always has trouble with his people after performance appraisals. They quit, call in sick for a week, or sabotage operations. During a conversation with Terry, the vice-president of human resources, about the performance evaluation process, the director complained, "I have a bunch of babies working for me. They all expect me to tell them what good performance is. Part of their job is figuring out what they are supposed to do." What would be the best response from Terry?
   a. Commiserate. Agree that the director's employees are babies.
   b. Help the director develop corrective action steps for his employees.
   c. Tell the director that performance standards should be set with employees, and objectives should be clearly agreed to.
   d. Tell the director to set clear performance expectations for his employees. It is his job, not theirs.
   e. Show the director the performance objectives Terry uses for her employees. Suggest that the director use those objectives.

3. Marie is a marketing analyst. Her boss periodically observes her work on specific parts of her job (client calls, conducting meetings, attending seminars, etc.) and writes down, using specific behavioural descriptions, what he sees her doing. What appraisal technique is he using?
   a. graphic rating scale
   b. critical incident
   c. BARS
   d. checklist appraisal
   e. forced-choice comparison

4. Compare the group order ranking and the individual ranking techniques for performance evaluation.
   a. The techniques are the same.
   b. The problem with individual ranking is that you may be forced to identify the "best of the best" in one set of employees and the "best of the worst" in another set. Group order ranking does not have this problem.

   c. The problem with group order ranking is that you may be forced to identify the "best of the best" in one set of employees and the "best of the worst" in another set. Individual ranking does not have this problem.
   d. Individual ranking forces the evaluator to compare all employees to each other. Group order ranking does not.
   e. Individual ranking allows no ties. Group order ranking allows ties.

5. If you had an MBO agreement with your professor about what to do to get an A in this class, which would be the best (in terms of MBO standards) objective?
   a. Get an A for doing the best you can.
   b. Get an A for excellent work on tests, quizzes, and projects.
   c. Get an A for a score of 96 or better on this test.
   d. Get an A for interesting contributions to class.
   e. Get an A if you are in the better part of the class.

6. Tony rates Al, an average worker, "excellent" on all of his performance evaluations. The rest of the staff suspect that Al gets high ratings because he graduated from the same prestigious university and was a member of the same fraternity as Tony. What rating error has the staff identified?
   a. similarity error
   b. halo error
   c. leniency error
   d. central tendency
   e. inflationary pressures

7. According to attribution theory, if, in a manager's judgement, an employee's poor performance is attributable to external factors,
   a. the employee will be more harshly rated.
   b. the employee will be favourably rated.
   c. the manager's perception will be jaded by impression management influence.
   d. there exists an internal focus of control.
   e. the poor performance will be viewed in more positive terms.

8. Which of the following is an example of an upward appraisal?
   a. A manager refers to earlier performance appraisals of subordinates before evaluating them.
   b. Peer evaluation is employed.
   c. Several managers form teams to evaluate all their employees collectively.
   d. Subordinates evaluate their managers.
   e. Managers evaluate employees' traits rather than their behaviours.

9. The 360-degree appraisal process
   a. provides feedback from a variety of individuals who have knowledge of an employee's performance.
   b. works best in large organizations.
   c. aids in developing competitive intelligence about competing organizations.
   d. diminishes the effect of development in the performance appraisal process.
   e. all of the above.

10. Sarah, vice-president of a large transnational firm, explains that because of cultural and language differences between the parent and most subsidiary countries, her organization has chosen to evaluate performance only "by the numbers." Gross sales figures and factory productivity levels are used. What is wrong with this approach?
    a. Nothing. Most firms are using this technique for international performance evaluation.
    b. Each country's accounting practices must be considered when recording sales. (For example, some countries record consignments as sales.)
    c. Language differences affect factory productivity levels.
    d. Sales figures cannot be easily converted to a common currency designation.
    e. The effort is redundant. Either gross sales or factory productivity levels should be sufficient.

11. Good performance management systems are designed to provide
    a. performance information and salary updates.
    b. disciplinary action and salary updates.
    c. feedback, development, and documentation.
    d. training, documentation, and salary updates.
    e. communication and documentation.

12. Performance management systems must satisfy the needs of
    a. employees, appraisers, organizations.
    b. employees, customers, supervisors.
    c. customers, managers, human resources professionals.
    d. employees, organizations, customers.

e. human resources professionals, supervisors, managers.

13. The three approaches for performance appraisal are:
    a. absolute standards, tangential standards, nominal standards.
    b. absolute standards, relative standards, objectives.
    c. absolute standards, objectionable standards, peer review.
    d. absolute standards, relative standards, peer review.
    e. relative standards, peer review, objectives.

14. MBO is likely to be ineffective in
    a. global organizations.
    b. hierarchical organizations that are implementing TQM.
    c. service-sector organizations.
    d. manufacturing plants with more than three production facilities.
    e. hierarchical organizations where managers traditionally do not trust subordinates and do not delegate.

15. Advantages of MBO include all of the following except
    a. employees have greater commitment to objectives they set.
    b. employees know what is expected of them.
    c. MBO provides a basis for performance evaluation.
    d. MBO is a time-saving way to set goals.
    e. employees know that performance is defined in terms of successfully meeting stated objectives.

16. Under which condition should an expatriate be evaluated by the host-country management instead of by parent-country management?
    a. When the evaluation forms are not properly translated.
    b. When a hostile cultural environment exists.
    c. When the home office is so remote that it cannot be fully informed about overseas operations.
    d. When the economic base of the parent country differs drastically from the host company.
    e. When the expatriate is from the parent country.

Chapter Thirteen

REWARDS AND COMPENSATION

LEARNING OBJECTIVES

AFTER READING THIS CHAPTER, YOU WILL BE ABLE TO:

1. Describe the link between rewards and motivation.
2. Explain the various classifications of rewards.
3. Discuss why some rewards are membership-based.
4. Define the goal of compensation management.
5. Discuss job evaluation and its four basic approaches.
6. Explain the evolution of the final wage and salary structure.
7. Describe competency-based compensation programs.
8. Discuss why executives are paid significantly higher salaries than other employees in an organization.
9. Describe the issues around the practice of pay secrecy.
10. Identify what is meant by the balance-sheet approach to international compensation.

In 1998 Chapters Inc. launched the Total Rewards Package in its 350 Chapters, SmithBooks and Coles bookstores across Canada.[1] The package is targeted at all of the company's 5,000 employees (not just managers and executives), and it provides competitive pay levels as well as benefits such as vacations, pensions, sick days, and group insurance. Among the package's features is an on-the-spot recognition and rewards program called Dream Points.

The most popular feature of the package, according to HR Manager Mary-Alice Schmidt, is the Master Bookseller designation. It is intended to reward the top performing booksellers, those "people who love selling books and do it well," says Schmidt. The designation comes after employees complete a screening and certification process. It carries with it the somewhat intangible reward of recognition and praise, together with the much more tangible one of a pay increase of about 20 per cent.

In addition, the company (which went public in December 1996) instituted a share purchase plan which allows all employees who work twenty or more hours per week to allocate as much as 10 per cent of their pay to buying company shares. Once they have been in the plan for six months, they can buy shares at a 15 per cent discount from the market rate, and they can sell their shares twice a year free of brokerage charges.

Employee reaction to the Total Rewards Package is extremely positive. In particular, employees like the fact that the company appears to be focusing on all employees and not only on those in management or those being trained for management.

Chapters Total Rewards Package compensates its top performing booksellers with recognition and praise and pay increases.

Introduction

"What's in it for me?" is a question every person consciously or unconsciously asks before engaging in any form of behaviour. Our knowledge of motivation tells us that people do what they do to satisfy some need. Before they do anything, therefore, they look for a pay-off or reward.

The most obvious reward employees get from work is pay, and we will spend the major part of this chapter examining pay as a reward as well as how compensation programs are created. However, as the chapter opener suggests, rewards also include promotions, desirable work assignments, and a host of other less obvious pay-offs—a smile, peer acceptance, a kind word of recognition and, in one company, even a professional massage![2]

The Linkage to Motivation

The place of rewards in our motivation model was made clear in Chapter 11. Since people behave in ways that they believe are in their best interest, they constantly look for pay-offs for their efforts. A well-designed organizational reward system demonstrates how good job performance can lead to organizational goal attainment which, in turn, leads to satisfying the individual goals or needs of the employee (see Figure 13-1).

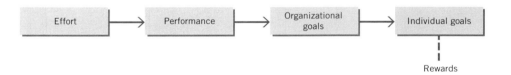

Figure 13-1

Rewards and the Link to Motivation

Organizations, then, use rewards to motivate people. They rely on rewards to motivate job candidates to join the organization, and they certainly rely on rewards to get employees to come to work and perform effectively once they are hired.[3]

In the following section, we will review the various types of rewards over which managers have discretion and look at the properties of effective rewards, with particular emphasis on using rewards in ways that are consistent with the motivation model.

Types of Organizational Incentives

There are a number of ways to classify rewards. We have selected three of the most typical dichotomies: intrinsic versus extrinsic rewards, financial versus non-financial rewards, and performance-based versus membership-based rewards. As you will see, these categories are far from being mutually exclusive, yet they all share one common thread—they help us to understand how rewards help maintain employee commitment.[4]

Intrinsic versus Extrinsic Rewards

Intrinsic rewards are the satisfactions one gets from the job itself. These satisfactions are self-initiated rewards such as having pride in one's work, having a feeling of accomplishment, or being part of a team. Job enrichment, for instance, discussed in Chapter 11, can offer intrinsic rewards to employees by making work seem more meaningful.[5] **Extrinsic rewards**, on the other hand, include money, promotions, and benefits, all of which are external to the job and come from an outside source. In most but not all cases, these rewards are given by management or other superiors. For example, in many universities, it is student organizations and not deans or presidents that give best teacher awards to professors. Thus, if an employee experiences feelings of achievement or personal growth from a job, we would label such rewards as intrinsic. If the employee receives a salary increase or a write-up in the company magazine, we would label these rewards as extrinsic. The general structure of rewards has been summarized in Figure 13-2.

Intrinsic Rewards Rewards one receives from the job itself, such as pride in one's work, a feeling of accomplishment, or being part of team.

Extrinsic Rewards Rewards one gets from the employer, usually money, a promotion, or benefits.

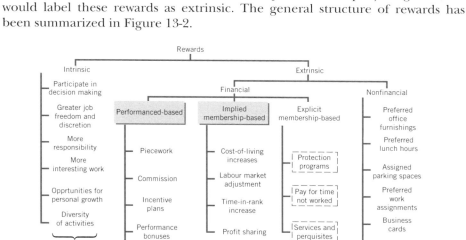

Figure 13-2
Structure of Rewards

Financial versus Non-Financial Rewards

Rewards may or may not enhance the employee's financial well-being. Financial rewards can be either direct—wages, bonuses, profit sharing, and the like—or indirect—supportive benefits such as pension plans, paid vacations, paid sick leaves, and employee discounts.

Non-financial rewards cover a smorgasbord of desirable extras that do not increase the employee's financial position. Instead of making the employee's life better off the job, non-financial rewards attempt to make it better on the job. The non-financial rewards that we will identify represent a few of the more obvious; however, the creation of these rewards is limited only by managers' ingenuity and ability to assess the pay-offs available within their jurisdiction that individuals within the organization find desirable.

The old saying, "one man's meat is another man's poison" clearly applies to the subject of rewards, and most particularly to non-financial awards. What one employee views as "something I've always wanted," another might find useless or undesirable. Therefore, care must be taken in providing the right non-financial reward for each person. Yet proper selection can lead to significant benefits to the organization through increased performance.

Some workers are very status-conscious. A panelled office, a carpeted floor, a large walnut desk, or a private bathroom may be just what stimulates an employee to top performance. Similarly, status-oriented employees may value an impressive job title, their own business cards, their own administrative assistant, or a well-located parking space with their name clearly painted underneath the "Reserved" sign. Similarly, if lunch is normally from noon to 1:00 p.m., the benefit of being able to take lunch at another, more preferred time can be viewed as a reward. Having a chance to work with congenial colleagues, winning a desired work assignment, or being able to work without close supervision are all non-financial rewards within management's discretion and, when carefully used, can provide stimulus for improved performance.

Some organizations make very effective use of non-financial rewards: Earl's, a Western Canada restaurant chain, is constrained by its very competitive market and thus pays relatively low wages to its mainly young and somewhat transient workforce. But it has been able to use non-financial rewards creatively to stimulate enthusiasm and performance in its employees.[6]

Performance-Based versus Membership-Based Rewards

The rewards that the organization allocates can be said to be based on either performance or membership criteria. While managers in most organizations will argue vigorously that their reward system pays for performance, this isn't always the case. Few organizations actually reward employees based on performance—a point we will discuss later in this chapter. Without question, the dominant basis for reward allocations is membership in the organization.

Performance-Based Rewards
Rewards that are based on the job performance of individuals or teams.

Performance-based rewards are exemplified by the use of commissions, piecework, pay plans, incentive systems, group bonuses, merit pay, or other forms of pay-for-performance plans. On the other hand, **membership-based rewards** include cost-of-living increases, benefits, and salary increases attributable to labour-market conditions, seniority or time in rank, credentials (such as a university degree or a college diploma). The key point here is that membership-based rewards are generally extended irrespective of an individual's, group's, or organization's performance. The difference between the two is not always obvious. In practice, performance may be only a minor determinant of rewards despite theories that hold that high motivation depends on performance-based rewards.

Membership-Based Rewards
Rewards that go to all employees regardless of performance.

What Is Compensation Management?

Why do aerospace engineers who design airplanes for Bombardier Aerospace earn more than Bombardier's security guards? Maybe your first answer will be that the engineers are more skilled and thus should earn more. But what about the industrial engineers who design the manufacturing processes that Bombardier uses to make those airplanes? Should they make more or less than the aerospace engineers who design the airplanes? The answer to these questions lies in job evaluation.

Job Evaluation The process of determining the value of each job in relation to the other jobs in the organization.

Job evaluation is the process whereby an organization systematically establishes the relative value of its various jobs by comparing them to determine each job's appropriate worth. In this section, we will discuss the broader topic of compensation, narrow our discussion to job evaluation methods, and conclude with a review of an increasingly controversial topic—executive compensation.

Employees exchange work for rewards. Probably the most important reward, and certainly the most obvious, is money. Why don't all employees earn the same amount of money? The search for this answer moves us directly into the topic of compensation management.

The goals of **compensation management** are to design a cost-effective pay structure that will attract, motivate, and retain competent employees and that also will be perceived as fair by these employees. Fairness is a concept that frequently arises in the administration of an organization's compensation program. To minimize costs, organizations generally seek to pay the least possible, so, to them, fairness means a wage or salary that is adequate for the demands and requirements of the job. Of course, fairness is a two-way street: employees also want what they see as fair compensation. As we pointed out in our earlier discussion of motivation in Chapter 11, if employees perceive an imbalance in the relation of their efforts to the reward, they will act to correct the inequity. Therefore, the search for fairness is pursued by both employers and employees.

Compensation Management The process of managing a company's compensation program in a cost-effective manner.

Government Influence on Compensation

In Chapter 3, we described how government policies and regulations shape and influence HRM. Governmental influence, however, is not equally felt in all areas of human resources management. Collective bargaining and the employee selection process, for example, are heavily constrained by laws and regulations. On the other hand, there is little direct governmental influence on areas such as how to conduct employee orientations or on strategic human resources planning (but of course, that planning may be addressing governmental requirements as in the development of plans to increase the hiring of minorities). Compensation management is one of the areas that is highly regulated. Governments set minimum wages and stipulate benefits that employers must provide, and governments pass pay equity legislation. We will discuss some of these governmental influences on compensation mangement, but you must bear in mind that we will only be touching on some of the major influences.

In all Canadian jurisdictions, legislation stipulates that employees must be paid time-and-a-half for any hours worked in excess of a stated weekly maximum, usually around forty hours. Some employees are exempt from this stipulation, and while there are slight differences from one jurisdiction to another, in all cases the exempt employees include supervisors, managers, and employees whose hours of work cannot be controlled (e.g., travelling sales representatives). That is what the terms *exempt* and *non-exempt* employees mean.

Furthermore, Canadian governments also legislate a minimum wage. Again, the amounts vary somewhat from one jurisdiction to another, and the different provinces make special adjustments. For example, Quebec has a different, lower rate, for employees who earn tips, while Ontario has a different, lower rate for students under eighteen (see Table 13-1).

Human rights legislation protects employees from discrimination. The legislation clearly prohibits discrimination in hiring decisions and by extension, in pay decisions, on the basis of race, colour, national origin, religion, age, or sex, and, in some jurisdictions, sexual orientation. More specifically related to pay, **equal pay legislation** requires that men and women be paid the same if they are performing identical or substantially similar work. The legislation covering most Canadian workers (federal, Manitoba, Nova Scotia, New Brunswick, Ontario, Prince Edward Island, Quebec) goes further: jobs deemed to be equal in

Equal Pay Legislation Laws that require that men and women be paid the same if they are performing identical or substantially similar work, and in some jurisdictions, if they are performing work of equal value.

TABLE 13-1 Minimum Wages in Canada

Province or Territory	Hourly Rate	Effective Date
Newfoundland		
General	$ 5.25	17-Jul-96
Prince Edward Island		
General	$ 5.75	17-Jul-96
Nova Scotia		
Inexperienced workers	$ 5.05	Feb-97
Experienced workers	$ 5.50	Feb-97
New Brunswick		
General	$ 5.50	01-Jul-96
Quebec		
General	$ 6.80	01-Oct-97
Liquor Server	$ 6.05	01-Oct-97
Carved-Wood Workers	$ 8.90	01-Oct-97
Ontario		
General	$ 6.85	01-Jan-95
Liquor Server	$ 5.95	01-Jan-95
Student	$ 6.40	01-Jan-95
Harvest Workers	$ 6.85	01-Jan-95
Homeworker	$ 7.54	01-Jan-95
Manitoba		
General	$ 5.40	17-Jul-96
Saskatchewan		
General	$ 5.35	17-Jul-96
Alberta		
General	$ 5.00	01-Oct-98
British Columbia		
General	$ 7.15	01-Apr-98
Yukon Territory		
General	$ 6.86	17-Jul-96
Northwest Territories		
General	$ 6.50	17-Jul-96

Notes:

General

Employees under federal jurisdiction are entitled to the minimum wage according to the province/territory in which they work.

Ontario

Student minimum wage applies to student workers who are under eighteen years of age, and work less than twenty-eight hours per week. Any student working more that will receive the general minimum wage.

Nova Scotia

Inexperienced workers are those who have worked less than three months in a position.

Alberta

The minimum wage will increase by $0.25 on April 1, 1999 and $0.25 on October 1, 1999.

Newfoundland

Minimum wage is paid to any worker who is above age sixteen.

value must be paid at the same rate. In essence, the legislation is an effort to correct the historic imbalance in pay between men and women. (The total after-tax income of women in Canada was 52 per cent of that of men in 1985, rising to 60 per cent in 1995.[7]) Again, there are differences between the laws in the different jurisdictions, but the general principle is constant: salaries and wages must be established on the basis of skill, responsibility, and working conditions, while individual salaries may differ on the basis of performance and seniority. In addition, Canadian legislation typically requires that employers equate the pay of female-dominated jobs (those where most employees are women) with that of male-dominated jobs. In Ontario, an analysis found that the skills, knowledge, and working conditions of nursing assistants (almost all of whom were women) in hospitals were comparable to those of plumbers (almost all men) working in the same locations. Accordingly, the nursing assistants received a 17 per cent raise to bring up their salaries to the level of the plumbers' salaries.[8]

In July 1998, the Canadian Human Rights Tribunal ruled that the federal government had been, for the past thirteen years, underpaying its female workers (compared to men) in violation of the 1978 Canadian Human Rights Act. The ruling affected almost 200,000 current and former workers, and the tribunal further ruled that the government should adjust the employees' pay retroactively.[9] This settlement would cost the government $3 billion (according to the Public Service Alliance of Canada) or as much as $5 billion (according to government sources). Not surprisingly, the government decided to appeal the decision.[10]

The government's arguements were weakened by a November 1998 ruling by the Federal Court of Appeal that seven complaints—filed by unions representing some 20,000 mostly female Bell Canada telephone operators—should be heard by the Canadian Human Rights Tribunal. The telephone operators claimed that they had been underpaid since 1992 in comparison with mostly male technicians.[11]

How does one determine the value of jobs so that one can compare ones as dissimilar as those of plumbers and nursing assistants? The answer to this question is job evaluation, which we will discuss now.

Job Evaluation and the Pay Structure

The essence of compensation management is the establishment of fair and equitable criteria for valuing jobs and the consequent pay structure. Let us turn now to a definition of job evaluation and a discussion of how it is done.

What Is Job Evaluation?

In Chapter 5, we introduced job analysis as the process of describing the duties of a job, authority relationships, skills required, conditions of work, and additional relevant information. We stated that the data generated from job analysis could be used to develop job descriptions and specifications as well as to do job evaluations (but see "What If : HRM in a De-Jobbed Organization"). By job evaluation, we mean using the information in job analysis to determine systematically the value of each job in relation to all jobs within the organization. In short, job evaluation seeks to rank all the jobs in the organization and

What If:

HRM in a De-Jobbed Organization

Job evaluation, the systematic examination of the relative value of jobs in organizations, is designed to specify the relative value of each job to the organization. Similar to the discussion of job analysis, the process of job evaluation is contingent on having accurate and complete job descriptions. Without these prerequisites, however, job evaluation becomes a process of subjectively determining how much to pay any position. In today's increasingly flexible organizations with increasingly flexible jobs, accurate and complete job descriptions may no longer be possible. The question becomes, without the job analysis serving as the foundation of the job evaluation process, has job evaluation been rendered obsolete? In its current form, more than likely yes.

However, job evaluation is unlikely to disappear altogether. Rather than being based on the job analysis process and job descriptions, job evaluation is likely to change its focus. That is, rather than focus on the jobs themselves, the process may focus on individual workers. How so? Consider the following. There is a movement today to rethink how employees are paid. Rather than focusing on the value of the job to the company, this new process looks at what value the individual adds to the organization. For example, under this new job evaluation method, employees will be paid according to the degree of skill, knowledge, and specific behaviours they bring to the job. Those who possess these competencies to a greater degree will be paid a higher wage rate. Consequently, pay systems will move away from the traditional approach of paying the job towards paying the person or, more accurately, the competencies of the person.

When you consider such a system, paying employees according to what they add to the organization is consistent with most aspects of HRM we've discussed. The specific competencies required of employees should be detailed in the strategic human resources planning process. In this manner, organizations are paying specifically for those things that will help them achieve their goals. Likewise, knowing that the organization rewards competencies rather than other factors helps individuals to better manage their career growth. Those who wish to be paid more know what is required for the next step. Furthermore, such a process is critically linked to the motivation process in that performance dictates the rewards one receives. Traditional job evaluation techniques, then, may not be losing ground in today's organizations. Rather, they may be changing to more appropriately reflect the new workforce we employ. When you consider the contingent workforce that exists and the number of consultants employed for projects, paying people for their value added makes more sense. For example, have you ever wondered why some consultants can command $250 per hour while others may struggle to get $25? The answer lies in the skills, knowledge, and behaviours that each brings to the client organization. Those who possess special competencies are worth more to an organization and as such, are paid accordingly. Wouldn't you prefer to be compensated based on what value you bring to the organization? In many respects, that is precisely what employees have been wanting for years—fair and equitable payment for the services they render.

place them in a hierarchy that will reflect the relative worth of each. This is a ranking of jobs, not people. Job evaluation assumes normal performance of the job by a typical worker. So, in effect, the process ignores individual abilities or the performance of the job holder.

The ranking that results from job evaluation is a means to an end, not an end in itself. It should be used to determine the organization's pay structure. Note that we say should; in practice, this is not always the case. External labour market conditions, collective bargaining, and individual differences may require a compromise between the job evaluation ranking and the actual pay structure. Yet even when such compromises are necessary, job evaluation can provide an objective standard from which modifications can be made.

Isolating Job Evaluation Criteria

The heart of job evaluation is the determination of what criteria will be used to arrive at the ranking. It is easy to say that jobs are valued and ranked by their relative job worth, but there is far more ambiguity when we attempt to state what it is that makes one job higher than another in the job structure hierarchy. Most job evaluation plans use responsibility, skill, effort, and working conditions as major criteria,[12] but each of these, in turn, can be broken down into more specific terms. Skill, for example, is often measured "through the intelligence or mental requirements of the job, the knowledge required, motor or manual skills needed, and the learning that occurs."[13] Other criteria can and have also been used: supervisory controls, complexity, personal contacts, and the physical demands needed.[14]

You should not expect the criteria to be constant across jobs. Since jobs differ, it is traditional to separate jobs into common groups. This usually means that, for example, production, clerical, sales, professional, and managerial jobs are evaluated separately. Treating like groups similarly allows for more valid rankings within categories but still leaves unsettled the importance of how to compare between categories. Separation by groups may permit us to say that the position of die design engineer in the production group requires more mental effort than that of a production supervisor and hence, it gets a higher ranking. However, it does not readily resolve whether greater mental effort is necessary for die design engineers than for office managers.

This is a major problem under pay equity legislation, which usually requires that comparisons be made between jobs that belong to different groupings.

Methods of Job Evaluation

There are four basic methods of job evaluation currently in use: ranking, classification, factor comparison, and point method.[15]

Ranking Method The ranking method requires a committee, typically composed of both management and employee representatives, to arrange jobs in a simple rank order, from highest to lowest. No attempt is made to break down the jobs by specific criteria. The committee members merely compare two jobs and judge which one is more important or difficult. Then they compare another job with the first two and so on until all the jobs have been evaluated and ranked.

The most obvious limitation to the ranking method is its sheer unmanageability when there are a large number of jobs; imagine the difficulty of trying to rank hundreds or thousands of jobs in the organization. Other drawbacks to be con-

Ranking Method A method of evaluating jobs by placing them in order, from most to least valuable.

Classification Method Method of job evaluation that involves placing jobs into predetermined classes based on skills, knowledge, and abilities required.

sidered are the subjectivity of the method—there are no definite or consistent standards by which to justify the rankings—and because jobs are only ranked in terms of order, we have no knowledge of the distance between the ranks. The advantage is that it is quick and cheap, but it is best used in small organizations.

Classification The classification method was made popular by the US Civil Service Commission which sought to establish classification grades. These classifications are created by identifying some common denominator—skills, knowledge, responsibilities—with the desired goal being the creation of a number of distinct classes or grades of jobs. Examples might include shop jobs, clerical jobs, sales jobs, and so on, depending, of course, on the type of jobs the organization requires.

Once the classifications are established, they are ranked in an overall order of importance according to the criteria chosen, and each job is placed in its appropriate classification. This latter action is generally done by comparing each position's job description against the classification description.

The classification method shares most of the disadvantages of the ranking approach plus the difficulty of writing classification descriptions, judging which jobs go where, and dealing with jobs that appear to fall into more than one classification. While the classification system was used with apparent success in classifying millions of different jobs in the US civil service, legislative demands in that country (as in Canada) required an approach that permitted a more quantitative evaluation of jobs. The classification system is being replaced by a point system developed in the mid-1970s by the US government.[16]

Factor Comparison Method
A method of job analysis in which job factors are compared to determine the worth of the job.

Factor Comparison Method The factor comparison method is a sophisticated, quantitative ranking method. The evaluators select key jobs in the organization as standards. Those jobs chosen should be well known, with established pay rates, and they should consist of a representative cross-section of all jobs that are being evaluated. Generally, fifteen to fifty key jobs are selected by the committee.[17]

What factors in the key jobs will the other jobs be compared against? These criteria are usually five: mental, skill, and physical requirements; responsibility; and working conditions. Once the key jobs are identified and the criteria chosen, committee members rank the key jobs on the criteria. The next step is the most interesting dimension in the factor comparison method. The committee agrees on the base rate (usually expressed on an hourly basis) for each of the key jobs and then allocates this base rate among the five criteria (see Table 13-2). For example, in one organization, the job of maintenance electrician was chosen as a key job with an hourly rate of $17.40. The committee allocated $4.25 to mental effort, $5.15 for skill, $2.50 for physical effort, $3.50 to responsibility, and $2.00 for working conditions. These amounts then became standards by which other jobs in the organization could be evaluated.

The final step in factor comparison requires the committee to compare its overall judgements and resolve any discrepancies. The system is in place when the allocations to the key jobs are clear and understood, and a high degree of agreement has been reached among committee members about how much of each criterion every job has.

Drawbacks to factor comparison include its complexity; its use of the same five criteria to assess all jobs when, in fact, jobs differ across and within organizations; and its dependence on key jobs as anchor points. "To the extent that one or more key jobs change over time either without detection or without

TABLE 13-2 Factor Comparison Method (Selected Positions)

Jobs	Hourly Pay Requirements	Mental Requirements	Skill Requirements	Physical	Responsibility	Working Conditions
Maintenance Electrician	$17.40	$4.25	$5.15	$2.50	$3.50	$2.00
Inventory Control Specialists	14.95	4.05	4.65	2.00	3.25	1.00
Warehouse Stocker	12.60	2.75	3.50	1.80	2.30	2.25
Administrative Assistant	11.15	3.25	3.00	1.00	2.65	1.25
Maintenance Electrician Helper	10.45	2.65	2.00	2.20	1.60	2.00

correction of the scale, users of the job comparison scale are basing decisions on what might be described figuratively as a badly warped ruler."[18] Another disadvantage is that changes in actual wages, particularly if the wages of some of the jobs move differently from others (as a result of market pressures, for instance), require recomputing the wages of all jobs. On the positive side, factor comparison requires a unique set of standard jobs for each organization, so it is ideal for the tailor-made approach. As such, it is automatically designed to meet the specific needs of each organization. Another advantage is that jobs are compared with other jobs to determine a relative value, and since relative job values are what job evaluation seeks, the method is logical.

Point Method The last method we will present breaks down jobs based on various identifiable criteria (such as skill, effort, and responsibility) and then allocates points to each of these. Depending on the importance of each criterion to performing the job, appropriate weights are given, points are totalled, and jobs with similar point totals are placed in similar pay grades.

An excerpt from a **point method** chart for clerical positions is shown in Figure 13-3. Each clerical job would be evaluated by deciding, for example, the level of education required to perform the job satisfactorily. The first degree might require the equivalent of skill competencies associated with ten years of elementary and secondary education; the second might require competencies associated with four years of high school; and so forth.

The point method offers the greatest stability of the four approaches we have presented. Jobs may change over time, but the rating scales established under the point method stay intact. Additionally, the methodology underlying the approach contributes to a minimum of rating error. On the other hand, the point method is complex, making it costly and time-consuming to develop. The key criteria must be carefully and clearly identified, degrees of factors have to be agreed upon in terms that mean the same to all raters, the weight of each criterion has to be established, and point values must be assigned to degrees. While it is expensive and time-consuming to both implement and maintain, the point method appears to be the most widely used method. Furthermore, it can be effective for addressing the comparable worth issue.[19] The Canadian federal government uses the point method for job evaluation, and as mentioned earlier, the US civil service is moving to the point method. The Hay System, a proprietary method that is very popular for the evaluation of management-level jobs, is also a point method that uses four criteria (factors) although its origins can be traced to the factor comparison approach.

Point Method Breaking down jobs based on identifiable criteria then allocating points to each.

Figure 13-3
Excerpts from a Point Method

Job Class: Clerk

Factor	1st Degree	2nd Degree	3rd Degree	4th Degree	5th Degree
Skill					
1. Education	22	44	66	88	110
2. Problem solving	14	28	42	56	70
Responsibility					
1. Safety of others	5	10	15	20	25
2. Work of others	7	14	21	28	35

2. Problem solving:
This factor examines the types of problems dealt with in your job. Indicate the one level that is most representative of the majority of your job responsibilities.

Degree 1: Actions are performed in a set order per written or verbal instruction. Problems are referred to supervisor.

Degree 2: Solves routine problems and makes various choices regarding the order in which the work is performed within standard practices. May obtain information from varied sources.

Degree 3: Solves varied problems that require general knowledge of company policies and procedures applicable within area of responsibility. Decisions made based on a choice from established alternatives. Expected to act within standards and established procedures.

Degree 4: Requires analytical judgment, initiative, or innovation in dealing with complex problems or situations. Evaluation not easy because there is little precedent or information may be incomplete.

Degree 5: Plans, delegates, coordinates, and/or implements complex tasks involving new or constantly changing problems or situations. Involves the origination of new technologies or policies for programs or projects. Actions limited only by company policies and budgets.

Source: Material reprinted with permission of The Dartnell Corporation, Chicago, IL 60640.

Establishing the Pay Structure

Once the job evaluation is complete, its data become the nucleus for the development of the organization's pay structure.[20] This means pay rates or ranges will be established that are compatible with the ranks, classifications, or points arrived at through job evaluation. Any of the four job evaluation methods can provide the necessary input for developing the organization's overall pay structure. Each has its strengths and weaknesses, but because of its wide use, we will use the point method to show how point totals are combined with wage and salary survey data to form wage and salary curves.

Wage and Salary Surveys Many organizations use surveys to gather factual information on pay practices within specific communities and among firms in their industry.[21] This information is used for comparison purposes. It can tell management if the organization's wages or salaries are in line with those of other employers and, in cases where there is a short supply of individuals to fill certain positions, may be used to actually set wage or salary levels.[22] Where does an organization get wage and salary data? Many industry and employee associations conduct surveys and make their results available to members, but organizations can conduct their own surveys, and many large ones do.

KPMG Canada, a major consulting firm, conducts an annual survey of salaries for over 200 different benchmark positions—from junior clerical jobs to chief executives—across Canada. The reports are available to the general public (for a price) in mid-September, but participating organizations (those that supply information on the salaries and wages they pay) receive a very substantial discount. Data are gathered via questionnaires. The company has developed Windows-based data entry software (which can be downloaded through the World Wide Web) that makes it easier for companies to supply information.[23]

It is not uncommon for the HRM director of a large company to regularly share wage and salary data on key positions with her counterparts at similar organizations. This could be done at the local level (for example, data could be shared by the directors of firms such as 3M, General Motors, and London Life in London, Ontario) or at the regional or national level which would happen if auto parts maker Magna International were to conduct a national salary survey. In these cases, key jobs such as maintenance engineer, computer programmer, or administrative assistant are identified and comprehensive job descriptions are shared so that comparisons can be made with jobs in the other organizations. A mailed questionnaire is the usual approach, but personal or telephone interviews are also common.

When organizations do their own wage and salary surveys, they are not limited in what they can ask. In addition to the average wage or salary for a specific job, other information frequently requested includes entry-level and maximum wage and salary rates, shift differentials, overtime pay practices, vacation and holiday allowances, the number of pay periods, and the length of the normal workday and work week.

When one of your authors was responsible for compensation management for the subsidiary of a large multinational company, a group of a dozen or so compensation managers of the largest companies in the country used to meet regularly to exchange such compensation information. Having such information available allowed the companies to react quickly to changes in a dynamic wage market.

Wage and Salary Curves   When management arrives at point totals from job evaluations and obtains survey data on what comparable organizations are paying for similar jobs, then a wage and salary curve can be developed from the data. An example of a wage curve is shown in Figure 13-4. This example assumes the use of the point method and plots point values and wage data. A separate wage curve can be constructed based on the company's actual wages and compared with the survey-based curve for discrepancies.

A completed wage or salary curve tells management the average relationship between points of established pay grades and wage or salary base rates. Importantly, it can identify jobs whose pay is out of the trend line. When a job's pay rate is too high, it should be identified as a "red circle" rate. (The term comes from the practice of drawing a circle in red ink around the particular wage or salary.) This means that pay is frozen, or below-average increases are granted until the structure is adjusted upward to put the circled rate within the normal

Wage and Salary Surveys
The process of gathering and interpreting information regarding the wages or salaries paid in the relevant labour market.

Wage and Salary Curves   The result of the plotting of points of established pay grades against wage or salary base rates to identify the general pattern of wages or salaries and find individuals whose wage or salaries are out of line.

range. Of course, there will be times when a wage or salary rate is out of line but not red circled. The need to attract or keep individuals with specific skills may require a wage or salary rate outside the normal range. To continue attracting these individuals, however, may ultimately upset the internal consistencies supposedly inherent in the wage or salary structure. It is also possible that a wage or salary rate may be too low. Such undervalued jobs carry a "green circle" rate, and attempts should be made to grant these jobs above-average pay increases.

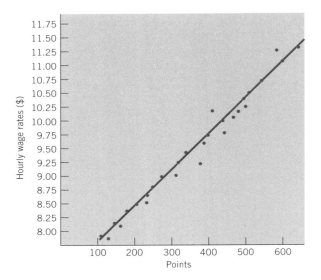

Figure 13-4
A Wage Curve

Wage and Salary Structure
Organizing jobs into pay grades and assigning wages or ·salaries to each grade. Frequently each grade is assigned a pay range.

The Wage and Salary Structure   It is only a short step from plotting a wage and salary curve to developing the organization's **wage and salary structure**. Jobs that are similar—in terms of classes, grades, or points—are grouped together. For instance, pay grade 1 may cover the range from 0 to 150 points, pay grade 2 from 151 to 300 points, and so on. As shown in Figure 13-5, the result is a logical hierarchy of wages.[24] The more important jobs are paid more, and as individuals assume jobs of greater importance, they rise within the wage hierarchy.

Irrespective of the determinants, notice that each pay grade has a range and that the ranges overlap. Typically, organizations design their wage and salary structures with ranges in each grade to reflect different tenure in positions as well as different levels of performance. While most organizations create a degree of overlap between grades, employees who reach the top of their grade can only increase their pay by moving to a higher grade.

Some Special Cases of Compensation

As traditional organizations are rapidly changing in the dynamic world in which we live, so, too, are compensation programs. Most notably, organizations can no longer continue to increase wages or salaries by a certain percentage each year (a cost-of-living raise) without also achieving some comparable increase in performance. Accordingly, more organizations are moving to one or more of numerous varieties of pay-for-performance systems. These may include incentive compensation plans, competency based compensation, and team-based compensation.

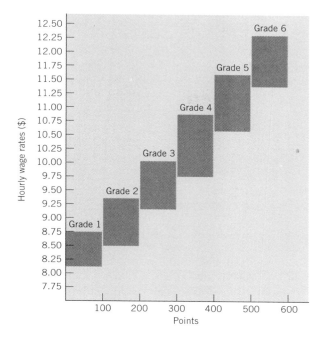

Figure 13-5
A Wage Structure

Incentive Compensation Plans

In addition to the basic wage and salary structure, organizations that are sincerely committed to developing a compensation system that is designed around performance will want to consider the use of incentive pay. Generally given in addition to, rather than in place of, the basic wage or salary, incentive plans should be viewed as an additional dimension to the wage and salary structure we have described. Incentives can be paid based on individual, group, or organization-wide performance, all of which are pay-for-performance concepts.

Individual Incentives   Individual incentive plans pay off for individual performance.[25] For the 1990s, these plans have been the biggest trend in compensation management in North America. A survey of 314 Canadian firms conducted in 1997 revealed that 74 per cent of employers paid their employees on the basis of individual and company performance, a marked increase over the 40 per cent that reported doing so in a survey four years earlier.[26] Popular individual incentive plans include merit pay, piecework, time-savings bonuses, and commissions.

One popular and almost universally used incentive system is **merit pay**.[27] Under a merit pay plan, employees who show "merit" have a sum of money added to their base salary. Merit pay should differ from cost-of-living increases in that their size is attributable solely to performance. Those who perform better should receive more merit pay. Often, though, this is not the case, and merit pay is just a substitute for cost-of-living raises.[28] Just as with the cost-of-living raise, merit monies become permanent additions to the base salary, becoming, in essence, the new base from which future percentage increases are calculated. The problem with merit pay plans administered in this way, as with a cost-of-living system, is that pay increases are always expected. Under these traditional systems, if the company has a bad year or employees don't produce, wage increases are still expected.

Merit Pay   An increase in pay based on some overall measure of individual performance, usually awarded at regular periods such as annually or bi-annually.

Piecework Plan A compensation plan whereby employees are typically paid for the number of units they actually produce.

Organizations are attempting to deal with this problem in different ways, sometimes within a more or less traditional merit pay approach, for example, by linking pay increases to increases in productivity.

While the merit pay approach is the most widely used, the best-known incentive is undoubtedly piecework. Under a straight piecework plan, the employee is typically guaranteed a minimal hourly rate for meeting some pre-established standard output. For output over this standard, the employee earns so much for each piece produced. Differential piecework plans establish two rates—one up to standard and another when the employee exceeds the standard. The latter rate, of course, is higher to encourage the employee to beat the standard.

Individual incentives can be based on time saved as well as output generated. For example, at the Jacobs Engineering Group, engineers are not given annual pay raises. Rather, based on their performance, they are given an incentive bonus. For the past few years, this bonus has averaged more than 5 per cent of their annual salary—greater than the cost-of-living adjustments would be if tied to inflation.[29] As with piecework, the employee can expect a minimal guaranteed hourly rate, but in this case, the bonus is achieved for doing a standard hour's work in less than sixty minutes. Employees who can do an hour's work in fifty minutes obtain a bonus that is some percentage (say 50 per cent) of the labour saved.

Sales personnel frequently work on a commission basis. Added to a lower base wage, they get an amount that represents a percentage of the sales price. On encyclopedias, it may be a hefty 25 or 30 per cent, while on sales of multi-million-dollar aircraft or city infrastructure systems, commissions are frequently 1 per cent or less.

Individual incentives work best where clear performance objectives can be set and where tasks are independent.[30] At Interlink Freight Systems, an incentive compensation system was established for pick-up and delivery drivers. The system was designed by management and the Transportation Communications International Union with assistance from KPMG Canada. Key performance indicators were identified through testing and use of historical data. The pilot test indicated that average driver productivity increased by 21 per cent, and nearly half the drivers were earning more than under the traditional hourly pay structure. Therefore, the company implemented the system nationally.[31]

However, if tasks are not independent, or if performance objectives cannot be set clearly, individual incentives can create dysfunctional competition or encourage workers to cut corners. Co-workers can become the enemy, individuals can create inflated perceptions of their own work while deflating that of others, and the work environment may become characterized by reduced interaction and communication between employees. Quality and safety may also be compromised if corners are cut.

A potentially negative effect with performance incentives is that you may get what you pay for. Since the incentives are tied to specific goals (which are only part of the total outcomes expected from a job), people may not perform the unmeasured and thus not unrewarded activities in favour of the measured, rewarded ones. For example, let us suppose that the instructor of a given course believes that classroom participation and independent library research are two important ways in which students enhance their learning. The instructor tells you this, and it's even clearly spelled out in the course outline. However, all the course's marks will come from multiple-choice tests based on the textbook. The instructor will, indeed, get what he is paying for: most students will focus on studying from the textbook and spend little time in the library or paying attention to classroom discussions.

Group Incentives Each of the individual incentives we described can also be used on a group basis; that is, two or more employees can be paid for their combined performance. Group incentives are desirable when employees' tasks are interdependent and require cooperation.[32]

Plant-Wide Incentives The goal of **plant-wide incentives** is to direct the efforts of all employees towards achieving overall organizational effectiveness. This type of incentive produces rewards for all employees based on organization-wide cost reduction or profit sharing. An organization-wide incentive can be combined with individual incentives. Employees of the Royal Bank of Canada, for instance, receive bonuses if the bank meets its financial targets and they meet their individual goals.[33] Another name for these incentive plans is **gainsharing** because employees share in the organization's financial gains. Lincoln Electric, mentioned in the previous chapter, has had a year-end bonus system for decades which in some years has provided an annual bonus "ranging from a low of 55 per cent to a high of 115 per cent of annual earnings."[34] The Lincoln Electric plan pays off handsomely when employees beat previous years' performance standards. Since this bonus is added to the employees' salaries, it has made the Lincoln Electric workers the highest-paid electrical workers in the United States.[35]

One of the best-known organization-wide incentive systems is the **Scanlon Plan**.[36] Developed in the 1930s by Joseph Scanlon, president of a United Steelworkers of America local, it seeks to bring about cooperation between management and employees through the sharing of problems, goals, and ideas. (It is interesting to note that many of the quality circle programs instituted in the 1980s were a direct outgrowth of the Scanlon Plan.[37]) Under Scanlon, each department in the organization has a committee composed of supervisor and employee representatives. Suggestions for labour-saving improvements are funnelled to the committee, and, if accepted, cost savings and productivity gains are shared by all employees, not just the individual who made the suggestion. About 80 per cent of the suggestions prove practical and are adopted.

Wescast Industries, an Ontario auto parts manufacturer, in partnership with the Canadian Auto Workers union implemented a Scanlon approach in 1989 and attributes much of its success to this plan: sales increased from $27 million to $198 million, the number of plants rose from one to six, and the number of employees grew from 250 to over 1,150.[38]

Another incentive plan that gained momentum in the early 1990s is called **IMPROSHARE**.[39] IMPROSHARE, which is an acronym for "Improving Productivity through Sharing," uses a mathematical formula for determining employees' bonuses.[40] For example, if workers can save labour costs in producing a product, a predetermined portion of the labour savings will go to the employees. Where IMPROSHARE exists, productivity gains up to 18 per cent have been identified, with most of the gains coming from reduced defects and less production down time.[41]

Gainsharing is not limited to the private sector. The township of Pittsburgh, Ontario (population 11,500) established a gainsharing plan in 1993 for its workforce of forty-five full-time employees based on each employee submitting at least five cost-saving suggestions per year. Over two years, the township awarded gainsharing dividends of $700 and $875 to every employee, reduced its operating budget by 14 per cent, had no increases in property taxes, and had no staff lay-offs.[42] The Workers' Compensation Board of British Columbia and its union agreed to establish a gainsharing program beginning in 1998 to give staff a share of the savings generated by staff productivity improvements.[43]

Plant-Wide Incentives An incentive system that rewards all members of the plant based on how well the entire group performed.

Gainsharing Plant-wide incentive plans in which workers share in the organization's financial gains.

Scanlon Plan An organization-wide incentive program that distributes cost savings and productivity gains among all employees and emphasizes cooperation between management, union, and employees.

IMPROSHARE "Improving Productivity Through Sharing," an incentive plan that allocates employee bonuses through a mathematical formula based on cost or other savings.

In the private sector, profit-sharing plans such as the Royal Bank of Canada's plan mentioned earlier are becoming more common. They allow employees to share in the success of the firm by distributing part of the company's profits back to the workers. In a way, employees become owners of the company. Profit-sharing plans are considered to increase employees' commitment and loyalty to the organization. When employees encounter problems with customers or with the work process, it is in their best interest to take corrective action since they will be sharing in the benefits.

On the negative side, employees often find it difficult to relate their efforts to the profit-sharing bonus. Their individual impact on the organization's profitability may be minuscule. As well, factors such as economic conditions and actions of competitors—which are outside the control of the employees—may have a far greater impact on the company's profitability than any actions the employees take themselves.[44]

All the plant-wide incentives suffer from a dilution effect. It is hard for employees to see how their efforts contribute to the organization's overall performance. These plans also tend to distribute their pay-offs at wide intervals; a bonus paid in March 2000 for employees' efforts in 1999 loses a lot of its reinforcement impact. Finally, we should not overlook what happens when organization-wide incentives become both large and recurrent. When this happens, it is not unusual for the employees to begin to anticipate and expect the bonus as a matter of course and adjust their spending patterns in the assumption that the bonus will be a certainty. The bonus thus loses much of its motivating properties because employees see it as simply a membership-based reward.[45]

Competency-Based Compensation

So far in our discussion of establishing pay plans, we've implied one specific aspect of the process. That is, we pay for jobs. People who hold those jobs just happen to get the salary assigned to that position. That assumption, however, may be changing. Organizations like consulting firm Towers Perrin are advocating something radically different.[46] Rather than thinking of the job as the most critical aspect to the organization, such organizations view the people as an organization's competitive advantage. When that happens, compensation programs become ways of rewarding competencies or the "skills, knowledge, and behaviours"[47] employees possess. Let's look at how this system works.

Competency-Based Compensations Organizational pay system that rewards the employee's skills, knowledge, and behaviours.

The premise behind competency-based compensation programs is that individuals progress through a four-stage model of development—*apprentice, doer, mentor,* and *strategic leader*—sometimes referred to as job families.[48] During the first stage, *apprentice,* workers are dependent on the assistance of others. They perform their work under direct supervision and are considered new learners to the job. Salaries in this stage are the lowest. At the *doer* stage, employees begin to learn the job for which they were hired. They contribute significantly to achieving unit goals and have assumed some sense of independence and autonomy in performing their work. In other words, at the doer stage, we have an empowered employee. Hence, Stage II employees have greater competencies and thus are compensated at a greater rate than apprentices. At Stage III, the *mentor* stage, the employee now accepts greater responsibility for achieving unit goals. This may include developing others, setting unit goals, and having the responsibility and being held accountable for the unit's performance. In other words, the mentor becomes the facilitator and leader of the unit. Because of these added responsibilities, mentors are paid a higher salary than doers. The final stage is the *strategic leader.* Whereas the mentor has unit responsibilities, the strategic leader has organizational responsibilities. This means establishing the organization's direction as well as having responsibility for achieving those goals. The highest rate of pay, therefore, goes to individuals possessing strategic leader competencies.

What in essence has occurred is a pay scheme based on the specific competencies an employee possesses. These may include knowledge of the business and its core competencies, skills to fulfil these core requirements, and demonstrated employee behaviours such as leadership, problem solving, decision making, and planning.[49] Based on the degree to which these competencies exist, pay levels are established. For example, all individuals who are evaluated at the apprentice stage would be paid according to some pre-set level. In competency-based pay plans, these pre-set levels are called broadbanding (see Figure 13-6). That is, those who possess a level of competencies within a certain range will be grouped together in a pay category. Pay increases, then, are awarded for growth in personal competencies as well as the contribution one makes to the organization. Accordingly, career and pay advancement will not be tied to a promotion per se, but rather to how much more one is capable of contributing to the organization's goals and objectives.

You will recall that a few pages ago, in discussing the point method of job evaluation, we talked about assigning points to factors such as skill, experience, and working conditions. There seems to be something similar here. However, the point method looked specifically at the job and its worth to the company. Competency-based pay plans assesses these "points" based on the value added by the employee in assisting the organization in achieving its goals.

As more organizations move towards competency-based pay plans, HRM will play a critical role. Just as we discussed in Chapter 5 on strategic human resources planning, once the direction of the organization is established, attracting, developing, motivating, and retaining competent individuals becomes essential. This will continue to have implications for recruiting, training and development, career development, performance appraisals, as well as pay and reward systems.[50] Not only will HRM ensure that it has the right people at the right place, but it will have assembled a competent team of employees who will add significant value to the organization.

Team-Based Compensation

You've just been handed a copy of the syllabus for the business policy course you're taking this semester, and your eyes glance quickly at how the final grade will be calculated: two tests (a mid-term and a final) and a class project. Intrigued, you read further about the class project. You and four other classmates will be responsible for thoroughly analysing a failing company. The group is to make recommendations about the company's financial picture, human resources, product lines, competitive advantage, and strategic direction in a case paper of at least fifty double-spaced pages and make a thirty-minute presentation to the class about your suggested turnaround. The case paper and presentation account for 50 per cent of the course grade, and each member of the group will receive the same grade for the project. Not fair? Too much riding on the efforts of others? Welcome to the world of team-based rewards.

In today's changing organizations, much more emphasis has been placed on involving employees in most aspects of the job that affect them. When organizations group employees into teams and empower them to meet their goals, teams reap the benefits of their productive effort. That is, team-based rewards are tied to team-based performance, and that translates directly into their compensation. A

Broadbanding Grouping together several grades into wider bands, thus encouraging growth in personal competencies.

The more competencies an individual possesses the higher the stage they will attain and the larger their salary or wage will be.

Team-Based Rewards Rewards based on how well the team, not the individual employee, performed.

Meet

Keith MacAulay
Department Manager,
Sport Chek

Before 1997, employees at Sport Chek sporting goods stores were all paid straight wages. When the Sport Chek's parent company, the Forzani Group, decided to change all its stores to a commission plan, employees first greeted the concept with apprehension.

"There was some concern" that they would lose money or that the system wouldn't be fair, explains Keith MacAulay, department manager at the Crossroads Centre Sport Chek store in Winnipeg. As is often the case, the decision to change the compensation plan was made at the head office, but it was up to front-line managers such as MacAulay to implement it.

He listened sympathetically to his staff's concerns and helped them work out what the new system meant in real terms. "The grumbling stopped within a few months. It's worked out that just about everyone gets more money—employees are better paid, and profits went up."

Under the old system, MacAulay explains, employees were protected during slow periods, but during really busy times, they could be taken advantage of. "You might work like crazy, sell $5,000 worth of goods on a really busy day, and still take home just your regular wage."

Today, all Sport Chek employees, aside from cashiers and technical staff, are paid on a commission basis. The system has three levels. Part-time staff are on a straight commission. "You get 6 per cent of what you sell, period," says MacAulay, provided, of course, that it comes out to more than minimum wage. If the commission does not work out to more than minimum wage, then the staff member is paid minimum wage for the hours he or she worked. Full-time staff get a base amount per day plus a sliding-scale commission. The higher your sales, the greater the percentage of them you get to keep. Managers, too, receive a base salary and a small commission on sales they make, but they are also paid a portion of total store sales.

"So it's in my interests to make sure the store does well as a whole," points out MacAulay. That's why you can always find him out on the floor, amid the racks of shoes, biking shorts, and in-line skates, helping out his staff. With the right compensation plan, he finds, everybody wins.

---

benchmarking study by the Public Service Commission of Canada found that several major organizations in Ontario and Quebec were implementing team-based pay. [51] Several large multinational companies are also implementing team-based pay, including the Bank of Montreal,[52] American Express, and General Motors.[53]

Under a team-based compensation plan, team members who have worked on achieving and exceeding established goals often share equally in the rewards (although, in the truest sense, teams allocate their own rewards). By providing for fair treatment of each team member, group cohesiveness is encouraged.[54] This does not occur overnight; it is a function of several key components being in place.[55] For instance, for teams to be effective, they must have a clear purpose and goals. They must understand what is expected of them and that their

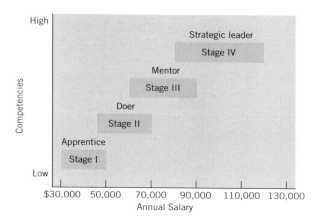

Figure 13-6
Competency-Based Pay Scale

effort is worthwhile. Teams must also be provided with the necessary resources to complete their tasks because their livelihood may rest on accomplishing their goals and a lack of requisite resources may doom a team effort before it begins. Finally, there must be mutual trust among the team members. They must respect one another, effectively communicate with one another, and treat each member fairly and equitably. Without these key components, serious obstacles to teams may exist, and this might defeat the purpose that group cohesiveness can foster.

Executive Compensation Programs

Executive pay is merely a special case within the topic of compensation, but it does have several twists that deserve attention. First, the base salaries of executives are higher than those of lower-level managers or operative personnel, and we want to explain why this is so. Second, executives frequently operate under bonus and stock-option plans that can dramatically increase their total compensation. In 1997, the CEOs of fifty Canadian firms earned between $2 million and $27 million in bonuses, exercised stock options, and other compensation, on top of salaries that ranged from $100,000 to $2.2 million.[56] We want to look briefly at how such compensations come about and why. Finally, executives receive perquisites or special benefits that others do not. What are these, and what is their impact on executive motivation?

Salaries of Top Managers

The salaries of the top managers in Canada's largest companies can certainly be impressive. In 1997, for example, Michael Brown president and CEO of Thomson Corp., had a salary of $2,215,040, while the president and chief operating officer of Northern Telecom, J.A. Roth, had a salary of $2,449,600,[57] and Bombardier's Laurent Beaudoin's salary was an even $1 million.[58] (This does not include the supplementary compensation we mentioned above and will discuss in more detail below.) A survey of thirty-nine large Canadian companies by William Mercer Ltd. revealed an average base salary of $607,000 for Canadian chief executives but a total pay package of $1.6 million.[59] When one considers that the average 1995 income of all Canadian workers, according to Statistics Canada, was $29,769,[60] these salaries certainly look like a *lot* of money.

How do organizations justify such extraordinary salaries for their executives (see "Ethical Decisions in HRM")? The answer is quite simple: economics and motivation.[61] In economic terms, we know that top managers are expected to demonstrate good decision-making abilities—a rare commodity. As a result, the supply of qualified senior executives is scarce, and organizations have to bid up the price for this talent. They must keep their salaries in line with the competition or potentially lose an executive to another organization.

There is additional competitive concern in Canada that top talent could be lost to the United States which boasts the highest executive salaries in the world. The Mercer study mentioned above revealed an average US CEO salary of US$790,000—US$3.17 million when bonuses and long-term incentives are included.[62] That was approximately $1.1 million and $4.3 million in Canadian dollars at the exchange rates prevailing in 1997. In other words, Canadian CEOs earn only 37 per cent of what their American equivalents do. This is without considering extreme cases like the US$203 million that Disney's Michael Eisner earned in 1993.[63]

In general, there is agreement that people higher in the corporate hierarchy should be paid more. After all, they have more responsibilities and their actions and decisions have a direct impact on the organization's performance. The difficulty arises in determining how much more they should be paid. As we have seen, competitive criteria (what other top managers are paid) enter into the equation. Also, one would expect the executives of larger and more profitable companies to be paid more, but the relationship is not always so clear. The top earners of 1997 were Power Financial Corp.'s president and CEO Robert Gratton (total earnings of $27.4 million) and Onex Corp.'s chairman and president Gerald Schwartz (total earnings of $18.8 million). But Power Financial had revenues of $8.3 billion (up 23 per cent from the previous year) and profits of $603 million (up 61 per cent), while Onex had revenues of $11.2 billion (up 27 per cent) but profits of only $54.4 million (*down* 37 per cent).[64] Another criterion might be the value of the organization's stock: if it rises, then the CEO is doing a good job and deserves a higher salary. It has been suggested that on this basis, the CEOs of many of Canada's largest corporations are probably being overpaid while the CEOs of smaller, more dynamic companies are being underpaid.[65]

Finally, high compensation serves both to attract managers to those positions, and presumably encourages them to perform well. But it also attracts ambitious and competent people to the lower-level jobs, stimulating them to work hard so they can move up the corporate ladder and finally earn those enormous salaries.

Supplemental Financial Compensation

The average compensation of the CEOs of TSE 300 firms was in excess of $700,000 in 1996.[66] This figure includes their total compensation—base salary plus bonuses and stock options. Bonuses and stock options dramatically increase the total compensation that executives receive. Much of this additional compensation is obtained through a deferred bonus—that is, the executive's bonus is computed on the basis of some formula, usually taking into account increases in sales and profits. This bonus, although earned in the current period, is distributed over several future periods. Therefore, it is not unusual for an executive to earn a $500,000 bonus but have it paid out at $50,000 a year for ten years. The major purpose of such deferred compensation, aside from possible tax advantages, is to tie the executive more closely to the organization and increase the cost of leaving. In almost all cases, executives who voluntarily terminate their employment must forfeit their deferred bonuses. One of the main

Ethical Decisions in HRM:

Are Executives Overpaid?

Are executives overpaid? Is an average salary of almost $1 million justifiable? In any debate, there are two sides to the issue. In support of these salaries is the fact that these individuals have tremendous responsibilities, not only to manage the organization today, but to keep it moving into the future. Their jobs are not 9-to-5 jobs, but rather six to seven days a week, often ten to fourteen hours a day. If jobs are evaluated on the basis of skills, knowledge, abilities, and responsibilities, executives surely should be highly paid. Furthermore, there is the issue of motivation and retention. If you want these individuals to succeed and stay with the company, you must provide a compensation package that motivates them to stay. Incentives based on various measures also provide the impetus for them to excel.

On the other hand, most of the research done on executive salaries questions the linkage to performance. Even in down years, executives are paid handsomely. Canadian chief executives average over $700,000 per year in total compensation. That is some twenty-four times the average income of Canadian workers, and in some organizations, the difference between top and bottom is even more remarkable: the CEOs of Canada's six major banks averaged well over $3 million in total compensation in 1997. That is over 100 times the salary of the banks' lowest paid workers. Some people are concerned. Shareholder rights activist Yves Michaud successfully sued two of the banks to force them to put his proposal—to cap top executives' pay at twenty times the average bank employee's earnings—to a vote at the banks' annual meetings. (It was defeated.)

One argument for the pay levels of Canadian CEOs is that American top executives earn even more: on average, over US$3 million. In fact, American company executives are regarded as some of the highest paid people in the world. It is estimated that these individuals make nearly 150 times the salary that their employees do. The average CEOs make almost $1,500 an hour, whereas the average worker makes just over $10 an hour. It is argued that this enormous difference reinforces the attitude that employees of the organization are second-rate.

Are our executives overpaid? What's your opinion?

Source: Andrew Coyne, "By All Accounts, It's Tough To Judge a Banker's Worth," *The Ottawa Citizen* (January 16, 1997); David Berman, "Do They Deserve It?" *Canadian Business* (September 26, 1997), pp. 31-33; Ford S. Worthy, "Still Making Out on Wall Street," *Fortune* (April 6, 1992), p. 71; See also Judith H. Dobrzynski, "CEO Pay: Something Should Be Done—But Not by Congress," *Business Week* (February 3, 1992), p. 29; and Michael A. Verespej, "Pay-for-Skills, Its Time Has Come," *Industry Week* (June 15, 1992), p. 29.

---

reasons why there are so few voluntary resignations among the ranks of senior management at General Motors, for example, is that these executives would lose hundreds of thousands of dollars in deferred income.

Interestingly, another form of bonus, the "hiring bonus," has arisen in the last decade, purposely designed to help senior executives defray the loss of de-

Stock Options An incentive plan that permits executives to purchase company shares at some time in the future at the price set at the moment the option is granted, thus encouraging them to work towards increasing the value of the company's shares.

Golden Parachute An approach to protecting executives in the case of a hostile turnover by providing either severance pay or guaranteed positions.

Perquisites Benefits that are made available to executives; commonly called "perks."

ferred income. It is now becoming increasingly popular to pay senior executives a hiring bonus to sweeten the incentive for them to leave their current employer and forfeit their deferred bonuses and pension rights. These bonuses often do provide deferred income to compensate for loss of pension rights.

Stock options also have been a common incentive offered to executives. They generally allow executives to purchase a specific amount of the company's stock at a fixed price at some time in the future. Under the assumption that good management will increase the company's profitability and, therefore, the price of the stock, stock options are viewed as a type of performance-based incentive. It should be pointed out, however, that the use of stock options is heavily influenced by the tax laws: changes to tax regulations can make stock options less attractive.

Another challenge to stock options is that, if executives do not exercise their options, they do not lose money directly if the share price drops, as they would if they owned the shares. So some companies, such as AT&T and General Motors, are now requiring their senior executives to actually own a certain number of shares and thus have a stronger commitment to the company's success.[67]

A benefit for top executives that has become popular with the growth of mergers, takeovers, and downsizing is the golden parachute. This was designed by top executives as a means of protecting themselves from a merger or hostile takeover. These "parachutes" provide either a severance salary to the departing executive or a guaranteed position in the newly created (merged) operation.

Supplemental Non-Financial Compensation: Perquisites

Executives are frequently offered a smorgasbord of perquisites not offered to other employees. From the organization's perspective, the logic of offering these perks is to attract and keep good managers and to motivate them to work hard in the organization's interest. In addition to the standard benefits offered to all employees (see Chapter 14), some benefits are reserved for privileged executives. They include such things as an annual physical examination and interest-free loans of millions of dollars which can be worth $100,000 a year or more. Popular perks include the payment of life insurance premiums, club memberships, company automobiles, liberal expense accounts, supplemental disability insurance, supplemental retirement accounts, post-retirement consulting contracts, and personal financial, tax, and legal counselling.[68]

Pay Secrecy

Pay Secrecy The practice of keeping information on pay strictly confidential.

At this point we would like to introduce a brief comment on the issue of pay secrecy. The practice in Canada (as in much of the world) has usually been to consider pay confidential—a matter between the employee, the employee's superiors (and, of course, the HRM and payroll units), and Revenue Canada. There are, of course, exceptions to this practice: wages in unionized companies are a matter of public record and are clearly spelled out in the labour contract. At the other end of the scale, regulations of the Ontario Securities Commission specify that the total compensation of the five highest-paid employees of companies traded on the Toronto Stock Exchange must be revealed in the companies' annual statements. (A similar requirement was set out by the Securities Exchange Commission for the New York Stock Exchange.) In Ontario, the compensation of all public sector employees earning more than $100,000 a year must be made public.

Most specialists believe that pay secrecy is a bad idea because it hides the link between pay and performance and can lead to dissatisfaction with pay. Employees will still speculate on how much others are earning and will tend to assume that other workers are getting more than they really are. Further, if they do not see that the good performers are earning more than the bad performers, they will have no reason to believe that management does, indeed, reward performance. A very old story had a boss telling a new employee: "Now remember, salaries are confidential. You should not discuss your salary with anyone." The employee responded: "Don't worry, boss. I'm as ashamed of my salary as you are!" The only justification for pay secrecy is bad pay administration practices, and that's a pretty weak excuse.

Stock options are a common incentive used to attract top managers. The executives have the option of buying stock at a set price any time in the future.

International Compensation

Probably the most complex function of international human resources management is the design and implementation of an equitable compensation program in a multinational organization.[69] The first step in designing an international compensation package is to determine if there will be one policy applying to all employees or whether parent-country nationals (PCNs), host-country nationals (HCNs), and third-country nationals (TCNs) will be treated differently. Currently, it is common to differentiate among types of expatriate assignments (temporary or permanent transfer) or employee status (executive, professional, or technical). It is also necessary to thoroughly understand the statutory requirements of each country to ensure compliance with local laws.[70] International compensation packages in Canada generally utilize the "balance-sheet approach" which considers four factors: base pay, differentials, incentives, and assistance programs.[71]

Base Pay

Ideally, this is equal to the pay of employees in comparable jobs at home, but the range of pay scales in many countries is far narrower than in Canada. Thus, where a middle manager in a Canadian factory might earn $70,000 a year, the same manager in a US factory might earn US$60,000 (almost $90,000) a year, and in Germany, $120,000. However, a US higher-level executive might earn US$500,000, her counterparts in Canada $300,000, and in Germany $230,000. How can human resources managers satisfy the middle manager who earns a third less than the counterpart where he works while also satisfying the German executive who earns less than her Canadian or American counterpart?

In addition to considerations of fairness among overseas employees, foreign currencies and laws must be considered. Should expatriates be paid in Canadian dollars, the local currency, or a combination of the two? How will the organization deal with changes in currency values? Are there restrictions on either bringing in or taking out dollars or the local currency? If so, how will savings be handled? Should salary increases be made according to the same standards used for domestic employees or by local standards? Will the expatriate pay Canadian or foreign income taxes?

Taxation is a major factor in calculating equitable base pay rates. If there are substantial differences in tax rates (for instance, in Sweden where income taxes are about 50 per cent), will the base pay be adjusted for the actual loss of net income? What about assignments to the United States where income tax rates are lower than in Canada? What happens when the employee returns to Canada with its higher taxes?

While Canada has negotiated agreements with many countries to determine which country will collect the income taxes, there are still new administrative requirements for the organization with regard to such taxes. Almost all multinational corporations have some tax protection plan so that the expatriate doesn't pay more in taxes than if she were in her home country.

Differentials

The cost of living is not the same around the world. A litre of gasoline may cost $0.60 in Toronto, but it's $1.70 in Lyon. The Big Mac meal that sells for less than $5 in Vancouver will cost you over $9 in Geneva. Pay differentials are intended to offset the higher costs of overseas goods, services, and housing. To set appropriate differentials, information can be obtained from a variety of sources, including the Canadian Department of Foreign Affairs, Industry and Trade. On a more anecdotal level, *The Economist* regularly publishes its Big Mac index, comparing the price of a standard product—the Big Mac—in dozens of cities around the world.

Incentives

Not all employees are willing to be separated from family, friends, and the comforts of home for long periods of time. Thus, inducements to go on foreign assignments are regularly offered. These may include monetary payments or services such as housing, car, chauffeur, and other incentives. How should a hardship premium be paid? As a percentage of salary? In a lump-sum payment? In the home or the foreign currency? If foreign housing is provided, what happens to the vacant home back in Canada? How is the family housed when they eventually return? Incentives require careful planning before, during, and after the overseas assignment.

Assistance Programs

As with any relocation, the overseas transfer requires a lot of expenditures for the employee's family. Some of the assistance programs commonly offered by multinational corporations include: household goods shipping and storage; major appliances; legal clearance for pets and their shipment; home sale/rental protection; automobile protection; temporary living expenses; travel, including pre-relocation visits and annual home leaves; special/emergency return leaves; education allowances for children; club memberships (for corporate entertaining); and security, including electronic systems and bodyguards.

Clearly, the design of a compensation system for employees working overseas is complex and requires enormous administrative expertise, particularly when an organization has expatriates posted in forty or fifty different countries.

Designing and implementing an equitable compensation program in a multinational organization is probably the most complex function of international HRM.

Study Tools and Applications

Summary

This summary relates to the Learning Objectives provided on p. 376.
After having read this chapter, you should know:

1. Rewards are the final link in the motivation model. After the effort has been expended, successful performance happens, organizational goals are achieved, and individuals are now ready to have their individual goals met. These goals or rewards can come in a variety of types.
2. Rewards can be classified as (1) intrinsic or extrinsic, (2) financial or non-financial, or (3) performance-based or membership-based.
3. Some rewards are membership-based because one receives them for simply belonging to the organization. Employee benefits are an example of membership-based rewards—every employee gets them irrespective of performance.
4. Compensation management seeks to design a cost-effective pay structure that will not only attract, motivate, and retain competent employees, but also be perceived as fair.
5. Job evaluation systematically determines the value of each job in relation to all jobs within the organization. The four basic approaches to job evaluation are: the ranking method, the classification method, the factor comparison method, and the point method.
6. The final wage and salary structure evolves from job evaluation input, wage and salary survey data, and the creation of wage and salary grades.
7. Competency-based compensation views employees as a competitive advantage in the organization. Compensation systems are established in terms of the knowledge and skills employees possess and the behaviours that they demonstrate. Possession of these three factors is evaluated and compensated according to a broadbanded salary range established by the organization.
8. Executive compensation is higher than that of rank-and-file personnel and also includes other financial and non-financial benefits not available to other employees. This is done to attract, retain, and motivate executives to higher performance levels.
9. Pay secrecy can lead to dissatisfaction with pay by obscuring the relationship between performance and rewards.
10. The balance-sheet approach to international compensation takes into account base pay, differentials, incentives, and assistance programs.

Key Terms

broadbanding
classification method
compensation management
competency-based compensation
equal pay legislation
extrinsic rewards
factor comparison method
gainsharing
golden parachute
IMPROSHARE
intrinsic rewards
job evaluation
membership-based rewards
merit pay

pay secrecy
performance-based rewards
perquisites
piecework plan
plant-wide incentives
point method
ranking method
Scanlon Plan
stock options
team-based rewards
wage and salary curves
wage and salary structure
wage and salary surveys

EXPERIENTIAL EXERCISE:

Determining Pay Increases

For most people, their annual pay raise may be the most concrete information they have on how the organization evaluates their performance. Therefore, whether you as a manager intend it or not, a pay raise will be seen by the employee as a reward for last year's work performance. Conversely, the employee may perceive no raise or a minimal one as a punishment. In behavioural terms, with the size of the pay raise, you either positively or negatively reinforce last year's performance. Therefore, the pay raise can either be motivating or demotivating, depending on how the employee views the connection between good performance and financial issues. Issues of fairness, equity, and the motivation process are thus involved in people's reaction to pay decisions.

Purpose

1. Provide practice in making salary decisions.
2. Evaluate and weigh different sources of information about employee performance.
3. Develop skills in applying motivation theory to compensation decisions.

Step 1

Read the instructions on the "Employee Profile Sheet" (provided by your instructor), and then individually decide on a percentage pay increase for each of the eight employees.

Step 2

Form teams of three to five members. Each team member should report his or her recommendations for pay increases, and the team should reach consensus on pay increases for the eight employees. Your team should also justify these raises, explaining the criteria for these choices.

Step 3

Each team will turn in to the instructor their recommended increases and the new salaries for each of the eight employees. Your instructor will record and post them. Each group will then briefly explain the criteria for their decisions. Specifically: what factors affected your pay raise decisions? What are the reasons for basing pay raises on each of these factors? What do you believe the behavioural effects will be for basing pay increases on these factors?

Step 4

The entire class will discuss briefly the differences between the pay raises and the factors that went into these decisions. Particular attention should be directed to employees for whom there was a wide variation in pay increases recommended by the different teams.

Source: Based on "Motivation Through Compensation," in Roy J. Lewicki, Donald D. Bowen, Douglas T. Hall, and Francine S. Hall, *Experiences in Management and Organizational Behavior* (New York: John Wiley, 1988), pp. 49-51. Used with permission.

CASE APPLICATION:

Husky Injection Molding Systems

Headquartered in Bolton, Ontario, Husky is a successful manufacturer of injection moulding machinery.[72] The company grew at 25 per cent annually from 1985 to 1995 and is credited with making significant contributions to the success of Canada's plastics industry. Its record in human resources management is just as remarkable. In the opinion of management consultant and author Jim Collins, this is because of the value system of Husky's founder Robert Schad.

The company's 1,700 employees work in sixteen different countries in an atmosphere of egalitarianism. Executive offices are small and Spartan; dress is casual. All employees share the same parking lots, dining rooms, and washrooms. The company pays wages and salaries that are among the highest in the industry and has profit-sharing and share-purchase plans (currently 25 per cent of shares are owned by employees). While the company is still privately owned (65 per cent of the shares are owned by Schad and his family and 10 per cent by Komatsu, a Japanese heavy equipment maker), employees receive an annual report as well as a monthly newsletter that provides details of the company's performance.

Husky's headquarters are spotlessly clean and well lit. The building is entirely air-conditioned and smoke-free (Schad made his plants smoke-free long before it was mandatory or even fashionable). The company cafeterias serve healthy meals at subsidized prices; herbal teas are free and there are no vending machines. Employees receive a $500 annual benefit for vitamins. A fitness centre, medical doctor, chiropractor, naturopath, nurse, and massage therapist are available. The company's $5-million childcare centre is one of the best of its kind. And the company pays 100 per cent of the tuition and book costs of employees who attend a college or university.

Husky is a high-pressure work environment; Schad is a demanding boss who has been known to chew out employees for poor performance. It is said that in the company's early days, Schad would walk through the shop, checking that the draftsmen's T-squares were just so; if they weren't, he'd knock them onto the floor.

The company does well financially, but other indicators are encouraging too: absenteeism is 2.4 days per year per employee versus an industry average of nine days. Husky spends $153.70 per employee on drugs compared to the industry average of $459.02. There are also fewer Workers' Compensation Board claims and more accident-free days than the industry average.

Questions

1. Evaluate Husky's reward system. What are its strong points?
2. Although Husky is a very demanding work environment, most employees appear to be happy to work there. What contributes to this feeling?
3. There is no information in this case on the pay of Husky executives. Would you expect it to be much higher than that of lower-level employees? Why or why not?

How well did you fulfil the learning objectives?

1. Employees respond to organizational rewards for all of these reasons except
   a. people behave in ways that they believe are in their best interest.
   b. people constantly look for pay-offs for their efforts.
   c. people expect that good job performance will lead to organizational goal attainment that will lead to satisfying individual needs or goals.
   d. organizations use rewards to motivate employees.
   e. employees often respond to peer pressure.

2. What is the difference between financial and non-financial rewards?
   a. Financial rewards (such as salary) are taxable. Non-financial rewards (such as daycare spending accounts) provide tax shelters.
   b. Financial rewards are a matter of public record. Non-financial rewards are not a matter of public record.
   c. Financial rewards make life better off the job. Non-financial rewards make life better on the job.
   d. Financial rewards are fixed according to a compensation schedule. Non-financial rewards are variable in nature.
   e. Financial rewards provide the same motivation levels for all employees. Non-financial rewards provide differing levels of motivation.

3. Good organizational reward systems have all of the following qualities except
   a. they are individualized to reflect differences in what employees consider important to them.
   b. they are perceived as equitable.
   c. they are visible and flexible.
   d. they are based on seniority.
   e. they are allocated at a relatively low cost.

4. In the context of a compensation system, fairness means all of the following except
   a. a wage adequate for the demands of the job, from the organization's perspective.
   b. employees' perception of an appropriate balance in terms of their effort-rewards ratio compared to a relevant standard.
   c. employees' perception that they are treated better than similar workers in competing organizations.
   d. pay rates are established according to a job's comparative worth.
   e. reasonable cost minimization by organizations.

5. A compensation analyst for a large firm is completing a job evaluation for her organization. Identifiable criteria for jobs (skill, effort, responsibility) were deter-

mined, and points were assigned based on weighting factors. Several degrees of competency were identified for each of the job criteria. All jobs were then categorized according to these rating scales. What job evaluation method was used?
   a. Ranking.
   b. Classification.
   c. Factor comparison.
   d. Point method.
   e. Core specification.

6. Rachel works for a textile manufacturer as a seamstress. She is paid five cents for each sleeve she sews an hour, up to 100 sleeves. She is paid nine cents for each sleeve she produces over the first 100. What kind of compensation system is used?
   a. Piecework.
   b. Time-saving bonus.
   c. Commission.
   d. Scanlon Plan.
   e. IMPROSHARE.

7. Last year, an aerospace engineer made $110,000. His annual base pay was $100,000. The remainder was calculated based on his ability to work faster than the standard hour's work. What kind of compensation system was used?
   a. Piecework.
   b. Time-saving bonus.
   c. Commission.
   d. Scanlon Plan.
   e. IMPROSHARE.

8. Competency-based compensation systems can best be described as
   a. paying employees according to their knowledge, skills, and demonstrated behaviours.
   b. paying employees according to how educated they are and the number of advanced degrees they possess.
   c. pay systems that promote team-based incentives.
   d. incentive systems whereby strategic goals of the organization are replaced by the value-added nature of employee skills.
   e. paying employees according to a piecework system whereby a sophisticated formula is used to determine the dollar value of the employee's bonus.

9. Team-based compensation programs reward employees for achieving unit and organizational goals. Under which situation would a team-based compensation most likely function well?
   a. A situation where a team of workers perform mutually exclusive, independent tasks.
   b. A situation where a team of workers have mutual distrust for one another.

c. A situation where work tasks are woven together such that the work of any one individual is difficult to assess.

d. A situation where competition among employees is encouraged and fostered.

e. A situation where group values conform to limiting production.

10. Canadian organizations justify high salaries for their executives in all of these ways except

a. good decision-making ability is not widely represented in the workforce.

b. global competition requires that Canada match the salaries given to executives in other countries.

c. organizations must pay high prices for scarce executives.

d. high salaries are necessary to keep executives from going over to the competition.

e. high executive salaries attract good workers throughout managerial levels of an organization.

11. Bill, a Canadian computer programmer, reluctantly moved his family to Saudi Arabia for a three-year assignment with his firm. A hardship premium, equal to his annual Canadian salary, was deposited in a Canadian account for each six months of his assignment. What kind of pay factor was used?

a. Base pay.

b. Differentials.

c. Bonuses.

d. Incentives.

e. Assistance programs.

12. All of the following questions should be addressed when considering base pay for expatriates except:

a. Is the cost of living the same in the host country as in Canada?

b. Will the expatriate pay Canadian or foreign income tax?

c. Should expatriates be paid in Canadian dollars or local currency?

d. Are there restrictions on taking money into or out of the host country?

e. Should salary increases be made according to local standards or Canadian standards?

13. Membership-based rewards include all of the following except

a. cost-of-living allowances.

b. benefit provisions.

c. pay increases for seniority.

d. pay increases for completion of a college or university degree.

e. commissions.

14. Compensation management is

a. more heavily influenced by government policies than is strategic human resources planning.

b. less influenced by government policies than is strategic human resources planning.

c. less influenced by government policies than is orientation.

d. influenced at the provincial but not the national level.

e. influenced at the national but not the provincial level.

15. Canadian executives

a. are the highest paid in the world.

b. earn, on average, about one hundred times what the average Canadian worker does.

c. should have their earnings capped at twenty times the average pay of workers in their companies.

d. earn, on average, about 37 per cent of what comparable American managers earn.

e. earn, on average, about 67 per cent of what comparable American managers earn.

16. Pay adjustments designed to maintain the standard of living for an expatriate that she would enjoy at home are called

a. Base pay.

b. Differentials.

c. Bonuses.

d. Incentives.

e. Assistance programs.

Chapter Fourteen

EMPLOYEE BENEFITS

LEARNING OBJECTIVES

AFTER READING THIS CHAPTER, YOU WILL BE ABLE TO:

1. Describe the growth in employee benefits.
2. Discuss why employers offer benefits to their employees.
3. Explain the link of benefits to motivation.
4. Distinguish between the main types of benefits: employee security, pay for time not worked, and services.
5. Describe the role of federal and provincial governments in the provision of employee benefits.
6. Describe the working of the Canada/Quebec Pension Plan.
7. Distinguish between different forms of pay for time not worked.
8. Discuss the advantages and disadvantages of flexible benefit plans.
9. Identify new trends in employee benefits such as wellness programs and family-friendly benefits.
10. Discuss the role of benefits within the organization's overall HRM strategy.

It is not surprising that one of the most popular benefits for Sony Music Canada's employees is the opportunity to purchase Sony products—from television sets to the latest CDs—at a discount from the employee store in the company's Don Mills headquarters.[1] It was quite a challenge to develop a modern benefits package: on the one hand, Sony Music is a global company with employees from around the world working on projects in an extremely dynamic industry; on the other, it is a relatively small Canadian company with just 360 employees.

A comprehensive employee survey was the first step. The survey revealed that employees wanted more choices so that they could choose the benefits that best suited their needs and lifestyle. The ideal would have been a fully flexible benefits plan, including benefit credits, but that was not feasible for a plan with fewer than 400 members. So, together with benefits consultant Towers Perrin and insurance underwriter Sun Life, Sony developed a program called *Benefits Options* with a required core and three modular, optional benefits choices.

Focus groups were used to involve employees in the design of the program and the communication materials. At the launch in January 1997, employees received a guide to the program and information through e-mail as well as invitations to attend "lunch-and-learn" seminars and information sessions. Information is very important in a flexible plan because employees must make choices regarding their coverage, including varying reimbursement levels. The company's quarterly newsletter carries information on health and wellness designed to help employees make good choices.

The new plan is much more cost-effective than the traditional benefits plan it replaced. The company is not spending any more money than before but is providing a selection of benefits that fits employees' needs much better. "We are definitely getting better value for our benefits dollar," says Vanessa Lewerentz, Sony's manager of compensation and benefits.

●

Employee Benefits Membership-based, non-financial rewards, such as insurance, pensions, vacations, and other services, designed to attract and retain employers.

Introduction

When an organization is designing its overall compensation program, one of the critical areas of concern is what benefits should be provided. Today's workers expect more than just an hourly wage or a salary from their employer; they want additional considerations that will enrich their lives. These considerations in an employment setting are called employee benefits.[2]

Employee benefits have grown in importance and variety over the past several decades. Once a small additional cost to the employer—which is why you will still come across the term "fringe benefits"—they are now an important part of the total compensation package. Benefits administration has developed into a complex business activity. Employers realize that the benefits provided to employees have an impact on whether applicants accept their job offers, or, once employed, whether workers will continue to stay with the organization. Benefits, therefore, are necessary components of an effectively functioning compensation program.

The irony, however, is that while benefits must be offered to attract and retain good workers, benefits as a whole do not directly affect a worker's performance. Benefits are generally membership-based, offered to employees regardless of their performance levels. While this does not appear to be a logical business practice, there is evidence that the absence of adequate benefits and services for employees contributes to employee dissatisfaction and increased

TABLE 14-1   A Classification of Employee Benefits in Canada

Type of benefit	Comments
Employee Security	
Workers' compensation	Legally required
Employment insurance	Legally required (called Unemployment Insurance until 1997)
Health insurance	Legally required: provincial health and hospital insurance plans
	Voluntary: private health insurance plans
Pensions	Legally required: Canada/Quebec Pension Plans
	Voluntary: Registered Pension Plans, Group RRSPs (regulated by federal and provincial laws)
Other group insurance	Voluntary: group life insurance, etc.
Pay for Time Not Worked	
Vacations	Legally required
Paid holidays	Legally required
Personal days off	Voluntary
Other leaves	Some are legally required (e.g., maternity leave)
Breaks	
Services	
Employee Assistance Programs	
Wellness Programs	
Counselling	
Subsidized Meals	
Discounts on company products and services	
Education support	A tax-free benefit only if the education program is directly job-related
Other	Voluntary and limited only by the imagination

absenteeism and turnover.[3] Accordingly, because the negative impact of failing to provide adequate benefits is so great, organizations spend tens of billions of dollars annually to ensure that valuable benefits are available for each worker.

Over the decades, the nature of benefits has changed drastically, and the benefits offered in the early 1900s clearly were different from those offered today. Then, much emphasis was placed on time off from work. As the first personnel departments arrived on the scene, their main emphasis was to ensure that workers were happy and healthy. This meant that their responsibility was to administer such benefits as scheduled vacations, company picnics, and other social activities for workers. Later, around the late 1930s, the practice of having employees complete a sign-up card for some type of health insurance came about. Those simple days are long gone. Legislation, labour unions, and the changing workforce have all led to growth in benefit offerings. Today's organizational benefits are more widespread, more creative, and clearly more abundant. As indicated in Table 14-1, the benefits offered in the 1990s clearly are designed to ensure something of value for each worker.

The High Cost of Benefits

Most of us are aware of inflation and the impact it has had on the wages and salaries of virtually every job in Canada. It seems incredible that only sixty years ago, a worker earning $100 a week was ranked among the top 10 per cent of wage earners in Canada. Although we are aware that hourly wages and monthly salaries have increased in recent years, we often overlook the more rapid growth in benefits offered to employees. Since the cost of employing workers includes both direct compensation and the corresponding benefits and services, the growth in both benefits and services has resulted in dramatic increases in labour costs to organizations. In 1953, the cost of employee benefits was about 15 per cent of payroll. By 1992, according to a Conference Board of Canada survey, the average cost of benefits was 26.9 per cent of payroll, and some organizations reported as much as 52 per cent.[4]

Employers have also found that benefits present attractive areas of negotiation when large wage and salary increases are not feasible. For example, if employees were to purchase life insurance on their own, they would have to pay for it with net dollars, that is, with what they have left after paying taxes. If the organization pays for it, the benefit is non-taxable.

Benefits for the Twenty-First Century

There has been a dramatic increase in the number and types of benefits offered and an equally sensational increase in their costs. What has triggered the sweeping changes in benefits that will carry us into the new millennium? The answer to that question lies, in part, in the demographic composition of the workforce.

Benefits offered to employees reflect many of the trends existing in our labour force. As the decades have witnessed drastic changes in educational levels, family status, and employee expectations, benefits have had to be adjusted to meet the needs of the workers.[5] What specifically have we seen over the past few decades with respect to demographic changes? Let's explore a few factors to show why the benefits offered today are different from those of thirty years ago.

In Chapter 2, we discussed the changing workforce; now let's look at this issue with an eye on benefits. As recently as the early 1960s, the workforce was comprised of a relatively homogeneous group—predominantly males. This typical male had a wife who stayed home and cared for their children, thus necessitating a relatively standard benefit. In other words, most of these workers required a retirement plan, sick leave, vacation time, and health insurance. Providing these to workers was customary and, for the most part, uncomplicated. However, the typical worker of the early 1960s is rare in today's workforce. Dual-career couples, singles, singles with children, and individuals caring for their parents (elder care) are now widely prevalent in the workforce. Just as important, if still somewhat controversial, is the issue of benefit coverage for an unmarried worker's significant other. As a result of such events, organizations must be able to satisfy diverse benefit needs. Consequently, organizational benefit programs are being forced to take on different focuses in order to achieve the goal of something of value for each worker (see "What If: HRM in a De-Jobbed Organization").

The Link to Motivation

Wait a minute! The link to motivation? In the last chapter and even a few paragraphs ago, we stated that benefits are membership-based and are provided to employees regardless of performance. How, then, can they be linked to motivation?

Let's review the motivation process we discussed in Chapter 11 (see Figure 14-1). Benefits may become a critical link to this process if organizations tailor them to meet the specific needs of employees. For instance, if all employees are given the same benefits package regardless of their situation or needs (the traditional approach), then, yes, benefits may have little effect on their motivation. But, if employees have the opportunity to pick and choose the benefits most useful to them, then behaviour can be influenced. Let's explain this using a classroom analogy.

FIGURE 14-1

Benefits and the Link to Motivation

Your professor has laid out a syllabus that attempts to meet your specific needs. In it, the instructor informs students that his policy is to permit each student to drop one test score—their lowest grade of the four exams scheduled in the course. While that consideration (benefit) may be available to everyone, it may not be appealing enough to you. After all, you still have to take all four exams, and, generally, you have done well in classes like this. Getting four As on the exams and getting to drop one for final grade determination may not meet your individual goal. Hence, its effect on your performance may be minimal. However, this professor is well known and respected in the surrounding business community. You know that a letter of recommendation from him to specific company representatives could provide you with the edge you need to land that great job you want after graduation. However, he doesn't write letters of recommendation freely. Instead, you notice on his syllabus that he will write letters only for students in the top 5 per cent of the class. This benefit is of value to you, so you will perform so as to be included in that select group and fulfil your individual goal.

What If:

HRM in a De-Jobbed Organization

Benefits in a de-jobbed organization—even the sound of that is something of an anomaly. Unquestionably, there are those in the contingent workforce who would argue that working part-time or even on a temporary basis better serves their personal needs. That is really not the point. The issue is what major changes those who are thrust into this de-jobbed arena will expect. For several areas of HRM, we have been laying out the what ifs, but none will hit home more than the area of benefits.

Our workforce is comprised of several generations of workers, many of whom enjoyed the richness that benefits administration had to offer. We felt comfortable that our health insurance would cover us in the event of a catastrophic illness. We knew that some retirement would be ours, as long as we put in the many years of hard work. We also planned our vacations to coincide with our children being out of school. But those benefits, and many others that we have grown accustomed to, simply may be a thing of the past.

For one thing, we will be working when the organization needs us, and our income will be determined largely by the actual work we perform. We will not have the luxury of having sick leave, for if we are not available to work on our projects, we won't get paid. Like the consultant who gets paid based on the number of hours actually worked, if you can't work today, you simply don't get your fees. Vacations, too, will become yesterday's dream. A vacation will likely be hard to plan because it will occur when you are between jobs. One project finishes up on Friday, and the next one doesn't begin for two weeks. Well, then, there's your vacation.

Similar analogies can be drawn to such benefits as leaves of absences, long-term disability, and other paid time off from work. They simply won't exist in their current form—that is, employer offered. Rather, as independent contractors, we will be expected to provide our own coverage through our own insurance plans. And don't forget about retirement. Over the past decade, we've been hearing that we need to save more for our own retirement—to augment the retirement income we may get from CPP and our company's pension plan. That advice will become even more important in the future when we, as individuals, have full responsibility for funding our retirment income, especially if reforms to the CPP are not enough to solve the expected funding challenges.

The days of having something added to make organizational life sweeter may be ending. As employees, we've always wanted benefits that best fit our needs. Benefits in the de-jobbed organization will permit just that, but how? Simply, we will personally buy only what we want. This is clearly not the vision that flexible-benefit advocates had in mind, but organizational life, like life in general, continues to evolve.

Source: Based on William Bridges, "The End of the Job," *Fortune* (September 19, 1994), pp. 72-73.

In the same way, it is possible for organizations to use their benefits programs to motivate their employees. We will discuss this in more detail later in this chapter, but first we will take a look at the different types of benefits that organizations currently provide their employees.

As we mentioned earlier, the area of compensation is one that is strongly affected by government regulation, and this is particularly the case with the benefits component of compensation. As we go through the different benefits, we will see that some are required by statute, while others are voluntary, although governments may regulate how many of the latter are provided.

This, in part, reflects the fact that society considers benefits important and, in part, responds to history. The growth in benefits in Canada may be traced to government controls. During World War II, when the Canadian government instituted wage and price control in 1941, employers could not give their workers pay increases, so instead they offered "fringe benefits" such as paid vacations to attract or retain workers.[6] Eventually, many of these benefits were enacted into legislation.

We will classify benefits into three groups: employee security, pay for time not worked, and services. Let us look at each of these in turn.

Ethical Decision in HRM:

Benefits and the Contingent Workforce

Hiring contingent workers can be a blessing for organizations. Contingent workers provide employers with a rich set of diverse skills on an as-needed, cost-effective basis. Likewise, workers who wish to work less than full-time are also given the opportunity to keep their skills sharp while, at the same time, balancing their commitment to personal matters and career.

Unfortunately, many contingent workforce members are not there by choice. Jobs have disappeared all too frequently, and the trend is growing. In fact, by the beginning of 1994, about 30 per cent of the North American workforce was made up of contingent workers, including part-time employees, people who contract directly with companies for specific projects, and temporary workers. Furthermore, many of these workers receive a lower rate of pay and accompanying benefits than full-time, core employees. For example, in Canada, 68 per cent of full-time workers have access to a private health plan, against only 18 per cent of part-timers. The gap is only slightly lower in pensions: 58 per cent of full-time workers have a private pension plan, compared to 19 per cent of part-timers.

So, is the movement towards contingent workers a management windfall that exploits workers? Should organizations be required to provide full benefits to its contingent workforce? Is legislation necessary to mandate this coverage? Or, do we simply argue that no change is necessary because many contingent workers choose their employment status, thereby reaping other benefits from blending personal and career factors? What's your opinion?

Source: J. Fierman, "The Contingent Work Force," *Fortune* (January 24, 1994), pp. 30-36, and Bruce Little, "Middle Kingdom: The Full-Scale Advantage of Full-Time Work," *The Globe and Mail* (July 14, 1997), p. A6.

Employee Security

Under this heading, we will consider programs that are intended to protect employees' income and well-being. They are by far the most important components of any benefit package in terms of cost.

Workers' Compensation

Workers' compensation is intended to cover employees for disability, injury, or death caused by a work-related accident. It is essentially a no-fault insurance program administered by the Workers' Compensation Boards in each province or territory, funded by premiums collected from the employers. The premium rate depends upon the risk factor in each industry: an accounting firm will pay a lower rate than a mining firm, for example. The trend in recent years has been to link premiums to individual firms' performance and thus to encourage and reward better safety practices in the workplace. In Ontario, firms with accident rates better than the industry average have their premiums reduced up to 10 per cent, while firms with very poor records could receive a surcharge of up to 50 per cent.[7] A new emphasis on workplace safety is reflected in the renaming of Ontario's Workers' Compensation Board as the Workplace Safety and Insurance Board on January 1, 1998.[8]

Workers' Compensation Payment to workers (or their heirs) for death or disability resulting from job-related activities.

Employment Insurance

The *Unemployment Insurance Act* was passed by the Canadian Parliament in 1940. It has been amended several times and in July 1996, a new **Employment Insurance** system came into effect. The system is intended to provide temporary income support to the unemployed so that individuals can locate jobs that suit their knowledge, skills, and abilities. Employees on strike or who have been locked out are not covered by EI.

EI is administered by the federal government and funded by contributions from both employers and employees. Premiums are tax deductible, and the benefits are considered taxable income by Revenue Canada. Unemployed workers qualify for EI if they have made contributions during a qualifying period, and they receive benefits after a waiting period, as stipulated in the act. There is a time limit on how long a person can receive EI benefits, which depends on both how long the individual has worked and the unemployment rate in the region. In general, benefits are 55 per cent of the person's insured earnings, to a maximum of $413 per week (in 1997). There are also special EI benefits for workers who are on maternity leave, sick, or injured.

Employment Insurance Administered by the federal government, it is intended to provide temporary income support to the unemployed while they search for jobs.

Some companies, particularly in the automotive industry, provide **supplemental unemployment benefits (SUBs)** to their laid-off workers. With a SUB, laid-off workers receive 95 per cent of their regular income, thus being encouraged to wait out the lay-off period and return to their employer rather than seek other jobs. The value to the employers is that they retain skilled and trained workers over periods of temporary lay-offs, which is important in a cyclical industry such as the automotive industry.

Supplemental Unemployment Benefits (SUBs) Payments available to laid-off workers in certain industries (particularly the automotive industry) that supplement the payments they receive from Employment Insurance.

Health Insurance

Health insurance is intended to provide individuals with the means to pay for medical services, hospital care, and the like. In Canada, we must consider two sources of insurance: the public and the private.

Health Insurance An insurance policy intended to provide individuals with the means to pay for medical services, hospital care, and the like.

●

Public Health Insurance
Health insurance available
to all residents of Canada
through programs adminis-
tered by the provinces and
territories with assistance
from the federal government.

Canada Health Act An act of
Parliament specifying the
conditions that provincial
health and hospital insurance plans must meet in order to receive assistance
from the federal government.

Private Health Insurance A
health insurance plan that
supplements public health
and hospital insurance coverage and is administered
through private insurance
companies.

Canada Pension Plan (CPP)
Public pension plan that operates throughout Canada
(excluding Quebec), providing pensions for workers
upon retirement.

Quebec Pension Plan (QPP)
Public pension plan that operates in Quebec providing
pensions for workers upon
retirement. The QPP is coordinated with the Canada
Pension Plan, and they operate virtually as one plan.

Public health insurance is available to all residents of Canada through health
and hospital insurance programs administered by the provinces and territories,
with assistance from the federal government. To receive federal assistance,
provinces must comply with the *Canada Health Act,* which requires that the plan
be administered on a non-profit basis by a public agency, must provide comprehensive coverage of hospital and medical service, must be universally available to
all residents of the province, and must be portable. Portablility means that coverage must be provided for people temporarily out of their province, and the waiting period for new residents must not exceed three months.[9] In some provinces
(Alberta and British Columbia), individuals must pay premiums, while in others
(Newfoundland, Ontario, and Quebec) there is a specific tax on employers.[10]

Provincial health and hospital insurance plans typically cover all doctor's fees,
hospital stays in public wards, nursing, laboratory services, use of operating
facilities, and emergency treatment. There is some variation from one province
to another as to details of the coverage as well as to the extent to which medical
expenses incurred outside of the province are reimbursed.

Practically all Canadian employers provide extended health insurance to their
employees.[11] About twenty million Canadians are covered by these private health
plans; total expenditure on private health insurance totalled more than $22 bil-
lion in 1996, almost one-third of total health care expenditures in Canada.[12] Private plans supplement the public health and hospital insurance and usually pay
for such expenses as semi-private or private rooms in hospitals, paramedical and
nursing services, prosthetics and other medical equipment, and prescription
drugs. Almost half of these plans are contributory (i.e., the employee pays part of
the costs), while the employer pays all of the costs in the rest.[13]

Most organizations now offer dental care plans which are separate from the
health care plans. Almost all dental plans cover major restorative care (crowns,
fixed bridges, dentures) as well as basic preventive care, while a majority of
plans also cover orthodontic care. Most of these plans are contributory. In almost all cases, plans are compulsory (all employees are covered) and provide
coverage to the employee's dependents. In order to control costs, there is usually a deductible for prescription drug reimbursements as well as for many types
of dental care.

Pensions

Pension plans are intended to provide workers with an income after they
have retired from the workforce and are the most complex of all employee benefits. As with health coverage, there are public and private plans.

Public Pension Plans The Canada Pension Plan (CPP) operates throughout
Canada except for Quebec, which has the similar Quebec Pension Plan (QPP).
Both plans are coordinated through a series of agreements, and benefits are received from the pension credits accumulated under either plan as if there was
only one plan.[14] The CPP and QPP were implemented on January 1, 1966 and
have been modified several times. The last change was on January 1, 1998, in
part to deal with fears that the funding would not be sufficient to meet pension
obligations early in the twenty-first century.[15] It transformed the CPP from pay-
as-you-go-financing (entirely from premiums) to fuller funding through income from investments of the Canada Pension Plan Fund.

The CPP is financed through contributions from employers, employees,
self-employed persons, and interest from the Canada Pension Plan Fund. All

persons who earn more than the year's basic exemption (YBE, frozen at $3,500) are covered. Contributions are made on the difference between the YBE and the year's maximum pensionable earnings (YMPE), which is linked directly to the average wage in Canada. The contribution rate was initially set at 3.6 per cent, but in 1997, it was set to rise in steps to a rate of 9.9 per cent in 2003. The contribution is split equally between employer and employee (self-employed workers contribute the full amount).

Contributors are entitled to a pension from the CPP from age sixty if they have stopped working (substantially ceased to be in pensionable employed). If they are over sixty-five they may receive a pension from the CPP even if they continue to work. The pension amount is based on the worker's earnings to a maximum of 25 per cent of the YMPE. In 1998, the maximum benefit rate for a worker retiring at age sixty-five was $744.79 per month.[16] The pension may be paid to the surviving spouse of a contributor who dies, although if the surviving spouse is under age thirty-five, he or she must wait until age sixty-five to collect the pension unless he or she is disabled or raising children. This has been appealed by British Columbia resident Nancy Law to the Supreme Court on the grounds of age discrimination.[17] There are also provisions for the payment of pensions to workers who must retire because of disability.[18] In 1998, almost 2.5 million people were receiving pensions from the CPP and over 800,000 from the QPP for a total expenditure of $1.3 billion per month[19].

Private Pension Plans   Many organizations offer private pension plans to supplement the CPP and QPP[20]. These plans are regulated by a number of relatively strict and complex laws enacted by the different provinces. Private pension plans must also be registered with Revenue Canada for tax purposes—hence the name registered pension plans. According to Statistics Canada, about 42 per cent of all paid workers were covered by a registered pension plan in 1996.[21]

The law does not require employers to have a pension plan for their employees, but if they do have one, it must comply with the existing legislation. In general, the legislation requires that employees should be eligible for coverage in the plan after a relatively short period of time (usually no more than two years), and a certain level of portability. After five years of service (in Alberta) or only two (in Manitoba), contributions to the plan are vested in the employee. That means that if the employee changes jobs, all the contributions made to the pension fund by both the employee and the employer belong to the employee, who could then invest them in the pension plan provided by the new employer (if there is one) or in a Registered Retirement Savings Plan (RRSP).

Most registered pension plans are contributory, but the laws require that employers contribute at least 50 per cent. Pension legislation stipulates that plans be valuated every three years to ensure that there is enough money in the fund to meet pension obligations: if there is a shortfall, it must be covered by the employer. A surplus, on the other hand, may be used to improve the plan's provisions or to reduce the employer's contributions to the fund.

Registered pension plans may be one of three types: defined benefit, defined contribution, or hybrid. In a defined benefit plan, the employer commits to paying out a predetermined pension: for example, $20 a month for every year of service (flat benefit) or 2 per cent of pay per year of service (unit benefit). In a defined contribution plan, the pensions will vary in amount depending on the amount of contributions, the pension fund's investment income, and economic conditions at retirement. Hybrid or mixed plans combine characteristics of both.

Private Pension Plans Pension plans that supplement the CPP/QPP.

Registered Pension Plans Private pension plans must be registered with Revenue Canada for tax purposes—hence the name.

●

Canadian laws generally require that the plans be administered by a pension committee which must ensure that provisions of the plan and of the legislation are met. The committee must also provide all members (the employees covered by the plan) with annual personal pension statements, provide the provincial regulating agency with annual reports, have the actuarial reports prepared every three years, and so on. Bear in mind that plans are set up so that employees' contributions over their employment will produce a pension when they retire—five, ten, or even forty years later. This pension will be received by the retiree for the rest of his or her life. So if retirees live longer than was estimated when the plan was set up, adjustments will have to be made or the fund will run out of money.

Registered Retirement Savings Plans (RRSPs) are personal retirement savings plans that any individuals may contribute to, even if they also belong to a registered pension plan through their employer. (Revenue Canada establishes limitations on how much may be contributed to RRSPs.) They are the ideal mechanism for the self-employed and for individuals whose employer does not provide a pension plan. With the increase in the complexity of the legislation governing registered pension plans, group RRSPs are becoming attractive, particularly for small employers. Calgary law firm Walsh Wilkins established a group RRSP twenty years ago, long before they became fashionable. For the firm, administration is easy: all it has to do is to forward payroll deductions to the financial institutions chosen by the members. The group members (ten of the firm's support staff) are free to invest their money in any financial firm providing RRSPs. They meet yearly to make this and related decisions.[22]

Important pension issues are the integration of the pension plans' benefits with those provided by the CPP and QPP and provisions for a flexible retirement age. Legislation specifies that plans allow employees to retire as much as ten years before the normal retirement age. On the other hand, many plans allow employees to defer their retirement beyond normal retirement age and continue contributing, which will entitle them to a higher pension when they do retire. However, tax laws require individuals to start collecting their pension no later than age seventy-one, although they may continue to work. Many do: Revenue Canada reported that approximately 30 per cent of people aged sixty to sixty-nine who paid tax earned professional or employment income, and 14 per cent of those seventy to seventy-four did so too.[23]

Two additional old age pensions should be mentioned at this point. Canadians are entitled to a monthly Old Age Security Pension (OAS) at age sixty-five, and those with lower financial resources are also entitled to a Guaranteed Income Supplement (GIS). Both the OAS and GIS are funded from general tax revenues.

Group Life Insurance

Practically all employees in Canada are covered by a group life insurance plan paid for by their employer[24]. In some plans, the deceased's family receives a lump-sum payment; in others, the family receives a somewhat lower payment plus a survivor's pension. Coverage is usually based on the employee's pay, usually equivalent to one or two annual salaries. Optional plans allowing for more coverage or allowing employees to purchase coverage for their dependents are also common.

Other common types of group insurance are travel insurance (providing coverage for death or disability occurring during business travel) and group accidental death and dismemberment insurance.

Workers cannot work all the time; they must take time off to eat, rest, or attend to personal or family matters. As we mentioned earlier, legislation in every Canadian jurisdiction specifies the maximum number of hours that can be worked in a week and that there be a weekly day of rest. Legislation also specifies vacations, holidays, and some other leaves.

Vacations

Every employee in Canada who is covered by employment standards legislation is entitled to an annual vacation with pay. The first jurisdiction to make paid annual vacations compulsory was Ontario in 1944; Saskatchewan, Alberta, British Columbia, Quebec, and Manitoba followed within three years, and all jurisdictions had passed similar legislation by 1970.[25]

In all Canadian jurisdictions except Saskatchewan, employees are entitled to two weeks' annual vacation after each completed year of employment; in Saskatchewan, the entitlement is three weeks' vacation.[26] Several jurisdictions stipulate that employees are entitled to longer vacations after a number of years with the same employer: Saskatchewan awards four weeks after ten years' employment; Manitoba, three weeks after four years' employment; Alberta, British Columbia, Quebec, and the Northwest Territories, three weeks' vacation after five years' employment; while the *Canada Labour Code* awards three weeks' vacation after six consecutive years with the same employer.

Annual Vacation A period of several days or weeks when employees are away from work and which are intended to be used for rest and recreation.

TABLE 14-2 Statutory Paid Annual Vacations in Canada

Jurisdiction	Basic vacations	Additional vacations
Federal	Two weeks	Three weeks after six consecutive years with the same employer
Alberta	Two weeks	Three weeks after five years with the same employer
British Columbia	Two weeks	Three weeks after five continuous years with the same employer
Manitoba	Two weeks	Three weeks after four years
New Brunswick	Two weeks	
Newfoundland	Two weeks	Three weeks after 15 years of service with the same employer
Northwest Territories	Two weeks after one year	Three weeks after five years
Nova Scotia	Two weeks	
Ontario	Two weeks	
Prince Edward Island	Two weeks	
Quebec	Two weeks	If less than one year of service: one day per month to a maximum of two weeks Three weeks after five years
Saskatchewan	Three weeks	Four weeks after 10 years
Yukon Territory	Two weeks	

Source: Human Resources and Development Canada (http://labour-travail.hrdc-drhc.gc.ca/policy/leg/stand9-e1.html ff.; July 1998.

Employers usually award all their employees the same, or better, vacation periods than required by law, even if those workers are legally exempt. As a matter of fact, it is not uncommon for employers to offer (or to negotiate with their unions) longer paid vacation periods. As with statutory vacations, it is common practice that longer-serving employees are entitled to longer vacation periods. This practice of rewarding seniority helps to encourage retention.

Holidays

Statutory Holidays Days for which time off must be given with pay as specified in the statutes of the appropriate jurisdiction.

All Canadian jurisdictions specify a number of statutory holidays for which time off must be given with pay. The number of holidays varies from one jurisdiction to another, from a low of five to a high of nine.[27] They are shown in detail in Table 14-3. As with vacations, employers may choose to grant additional days: for example, employers in Nova Scotia would probably grant Thanksgiving Day even though the provincial legislation does not require it. Many educational and manufacturing organizations give their employees the days between Christmas Day and New Year's Day as paid holidays.

Personal Days

Many organizations grant between two and five days off per year to allow employees to meet personal or family obligations of different kinds. According to Statistics Canada, the average employee missed 3.3 days in 1993 due to family responsibilities.[28] Since flextime allows employees to arrange their work schedules

TABLE 14-3 Statutory Holidays in Canada

	Fed.	Alta.	BC	Man.	N.B.	Nfld.	NWT	NS	Ont.	PEI	Que.	Sask.	YT
New Year's Day	X	X	X	X	X	X	X	X	X	X	X	X	X
Alberta Family Day[a]		X											
Good Friday	X	X	X	X	X	X	X	X	X	X	X[b]	X	X
Victoria Day	X	X	X	X			X		X		X[c]	X	X
National Holiday (June 24)											X		
Canada Day	X	X	X	X	X	X[d]	X	X	X	X	X	X	X
First Monday in August[e]			X		X		X					X	
Discovery Day (Third Monday in August)													X
Labour Day	X	X	X	X	X	X	X	X	X	X	X	X	X
Thanksgiving Day	X	X	X	X			X		X	X	X	X	X
Remembrance Day	X	X	X	X			X	X				X	
Christmas Day	X	X	X	X	X	X	X	X	X	X	X		
Boxing Day	X							X					

Source: Human Resources Development Canada, *Employment Standards Legislation in Canada* (http://labour-travail.hrdc-drhc.gc.ca/policy/leg/e/index.html), July 1998.

a   Third Monday in February
b   Or Easter Monday, at the employer's discretion
c   Dollard Day, on the same date as Victoria Day
d   Memorial Day in Newfoundland
e   In the respective provinces, it's known as British Columbia Day, New Brunswick Day, and Saskatchewan Day

to their convenience, employees who enjoy flextime have little need for this type of time off. Consequently, some authors classify flextime as a benefit.[29]

Many organizations also offer paid sick leave. The arrangements vary enormously, from a limited number of days per year which cannot be accumulated, to allowing the unused sick leave to be accumulated for use at a later day or even cashed in upon retirement. (In organizations that grant sick days but not personal days, employees will frequently use sick days to deal with personal matters.) One example of tying these benefits to performance is that of Toronto law firm Fogler, Rubinoff. Staff receive their birthday off with pay if they have missed three days or less in the previous year.[30]

Other Leaves

All Canadian jurisdictions require that employers grant maternity leave of seventeen or eighteen weeks; several jurisdictions grant parental leave, and all grant voting leave. Maternity and parental leaves are unpaid, but employees are eligible for employment insurance benefits.[31] Again, organizations may grant more generous conditions for these purposes as well as for bereavement, marriage, or family problems (Quebec and Newfoundland stipulate paid bereavement leave). Employers must give time off for jury duty, and many organizations will pay for this time.[32]

Breaks

Most organizations provide a number of paid breaks in the working day: lunch and coffee breaks are the most common. Some, but not all, organizations will also pay for preparation or clean-up time required to don working clothes or to wash-up after completing the work day. (For several years, this issue has been a bone of contention between the Canadian Auto Workers and Chrysler.)

Services

Organizations and employees have shown creativity in a wide variety of benefits. Many of them are services that have been around for a very long time, while others are recent developments. In most cases, they are offered because employees want them, but in a few cases, it may well be the employer who is most interested in making them available. Services include: employee assistance programs, wellness programs, counselling, meals and housing, discounts on company's products and services, education, and other benefits. Let us take a brief look at them.

Employee Assistance Programs

Employee assistance programs (EAPs) originated to help employees deal with alcohol and drug abuse problems, providing counselling and rehabilitation that, on the one hand, benefitted the employee directly, and on the other, benefitted the employer by reducing the costs associated with substance abuse (absenteeism, lateness, and substandard performance). Today, EAPs deal with all types of problems, of which only 10 per cent are alcohol- and drug-related. One-third are marital or family problems; 25 per cent, psychological problems such as depression and anxiety; and up to 20 per cent involve work-related stress.[33]

Employee Assistance Programs (EAPs) Plans intended to help employees to deal with issues such as stress, depression, anxiety, family and marital problems, and substance abuse.

One of the major issues in EAPs is maintaining confidentiality. At firms like London Life, where stress (originating from family problems and as well as workplace) is one of the major reasons employees use the company's EAP, elaborate mechanisms are used to preserve confidentiality. While the company must know, for example, how many hours of therapy it must pay, say, a psychologist for, management does not want to know (nor should it) the identity of the employees with whom the therapist spent those hours.[34]

EAPs are growing more popular. Currently, about one-third of North American companies with 100 or more employees offer some form of EAP, and this figure will probably grow as more programs take advantage of technology. On-line psychological counselling, for example, is cheaper. The Ontario Psychological Association reports that the base rate for face-to-face counselling is $135 an hour, while one-on-one on-line counselling costs about $100 an hour and preserves confidentiality better.[35]

Wellness Programs

Wellness Programs Programs designed to help employees maximize their physical well-being.

If EAPs are primarily concerned with employees' psychological well-being, **wellness programs** are concerned with their physical well-being. They respond to both the employees' desire for good health—so fashionable in the 1990s—and employers' desire to control the costs of their health insurance programs. After all, a healthy person will not need to be hospitalized or take prescription drugs. Wellness programs may include provision of exercise facilities, nutrition programs, health information, or changing the company cafeteria's menu to include more healthy foods. For example, some companies have gone well beyond the legally required limitations on smoking and provided their employees with a variety of programs to help smokers stop. Such programs are impelled by figures from the Addiction Research Foundation that show that tobacco-related illness cost the Canadian government $9.5 billion a year and that smokers cost their health plans, on average, $1,500 a year in smoking-related expenses.[36]

The concern for controlling health care costs is fuelling growth in wellness approaches. Not only are companies starting their own programs, but other organizations have started programs that they offer to many employers. Health Alliance (a wholly owned division of Astra Pharma, a pharmaceutical firm) developed a program called Sharing a Healthier Future (SHF) which provides information as well as services to the employees of participating companies.[37]

Wellness programs are becoming popular as organizations come to see the benefits such as savings in health care costs.

Counselling

Counselling is usually provided within the context of EAPs and wellness programs. Other kinds of counselling are sometimes provided such as retirement planning (sometimes within the framework of the company's pension plan) and financial or investment counselling. The latter is especially of interest to higher income employees.

Preferences for counselling will vary from one employee to another. Older employees will be interested in pension-related and retirement planning matters, while younger employees will find counselling on personal development and child rearing more relevant to their needs.

Meals and Housing

Large companies frequently provide subsidized cafeterias, and companies with operations in isolated spots provide not only subsidized meals but housing as well. Some companies also have elaborate dining rooms that are restricted to upper-level management and clients, but this practice is disappearing with the trend to more egalitarian workplaces. In urban centres in Europe and Latin America, many companies provide their employees with vouchers that can be used to pay for meals at a variety of restaurants, thus providing subsidized meals without having to set up their own cafeterias. As long as these subsidies are not excessive, Revenue Canada will not tax this benefit.

Discounts on Company's Products and Services

Most organizations allow their employees, and frequently their dependants, to acquire the organization's products or services at a discount. For example, Ford workers get substantial discounts on Ford cars and trucks, Canadian Airlines personnel get free air travel, and University of Windsor faculty and staff get free tuition for their spouses and children.

Education

Many organizations provide education assistance. This varies widely from one to another, and some extend that assistance to the employees' dependents. For example, Chrysler Canada offers awards (based on academic excellence) to facilitate university studies by the children of active, retired, or deceased employees of the company or its dealerships.[38]

Some firms pay for tuition and books, while others provide time off and tuition loans. In some organizations, reimbursement is conditional on obtaining acceptable grades; in others, support is provided only for job-related programs. (If the educational program is job-related, the benefit is not taxable; if it is not, the benefit is considered taxable income. One could also argue that support for job-related programs of study is a training and development cost rather than a benefit.)

Other Benefits

The benefits that organizations can provide are limited only by the imagination of its management and employees. Long before wellness programs even existed, many companies provided recreational facilities and programs or supported employee teams. Sometimes, this creativity produces somewhat extreme offerings: Newbridge Networks Corp. of Kanata, Ontario, announced it would build a variety of facilities for its employees including a hotel, an eighteen-hole golf course, tennis and racketball courts, and a day care centre.[39] Perhaps they were inspired by Microsoft's 300-acre campus in Redmond, Washington, where members of a project team, in need of a break, might go outside for a game of basketball.[40]

Managers and executives frequently have special benefits, usually called **executive perquisites** or **perks**. These can include such niceties as a company car, club memberships, and executive lifestyle management plans (such as that provided by Toronto's King Health Centre which includes all aspects of medicine, non-medical specialists, such as nutritionists and fitness experts, and even a golf clinic with computerized equipment worth $45,000.[41] Other popular perks include reimbursement of a spouse's expenses when accompanying the executive on business trips, generous expense accounts, and assistance with the minor problems of life such as purchases and home repairs.

In Chapter 13 we discussed the concerns that have been raised regarding excessive executive pay. Similar criticisms have been levelled at executive perks.

Executive Perquisites Perks Benefits made available to executives and managers but not to lower-level employees.

Again, there is a tension between the desire for a more egalitarian workplace and the need to provide senior managers with compensation packages comparable to those offered by competing organizations. Revenue Canada, too, has shown an interest in perks, making many of them taxable benefits—which, of course, makes them less attractive.

Major Issues in Benefits

From a quick survey of the benefits scene, we have found that not all employers offer all of these benefits. As a matter of fact, many Canadian workers only receive the legally required benefits. Increasing pressure to offer benefits is just one of the many issues facing managers and benefits administrators. We will now consider some of the major issues in employment benefits in Canada, such as flexible benefits, domestic partners, family-friendly benefits, community benefits, and international benefits.

Flexible Benefits

In traditional benefit plans, all employees receive the same benefits coverage. This is the simplest, and still the most common, way of providing benefits, but it has two important disadvantages: cost and desirability of benefits. First, as the costs of the offered benefits increase or as new benefits are added to the package to address employee needs, the total cost of benefits escalates rapidly.

Second, not all the benefits on offer are equally valued by all employees, thus diminishing their motivating or impact (for example, tuition refunds for employees' children are of no value to a childless worker). Changes in workplace demographics also have had an impact on benefit desirability. With dual-income households becoming the norm rather than the exception (in 1967, 67 per cent of Canadian families had only one wage earner, while by 1992, both spouses were employed in 61 per cent of families[42]), a second health insurance plan is of little use, and people would prefer to receive something else rather than a program they would never use.

An answer to these two concerns is flexible benefits, first introduced to Canada by Cominco, a Vancouver-based mining company.[43] Under this approach employers would allocate a certain sum of money for employee benefits, and each employee would choose those benefits he or she found most useful, up to the cost limit.

How flexible can a flexible benefits program be? In a fully flexible benefit program, employees would be assigned an amount of money that they could allocate to the benefits they wish to have (such as vacation time or health insurance), and any unused "benefits money" could be exchanged for cash. In practice, companies are forced by legal and cost considerations to offer programs that are less than fully flexible. This is because, as we have seen, certain benefits are mandated by law, and also, because, to be affordable some benefits must cover all, or most, employees. For example, consider a drug plan. If only people who spend $100 a month on prescription drugs sign up, then the premiums would have to be $1,200 a year just to cover the expenses, let alone the administration costs. So the usual compromise is to have a semi-flexible benefit plan where there is a core of mandatory benefits and optional benefits from which employees can pick and choose their maximum benefits allowance. Some organizations use a modular

Flexible Benefits Benefits programs that allow employees to pick the benefits that best meet their needs.

plan where employees may choose between two or more different, fixed combinations of benefits; each combination (module) is designed to cost the company approximately the same.

The principal advantage of flexible benefits is that if employers offer a wide variety of benefits from which employees can pick the ones most useful to them, the total benefits bill will be substantially lower than if the company were to provide the entire selection to all employees. Furthermore, the fact that employees are getting benefits they value should make them feel better about their organization, and because they can worry less about issues such as health coverage, they can even be able to dedicate more energy to their performance.

Disadvantages of flexible benefits include, primarily, the cost of developing such a plan, (which can be quite high) and higher administration costs once the plan is implemented (tracking employee choices, estimating benefits usage, informing employees of their options, and dealing with employees making changes to their selections every year). Computer-based technology is extremely helpful in this regard, both for administration by the employer as well as to help employees make good choices.

We can expect flexible benefit plans to become more popular in Canada because governments are reducing their support in such areas as health insurance and because there is much room for growth. In 1995, only some 20 per cent of major Canadian employers had flexible benefits plans in place, compared with 85 per cent in the United States.[44]

Domestic Partners

When employers first started extending benefit coverage to employees' dependants, the procedure was straightforward: an employee's spouse and children (if any) were covered, and that was that. But the number of unmarried couples living together, and, in consequence, so have the demands from employees that coverage be extended to such partners. Employers seem to be moving in this direction, and the recommendation of benefits consultants such as William M. Mercer Ltd. is that they should do so.[45]

The still somewhat controversial matter of benefits coverage for partners of the same sex can be seen as an extension of this issue, and Mercer's recommendation is the same: that employees be allowed to designate any person to receive "spousal equivalent benefits." Revenue Canada now allows same-sex spousal benefits to be given in private health services plans but not pension survival benefits. A number of court cases in recent years have dealt with these issues since employment discrimination based on sexual orientation is prohibited in all Canadian jurisdictions except for Alberta, Newfoundland, and Prince Edward Island. (But this lack of protection is open to challenge under the *Canadian Charter of Rights and Freedoms*.)

In two Ontario cases, the courts indicated that employers should modify their benefit plans to provide gay and lesbian employees benefits equivalent to those received by heterosexual employees, but they noted that due to the *Income Tax Act* restrictions, a different mechanism would be needed to provide same-sex survivor pension benefits.[46] Similar rulings came from two federal cases[47] and a case adjudicated by the Manitoba Human Rights Commission in 1998.[48] In April 1998, the Ontario Court of Appeals ruled that excluding same-sex partners from the *Income Tax Act*'s definition of "spouse," as applied to registered pension plans, is unconstitutional under the *Canadian Charter of Rights and Freedoms*.[49] The tendency clearly seems to be to eliminate any differences in the treatment of heterosexual and homosexual employees.

Family-Friendly Benefits Flexible benefits that support care for the employee's family.

Family-Friendly Benefits

A major trend is the push for family-friendly benefits, which are those that support care for the employee's family. We have mentioned some of them already: flexible work schedules, child care, health insurance coverage for dependants, parental leave, and tuition support for dependants. The reason for the trend to family-friendly benefits is that, as we mentioned earlier, there are more dual-career couples than ever before, and this means that there are fewer stay-at-home parents to look after the children. The plight of the single parent (another growing demographic category) is even more serious, and longer life-spans mean that there also are more elderly persons requiring assistance from their working children.

While flexible working hours are perceived as helpful in these circumstances, so is job-sharing, which is attractive to workers who want to spend more time with their small children. The Royal Bank of Canada's work-family program, with 1,100 employees sharing jobs, is the largest of its kind in Canada.[50] Such programs, and family-friendly benefits in general, are likely to grow, partly because they are very important to employees. The WorkCanada 1995 survey by consulting firm Watson Wyatt revealed that one of the key factors in increasing employee commitment was the existence of company policies that helped employees balance work and family responsibilities.[51] The same survey revealed that there was much room for improvement: while 53 per cent of the top managers surveyed believed that their company policies allowed employees to balance their jobs and their home duties, only 37 per cent of hourly workers agreed.[52]

Communicating Benefits

Communicating with employees is extremely important and seldom more so than in the case of benefits. Even traditional benefit plans have become quite complex. Employees need to know such things as how much vacation time they are entitled to or if their health insurance plan provides coverage if they travel to visit their relatives in Houston, Hamburg, or Hong Kong. Communication is also important if the company wants to know how employees feel about their benefits coverage, and it becomes absolutely critical if the company is making major changes to its benefit coverage as well as for flexible benefit plans.

In general, employees frequently do not know the full extent of the benefits they are entitled to and are even less aware of the actual cost of these benefits. This leads to their undervaluing their benefits coverage. This, in turn, has a negative impact on employees' satisfaction with them and thus, on their commitment to their employer. For a small test, take a look at your own family or that of a close friend. What benefits would the family be entitled to if the primary breadwinner were run over by a bus? Which family members (if any) have this information?

Technology has come to the aid of the benefits administrator. London Life, for instance, had established a computer-based system that allowed employees to inquire about aspects of their benefits coverage via computer terminals long before the World Wide Web had come into existence.[53] The Hudson Bay Company, with over 400 locations across Canada, uses its computer network to provide its employees with benefits-related information. "Because we have so many locations across the country, the key for us is to make available to our people as much information as possible," says Emree Siaroff, the company's manager of programs and benefits.[54]

Generational differences appear to matter for communications as well as for benefit preferences. While people over the age of forty or so prefer a linear communication style (like reading a book), younger people prefer to get their information on a random access basis (like "channel surfing" on TV). So, while benefits information booklets work well for baby boomers, generation Xers prefer CD-ROMs. This is an important consideration, given that demographic projections suggest that most workplaces will have about equal numbers of baby boomers and generation Xers by 2003.[55]

The Alberta Energy Company Ltd.'s (AEC) intranet site appears to meet the benefit information needs of its 700 employees at a very low cost.[56] It provides practically all the information an employee might need—from pension and benefits information to wellness program news. On the other hand, when the Bank of Nova Scotia implemented its new flexible benefits program, Flexbenefits, in 1997, it used a very elaborate communication strategy over eleven months.[57] This included printed materials (magazines, leader's guides, plan booklets) in English, French, and Braille; a video with closed captioning; software; and personal presentations by Kate Hart, assistant general manager of benefit products, and her team at eighty locations across Canada. Employees were involved in producing the materials—not just in listening to the message—and this contributed to the communications program's success. At a cost of about $40 per employee, the program contributed to achieving a 99.6 per cent enrolment in the Flexbenefits program by Scotiabank's 27,000 employees (400 of them outside Canada). But these things cannot be done on the cheap: the total cost was $1.1 million.

International Benefits

In Chapter 13, we briefly discussed aspects of international compensation. You will by now have realized that international benefits present even greater challenges for organizations partly because legal environments differ, sometimes quite substantially, from one country to another. Organizations have to deal with these differences when they move staff from one country to another, when they analyse the cost structure of different organizational units, and when they do their human resources and budgetary planning encompassing their international activities.

Let us look at a very few of these differences. For example, German workers are entitled to five weeks' vacation, while in the United States, there is no statutory vacation requirement (although most employers give two weeks' annual vacation with pay). Imagine that a company based in Hanover, Ontario is sending two technicians abroad on two-year assignments: one to Hanover, New Hampshire, and the other to Hanover, Germany. The company's collective agreement entitles them to three weeks' vacation. How many weeks' vacation will they be entitled to on their foreign assignment? Paid holidays also vary across the world. In the United Kingdom, employees average nine paid holidays per year, the average is ten in the United States, eleven in Brazil, seventeen in Japan, and nineteen in Mexico.[58]

Balancing these differences in benefits is not only important to expatriates, companies with plants in other countries have to face this question too. It affects matters as simple as planning international meetings or travel because of different holidays—do not try to call the French subsidiary on July 14 or schedule a meeting in Rio de Janeiro on the week before Ash Wednesday—and as complex as matching pension plan requirements. The impact on costs can be

HRM Skills:

Managing Employee Benefits

Successful benefits programs do not just happen. They have to be managed. Here are some suggestions.

Know your compensation strategy. Remember, benefits are part of your overall compensation package. What are you trying to achieve with your compensation strategy? What kind of employees are you trying to attract and retain? Would you be better off tying employee remuneration to your company's performance through bonuses and letting them purchase their preferred coverage on their own?

Be aware of your workforce. What is your workforce like? Is it composed primarily of young people? Is it multiethnic and multicultural? Is there a large proportion of employees nearing retirement? This will affect what benefits your employees will need and want, but you should go further. How is your workforce going to evolve? Will you be adding employees, and, if so, what will they probably be like?

Be aware of your employees' preferences. What benefits do your employees value? A careful analysis of the information you gathered to answer the questions in the previous topic will help, but nothing will give you better information than asking the employees themselves. In a small organization, you can ask them all; in larger companies, you will have to conduct surveys, use focus groups, or some combination of the two. Remember that your workforce will change, and so will your employees' preferences.

Communicate. Communicate continually with your employees: when they are brought into the benefit program; as users of the different benefits, and every time you make any changes. Let employees know what benefits they are eligible for and how much those benefits cost. Don't forget, communication is a two-way street. Don't just tell them about the benefits package; ask them what they like and don't like (as we mentioned above). Better yet, involve employees in the design and administration of the benefits.

Monitor the program. Keep track of what benefits are used and to what extent. Keep track of the costs. Look at the trends: is usage growing or dropping? Are the trends compatible with the changes in your workforce? If a benefit is underutilized, should it perhaps be dropped? If usage of another program is growing, must new resources be made available, or can costs be controlled in some way?

Monitor the environment. What are the developments in benefits? What are the expected changes in legislation that will affect benefits? What are other employers offering? You should keep abreast of the developments by reading the specialized press and perhaps by participating in nationwide surveys such as KPMG's Employee Benefits Costs Survey.

Get help. You should not try to reinvent the wheel. Very few organizations (if any) have enough in-house expertise to manage all aspects of a benefits program. There are a number of specialized firms that can help. Small organizations can profit from their industry associations, and HRM professionals can always seek advice from their provincial HR association (for example, the FastFacts service offered by Ontario's HRPAO).

quite direct: US manufacturers have argued that Canadian firms have an unfair cost advantage because Canadian public health insurance programs mean it is much cheaper to provide health benefits for Canadian employers than for US companies. At the other end of the Americas, the Argentine government proposed amending labour legislation to reduce the cost of benefits and, in particular, to make it cheaper to fire redundant workers in order to make the country more attractive to foreign investors. The bottom line is that benefits administrators in international organizations must remain aware of the differences as well as of the changes that are continually taking place.

Issues in the Administration of Benefits

As you can see, there are many challenges regarding benefits administration. The first is to integrate employee benefits in the organization's overall HRM strategy. This will require, first, determining what role benefits will have in the organization's overall compensation strategy. For example, an organization may decide to pay high wages and let employees purchase whatever benefits they wish themselves or to provide a rich array of benefits. Second, the company must decide on the process that will be used to design the organization's plan, in particular, what will be the level of employee participation. A third consideration is to identify which benefits are to be included (will the firm use a flexible benefits system?). Fourth, what will be the structure of each benefit (what will the benefit be? who will pay for it? will it be required or optional? who will be covered?). Finally, procedures must be developed for administering, communicating, and evaluating the system.[59]

We should point out that, given the complexity of many benefits, most organizations today outsource some, if not most, of their benefits administration. This has been true for a long time: the management of many firm's health insurance plans, for instance, was done by insurance carriers. Today, things are going even further. A BC Hydro employee who phones to ask if the company's dental plan covers a hockey accident will be unaware that she is speaking to an operator in Toronto.[60] The Morneau Technology Centre (run by Morneau Sobeco Coopers & Lybrand) answers some 200,000 benefit-related calls every month. The other three major specialists in pension and benefits administration (Hewitt Associates L.L.C., Towers Perrin, and William M. Mercer Ltd.) are hard-pressed to keep up with employer demand. Hewitt opened a benefits call centre in Toronto in 1996, Towers Perrin opened its National Benefits Centre in Mississauga in the fall of 1997, and Mercer followed its long-standing Vancouver centre with new locations in Calgary, Toronto, and Montreal.[61] Other large firms using outsourcing include Imperial Tobacco, Canadian National Railways, and Bank of Montreal. According to Karen Duchene, the Morneau Technology Centre's manager, smaller organizations are pooling into associations to take advantage of the call centres.[62]

The increasing complexity of benefits has led to the outsourcing of benefits administration. Pension and benefits specialists have established call centres (such as this one) to handle enquiries across the nation.

Meet

Murray Ceulemans
Group Extended Health/Dental Claims,
The Co-operators

Today, an organization wishing to offer group insurance coverage to its employees faces a dizzying range of options. Whatever your requirements, the perfect plan is available ... for a price.

Explains Murray Ceulemans, who oversees the Group Extended Health/Dental Claims operation at the Regina office of the Co-operators, which provides group insurance to many companies across Canada. "When a large employer 'goes to market' seeking a benefits package for its employees, competing insurers will usually tailor a package to meet their specific needs."

The insurer may also set up a partnership or third-party arrangement to meet some of those needs. For example, the Co-operators sometimes contract with a Francophone administration company to deal with an organization's Quebec branch; they also offer a "pay direct" drug plan in partnership with Green Shield Canada, under which an employer can issue cards that allow its workers to pay out of pocket for drugs only the deductible portion of cost for which they are responsible.

Very small business? No problem. The Co-operators have a standard "Business Advantage package" geared for small companies, which, for an affordable cost, includes life and disability coverage as well as a basic dental and extended health care plan, including a drug plan.

"We're always developing new products and enhancing old ones," says Mr Ceulemans, citing as an example a new emergency out-of-country benefit that provides reimbursement of certain nonmedical travel expenses, such as return of vehicle, living allowances, and transportation costs incurred as a result of a medical emergency.

But as the options available have widened in recent years, the overall cost of benefits have also risen. There are many reasons for this rise, Mr Ceulemans theorizes. "For one thing, provincial health plans have been cutting costs by reducing or de-insuring services. As a consequence, responsibility for some of these costs have shifted to private plans. If you reduce the average length of hospital stays, people may need private nursing care when they come home. If your plan covers that, then the plan's cost goes up. In recent years I've seen some companies put a cap on private duty nursing care, since those costs have risen significantly."

The development of new, expensive drugs to treat some very serious conditions, such as multiple sclerosis, is another contributor to rising costs. Then there are changing habits. "People tend to travel more now, so we see more out-of-country medical claims," says Mr Ceulemans. "And they use more dental services. Today's dentists are far more diligent in ensuring that their patients take full advantage of the coverage provided by their dental plans."

In this age of spiralling benefit costs, some companies are scaling back the benefits they offer. But others are increasing them nonetheless, regarding these costs as an investment. "If you want to get really good staff and keep them," explains Mr Ceulemans, "then a good benefits package is one arrow in your quiver. I can think of one very high-tech firm, for example, that includes even its casual staff in the group insurance plan. It makes the company more attractive."

430

As we have seen, the area of employee benefits is one of increasing complexity. Organizations must respond to the changing needs and preferences of the changing Canadian workforce as well as to changes in the legal environment of pay and benefits.

As different benefits become more commonplace, a well-rounded benefits package becomes an important tool for attracting and retaining employees. This presents a particular challenge for small and medium-sized organizations, which are unable to fund specialized benefits departments or even to supply the critical mass of employees necessary to make certain benefits possible. The opening example illustrated this in the case of Sony Music Canada, which has less than 400. One solution to the problem of size is to join with other employers in consortia or to enrol in commercially available programs offered by benefits underwriters.

In every case, it is crucial that benefits be viewed as an important component of the organization's total reward system and not as an isolated item. Thus, the benefits package must be integrated into the organization's HRM strategy which, as we have seen, must match the organization's overall strategy.

Finally, we have seen that while benefits are useful for attracting and retaining employees, it is very difficult to link benefits to individual employees' motivation and performance. However, it is possible to evaluate the impact of a benefits program to the organization's overall performance by analysing factors such as costs, turnover, absenteeism, and employee satisfaction. This analysis should be a regular part of the organization's HRM activity.

Study Tools and Applications

Summary

The summary relates to the Learning Objectives provided on p. 408.
After having read this chapter, you should know:

1. Employee benefits have grown from a relatively unimportant component of the compensation package ("fringe benefits") to being, on average, almost 27 per cent of payroll in Canada (52 per cent in some organizations). The origin of these benefits can be traced to wage and price controls established during World War II.

2. Employers offer benefits to attract and retain employees. Furthermore, certain benefits are required by law. Employees expect benefits, and these should be offered in a way that provides value and meaning to the employees.

3. Since benefits are usually membership-based, the link to individual motivation and performance is not strong. However, benefits are linked to commitment, satisfaction, and retention, particularly in flexible benefit approaches that allow employees to choose the benefits they really value and want.

4. Employee security benefits are designed to protect employees' well-being and include such programs as health insurance, pensions, workers' compensation, employment insurance, and other types of insurance. Pay for time not worked is intended to allow employees time off for recovery and relaxation, and it includes vacations,

holidays, and other types of leaves and breaks. Services include several other benefits such as employee assistance programs, wellness programs, a variety of subsidized services, and perquisites.

5. The federal and provincial governments' roles include, first, establishing certain benefits that must be provided to all employees such as vacations, holidays, employment insurance, and the Canada/Quebec Pension Plan. Second, governments establish rules regarding the way certain benefits can be provided, such as pensions and health insurance. Finally, governments also establish certain programs that are available to the population as a whole, such as provincial health and hospital insurance programs.

6. The Canada Pension Plan operates in all of Canada except Quebec, which has the Quebec Pension Plan. Both plans are coordinated in such a way that they are essentially the same. They are funded by a contribution of a percentage of the year's maximum pensionable earnings (YMPE), paid in equal parts by employer and employee. Upon retirement, the employee will receive a pension to a maximum of 25 per cent of the YMPE, which is equivalent to the average industrial wage. In 1998, amendments were made to the CPP to ensure that it is adequately funded in the future.

7. The principal types of pay for time not worked include annual vacations and holidays, which are required by statute in all Canadian jurisdictions, although employers may make more generous allowances. In addition, many organizations provide for personal and sick leaves and breaks. Maternal and parental leaves, required by statute, are unpaid, but employees are eligible for employment insurance.

8. The major advantages of flexible benefit plans are, first, they allow employees to receive those benefits that are of most value to them, and, second, they help to contain the increasing cost of benefits. The major disadvantages are the cost of developing the plan and higher administration costs than for traditional benefits.

9. The newer trends in benefits include growth in flexible benefits as well as in such support services as employee assistance plans (EAPs) and wellness programs, family-friendly benefits, and broader definitions of which domestic partners are eligible for benefit coverage. On the administrative side, greater use of information technology for administration and communication and the growth of outsourcing are worth mentioning.

10. Benefits should be seen as an important component of the organization's compensation program. The operative term should be "total rewards." Management should evaluate the contribution of the benefits program to the organization's performance using such indicators as costs, absenteeism, turnover, and employee satisfaction.

Key Terms

annual vacation

Canada Health Act

Canada Pension Plan (CPP)

Employee Assistance Programs (EAPs)

employee benefits

Employment Insurance

executive perquisites

family-friendly benefits

flexible benefits

group life insurance

health insurance

private health insurance

private pension plans

public health insurance

Quebec Pension Plan (QPP)

registered pension plan

Registered Retirement Savings Plans (RRSPs)

statutory holidays

supplemental unemployment benefits (SUBs)

wellness programs

Workers' Compensation

Flexible Benefits Choices

Form into groups of three to five members, and using Table 14-4, determine the mix of benefits that would best fit your needs. After doing so, answer the following questions in your group.

1. Explain the reasons for the choices you made. What compelled you to make those specific choices?
2. Compare what you have chosen with the members of your group. Are there similarities? In which benefit coverage? Are there differences? In which benefit coverage?
3. How can you best explain the reasons for the differences—that is, what factors from Question 1 affected the differences in benefits selection?
4. Do you think your benefits selection choices will be the same five years from now? Ten years? Explain.

TABLE 14-4   Sample Flexible Benefit Selection Sheet

| Name: Manny Choices[1] | Years of Service: 3 |
Annual Earnings: $ 35,000	Credits to Spend: 2500[2]
Health Care	
Provincial Health Insurance	Core
Dominion Health Plan[3]	850
Dominion Dental Plan[4]	200
Dominion Vision Plan	180
Life Insurance	
1 x Annual Earnings[5]	Core
2 x Annual Earnings	252
3 x Annual Earnings	504
Retirement	
CPP	Core
Company Registered Retirement Savings Plan	1,000
Group RRSP	400
Vacation	
2 weeks[6]	Core
3 weeks	673
4 weeks	1,346
Paid Holidays	
9 days	Core
Personal Days	
1 day	Core
2 days	134
3 days	268
Other	
Workers' Compensation	Core
Employment Insurance	Core

[1] Numbers assigned here are for an employee with no dependants. For family coverage for dependents, see note below.
[2] Credits available for flexible benefits are computed based on total benefit rate of 32 per cent of salary, minus the required core.
[3] Add 150 credits for one dependant; 300 credits for two or more dependants.
[4] There is no additional cost for dependants in dental or vision plans.
[5] Computed at 7.2 cents per $1,000 of life insurance.
[6] Core increases to 3 weeks after 4 years' seniority, with the corresponding reduction in available flex credits.

CASE APPLICATION:

Wellness Workout at Northern Telecom

After years of conducting customer satisfaction studies, in 1994, Northern Telecom Limited (Nortel), the telecommunications giant headquartered in Brampton, Ontario, started doing annual surveys of its 70,000 employees worldwide.[63] An analysis of the relationship between employee satisfaction and customer satisfaction convinced management that there was, indeed, a positive correlation between these measures. Thus, senior management was easily convinced that enhancing employee satisfaction was good for the company. Improving employee benefits was one way to increasing employee satisfaction.

While Northern Telecom is one of Canada's largest companies (its 1997 sales of $22 billion ranked it fourth, after GM Canada, BCE, and Ford Canada[64]), the company is concerned with saving money, by controlling health benefit costs, for example. An answer to both concerns (improving the benefits program and controlling health benefit costs) was the development of what many consider the most comprehensive corporate wellness program in Canada. The company chose the name Aralia (a genus of ivy) to symbolize its commitment to a healthy workforce and hired wellness expert Sue Brown to develop the program. One of her first steps was to carry out a needs assessment survey to find out what the employees wanted.

In the process of consolidating four locations and renovating its headquarters, the company set space aside for the Aralia wellness centre. The 3,500 employees at headquarters now have access to over twenty programs designed to improve and maintain their health. The 4,200-square-foot centre holds a multimedia library, multimedia stations with on-line information, two relaxation areas, and physio and massage therapy rooms. In addition, it has offices for occupational health nurses, a physician, and administrative staff. In a 16,000-square-foot fitness centre, seven staff members run aerobic, cardiovascular, and weight training workouts. There are also programs for parenting, asthma self-management, relaxation training, and so on.

To run such a large variety of services and programs, Aralia partnered with a variety of wellness specialists including Relaxation Responses' Ely Bley, Toronto's Women's College Hospital, Montreal's Abbot Laboratories, and Mississauga's Glaxo Wellcome. "We have to tender out the programs because we couldn't possibly have the personnel to implement them ourselves," says Brown.

A year after the program was implemented, it was still too early to evaluate its success, but preliminary data showed enthusiastic employee participation and positive feedback. However, the company intends to have the program evaluated by an independent research scientist. As Brown says, "We'll be able to see, for example, if the ulcer care program lowers the company's drug claims in the long term." The subjective benefits such as staff morale will be measured through Nortel's annual employee satisfaction surveys. This information will be shared with other Nortel locations so that they can develop their own programs for their own employees' needs.

Questions

1. Analyse the Aralia program in terms of its impact on Nortel's headquarters employees' motivation and productivity.
2. What are the main things that Nortel appears to have done well in developing this program?

3. What type of benefit is Aralia? In your view, how does Aralia fit in with Nortel's strategies (in compensation, in HRM, and as an organization)?
4. Northern Telecom is one of Canada's largest companies, and it has abundant resources. Can smaller organizations learn from the Aralia program? How?

Testing Your Understanding

How well did you fulfil the learning objectives?

1. Employee benefits are important in today's organizations for all of these reasons except
   a. employees expect more than monetary rewards from their jobs.
   b. benefits packages are instrumental in recruiting the best workers for an organization.
   c. benefits packages increase employee productivity.
   d. benefits packages help to retain good workers in an organization.
   e. benefits packages are designed to meet the needs of a wide variety of workers.

2. According to a Conference Board of Canada survey, in 1992, the average cost of benefits was
   a. 14.9 per cent of payroll.
   b. 20.9 per cent of payroll.
   c. 26.9 per cent of payroll.
   d. 32.9 per cent of payroll.
   e. 51.9 per cent of payroll.

3. Employment insurance is intended to
   a. cover employees for disability or injury caused by work-related accidents.
   b. provide training for school leavers so they may enter the workplace.
   c. provide additional benefits for employees who are locked out.
   d. provide temporary income support to the unemployed.
   e. ensure that employers have a sufficient supply of skilled labour.

4. Public health insurance is provided to all Canadian residents
   a. through health and hospital insurance programs administered by the provinces and territories.
   b. through a health and hospital insurance program administered by the Canada/Quebec Health Authority.
   c. and covers doctors' fees, hospital stays in semi-private wards, nursing, and use of operating facilities.
   d. and covers doctors' fees, hospital stays in semi-private wards, nursing, use of operating facilities, and prescription drugs.
   e. and covers doctors' fees, hospital stays in public wards, nursing, use of operating facilities, and prescription drugs.

5. Total expenditures on private health insurance in Canada are around
   a. $ 1 billion per year.
   b. $ 10 billion per year.
   c. $ 19 billion per year.
   d. $ 22 billion per year.
   e. $ 25 billion per year.

6. The Canada Pension Plan is funded through income from investments of the Canada Pension Plan Fund and
   a. contributions from employers.
   b. a tax on all employers with more than forty-nine employees.
   c. contributions from employees.
   d. contributions from employers and employees.
   e. contributions from employers, employees, and the self-employed.

7. Contributors are entitled to a pension from the Canada/Quebec Pension Plan
   a. once they have maximized their contributions to the pension plan fund.
   b. starting at age fifty-five.
   c. starting at age sixty.
   d. starting at age sixty-five.
   e. starting at age sixty for men and sixty-five for women because women live longer than men.

8. In a defined benefit pension plan,
   a. the employer commits to paying out a pension the amount of which will be greater if the pension fund's investments have done well.
   b. the employer commits to paying out a pension that is a flat sum for every year of service plus a supplement based on the pension fund's performance.
   c. the employer commits to paying out a pension that is a percentage of the employee's contributions plus a supplement based on the pension fund's performance.
   d. the employer commits to paying out a pension that is a flat sum for every year of service or a percentage of pay per year of service.
   e. pensions are payable for a defined number of years after retirement.

9. Every Canadian worker is entitled to an annual vacation of
   a. one day for each year's seniority.

b. a minimum of two weeks, except in Saskatchewan where the minimum is three weeks.

c. a minimum of three weeks, except in Saskatchewan where the minimum is four weeks.

d. a minimum of two weeks, except for miners and sailors.

e. a maximum of four weeks.

10. Employee assistance programs

a. are intended to help employees deal with alcohol and drug abuse problems.

b. are intended to assist employees with health problems.

c. help employees deal with a variety of problems including marital or family problems.

d. are intended to provide psychological assistance to troubled employees.

e. are an extension of a holistic approach to employee well-being.

11. A major advantage of flexible benefit plans is that

a. they ensure that all employees get equivalent coverage.

b. they are simple to administer.

c. they have higher administrative costs than traditional benefit plans.

d. they are particularly adaptable to small firms' needs.

e. they allow employees to choose the benefits they prefer.

12. A major disadvantage of flexible benefit plans is that

a. they prevent employees from having comparable coverage.

b. they are simple to administer.

c. they have higher administrative costs than traditional benefit plans.

d. they are particularly adaptable to small firms' needs.

e. they allow employees to choose the benefits they prefer.

13. An important recent trend in benefits is

a. the push for family-friendly benefits.

b. the combination of EAPs with wellness programs.

c. the increase in executive perks.

d. the narrowing of the definition of "domestic partner."

e. the increase in paid time off.

14. Modern information technology

a. is of little use to benefits administrators because people skills are more important.

b. has been relatively useful in the implementation of flexible benefit programs.

c. has been useful in the administration and the communication aspects of benefits.

d. has only been useful since the development of the Internet.

e. has completely changed benefits administration.

15. When one compares internationally, one notices that

a. employee benefits are remarkably uniform across the globe.

b. international conventions ensure the portability of benefits for expatriate employees.

c. public health insurance programs give US companies an unfair cost advantage.

d. benefits vary substantially from one country to another.

e. international differences in benefits are somewhat less than international differences in pay.

16. One reason for the outsourcing of benefits administration is

a. the growing complexity of many benefits

b. the privatization of government benefits.

c. the simplification of legal requirements.

d. the growing sophistication of Canadian workers.

e. the development of university-level HRM programs.

Chapter Fifteen

HEALTH AND SAFETY

LEARNING OBJECTIVES

AFTER READING THIS CHAPTER, YOU WILL BE ABLE TO:

1. Describe occupational health and safety legislation in Canada and how it is enforced.
2. Understand the general responsibilities of the employer, manager, and employee in their respective occupational health and safety duties.
3. Describe the leading causes of workplace accidents and what companies can do to ensure job safety.
4. Explain what companies can do to maintain a healthy working environment.
5. Discuss current workplace health-related issues such as smoke-free policies and repetitive strain injuries (RSIs).
6. Understand what stress and burn-out are and identify their symptoms in the workplace.
7. Describe the value of employee assistance programs (EAPs) and wellness programs to the organization.
8. Recommend special health and safety procedures for employees who accept international assignments.

Early in the morning of May 9, 1992, residents of the tiny community of Plymouth, Nova Scotia, were awakened by a violent explosion. The explosion, caused by a build up of dust, came from the Westray coal mine. Twenty-six miners were killed instantly.

An inquiry was convened to report on the accident. In the inquiry report, Justice Peter Richard exonerated all twenty-six victims from any responsibility whatsoever. He placed the blame on mine managers for ignoring safety rules and on provincial inspectors for failing to protect workers. The disaster, he said, was a "story of incompetence, of mismanagememt, of bureaucratic bungling, of deceit, of ruthlessness, of cover-up, of apathy, of expediency and of cynical indifference."[1]

The evidence presented to the inquiry revealed that Westray management had violated the fundamental principles of safe mining practices. The philosophies and procedures that management espoused on paper—most notably in its employee handbook—were not put into practice. The inquiry found that Curragh, Inc., the company that owned the mine, had clearly rejected industry standards, provincial regulations, and common sense. In fact, the report concluded that management had sent the message that the Westray operation was to produce coal at the expense of workers' safety.

The effects of the Westray disaster linger. More than six years after the accident took place, families of the deceased miners are outraged when criminal charges against two mine managers were withdrawn. Many feel that their right to justice has been denied. A severance package worth $1.8 million from the Nova Scotia government will bring some relief to employees who lost their jobs when the mine was shut down. However, the anguish and suffering endured by the survivors cannot be compensated. For them, a memorial has been erected above the long, snaking mine tunnels where eleven bodies still remain.[2]

The Westray mine disaster is an example of what can happen when workplace safety precautions are ignored.

Introduction

Not all workplace accidents are as devastating as the Westray mine disaster. However, the number and severity of accidents that occur in Canada may surprise you. In 1996, 377,885 workers were injured on the job and 705 died.[3] That means that, on average, someone is injured on the job every nine seconds and that one in every fifteen workers risks having an accident in the coming year.[4]

Employers and managers have a legal responsibility, if not a moral one, to ensure that the workplace is free from unnecessary hazards, and that conditions surrounding the workplace are not hazardous to employees' physical or mental health. Heartless as it sounds, employers must be concerned about employees' health and safety if for no other reason than that accidents cost money. Accidents in the workplace drain the Canadian economy of an estimated $10 billion in direct and indirect costs.[5]

From the turn of the century through the late 1960s, remarkable progress was made in reducing the rate and severity of job-related accidents and diseases. Yet it was not until the mid-1970s, in Saskatchewan, that an effort was made to consolidate existing health and safety laws from various industries into one comprehensive law that would address principal economic sectors such as industry, construction, and mining.

Occupational Health and Safety Legislation

Any discussion of employee health and safety today is different from what it would have been three decades ago. The passage of health and safety laws dramatically changed the role that management must play in ensuring that the physical working conditions meet adequate standards. We might say that occupational health and safety legislation committed the employer to health and safety programs in the same way that human rights legislation has committed the employer to promoting shared dignity and respect.

Occupational Health and Safety Legislation Standards set to ensure safe and healthy working conditions and provide stiff penalties for violators.

The Purpose of Legislation

As you will learn in Chapter 17, labour legislation in Canada falls under both federal and provincial jurisdictions, and the same is true with health and safety legislation. Laws have been enacted to apply to most, if not all, Canadian businesses. These laws have established comprehensive and specific health standards; they authorize inspections to ensure that standards are met, and they empower the federal or provincial authorities to monitor compliance in procedures such as keeping records of illness and injuries, designating safety representatives, or establishing joint management and employee health and safety committees.

Established federal and provincial health and safety standards are quite complex. Standards exist for such diverse conditions as noise levels, air impurities, physical protection equipment, the height of toilet partitions, and the correct size of ladders. More recently, there has been research into repetitive strain injuries, video display terminal use and eye strain, and the development of training and education programs.

In many cases, the regulations to the act or code are as extensive as the legislation itself and in some cases, more so. Nevertheless, employers are responsible for knowing these standards and ensuring that all that apply to them are followed. Table 15-1 outlines legislation in each jurisdiction and the bodies responsible for enforcing it. While each statute differs in its approach to assigning responsibility for health and safety in the workplace, the basic concepts of shared responsibility, clearly assigned health and safety duties, and workers' rights are present in most legislation.

TABLE 15-1   Occupational Health and Safety Legislation in Canada

Jurisdiction	Legislation	Responsible
Federal	Canada Labour Code	Occupational Safety and Health Branch–Department of Human Resources Development
Alberta	Occupational Health and Safety Act	Occupational Health and Safety Division
British Columbia	Workers Compensation Act Workplace Act	Workers' Compensation Board
Manitoba	Workplace Safety and Health Act	Workplace Safety, Health and Support Services Division
New Brunswick	Occupational Health and Safety Act	Workplace Health, Safety, and Compensation Commission
Newfoundland	Occupational Health and Safety Act	Occupational Health and Safety Division–Department of Employment and Labour
Nova Scotia	Occupational Health and Safety Act	Occupational Health and Safety–Department of Labour
Ontario	Occupational Health and Safety Act	Operations Division–Ministry of Labour
Prince Edward Island	Occupational Health and Safety Act	Occupational Health and Safety Division–Department of Provincial Affairs and Attorney General
Quebec	An Act Respecting Occupational Health and Safety	Commission de la santé et de la sécurité du travail
Saskatchewan	Occupational Health and Safety Act	Occupational Health and Safety Division–Department of Labour
Northwest Territories	Safety Act	Department of Safety and Public Services
Yukon	Occupational Health and Safety Act	Department of Justice

Source: Compiled from *1998 Canadian Master Labour Guide,* 12th edition (Toronto: CCH Canadian Limited, 1998), p. 1002, 1019–21.

Shared Responsibility A system where employers and employees share the responsibility for health and safety in the workplace.

Workers' Rights The employer's right to direct workers and control the production process must be counterbalanced by rights for the employees. Basic rights include the right to participate, the right to know, the right to refuse work, and the right to stop work.

Shared Responsibility   The concept of shared responsibility means that employers and employees share the responsibility for occupational health and safety. This partnership assumes that the best way to identify problems and develop solutions is to consult the people who actually use the workplace. To work well, this system should involve everyone—from the CEO to the worker—and should establish a complete, unbroken chain of responsibility and accountability.

Workers' Rights   Workers' rights act as a balance to the employer's right to direct workers and control the production process. Basic rights include:

a. The right to participate in the process of identifying and resolving health and safety concerns either as members of joint health and safety committees or through representatives.
b. The right to know about potential hazards and to receive information about machinery, equipment, working conditions, processes, and hazardous substances. The Workplace Hazardous Materials Information System (WHMIS) plays a key role in educating employees about handling materials controlled by the federal *Hazardous Products Act* (see Figure 15-1).
c. The right to refuse work that may be dangerous to their own health and safety or to that of another worker.
d. As members of a joint health and safety committee, workers have the right to stop work if they determine that the work is dangerous to anyone.

Workplace Hazardous Materials Information System (WHMIS) This process plays a key role in educating employees about handling materials controlled by the federal *Hazardous Products Act.*

FIGURE 15-1 Designation of Hazardous Materials

There are six classes of controlled products:

Class A—Compressed Gas

Class B—Flammable and Combustible Material

Class C—Oxidizing Material

Class D—Poisonous and Infectious Material

Division 1—Material Causing Immediate and Serious Toxic Effects

Division 2—Material Causing Other Toxic Effects

Division 3—Biohazardous Infectious Material

Class E—Corrosive Material

Class F—Dangerously Reactive Material

Source: Hazardous Products Act, R.S.C. 1985, c. 24 (3rd Supp.), Schedule II, s.2.

Health and Safety Duties   Each statute assigns specific health and safety duties to employers, managers, and workers. In Ontario—which has Canada's largest workforce—the directors of an organization are expected to ensure that the organization complies with all applicable legislation and regulations. Employers are expected to protect the health and safety of workers and to properly investigate workplace accidents. Workers are generally expected to work safely.[6]

Health and Safety Duties Specific duties that the law assigns to managers, employers, and workers to help ensure a safe and healthy workplace.

Enforcing Occupational Health and Safety Legislation

A government health and safety officer may enter a workplace at any time, without prior notification, to see if the requirements of health and safety legislation are being met. The officer has the power to:

- require, inspect, and copy any drawing, record, or report;
- conduct or take tests of any equipment, article, or substance found on the premises; and
- make such examinations deemed necessary for determining the cause of any accident or ill health of a worker.[7]

The examination may lead the officer to make a wide variety of orders. For example, the officer may order an employer or a worker to stop work, store and handle substances properly, install first-aid equipment, or stop emitting contaminants.

Penalties for Statutory Violations

Employers, managers, and workers may be prosecuted in the courts, although this measure is generally viewed as a last resort. Across Canada, the guilty party may either be fined, serve a jail term, or both. The amount of fines varies between jurisdictions. In the Northwest Territories, for example, an employee may be fined up to $50,000 and spend six months in jail, while a corporation may be fined a maximum of $500,000.[8] In Ontario, the maximum fine for a corporation is also $500,000, but an individual can be fined as much as $25,000 or serve a twelve-month jail term.[9] All jurisdictions do offer an appeals process.

Job Safety

If businesses are concerned with efficiency and profits, you may ask, why would they do more than the minimum required by law? The answer is the profit motive itself. The cost of accidents can be, and for many organizations is, a substantial additional cost of doing business.

A 1996 report by the Industrial Accident Prevention Association of Ontario estimated that disability claims cost Canadian companies up to $78,000 per injury per employee. The cost of claims is both direct and indirect. Besides paying a specific sum to the employee the company also experiences clerical and administrative costs, production delays, loss of expertise, production and material damage, and legal costs.[10]

Accident Causes and Preventative Measures

The cause of an accident can be generally classified as either human or environmental. Human causes are directly attributable to human error brought about by carelessness, intoxication, daydreaming, inability to do the job, or other human deficiency. In contrast, environmental causes are attributable to the workplace and include the tools, equipment, physical plant, and general work environment. Both of these sources are important, but in terms of numbers, the human factor is responsible for the vast majority of accidents. No matter how much effort is made to create a work environment that is accident-free, a low accident rate record can only be achieved by concentrating on the human element.

One of the main objectives of safety engineers is to scrutinize the work environment to locate sources of potential accidents. In addition to looking for

Meet

Barbara Crosby
Co-chair of JOSH Committee,
Revenue Canada
Charlottetown Tax Services Office

Answering tax-related questions and conducting audits isn't particularly dangerous work. And indeed, serious accidents are rare among the 100 or so employees at the Tax Services Office in Charlottetown, PEI. But that doesn't mean that health and safety issues aren't given a high priority at the office.

Barbara Crosby is co-chair of the office's joint Occupational Health and Safety (JOSH) Committee. The assistant director of client services, she alternates chairing its meetings with her co-chair, a union member. The committee has a high profile in the organization.

It conducts regular safety "walk-throughs" of the office's two sites. "If you look at something long enough, day after day, it starts to seem normal," says Ms Crosby. "We can take a fresh look at someone's cubicle and point out that the tangle of wires under the desk could well trip someone." The committee also acts as a liaison with the fire marshall's office ("Did you know there are three different kinds of fire extinguisher?" asks Ms Crosby); ensures that special equipment, such as an emergency evacuation chair for handicapped employees, is in place and maintained; and produces a folder of emergency and first-aid information for employees, such as checklists for dealing with an injury—or a bomb threat (the office is a federal government agency, after all).

The JOSH committee also handles any complaints about health or safety that an employee's supervisor wasn't able to resolve satisfactorily, and consults with management on ergonomic issues. For example, "We're gradually replacing people's keyboards with the new "natural" ones that have two parts and elevate your wrists," says Ms Crosby.

But for the most part, the committee focuses on health promotion. It sponsors frequent "lunchbox sessions" on topics from nutrition to heart-and-stroke awareness to stress reduction. "We recently had a physiotherapist come in to talk about sitting properly, and teach some exercises people could do to help avoid sore necks and backs," says Ms Crosby. "We felt this topic was so important that we got permission from management to hold the sessions during working hours rather than lunchtime, and we encouraged everyone to attend." The committee played a similar advocacy role in getting management to approve a flexible-hours policy to make it easier for employees to fit a workout into their work day.

Does all the JOSH committee's work have tangible results? "I think our role is to educate, to pique people's interest," says Ms Crosby. "And changes do happen, gradually." It's hard to prove that a particular change is a direct result of the JOSH committee's efforts, but several employees have quit smoking recently; several others have joined fitness clubs; a few people who were on workers' compensation with carpal tunnel syndrome have returned and are working well with the new keyboards. All the lunchbox sessions are well attended. It certainly seems as if the committee is doing something right.

And as Ms Crosby points out, "There's bound to be benefits for the employer as well as the employee, because if people fee better, they work better."

such obvious factors as loose steps, oil on the walkway, or a sharp protrusion on a piece of equipment at eye level, safety engineers will seek those that are less obvious. Standards established by applicable health and safety legislation provide an excellent reference to guide the search for potential hazards.

What traditional measures can we look to for preventing accidents? The answer lies in education, skill training, engineering, protection devices, and regulation enforcement. We have summarized these in Table 15-2.

TABLE 15-2 Accident Prevention Means

Education	Create safety awareness by posting highly visible signs that proclaim safety slogans, placing articles on accident prevention in organization newsletters, or exhibiting a sign proclaiming the number of days the plant has operated without a lost-day accident.
Skills Training	Incorporate accident prevention measures into the learning process.
Engineering	Prevent accidents through both the design of the equipment and the design of the jobs themselves. This may also include eliminating those factors that promote operator fatigue, boredom, and daydreaming.
Protection	Provide protective equipment where necessary. This may include safety shoes, gloves, hard hats, safety glasses, and noise mufflers. Protection also includes performing preventive maintenance on machinery.
Regulation Enforcement	The best safety rules and regulations will be ineffective in reducing accidents if they are not enforced. Additionally, if such rules are not enforced, the employer may be liable for any injuries that occur.

Ensuring Job Safety

One way management can be assured that rules and regulations are being enforced is to develop some type of feedback system. This can be provided by inspection of the work surroundings. Management can rely on oral or written reports for information on enforcement. Another approach is to get first-hand information by periodically walking through the work areas to make observations. Ideally, managers will rely on reports from supervisors on the floor and employees in the work areas and support these by their own personal observations.

Although safety is everyone's responsibility, it should be part of the organization's culture and a paramount accountability for members of management (see Table 15-3). Top management must also show its commitment to safety by providing safety devices and maintaining equipment. Furthermore, safety should become part of every employee's performance appraisal. Holding employees accountable for evaluating their performance sends the message that the company is serious about safety. Although a responsibility created for the most part by statute, health and safety committees serve a vital role in helping the company and its employees implement and maintain a good health and safety program.

A Safety Issue: Workplace Violence

Inasmuch as there is growing concern for job safety for workers, a much greater emphasis today is being placed on the increasing violence that has erupted on the job. No organization is immune from this, and the problem appears to be getting worse. Far too many employers are experiencing workplace aggression between co-workers with unnecessary and costly disruptions to morale and productivity, as well as costly lawsuits.

Violent acts committed on the job have traditionally been viewed as a criminal matter and as such, have received little attention as an occupational health and safety issue. However, British Columbia and Saskatchewan have attempted to address the issue of violence in the workplace. For example, violence in the workplace

TABLE 15-3 Management's Responsibility for Safety

Every member of management will ensure that:

1. Each employee has had a thorough initial review of all rules related to his or her job and that he or she knows and understands them. Every manager will also make sure that a complete review of all rules is held with each employee on an annual basis and that all rules are enforced.

2. Any unsafe practice or condition reported by an employee is promptly placed in the hazard report system and followed up promptly. He or she will conduct and record the results of a formal inspection of the entire physical plant area under his or her responsibility not less than once every two months and develop a system to make sure that all critical parts in this area are inspected as necessary or required.

3. Each employee received well-planned, proper job instruction (PJI) with every new or different job assigned to him or her and that safety tips are given frequently during routine contacts on a day-to-day basis.

4. Each new employee receives an adequate, complete indoctrination to his or her job on all aspects of safety and efficiency before being permitted to work ... and that several follow-up contacts are made with him or her during this probationary period to determine that the employee knows and is following all required standards.

5. Each employee under his or her supervision attends a weekly safety meeting that has been properly planned and presented by the manager.

6. All employees know, understand, and practise the principles of good housekeeping and that the "order" of his or her area of responsibility reflects this desired goal at all times.

7. All employees are properly issued required protective equipment and motivated to wear it as prescribed at all times.

8. Every accident resulting in personal injury or property damage is promptly and efficiently investigated with results reported on the supervisor's report form before the end of the shift on which the accident occurred.

9. Each employee in his or her charge is recognized frequently on a personal basis when he or she demonstrates behaviour that is safe or desired ... and that this recognition should reflect the supervisor's personal enthusiasm, constant interest, and deep concern for the safety and welfare of his or her employees.

10. His or her personal example of safe behaviour sets the best possible example for everyone with whom he or she comes in contact.

Source: Adapted from Frank E. Bird, Jr., and George L. Germain, *Practical Loss Control Leadership*, 2nd Edition (Loganville, GA: International Loss Control Institute, 1992), p. 30. Reproduced with permission.

is defined in British Columbia's occupational health and safety regulation as: "the attempt or actual exercise of a person, other than a worker, of a physical force so as to cause injury to a worker, and includes any threatening statement or behaviour which gives a worker a reasonable cause to believe that the worker is at risk of injury."[11] In British Columbia, employers have a duty to ensure that a worker who is injured or suffers some other adverse effect as a result of an incident of violence is advised to consult a physician of their choice for treatment or referral.[12]

The issue for companies is how to prevent the violence from occurring on the job.

Because the circumstances of each incident are different, a specific plan of action for companies to follow is difficult to detail. However, several suggestions can be made.[13] First, the organization must develop a plan to deal with the issue. This may mean reviewing all corporate policies to ensure that they are not adversely affecting employees. In fact, there was a common factor in most instances of workplace violence, and that was that the employees involved felt that they had not been treated with respect or dignity. They were either laid off without any warning or treated too harshly (in their mind) in the discipline process. Sound, HRM, practices can help to ensure that employees are handled with care and sensitivity, even in the most difficult of cases such as terminations.

Organizations must also train their management personnel to identify troubled employees before a problem results in violence. Employee assistance programs (EAPs) can be designed specifically to help these individuals. As we'll see shortly in our discussion of EAPs, an individual rarely goes from being happy to assaulting co-workers overnight. Furthermore, if supervisors are better able to spot the types of demonstrated behaviours that may lead to violence, then those who cannot be helped through the EAP can be removed from the organization before others are harmed. Organizations should also implement stronger security mechanisms. For example, many women who are assaulted at work, following a domestic dispute, are attacked by someone who didn't belong on company premises. Well-lit parking lots and corridors as well as monitored entry and exit points go a long way to adding protection. Moreover, weapons such as guns and knives must not be allowed on the premises.

Sadly, no matter how careful the organization is and how much it attempts to prevent workplace violence, some will still occur. In those cases, the organization must be prepared to deal with the situation and be prepared to offer whatever assistance it can to deal with the aftermath.

Maintaining a Healthy Work Environment

Unhealthy work environments are a concern to us all. If workers cannot function properly at their jobs because of constant headaches, watering eyes, breathing difficulties, or fear of exposure to materials that may cause long-term health problems, productivity will decrease. Consequently, creating a healthy work environment not only is the proper thing to do, but it also benefits the employer. Often referred to as sick buildings, work environments that contain harmful materials such as airborne chemicals, asbestos, or other indoor pollution have forced employers to take drastic steps. For many, this has meant having to deal with asbestos in older buildings. Because extended exposure to asbestos has been linked to lung cancer, companies are required by various environmental protection and occupational health and safety agencies to remove it or at least seal it so it cannot escape into the air.

These problems that traditionally have been found mainly in manufacturing environments have recently become a concern for many school boards across Canada, particularly with respect to their portable classrooms. Many have had to refurbish or close the portable classrooms altogether.

Sick Buildings An unhealthy work environment caused by harmful materials such as airborne chemicals, asbestos, or other indoor pollutants.

TABLE 15-4 Suggestions for Keeping the Workplace Healthy

1. **Make sure workers get enough fresh air**. The cost of providing it is peanuts compared with the expense of cleaning up a problem. One simple tactic is to unseal vents closed in overzealous efforts to conserve energy.

2. **Avoid suspect building materials and furnishings**. A general rule is that if it stinks, it's going to emit an odour. Substitute tacks for smelly carpet glue and natural wood for chemically treated plywood.

3. **Test new buildings for toxins before occupancy**. Failure to do so may lead to potential health problems. Most consultants say that letting a new building sit temporarily vacant allows the worst fumes to dissipate.

4. **Provide a smoke-free environment**. If you don't want to ban smoking entirely, then establish an area for smokers that has its own ventilation system.

5. **Keep air ducts clean and dry**. Water in air ducts is a fertile breeding ground for fungi and other harmful irritants.

6. **Pay attention to workers' complaints**. A designated employee should record dates and particulars.

Source: Faye Rice, "Do You Work in a Sick Building?" *Fortune* (July 2, 1990), p. 88. Reproduced with permission.

Although specific problems and their elimination go beyond the scope of this text, Table 15-4 lists some suggestions for keeping the workplace healthy. One in particular, which has received noteworthy legislative consideration, is the smoke-free environment.

The Smoke-Free Environment

Should smoking be prohibited in a public place of business, even, say, in a bar, where owners claim that banning smoking could put them out of business? The dangers and health problems associated with smoking have been well documented and are reflected in increased health insurance and operational costs. Smokers have been found to be absent more than non-smokers and have lower productivity due to smoke breaks. They also cause damage to property with cigarette burns and fires. Their habit means more routine maintenance (ash/butt clean-up), and it also creates problems for other employees through second-hand smoke. Smoke-free policies are one means to control the problems associated with smoking; this is reinforced by society's renewed emphasis on wellness, which has resulted in smoke-free policies such as legislated smoking-area prohibitions in several parts of Canada.

Smoke-Free Policies Organization policies that prohibit smoking on company premises.

Repetitive Strain Injuries (RSIs)

Whenever workers perform a continuous motion such as typing without proper workstation design (seat and keyboard height adjustments), they run the risk of developing repetitive strain injuries (RSIs), referred to as cumulative trauma disorders. Symptoms of these complaints include headaches, dizziness, and even nerve damage. The most common area affected is the wrist where nerve damage can lead to pain, weakness, and loss of feeling, a condition known as carpal tunnel syndrome. Carpal tunnel has been found to be directly linked to poor office design and the way that work is performed. These injuries cost Canadian companies millions of dollars every year.

One chief means of reducing the potential effects of cumulative trauma disorders is through the use of ergonomics. Ergonomics involves fitting the work environment to the individual rather than the other way around. Every employee is different in shape, size, height, and so on, yet, too often, we expect each worker to adjust to "standard" office furnishings. Instead, recognizing and acting on these differences, ergonomics looks at customizing the work environment such that it is not only conducive to productive work, but keeps the employee healthy.

When we speak of ergonomics, we are primarily addressing two main areas: the workplace and its equipment and furniture. Organizations are reviewing their office settings, their work environment, and their space utilization in an effort to provide more productive atmospheres. This means that new furniture is being designed and purchased to reduce back strain and fatigue. Properly designed and fitted office equipment, like adjustable desk add-ons for a keyboard or computer monitor stand, can help reduce repetitive strain injuries. Furthermore, organizations are using colours such as mauves and greys that are more pleasing to the eye and experimenting with lighting levels to lessen employee exposure to harmful eye strain associated with today's video display terminals.

Repetitive Strain Injuries (RSIs) Injuries caused by continuous and repetitive movements, usually of the hand and arm, as in typing.

Cumulative Trauma Disorder An occupational injury that occurs from repetitively performing similar physical movements.

Ergonomics The process of matching the work environment to the individual.

Triumph! The "psyching up" that an athlete goes through can be stressful, but it can also lead to maximum performance.

Ethical Decisions in HRM:

Smokers' Rights

It has been well documented that smoking can create health problems. Accordingly, insurance premiums on health as well as other insurance like life are significantly higher to those who light up. In most cases, employers have passed these increased premium costs on to the worker. Companies have become more stringent in developing policies on smoking, and many have banned it altogether on company premises. Clearly, the smoker today is disadvantaged, but how far can that go?

Can an organization refuse to hire someone simply because he or she smokes? Depending on the organization, the requirement of the job, and the jurisdiction in which one lives, they might. Even so, employers may take this one step further. Companies may, in fact, be able to terminate an individual for smoking off the job—on an employee's own time.

Do you believe companies have the right to dictate what you do outside of work? If an organization can take such action against employees for smoking and justify it on the grounds that it creates a health problem, what about other things we do? Eating too much fatty food can create a health problem, so should we be susceptible to discipline for being caught eating fast food? Some members of the medical community cite how one or two alcoholic drinks a day may in fact be therapeutic and prevent the onset of certain diseases. Yet, alcohol can be damaging to humans. Accordingly, should we be fired for having a glass of wine with dinner or drinking a beer at a sporting event?

What do you think? How far should we permit wellness regulation in our organizations?

Stress

Stress A condition in which you have either the opportunity to gain something that is important to you but the outcome is uncertain or you are prevented from gaining something by constraints and demands placed on you.

Stress seems to be the buzzword of the nineties, but what is it? A classic definition of stress describes it as a condition in which you have the opportunity to gain something that is important to you but the outcome is uncertain. Or, it may be that you are prevented from gaining something because of restrictions or demands placed on you.[14] In the case of an opportunity, stress can have a positive effect. For example, the "psyching-up" that an athlete goes through can be stressful, but it can also lead to maximum performance. When constraints or demands are placed on you, however, stress can become harmful.

Constraints are barriers that keep you from getting what you want. Buying a new car may be your desire, but if you cannot afford the down payment, you are stopped from buying it. Accordingly, constraints inhibit you in ways that take the control of a situation out of your hands. If you cannot afford the car, you walk or take the bus.

Demands, on the other hand, may cause you to give up something you desire. If you wish to attend a concert on campus Thursday night but have a major exam Friday morning, the test may take precedence. Thus, demands preoccupy your time and force you to shift priorities.

Constraints and demands can lead to potential stress. When they are coupled with outcomes that are both uncertain and important to you, potential stress becomes actual stress. Regardless of the situation, if you remove the uncertainty or the importance, you remove stress. For instance, you may have been constrained from buying the car because of your budget, but if you know you will get a company car with your first job after graduating from college or university, the uncertainty element is significantly reduced. Accordingly, if you are auditing a class for no grade, the importance of the major examination is reduced. However, when constraints or demands have an impact on an important event and the outcome is unknown, pressure is added—pressure resulting in stress.

Causes of Stress

Stress can be caused by a number of factors called stressors, which can be grouped into two major categories: personal factors and organizational factors. Both of these categories directly affect the person and, ultimately, the job. For the moment, we will postpone our discussion of organizational factors and cover them in the "burn-out" section of this chapter. However, because personal factors affect and are affected by organizational factors, we will address them now.

Almost anything can cause stress, and while each individual can tolerate different levels, once the stressors become too great, everyone exhibits some behaviour change. Stress can be either positive or negative. It is said to be positive when the situation offers an opportunity for one to gain something. Certainly we all know that the death of a family member, a divorce, or being fired can cause major stress, but so can getting married, the birth of a child, or landing that new job. For example, remember the time you finally got that date with the person of your dreams? Was it a happy time? Yes. But what did you go through to get ready for it? You debated over what clothes to wear, where to go, how you looked, and so on. You were nervous, but all in all, you had a good time on the date, even though it caused you a lot of stress.

While we are not attempting to minimize stress in people's lives, it is important to recognize that both good and bad personal factors may cause stress. Of course, when you consider the changes that are occurring in Canadian companies such as globalization, downsizing, etc., it is little wonder that stress is so rampant. And stress on the job knows no boundaries. In Japan, a Fukoku Life Insurance Company study identified worker stress in 70 per cent of employees.[15] In fact, the Japanese have a concept called *karoshi*, which means death from overworking. Many literally work themselves to death.

Stressors Anything that causes stress in an individual.

Symptoms of Stress

In North America, stress is seldom the cause of death, but there are a number of symptoms of job stress. These are of three types: physiological, psychological, or behavioural.[16]

The physiological symptoms of stress are often difficult to detect with the naked eye because they relate to the medical changes that occur inside the individual. Such changes as increased heart and breathing rates, higher blood pressure, headaches, and even heart attacks can be brought on by stress but are not easy to spot early.

Physiological Symptoms Characteristics of stress such as increased heart and breathing rates, higher blood pressure, and headaches.

Psychological Symptoms Characteristics of stress such as tension, anxiety, irritability, boredom, and procrastination.

Behavioural Symptoms Symptoms of stress characterized by decreased productivity, increased absenteeism and turnover, and possibly even substance abuse.

Burn-out Chronic and long-term stress can lead to emotional and/or physical exhaustion and a decline in work productivity.

Has another tight deadline given you a headache? That may be a symptom of stress. Other physiological symptoms include high blood pressure and increased breathing and heart rates.

The **psychological symptoms** of stress manifest themselves as tension, anxiety, irritability, boredom, and procrastination. Alone or in combinations these can cause harm to an individual in an organization. They can, for example, lead to significant job dissatisfaction.

It's the third group, the **behavioural symptoms**, that has the greatest effect on the organization because they are reflected in terms of decreased productivity, increased absenteeism and turnover, and even substance abuse. Where one or more of these symptoms persists for a prolonged time, even greater problems may arise for both the individual and the company. This extended, chronic stress is commonly referred to as burn-out.

Chronic Stress: Burn-out

Worker **burn-out** costs the North American industry billions of dollars. According to the Conference Board of Canada, the cost of stress in Canada can reach $12 billion a year.[17] The board found that Canadian workers take an average of five days per year off for stress and personal problems, a figure that has doubled over the past three decades. Burn-out is a multifaceted phenomenon, the by-product of both personal and organization variables. It can be defined as a function of three concerns: (a) emotional and/or physical exhaustion, (b) lowered job productivity, and (c) automatized or machine-like performance of duties.[18]

Causes and Symptoms of Burn-out   The factors contributing to burn-out can be identified as follows: general characteristics of the organization such as work ethic and size; perceptions of how the organization is managed and relations among co-workers; perceptions of the role of employees in the organization; individual characteristics such as age and seniority; and the perceived outcomes of working for the organization, which are evident in level of job satisfaction and employee turnover rate. Table 15-5 summarizes these factors.[19] While these variables can lead to burn-out, their presence does not guarantee that burn-out will occur. Much of what actually happens depends on the individual's ability to work under and handle stress. Stressful conditions, therefore, may result in stress itself or in problems that arise from this stress.[20]

Reducing Burn-out   Recognizing that stress is a fact of life and must be channelled properly, organizations need to establish procedures for reducing these stress levels before workers burn out. Although no clear-cut remedies are available, four techniques have been found to be useful:

1. **Identification**. This is the analysis of the incidence, prevalence, and characteristics of burn-out in individuals, work groups, subunits, or organizations.

2. **Prevention**. Attempts should be made to prevent the burn-out process from getting underway before it begins.

3. **Mediation**. This involves procedures for slowing, halting, or reversing the burn-out process.

4. **Remediation**. Techniques are needed for individuals who are already burned out or are rapidly approaching the end stages of this process.[21] An employee who exhibits signs of burn-out should still be showed respect and be encouraged to seek appropriate help such as counselling, family and peer support, or medical treatment.[22]

The key point here is that accurate identification is made and then, and only then, is a program tailored to meet that need. Because of the costs—both personal and financial—associated with burn-out, many companies are implementing a full array of

TABLE 15-5 Variables Found to Be Significantly Related to Burn-out

Organization Characteristics	Perceptions of Organization	Perceptions of Role	Individual Characteristics	Outcome
Caseload	Leadership	Autonomy	Family/friends support	Satisfaction
Formalization	Communication	Job involvement	Sex	Turnover
Turnover rate	Staff support	Being supervised	Age	
Staff size	Peers	Work pressure	Tenure	
	Clarity	Feedback	Ego level	
	Rules and procedures	Accomplishment		
	Innovation	Meaningfulness		
	Administrative support			

Source: Baron Perlman and E. Alan Hartman, "Burnout: Summary and Future Research," *Human Relations,* Vol. 25, No. 4 (1982), p. 294. Reproduced with permission.

programs to help alleviate the problem. Many of these programs are designed to do two things: make the job more pleasant for the worker and increase productivity.

Employee Assistance Programs (EAPs)

No matter what kind of organization or industry one works in, it is certain that employees will have personal problems at times. Whether it is job stress, legal, marital, financial, or health-related, there is one thing they have in common—if an employee experiences a personal problem, sooner or later it will have an impact in the workplace in terms of lowered productivity, increased absenteeism, or turnover.[23] To help employees deal with these personal problems, more and more companies are implementing employee assistance programs (EAPs).

Let us see how this works. Suppose you have a worker, Beverly, who has been with you for a number of years. Beverly has been a solid performer throughout her tenure, but lately something has happened. You notice Beverly's performance declining: The quality of her work is diminishing, she has been late three times the past five weeks, and rumour has it that Beverly is having marital problems. You could, and would, have every right to discipline Beverly according to the company's discipline process. But it is doubtful discipline alone would help; consequently, you may end up firing Beverly. If you do, you will have lost a once-good performer, and must fill her position with another—a process that may take eighteen months to finally achieve the productivity level Beverly had. However, instead of firing Beverly you decide to refer her to the company's EAP. This confidential program works with Beverly to determine the cause(s) of her problems, and seeks to help her overcome them. Although Beverly meets very frequently at first with the EAP counsellor, you notice that after a short period she is back on the job, improving her performance. And after four months, she is performing at the level she once did. In this scenario, you now have a fully-productive employee back in four months, as opposed to possibly eighteen months had you fired and replaced Beverly.

In Chapter 14, we identified EAPs as an integral part of the progressive company's benefits program, but it is important to recognize that this employee benefit is also a valuable tool for the company itself. Many companies have

Employee Assistance Programs (EAPs) Plans intended to help employees deal with issues such as stress, depression, anxiety, family and marital problems, and substance abuse.

found EAPs useful in helping to control rising health insurance premiums—especially in the areas of mental health and substance abuse.[24] The EAP is an operation that is designed to help employees deal with such problems as "alcohol and chemical dependency, emotional problems, stress, pre-retirement planning, marital problems, careers, finances, legal matters, or termination."[25] In addition, EAPs are becoming involved in everything from helping employees who have AIDS to counselling on cultural diversity issues.[26]

No matter how beneficial EAPs may be to an organization, employee participation cannot be taken for granted. Employees must be convinced that EAPs are worthwhile. For employees to accept EAPs, a few criteria must exist: "familiarity with the program, and the perception of the trustworthiness and opportunity for personal attention."[27] Accordingly, employees must be thoroughly informed regarding how the EAP works, how they can use its services, and how confidentiality is guaranteed. Furthermore, supervisors must be properly trained to recognize changes in employee behaviour, when to refer them to the EAP, and how to do that in a sensitive and confidential manner.

Although EAPs can help employees when problems arise, companies have given support to finding ways to short-circuit some factors that may lead to those personal problems. In doing so, many organizations have actively begun to promote wellness programs.

Wellness Programs

Wellness Programs Programs designed to help employees maximize their physical well-being.

When we mention wellness programs in any organization, we are talking about anything that is designed to keep employees healthy. These programs are varied and may focus on such things as smoking cessation, weight control, stress management, physical fitness, nutrition education, high blood pressure control, and so on. Wellness programs are designed to help cut employer health costs and to lower absenteeism and turnover by preventing health-related problems before they develop. Absenteeism costs the North American economy an estimated $50 billion annually,[28] so wellness programs make economic sense. For instance, it is estimated that over a ten-year period, the Adolph Coors Company saved almost US$2 million in decreased medical premium payments, reduced sick leave, and increased productivity. For Coors, that represents a more than $6 return for every $1 spent on wellness.[29] Not all wellness programs will produce such dramatic results, of course, and as with EAPs, they will only work if employees see them as worthwhile.

International Health and Safety

It is important to know the health and safety environments of each country in which an organization operates. Generally, corporations in Canada, western Europe, Japan, and the United States put great emphasis on the health and welfare of their employees. However, most businesses in less-developed countries have limited resources and thus cannot establish the same kind of awareness or protection programs.

Most countries have laws and regulatory agencies that protect workers from hazardous work environments. It is important for Canadian firms to learn the often complex regulations that exist, as well as the cultural expectations of the local labour force. Manufacturers, in particular, where there are a myriad of potentially hazardous situations, must design and establish facilities that meet the needs, expectations, and attitudes of the local employees—not necessarily those of Canadians.

The Union Carbide pesticide plant in Bhopal, India, provides a dramatic example of the impact of local cultural attitudes toward health and safety. Union Carbide built its plant with all the safety devices that would be available in a comparable plant in North America, as well as with the expectation that managers and employees who worked there would react to an emergency like North American workers. However, in the early morning of December 3, 1994, poisonous vapours spewed forth from the plant and killed 2,000 people while injuring more than 200,000. The company argued that local management and workers had violated the company's safety procedures.[30] It appears that company headquarters had not fully considered normal work practices in the country.

International Health Issues

For corporations preparing to send executives or other employees on overseas assignments, a few basic health-related items appear on every checklist.

1. An Up-to-date Health Certificate. Often called a "shot book," this is the individual's record of vaccinations against infectious diseases such as cholera, typhoid, and smallpox. Each country has its own vaccination requirements for entry inside its borders, and updated information can be obtained from the Department of Foreign Affairs' *Travel Information and Advisory Reports* regarding the situation in particular countries.

2. A General First Aid Kit. This should include all over-the-counter medications such as aspirin, cold and cough remedies, and so on, the employee or family members would usually take at home, but that might not be available at the overseas drugstore. In addition, any prescription drugs should be packed in twice the quantity expected to be used. In case of an accidental dunking, overheating, or other problem, it is wise to pack the two supplies of drugs separately. It also is advisable to know the generic name—not the trade name—of any prescription drug. Finally, if necessary, include special items such as disinfectant solutions to treat fresh fruit or vegetables, and water purifying tablets.

3. Emergency Plans. Upon arrival at the foreign destination, check out the local medical and dental facilities and plan on what care can be expected in the host country or where the closest appropriate medical care is. This might include evacuation of a sick or injured employee or family member to another city or even another country. For example, expatriates in China often prefer to go to Hong Kong for regular medical checkups. It is always wise to take along copies of all family members' medical and dental records.

International Safety Issues

Safety for the expatriate executive has become increasingly an issue of security, both while traveling and after arrival. Again, DFAIT's provides travel advisories in its *Travel Information and Advisory Reports*; in November 1998 DFAIT recommended that Canadians avoid all non-essential travel to eighteen different countries, including Albania (civil unrest, gang violence), Burundi (civil unrest), Honduras (civil unrest and natural disaster in the aftermath of hurricane Mitch) and Montserrat (volcanic activity). DFAIT's country reports will include other relevant safety information for Canadians.

Safety begins before the trip, and depends on carefully researching the destination country as well as the travel arrangements; travellers to certain parts of the world, for example, try to avoid flying on US airlines because they believe they are more susceptible to terrorist attacks than, say, Canadian or Asian airlines. Ostentatious behaviour attracts pickpockets, thieves, and kidnappers, whether in the airport, on the plane, or after arrival. In high-risk locations many corporations now provide electronic safety systems, floodlights, and the like for home and office, as well as bodyguards or armed chauffeurs—but individual alertness is the key factor. It is suggested that kidnappers select their potential targets by seeking someone who is valuable to either a government or corporation, with lots of family money or a wealthy sponsor, and where there is opportunity to plan and execute the kidnapping.

In general, companies have a responsibility to provide expatriate employees with full information on health and safety conditions in the country of assignment, and to provide reasonable means to deal with the problems that may exist. In early 1999 an assignment to Christchurch, New Zealand, for instance, was likely to pose fewer health challenges than one to Asmara, Eritrea, and many less safety concerns than a posting in Lagos, Nigeria.

Study Tools and Applications

Summary

This summary relates to the Learning Objectives provided on p.437.
After having read this chapter, you should know:

1. Occupational health and safety legislation falls under both federal and provincial jurisdictions. Basic concepts include shared responsibility, workers' rights, and health and safety duties. Government inspectors may may check a workplace at any time to see if standards are met. Organizations and individuals may be fined or jailed for violating health and safety legislation.

2. Federal and provincial occupational health and safety legislation assigns specific duties to employers, managers, and employees. In Ontario, for example, the directors of an organization ensure that laws and regulations are followed, the employer is responsible for providing a safe work environment and properly investigating accidents, and the employee is expected to work safely.

3. The leading causes of accidents are human or environmental factors. Traditional measures for preventing accidents include education, skill training, engineering, protection devices, and regulation enforcement. Job safety programs should include everyone in the company—from top management to workers. Joint health and safety committees play a vital role in implementing effective programs.

4. Creating a healthy workplace involves removing any harmful substance, including asbestos, cigarette smoke, and other synthetic pollutants.

5. Two current health-related issues in the workplace are smoke-free policies and repetitive strain injuries. Smoke-free policies in the workplace help to control the problems associated with smoking such as increased health insurance costs, damage to property, reduced productivity, and the effects of second-hand smoke. Repetitive strain injuries (RSIs) or cumulative trauma disorders can be prevented by introducing ergonomically designed furniture and equipment into the workplace.

6. Stress is a condition in which you have the opportunity to gain something that is important to you but the outcome is uncertain. In this case, stress may have a positive effect and lead to maximum performance. If constraints or demands are placed on you

that prevent you from gaining something, stress can be harmful. In the workplace, stress is caused by both personal and organizational factors. Its symptoms may be physiological, psychological, or behavioural. Chronic stress results in burn-out or exhaustion. Signs of burn-out in an employee include emotional and/or physical exhaustion, lowered job productivity, and automatized or machine-like performance of duties.

7. Employee assistance and wellness programs are designed to offer employees a variety of services that will help them to become mentally and physically healthy which, in turn, helps to contain the organization's health care costs.

8. If an organization operates in countries other than Canada, the United States, Western Europe, or Japan it may not be able to establish the same level of health and safety standards for all of its locations. Employees assigned to work abroad should carry a "shot book" and a first aid kit, including any prescription drugs. They should consult the Department of Foreign Affairs *Travel Information and Advisory Report* about their destination before leaving and develop an emergency plan once they arrive.

Key Terms

behavioural symptoms

burn-out

cumulative trauma disorder

employee assistance programs (EAPs)

ergonomics

health and safety duties

occupational health and safety legislation

physiological symptoms

psychological symptoms

repetitive strain injuries (RSIs)

shared responsibility

sick buildings

smoke-free policies

stress

stressors

wellness programs

workers' rights

Workplace Hazardous Materials
    Information System (WHMIS)

EXPERIENTIAL EXERCISE:

Stress and Life Events

The list of life events provided in Table 15-6 is designed to give you some indication of the level of stress in your life. Look at each item, noting those that apply to you. When you have finished, determine your sum total of points and answer the following questions:

1. What does this assessment tell you about the level of stress in your life? Do you feel you are managing your stress well? Explain.

2. What are the main factors that contribute to your stress?

3. What would you suggest you do to lessen this effect of stress?

4. If many of your stressors were job-related, would you consider giving up your job or possibly changing your lifestyle to a more calm state? Explain why or why not.

CASE APPLICATION:

Violence in the Workplace

On the last Sunday Theresa Vince was scheduled to work before taking early retirement from Sears Canada in Chatham, Ontario, her boss, store manager Russell Davis, asked her to stay after the store closed. Neither left the store that night. Police discovered their bodies in Davis's office. The manager had shot his employee in the head and chest and then shot himself. A coroner's inquest was called to look into the deaths and the circumstances that led to the shootings.

The inquest heard that Vince had decided to take early retirement after complaining to a human resources manager at Sears that Davis was sexually harassing her. In the months before the shooting, she had lost weight, couldn't sleep, and found that she no longer enjoyed her work.

The company maintained that its sexual harassment policy was a good one, and that it had been followed by both the company and its employees. Ms Vince, according to Sears, had wanted to handle matters on her own. No one could have predicted the tragedy that took place.

The inquest, however, revealed that the human resources manager had not even bothered to investigate the complaint. There was no documentation of it, and no attempt had been made to interview other employees about it—including Russell Davis.

TABLE 15-6 Life-Event Stress Sheet

Live Events	Mean Value	Live Events	Mean Value
1. Death of spouse	100	25. Outstanding personal achievement	28
2. Divorce	73	26. Spouse beginning or ceasing work outside of home	26
3. Marital separation from spouse	65	27. Beginning or ceasing formal schooling	26
4. Detention in jail or other institution	63	28. Major change in living conditions (e.g., building a new home, remodelling, deterioration of home or neighbourhood)	25
5. Death of a close family member	63		
6. Major personal injury or illness	53		
7. Marriage	50	29. Revision of personal habits (dress, manners, associations, etc.)	24
8. Being fired from work	47		
9. Marital reconciliation with spouse	45	30. Troubles with the boss	23
10. Retirement from work	45	31. Major changes in working hours or conditions	20
11. Major change in the health or behaviour of a family member	44	32. Change in residence	20
		33. Changing to a new school	20
12. Pregnancy	40	34. Major change in usual type and/or amount of recreation	19
13. Sexual difficulties	39		
14. Gaining a new family member (e.g., through birth, adoption, parent moving in, etc.)	39	35. Major change in church activities (e.g., a lot more or a lot less than usual)	19
15. Major bankruptcy readjustment (e.g., merger, reorganization, bankruptcy, etc.)	39	36. Major changes in social activities (e.g., clubs, dancing, movies, visiting, etc.)	18
16. Major change in financial state (e.g., a lot worse off or a lot better off than usual)	38	37. Taking on a loan (e.g., purchasing a car, TV, freezer, etc.)	17
17. Death of a close friend	37		
18. Changing to a different line of work	36	38. Major changes in sleeping habits (a lot more or a lot less sleep, or change in part of day when asleep)	16
19. Major changes in the number of arguments with spouse (e.g., either a lot more or a lot less than usual regarding child rearing, personal habits, etc.)	35		
		39. Major change in the number of family get-togethers (e.g., a lot more or a lot less than usual)	15
20. Taking on a significant mortgage (e.g., purchasing a home, business, etc.)	31	40. Major changes in eating habits (a lot more or a lot less food intake, or very different meal hours or surroundings)	15
21. Foreclosure on a mortgage or loan	30		
22. Major change in responsibilities at work (e.g., promotion, demotion, lateral transfer)	29	41. Vacation	13
		42. Christmas	12
23. Son or daughter leaving home (e.g., marriage, attending university, etc.)	29	43. Minor violations of the law (e.g., traffic tickets, jaywalking, disturbing the peace, etc.)	11
24. In-law troubles	29		

Source: Adapted from T.H. Homes and R.H. Rahe, "The Social Readjustment Rating Scale," *Journal of Psychosomatic Research* (Pergamon Press, Ltd., 1967), pp. 217–18. Reproduced with permission. All rights reserved.

Later it was determined that Mr Davis had been working under enormous pressure. A week before the shootings, he was given an ultimatum to improve his performance, quit, or be fired by the company.[32]

Questions

1. What recommendation would you make to the employer to deal with the situation and to avoid a similar event in the future?

2. What recommendation would you make to employers in general?

3. What recommendation would you make to the provincial government and, in particular, to those responsible for health and safety legislation?

Testing Your Understanding

How well did you fulfil the learning objectives?

1. Occupational health and safety laws place the responsibility for ensuring that health and safety standards are met on
   a. the employer.
   b. the manager.
   c. the employee.
   d. all of the above.

2. In most jurisdictions, common powers of an inspector include the right to
   a. require, inspect, and copy any drawing, record, or report.
   b. conduct a test of any equipment, article, or substance found on the premises.
   c. make such examination as he or she deems necessary for determining the cause of any accident or ill health occurring to a worker.
   d. all of the above.
   e. none of the above.

3. A chemical engineer for a pharmaceutical plant was blinded when a pipe he was adjusting cracked and spewed hot vapour into his face. He wasn't wearing safety glasses or a hard hat, although both were specified for the job he was doing. The report on the accident indicated that the engineer knew about the safety equipment, but that for the past five years, he had gotten along quite well without the cumbersome gear. What means of preventing accidents was not being used effectively in this situation?
   a. Education.
   b. Skills training.
   c. Engineering.
   d. Protection.
   e. Regulation enforcement.

4. In academic life, the year that tenure is decided for a professor is usually a very stressful one. The tenure decision means that a professor can either stay at that university until retirement or must leave within a year to find employment elsewhere. Bob, an untenured assistant professor, cut a "deal" with the provost and the dean, two key decision makers in his tenure process, well in advance of the decision. Bob was not stressed during his tenure decision year due to the lack of which stress contributor?
   a. Constraints.
   b. Demands.
   c. Outcome importance.
   d. Outcome uncertainty.
   e. Burn-out.

5. Why do companies use EAPs?
   a. Occupational health and safety laws require EAPs.
   b. EAPs have been shown to assist employees with job stress as well as legal, marital, financial, and health problems.
   c. EAPs are more popular with employees than traditional health insurance coverage.
   d. Human rights compliance require either EAPs or wellness programs.
   e. EAPs are required in most health insurance packages.

6. Which one of the following is not a recommended measure for preventing workplace violence?
   a. Have police agencies from the local area frequently visit the facility.
   b. Train supervisors to identify troubled employees and refer them for help.
   c. Install security measures such as guards and electronic detection equipment.
   d. Establish an employee assistance program.
   e. Instruct employees on what to do if someone becomes violent.

7. Indirect costs of accidents that must be borne by the employer include all of the following except
   a. wages paid for time lost due to injury.
   b. damage to equipment and material.
   c. the workers' compensation premium.
   d. personnel to investigate and report accidents.
   e. lost production due to stoppages and changeovers.

8. Burn-out is defined as a function of all of these concerns except
   a. machine-like performance of duties.
   b. boredom.
   c. emotional exhaustion.
   d. physical exhaustion.
   e. lowered job productivity.

9. Which of the following would qualify as smoke-free environments?
   a. Smoking is prohibited in portions of the employee cafeteria.
   b. Smoking is prohibited in meetings, conferences, and training sessions.
   c. Smoking is prohibited in all areas of the building except private offices.
   d. Smoking is prohibited on all company premises.
   e. All of these.

10. Causes of accidents can be generally classified as
    a. human error.
    b. environmental problems.
    c. ineffective legislation.
    d. a and b.
    e. all of the above.

11. An employee who accepts an international assignment should rely on
    a. the employer to research potential threats to health and safety.
    b. the Department of Foreign Affairs to notify each traveler about health and safety risks.
    c. his or her own awareness of health and safety issues.
    d. colleagues to give tips about leading the life of a high-profile dignitary.
    e. a, b, and c.

12. Silvana sews clothes for a fashion manufacturer. A few months after starting the job, she noticed that her wrists felt "stiff". Now she finds it difficult to grip the cloth, never mind doing finer needlework. Worried about the quality of her work and lowered productivity, Silvana asks her manager for advice. Silvana's manager should:
    a. Recommend that Silvana see a physician.
    b. Tell Silvana to stop whining and get back to work.
    c. Examine Silvana's work station to see if it can be adjusted to "fit" Silvana better.
    d. Ask the HR department to educate employees about repetitive strain injuries (RSIs).
    e. a, c, and d.

13. A health and safety committee
    a. is set up to satisfy the requirements of occupational health and safety legislation.
    b. must show quantifiable results (for example, 30 per cent reduction in minor burns to welders over one year) or it is dissolved.
    c. functions best if membership is limited to workers.
    d. is liable for damages if an accident occurs in the workplace.
    e. a and b.

14. Presta Global Inc., a placement firm, supplies companies throughout the world with highly-trained technical experts from Canada. As an HRM consultant to Presta Global, you recommend that
    a. the firm promise applicants health and safety standards equal to those in Canada.
    b. the firm send an armed guard with every placement.
    c. placements should travel light and wait until they get settled to stock up on anything.
    d. the firm add value to its services by offering an international health and safety information program to placements.
    e. none of the above.

15. Raj, twenty-eight, manages the accounting division of a prestigious retail firm. Everyone who knows and works with Raj thinks of him as a young, bright, and aspiring professional. Raj, however, feels that he is sinking quickly under the strain of supervising thirty employees while trying to contribute something "significant" to the company. Which of the following variables are related to Raj's burn-out?
    a. Organization characteristics.
    b. Perceptions of the organization.
    c. Perceptions of role.
    d. Individual characteristics.
    e. Outcome.

Chapter Sixteen

COMMUNICATION PROGRAMS

Almost every successful organization has a rich history associated with it. Thriving companies usually got started through the entrepreneurial spirit of a well-focused risk taker. And although such organizations such as Eaton's, Hiram Walker, Ford, and Microsoft can be traced to their inspirational founders, it's hard to fathom that these giants were once run out of someone's basement. For instance, unless you've read a profile of Bill Gates, you probably can't imagine that this software genius started his company in his home. Inspirational founders get nowhere, however, unless they can communicate their inspiration to their employees. Sometimes, this communication calls for dramatic, unusual, and even controversial efforts such as the mystical "love-in" at Calgary Co-operative Association Ltd.[1]

Several hundred employees of the grocery store chain found themselves gathering into circles around plastic tubs filled with kitty litter and pot-pourri, holding small unlit candles. One by one, they stepped forward, lit their candles, and spilled out heartfelt pledges for their personal and working lives. They leaned over the tubs, stuck in the lit tapers, and huddled around the glowing tubs to the strains of "Amazing Grace." This experience was the climax of an impassioned communication effort by Gene Syvenky, CEO of Calgary Co-op, who had been brought in by the board to maintain market share in the cutthroat business world of food retailing. Syvenky is a firm believer in lifelong learning and the need to make employees nimble and eager for a range of jobs and able to make decisions for themselves. Syvenky sneers at the popular slogan, "Life's a bitch, and then you die." He says, "If that's your philosophy, I don't want you here."

The love-in was organized by mystical consultant Lance Secretan. As part of its communication efforts, Calgary Co-op has also hired other inspirational forces including a ritual drummer from California who played to 400 employees in an attempt to transform their rhythms. Why has Gene Syvenky put so much effort into communication, particularly when the media used are so unusual? It's because he has a vision of outstanding customer service which he wants to pass on to his employees. He believes that an enthusiastic workforce is a critical competitive edge if Calgary Co-op is to hold its market share against formidable competition from larger chains.

Introduction

For fifteen chapters, we have been discussing a variety of HRM activities. Inherent in all of these activities is one common theme—effective communication. Although we may not have elaborated specifically on how HRM involves itself in the communication process, we have addressed its importance on several occasions. For example, in Chapter 2, the discussion of worker diversity identified the need for better communication with employees, especially those who do not speak the native language. Communication in workforce diversity also means letting these individuals know that they are welcome in the corporation and that the company will make every attempt to provide equal opportunity for them.[2]

We also addressed the need to communicate with respect to recruiting and selection (in terms of understanding what the job entails and realistic job previews), in orientation (acclimating employees to HRM activities and policies), and training (understanding how to do the job). Yet probably the most critical HRM activities emphasizing communication came in the discussion of motivation, performance evaluations, benefits, and health and safety. In motivation, we discussed the need to be able to illustrate the relationship between one's efforts and individual goal attainment. In that discussion, we highlighted the need for performance goals to be communicated—goals that, when met, will lead to the achievement of organization-wide objectives. The specific means to achieve these goals and how the interaction between an employee and manager can affect performance outcomes was discussed in performance evaluations. When these outcomes are positive, individuals should be rewarded; when they are not, effort must be made to correct the problem. For that, we introduced employee counselling which relies heavily on effective communication.

For benefits and health and safety, we discussed not only the importance of informing employees of the benefits offered them and availability of wellness and employee assistance programs (EAP), but also the legal issues of providing certain information. With respect to benefits, HRM is responsible for providing employees with a summary description of their benefit plans which describes in understandable terms employee rights under their pension plan requirements and updated benefits accumulation. Likewise, health and safety legislation requires employers to notify employees of potential dangers and protective measures when exposed to workplace hazardous chemicals or toxins. All terms of employment set out in company communication must comply with the provisions of the relevant *Employment Standards Act* and *Human Rights Code*.[3]

As we move into the twenty-first century, we recognize that our companies will be different. Factors like global competition, computerization, and the Internet are forcing companies to rethink how they are organized. We've witnessed extensive delayering, mergers, and acquisitions through the mid-1990s, which increases employee stress greatly. One way of allaying such stress is to reduce the uncertainty that surrounds the situation—in our terms, effective communication. Such communication is particularly effective if it comes directly from top management. Think back to the example mentioned in Chapter 5 of Michael O'Brien, CEO of Sunoco Canada, who left a message on the voice mail of all employees congratulating them for passing the milestone that marked the end of a dramatic three-year turnaround for the company.[4]

We know the years ahead will continue to witness change in our companies.[5] Our movement towards leaner structures, continuous improvement, employee involvement, and work teams will work best if there is effective communication.

Communication The transference of meaning and understanding.

Where good communication programs are operating, benefits accrue to the company. For instance, Xerox Canada discovered that employee empowerment and effective communication played a key role in improving its bottom line.[6] According to Mel Thompson, director of organizational effectiveness, "We have to be able to communicate regularly—daily, in fact. The successful teams are communicating all the time."

Innovations in technology now allow us to communicate more quickly and efficiently than ever before, but our ability to communicate has not kept up with the rate of change in organizations and technology. Today, companies that need the input and commitment of empowered employees are opening up communication and making it interactive rather than one-sided. Corporate leaders are recognizing that communication is an essential part of the changing corporate climate. As John Hempsey, executive vice-president of Thomas Cook, explains, "When I speak to employee groups, it is my job to convey my enthusiasm, integrity and sincerity. I must personify the values of this company."[7]

This use of communication is well illustrated in the determination of the executives of the new DaimlerChrysler that was formally instituted in November 1998 to ensure that their company is not one of the 70 per cent of all mergers that fail to thrive.[8] The communication technology at their disposal is impressive. For instance, there is equipment in a series of rooms in Stuttgart, Germany which enables employees in Germany and their counterparts in North America to chat together and share whiteboard sketches. Technology is only part of the story, however, and management have devoted considerable time and effort to cross-culture communication. The HRM departments on both sides of the Atlantic play a key role in educating employees about one another. As well as language classes, Daimler-Benz workers can attend seminars on "Job Interviews with Americans" while Chrysler workers are offered seminars on "German Social and Business Etiquette."

Achieving these goals is not easy. Effective communication does not just happen; rather, it evolves after careful thought, implementation, and evaluation. For much of that, we rely on HRM. Although we've highlighted many throughout the text, there are still a few that need to be revealed. Specifically, in this chapter, we want to focus on HRM's role in the communication process, look at the purpose of employee handbooks and newsletters, examine the role of electronic media, and close with a discussion of suggestion systems and complaint procedures that exist in companies. Let's now turn our attention to HRM communication programs.

HRM Communication Programs

The Purpose

Human resources management communication programs are designed to keep employees abreast of what is happening in the organization and knowledgeable of the policies and procedures affecting them.[9] Whereas public relations departments are created to keep the public informed of what an organization does, HRM communication focuses on the internal constituents—the employees.[10] As we mentioned in Chapter 1 regarding the role of the employee relations department in the maintenance function, communication programs serve as a basis for increasing employee loyalty and commitment.[11] By building into the corporate culture a systematic means through which information is free-flowing, timely, and accurate, employees are better able to perceive that the organization values them.[12] Such a system builds trust and openness among organizational members, even assisting in the sharing of organizational problems.[13]

One of the most important points to make in communicating is that in contrast to the popular adage, no news is *not* good news. As Brian Dalzell, president of The Performance Advantage Inc. in Brampton, Ontario, puts it: "From my point of view, everything you find out is good news…. Better you know how [employees] feel than to think they feel better than they do."[14] Dalzell argues that the same truth holds in communicating the other way. Managers who do not communicate "bad news" back to employees make a big mistake. "They naively think that by withholding the information, they're stopping people from being contaminated with the news. What they're missing is that the employees already know."

HRM communication has the ability to bring about many positive changes in an organization. This is particularly true in the area of corporate recognition programs. What an organization recognizes, who it recognizes, and how it does so send powerful messages to current and prospective employees, to customers, and to the community about the organization and what it values. Such diverse organizations as the Blue Jays, Labatt Breweries, Star Data Systems Inc., and the Ontario Government use communication as a tool to make recognition part of their corporate culture.[15] Some of these programs take some interesting turns, such as Labatt's Bloopers Award which recognizes employees who took a well-thought-out chance that didn't work out.[16]

Guidelines for Supporting Communication Programs

Effective human resources communication does not just happen; it has to be consciously planned for, and supported by, all organization participants. You might ask: But can plans be made in today's world of dramatically changing new technology? Has the arrival of the Internet and mobile phone, for example, which have so revolutionized the way we communicate with each other, made it impossible to set guidelines for supporting communication programs? The answer is, most certainly not! If anything, new technology offers greater freedom to the organization in setting up effective communication programs, though such programs may look somewhat different from those of earlier generations. Building effective human resources communication programs, whatever technology is employed, involves a few fundamental elements. These include: top-management commitment, effective upward communication, determining what to communicate, allowing for feedback, and information sources. Let's look at each of these.

Top Management Commitment   Before any organization can develop and implement an internal organizational communication program, it must have the backing, support, and "blessing" of the managing director or CEO.[17] Any activity designed to improve work environments must appear to employees as being endorsed by the company's top management. In doing so, these programs are given priority and are viewed as significant components of the corporate culture.[18] Just as it is critical for employees to see top management supporting communication, so, too, is it crucial for them to see communication operating effectively at all levels. In other words, effective communication is not just top management sending information down throughout the company; it also means that information flows upward and laterally to other areas in the organization.

The revolution in modern communications technology offers organizations greater freedom in setting up effective communication programs

Effective Upward Communication   The upward flow of communication is particularly noteworthy because it is often the employees—the ones closest to the work—who have vital information that top management should know. For instance, let's take a situation that occurs in HRM.[19] Legislation at any level—federal, provincial, or local—is always changing and may place new HRM demands on organizations. Unless top management is made aware of the implications of these requirements—such as knowing how to ensure that sexual harassment charges are thoroughly investigated—there could be severe repercussions. Thus, that information must move upward in the company.

A similar point could easily be made for any part of an organization, and in keeping with the spirit of employee empowerment as employees are more involved in making decisions that affect them, that information must be communicated "up the line." Furthermore, it's important for top management to monitor the pulse of the organization regarding how employees view working for the company. It is crucial to get that information, whether it is obtained from walking around the premises, through formal employee suggestions, or by employee surveys. In fact, on the latter point, with the advent of technology, some of the employee satisfaction measures can be captured in almost real time. Of particular significance is the growth of the World Wide Web and company intranets (which we will discuss later) that allow for on-line surveys that are easier for employees to use, easier to analyse, and immediately available for company use.

Determining What to Communicate   At the extreme, if every piece of information that exists in our organizations were communicated, no work would ever get done. People would be spending their entire days crushed under information overload. Employees, while wanting to be informed, are not concerned with every piece of information such as who just retired, who was promoted, or what community group was given a donation yesterday.[20] Rather, employees need pertinent information addressing those things they need to know to do their jobs. This generally means information on where the business is going (strategic goals),[21] current sales/service/production results, new product or service lines, and human resources policy changes.[22]

One means we advocate is a "what if, so what" test. When deciding the priority of the information to be shared, managers should ask themselves: *What if* this information is not shared—will my employees still be able to do their jobs as well? Will they be disadvantaged in some way by not knowing? If the answers are no, then that may not be a priority item. The *so what* part of the test asks: Will employees feel ambivalent about the information? Will they see it as an overload of meaningless information? If the answers are yes, then that, too, may not be priority information. That's not to say that this information may never be exchanged; it only means that it's not important for employees to get it immediately.

For example, let's assume we have two pieces of information to share. One item is that the company's health insurance plan is changing its health carrier from Blue Cross to Green Shield. Would this meet our what if, so what test? What if we didn't communicate this in a timely fashion? Would the employees be affected? When you are talking about their welfare, you bet they would. As we discussed in terms of individual goals being met for motivation purposes, such a change matters, thus passing the so what test.

Contrast the benefit change with information regarding the information systems department installing a Novell computer network. Will employees be adversely affected if the information is delayed a day or a week? Probably not, but this delaying of information must be considered on an individual basis. While many employees may not need the information on the network immediately, certain areas of the company such as purchasing and systems maintenance would find it a necessity.

Allowing for Feedback   We cannot just assume that our communication programs are achieving their goals. Consequently, we must develop into the system a means of assessing the flow of information and for fostering employee feedback. How that information is generated may differ from organization to organization. For some, it may be a casual word-of-mouth assessment. Others may use employee surveys to capture the data or provide a suggestion box where comments can be given. For others, there is a formalized and systematic communication audit program.

No matter how that information is gathered, employees must be involved or else measurement of the effectiveness of the communication program may be difficult.[23] You may also destroy the benefits by appearing to be less committed to employees. David Sissons, vice-president and director of research services in the Toronto office at management consultants the Hay Group, points out that it takes real effort to ensure "honest, unfiltered feedback" from employees, but that he is encouraged to report that "there are fewer and fewer cases" of Canadian organizations simply shelving the results of surveys and other feedback from their employees.[24]

Information Sources   HRM communication should serve as a conduit in promoting effective communication throughout the organization. Although HRM plays an important role in bringing this to fruition, they are not the only, or even the main, source of information. For that, we have to turn to the employee's immediate supervisor. If successful programs can be linked to the immediate supervisor, then HRM must ensure that these individuals are trained in how to communicate properly. Even the health insurance change cited earlier would likely result in a number of questions for a supervisor if implemented. Thus, HRM must make every effort to supply these supervisors with accurate data to deal with the front-line questions. From an HRM point of view, where is information best conveyed? Note that these items are areas that HRM can influence directly by either providing the training, publishing periodicals and newsletters, posting on the Web, or through word-of-mouth dissemination of factual data.

Although these sources are varied and serve vital purposes, there is one medium that is central to providing information to employees: the employee handbook.

A Guide for Employees: The Employee Handbook

During the orientation of new employees, we inform them of a number of important facts regarding employment in the organization, but we must recognize that stating this information once will not be enough. There's often too much for the employee to absorb, especially during the excitement of the first day on the job. So a permanent reference guide is needed. This reference guide for employees is called the employee handbook, which Eric Roher, a Canadian labour lawyer, describes as a key element in the introductory "tango" between a prospective employee and an employer.[25] An employee handbook can be posted on an organization's Web page, but it is usually still produced in hard copy form to ensure distribution to all employees.

Employee Handbook A central information source outlining the important aspects of employment an employee needs to know.

The Purpose of an Employee Handbook

An employee handbook is a tool that, when developed properly, serves both employee and employer. We will describe a handbook in the form of an actual book, but many organizations now present their handbooks in electronic form. For the employee, a well-designed handbook provides a central information source that conveys such useful information as what the company is about, its history, employment practices, and employee benefits. The handbook, then, gives employees an opportunity to learn about the company and what the company provides for them in a way that permits each employee an opportunity to understand the information at his or her own pace.[26] By having this resource available, questions that may arise over such benefits as vacation accrual, matching contributions, pension fund investment strategies, and so forth can be more easily answered. Serving as an easy reference guide, the employee handbook can be used by employees whenever necessary.[27] Table 16-1 lists the key information in an employee handbook, whether electronic or paper.

Beyond just being a source of information, employee handbooks also deliver some other benefits. It has been found that they assist in creating an atmosphere in which employees become more productive members of the organization and increase their commitment and loyalty to it.[28] Furthermore, a good handbook also helps create a sense of security for employees.[29] By being thorough in its coverage, an employee handbook will address various HRM policies and work rules, setting the parameters within which employees are expected to perform.[30] For example, the handbook may express information on discipline and discharge procedures and a means of redressing disciplinary action should the employee feel that it was administered unfairly. The handbook, then, serves to ensure that any HRM policy will be fair, equitable, and consistently applied.[31]

Employers, too, can benefit from using an employee handbook. In addition to any benefits accrued from having a more committed and loyal workforce, handbooks can also be used in recruiting.[32] Remember, we advocated the use of realistic job previews for helping to "sell" recruits on the organization; a well-written employee handbook, can be useful in providing some of the necessary information an applicant may be seeking. Although employee handbooks are designed to "educate, inform, and guide" employees in the organization,[33] a word of caution is in order. In Chapter 4, in our discussion of employee rights, we addressed the issue of implied contracts. Recall that an implied contract is anything expressed, verbally or in writing, that may be perceived by the individual to mean that she or he can't be terminated. For example, telling an employee that as long as her performance is satisfactory, she will have a job until retirement could be construed as an implied contract. Over the years, the courts have viewed various statements made in employee handbooks as binding on the company.[34] To avoid this, legal advocates and HRM professionals recommend a careful choice of words in the handbook as well as a disclaimer.[35] Figure 16-1 includes an example of a disclaimer from one business. (Note that the particular arrangements for an employee to leave the organization mentioned in this example may not be legally applicable in all jurisdictions. This all-encompassing disclaimer would still probably not be enough to prevent courts from taking the employee handbook as an implied contract.) The implied legal value of handbooks can, on the other hand, be used to the organization's advantage. Employers must clearly communicate the policies they want followed in the handbook. If they do not, they run the risk of having the courts rule that these implicit policies are not part of the contractual agreement between the parties; in other words, polices not included in written handbooks cannot be enforced.[36]

TABLE 16-1 Key Information in an Employee Handbook

A well-designed, well-written employee handbook should convey such information as:

1. **What the organization expects from its employees.** Employees need to be informed of company policies. This includes such items as work hours, employee conduct, performance evaluations, disciplinary process, moonlighting, vacations, holiday, and sick and personal leave.

2. **What the employee can expect from the organization.** What benefits does the employee receive? These should be detailed enough so that the employee fully understands the "fringes" of the job. The company's HRM policies regarding salary increases, promotions, and so on also need to be conveyed.

3. **The history of the organization.** The history section provides an opportunity to help employees understand where the organization has been and where it is heading. This section puts the company in perspective, and it also includes the philosophy/culture of the organization.

4. **A glossary section.** Words have different meanings to different people, and they may differ depending on the context used. To eliminate confusion, the terms used in the handbook should be defined.

This handbook is not a contract, expressed or implied, guaranteeing employment for any specific duration. Although [the company] hopes that your employment relationship with us will be long-term, either you or the company may terminate this relationship at any time, for any reason, with or without cause of notice.

Figure 16-1
Sample Employee Handbook
Disclaimer

Before we move into the specific components of a handbook, there is one other important aspect for management to consider. An employee handbook is of little use if employees don't read it. To get them to do that, we recommend that the handbook should first of all be relevant to employees' needs.[37] Providing information that is seen as unnecessary and irrelevant or that is unclearly worded or has excessive verbiage[38] will almost guarantee that employees will ignore it. That is why employers must use feedback mechanisms to assess how employees perceive the usefulness of employee handbook information, gather their input, and make modifications where necessary. HRM should not assume that once developed and distributed to employees, the employee handbook is complete; it should be viewed as something to be updated and refined on an ongoing basis. Employers often find that using some sort of electronic medium, such as the Internet, allows for more flexibility in corrections, updates, and additions. We will discuss electronic media later in this chapter.

As a second requirement, it is essential that the handbook be well organized to make it easy to find the needed information.[39] Just as this book has a table of contents and an index to help you find specific information more quickly, so, too, should the employee handbook. HRM must remember that the handbook has to be helpful to employees, so it should be easy to use. It is probably wise to have the handbook available in both an electronic and a hard copy format. In Table 16-2, we have summarized some guidelines for making employee handbooks more employee-friendly.

TABLE 16-2 Suggestions for Making Employee Handbooks More Employee-Friendly

Use simple language that can be understood by all employees.

Keep sentences short—twenty words or less.

Keep discussion of each item to less than one page.

Use graphics wherever possible.

Use wide margins (top, bottom, and sides).

Keep the handbook under thirty-five pages.

Source: Adapted from James W. Wimberly, Jr., "How to Prepare and Write Your Employee Handbook," in Commerce Clearing House, *Topical Law Reports* "Handbook: The Format—How You Want It to Look" (Chicago: Commerce Clearing House, Inc., October 1990), p. 5410.

Employee Handbook Contents

Although there are no right or wrong ways of putting together the contents of an employee handbook, there is a recommended format.[40] As a means of facilitating this discussion, we will present an outline from the employee handbook (see Table 16-3) of an actual tree maintenance and trimming company that we will call Acme Tree Service. Let's elaborate on these components.

Introductory Comments   In this section, the company conveys various introductory information to the employees. Acme Tree Service begins by having its top management send a letter of greetings to the employees welcoming them into the organization. The purpose of this letter is to describe to employees what the company is about, its mission, and goals. Furthermore, the company conveys to its employees the corporate value of customer satisfaction and how, by achieving that goal, the firm can provide those things that employees desire (e.g., job security, pay increases, better benefits).

These introductory remarks also tell new employees that they are valuable assets to the organization. By making employees feel important, letting them know the roles they play, and conveying what the company will do to help them grow as employees, the organization fosters an environment where effective worker performance, loyalty, and commitment can be realized.

There is often a final component to this introductory section: a brief history of the organization. Although not all employees will value this information, it does provide them with a better understanding of how the company progressed to its current state. It is also another means of expressing the company philosophy which the organization wishes to share with its employees.

What You Should Know   This section is designed to inform all employees of the rules and policies regarding employment in the company. Those items of importance to employees—such as attendance, work hours, and so forth—are plainly presented so that there is no misunderstanding by employees. For example, in this company, specific information regarding the length of one's lunch period, pay days, work hours, and how employees will be evaluated is laid out in such clear terms that confusion is avoided.

In Chapter 12 on performance appraisals, we discussed the need for managers to state explicitly what is required of employees. If, for example, you expect employees on the job by 8:00 a.m., tell them so, and hold employees accountable for

TABLE 16-3 Sample Employee Handbook Table of Contents

being on time. The handbook, then, reinforces those work behaviours a company expects of its employees.

Your Benefits   No matter how much value we place on the introductory remarks of any employee handbook, the section on employee benefits is probably the most widely read and most important to employees. This section should explain thoroughly the benefits employees receive, when they are eligible (if not immediately upon employment), and what (if any) costs the employee might incur. As we explained in Chapter 14 on employee benefits, although these benefits are membership-based, they are important to keep employee morale high. Hence, we must make every effort to convey the full slate of benefits to employees in such a manner that they know what they have and how they can use them.

Your Responsibility, Safety, and Operating Procedures Just as employers are responsible for creating a safe and healthy workplace, workers must also do their part. Accordingly, these final sections provide information regarding equipment, operating procedures, company policies on reporting accidents, alcohol and substance abuse, and personal conduct, among other things. The important point is that everything is explained in such straightforward terms that employees know what is required of them. Furthermore, the consequences of failure to comply with these policies is thoroughly explained.

Other Vehicles for Employee Communication

There are a number of other means of employee comunication available besides the employee handbook. The four most popular are: electronic media, bulletin boards, company newsletters, and company-wide meetings. We will discuss electronic media as a separate category, but students should note that there is considerable overlap between this and the other categories. With the rapid growth in the Internet, World Wide Web (WWW), and the intranet, electronic media can also be used to supplement, or even replace, the other communication vehicles.

Electronic Media

Technology has served organizational communication well. Whether it's an interactive video for employees, access to on-line information, or the use of a company intranet, technology is enhancing the effectiveness of communication. The impact of this technology is no more evident than in HRM.

Whenever a company wishes to provide employees with up-to-date or even real-time information regarding their pay and benefits, nothing serves that purpose better than the electronic media. For a number of companies such as Ford of Canada, AT&T, and IBM, this has meant developing an in-house television station.[41] Through their television stations, these companies are able to send information faster and with less chance of distraction. Perhaps the most dramatic development in employment communication over the past few years has been the explosive growth of information from the Internet and World Wide Web in company-specific intranets. This technology has several particular advantages as a communication medium: it is immediate, highly flexible, can be easily tailored to individual needs, and has the graphics and multimedia to make if far more interesting than the static, one-dimensional modes of traditional communication. Many Canadian organizations rely on intranets for communicating with their employees. For example,[42] the HR home page on the intranet of Motorola's Wireless Data Group offers policies, procedures, training resources, and calendars—just about anything employees need to know. Hewlett-Packard (Canada) Inc. has produced an electronic pension booklet and a pension modelling tool that employees can download from the company's intranet. The HR home page on this intranet gets twice as many hits as any other department—a reflection of the value employees place on this communication source. The intranet is particularly useful in the public sector in Canada since it is such a cost-effective means of communication. Ontario's Ministry of Education and Training, Ministry of Public Works, and Government Services Canada are additional examples of organizations that have introduced comprehensive intranets to communicate all the HR information employees typically need to access. A value of intranets and the Internet is that they are accessible twenty-four hours a day.

Electronic Media Technological devices, such as radio, TV, and computer networks, that enhances communication.

Intranet An organization-specific information network often including an Internet-based set of Web pages.

Meet

Marie Szklarz
HR Communication Consultant

If your idea of communication in human resources is an occasional company newsletter and a once-a-year staff meeting, you've never met Marie Szklarz. A Calgary-based human resources consultant and researcher specializing in communication issues, she sees communication within an organization as a complex "living process."

"Only about 10 per cent of messages about what is important in an organization are transmitted through formal means such as meetings, newsletters, videos, or the company intranet," she explains. "The most influential messages about an organization—about 60 per cent—come from the leadership style and personal behaviour of their managers. Employees get the remaining 30 per cent or so from observing the organization's systems—how people are rewarded, how the hierarchy is organized, etc."

For employee communication to be successful, all three of these methods must be in sync. "For example," says Ms Szklarz, "if your company's training videos stress the importance of cross-functional teams but the leaders in the organization do most of their work alone, and the pay structure recognizes only the contribution of individuals, you're sending a very mixed message."

So when a company asks for her help in creating a communication strategy—often connected with introducing a change in the organization such as a new compensation system—she makes sure they see this bigger communication picture.

She also makes sure they're not making decisions in the dark. "Research is the fundamental stepping stone to communication in business," she explains.

It's a truism that communication should go both ways, but all too often, companies implement policies without any real understanding of the potential effect on employees.

Effective communication can make all the difference in whether a new program flies or flops. Ms Szklarz gives the example of a gas marketing company that faced the most difficult communication challenge of all: it was going out of business. By paying serious, careful attention to communication issues, the company's management was able to make the process a smooth and non-acrimonious one.

"The company held a series of focus groups to find out what the employees' chief concerns were," she recounts. "Then they based the communication program on this information. For example, they found that it was important to employees that their CEO be very visible during this process, and that information be distributed on a timely basis. So he made a point of meeting with them regularly, even if there was no news. The perception of his involvement was crucial."

When there was news, employees wanted to be kept completely up to date on it. So even if that meant sending daily bulletins and calling frequent assemblies, that's what the senior executives did.

Whether it's delivering bad news, good news, or just news, the right communication program—the right communication attitude—can make all the difference between success and disaster.

"Communication enables a company to get the work done," says Ms Szklarz. "It's all about touching the hearts and minds of employees and inspiring the behaviours you need to realize your vision."

Bulletin Board A means a company uses to post information of interest to its employees. This can be a traditional physical board or and electronic one.

Company Newsletter A means of providing information for employees in a specific recurring periodical.

Figure 16-2
Company Newsletter Message

Bulletin Boards

A bulletin board in any organization serves several purposes in communicating with employees. Bulletin boards are generally centrally located in the organization where a majority of employees will have exposure to them. In some organizations, these bulletin boards are found near company cafeterias, or by the main office, or displayed near an entrance. More and more organizations, however, supplement hard-copy displays with electronic bulletin boards. These are particularly useful for late breaking news and are frequently given a prominent place on the company intranet.

The information posted on a bulletin board will vary among organizations. Job postings, upcoming company-sponsored events, new HRM policies, and the like may be posted in this highly visible location to help "get the information out." Furthermore, if employees know that important information is placed on these boards, they will be more inclined to read them. Bulletin boards may also extend beyond employer-related business; that is, employees can post information for other employees to see. For example, companies may permit employees to advertise personal belongings for sale or promote a charitable event an employee is associated with. Although the information employees place on the bulletin board is given great latitude, most organizations require such information to have HRM approval before it is posted. By following this procedure, inappropriate or offensive information can be eliminated before any problems arise.

Company Newsletters

The company newsletter (or newspaper) is designed to provide sound internal communication to employees regarding important information they need to know, activities happening in the organization, and anything else of interest.[43] Just as a town's daily newspaper discusses current events, sports, and human interest stories, so, too, should the company newsletter. Company newsletters provide employees with a written record they can keep and refer to in the future. Furthermore, some information—things that are very technical and detailed—may be better communicated in writing.

Message From our Managing Director

1998 is shaping up to be another very positive year for Air Canada Cargo. Strong demand on our Atlantic services and a confidence that we are prepared for Year 2000 have left an impression of readiness in the Cargo environment. We don't wait for challenges here, we confront them head on. As you read the articles within this newsletter, you'll see that we are dealing directly with some of the issues facing us today. The cargo industry is a network, an interconnected web that links the customer to the services they need. The stories that follow feature some of Air Canada's important envoys in that network. These people are working at creating a better structure for the way Air Canada Cargo does business; a method that will result in increased customer satisfaction, more effective transport of the precious shipments trusted to us every day and a proven way to aggressively meet the challenges of the new millenium.

AIR CANADA

While there is no definitive design for company newsletters, they should focus on activities of concern to employees, problems the company may be experiencing, successes the company has enjoyed, updates on newsworthy company items (such as company-sponsored sporting events and United Way campaigns), and stories about employees (those receiving awards, recognition, retiring, and so forth) (see "Ethical Decisions in HRM"). Company newsletters can also be enhanced with question-and-answer sections and employee articles.[44] Newsletters are ideal for upbeat communication from management at the start of a new work term. Figure 16-2 illustrates the New Year's message to employees from Claude Morin, the managing director of Air Canada Cargo. This was posted on the Air Canada Web site to ensure it reached the widest audience of employees, customers, and suppliers.

Ethical Decisions in HRM:

The Whole Story

Effective communication in organizations is built on the premise that appropriate and accurate information must be conveyed. Organization members should be afforded the respect and dignity that factual information can deliver. At what point is it best to withhold information from employees?

We've addressed a so what test—if it really matters to individuals, the information should be conveyed. But reality tells us that even factual information can, at times, be difficult to deliver and may best be withheld for a number of reasons. For example, confidentiality is a must in matters that affect employees personally. Assume, then, that you have just been informed by one of your employees that he has Hodgkin's disease, a treatable form of lymph node cancer. Consequently, he may be absent frequently at times, especially during his chemotherapy treatments. Yet, he doesn't anticipate his attendance to be a problem nor that it will directly affect his work. After all, some of his duties involve direct computer work, so he can work at home and forward the data electronically to the appropriate people.

On several occasions, the employee has either called in sick or has had to leave early because he felt ill. Your employees are beginning to suspect something is wrong and have come to you to find out what it is. There are even rumours going around that the employee might be HIV-positive, and that is causing quite a stir. You simply and politely decline to discuss the issue about an employee with other individuals. However, a number of your employees think that you are giving this individual preferential treatment. You know that if they only knew what was going on, they'd understand, but you can't disclose the nature of the illness. On the other hand, continued "favouritism" will surely be a disruptive force in your department. You are stumped. What do you do? Should employees be given the whole story? What's your opinion?

Company-Wide Meetings

Every so often, there is a need to inform all employees at once in a face-to-face encounter. Should an organization be facing a merger, going into a new product line, or changing its culture, for example, it may be useful for the CEO to address all employees en masse. In doing so, the CEO can add emphasis to this new direction while simultaneously answering questions and addressing concerns.

Research suggests that HR professionals, while widely using electronic media such as e-mail, prefer face-to-face meetings for communication purposes.[45] Certainly, the ideal company-wide meeting is an actual face-to-face gathering of all employees in some type of "town hall" assembly. However, this may not always be possible in large or disparate companies, and it can be expensive to arrange. In such cases, the immediacy and broad scope of electronic media offer a cost-effective alternative. The organization can use videoconferencing technology or offer simultaneous broadcasting of the top manager's message to all employees. For example, public institutions such as Canada Post and the CBC used live television to pass on the latest restructuring news from Ottawa to all employees across Canada.[46]

In addition to opening up the channels of communication for employees, **company-wide meetings**, whether face to face or electronic, permit all employees to have the same information at once. For many operations, this reduces the grapevine rumours that may occur, especially when the company is facing difficult times or significant changes.[47]

Company-Wide Meetings
Meetings used to inform all employees of various company issues.

Communication and the Off-Site Employee

Communication in many of today's organizations no longer follows the traditional downward or upward flows so typical of hierarchical organizations. Instead, as our work as well as our workforce changes, communication mechanisms must also adapt. As we described in Chapter 2, one trend today is the movement to the off-site worker. Individual needs coupled with technology advancements have enabled some people to work at home. This has flattened the organizational hierarchy. How, then, can effective communication be fostered with off-site employees? The answer lies in the technology that has become routine today—the Internet, e-mail, fax machines, and the computer modem.

If any of you have watched an eight-year-old child send an e-mail, you will realize how quickly the Internet and e-mail, in particular, are becoming a part of everyday life. According to a study conducted among 972 executives, managers, professionals, and administrative staff in Fortune 1,000 companies, the average worker is sending and receiving, on average, a remarkable 178 messages a day.[48]

With the use of home computer systems, employees can remain in close contact with their employers even though they are far away. For instance, modems and scanners can be used to receive and transmit data between teleworking employees and computers at a company location. Data downloaded to an employee can be manipulated, passed on to colleagues, and then sent back to the organization in its final form. Where electronic data won't do, fax machines can send documents in hard copy formats almost instantaneously to anywhere in the world. **E-mail** allows written messages to be sent between parties with computers that are linked together with an appropriate software. It is fast, cheap, and permits the reader to retrieve the message at his or her convenience. E-mail is the most used (though not most preferred—face to face

Computers have become an integral part of modern communication. The technology—the Internet, e-mail, fax machines, and the modem—have changed fundamentally the way we communicate.

E-mail Electronic mail that can be sent or received over the Internet or private networks.

remains the most preferred) communication technique according to respondents in a survey of HR practitioners.[49] Increasingly common is the use of tele-conferencing which enables groups of employees to communicate with each other simultaneously while in different locations. Finally, the Internet allows for electronic bulletin boards, user groups, and even quite complex technical communication. In the survey of HR practitioners mentioned above, 48 per cent of respondents have job postings on their company Web site.

Mechanisms for Effective Upward Communication

We know that communicating with our employees is important in whatever form, but there still remains one final aspect to be addressed: Is there a mechanism in the organization that allows employees to raise their concerns? In this section, we'll look briefly at employee complaint and suggestion systems.

Any communication system operating in an organization will only be effective if it permits information to flow upward. For HRM, enabling this process revolves around two central themes: complaints procedures, and suggestion programs and employee surveys.[50]

Complaints Procedure

An organization's complaints procedure is designed to permit employees to question actions that have occurred in the company and to seek the company's assistance in correcting the problem. For example, if the employee feels that her boss has inappropriately evaluated her performance or believes that her boss' behaviour is counter-productive, a complaints process allows for that information to be heard. Typically under the direction of employee relations specialists, complaints are investigated and decisions made regarding the validity of the alleged wrongdoings.

Complaints procedures implemented in non-unionized organizations are called by a variety of titles, but most follow a set pattern. Given the structure of HRM laid out in Chapter 1, a non-unionized complaints procedure may consist of the following steps:

Step 1: Employee–Manager This is generally regarded as the initial step to resolve an employee problem. Here, the employee tries to address the issue with her manager, seeking some resolution. If the issue is resolved here, nothing further need be done. Accordingly, this is considered an informal step in the process. Depending on the problem, this step may be skipped altogether should the employee fear retaliation from the manager.

Step 2: Employee–Employer Relations Representative Not getting the satisfaction desired in Step 1, the employee then proceeds to file the complaint with the employee relations representative. As part of his or her job, the ER representative investigates the matter, including gathering information from both parties, and renders a decision. Although this is the first formal step, the employee may continue upward should the recommended solution be unsatisfactory.

Step 3: Employee–Department Division Head If employee relations fails to correct the problem or if the employee wishes to exercise her rights further, the

Complaints Procedure A formalized procedure in an organization through which an employee may seek resolution of a work problem.

next step in the complaints procedure is to meet with the senior manager of the area (e.g., vice-president). Once again, an investigation will take place and a decision rendered. It is important to note, however, that if employee relations found no validity in the individual's charge, they are not responsible for providing continued assistance to the employee.

Step 4: Employee–President The final step in the process involves taking the issue to the president. Generally, although employee rights may be protected under law, the president's decision is final.

The procedure just described and portrayed graphically in Figure 16-3 is a generic one. In large organizations, more levels of management will be involved. In unionized settings, the complaints procedure is known as the grievance procedure and is specified in the collective agreement. We will be discussing this in more detail as part of collective bargaining in Chapter 18.

It is important that the complaints process be known to employees. They should be informed of it during orientation, and it should be clearly featured in employee handbooks. In unionized settings, the grievance procedure is spelled out in the collective agreement which usually is distributed to all affected employees.

Note: This is a sample process and will be affected by the laws of the relevant jurisdictions. For example, complaints regarding gender or racial discrimination may be taken to the appropriate Human Rights Commission outside the organization.

Figure 16-3
A Sample Complaints Procedure in a Non-Unionized Work Environment

Suggestion Programs and Employee Surveys

Suggestion Program A process whereby employees have the opportunity to tell management how they perceive the organization is doing.

Similar to the complaints procedure, a suggestion program is designed to allow employees opportunities to tell management what it is doing inefficiently and what the company should do from an employee's point of view. In particular, suggestion programs give employees the chance to tell management "what they are doing right and what they are doing wrong."[51] In many companies, in conjunction with quality improvement programs and employee involvement, management welcomes such suggestions. In fact, as we discussed in Chapter 13, companies such as Lincoln Electric and those that use plans such as Scanlon or

IMPROSHARE actually monetarily reward individuals for their suggestions that are implemented. Although employees value these rewards, the most important aspect of a suggestion program is for individuals to witness management action.

Whether the suggestion is useful or not, employers must recognize those employees who make suggestions and let them know the results. Even if the idea isn't appropriate for the company, employees still should be told what management decided to do and why. Failure to do so will more than likely lead to a decline in suggestions. In the spirit of good employee communication, useful suggestions should be rewarded and recognized in the company's Web pages or newsletter.

In addition to having suggestion programs, many organizations carry out employee surveys to find out what employees are thinking. These are important elements of upward communication provided they are both confidential and anonymous so that employees can express their feelings—including criticisms of management—without fear of reprisals. To ensure anonymity, some organizations have external consultants carry out employee surveys. However, with adequate safeguards, they can also be done inside the company, usually with the help of human resources professionals.

Employee Surveys Systematic studies of the attitudes and perceptions of employees to ascertain how they feel about various aspects of their work and their environment.

A Concluding Word

New electronic media, particularly the Internet, are resulting in a revolution in the way communication programs operate and need to be managed. This is perhaps particularly true of Canada where our geographic distances and distinctive competence in communication technology have encouraged the growth of leading-edge communication programs. These programs will have to include new guidelines for effective communication that use electronic media. For example, all users of e-mail must be careful not to allow the immediacy of the technology to prevent the planning and a forethought that was put into the typed or handwritten communication of a previous generation. Many an employee has discovered, to their cost, that their immediate e-mail reaction to a situation has been instantly sent to everyone on a group mailing list. Each method of communication requires an understanding of a specific set of rules. In the past, organizations learned to live by a set of rules in oral exchanges, but those rules do not necessarily apply to electronic communication.

At the time of writing, it is still very difficult to predict where the exponential growth in Internet use and mobile communication technologies will end up. New technology is creating a whole sheaf of new careers and new media which were totally unknown to earlier generations—even as recently as a decade ago. We can confidently predict, however, that communication will become more and more important as part of strategic HRM programs in Canadian organizations. We need to be conscious of how changing audiences and changing organizations are affecting our ability to communicate. Above all, in this age of high-speed electronic communication, human resources professionals must not forget the importance of face-to-face communication.

Summary

This summary relates to the Learning Objectives provided on p. 459.
After reading this chapter, you should know:

1. Effective communication is fundamental to the effective operations in HRM activities in that it enables understanding to occur between the organization and its employees, assists in recruiting and selection, and specifies what activities must be done to successfully perform one's job. Effective communication also implies keeping employees informed of happenings in the organization.

2. Communication in benefits administration and health and safety is mandated by law. In benefits administration, employers must provide employees with a summary pension plan description. In health and safety, employees must be given information concerning such things as exposure to hazardous and toxic materials.

3. Human resources management communication programs are designed to keep current employees abreast of events occurring in the organization including the various policies and procedures that affect them.

4. Effective communication can affect corporate culture because open, frank discussions indicate a culture where employees are valued.

5. The CEO of an organization is the one individual responsible for setting the foundation from which the culture is built. If this person promotes and practises open communication, then that activity will filter down through the company.

6. A communication program should, at the minimum, inform employees what is expected of them, what they can expect from the company, and what the various personnel policies are.

7. The employee handbook is a tool that provides one central source of organizational information for employees regarding the company and its HRM policies.

8. Although employee handbooks differ, most include introductory comments about the organization, information about what employees need to know about the workplace, their benefits, and employee responsibilities.

9. Four popular means of communicating are: electronic media (especially the intranet), bulletin boards, company newsletters, and company-wide meetings. The fastest-growing communication media is the Internet in which are included the World Wide Web, intranet, and e-mail.

10. A critical component of an organizational suggestion program is the recognition that employees' suggestions will be heard. Failure to pay attention to employees' suggestions will reduce the value and credibility of the program.

Key Terms

bulletin board	e-mail
communication	employee handbook
company newsletter	employee survey
company-wide meetings	intranet
complaints procedure	suggestion program
electronic media	

EXPERIENTIAL EXERCISE:

The Student Handbook

In any communication program, there is a need to ensure that the information conveyed is appropriate and necessary. For this exercise, you will need to obtain a copy of your school's student handbook. This may be hard copy downloaded from the school's Web page or one obtained from the student affairs or registrar's office. In your group, go through this publication and analyse the information. To assist your analysis, use the information in this textbook about employee handbooks.

After analysing the material, identify information that your group feels is useful, and explain why. Also, point out areas that you feel may be missing or need to be expanded. How should that be done?

CASE APPLICATION:

Communicating Railway Safety[52]

In many organizations, safety is sometimes a difficult topic to communicate and certainly a tough area in which to get employees enthusiastically involved. This was particularly true of Canada's railways where safety was left to government regulators and only communicated to employees in the form of edicts and pronouncements from on high. All this is changing with a new emphasis on self-regulation in the current revisions to the *Railways Safety Act* (RSA) in Canada. Faye Ackermans, general manager of safety and regulatory affairs for CP Rail, gives a flavour of the changes that have occurred in involving employees in a proactive approach to safety. "We are not just dealing with safety administratively, but by taking a more holistic view, we are ensuring that employees follow the rules."

In the past, CN and CP Rail were expected to attend lengthy quasi-judicial, "show cause" meetings with regulators in the House of Commons' railway committee room, with both sides surrounded by a platoon of high-priced lawyers. "Our meetings are now informal, low-key, and effective," says Ackermans, "and much cheaper without the lawyers." In the past, changes occurred at glacial speed and only after an endless string of public meetings. For example, the elimination of cabooses in the mid-80s took eight years, both because of union resistance to possible job losses and the slow process of regulatory approval. Ackermans is proud to point out that most straightforward safety approvals today come in less than sixty days.

The new RSA legislation places much more emphasis on self-regulation and involvement of all major stakeholders in railway safety. This has brought about a shift in the communication culture in CN and CP. "At the beginning," recalls CN's Achille Ferrusi, vice-president of safety and regulatory affairs, "Transport Canada inspectors were struggling with their new roles. Then they started to realize that they did not have as much power or as much support from their colleagues as before. Finally, they began working more cooperatively with us." Much of that cooperative spirit developed from improved communication between the railways and regulators and also between the companies and employees. "We had to tell our employees that 'Big Brother' was gone," says CP's Ackermans, "and assure ourselves that we could operate safely. We had to raise safety awareness by impressing upon our employees that accidents cost a lot of money…. Our message now is 'do it safe no matter what the regulations say.'" The exciting outcome of this communication effort is that safety is now a line rather than a staff function. At both CN and CP, the division overseeing safety reports directly to the executive in charge of operations.

Questions

1. Describe how communication programs such as the one implemented in CN and CP have helped shape a new culture in Canada's railways.
2. What are the pros and cons of employee involvement in the communication of something as fundamental as safety?
3. How does effective communication influence worker performance and productivity?
4. How does the line responsibility for safety affect the role of HRM in communicating safety?

Testing Your Understanding

How well did you fulfil the learning objectives?

1. Effective communication is an important contributor to successful workforce diversity because
   a. it lets minority workers know that the company will make every attempt to provide them equal opportunity in the organization.
   b. it ensures realistic job previews.
   c. it helps employees understand how to do their jobs.
   d. it helps employees understand the relationship between their efforts and individual goal attainment.
   e. it helps to increase positive outcomes for interactions between managers and their employees.

2. Human resources management communication programs are designed to
   a. keep employees knowledgeable about policies and procedures affecting customers.
   b. keep customers informed about policies and programs designed to increase service.
   c. keep employees knowledgeable about policies and programs affecting them.
   d. keep customers informed about policies and programs affecting employees.
   e. improve interactions between employees and their managers.

3. How does HRM communication affect corporate culture?
   a. HRM communication does not affect corporate culture.
   b. HRM communication can be used to state corporate culture effectively.
   c. HRM communication often replaces corporate culture in large, hierarchical organizations.

   d. A free-flowing, timely, and accurate HRM communication system can help to build trust.
   e. A free-flowing, timely, and accurate HRM communication system can help to improve productivity.

4. A CEO of a 300 employee electronics manufacturer had just been convinced by her vice-president of human resources that an "open door" management policy would help to improve worker morale. Agreeing to the idea, how can she best show support for this program?
   a. Support can be shown by opening her own door to employees.
   b. Support can be shown by making a video to endorse the program, to be shown to all employees.
   c. Support can be shown by announcing the program herself over the company address system.
   d. Support can be shown by writing a column endorsing the new system for the next issue of the company newsletter.
   e. Support can be shown by feigning ignorance of the new program.

5. Why is upward communication important in empowered organizations?
   a. Upward communication is the definition of an empowered workforce.
   b. Empowered employees make more decisions about how to do their work. These decisions need to be communicated to top management.
   c. Workers feel empowered when they can communicate with top management.
   d. There is no upward communication in empowered organizations. Top management has been removed,

and most decisions are made by individuals closest to the problem.

e. Customer information and satisfaction are top priorities in an empowered organization.

6. A well-written employee handbook will provide all of these benefits to the organization except
a. create an atmosphere in which employees become more productive.
b. create an atmosphere in which employee commitment is increased.
c. create a sense of security for employees.
d. provide an implied employment contract.
e. provide a source of information for many employee work-related questions.

7. A small, family-run electronics firm has just been acquired by an aggressive transnational organization. What is the best way to inform employees?
a. Employee handbook.
b. Bulletin board.
c. Company-wide meeting.
d. Company newsletter.
e. Electronic media.

8. If you have a complaint about the grade you receive in this course, who should you go to first?
a. The professor.
b. The department chairperson who is the "boss" of the professor.
c. The dean of the school in which the professor teaches.
d. Your academic advisor.
e. Another professor.

9. Compare suggestion programs and complaints procedures.
a. Suggestion programs are found only in union shops. Complaints procedures are found only in non-union shops.
b. Both suggestion programs and complaints procedures allow the upward flow of information in an organization.
c. Suggestion programs allow employees to tell management what it is doing right. Complaints procedures allow employees to tell management what it is doing wrong.
d. Suggestion programs target individual performance. Complaints procedures target group performance.

e. Suggestion program events are initiated by managers. Complaints procedures events are initiated by employees.

10. Effective communication is an important contributor to the recruiting and selection process because
a. it lets minority workers know that the company will make every attempt to provide them equal opportunity in the organization.
b. it helps to increase positive outcomes for interactions between managers and their employees.
c. it helps employees understand how to do their jobs.
d. it helps employees understand the relationship between their efforts and individual goal attainment.
e. it ensures realistic job previews.

11. Diane has just been promoted to director of HRM communication. She is writing a mission statement for her department. What item should be included?
a. Keep employees knowledgeable about policies and programs affecting them.
b. Keep customers informed about policies and programs designed to increase service.
c. Keep employees knowledgeable about policies and procedures affecting customers.
d. Keep customers informed about policies and programs affecting employees.
e. Improve interactions between employees and their managers.

12. If new HRM communication programs are endorsed by top management,
a. they are bound to fail.
b. they are viewed as significant components of corporate culture.
c. they are accepted more slowly by the rest of the organization.
d. they are viewed with suspicion by the rest of the organization.
e. they replace the authority of the top management.

13. All of the following questions are appropriate for managers to use in determining how to filter information to their employees except:
a. Will my employees be able to do their jobs as well if this information is not shared?
b. Will my employees be disadvantaged in some way by not knowing this information?
c. Will employees care about the information?

d. Will my employees think badly of me for telling them?
e. Will my employees view this information as information overload?

14. Employee handbooks should convey all of this information except
   a. specific wage and salary information.
   b. what the company expects of its employees.
   c. what the company history is.
   d. why individuals would want to work for the company.
   e. what the company's mission is.

15. There has been a lot of confusion lately about the corporate policy on sexual harassment. One of the human resources managers is willing to write a question-and-answer column to deal with the subject. What is the best way to share this column?
   a. Employee handbook.
   b. Bulletin board.
   c. Company newsletter.
   d. Company-wide meeting.
   e. Electronic media.

Chapter Seventeen

INTRODUCTION TO LABOUR RELATIONS

LEARNING OBJECTIVES

AFTER READING THIS CHAPTER, YOU WILL BE ABLE TO:

1. Define the role and functions of a union.
2. Explain how Canadian law evolved to recognize unions and collective bargaining as lawful endeavours.
3. Explain how the passage of the US *Wagner National Labor Relations Act* (known as the *Wagner Act*) of 1935 influenced Canadian labour law.
4. Explain how the Canadian public sector came to be unionized beginning in the late 1960s.
5. Identify how the main Canadian labour federation—the Canadian Labour Congress (CLC)—is structured, and explain its role and functions.
6. Explain how national unions are typically structured, and identify the division of authority between the national and its various locals.
7. Describe the union organizing process.
8. Describe some of the tactics that are used by employers against unions in the course of an organizing drive.
9. Explain what is meant by the union's duty of fair representation.
10. Explain some of the challenges that are facing Canada's labour movement as we move into the next millennium.

The history of the labour movement in both Canada and the United States is rich in character. The Canadian labour movement and governmental policy regarding labour unions and collective bargaining has been strongly influenced by events south of the forty-ninth parallel. For many years, whenever workers tried to unite and defend themselves against various management practices, employers, with the backing of the courts and the government of the day usually were able to successfully quash such employee efforts. In the mid-1800's, Canadian common law held that unions were unlawful combinations designed to restrain trade, and, as such, unionized employees could not rely on the courts to recognize agreements reached with employers. Indeed, employers frequently obtained court injunctions against organizing activity by trade unions. The common law viewed any concerted effort by a trade union to increase the wages and enhance the working conditions of their members as an unlawful conspiracy. Indeed, it was only in 1872 that the *Canadian Trades Union Act* declared that usual trade union activities were not an unlawful restraint of trade, but the *Criminal Code* was not amended to permit peaceful strikes and picketing until 1934.[1]

Although North American legislators did not enact legislation that formalize an employers' obligation to engage in collective bargaining with their unionized employees until the mid-1940s, legislation that recognized the fundamental reality of trade unions was in place in both countries in the early 1920s. Despite the presence of such laws, however, during the first half of this century, the relationship between labour and management was frequently characterized by conflict and, at times, open hostility to the point of workers losing their lives as a result of labour–management disputes. Yet by 1970s, management began to recognize that unions might not be the "enemy." Rather, global competition, technological change, and the like made both sides recognize that they needed to be more cooperative. Fighting each other served no useful purpose and even threatened the survival of both. Something drastic was needed—new ideas on how to increase production and improve quality. Employees had to have more of a say in what affected their jobs, and joint labour–management problem solving had to establish, implement, and achieve common goals. As a result, the 1970s witnessed the birth of joint committees comprising both labour and management to identify problem areas in the organization and jointly determine and implement a solution. Finally, the confrontational days of yesteryear could be put to rest—perhaps. Sadly, that did not materialize in all cases.

There are a number of reasons why a new and more cooperative labour–management relationship was not fully accepted by the key stakeholders in all cases. These reasons include the changing world of work, the growth of international trade and the reduction in trade barriers (such as the *North American Free Trade Agreement*), and the historical record of mutual mistrust that characterize some bargaining relationships.

Introduction

A **union** is an organization of employees acting collectively, who seek to promote and protect their mutual workplace interests—wages, benefits, and working conditions—through collective bargaining. However, before we can examine the collective bargaining process, it is important to understand what unions are, how they developed over the years, and to identify the various legislative and administrative rules that govern collective bargaining. At the outset, it should be clearly recognized that unionized workplaces impose constraints on HRM practices that do not exist in a nonunion firm. For the most part, in a non-union firm, management is free to determine (subject to legislative standards of employment, health and safety, and human rights) the wages, benefits, and working conditions of employees. In a unionized firm, on the other hand, management cannot act unilaterally; it must bargain with the union with respect to all matters affecting employees' wages, benefits, and working conditions.

Although unions in the United States represent only about 11 per cent of the workforce, in Canada, that figure is nearly 40 per cent of the non-agricultural workforce. However, the proportion of unionized workers varies widely by geographic region and by industrial sector.[2] For example, while the civil service (at both the federal and provincial levels) is heavily unionized—about 80 per cent—unions have little if any presence in banking and financial services, agriculture, or trade (see Figure 17-1). The **union density rate** (that is, the percentage of employees who are represented by unions) is highest in the provinces of Newfoundland, British Columbia, and Quebec and lowest in Alberta and Prince Edward Island.

Union An organization that exists to represent, and bargain on behalf of, a group of employees as their agent with respect to the employees' terms and conditions of employment.

Union Density Rate The percentage of the workforce represented by union members and employees covered by collective bargaining agreements.

Workers—particularly those in competitive or risky occupations—often look to a union to represent their interests.

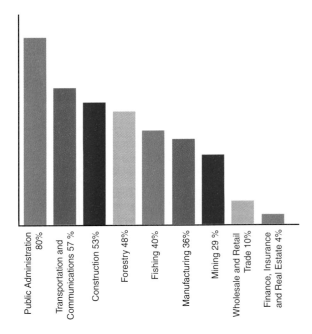

Figure 17-1
Union Density Rates
by Industry

Collective Bargaining Agreement The employment agreement reached between the union and employer, setting out terms and conditions of employment.

However, the influence of unions extends beyond those sectors where they have a strong presence. First, since many major Canadian industries are heavily unionized (for example, automobile manufacturing and transport and communications), unions have a major effect on the overall economy. Second, any gains made by unions typically spill over into other non-unionized sectors of the economy.

HRM activities in a unionized organization centre on the negotiation and administration of a collective bargaining agreement. A **collective bargaining agreement** (or collective agreement) is a binding contract agreed to by both management and the labour union which stipulates things such as wages, hours of work, and the terms and conditions of employment for those covered by the agreement. The presence of a union imposes a duty on both the union and management to negotiate a collective agreement; management no longer has the unilateral authority to determine how much employees will be paid, the benefits they will receive, or the schedules that they will work. These matters must be determined jointly through collective bargaining.

In order to better understand the environment within which labour relations activities are conducted, it is important to know the various legislative and other legal rules that govern the union–management relations.

Canadian Labour Law

Labour–management relations are undoubtedly affected by such things as the overall state of the economy, the business cycle, and the Canada's foreign trade. However, the legal framework governing labour–management relationships also plays a crucial role in defining that relationship. In this section, major developments in Canadian labour law will be discussed including the key labour legislation and judicial decisions.[3] We have also provided a quick reference guide to these laws in Table 17-1.

In Canada, eleven separate governments have authority over labour relations. Thus, rules vary from province to province, causing some confusion but allowing for experimentation and local solutions to particular labour relations problems.

TABLE 17-1: Summary of Major Labour Legislation and Judicial Decisions

IDIA (1907)	Mandated conciliation of labour disputes and prohibited strikes and lockouts during the mediation process.
T.E.C. v. Snider (1925)	Limited the federal government's presence in labour relations in favour of the provinces.
Wagner Act (1935)	First US collective bargaining legislation. It was a model for subsequent Canadian legislation.
P.C. 1003 (1944)	Federal wartime emergency regulations that created a "Wagner-style" legislative regime.
Public Service Staff Relations Act (1967)	First general public sector collective bargaining law outside Quebec.
RWDSU v. Dolphin Delivery (1986)	Recognized picketing as constitutionally protected free expression.
The "Labour Trilogy" (1987)	Recognized legislators' unfettered right to structure Canada's labour relations systems including the right to limit or even deny access to collective bargaining.
Lavigne v. OPSEU (1991)	Refused to adopt the US rules fettering unions' right to spend union dues for political purposes.

While Canadian labour law has been strongly influenced by US legislation, over the years, Canadian lawmakers have put into place a rather unique legislative framework that differs in many important aspects from the US model. One of the most important distinguishing characteristics of Canadian labour law compared to that of the US is that there is no single national collective bargaining law. Canadian labour law is divided among the the provinces or the federal government depending upon which has constitutional authority over the employer or industry in question. Today, only about 10 per cent of the Canadian workforce falls under the legislative authority of the federal government. This includes such areas as the federal civil service, banks, airlines and railways, and broadcast and telecommunication firms. At the provincial level, while there are broad similarities in labour legislation from province to province, there are also important differences. For example, in some provinces, unions can be certified by demonstrating sufficient support through signed **union membership cards**, while in other provinces, a union can only be certified after a **representation vote**. Some provinces limit management's ability to continue operations during a strike or lockout, while others allow management to go so far as to hire replacement workers (scabs) to perform the work of those employees who are locked out or are on strike.

It was not always the case that the primary legislative authority over labour relations rested with the provinces rather than with the federal government. Following a 1906 coal miners' strike in Lethbridge, Alberta, the federal government enacted the *Industrial Disputes Investigation Act* of 1907 (the IDIA).[4] Although there had been previous federal and provincial legislation, none provided for compulsory conciliation.[5]

The IDIA, which only applied to certain sectors (mining, transportation and communication, and public utilities), mandated that before there could be a lawful strike or lockout, the parties were required to participate in a conciliation process before a tripartite board (made up of an employer and employee representative and chaired by a neutral third party). The IDIA also required management to recognize the union's authority to represent all bargaining unit

Union Membership Cards A card signed by an employee authorizing the union to act on his or her behalf; relied on by the union when applying to be certified an an exclusive bargaining agent.

Representation Vote The vote conducted by the labour relations board to determine if a union has majority support among bargaining unit employees.

employees once it had demonstrated majority support, thereby eliminating the need for the union to call a "recognition strike" simply to force the employer to the bargaining table. The conciliation board was charged with the responsibility of meeting with the parties, inquiring into the merits of the dispute, and recommending an appropriate settlement. During the conciliation process, not only were strikes and lockouts prohibited, but so were any unilateral changes in the employees' wages or working conditions by management. The IDIA was important in at least three broad respects:

1. It represented a marked departure from past governmental policy by demonstrating that legislators were no longer prepared to leave private labour relations disputes solely in the hands of the parties or the courts. Legislative intervention was thought to be appropriate in order to safeguard the broader public interest.

2. It represented the first occasion where government imposed on employers, in essence, a duty to bargain with the union.

3. The tripartite model, as embodied in the IDIA, was to become a preferred model for dealing with labour–management disputes.

Paradoxically, a constitutional challenge to the IDIA, one of the first pieces of national labour relations legislation, led to the multijurisdictional patchwork that is now the Canadian labour law landscape. The case of *Toronto Electric Commissioners v. Snider*,[6] a case decided by the British Privy Council (then Canada's final appeal court), held that the IDIA could not apply to a labour relations dispute involving the Toronto municipal transit system. The Privy Council ruled that labour laws were purely a local, not a federal, concern. Thus, the seeds were sown for provincial, rather than federal, jurisdiction over the vast majority of the Canadian workforce.

In 1935, the US Congress passed the *National Labor Relations Act*,[7] often referred to as the *Wagner Act* after its legislative sponsor. For the very first time in North America, the *Wagner Act* enshrined unions and the collective bargaining process into the public policy fabric. The *Wagner Act* guaranteed workers the right to organize and join unions, to bargain collectively, and to act in concert to pursue their workplace objectives. The *Wagner Act* specifically required employers to bargain in good faith with respect to employees' wages, hours of work, and other terms and conditions of employment. The *Wagner Act* also declared that certain management actions were **unfair labour practices**. These unlawful acts included such things as obstructing employees from joining unions, refusing to bargain or bargaining in bad faith, and discriminating against employees for engaging in union activities. The *Wagner Act* also established a separate administrative tribunal—the *National Labor Relations Board* (NLRB)—to enforce and administer the act. **Labour relations boards**, both in Canada and the US, determine appropriate **bargaining units**, conduct union representation elections, and interpret and apply the law with respect to unfair labour practices.

Although the *Snider* case gave the provincial legislatures the constitutional authority to enact comprehensive collective bargaining legislation, few provinces chose to do so until after World War II. It was the federal government, acting under its wartime emergency powers, that first enacted (in 1944) comprehensive collective bargaining legislation via wartime regulations brought in under amendments to the *War Measures Act*. These regulations—the Wartime Labour Relations Regulations and more generally known as **P.C. 1003**—essentially replicated the main features of the *Wagner Act*.

The effect of P.C. 1003 was immediate and dramatic. Canadian union membership doubled in very short order; many unions, now freed of the burdens of

Wagner Act Also known as the US *National Labor Relations Act* of 1935, the *Wagner Act* gave employees the legitimate right to form and join unions and to engage in collective bargaining.

Unfair Labour Practices A violation by the employer or the union of the rules set out in the collective bargaining legislation; the violation can be remedied in a variety of ways by the labour relations board.

National Labor Relations Board Established to administered and interpret the *Wagner Act*, the NLRB has primary responsibility for conducting union representation elections in the US.

Labour Relations Boards The quasi-judicial administrative tribunal charged with administering and enforcing collective bargaining legislation.

Bargaining Unit The particular group of employees that is represented by a single trade union in negotiations with the employer; the structure of the unit is determined by the labour relations board.

P.C. 1003 The 1944 emergency wartime regulations that established Canada's first collective bargaining regime.

having to call recognition strikes simply to get management to the bargaining table, negotiated binding collective bargaining agreements that served the twin purposes of providing better pay and working conditions for employees and more stable production efficiency for employers. Perhaps most importantly, the right to join trade unions and to engage in collective bargaining came to be recognized as legitimate rights for all working Canadians. P.C. 1003 was the model for all subsequent provincial collective bargaining legislation in the first few years after the war ended.

Although the basic structure of collective bargaining legislation, modelled on the US *Wagner Act*, has remained unchanged since the early 1950s, proposals to alter collective bargaining laws are frequently on the legislative agenda. Some of the current issues include the way unions are required to demonstrate majority support. For example, in British Columbia, signed union membership cards submitted to the labour board are accepted as demonstrating majority support,[8] while in neighbouring Alberta, a representation election must always be held prior to a union being certified as a bargaining agent. Other contentious issues include whether or not there should be restrictions on the employer's ability to hire replacement workers during a strike or lockout; how far a union's right to picket should extend (for example, where the struck employer is a subcontractor on a larger construction project); whether lower-level managers should be prohibited from unionizing; whether employees in "essential services" should be prohibited

A knowledge of legislation provides the fastest way around the complex world of Canadian labour relations.

from striking or in some way limited; and whether all unionized employees and employers in a given sector (for example, construction, health care, forestry) should be required to bargain for a single sectoral agreement as they do in Japan and other places. Different jurisdictions have approached these issues in different ways, and, in that sense, Canadian labour relations are akin to a large laboratory where various labour relations experiments are ongoing.

Unions in the Public Sector

In the late 1940s and early 1950s, the federal and provincial governments enacted substantially similar collective bargaining laws which, for the most part, only affected employees in the private sector. It was only in the late 1960s that government employees were included in collective bargaining legislation. The watershed year for public sector employees was 1967, and, as it had in the past, the federal government once again took a lead role (although it should be noted that Quebec had given its public sector employees collective bargaining rights two years earlier).

Public Service Staff Relations Act The first major public sector bargaining law enacted by the federal government in 1967.

In 1967, in response to continuing pressure from its civil servants, the federal government introduced the *Public Service Staff Relations Act*.[9] Historically, Canadian governments had been reluctant to give full collective bargaining rights to public sector employees because to do so would be incompatible with the government's fiscal responsibilities—the government alone should decide how tax money should be spent. If government employees wish to have input into spending decisions, that input should be given via the ballot box and not across a bargaining table. While this idea still holds sway in the United States where comparatively few public sector employees have meaningful collective bargaining rights, the theory has been completely abandoned in Canada. Indeed, the prominent role of public sector unions is demonstrated by the fact that three of Canada's five largest unions represent public sector employees.

Following the enactment of the *Public Service Staff Relations Act*, most other jurisdictions rapidly followed suit and by the mid-1970s, most public sector and quasi-public sector employees—teachers, police officers, firefighters, and hospital employees—were given full collective bargaining rights. Not surprisingly, however, there is no single public sector collective bargaining model. In some jurisdictions, the public sector is governed by a general collective bargaining law, while in others, special legislation covers particular public sector employees. For example, in some provinces public education is governed by a separate collective bargaining law. Most public sector employees have the right to strike, but, in some cases known as interest disputes (which involve wages and working conditions), a neutral third party attempts settlement through a process known as interest arbitration.

Interest Dispute/Arbitration An interest dispute is a dispute about the terms and conditions of employment; interest arbitration is the process whereby a third party neutral issues a binding decision regarding the dispute.

The Impact of the Charter on Labour Relations

In 1982, the *Canadian Charter of Rights and Freedoms*[10] was included in a new patriated Canadian *Constitution Act*. It remains to be seen precisely how much impact the *Charter* will ultimately have on labour relations. Thus far, its influence appears to have been rather modest, but it must be remembered that *Charter* jurisprudence is an ongoing developmental process. In *R.W.D.S.U. v. Dolphin Delivery Ltd.*,[11] the Supreme Court of Canada held that while peaceful union

Meet

Tomi Eeckhout
Director of Labour Relations
British Columbia Institute of Technology

"You never know what's around the corner." That's how Tomi Eeckhout describes a "typical" day at his job as Director of Labour Relations at the British Columbia Institute of Technology (B.C.I.T.). "You don't have much control over the work."

Despite this fact—or perhaps because of this fact—he loves his job. "On a day-to-day basis, you're a little bit of a lawyer, a little bit of a psychologist, a little bit of a social worker, and a little bit of an etiquette expert. You do everything. You don't have time to be bored." B.C.I.T.'s employees belong to three different bargaining units, and Mr Eeckhout oversees the college's relations with all of them, aided by two labour relations officers. There's no doubt that the task can be complex. One unit consists of support staff, such as administrators and maintenance workers. The second is mostly vocational instructors—those who teach in apprenticeship-type programs such as carpentry or mechanics. Both of these units are affiliated with the BC Government Employee's Union, which connects them ultimately to the Canadian Labour Congress. The members of the third bargaining unit, an independent union, are mostly instructors in technology-related fields, such as engineering and computers.

A decision made in one area can have repercussions for other agreements or departments, explains Mr Eeckhout. "To be effective in labour relations, you have to have a good sense of the organization as a whole. You really need to be able to see the big picture."

Basically, Mr Eeckhout sees himself as a problem solver. Whether it's settling a minor workplace issue, processing a more serious grievance, or negotiating a collective agreement, the goal is to find a solution that works.

Before he got an M.B.A. and eventually chose his career path, he got a math degree, and in an indirect way this early training serves him well. "Math does require you to think analytically," he points out.

Mr Eeckhout's background is somewhat unusual in another way, too; before coming to work for management at B.C.I.T., he spent six years as a business agent for a large public-service union. So he really knows the field from every angle. "I've been in labour relations for my whole career," he says. "And whether you're on the union or the management side, the core parts of the job are the same. You're dealing with very complex issues."

Above all, he says, "You're in the people business. You're responsible for one of the most important aspects of people's lives—their jobs."

---

picketing was constitutionally protected under the "freedom of expression" guarantee contained in section 2(b) of the *Charter*, such picketing could nonetheless be restricted or even entirely prohibited if it was directed at neutral third parties (so-called secondary picketing). A year later, in the Labour Trilogy,[12] the Supreme Court of Canada dealt a further blow to the labour movement when it decided that while the right to join labour unions is constitutionally protected, collective bargaining and the right to strike are not. Thus, legislatures remain free to determine not only who shall have collective bargaining rights, but also the particular form that those rights will take.

Labour Trilogy The three 1987 decisions issued by the Supreme Court of Canada all holding that collective bargaining and the right to strike were not constitutionally protected activities.

In something of a modest victory for the labour movement, in *Lavigne v. Ontario Public Service Employees' Union*,[13] the Supreme Court of Canada held that unions were free to spend union dues as they saw fit and not just on collective bargaining and related activities such as contract administration. The Supreme Court of Canada rejected the so-called fair share doctrine, which is part of US labour law, under which unions cannot spend union dues on, for example, political lobbying activities unless the bargaining unit membership consents.[14]

Having examined some of the relevant legislative and judicial history affecting the modern labour movement, we now turn to a discussion about the contemporary Canadian labour institutions.

The Structure of the Canadian Labour Movement

The Canadian Labour Congress (CLC) The Canadian equivalent of the U.S.-based AFL-CIO; approximately 60% of Canadian unions are affiliated with the CLC making it the largest Canadian labour federation.

AFL-CIO The American Federation of Labor and the Congress of Industrial Relations; the U.S.-based labor federation with which some Canadian unions are affiliated.

Have you ever given much thought to how organized labour in Canada is structured? Or what roles the Canadian Labour Congress (CLC) and its provincial affiliates play in labour–management relationships? Do you know what relationship exists between the CLC and its affiliates? Are you aware that although many unions are affiliated with the CLC, some are not, and that there exists a number of other labour federations? Finding answers to questions such as these is the focus of this section on union structures.

In many respects, Canadian labour federations are modelled on the structure found in the United States, the apex of which is the AFL-CIO.[15] While the CLC represents the majority of all Canadian labour unions (about 60 per cent), some unions have decided not to affiliate with the CLC. About 23 per cent of Canadian unions are affiliated with the US-based AFL-CIO (mostly unions that began in the United States and then filtered north). The Canadian Federation of Labour represents about 5 per cent of Canadian unions, and another 15 per cent belong to other federations. Figure 17-2 represents the organizational affiliations of labour unions in Canada.

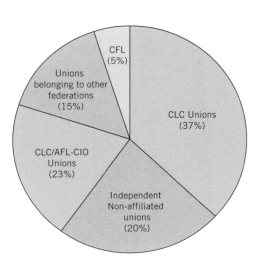

Figure 17-2
Affiliations of Canadian
Labour Unions

Certainly, as the largest and best-known labour federation, the CLC is often looked upon as the "voice of labour." The CLC represents about 2.5 million Canadian workers in about ninety different unions. The CLC does not have any particular institutional authority over its member unions; rather, its function is more in the realm of coordination (particularly by sorting out jurisdictional disputes among member affiliates) and national and international political action on behalf of its membership. The CLC is governed by a national elected executive council. The CLC structure is, for the most part, replicated by provincial labour federations. In addition to the CLC, other labour federations include the Canadian Federation of Labour (comprised mainly of construction unions) and the Quebec-based Confédération des syndicates nationaux (CSN) and Centrale de l'enseignement du Québec (CEQ).

Unions that are affiliated with a labour federation expect to receive various services from that federation in return for their fees. Such services can include political lobbying, assistance in contract negotiation, educational programs, and undertaking and disseminating relevant research. Unions affiliate with labour federations because they perceive value in so doing. The primary focus of any labour federation is to promote and assist the labour movement generally and the particular interests of its member affiliates. However, as noted earlier, a labour federation is not a union, and the day-to-day work of a union—negotiating and administering collective agreements on behalf of their members—falls to the individual member unions and, more particularly, to the individual locals of those unions.

National and International Unions

The governance of unions derives from the activities and chartering body policies of the national or international union, which is a federation of local unions.[16] These unions operate under the direction of a national union president and the executive committee (usually the secretary, treasurer, and vice-presidents) who set policies to govern the activities of its locals at the union's convention. At these conventions, delegates, usually elected from the local unions in proportion to the size of the local's membership, convene to decide on various policy issues such as establishing the parent union's constitution, the amount of dues each member will pay, and the election of officers. At these conventions, usually held biannually, national union policies are created, reaffirmed, revised, or dropped.

National or international union
The national or international union body that charters local unions and provides institutional support for collective bargaining and contract administration.

The national union, however, has other roles in the labour relations process—it is instrumental in organizing workers. Through its organizing efforts, existing locals may be expanded or new locals added. The national union also serves as the liaison to its locals by providing economic data, collective bargaining information, advice, and other services regarding labour–management relationships. Increasingly, the national union is responsible for strategic planning activities, essential if the union is to grow and prosper in a world characterized by a diverse workforce and global trade.[17] National unions typically have a regional vice-president who is responsible for serving and facilitating the actions of the local unions. This is especially true during contract negotiations when a vice-president of the national union may assist the local union in preparing for negotiations, bargaining with management, and implementing and administering the contract. National and local unions do not always agree, however, about how negotiations should be conducted or, indeed, what constitutes an acceptable bargain.[18] To a large extent, the national union functions much as a labour federation when providing services to its locals. More concerned with labour matters that directly affect their industry or trade, these unions support the efforts and the daily administration of the local unions. This is done through lobbying and by providing bargaining support, educational programs, and other special services.

The Local Union

The heart of day-to-day activities in labour–management relations exists at the **local union** level. It is at this level that workers have their greatest association with the union. No matter what the affiliation with a national union or labour federation, the local union provides the grass-roots support for the workers. Local unions operate much like any other business. They are usually guided by a president, a secretary–treasurer, and an executive board (all elected representatives) to serve and meet the needs of the rank and file.[19] It is this executive committee's responsibility to ensure that the day-to-day operations are handled effectively and efficiently. This means that it is a primary duty of the local union to collect union dues,[20] forward a portion of those dues—this varies among unions—to the national union, and to work with local management in negotiating, implementing, and administering the contract. In other words, its primary purpose is to represent the workers effectively.

In most cases, the national union vests its various union locals with two major responsibilities: contract negotiation and contract administration. A central component of the latter responsibility includes the filing of **grievances** and representing union members in the grievance arbitration process. The local union, usually with assistance from the national union, engages in collective bargaining with management on behalf of the bargaining unit employees. It is the local's responsibility to be aware of, and to try to achieve through negotiations, the bargaining goals of the local membership. This means that the local union, and more particularly the local bargaining committee, must be well informed about its members' expectations or else it might face the embarrassment of having a tentative collective agreement rejected by the broader local membership when that agreement is presented to the members for ratification. Thus, prior to and during the course of negotiations with management, the union executive will regularly seek input from the membership, usually through membership meetings, telephone hotlines, and surveys. After negotiations have been completed and a proposed collective agreement has been concluded, it is the responsibility of the local officers to present the package to the local members for ratification. Most often, the bargaining committee and the local executive will recommend acceptance of the agreement; however, from time to time, they will advice rejection of the proposed agreement. In the latter scenario, the bargaining committee and the union executive are seeking a mandate to either continue negotiations or to call a strike vote.

It will primarily fall to the local union to ensure that the collective bargaining agreement is honoured on a day-to-day basis. This responsibility is known as contract administration. An elected workplace agent, usually called the **shop steward**, is the person most responsible for ensuring that the contract is being followed correctly on an ongoing basis. Any deviations from the contract's language or problems arising from its implementation may result in a grievance being filed and, ultimately, a hearing before a neutral third-party decision maker known as an arbitrator. The local union is responsible for processing the grievance and ensuring that it is adjudicated appropriately.

Local Union Typically, the union that is certified to represent a particular group of employees; provides the grassroots support for union members in their daily interactions with the employer.

Grievance A formal protest filed by the union alleging that the employer has violated a provision of the collective bargain

Shop Steward The union representative, typically elected, who is responsible for administering the collective agreement at the level of the shop floor.

How Are Employees Unionized?

Unions don't just appear. Employees must go through a formal process in order to have a union designated as their certified bargaining agent. This process is known as an **organizing drive**. Not only must the union demonstrate that it has majority support among the employees, but it must also show that the proposed bargaining unit—for example, all non-managerial employees[21] at a particular plant or in a particular occupational category—would be an appropriate one.

Figure 17-3 contains a simple flow chart showing how a union organizing drive generally proceeds. It should be noted that this process varies among the eleven Canadian jurisdictions. For example, in British Columbia, a union may be automatically certified without a representation vote provided it can prove to the labour board, through signed membership cards, that not less than 55 per cent of the bargaining unit employees support the union. In Alberta, a representation vote must be held in every case so long as the union can show that at least 40 per cent of the bargaining unit employees have signed a union membership card.

Organizing Drive The process whereby a union seeks to be designated as the employees' bargaining agent; usually, the union will solicit employees' signatures on union membership cards which in turn will be presented to the labour relations board for verification.

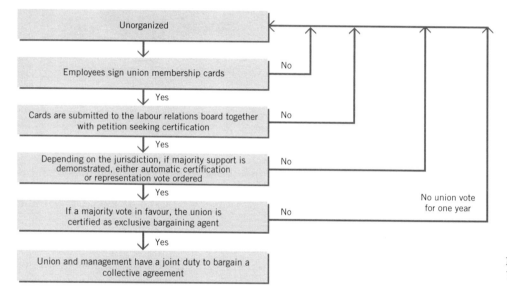

Figure 17-3
Union Organizing Process

Efforts to organize a group of employees (note that across Canada, managerial employees are generally prohibited from unionizing) may begin by employees requesting a union to visit the organization and solicit members, or the union itself might initiate a membership drive. Either way, the union must secure signed authorization cards from the employees it wishes to represent. Employees who sign the cards indicate that they wish the particular union to be their representative in negotiating with the employer.

A union is not required to show majority support before petitioning the labour board for a representation vote to be held, but unions will rarely file petitions for certification unless a clear majority of the bargaining unit have already signed membership cards. It is simply a matter of mathematics and business efficacy: In order to be certified, the union must be supported by a majority of eligible employees voting in a secret ballot election. To ensure that, the union has to have signed up substantially more than a simple majority of the bargaining unit employees to make up for those who might change their minds.

The attrition between card signing and representation vote has been demonstrated by research conducted in the United States.[22] It shows that when more than 75 per cent of the eligible workers sign the authorization card, the union

A union organizing a new workplace must ensure that it has a significant majority of workers' support before asking for a recognition vote.

has a 60 per cent chance of winning the election; when the signatures total between 60 and 75 per cent, the chances of winning drop to 50–50. And when only 30 per cent have signed, unions have only an 8 per cent chance of winning a certification election.[23]

Why the significant drop in numbers? Even when a sizeable proportion of the workers sign union membership cards, unless the jurisdiction permits automatic certification, the victory is by no means guaranteed. Management will not sit idly by during the organization drive; in fact, in most organizations, management can be expected to resist unions (see "Ethical Decisions in HRM"). Although it does not have an unfettered right to campaign against the union—if it does so too actively, it may risk being charged with unfair labour practices—management undoubtedly will use a variety of tactics—some subtle,[24] some very blatant—in order to defeat the union. One heavy-handed method is to fire the union ringleaders. It is clearly illegal but hardly unknown. Union organizers also realize that some employees who initially signed union membership cards might change their minds and vote against the union. For these and other reasons, unions usually will not file a petition for certification without already confirming that a substantial majority of the employees are union supporters.

Certification The exclusive right, granted by the labour relations board, authorizing a union to represent a particular group of employees.

Duty of Fair Representation The union's duty to ensure that it represents all of the bargaining unit employees in good faith and without discrimination.

Upon certification, either by way of a card count or following a representation election, the union is designated as the exclusive agent for the bargaining unit employees. The union must represent all employees in the bargaining unit, not just union supporters. And once a collective agreement is concluded, it governs all bargaining unit employees who are equally entitled to receive the benefits of that agreement. Indeed, if a union discriminates against a bargaining unit employee, say, because that individual is not a union supporter, the union can be sanctioned by the labour board for failure to meet its duty of fair representation and could be ordered to pay financial compensation to the aggrieved union member.

Ethical Decisions in HRM:

Anti-Union Organizing Strategies

You recognize that your employees are not happy over recent events in your organization. You had to make significant personnel cuts, restructuring the reporting relationships due to the elimination of several offices, and you announced that there will be no pay increases this year. You know there have been rumblings, but you never expected it to lead to a union organizing drive. After all, you've generally had a mutually respectful relationship with your employees over the past several years. Then you notice non-union literature in your parking lot, and you witness something hush-hush going on between employees. In fact, one of your supervisors mentions that he overheard several workers talking about joining a union. Not wanting to take any chances, you contact your labour lawyer, who suggests that you take some immediate steps.

First of all, you begin to send information to employees about all the good things you have done and how you value their input. You stress how you prefer to solve problems one on one rather than through a third party. You even indicate that you feel the worst is behind you, but you can't make absolute promises. Unfortunately, these actions appear to be having little effect on the union organizing activity around your facility.

You call a meeting of all employees and tell them that although it is their right to join a union, you feel that you must speak your mind. You explain that when a union organizes employees, there is an increase in administrative costs to the company, and in the financial shape your organization is in, if you were to incur more costs, it would create significant financial hardships. Thus, you tell them that if they unionize and costs go up, you will have no choice but to close the business and move to someplace where costs won't be so high.

In the meantime, you hire consultants to guide you on steps to take to avoid being unionized. You are more than willing to spend tens of thousands of dollars to keep the union out even though it's an expense you prefer not to have. By and large, it looks as if your investment pays off. When the election is finally held, 73 per cent of those voting reject the union.

You successfully defended your turf, but at what expense? You pressed hard to save the company from being unionized, spending a lot of money and leaving the impression that you would close down the facility if the union election ultimately added to your administrative costs. Were your union avoidance tactics legal? The union now files a series of unfair labour practices charges relating to your actions during the organizing drive. Have you committed any unfair labour practices, and, if so, what might the labour board do? Aside from the legal issue, were your tactics ethical and in the best interest of the company and its employees? What is your opinion?

Once a union has been certified, it does not follow that it will represent the bargaining unit employees forever. If they become dissatisfied with the union's representation, the employees may seek to have another union represent their interests or to abandon unionization altogether. The former process is known as a change in representation; the latter is known as revocation of certification or decertification. Typically, decertification mirrors the process that saw the union certified through a representation vote in the first place. The dissatisfied employees present the labour board with a petition for decertification, signed by an appropriate proportion of the bargaining unit employees—for example, in British Columbia, 45 per cent. A decertification vote will be held, and the outcome, as with certification votes, is determined by majority vote. It should be noted that the employer cannot play any active role in a decertification campaign; to do so is to commit an unfair labour practice. The choice of whether or not to be represented by a union is solely the employees'. Even though that choice undoubtedly affects managerial prerogatives and rights, the fact remains that the employees' decision must not be affected by any threats or promises of punishment or reward on the part of management.

Not all organizing drives are, of course, successful, at least not the first time out. However, once a union is certified, often its real work is just beginning: the negotiation of a collective bargaining agreement. We shall examine the specific issues surrounding contract negotiations in our next chapter on collective bargaining.

It should also be noted that while most workplaces become unionized as a result of a union organizing drive, there are at least two other ways a union can be designated as the bargaining agent for a particular group of employees. An employer can voluntarily agree to accept a union that has apparently demonstrated that it is supported by a majority of the bargaining unit employees and then proceed to negotiate a collective agreement. This process, known as **voluntarily recognition**, is relatively rare but not unknown. Management cannot, however, purport to voluntarily recognize a more compliant union in order to defeat an organizing drive by a union perceived to be more militant. In such a case, another union might challenge the voluntary recognition agreement which could be set aside by the labour relations board if the board was satisfied the union that was voluntarily recognized did not have majority support.

Another route to unionization is through a process known as **successorship**. In this case, the employer acquires most or all of the assets or operations of a previously unionized firm. In essence, the union certification (and any collective bargaining agreement that is in force) operates as a form of lien or charge on the assets and thus, as with any such lien, the purchaser is bound by the charge. Thus, after acquisition, if the new employer is declared by the labour board to be a successor to the predecessor firm, both the union certification and the collective agreement will automatically transfer to the new firm. In addition, the former employees of the former firm can rely on the collective agreement to secure rights and benefits (including the right to employment) with the successor firm.

Voluntary Recognition The process whereby an employer recognizes a union as the bargaining agent for a group of employees even though that union has not been officially certified by the labour relations board.

Successorship The process whereby the labour relations board declares that new employer, say a purchaser of the business, is bound by the former employer's certification and collective bargaining agreement.

Critical Issues for Unions Today

Union Avoidance

Management rarely welcomes a union into its midst, but in the course of an organizing drive, management often has relatively few lawful tools at its disposal with which to attack the union. Historically, union drives were snuffed out by simply firing the organizers and intimidating the rest of the workforce. These sorts of bullying tactics, while sometimes seem even today, rarely have the desired effect. Indeed, such hard-core tactics often do nothing more than strengthen the employees' resolve to organize by demonstrating the need for a union to protect their interests against management's capricious behaviour. Today, management may still wish to avoid unionization,[25] but their tactics and strategies have changed, and unions have to change their tactics in response.

Individual employers and employer associations frequently engage in lobbying efforts to convince the government to amend the existing labour laws to make them more friendly to business. Of course, organized labour also lobbies government. Thus, there is a continual push and pull on government to change labour legislation. Often, this sort of activity can result in intense public debate, as has been the case recently in Ontario in the education sector and in British Columbia in the construction industry.

Employers may lobby government to declare certain segments of their operations "essential services," and, thus, the employees so designated may only have a limited or even no right to strike. Generally speaking, labour boards take a conservative view about what constitutes an "essential service"—usually some threat to public safety or health must be demonstrated before employees will be designated essential. Once a labour dispute becomes a strike or lockout, governments may be lobbied to pass back-to-work legislation. Of course, lobbying to change labour legislation is primarily the concern of unionized employers. Non-union employers who wish to retain that status can defeat an organizing drive before it is under way by simply keeping its workers reasonably satisfied with their pay and working conditions. Some non-union employers have gone so far as to give their employees many of the benefits that unionized workers enjoy. Such actions go beyond merely matching union wage and benefit scales and can include setting up internal dispute resolution procedures, giving employees job protection guarantees, and establishing formalized channels for employee input into key strategic decisions.[26]

Unionizing the Non-Traditional Employee

While the percentage of workers who are unionized is more than three times higher in Canada than in the United States, Canadian unions are not without their challenges. The relative strength of the Canadian labour movement is attributable, in large measure, to the high level of public sector unionism—a source of strength to be sure, but also one that masks the relative weakness of unions in the private sector. Historically, unions have served the needs of a predominantly White, male workforce. Can unions meet the particular needs of the contemporary Canadian workforce, one that is dramatically more diverse than it was even two decades ago? For example, despite the dramatic increase of women in the labour force over the past three decades, unions have had only modest success in bargaining terms and conditions of employment that are of particular interest to women, such as family responsibility leave and day care provisions.[27]

In years past, unions' strongest presence was in manufacturing and the primary industries such as forestry, fishing, and mining. However, these sectors are declining now that the Canadian economy is in transition to a more service-based economy. Unfortunately for unions, the service sector (other than the public sector) has been one of their weakest areas. For example, despite their very significant role in the Canadian economy, financial institutions are virtually unorganized. Further, due to the very high rate of unionization in the public sector, future union gains will have to come from organizing activity in the service sector side of the private sector. If there is to be a vibrant private sector union presence, unions must reach out and fulfil the needs of these service sector employees. There have been recent signs of renewed vigour such as the recent certifications in British Columbia of a group of Starbuck's coffee houses and a McDonald's fast food franchise.

As the world of work continues to evolve radically, it is safe to assume that unions will target a broader, more diverse group of employees. The same things that unions "sold" fifty years ago to get people interested—wages, benefits, job security, and having a say in how employees are treated at work—are the same things that concern employees as we enter the new millennium. The restructuring, delayering, and the downsizing that are now common in Canadian corporations have forced affected workers to pay closer attention to what unions promise and are able to deliver.

International Labour Relations

Labour relations practices and the union density rate vary greatly among industrialized nations (see Table 17-2). In almost every case, the relationships among management, employees, and unions (or other administrative bodies) are the result of long historical development. For example, the business approach to unionism, which emphasizes economic over social objectives, is uniquely North American. In Europe, Latin America, and elsewhere, unions have often evolved out of a left-wing philosophy of the class struggle, resulting in labour being more politically involved. The Japanese Confederation of Shipbuilding and Engineering Workers' Union only recently began dropping its socialist slogans and rhetoric to pursue a "partnership" with management.[28] This fundamental difference in perspective sometimes makes it difficult for Canadian expatriates to understand how the labour relations process works in other parts of the globe because even the same terms can have very different meanings. For example, in Canada and the United States, collective bargaining generally refers to the negotiations that occur between the union and management with respect to wages and conditions of employment in a bargaining unit. However, in Sweden and Germany, collective bargaining refers to negotiations between the employers' organization and a trade union for an entire industry. While this so-called sectoral bargaining is not unknown in Canada, the vast majority of private sector negotiations occur at the level of the firm rather than of the industry or sector.[29] In the United States and Canada, arbitration usually refers to the settlement of individual contractual disputes, while in Australia, it is part of the contract bargaining process (a process that it known in Canada as "interest arbitration," to distinguish that process from "rights" or "grievance" arbitration).

TABLE 17-2 Unionization Around the World

Country	Percentage of Workers Unionized
Sweden	91%
Finland	79%
Canada	34%
United Kingdom	33%
Germany	29%
United States	14%
France	9%

Source: "Workers Drift Away from Unions," *BBC News* (November 22, 1997).
http://news.bbc.couk/hi/english/business/; Statistics Canada, *1997 Directory of Labour Organizations in Canada* (Ottawa: 1998), p.xvi.

Not only do other countries have a different history of unionism, national governments have differing views of their role in the labour relations process. This role is often reflected in the nature and type of the regulations in force. While the United States government generally takes a hands-off approach towards intervention in labour–management matters, that is clearly not the case in Canada where government involvement in labour relations disputes is a well-established norm.[30] This is also the case in Australia. Thus, not only must the multinational corporate industrial relations office be familiar with the separate laws of each country, it must also be familiar with the environment in which those statutes are implemented.

Understanding international labour relations is vital to an organization's strategic planning. Unions affect wage levels[31] which, in turn, affect competitiveness in both labour and product markets.[32] Unions and labour laws may limit employment-level flexibility through security clauses that tightly control lay-offs and terminations (or redundancies). This is especially true in countries such as Canada, England, France, Germany, Japan, and Australia, where various laws place severe restrictions on employers. It is not so in the United States. Indeed, twenty-one US states have passed so-called right-to-work laws which state that employees cannot be forced to join a union even though their employer is unionized. Not surprisingly, in the right-to-work states, unions have virtually no presence.[33]

Differing Perspectives Towards Labour Relations

If labour relations can affect the strategic planning initiatives of an organization, it is necessary to consider the issue of headquarters' involvement in host-country international union relations. The organization must determine whether labour relations should be controlled globally from the parent country, or if it would be more advantageous for each host country to administer its own operation. There is no simple means to decide this. Frequently, the decision reflects the relationship of the home market with the overseas one. For instance, when domestic sales are larger than those overseas, the organization is more likely to regard the foreign office as an extension of the domestic operations. This is true for many United States multinational organizations because the home market is so vast. Thus, American firms have been more inclined to keep labour relations centrally located at corporate headquarters. By contrast, Canada and many European countries have small home markets with comparatively larger international operations and are thus more inclined to adapt to host-country standards and have the labour relations decentralized.[34]

Another divergence among multinational companies in their labour relations is the national attitude towards unions. Generally, American multinational corporations view unions negatively and try to avoid unionization of the workforce.[35] Canadians and Europeans, on the other hand, have had greater experience with unions, are accustomed to a larger proportion of the workforce being unionized, and are more accepting of the unionization of their own workers. In Japan, as in other parts of Asia, unions are often closely identified with an organization and more loyal to the enterprise's goals than is the case in the United States where unions demand member loyalty, and their relationship with the organization tends to be more adversary. This may explain the extreme lengths to which Japanese auto manufacturers go in selecting plant sites in Canada[36] and the United States[37] and the tactics they utilize in order to avoid unionization of their workforces.[38]

The European Union

The new European Union is made up of a dozen or more individual labour relations systems.[39] For both the member nations and other countries doing business in Europe, it is important to understand the dynamics of what will necessarily be a dramatically changing labour environment.[40]

Labour relations in the emerging European Union are dynamic since a dozen or more individual labour relations systems are being merged into one.

Legislation about workers' rights is continually developing,[41] which has far-ranging implications for all employers. While the French and Germans lean towards strong worker representation in labour policy reflecting their cultural histories, the United Kingdom and Denmark oppose them. Many basic questions remain to be answered with the implementation of the free movement of labour across national boundaries. For example, with the increase in production that accompanies the opening of this market, workers and their union representatives are going to want their fair share. And what is this fair share? For starters, European unions want a maternity package that provides 80 per cent of salary for a fourteen-week period. They are also seeking premium pay for night work, full benefits for workers who are employed more than eight hours a week, participation on companies' boards of directors, and an increase in the minimum wage level to two-thirds of each country's average manufacturing wage.[42] Some of these demands will be difficult to obtain, but companies doing business overseas must be aware of what is happening in pending labour legislation and fully understand and comply with the host country's laws and customs.

Study Tools and Applications

Summary

This summary relates to the Learning Objectives provided on p. 483.

After having read this chapter, you should know:

1. A union is an organization of workers, acting collectively, seeking to promote and protect their mutual interests through collective bargaining.
2. How Canadian law evolved to recognize unions and collective bargaining as lawful endeavours.
3. How the US *Wagner (National Labor Relations) Act* of 1935 influenced Canadian labour law. The *Wagner Act* (and subsequently, the Canadian versions of that law beginning with P.C. 1003) gave unions the right to exist and identified unfair labour practices by employers.
4. How the Canadian public sector came to be unionized commencing in the late 1960s and how public sector bargaining has affected the Canadian labour movement.
5. How the main Canadian labour federations are structured as well as their role and functions. The main national labour federation is the CLC; in addition, many Canadian unions are also affiliated with the US-based AFL-CIO.
6. How national unions are structured and the division of authority between the national and its various locals.
7. The union organizing process officially begins with the signing of a union membership card. If a majority of potential union members show their intent to vote for the union by signing the membership card, the labour board will either automatically certify the union or conduct a representation election. In a representation election, if 50 per cent plus one vote are in favour, the union will be certified as the exclusive bargaining agent for all employees in the bargaining unit.
8. Union avoidance refers to the tactics and strategies that management may resort to in order to ensure that the workforce does not unionize.
9. Upon certification, a union must fairly represent the interests of all employees in the bargaining unit, not merely those who are strong union supporters or who vote for the union in a representation vote.
10. As we approach the year 2000, unions will have to adapt their strategies and tactics to account for the declining employment in the sectors of their traditional strength—such as resources and manufacturing—and the growth of service sector employment. Further, traditional union demands do not always adequately meet the needs of an increasingly diverse workforce; how will unions adjust to the realities of the new workplace?

Key Terms

AFL-CIO	organizing drive
bargaining unit	P.C. 1003
certification	*Public Service Staff Relations Act*
Canadian Labour of Congress (CLC)	representation vote
collective bargaining agreement	shop steward
duty of fair representation	successorship
grievance	unfair labour practice
interest dispute/arbitration	union
Labour Trilogy	union density rate
labour relations board	union membership card
local union	voluntary recognition
national/international union	*Wagner Act*
National Labour Relations Board	

EXPERIENTIAL EXERCISE:

Conflict Resolution

Introduction

A great deal of human activity in business situations is concerned with resolving conflicts. Individuals or groups have different needs, preferences, and priorities, and somehow, these must be resolved if they are to work together. Negotiation is one major process parties use to resolve their conflicts and manage disputes.

Procedure

Step 1: 15–20 MINUTES

The class will divide into groups of four. In each group, two students will represent Campus Travel Agency, and the other two will represent Great Northern Airlines. Each pair should read the information on their role provided by the instructor and work together to understand the information. They should try to set a negotiating goal (the deal they would like to achieve) and a bottom line (a minimally acceptable deal) as a team.

Step 2: 15-20 MINUTES

After pairs are prepared to negotiate, they should meet with their opponent(s). Each pair or foursome should attempt to negotiate an agreement that specifies:

- The number of tickets to be sold
- The percentage of commission that will be paid to Campus Travel Agency
- Any other elements to the agreement.

Great Northern Airlines should prepare to make the first offer on ticket price. You are NOT REQUIRED to agree. If you believe the other side is being unfair or unreasonable, you can take your business elsewhere. The instructor will signal when time is up. The Campus Travel representative(s) should tell the class about the progress and any outcome of their negotiations. If no deal is achieved, report the last offers on the table before negotiations ended and the reasons why negotiations broke down.

Step 3: 30 MINUTES

The instructor will ask for and record the results of the negotiations from each group of students. In addition, the instructor will ask for comments about the process of negotiation and the strategy and tactics used by various negotiators. Comparisons will be made, and the instructor will use these data to highlight the dynamics of the negotiation process.

Discussion Questions

1. What was the outcome that you negotiated in this situation? How did you feel about this as you were agreeing to it?
2. How does your settlement compare to the others' in the room? How do you feel about this settlement now that you have had a chance to compare it to what others did?
3. How does your outcome compare to the goal you set before negotiations began? Did you achieve your goal? Why or why not?
4. What strategy or tactics did you attempt to use to achieve your outcome? Did they work?
5. What strategy or tactics did your opponent(s) try? Did they work?

Source: Based on "Negotiation and Conflict," In Roy J. Lewicki, Donald D. Bowen, Douglas T. Hall, and Francine S. Hall, *Experiences in Management and Organizational Behavior* (New York: John Wiley, 1988), pp. 100-2. Used with permission.

CASE APPLICATION:

Organizing the Service Sector: The Starbuck's Organizing Drive

As traditional union strongholds, the resource and manufacturing industries continue to shed their unionized workers due to restructuring and productivity gains earned through mechanization, unions have turned to nontraditional markets in their drive for new members. Perhaps the largest untapped "market" is the lower-wage service sector—the sector characterized by what has been called "McJobs" (entry-level jobs characterized by relatively low wages and benefits).

In 1996, the Canadian Auto Workers successfully organized eight Vancouver area Starbuck's coffee houses and the Vancouver distribution centre—Starbuck's at that time had 970 North American outlets (91 in BC), none of which was unionized. A key issue was wages (employees started at the statutory minimum $7 per hour; the average hourly wage was $8.40). Although Starbuck's earned a 1996 profit of $US 42 million on sales of $US 696 million, the company expressed concern about its ability to absorb increased labour costs.

After certification, the business of collective bargaining began and dragged on through the fall of 1996 and into the winter of 1997 without an agreement being reached. By spring, the CAW had a 92 per cent strike mandate and even with the assistance of a mediator, the parties were still unable to reach an agreement—a May 15th strike deadline loomed. The sticking point in the negotiations concerned starting wages—the CAW seeking to increase the starting wage from $7 per hour to $10 and $12.50 per hour over two years. On May 16th, the employees reported for work but refused to wear their normal uniform as a form of "job action"; the employees also passed out leaflets to customers explaining their position. In mid-July the employees voted, by a margin of 95 per cent, to accept Starbuck's offer to raise starting wages by 75 cents per hour. Immediately, Starbuck's announced that it would be giving all of its workers the same deal that the unionized employees negotiated: according to a company spokesperson, "We have always had a philosophy of treating all our employees equally".

Questions

1. Why are the Canadian Auto Workers trying to organize coffee shop employees?

2. Who "won" this labour dispute? Explain.

3. Do you think that the CAW will be able to use this settlement as a springboard to organize the balance of Starbuck's Canadian workforce? Why or why not?

Testing Your Understanding

How well did you fulfil the learning objectives?

1. How do activities differ for human resource professionals in an organization that is unionized, and one that is not?
   a. Where a union exists, human resource professionals' responsibilities often consist mainly of following procedures and policies laid out in the labour contract. In a nonunion setting, human resource professionals are involved in a range of activities from planning through implementation of procedures and policies.
   b. In a union setting, human resource professionals spend most of their time in deciding wage rates. Where a union does not represent workers, human resource professionals are involved in a range of activities from planning through implementation of the whole array of human resource procedures and policies.

c. Where a union represents workers, human resource professionals have setting and monitoring the hours of work as their primary responsibility. Where they don't, human resource professionals are involved in a range of activities from planning through implementation of the whole array of human resource procedures and policies.

d. In a union setting, human resource professionals are responsible only for selecting and monitoring employee benefits packages, primarily health-care options. In a nonunion setting, human resource professionals are involved in a range of activities from planning through implementation of the whole array of human resource procedures and policies.

e. There is no difference between the two.

2. Canada's P.C. 1003:
   a. required employers to bargain in good faith with respect to wages and terms and conditions of employment.
   b. allowed unions to strike any time they had had a dispute with management.
   c. required employers to establish pension plans for their unionized employees.
   d. established collective bargaining rights for federal civil servants.

3. Compare national unions to the CLC.
   a. National unions are larger than the CLC.
   b. National unions are an alternative structure to the CLC.
   c. National unions are more concerned with labour matters that directly affect their industry or trade.
   d. CLC is more concerned with general worker welfare. The CLC is a national union.

4. Local union responsibilities include all of the following except
   a. collecting dues.
   b. working with local management in contract negotiations.
   c. processing any grievance that is filed.
   d. ensuring that the contract is being followed correctly.
   e. recruiting members from other local unions.

5. Legislative authority over labour relations
   a. is vested exclusively in the federal government.
   b. is vested exclusively in the provincial governments.
   c. is shared between the federal and provincial governments.
   d. is vested in local municipal governments.

6. Collective bargaining by public sector employees, including the right to strike
   a. has always been permitted under Canadian law.
   b. occurred in a piecemeal fashion starting in the late 1960s.
   c. first occurred when the Charter came into effect in 1982.
   d. remains unlawful across Canada.

7. Labour Relations Boards have the statutory authority to
   a. certify trade unions as exclusive bargaining agents.
   b. determine if the employer has committed an unfair labour practice.
   c. arbitrate all disputes arising under a collective bargaining agreement.
   d. all of the above.
   e. a and b only.

8. A union may be comprised of all but the following
   a. employees of a particular craft or occupation.
   b. managerial employees.
   c. employees made of up several job classifications.
   d. employees at more than one location of the employer.

9. The union's duty of fair representation means
   a. the union need only represent those employees who voted for the union.
   b. the union can charge union supporters lower dues than other bargaining unit employees.
   c. the union must fairly represent all bargaining unit employees.
   d. the union can only authorize a strike if 75% of its members agree.

10. A collective agreement
    a. is automatically imposed on the parties by statute as soon as the union is certified.
    b. sets out the terms and conditions of employment for all of the employer's unionized employees.
    c. can be unilaterally terminated by the union by giving reasonable notice to the employer
    d. none of the above.

11. Once a union is certified
    a. it can never be dislodged except in favour of another union.
    b. the employer can refuse to bargain with the union if it wishes.
    c. it can be decertified if a majority of the employees vote against the union.
    d. the employees are required to go on strike until an agreement is reached.

Chapter Eighteen

COLLECTIVE BARGAINING

LEARNING OBJECTIVES

AFTER READING THIS CHAPTER, YOU WILL BE ABLE TO:

1. Identify the objectives of collective bargaining.
2. Describe the components of collective bargaining.
3. Identify the steps in the collective bargaining process.
4. Describe the role of a grievance procedure in collective bargaining.
5. Explain the various types of union security arrangements.
6. Describe how power flows in organized labour.
7. Discuss what is meant by the term economic strike.
8. Identify the various impasse resolution techniques.
9. Discuss the four-quadrant diagram of labour-management relationships.

One of the fundamental issues in labour-management relationships is that both sides will come to the bargaining table and negotiate. Canadian legislation requires both union and management to negotiate in good faith. Good-faith bargaining requires both sides to willingly work towards a settlement. That is, their efforts must be viewed as having a positive influence on the process—towards the ultimate goal of reaching an agreement. But good-faith bargaining alone does not guarantee that an agreement will be reached. On the contrary, serious disagreements do arise at times, resulting in negotiations breaking off. That's all part of the process—and it's precisely what occurred between the National Hockey League Players Association and the National Hockey League in 1994.[1]

It is hard to imagine something more quintessentially Canadian than hockey. Indeed, in times when other national symbols are in disarray, many would consider hockey to be Canada's unifying force. Therefore, any interruption of hockey, particularly of an entire season, would not just disappoint a few million Canadians, but it would tamper with the social fabric of our entire country! Yet, this is exactly what did happen when the entire hockey season of 1994-95 was disrupted by the longest strike in NHL history.

Relations between the league and its players were governed by a collective agreement that expired in the autumn. NHL Vice-President Jeff Pash complained that the players had refused to meet for five months, and that contract talks were going nowhere. It seems hard to imagine that a major labour dispute could arise between such groups. Hockey, like other professional sports, does not seem to fit into the realm of traditional labour-management relations. Hockey players were very well paid and had enjoyed significant increases in salary. The problem was brought to a head by a sixteen-point roll-back

The 1994-95 NHL strike demonstrated that even wealthy players and owners can become involved in a labour dispute.

announcement by League Commissioner Gary Bettman. These were changes league management would introduce to the collective agreement unless a new pact was reached by the first of September 1994 when training camps for the new season would open.

The announcement proposed limitations to various benefits, eliminating salary arbitration and reducing the players' play-off pool to $2 million from $9 million in order to reduce team roster sizes and make two-way contracts mandatory. If the players had been indifferent to contract negotiations before, that changed overnight with the arrival of Bettman's proposals, and an immediate negative reaction was felt across the players association. When serious negotiations began, free agency and the salary cap became the major issues on the table. "It is certainly warfare," said Mike Gartner, president of the NHL Players Association. "They obviously want to fight. Why would they be doing something like this unless they were trying to provoke us?"

It took another four months, a long strike, and protracted negations before a collective agreement was reached and hockey nights in Canada resumed again. What this all revealed was that despite much talk about hockey being "part of the national fabric of Canada," as Mike Gartner put it, it was, in fact, a business like any other. The reality for the owners is wins and losses, scored in black and red ink respectively. Job security and salary dollars were the reality for the players. Ultimately, even our beloved national sport required agreement between the major parties involved. As the NHL strike showed, a breakdown in labour relations means that everyone loses—the players, the owners, and the fans.

Introduction

Tens of thousands of managers direct the activities of unionized employees who work under a collective agreement. Over four million Canadians are members of a union, and over half the entire Canadian workforce is covered by the provisions of a collective agreement.[2] Almost all employees in the public sector are covered by collective agreements, and when the thousands of smaller negotiations and non-industrial contracts are added to these figures, we can see that for a large segment of the workforce, HRM practices are determined substantially by the results of collective bargaining.

Some may view collective bargaining as a necessary evil in organizations unfortunate enough to be unionized, but it is also important to consider the positive side of collective bargaining—particularly from an HRM perspective. Collective bargaining can form part of a constructive policy of employee involvement on the part of proactive human resource managers. Employees are given the opportunity to influence their own work environment in a way that lessens the downside of such current practices as outsourcing, downsizing and offshore production. It may not be possible to avoid taking such difficult employment decisions, but it is important to ensure that they are addressed in a straightforward manner in collective bargaining.

The term collective bargaining generally refers to the negotiation, administration, and interpretation of a written agreement between two parties that covers a specific period of time. This agreement, or contract, lays out in specific terms the conditions of employment—what is expected of employees and what limits there are in management's authority. In the following discussion, we will take a somewhat larger perspective, also considering the organizing, certification, and preparation efforts that precede actual negotiation.

Collective Bargaining The employment agreement reached between the union and employer setting out the bargaining unit employees' terms and conditions of employment.

Most of us only hear or read about collective bargaining when a contract is about to expire or when negotiations break down. It took the major strike that grounded Air Canada for most of us to realize that the pilots who are responsible for our safety on every flight are themselves part of a union that does not always find it easy to reach a collective agreement with their employers. Similarly, teachers striking in Ontario, workers picketing logging operations in BC, or paralyzing General Motors in Ontario or hockey and baseball players striking remind us that organized labour deals with management collectively. The wages, hours, and working conditions of these unionized employees are negotiated for periods which are often two or three years long. Only when these contracts expire and management and the union are unable to agree on a new contract do most of us become aware of what an important part of HRM is collective bargaining.

Meet

Gordon MacDougall

Human Resource Officer,
Cape Breton Regional Municipality,
Nova Scotia

Ordinarily, once a collective agreement is established, it goes unchanged for the term of the contract, but sometimes an exceptional circumstance complicates things. One such circumstance is the amalgamation of several towns or other jurisdictions—an increasingly common phenomenon in many parts of the country. The Cape Breton Regional Municipality in Nova Scotia is a case in point.

The Nova Scotia provincial government amalgamated eight different Cape Breton Island municipalities, including Sydney, Glace Bay, and Louisbourg.

Gordon MacDougall, Human Resource Officer for the new Cape Breton Regional Municipality, explains, "There was no way we could operate without amending some of the language in the existing agreements."

Any successor employer who "inherits" several collective agreements faces difficulties administering these contracts. In the case of the Cape Breton amalgamation, major issues included assignment of employees, seniority, job postings, lay-offs, and recalls. Wage inequalities among workers doing exactly the same job were another problem. "You could have two police officers in a patrol car working side by side," says Mr MacDougall,

"one making $5,000 more than the other because he was part of a collective agreement with higher wages." Even regulations regarding working hours were different across the various agreements.

"To resolve these problems, we made an application to the Labour Relations Board of Nova Scotia to change some of the provisions of the collective agreements. This was the only way the new municipality to could become operational by the target date." Another round of negotiations ensued.

"Although the transition was not easy for either the employer or employees, positive gains have been made," Mr MacDougall points out. "Where the old municipalities had a total of twenty-four collective agreements with their workers, under the new structure the same area will have only five: firefighters, police officers, outside workers, inside workers, and crosswalk guards."

This is only a brief example of the many complexities associated with amalgamation and collective bargaining. The key to a successful collective agreement negotiation? "Always get your facts, and respect the other side's position," says Mr MacDougall.

Objective and Scope of Collective Bargaining

The objective of collective bargaining is to agree on an acceptable contract—acceptable to management, union representatives, and the union membership. What is covered in this contract? The final agreement will reflect the problems of the particular workplace and industry in which the contract is negotiated. The agreement may be very vague or highly specific. It may cover the obvious or what may appear to include ridiculous or irrelevant issues:

> Some maritime agreements specify the quality of meals and even the number of bars of soap, towels, and sheets that management must furnish the ship's crew. Such provisions are natural subjects for negotiation since they are vital to sailors at sea, but they would make no sense in a normal manufacturing agreement.... Detailed procedures respecting control over hiring are central to collective bargaining in industries with casual employment where employees shift continually from one employer to another as in construction or stevedoring. But in factory and office employment, new hiring typically is left to the discretion of management.[3]

What is important on one job may therefore have no bearing on another. This fact will definitely be reflected in the demands placed by the union on management and in the subject and terms of the agreement finally negotiated. Irrespective of the specific issues contained in various contracts, collective bargaining generally defines the work rules under which union members will work for a stipulated period of time, say two or three years. These work rules include any terms of conditions of employment including pay, work breaks, lunch periods, vacation, work assignments, and grievance procedures. We will examine these in more detail later, but first let's inspect our cast of characters.

Collective Bargaining Participants

Collective bargaining was described as an activity that takes place between two parties—in this context, management and labour. Who represents management and who represents labour? Given our previous discussion (in Chapter 17), would it be erroneous to add a third party—government?

Management's representation in collective bargaining talks depends on the size of the organization. In a small firm, for instance, bargaining is probably done by the president or owner. Since small firms frequently have no specialist who deals only with HRM issues, the president of the company often handles this. In larger organizations, there is often a sophisticated HRM department with full-time industrial relations experts. In such cases, we can expect management to be represented by the senior manager for industrial relations, corporate executives, and company lawyers, with support provided by legal and economic specialists in wage and salary administration, labour law, benefits, and so forth.

On the union side, we can expect to see a bargaining team made up of an officer of the local union, local shop stewards, and some representation from the international/national union.[4] Again, as with management, representation is modified to reflect the size of the bargaining unit. If negotiations involve a contract that will cover, say, 20,000 employees at company locations throughout Canada, the team will be dominated by international/national union officers, with a strong supporting cast of economic and legal experts employed by the union. In a small firm or for local negotiations covering special issues at the plant level for a nationwide organization, bargaining representatives for the union might be the local officers and a few specially elected committee members.

Watching over these two sides is a third party—government. In addition to providing the rules under which management and labour bargain, government provides a watchful eye on the two parties to ensure that the rules are followed. It stands ready to intervene if an agreement on acceptable terms cannot be reached or if the impasse threatens the well-being of the community, such as a national postal or rail strike or a provincial teacher's strike.

Are there any more participants? For the most part, no, with one exception—financial institutions.[5] Most people are unaware of the role of financial institutions' in collective bargaining. Although not directly involved in negotiations, these "banks" set limits on the cost of the contract. Exceeding that amount may cause the banks to call in the loans that had been made to the company. This results in placing a ceiling on what management can spend.

While there are a number of different groups involved in collective bargaining, our discussion will focus on labour and management. After all, it is the labour and management teams that buckle down and hammer out the contract.

Collective Bargaining Process

Let's now consider the actual collective bargaining process. Figure 18-1 contains a simple model of how the process might flow, including preparing to negotiate, negotiating at the bargaining table, and contract administration.

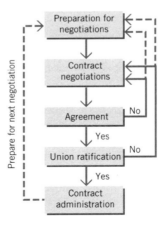

Figure 18-1
The Collective Barganining Process

Preparing to Negotiate

Once a union has been certified to represent the bargaining unit (see Chapter 17), both union and management begin the ongoing activity of preparing for negotiations. We refer to this as an ongoing activity because ideally, it should begin as soon as the union certification is achieved or a previous contract is agreed upon. Realistically, it probably begins anywhere from one to six months before the existing contract expires. We can consider the preparation for negotiation as composed of three activities: fact gathering, goal setting, and strategy development. Since we are interested in the role of collective bargaining in HRM, we will focus on the process from management's perspective.

Information is acquired from both internal and external sources. Internal data include grievance and accident records; employee performance reports; overtime figures; and reports on transfers, turnover, and absenteeism. External information should include statistics on the current economy, both at local and national levels; economic forecasts for the short and intermediate terms; copies of recently negotiated contracts by the union to determine what issues it considers important; data on the communities in which the company operates (such as cost of living); changes in cost of living, terms of recently negotiated labour contracts, and statistics on the labour market; and industry labour statistics to see what terms other organizations employing similar types of personnel are negotiating.

This information tells management where it is, what similar organizations are doing, and what it can anticipate from the economy in the near term. These data are then used to determine what management can expect to achieve in the negotiation. What can it expect the union to ask for? What is management prepared to concede?

With homework done, information in hand, and tentative goals established, management must put together the most difficult part of the bargaining preparation activities—a strategy for dealing with the union's demands (see Table 18-1). This includes assessing the union's power and specific tactics. But not all unions bargain from equal power bases. The labour market, economic conditions, rates of inflation, and recent contract settlements all affect the degree of union influence. Management's ability to tolerate a strike is also crucial. If demand for the company's product or service has been high, management may be reluctant to bear a strike, even one of short duration. On the other hand, if business has been slow, management may be considerably less willing to concede to union demands and may be prepared to endure a lengthy strike. Consequently, variations in power factors will affect the tactics used in bargaining.

TABLE 18-1 Bargaining Strategies

In most negotiations, there are two distinct strategies either the union or management can employ. These are called distributive bargaining and integrative bargaining.	
Distributive Bargaining:	A competitive, confrontational, win–lose strategy. Distributive bargaining occurs when one side wants to achieve some contract provision that the other side is opposed to. For instance, if management wants mandatory overtime, and the union does not—preferring instead to have more workers hired—negotiations will continue until one side prevails. That is, there will either be mandatory overtime (management wins) or there won't (union wins).
Integrative Bargaining:	(*sometimes also referred to as interest or mutual gains bargaining*) A cooperative strategy in which a common goal is the focus of attention. Integrative bargaining occurs when both the union and management must work together to solve a mutual problem. For instance, to remain competitive and secure jobs, both sides agree to relax some work rules and permit the automation of the production operations. Some workers will be trained on the new equipment, and those displaced by the technological improvements will be retrained to fill labour shortages elsewhere in the production process.

Distributive Bargaining

Integrative Bargaining

Negotiating at the Bargaining Table

Negotiation customarily begins with the union delivering to management a list of demands that is longer than those they really want or expect to achieve. By presenting extreme demands, the union creates significant room for haggling in later stages of the negotiation. It also disguises the union's real position, leaving management to determine which demands are adamantly sought, which are moderately sought, and which the union is prepared to quickly abandon. Examples of recent demands made by unions in negotiations include an immediate increase in the hourly wage, special adjustments for skilled workers, cost-of-living adjustments, early retirement, free dental care, free psychiatric care, improved quality of work life, increased relief time off the assembly line, more paid holidays, extended vacations, a shorter work week, and a guaranteed annual wage. In addition, demands for job security guarantees have been particularly important in times of restructuring and downsizing.

A wonderful example of an extreme demand occurred among stevedores at the time of the introduction of containerization in the early 1970s in Liverpool (UK). Unions requested a "pilfering allowance" to compensate their members for the benefits they had been able to make "on the side" through petty theft of items that were part of the open cargo arrangements prior to containerization.

A long list of demands often fulfils the internal political needs of the union. By seeming to back numerous wishes of the union's members, union administrators appear to be satisfying the needs of the many factions within the membership. In reality, however, these demands will be scaled down or abandoned if the union's negotiators believe it is expedient to do so. Not surprisingly, management's initial response is usually just as extreme. Management counters by offering little more and than the terms of the previous contract and sometimes even demands roll-backs. It is not unusual for management to begin by proposing a reduction in benefits and demanding that the union reduce or eliminate some of their work rules such as those on job transfer or outsourcing work.

These initial proposals are then considered by each party. This is a time of exploration, each party trying to clarify the other's proposals and to marshal arguments against one another. As should be expected, political activity tends to accelerate as each group plays out various roles. Management may say, "If we concede to the union's demands, we'll be bankrupt within six months." Union representatives may argue, "Company profits are at an all-time high, and our previous settlement has been eaten away by inflation. We must not only achieve a large raise to cover the next two years, but we must also be compensated for the loss in buying power during the past two years."

While both management and union representatives publicly emphasize their differences, the real negotiations go on behind closed doors. Each party tries to assess the relative priorities of the other's demands, and each begins to combine proposals into viable packages. What takes place, then, is the attempt to get management's highest offer to match the lowest demands that the union is willing to accept. Hence, negotiation is a form of compromise. When an oral agreement is achieved, it is converted into a written contract. Negotiation finally concludes with the union representatives submitting the contract for ratification or approval by its rank-and-file members.

Regardless of how negotiations proceed, there are several issues that are specific to each group. For management, we refer to these as management rights; for the union, union security arrangements.

While both union and management publicly emphasize the differences of their extreme demands, the real negotiations take place behind closed doors, out of the public eye.

Management Rights In terms of labour legislation, management and the union must negotiate over wages, hours, and terms and conditions of employment. Although this covers a wide array of topics, everything outside of these mandatory items is considered management rights.

Even though a unionized workforce may exist, management still retains its right to run the business. This means that management is generally unwilling to negotiate over items such as the products it will produce and sell, selling prices, the size of its workforce, or the location of operations. Needless to say, it is in management's best interest to have as many of the issues that affect them labelled as management rights. In this manner, they reserve the right to make unilateral decisions about those issues without having to consult or negotiate with the union. Unions, on the other hand, want to achieve a position where more and more is open to negotiations.

Just because something is a management right does not mean that it can never be part of negotiations. If it suits their purpose, management may take something that is rightfully theirs and place it into negotiations. For example, it might negotiate the location of a plant in return for wage level reductions. If and when that occurs, it is then removed from the "management right" category and will remain so until subsequent negotiations remove it from the contract. It is important to note, however, that under no circumstances is management required to discuss such issues with the union. Furthermore, management cannot be found "guilty" of negotiating in bad faith for failing to discuss management rights issues.

Union Security Arrangements The survival of a union depends on arrangements that can be reached with management to guarantee numbers of members and their financial contributions. Thus unions are very interested in achieving a union security arrangement that best suits their goals. Such arrangements range from compulsory membership in the union to giving employees the freedom to join the union or not.[6] The various types of union security arrangements—the union shop, the Rand Formula, and the open shop, as well as some special provisions under the realm of union security arrangements—are discussed below and summarized in Table 18-2.

The most powerful relationship legally available to a union is a union shop. This arrangement stipulates that employers, while free to hire whomever they choose, may retain only union members. That is, all employees hired into positions covered under the terms of a collective bargaining agreement must, after a specified probationary period of about thirty to sixty days, join the union or forfeit their jobs.

An agreement that requires non-union employees to pay the union a sum of money equal to union fees and dues ("checkoff") as a condition of continuing employment is referred to as the Rand Formula in Canada. This arrangement was designed as a compromise between the union's desire to eliminate the "free rider" (a non-union worker benefiting from union negotiations) and management's desire to make union membership voluntary. In such a case, if for whatever reason workers decide not to join the union (e.g., religious beliefs, values, etc.), they still must pay dues. Because workers will receive the benefits negotiated by the union, they must pay their fair share.

The least desirable form of union security, from a union perspective, is the open shop which is not often found in Canada. This is an arrangement in which joining a union is completely voluntary.

Management Rights Items that are not part of contract negotiations, such as how to run the company or how much to charge for products.

Union Security Arrangements Labour contract provisions designed to attract and retain dues-paying union members.

Union Shop Employers can hire non-union workers, but they must become dues-paying members within a prescribed period of time.

Rand Formula An arrangement in which all workers pay union dues.

Open Shop Employees are free to choose whether or not to join the union, and those who do not are not required to pay union dues.

TABLE 18-2 Union Security and Related Provisions

Union Shop	The strongest of the union security arrangements. Union shops make union membership compulsory. After a given period of time (generally thirty days), a new employee must join the union or be terminated. A union shop guarantees the union that dues-paying members will become part of the union.
Rand Formula	An arrangement in which all workers in a unit pay union dues. This is the second strongest union security arrangement, allowing workers the option of joining the union or not. However, because the gains that are made at negotiations will benefit those not joining the union, all workers in the unit must pay union dues.
Open Shop	The weakest form of a union security arrangement is the open shop. In an open shop, workers are free to join a union or not. If they do, they must stay in the union for the duration of the contract and pay their dues. Those who do not wish to join the union are not required to do so, and thus pay no dues. While an option in principle, the open shop is rarely offered in Canada
Dues Checkoff	Dues checkoff involves the employer deducting union dues directly from a union member's pay cheque. Under this provision, the employer collects the union dues and forwards them to the union treasurer. Generally, management does not charge an administrative fee for this service.

Dues Checkoff The employer withholds union dues from union members' pay cheques.

A provision that often exists in union security arrangements is a process called the **dues checkoff**. This is when the employer withholds union dues from the members' paycheques. Similar to other pay withholdings, the employer collects the dues and sends them to the union. There are reasons why employers provide this service and why the union would permit them to do so. Collecting dues takes time, so a dues checkoff reduces the down time by eliminating the need for the shop steward to go around to collect dues. Furthermore, recognizing that union dues are the primary source of income for the union, having knowledge of how much money there is in the union treasury can provide management with some insight as to whether or not a union is financially strong enough to endure a strike. Given these facts, why would a union agree to such a procedure? Simply, the answer is guaranteed revenues. By letting management deduct dues from a member's pay cheque, the union is assured of receiving their money. Excuses from members that they don't have the money or will pay next week are eliminated.

Contract Administration

Contract Administration Implementing, interpreting, and monitoring the negotiated agreement between labour and management.

Once a contract is agreed upon and ratified, it must be administered. There are four stages to contract administration: getting the information agreed to out to all union members and management personnel; implementing the contract; interpreting the contract and grievance resolution; and monitoring activities during the contract period.

Information Dissemination In terms of providing information to all concerned, both parties must ensure that changes in contract language are spelled out. For example, the most obvious would be hourly rate wage changes. HRM must make sure its payroll system is adjusted to the new rates as set in the contract. But it goes beyond just pay. Changes in work rules, hours, and the like must be communicated. If both sides agree to mandatory overtime, something that is new to the contract, all employees must be informed of how it will work.

Neither the union nor the company can simply hand a copy of the contract to each organization member and expect it to be understood. It will be necessary to hold meetings to explain the new terms of the agreement.

Implementing the Contract   During this stage of contract administration, the agreement both sides reached is implemented. All communicated changes now take effect, and both sides are expected to comply with the contract terms. During this phase, it is important to recognize the concept of management rights to which we referred to earlier. Normally, management is guaranteed the right to allocate organizational resources in the most efficient manner; to create reasonable rules; to hire, promote, transfer, and discharge employees; to determine work methods and assign work; to create, eliminate, and classify jobs; to lay off employees when necessary; to close or relocate facilities after an agreed-upon-notice such as sixty days; to institute technological changes; and so forth. Of course, good HRM practices suggest that whether the contract requires it or not, management would be wise to notify the union of major decisions that will influence its membership.

Grievance Procedures and Arbitration   Probably the most important element of contract administration relates to spelling out a procedure for handling contractual disputes. Almost all collective bargaining agreements contain formal procedures for resolving grievances of the interpretation and application of the contract (see "HRM Skills"). These contracts have provisions for resolving specific, formally initiated grievances by employees concerning dissatisfaction with job-related issues.[7]

Grievance procedures are typically designed to resolve complaints as quickly as possible and at the lowest level possible in the organization (see Figure 18-2). The

Grievance Procedures A complaint-resolving process contained in union contracts.

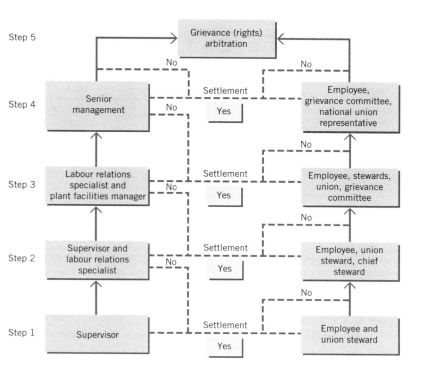

Figure 18-2
A Sample Grievance Process

HRM Skills:

Handling a Grievance

1. **Listen to the grievance being filed by an employee**. Although you may feel that the complaint has little merit or become defensive because it is something directed at you, listen attentively to what the employee says. Ask questions where necessary to ensure you fully understand what the employee is complaining about.

2. **Investigate the complaint**. Complaints may come in two forms: those that are based in fact, and those that are based in opinion and perceptions. Fully investigate the complaint. This means checking all relevant contract language concerning the issue and interviewing others who may shed light on the subject. If you are unsure about the contract language or what you uncover, seek assistance from someone in the labour relations department.

3. **Respond to the employee**. After you've fully investigated and understood the complaint, render your decision. You are either going to find the complaint valid or without merit. If it is a valid complaint, write to the employee (and the union) outlining the steps you will take to correct the situation. Remember, too, your labour contract may specify a time frame in which this decision must be given.

4. **Document all activities**. You're not dealing with something that can be taken lightly. It has a legal basis. As such, you must keep meticulous records of every activity of your investigation—from reviewing relevant contract language to interviews with key people—to show the thorough nature of what you did. If your decision is appealed to a higher level, you'll have accurate data on the steps you took.

5. **Expect the grievance to go to the next step**. The grievance process itself is designed to give the union several avenues to redress its complaint. Just because you found no merit to the complaint does not mean that the union will simply accept your decision. Instead, it is likely to appeal it to the next step in the grievance process. That's its right. Accordingly, this adds support for proper documentation of your activities.

Source: Adapted from Stephen P. Robbins, *Supervision Today* (Englewood Cliffs, N.J.: Prentice-Hall, 1995), p. 534-35.

first of five steps almost always has the employee attempt to resolve the grievance with his or her immediate supervisor.[8] If that is not successful, it is usually then discussed with the union steward and the supervisor. Failure at this stage usually brings in the individuals from the organization's industrial relations department and the chief union steward. If the grievance still cannot be resolved, the complaint passes to the facility's manager who discusses it with the union grievance committee. Unsuccessful efforts at this level give way to the organization's senior management and generally a representative from the national union. Finally, if those efforts are unsuccessful in resolving the grievance, the final step is for it to go to arbitration—called grievance (rights) arbitration.

In practice, most collective bargaining agreements provide for these five steps, culminating with the grievance (rights) arbitration as the final step to an impasse. Of course, in small organizations, these stages tend to be condensed, possibly moving from discussing the grievance with the union steward to taking the grievance directly to the organization's senior executive or owner and then, if necessary, to arbitration.

Monitoring In our discussion of the preparation for negotiations, we stated that both company and union need to gather various data. One of the most bountiful sources of information for both sides is that kept on a current contract. By monitoring activities, company and union can assess how effective the current contract was, when problem areas or conflicts arose, and what changes might need to be made in subsequent negotiations.

Grievance (Rights) Arbitration
The final step in the grievance procedure, when an external arbitrator resolves the dispute.

When Agreement Cannot Be Reached

Although the goal of contract negotiations is to achieve an agreement that is acceptable to all concerned parties, sometimes negotiations do break down, and an impasse occurs. These events can be triggered by internal issues in the union such as the desire to strike against the company or the company's desire to lock out the union knowing that striking workers can be replaced. Let's explore the following areas: where the power lies, strikes versus lockouts, and impasse resolution techniques.

Where the Power Lies

In the last chapter, we introduced you to the structure of organized labour in Canada. While that structure represents the overall framework of the union hierarchy, our discussion only briefly addressed the power the union local wields. We would like to take a closer look at union local power and show how it compares to the power of management.

The union local serves as the cornerstone of labour organizations. At the local level, decisions are made regarding which representatives are sent to the national convention, how governance will be established, and whether a contract is to be ratified. The union local holds much of the decision-making power in the union. While not always used to its fullest extent, the union local has, through the union hierarchy, a definite impact on all union activities including the Canadian Labour Congress (CLC).

Figure 18-3 is a graphic representation of the power flow in the labour hierarchy. For these labour organizations, the power flow flows from the bottom up. This means that those at the lowest level in the hierarchy—the locals—generate the power in the union and charge higher levels in the organization such as the national union and the Canadian Labour Congress to carry out their mission. In a sense, the union hierarchy is an inverted pyramid, with the bulk of power resting with the majority of the people instead of a chosen few. Accordingly, decisions made at the national level must reflect the wishes of those in charge. Failure to do so can result in turmoil or, at worst, organizational chaos.

Figure 18-3
Power Flows: Organized
Labour vs. Management

The power structure of unions is completely opposite to that of companies. Traditional organization structures of companies follow many of the classic management principles which establish clear hierarchical relationships and commensurate authority. In contrasting the labour and management structures, it is apparent that in one case, the majority is supposed to rule (union), whereas in the other, the minority (management) makes the decisions.[9] For the most part, these structures serve their respective organizations well. In unions, it is necessary for the expectations of all members to be heard, and accordingly, they must afford all members the opportunity to voice their concerns. In management, running an efficient and effective organization requires clear direction, clear lines of authority and accountability, and good communication flows.

If these particular structures appear appropriate for their respective organizations, why the need to discuss them? Because the balance of power shifts when the employees of an organization—who generally have no say in activities affecting their work lives—become unionized. These workers suddenly have greater power to deal with management over their concerns. In the majority of cases, this relationship with management does not cause a serious problem, but in those cases where one does exist, the power of the two groups often clashes, resulting in an impasse.

The critical element of differing structures and power bases can manifest itself during contract negotiations. When one looks at the composition of the negotiating teams, a fundamental question arises: if both sides are working together to reach a mutual agreement, why do some contracts fail to be ratified? The explanation may revolve around the cast of characters in these negotiations[10] and their power and authority to sign the contract. To all intents and purposes, those involved appear to be the appropriate individuals. However, one element is missing: the chief management negotiator in the private sector generally has the authority to "bind" the company to the agreements reached, but the same is not true of the union negotiator.

Throughout the negotiations, when the management's spokesperson agrees to any provision, it becomes part of the new contract. However, the union's chief representative serves the will of the members at negotiations and cannot automatically accept the contract or its provisions. A tentative contract must be submitted to the rank and file for their approval, and if ratification is achieved, the contract becomes legally binding. However, if the rank and file reject the contract or any of its terms, the chief spokesperson must return to the negotiations and try for a "better" contract.

Strikes versus Lockouts

There are only two possible preliminary results from negotiations. First, and obviously preferable, is agreement. When no viable solution can be found to the parties' differences, the other alternative is a strike or a lockout.

There are several types of strikes. The most relevant to contract negotiations is the economic strike which happens when the two parties cannot reach a satisfactory agreement before the contract expires. When that deadline passes, the union leadership can instruct its members not to work, thus leaving their jobs.[11] Although under today's legal climate, certain Canadian jurisdictions allow for the hiring of replacement workers, this is a risky strategy for employers, as employees often respond very negatively to these replacements whom they typically refer to as "scabs."

Another form of strike is the wildcat. A wildcat strike is one initiated by a group of workers but not sanctioned by union leaders; these often occur when enraged workers walk off the job over some perceived injustice or wrong. For example, if a union employee is disciplined for failure to call in sick according to provisions of the contract, fellow union members may walk off the job to demonstrate their dissatisfaction with management action. It is important to note that these strikes are illegal, because they take place while a contract is in force—an agreement that prohibits such activity. Consequently, wildcat strikers can be severely disciplined or even terminated.

The strike probably is still the union's most powerful weapon, but it is under some pressure today. Legislation is moving in the direction of limiting the right to strike; for example, Ontario's Bill 136 takes away the right to strike in a number of public sector areas.[12] Strikes are expensive for everyone, and the public support for strikes is increasingly uncertain, especially in the public sector. For example, in the era of public downsizing of the 1990s, taxpayers' sympathy was often with the government and against what were construed as "fat cat" public servants.[13] In addition, management hasn't been sitting idly by and, despite the risks, companies in the private sector have increasingly considered replacing striking workers.[14] On the other hand, continuing worker dissatisfaction over downsizing, pay cuts, restructuring, and the like, will encourage strike activity for the foreseeable future.

Just as the strike is the union's most powerful weapon, so the lockout is management's. A lockout, as the name implies, occurs when the organization denies unionized workers access to their jobs during an impasse. A lockout, in some cases, is management's predecessor to hiring replacement workers (see "Ethical Decisions in HRM"). In others, it's management's effort to protect their facilities and machinery and other employees at the worksite. There is likely to be an increase in management's use of the lockout in times when unions are under economic stress.

In either case, the strategy is the same. Both sides are attempting to apply economic pressure to their opponent in an effort to sway negotiations in their direction. When neither side will budge negotiations are said to reach an impasse. Should this occur, impasse resolution techniques are designed to help.

Economic Strike A work stoppage that results from labour and management's ability to agree on the wages, hours, terms, and conditions of a new contract.

Wildcat Strike An unauthorized and illegal strike that occurs during the terms of an existing contract.

Lockout A situation in labour-management negotiations whereby management prevents union members from returning to work.

Impasse A situation where labour and management cannot reach a satisfactory agreement.

Ethical Decisions in HRM:

The Striker Replacement Dilemma

Inherent in collective bargaining negotiations is an opportunity for either side to generate a power base that may sway negotiations in their favour. For example, when labour shortages exist or when inventories are in short supply, a strike by the union could have serious ramifications for the company. Likewise, when the situation is reversed, management has the upper hand and could easily lock out the union to achieve its negotiation goals. In fact, labour relations legislation and regulations attempt to ensure that the playing field is as fair as possible by requiring both sides to negotiate in good faith and permit impasses should they be warranted.

For decades, this scenario played itself out over and over again. Timing of a contract's expiration proved critical for both sides. For example, in the coal industry, having a contract expire just before the winter months—when coal is needed in greater supply for heating and electricity—worked to the union's advantage unless the coal companies stockpiled enough coal to carry them through a lengthy winter strike. This game, although serious to both sides, never appeared to be anything more than bargaining strategy that could show how serious both sides were. Some early labour legislation gave employers the right to hire replacement workers during a strike, but this was seldom done. In fact, often to settle a strike and for the organization to get back its skilled workforce, one stipulation in the new contract would be that all replacement workers be let go.

In the early 1980s that began to change. When US President Ronald Reagan fired striking air traffic controllers and hired replacements, businesses began to realize the weapon they had at their disposal. As part of a union-busting strategy, some organizations realized that using replacement workers could be to their advantage. The union members either came back to work on management's terms, or they simply lost their jobs. Period.

Undoubtedly, in any strike situation, management has the right to keep its doors open and keep producing what it sells. Often that may mean using supervisory personnel in place of striking workers or, in some cases, bringing in replacements. Does a law that permits replacement workers, create an unfair advantage for management in that it could play hardball just to break the union? Should a striker replacement bill (which would prevent permanent replacement workers or scabs from being hired) be passed? Should striking workers' jobs be protected while they exercise their rights under the law? What's your opinion?

Impasse Resolution Techniques

523
The Changing Labour–
Management Environment—
Are They Becoming More
Cooperative?

●

When labour and management cannot reach a satisfactory agreement themselves, they may need the assistance of an objective third party. This assistance comes in the form of conciliation and mediation, fact finding, or interest arbitration.

Conciliation and mediation are two very closely related resolution techniques. Both use a neutral third party who attempts to get labour and management to resolve their differences. Under conciliation, however, the role of the third party is to keep the negotiations going. In other words, this individual is a go-between, prodding and cajoling both sides to continue negotiating. Mediation goes one step further. The mediator attempts to define and establish the common ground that exists and make recommendations for overcoming the barriers that exist between the two sides. A mediator's suggestions, however, are only that—suggestions. They are proposals that are not binding on either party.

Fact finding involves a neutral third-party individual conducts a hearing to gather evidence from both labour and management. The fact finder then renders a decision as to how he or she views an appropriate settlement. Similar to mediation, the fact finder's recommendations are only suggestions and are not binding on either party.

The final impasse resolution technique is called interest arbitration. Under **interest arbitration**, a panel of usually three individuals—one each from the union and management and one neutral—hears testimony from both sides. After the hearing, the panel renders a decision on how to settle the current contract negotiation dispute. If all three members of the panel are unanimous in their decision, that decision may be binding on both parties. Interest arbitration is found more frequently in public sector collective bargaining, and its use in private sector labour disputes is rare.

Fact finding A process conducted by a neutral third party individual who conducts a hearing to gather evidence and testimony from the parties regarding the dif-

Interest Arbitration An impasse resolution technique used to settle contract negotiation disputes, where the arbitrator hears testimony and renders a decision.

The Changing Labour–Management Environment— Are They Becoming More Cooperative?

Several years ago, two researchers described the relationship that existed between unions and management over the decades.[15] They classified it as one that has four distinct quadrants through which the two groups pass (see Figure 18-4). Initially, the authors identified a period during which relations between labour and management were classified as the **confrontational stage**. The two groups opposed one another, and their actions were characterized as a "we–they" syndrome. Any gains "we" made must be at the expense of "them." Collective bargaining strategies for this phase, then, became a win–lose proposition (distributive bargaining) and led to such confrontational results as strikes and lockouts.

As this relationship matured, the groups moved into what was called the **cooperation stage** (integrative or "mutual gains" bargaining). While the we–they syndrome still dominated, reality set in; that is, faced with global competition, changing technology, and the like, the two groups cooperated with each other to fend off additional problems. For example, while organized labour has never been a friend to automation, unions have had to accept some of it to ensure competitiveness in the workplace. Without such cooperation, survival of the whole entreprise might have been threatened.

Confrontational Stage A labour-management relationship characterized as fighting one another until one or the other ultimately wins.

Cooperation Stage A labour-management relationship characterized as working together on a few specific issues.

●

To work together for common purpose because of legal requirements	To work together for common purpose to achieve best interests of both parties
2. Cooperation (Integrative)	**3.** Collaboration (Concession)
We–They	We–We
We–They	Us
1. Confrontational (Distributive)	**4.** Co-determination
To fight	Structured to work together for common purpose

Figure 18-4
Labour-Management
Relationships

Collaboration Stage A labour-management relationship characterized as working together for a common cause.

The third phase has been called the collaboration stage. Characterized as the "we–we" syndrome, this relationship now seeks gains for all concerned. For example, during the 1980s and early 1990s, unions made significant wage and benefit concessions in an effort to salvage floundering operations. In return for concessions, companies were to provide unions with more input in the decision-making process and other areas once reserved as management rights. Although continuing debate exists on the success of concession bargaining and resulting changes in management procedures, the fact remains that increasingly in Canadian labour practice, examples crop up in which organizational changes reflect the best interests of both management and unions. For example, Lafarge Canada Inc. introduced self-directed work teams and saved jobs at their cement plant in Brookfield, NS. The Westin Bayshore Hotel in Vancouver cross-trained employees as well as streamlined job classifications and duties so they could provide better services for guests.[16]

Co-Determination Stage A labour-management relationship characterized as separate but equal.

The final stage of labour–management relationships is called the co-determination stage. In this phase, management and unions act as one unit, exhibiting an "us" syndrome. Although prevalent in some European countries where the company is run by a board of directors comprised of union members, management personnel, and government representatives, this relationship has never materialized in North America.

The question remains, then: have industrial relations in Canada become more cooperative? There has certainly been some stormy collective bargaining in the recent past, for example, with General Motors, Air Canada, and in the continuing tough relations between the government and public service unions in such areas as education in Ontario. From an HRM perspective, however, we must recognize that a continued emphasis on a "we-they" syndrome serves little long-term purpose. There does seem to be a recognition of the reality that management and employees both have something to gain from mutual gains bargaining, particularly in times of global competition and technological change.

On this positive note, we conclude by looking at instances where cooperation has occurred and at the benefits that may be derived from it. For instance, when American Airlines bought into Canadian Airlines International, 700 management, clerical, and service agent jobs were lost. To help staff adjust to job loss, a joint management-labour committee was set up to determine what services were needed and to find suppliers to provide them. The committee, made up of representatives from management, the Canadian Auto Workers Union, and the International Association of Machinists and Aerospace Workers developed an action plan that included a transition centre for displaced employees. Employees could use company-supplied equipment and systems for skills assessment, counselling services, and advice on résumé writing. Both labour and management say the program has been a success based on the number of employees using the centre and the businesses seeking employees there.

The traditional union-management confrontational battles may never disappear completely, but the recent trend towards cooperation is demonstrated by the success at Canadian Airlines International.

Collaborative events such as those at Canadian Airlines are not isolated phenomena. This is just one of a number of examples of labour-management cooperation using a new tool kit put together by the Canadian Labour Market and Productivity Centre (CLMPC) to encourage joint approaches to workplace transition. Derwyn Sangster, the project director at CLMPC, points to a common theme to all the examples: "Both parties recognized that the best way to deal with a particular situation was a relatively collaborative approach versus an adversarial one."[17]

Study Tools and Applications

Summary

This summary relates to the Learning Objectives provided on p. 507.

After reading this chapter, you should know:
1. The objective of collective bargaining is to agree on a contract that is acceptable to management, union representatives, and the union membership.
2. Collective bargaining refers to the negotiation, administration, and interpretation of a written agreement between two parties that covers a specific period of time.
3. The collective bargaining process is comprised of the following steps: preparing to

negotiate, negotiating at the bargaining table, and contract administration.

4. The role of the grievance procedure is to provide a formal mechanism in labour contracts for resolving issues over the interpretation and application of a contract.

5. The various union security arrangements are the union shop which requires compulsory union membership; the Rand Formula which requires compulsory union dues; and the open shop which enforces workers' freedom of choice to select union membership or not.

6. In organized labour, power flows from the bottom to the top; that is, the power vested in labour organizations is at the local union level and flows upward to national or international unions and the Canadian Labour Congress.

7. An economic strike occurs when labour and management fail to reach an agreement on a new contract after the old contract expires. Although in some jurisdictions workers often can be replaced during such a strike, when these workers return to work, they cannot be disciplined for participating in strike activities.

8. The most popular impasse resolution techniques include: mediation (a neutral third party informally attempts to get the parties to reach an agreement); fact finding (a neutral third party conducts a hearing to gather evidence from both sides); and interest arbitration (a panel of individuals hears testimony from both sides and renders a decision).

9. The four-quadrant diagram depicting labour-management relationships consists of confrontation, cooperation, collaboration, and co-determination.

Key Terms

co-determination stage	grievance procedures
collaboration stage	impasse
collective bargaining	interest arbitration
confrontational stage	lockout
contract administration	management rights
cooperation stage	open shop
dues checkoff	Rand Formula
economic strike	union shop
fact finding	union security arrangements
grievance (rights) arbitration	wildcat strike

EXPERIENTIAL EXERCISE:

Third-Party Conflict Resolution

Purpose

1. To understand the criteria that third parties use when they intervene and attempt to resolve others' conflicts.
2. To practise mediation skills as a mechanism for resolving conflict between others.

Introduction

In addition to being involved in their own conflicts, managers are often called upon to intervene and to settle conflicts between other people. The two activities in this section are designed to explore how third parties may enter conflicts for the purpose of resolving them, and to practise one very effective approach to intervention. In the first activity, you will read about a manager who has a problem deciding how to intervene in a dispute.

Procedure

Step 1: Individually, read the following scenario.

THE SEATCOR MANUFACTURING COMPANY

You are senior vice-president of operations and chief operating officer of Seatcor, a major producer of office furniture. Joe Gibbons, your subordinate, is vice-president and general manager of your largest desk assembly plant. Joe has been with Seatcor for thirty-eight years and is two years away from retirement. He worked his way up through the ranks to his current position and has successfully operated his division for five years with a marginally competent staff. You are a long-standing personal friend of Joe's and respect him a great deal. However, you have always had an uneasy feeling that Joe has surrounded himself with minimally competent people by his own choice. In some ways, you think he is threatened by talented assistants.

Last week, you were having lunch with Charles Stewart, assistant vice-president and Joe's second in command. During your questioning, it became clear that he and Joe were engaged in a debilitating feud. Charles was hired last year, largely at your insistence. You had been concerned for some time about who was going to replace Joe when he retired, especially given the lack of really capable managerial talent on Joe's staff. Thus, you prodded Joe to hire your preferred candidate—Charles Stewart. Charles is relatively young, thirty-nine, extremely tenacious and bright, and a well-trained business school graduate. From all reports, he is doing a good job in his new position.

Your concern centres around a topic that arose at the end of your lunch. Charles indicated that Joe Gibbons is in the process of completing a five-year plan for his plant. This plan is to serve as the basis for several major plant reinvestment and reorganization decisions that would be proposed to senior management. According to Charles, Joe Gibbons has not included Charles in the planning process at all. You had to leave lunch quickly and were unable to get much more information from Charles. However, he did admit that he was extremely disturbed by this exclusion, and that his distress was influencing his work and probably his relationship with Joe.

You consider this a very serious problem. Charles will probably have to live with the results of any major decisions about the plant. More important, Joe's support is essential if Charles is to properly grow into his present and/or future job. Joe, on the other hand, runs a good ship, and you do not want to upset him or undermine his authority. Moreover, you know Joe has good judgement; thus, he might have a good reason for what he is doing.

Step 2

Decide for yourself how you would proceed to handle this issue. (Hint: You were the senior vice-president of operations. Exactly what would you do in this situation regarding the conflict between Joe and Charles? Also, why would you take this action (i.e., what are your primary objectives by intervening in this way)?

Step 3

In groups of three to five students, compare your individual responses to Step 2, and develop a group response to the scenario.

Step 4

Each group will present its solution to the rest of the class.

Step 5

Answer the following questions: How much agreement was there within the class about the way that the senior vice-president should approach the problem? How did this compare with your own preferred strategy?

Source: Based on "Third Party Conflict Resolution" in Roy J. Lewicki, Donald D. Bowen, Douglas T. Hall, and Francine S. Hall, *Experiences in Management and Organizational Behavior* (New York: John Wiley, 1988), pp. 107–10. Used with permission.

CASE APPLICATION:

Reorientation at Irving

One of the most difficult issues facing an organization that has gone through strike action is how to reintroduce employees who were on strike into the organization after it is over. A fine balance has to be achieved between learning from a strike by building better relations and singling out those who were on strike for anti-strike brainwashing. Rejoining employees have to be brought up to speed with their non-striking colleagues, but any hint of reprisals against strikers has to be avoided. This is not easily achieved, but it is essential if a new collective agreement is to survive.

Some of the difficulties involved in the post-strike adjustment process are illustrated in what took place at Irving Oil's Saint John refinery.[18] A bitter twenty-seven-month strike ended, and the company put the returning 106 refinery workers through a reorientation process to assist them in their return to work. According to Bob Chalmers, general manager of the refinery, the purpose of the program was to prevent any unresolved feelings over the strike affecting the significant performance improvements that the plant had achieved over the past two years.

Facilitators from the Boston Innovation Group led former strikers through a series of exercises designed to allow them to vent their feelings and clear the air as well as participate in team-building exercises designed to renew committed relationships with the company. Employees spent two weeks in a local hotel with facilitators from the consulting group. The widely divergent perspectives on the reorientation program on the part of the union and the company made reaching agreement difficult.

The union is very much against the program. "There seems to be a lot of pressure on them [participants] to agree that the union was wrong and had no credibility," says Larry Washburn, former president of the union local, who left the refinery once the collective agreement was finalized. Of particular concern is that the program is followed by a practical test at the refinery, lasting up to four weeks. Workers do not get full pay until they have gone through the whole program, and the worry is that this program may constitute illegal reprisal against participants in a strike.

Management, on the other hand, views the program as a positive attempt to reintegrate employees into teams that actually work together. This is in contrast to the continuing of what they see as the separate factions that led to the strike in the first place. Bob Chalmers comments, "I think it's very unusual for an organization like ours in the industry to invest this kind of money and this kind of effort after a strike."

Questions

1. Describe the relationship at Irving in terms of the four-quadrant diagram found in Figure 18-4. In what category would you place this relationship? Explain.
2. Is the reorientation program threatening the development of a new collective agreement or at least the inclusion of the returning employees in this agreement? Explain your position.
3. What recommendations would you make to management to achieve the integration of returning employees and the team-building objectives they have in mind for the program?

Testing Your Understanding

How well did you fulfil the learning objectives?

1. Issues that appear consistently throughout labour contracts are all of the following except
   a. wages.
   b. hours.
   c. grievance procedure.
   d. terms and conditions of employment.
   e. technology transfer.

2. Government is involved in labour negotiations in all of the following ways except
   a. to intervene if an impasse undermines the nation's well-being.
   b. to provide financial backing for the negotiators.
   c. to provide the rules under which labour and management bargain.
   d. to provide a watchful eye on the two parties to make sure the rules are followed.
   e. to intervene if an agreement on acceptable terms cannot be reached.

3. Management should gather all of the following internal information before collective bargaining negotiation except
   a. grievance and accident records.
   b. employee performance reports.
   c. cost-of-living changes.
   d. transfer, absenteeism, and turnover information.
   e. overtime figures.

4. Union contract negotiation
   a. is the attempt to get management's highest offer to match the lowest demands that the union is willing to accept.
   b. is conducted in public.
   c. begins with a written formal agreement and proceeds to verbal discussions of final details.
   d. is increasingly accompanied by union strikes.
   e. is most successful when a lockout results.

5. The concept of management rights typically includes all of the following except
   a. to create, eliminate, and classify jobs.
   b. to relocate facilities as needed with no advance warnings.
   c. to hire, promote, and transfer employees.
   d. to allocate organizational resources in the most efficient manner.
   e. to create reasonable rules.

6. Marti works for a company that has a union. She has refused, on religious grounds, to join the union. She must choose between forfeiting her job or paying a sum of money equal to union dues to the union to continue her employment. Marti works in a(n)

   a. closed shop.
   b. union shop.
   c. Rand Formula shop.
   d. open shop.
   e. dues checkoff shop.

7. A professional sports players' union has been trying to negotiate a new contract with the team owners through most of the off-season. Pre-season play is scheduled to begin next week, and the parties have agreed to have a panel of three individuals—a player, an owner, and a neutral third party—to hear testimony and render a decision about how to settle the contract dispute. If the three panel members agree, the decision will be binding on the players and the owners. What kind of impasse resolution technique is being used?
   a. Lockout.
   b. Grievance arbitration.
   c. Fact finding.
   d. Interest arbitration.
   e. Mediation.

8. Which of the following statements is true regarding the power structures in unions and traditional bureaucratic organizations?
   a. Power flows from top down in unions. Power flows from bottom up in traditional bureaucratic organizations.
   b. Power in the union rests in the Canadian Labour Congress governing body. Power in traditional bureaucratic organizations rests in the employees.
   c. With majority rule in the unions, all workers are given the opportunity to express their opinions. With minority rule in traditional bureaucratic organizations, effective and efficient performance requires clear direction and clear hierarchical lines of accountability and authority.
   d. Classic management principles consistently explain the power structures in both unions and traditional bureaucratic organizations.
   e. Classic management principles are not applicable to the power structures of either unions or traditional bureaucratic organizations.

9. Why are union contracts not ratified by union members after they have been negotiated?
   a. The negotiation process is considered binding on union members.
   b. The union representative doesn't carry the authority of all the union members to the bargaining table.
   c. Management participation is not considered binding during the negotiation process.
   d. Usually, arbitrators have to become involved in the negotiation process.

e. Usually, grievances have to be handled during the negotiation process.

10. Collective bargaining for Besborough Local 432 traditionally proceeds from the premise that the union and management are necessary partners in the success of the business. For example, two union members sit on the board of directors and strategic planning includes union members. The union does not strike. In fact, the union helps the company support lobbying efforts on behalf of the industry. What kind of relationship is evident in this union?
a. Confrontational.
b. Cooperation.
c. Collaboration.
d. Co-determination.
e. Co-dependency.

11. Collective bargaining for Biddicombe Local 131 traditionally proceeds from the premise that although the union and management generally have opposing interests, the union must make some concessions to management in the name of progress to survive. For example, last year, they agreed to change from calculations to spreadsheets because the work rate was so low that the firm was no longer competitive. What kind of relationship is evident in this union?
a. Confrontational.
b. Cooperation.
c. Collaboration.
d. Co-determination.
e. Co-dependency.

12. A union security arrangement is
a. a means to ensure some consistency in income.
b. a way to keep the press out of union negotiation meetings.
c. designed to prevent access of organized crime to union files.
d. a cooperative venture between workers and managers.
e. part of the health and safety provisions in most new union contracts.

13. John was hired last week as a chip frier at a fast food restaurant. After he successfully completes his thirty-day probationary period, he must either join the union or forfeit his job. John is working in a(n)
a. closed shop.
b. union shop.
c. Rand Formula shop.
d. open shop.
e. Dues checkoff shop.

14. Collective bargaining for Brampton Local 7 traditionally proceeds from the premise that the union and management have to work on the same side. For example, when the company had to cut its operating costs by

40 per cent a few years ago, the union took a hefty pay cut and gave up substantial benefits for a period of time to help with the cost containment measures. What kind of relationship is evident in this union?
a. Confrontational.
b. Cooperation.
c. Collaboration.
d. Co-determination.
e. Co-dependency.

15. Mike works in a florist shop that has a union, but he has chosen not to join it. His job is not contingent on union membership. Mike works in a(n)
a. closed shop.
b. union shop.
c. Rand Formula shop.
d. open shop.
e. dues checkoff shop.

16. Workers in an automotive plant are threatening to burn down the plant. Their union contract calls for 5 per cent pay raises each year for the three years of the contract. However, for the past two years, management has given them only 2 per cent a year increases, citing disastrous sales and earnings figures and potential bankruptcy as the reason. Last week, one of the union members read an article in a business weekly that announced the quarterly earnings for the firm: "Tenth Straight Record-Setting Quarter" read the headline. The article went on to announce a doubling of executive salaries for the third time in two years. The union steward has suggested that before burning the buildings, they let a third party try to resolve the wage dispute under terms of the existing contract. The issue completed its way through the grievance process of the company this morning. What kind of impasse resolution technique is being used?
a. Lockout.
b. Grievance arbitration.
c. Fact finding.
d. Interest arbitration.
e. Mediation.

17. A secretaries' union has been trying to negotiate a new contract with management for ninety days. The old contract expires in two weeks. To resolve the contract negotiation disputes, a third party has been hired to gather evidence from both the secretaries and the managers and present the findings to both parties. The recommendation will not be binding on either party. What kind of impasse resolution technique is being used?
a. Lockout.
b. Grievance arbitration.
c. Fact finding.
d. Interest arbitration.
e. Mediation.

Conclusion

THE FUTURE OF HUMAN RESOURCES MANAGEMENT IN A GLOBAL WORLD

As you come to the end of the text, it makes sense to take stock of what you have learned. By now you should have a good idea of the field of HRM and how it relates to the job of the manager—whether through the use of HR professionals in larger organizations or through the activities of senior line management in smaller organizations. While you may know what human resources professionals actually do in Canada today, this knowledge is incomplete. Without considering the future of Canadian HRM, you only have a partial understanding of what it means to manage people in an increasingly global world. In this conclusion, we show that the future for the field of HRM is likely to be quite different from the past, and that it is actually quite a challenge to define what constitutes HRM effectiveness.

The matter of HRM effectiveness is of interest to all who work in any type of organization because, after all, these institutions are composed of people who determine whether the individual organization will be successful or not. All members of the organization, then, have an interest in ensuring that HRM activities actually contribute to organizational effectiveness. Many of these HRM activities are carried out by managers and supervisors who are not HR specialists. For example, think of such issues as appraising employee performance, hiring new employees, and motivating workers. Even where HR specialists are used (such as conducting a salary survey or advising on the design of a pension plan), it is important that managers across the company understand the HRM discipline so that they can assess the value of the recommendations they receive. It is with this in mind that we now turn to an assessment of where the HRM field may go in the next few years.

Our intention is not to muddy the waters of what you have already covered in this book, but to alert you to the fact that in the future, HRM is likely to be quite a bit less predictable than our earlier material may have suggested. For example, think back to the discussion in Chapter 10 on the changing nature of careers and the shift from a position-based HRM to a contract or portfolio-based HRM.[1] If it does turn out in the future that more and more employees are employed in shifting contractual work and fewer and fewer hired for ongoing positions, the entire HR system will have to change to reflect the reality of this new contingent workforce.

Dimensions of Change

The old adage "change and decay in all around I see" seems particularly pertinent to the Canada of today. Megamergers are creating huge new financial institutions that, with the growth of electronic banking, no longer even require a physical presence in the landscape. Global partnerships in the auto industry are not only eliminating the differences between nationalities and cultures, but are also making it quite difficult to distinguish between foreign and domestic manufacturers. Downloading of government services, restructuring, and changing political alliances have even blurred the lines between the public and private sectors in Canada. At the risk of oversimplification, we suggest three primary dimensions of change that affect the future of Canadian HRM: new technology, quality and service, and globalization.

New Technology

The exponential growth in new technology, particularly information technology, is resulting in a profound change in the nature of work and HRM. Entire careers—such as the bank teller, telephone operator, or typesetter—are disappearing and being replaced by automated systems operated by a few high-skilled employees. Computer networking and reporting systems allow for transnational team projects structured without traditional supervisory channels and evaluation programs. HRM is shifting towards teleworking and self-managed review programs that make much more use of external specialists and consultants.

Quality and Service

Restructuring and changing demographics in Canada have produced organizational stakeholders with an increasing expectation of quality and service.[2] Customers are just as willing to buy the products of a quality supplier in Tijuana as from Toronto, and Tijuana may even be contacted first if their Web listing is more accessible to search engines. Customers calling for service from their local Sears in Vancouver may quite likely be making arrangements with an operator in New Brunswick. In this environment, HR functions that are not seen to add value to the organization and that do not offer exemplary service will simply not survive.[3] HR professionals will have little choice but to carry out regular assessments of effectiveness, both of the overall HR function and of the way people are managed throughout the organization.

Globalization

As we mentioned above, transnational mergers and alliances are making it increasingly difficult to determine where Canadian HR practices end and international HR practices begin. In the future, the distinction may become quite a moot point. For instance, top management in the new DaimlerChrysler organization now have to come up with an integrated HR system with congruent effectiveness criteria across the world. The good news is that Canadian HR professionals who have learned how to make the most of cultural diversity within Canada will have a genuine competitive advantage in the global arena.

Implications of Change for HRM

In a major study, forty-eight leading HR academics, consultants, and practitioners were asked to illustrate their view of "tomorrow's HR management."[4] All agreed that dramatic change from the status quo was the only possible course. A remarkable consensus emerged regarding the implications of this change for HRM, summarized in the following four points by David Ulrich:[5]

- HRM is under scrutiny, and this scrutiny is a good thing.
- HRM, as we have known it, needs to change.
- Changing HRM will represent important challenges and will require new competencies.
- If HRM does not meet the challenge of change, it is at risk of being disbanded.

Ulrich goes on to point out that while the importance of people in organizational effectiveness is widely accepted, the role of HR in achieving this effectiveness is much less clear. It is essential for HR professionals to find ways of demonstrating their contribution by "inserting" HR into the effectiveness equation. Even in the title of his book, *Tomorrow's HR Management*, HR appears to be inserted between tomorrow and management. Thus, while HR issues are gaining prominence, the actual role of the HR function is under change as never before.

Scott Adams, the author of the popular comic strip *Dilbert*, presents management in general, and HRM in particular, in a very negative light. Since he claims to base his strip on real incidents submitted by his readers, this is cause for concern. Unless the HR department is a serious, effective participant in the organization, it will be laughed away as irrelevant or even negative, as the reader of the comic strip does in seeing the antics of Catbert, the evil HR director. In his latest book, *The Joy of Work*, Adams presents an approach to work that is the exact opposite of what enlightened, effective HRM would promote.[6]

Evaluating HRM Effectiveness

In a world of change, there is an underlying requirement for the constant evaluation of HR effectiveness. The added value of HRM can only be demonstrated through *systematic* assessment against some kind of standard or benchmark. Such standards need to be broad in focus and dynamic rather than static since what we consider to be an effective organization depends on one's viewpoint. For example, organizations may be rational goal-seeking bodies, but they can also be viewed as political battle grounds of competing interest groups. In the first instance, effectiveness is judged in terms of rational objectives achieved; in the second, effectiveness may well be the achievement of one group's political objectives at the expense of another's.

In our own extensive research into HRM effectiveness,[7] we find that there is no one best way of managing human resources, but that a matching or "fit" perspective makes the most sense. In other words, effective HRM depends on the nature of the organization, its goals, and the strategies of its managers. Even when there is a congruent match between the organization and its HRM, it is not always easy to establish a causal link between HRM and effectiveness. Only a few studies[8] have demonstrated a link between HR management activities, employee attitudes, and organization performance. However, even then, it was not possible to establish that HRM alone made a significant impact. In general, successful organizations have both excellent overall management and HRM practices. A useful way to evaluate HRM effectiveness is through HR audits.

The Human Resources Audit

Just as organizations carry out an audit of their financial practices, it also makes sense to undertake periodic HRM audits. An HRM audit is the systematic evaluation of the total HRM program in the light of the organization's objectives. An audit needs to take place at three different levels of analysis: policy—overall blueprint or guidelines for HRM; procedures—action taken by HRM in the light of policy; and results—actual results achieved by HRM procedures. At each level of analysis, an HRM audit needs to cover a number of areas if the total HRM program is to be evaluated. This includes assessing the compatibility between HRM and organization goals, compliance with Canadian regulatory requirements, and evaluating the individual HR functions such as recruitment, training, and compensation.[9]

Given the complexity of human behaviour, it is not that easy to develop the measurement systems for an HRM audit. In our own work, we have made use of both quantitative questionnaires and indices as well as qualitative interviews and observation. The quantitative instruments give objectivity and standardization, but much of the in-depth explanation and understanding comes from the insights and detail that come out of the qualitative approaches.

It is crucial to recognize that the HR audit is not a single exercise so much as an ongoing process relying on continuous evaluation and research. There are a number of different points of comparison against which to judge findings. These include other firms' HR practices, what outside authorities recommend, legal regulations to be followed, HR statistical data already in place, and what objectives were set in a management by objectives (MBO) exercise.[10] There is still relatively little empirical HRM research in Canada, so organizations often have to build up their own data upon which to base their HR audit. We have found that this involves at least three steps:

1. Setting up a procedure for assessing the effectiveness of HRM activities by monitoring perceptions of key constituents such as managers, employees, and unions.

2. Setting up the means for making objective judgements of HRM effectiveness. This involves collecting hard data that can be used to develop future standards. The HR information system is key.

3. Periodically reassessing the measures of HR effectiveness as well as the congruence between HR and the organization as a whole and the alignment between objectives and organization context.[11]

Research in HRM

Among practising managers, the term "research" frequently carries the connotation of academic mumbo-jumbo or irrelevant findings that have little generalizability to practice. While this may sometimes be true, it need not be so. The research process and the findings it generates can provide valuable information to a manager. When we use the term *research*, we mean a systematic, goal-oriented investigation of facts that seeks to establish a relationship between two or more phenomena. Most of the conclusions presented throughout this book are based on systematic, goal-oriented research. For instance, in our discussion on selection, we presented the assessment centre as an effective procedure for identifying high performers. This assertion is not based on casual observation or intuition but rather on a number of research studies, the results of which led us to our conclusion.

Research, however, is not the sole province of scientists and academics. Keeping up to date in one's field is now, more than ever, a necessity. To that end, every effective manager should consider research—particularly human resources research—a mandatory and ongoing part of the job.

The Importance of Research in HRM

Research can lead to an increased understanding of, and improvement in, HRM practices. The following is a small sample of topics that can be better understood through HRM research.

- Workforce diversity
- Contingent workforce
- Wage surveys
- Effectiveness of various recruitment sources
- International HRM
- Test validation
- Health and wellness programs
- Effectiveness of training efforts
- Supervisors' effectiveness
- Development of weighted application blanks
- Recent community labour settlements
- Recent industry labour settlements
- Recent labour settlements negotiated by our union
- Workplace violence

This list suggests that HRM research can provide insights for managers as they attempt to increase employee productivity and satisfaction while reducing absenteeism and turnover. For instance, research findings make managers aware of changes. The department manager who annually surveys her employees' attitudes about their work, her supervisory practices, and the organization in general will develop long-term data allowing her to assess changes in her employees' perception of the organization's climate. Research can also identify potential problem areas. If our department manager notes an unexpected drop in her employees' satisfaction with a certain element of their work, she can take rapid action to correct it, preferably before it leads to resignations, increased absenteeism, shoddy workmanship, or other undesirable outcomes.

Managers derive other positive benefits from engaging in research. Managers who keep current with what colleagues are doing and with the latest HRM concepts and practices increase the probability that they will be more effective. In fact, engaging in some type of research into what is happening in the HRM discipline can be viewed as essential to one's survival as a manager over the long term. Research can also help managers determine the success of programs—such as training and development programs—for which they bear responsibility. For example, research can help determine whether a program's benefits justify its costs.

We should also remember that some of the research findings presented in a book such as this are not applicable to all situations. Research studies on the motivation needs of unionized stevedores in Halifax, for example, may have little practical application to someone managing a group of non-unionized social workers at Children's Aid in Brandon, Manitoba. Therefore, a manager should understand the appropriate methodology or approach for engaging in primary research. Such research can provide answers to the unique issues and problems that managers face in their specific environment.

Secondary Sources: Where to Look It Up

As we have noted, a manager's long-term survival may depend on staying current. We propose, therefore, that every manager should aim, at a minimum, to keep abreast of the field. What sources should a manager look to in order to keep up with the latest findings in HRM? The answer to that question depends on the level of sophistication desired. Research journals are directed to different audiences. Some journals assume the reader has a solid background in statistics and research methodology; their articles contain more details but are more difficult to read. Other journals are meant to be read quickly; their articles are condensed and simplified. In addition, excellent overviews of current research are now available in the Web pages of the major HR professional associations around the world.

The table below sets out some of the major research sources in HRM, separated into the more technical (for the specialist reader), and the non-technical (those focusing on translating the academic research into practical application). Note that we have placed the wide range of MCB University Press journals, based in the UK, in the technical grouping. They could also be in the non-technical group since they are practitioner-oriented. The table also includes some specifically Canadian sources and the Web sites of some of the major HR professional associations. In addition to the sources we have listed, other secondary sources include books and research reports from such institutions as the Conference Board of Canada, government publications from provincial HRM and labour departments, as well as the federal government's Human Resources Development Canada.

SOME MAJOR RESEARCH SOURCES FOR HRM

Technical Journals

Academy of Management Journal

Academy of Management Review

Administrative Sciences Quarterly

Behavioral Science

*Canadian Journal of Administrative Studies**

Education + Training

Electronic Resources review (Anbar)

Employee Relations

Employee Relations Select

Human Organization

Human Relations

Human Resource Management International Digest

Industrial Relations

*Industrial Relations/Relations Industrielles**

Industrial and Labor Relations Review

Journal of Applied Behavioral Science

Journal of Applied Psychology

Journal of Business Research

Journal of Human Resources

Journal of Management Development

Journal of Managerial Psychology

Journal of Industrial Relations

Journal of Social Psychology

Journal of Organizational Psychology

Journal of Vocational Behavior

Journal of Workplace Learning: Employee Counselling Today

Organizational Behavior and Human Decision Processes

Personal Psychology

Personnel Review

Psychological Bulletin

Training and Management Development Methods

Women in Management Review

Non-Technical Journals

Academy of Management Executive

Across the Board

*Benefits Canada**

Business Horizons

*Canadian Business**

*Canadian Business Review**

*Canadian HR Reporter**

*Canadian Occupational Safety**

Entrepreneur

*The Globe and Mail Report on Business Magazine**

HRMagazine

*HR Professional**

Human Resources Management in Canada

*Inc.**

Industry Week

*Occupational Health and Safety Canada**

Training

Training and Development Journal

Working Woman

A Few Useful Web Sites

Canadian Council of Human Resources Associations: http://www.chrpcanada.com/

Institute of Personnel Development: http://www.ipd.co.uk/homepage.html

Society of Human Resources (US): http://www.shrm.org

Anbar Management Resources: http://www.anbar.co.uk/management/home.htm

Since the World Wide Web is evolving with great speed, we have provided only these few sites—which may have changed by the time you read this!

*denotes a Canadian publication

HRM Tomorrow: What Will It Look Like?

HRM is under pressure to change, and there is a much closer examination of what HR effectiveness is all about. Despite the recognition that people are probably more important than ever as a source of competitive advantage, the way we managed human resources yesterday will not work in the new millennium. New global realities demand new structures and processes, and the question arises: What will HRM look like tomorrow? Of course, we don't know for sure, but one of the most useful pictures is provided in the wide-ranging analysis of Ulrich, to which we have already referred.[12] Although he has the larger organization in mind, what Ulrich says applies equally to smaller companies in which HRM is carried out by non-specialists. Ulrich draws all his material together around six prescriptive themes that suggest what the HRM professional of the future will need to achieve.

1. *Manage HRM like a business.* HRM departments need to become more business-focused, with clear objectives and outcomes against which their contribution is assessed. Note that this focus applies just as much to the public and non-profit sectors as it does to the private and profit-generating sectors.

2. *Play new roles.* HRM professionals will have to play many new roles organized around new "deliverables" (i.e., operationalized value-added contributions). HRM professionals will increasingly operate as change agents and business partners in the organization.

3. *Respect history while creating a future.* Excellence in HRM will entail building upon the best of HRM's past but not becoming hidebound in a traditionalism that prevents moving forward. Particularly important will be the ability to see the links between current strengths and future needs.

4. *Build an HRM infrastructure.* HRM professionals can only move forward from an effective base within the HRM function itself. Success in contributing to the organization can only come from an HRM function that has identified relevant and measurable competencies that demonstrably provide the basis for organization leadership.

5. *Remember the "human" in human resources.* Whatever else it does, the HRM function must never lose its people focus. Becoming a business partner without this people focus adds little to the people management of organizations.

6. *Go global.* The HRM world of tomorrow will be a global one in which practices in one culture or country will be directly affected by practices in others. This will entail a new world perspective of HRM professionals that has not been reflected in their performance up to now.

Ulrich shows what human resources professionals in the future will have to achieve, but what will the HRM function look like? James Peters suggests that HRM will have an entirely new vision, what he terms the "*new HR franchise.*"[13] This is depicted in Figure 1. Corporate HRM is headed by a person with a role similar to the practice director typically found in large consulting firms and responsible for coaching, peer reviewing, and facilitating the professionals in the HRM franchise. The *organization capability consultants*, comprised of experts in specific subjects, exist to assist particular operating units to improve overall organization effectiveness. Where particular help is needed, line managers can contract with *Solutions, Inc.* or seek a competitive bid from another consultancy external to this

Figure 1
The New HR Franchise

Source: James Peters, "A Future Vision of Human Resources," in David Ulrich, Michael Losey, and Gerry Lake (eds.), *Tomorrow's HR Management* (New York: John Wiley & Sons, 1997), p. 253. Used with permission.

organization. The third element of the HRM franchise, *Services, Inc.* is a compendium of outsourcing and in-sourcing solutions to the administrative needs of the enterprise. As before, if managers find a lower cost or higher service delivery elsewhere, they are encouraged to do so.

The figure above presents a larger organization with a corporate HRM function, but it also applies to a smaller organization with just one or two HRM professionals (or even no HRM professionals) in full-time employment. HRM activities will still break down into capability, service, and solutions areas, but they are likely to be implemented by contract-based specialists hired from outside.

How do we sum up where human resources is going? We can think of no better way to conclude than to leave you with a quote that seems to epitomize the change facing the field:

> The focus must shift from helping those who are drowning
> to moving upstream and finding out who is throwing them
> off the bridge and why.[14]

Appendix A

MAKING A GOOD FIRST IMPRESSION— WRITING YOUR RÉSUMÉ

One of the most trying and stressful situations that individuals face occurs when they begin the process of applying for a job. This is in part because there are no specific guidelines to follow to ensure success. However, we can offer some tips that could increase your chances of finding employment. Even though getting to the interview stage is a goal we all desire when we seek employment, obtaining that opportunity is not easy. As a rough guideline, expect the following:

100 targeted résumés, lead to
10 job interviews, which lead to
1 job offer.

Now, don't hold us to these numbers; they are merely a rule of thumb. The point, though, is that competition for jobs is fierce. Even so, there are things you can do to help increase your odds. After you have given some thought to your employment goals (e.g., what type of work you want to do—sales, HRM, accounting), start your job hunt early. Give yourself at least seven to nine months' lead time; that is, if you are looking for a job after graduation (May), you should begin your job search sometime around September of your senior year. You may not need the entire time, but you don't want to wait until March to begin, either.

How is starting early helpful? In two ways: First, it shows that you are taking an interest and that you are planning. You are not waiting until the last minute to begin, and this reflects favourably on a candidate. Second, this period coincides with companies' recruiting cycles. If you wait until March to start, some job openings may have already been filled. For specific information regarding the company recruiting cycles in your area, visit your career development centre, which should be able to give you helpful information.

Our discussion so far has centred on getting to the interview. But let's digress for a moment. Before you go to an interview, you should have some information that reflects positively on your strengths. This information is circulated in a résumé.

No matter who you are or where you are in your career, you will need a current résumé. Your résumé is typically the only information source that a recruiter will use in determining whether to grant you an interview. Therefore, it must be a sales tool; it must give accurate information that supports your candidacy, highlights your strengths, and differentiates you from others. Identifying these strengths can take a long time, but you must give them much thought and express them in ways that speak well of you. The information in the résumé must also be listed in a way that is easy to read. An example of the type of information that should be included is shown in Figure A-1. It is important to pinpoint a few key themes regarding résumés that may seem like common sense. First of all, your résumé must be printed on a quality printer. The style of font should be easy to read (e.g., `Courier` type font). Avoid any style that may be hard on the eyes, such as a script or italics font. Look at the résumé in Figure A-2. It contains exactly the same information as Figure A-1, but what a difference! A recruiter who must review two hundred résumés a day is not going to strain to read the script type; valuable information may not come across. So, use an easy-to-read font and make the recruiter's job easier.

FIGURE A-1 Sample Résumé

CONFIDENTIAL RÉSUMÉ OF:	CHRIS CONNOLLY 21 Main Street Vancouver, BC V6T 1A1 604-555-0028 (residence) 604-555-8000 (work)
CAREER OBJECTIVE:	Challenging opportunity to combine multidisciplinary skills of finance and management in a dynamic international environment.
EDUCATION:	University of British Columbia B.S., Business Administration, May 1996.
EXPERIENCE: 5/94 to present	Westinghouse Electronics Financial Analyst Assistant <u>Primary Functions</u> Responsible for developing monthly financial statements, analysing payroll data, and reconciling corporate bank statements. Serving as finance department liaison to the HRM Compensation Committee.
8/92 to 5/94	Anywhere Recreation Council Program Leader <u>Primary Functions:</u> Responsible for designing, planning, implementing, and evaluating recreational programs for teens aged 12-14. Responsible for a budget of $4,000. Three assistant staff members supervised.
SPECIAL SKILLS:	Fluent in Spanish and Japanese; computer-literate in word processing, database management, and spreadsheet applications.
SERVICE ACTIVITIES:	President, Student Government Association; Student Representative, Faculty Senate; Hugger, Special Olympics.
REFERENCES:	Furnished on request.

FIGURE A-2 Sample Résumé with a Font Change

Confidential *Résumé of:*	*Chris Connolly* *21 Main Street* *Vancouver, BC V6T 1A1* *604-555-0028 (residence)* *604-555-8000 (work)*
Career Objective:	*Challenging opportunity to combine multidisciplinary skills of finance and management in a dynamic international environment.*
Education:	*University of British Columbia* *B.S., Business Administration, May 1996.*
Expreience: *5/94 to present*	*Westinghouse Electronics* *Financial Analyst Assistant* *Primary Functions* *Responsible for developing monthly financial statements, analysing payroll data, and reconciling corporate bank statements. Serving as finance department liaison to the HRM Compensation Committee.*
8/92 to 5/94	*Anywhere Recreation Council* *Program Leader* *Primary Functions:* *Responsible for designing, planning, implementing, and evaluating recreational programs for teens aged 12-14. Responsible for a budget of $4,000. Three assistant staff members supervised.*
Special Skills:	*Fluent in Spanish and Japanese; computer-literate in word processing, database management, and spreadsheet applications.*
Service Activities:	*President, Student Government Association; Student Representative, Faculty Senate; Hugger, Special Olympics.*
References:	*Furnished on request.*

It is also important to note that some companies today are using computer scanners to make the first pass through résumés. In a matter of moments, computers can be programmed to scan each résumé for specific information like key job elements, experience, work history, education, or technical expertise.[1] The use of scanners, then, has created two important aspects for résumé writing.[2] The computer matches key words in a job description. Thus, in creating a résumé, typical job description phraseology should be used. Additionally (and this goes back to the issue of font type), the font used should be easily read by the scanner. If it can't, your résumé may be put in the rejection file.

Your résumé should be copied on good-quality paper (no off-the-wall colours—use standard white or cream). There are many definitions of good-quality paper, but you can't go wrong with a 20-bond-weight paper that has some cotton content (about 20 percent). Don't send standard duplicating paper—it looks as if you are mass mailing résumés. (You probably are mass mailing résumés—especially if you follow the "100 résumés" rule of thumb—but don't make it obvious.) To get your résumé in order, typed, and copied on good-quality paper, you should expect to spend about $40 (excluding envelope and postage costs). Typing costs about $10 per page, and the paper (including copying) will cost about $20. The cost might seem an expense you would rather not incur, but remember that your competition is probably doing it—if you have to spend a few dollars to make a few copies, consider it a wise investment.

The last point on résumés, one that shouldn't have to be mentioned, relates to proofreading. Because the résumé is the only representation of you the recruiter has, a sloppy résumé can be deadly. If it contains misspelled words or is grammatically incorrect, your chances for an interview will be significantly reduced. Proofread your résumé, and if possible, let others proofread it, too.

In addition to your résumé, you need a cover letter. Your cover letter should contain information that tells the recruiter why you should be considered for the job. The cover letter should not be an "oversell" letter, but one that highlights your greatest strengths and indicates how these strengths can be useful to the company. Your cover letter should also contain some information citing why the organization getting your résumé is of interest to you. Cover letters must be tailored to the organization; letters should be originals, not copies of a "To Whom It May Concern." One of the biggest turnoffs a recruiter may experience in reviewing résumés is the "To Whom It May Concern" letter. This tells the recruiter that you are on a fishing expedition and are sending out hundreds of résumés. This situation does not help your job hunting. A much greater impact is made when you write to a specific person. You might not have the recruiter's name and title, but with some work you can get it. Use whatever resources you can. Telephone the company in question and ask for it; most receptionists in human resources will give out the recruiter's name and title. If you just can't get a name, go to the library and locate a copy of the *Dun & Bradstreet "Blue Book,"* which lists the names and titles of companies' officers. A more current alternative is to search the company's Web site. If everything else fails, send your résumé to one of the officers, preferably the officer in charge of HRM or administration, or to the president. This is much better than "To Whom It May Concern."

We won't belabour the point about typing and proofreading the cover letter except to say that it also must be impeccable. Finally, sign each letter individually. A real signature has a better effect than a duplicated one.

Appendix B

THE CRITICAL MEETING— IMPROVING INTERVIEW SKILLS

If you are fortunate to have made it through the initial screening process, chances are good that you may be called in for an interview. Although you may be excited, some caution is in order. Remember that interviews play a critical role in determining whether you will get the job. Up to now, all the recruiter has seen is your well-polished résumé. In the following paragraphs, we'd like to offer some suggestions on how to increase your chances of making it through the interview. Although we'll address the initial interview with the recruiter, realize that multiple interviews are the norm rather than the exception; that is, getting through the recruiter is only stage one of an interview. Should you meet the recruiter's expectations, you can expect to be interviewed by at least two other people. These individuals are the manager of the area in which you will work and typically the senior management official in the division. Although this final interview is mostly protocol, keep in mind that no final decision will be made unless you get passing grades from all who interview you. Let's look at some ways of achieving that goal.

First of all, do some homework. If you haven't already done so in your search of whom to send résumés, go to your library and get as much information as possible on the organization. Don't fall into the trap one applicant did when he didn't even know what IBM stood for. Gather as much data as possible, so you sound like you know a bit about the company. This will be time well spent, as it creates a perception of you as an individual who is taking charge. Many an interviewer may look at you favourably if you have read about a recent company venture in such publications as *The Globe and Mail Report on Business Magazine, Canadian Business* or *Fortune*. In fact, the job you may be interviewing for may be directly related to that venture. So, go to the interview prepared!

The night before the interview, get a good night's rest. Eat a good breakfast to build your energy level, as the day's events will be grueling. As you prepare for the interview, keep in mind that your appearance is going to be the first impression you make. Dress appropriately. Even though appearance is not supposed to enter into the hiring decision, it does make an impression. In fact, one study suggests that 80 percent of the interviewer's perception of you in the interview comes from his or her initial perception of you, based primarily on your appearance and body language.[1] Therefore, dress appropriately and be meticulous in your attire.

Arrive at the interview location early. We don't mean two hours early, but about thirty minutes ahead of your scheduled interview. It is better for you to wait than to have to contend with something unexpected, like a traffic jam, that could make you late. Arriving early also gives you an opportunity to survey the office environment and possibly gather some clues about the organization. For instance, if the atmosphere is friendly and cheerful, this may indicate that the organization puts considerable emphasis on employee satisfaction. Again, any hint you can pick up to increase your chances, you should use. As you meet the recruiter, give him or her a firm handshake. Make good eye contact, and maintain it throughout the interview. Remember, your body language may be giving away secrets about you that you don't want an interviewer to pick up. Sit erect and maintain good posture.

At this point, you are probably as nervous as you have ever been. While this is natural, try your best to relax. Recruiters know you'll be anxious, and a good one will try to put you at ease. Being prepared for an interview can also help build confidence and reduce the nervousness. You can start building that confidence by reviewing a set of questions most frequently asked by interviewers. You can obtain a copy of these typically through the career development office of your college or university. More important, however, since you may be asked these questions, you should begin to develop responses to them. But let's add a word of caution here. The best advice we can give is to be yourself. Don't go into an interview with a prepared text and recite it from memory; have an idea of what you would like to say, but don't rely on memorized responses. They will only frustrate you when you lose your place and may ultimately make you look foolish.

You should try to go through several "practice" interviews if possible. Universities and colleges often have career days on campus, when recruiters from companies are on-site to interview students. Take advantage of them. Even if the job does not fit what you want, the process will at least serve to help you become more skilled at dealing with interviews. You can also practice with family, friends, career counselors, student groups to which you belong, or your faculty advisor.

There's another issue that should be considered with respect to interviewing. You must be prepared to deal with the stress, or pressure interview, and interviews in which potentially discriminatory questions are asked.[2] The point of these tactics is to "see how you react when you're pressured and to test your professionalism and confidence."[3] These questions may appear rude, or even demeaning. But remember, they are designed to rattle you.[4] If you lose control, chances of a job offer are slim!

When the interview ends, thank the interviewer for his or her time, and for giving you this opportunity to talk about your qualifications. But don't think that "selling" yourself has stopped there. As soon as you get home, type a thank-you letter and send it to the recruiter. You'd be amazed at how many people fail to do this! This little act of courtesy carries a big impact—use it to your advantage. Then sit back and wait to see what happens.

We have tried to convey our experience with this process in the hope that it will help you in your interview. It takes long and hard work to get a job. But you needn't do it alone. Visit your school's career placement office, whose professionals can help you work through all aspects of the selection process and give you a lot of supporting information. Consider getting a job your job! It's not an easy task, but it will be time well spent if you achieve your ultimate goal—employment.

Endnotes

Chapter 1

1. Howard Burns, "Lanier Puts Customers First, But Employees Aren't Far Behind," *London Free Press* (February 24, 1998), pp. D1&2.

2. For a comprehensive overview of management, see John R. Schermerhorn Jr., Julian Cattaneo and Andrew Templer, *Management: The Competitive Advantage* (Toronto: Wiley 1995), chapter 1. It is also worth noting that changes in the world of work reveal that these work functions may no longer be just the purview of managers but instead, be part of every worker's job responsibility.

3. While no specific date is identified regarding the "birth" of personnel departments, the generally accepted inception of personnel coincided with the growth of unions in Quebec in the late 1800s and the "best" movement during World War I.

4. They were seen as performing relatively unimportant activities. In fact, the personnel department was often seen as an "employee graveyard"—a place to send employees who were past their prime and couldn't do much damage.

5. See, for example, Augustine A. Lado and Mary C. Wilson, "Human Resource Systems and Sustained Competitive Advantage: A Competency-Based Perspective," *Academy of Management Review*, Vol. 19, No. 4 (1994), pp. 699–727.

6. Jeffrey Pfeffer, "Producing Sustainable Competitive Advantage Through the Effective Management of People," *Academy of Management Executive*, Vol. 9, No. 1 (1995), p. 55.

7. David Guest, "Personnel and HRM: Can You Tell the Difference?" *Personnel Management* (January 1989), pp. 48–51.

8. Norman Trainor, "Taking Lessons From the Royal Bank," *Canadian HR Reporter* (March 9, 1998), p. 8.

9. Sharon Lebrun, "People Policies Key to Sunoco Turnaround," *Canadian HR Reporter* (February 10, 1997), pp. 1 and 8.

10. Kathy Blair, "Hearing-Impaired Woman Told to Answer Phones," *Canadian HR Reporter*, (July 14 1997), p. 7.

11. Figures on union membership are from the *Directory of Labour Organizations in Canada*, Human Resources Development Canada (Ottawa: HRD Canada, 1996).

12. Although there has been much criticism of the Hawthorne studies regarding the conclusions they drew, this has in no way diminished the significance of opinions they represent in the development of the field of HRM.

13. Of course, we recognize that as with other HRM activities, staffing, is a continuous concern, and all functions occur simultaneously, but for the sake of explanation, we present each function as a linear process.

14. Brian O'Reilly, "The New Deal: What Companies and Employees Owe One Another," *Fortune* (June 13, 1994), pp. 44–52; and Stanley J. Modic, "Is Anyone Loyal Anymore?" *Industry Week* (September 7, 1987), p. 75.

15. As we will show in Chapter 5, during a period of downsizing, employment may also be the department handling the lay-offs.

16. See, for example, Nicholas J. Mathys, "Strategic Downsizing: Human Resource Planning Approaches," *Human Resource Planning* (February 1993), pp. 71–86.

17. It should be noted that compensation and benefits may be, in fact, two separate departments. However, for simplicity we will consider the department as a combined, singular unit.

18. Perquisites, or perks, are special offerings accorded to senior managers in an attempt to attract and retain the best managers possible. We will take a closer look at perks in Chapter 13, "Rewards and Compensation."

19. A strategic business unit, (or market-driven unit), often operates as an independent entity in an organization with its own set of strategies and mission.

20. Nicholas J. Mathys, "Strategic Downsizing: Human Resource Planning Approaches," *Human Resource Planning* (February 1993), p. 83.

21. See, for example, Commerce Clearing House, Human Resources Management, 1992 SHRM/CCH Survey (1992), pp. 1–12.
22. The idea for this exercise was derived from Barbara K. Goza, "Graffiti Needs Assessment: Involving Students in the First Class Session," *Journal of Management Education*, Vol. 17, No. 1 [(February 1993), pp. 99–106.] Your authors first used a version of this exercise in their text, Fundamentals of Management (Englewood Cliffs, N.J.: Prentice Hall, 1994), p. 22.
23. Adapted from, "Scotiabank Links Customer, Employee Satisfaction," *Canadian HR Reporter*, (January 26, 1998), p. 3.

Chapter 2

1. Based on Sharon Lebrun, "Eaton's HR Soldiers On," *Canadian HR Reporter* (April 7, 1997), pp. 1–2.
2. A multinational corporation is an organization that has significant operations in two or more countries. A transnational corporation is one that maintains significant operations in two or more countries simultaneously and gives each the decision-making authority to operate in the local country.
3. Victoria Curran, "Fasttalkers," *Canadian Business* (March 1997), pp. 22–23.
4. Because of the global nature of work, it is important for students to be bilingual. In terms of gaining employment, those who speak more than one language will have an advantage in the job market.
5. David North, "Is Your Head Office a Useless Frill?" *Canadian Business* (November 1997), pp. 78–80.
6. For a more comprehensive coverage of cultural dimension, see Geert Hofstede, *Cultural Consequences: International Differences in Work-Related Values* (Beverly Hills, Calif.: Sage Publications, 1980).
7. Cleta Moyer, "Diversity Management," *Human Resources Professional* (November 1995) pp. 21–22.
8. *HR Magazine* (January 1991), pp. 40–41.
9. *Ibid.*, p. 40.
10. William H. Wagel, *Personnel* (January 1990), p. 12.
11. Ann Crittenden, "Where Workforce 2000 Went Wrong," *Working Woman* (August 1994), p. 18.
12. Samuel, *Visible Minorities in Canada: A Projection* (Toronto: Canadian Advertising Foundation, 1994).
13. These statistics, drawn from Statistics Canada, are noted in the summary in Luis Gomez-Mejia, David Balkin, Robert Cardy, and David Dimick, *Managing Human Resources* (Scarborough, Ont., Prentice-Hall, 1997), pp.146–68.
14. The baby boom generation refers to those individuals born between 1947 and 1964.
15. David Foot & Daniel Stoffman, *Boom, Bust and Echo* (Toronto: Macfarlane, Walter & Ross, 1996).
16. Cleta Moyer, "Diversity Management," *Human Resources Professional* (November 1995), pp. 21–22.
17. Faye Rice, "How to Make Diversity Pay," *Fortune* (August 8, 1994), p. 79.
18. Helen LaFountaine and Greg Kozdrowski, "Today's Workplace: A United Nations of Needs," *Canadian HR Reporter* (14 July, 1997), pp. 17–18.
19. *Ibid.*
20. For a good review of family-friendly companies, see Milton Moskowitz and Carol Townsend, "100 Best Companies for Working Mothers," *Working Mother* (October 1994), pp. 21–68.
21. Sue Shellenbarger, "Flexible Workers Come Under the Umbrella of Family Programs," *The Wall Street Journal* (February 8, 1995), p. B1.
22. See, for example, Suneel Ratan, "Why Busters Hate Boomers," *Fortune* (October 4, 1993), pp. 56–70.
23. Linda Thornburg, "The Age Wave Hits: What Older Workers Want and Need," *HR Magazine* (February 1995), pp. 43–44.

24. Charles E. Cohen, "Managing Older Workers," *Working Woman* (November 1994), pp. 61–62.

25. "Office Hours," *Fortune* (November 5, 1990), p. 184.

26. The Wyatt Communicator, p. 11.

27. Conference Board of Canada, "The Economic Benefits of improving Literacy Skills in the Workplace," excerpted in *Canadian HR Reporter* (May 19, 1997), pp.16–17.

28. *Ibid.*

29. Commerce Clearing House, "Employers to Bear Burden of Adult Literacy," *Human Resources Management: Ideas and Trends* (November 10, 1993), p. 182.

30. "Employee Literacy," *Inc.* (August 1992), p. 81.

31. *Ibid.*

32. Jamie Harrison, "Molson Opens Learning Centre," *Canadian HR Reporter* (January 26, 1998), pp.1–2.

33. Anita Lahey, "Seeing Skills More Clearly," *Canadian HR Reporter* (May 19, 1997), pp. L11–L12.

34. Canadian Human Rights Commission, "Equity Competing with Downsizing," *Canadian HR Reporter* (April 7, 1997), p. 1.

35. Brenton S. Schlender, "Japan's White Collar Blues," *Fortune* (March 12, 1994), pp. 97–104.

36. Joann S. Lublin, "Don't Stop Cutting Staff, Study Suggests," *The Wall Street Journal* (September 27, 1994), p. B1.

37. We recognize that this number is not an accurate reflection of the cost savings. In addition, one would have to add in the costs of employee benefits saved and subtract any monies used to "buy people out." The $35 million figure is for illustration purposes only.

38. Anne B. Fisher, "Welcome to the Age of Overwork," *Fortune* (November 30, 1992), p. 64.

39. See Marjorie Armstrong-Stassen and Janina C. Latack, "Coping with WorkForce Reduction: The Effect of Layoff Exposure on Survivors' Reactions," In Jerry L. Wall and Lawrence R. Jauch, eds., *Academy of Management Best Papers Proceedings 1992*, Las Vegas (August 9–12, 1992), pp. 207–12. See also Terence Krell and Robert S. Spich, "A Tentative Model of Lame Duck Situations in Organizations," *Proceedings of the 1992 Conference of the Midwest Society for Human Resources/Industrial Relations* (March 25–27, 1992), pp. 161–75.

40. See, for example, Joann S. Lublin, "The Layoff Industry Learns that the Ax Can Be a Real Grind," *The Wall Street Journal* (November 28, 1994), pp. A–1; A–8.

41. *Ibid.*; and "A Comeback for Middle Managers," *Fortune* (October 17, 1994), p. 32.

42. Alan C. Fenwick, "Five Easy Lessons: A Primer for Starting a Total Quality Management Program," *Quality Progress*, Vol. 24, No. 12 (December 1991), p. 63.

43. Fenwick, p. 63.

44. David Greising, "Quality: How to Make It Pay," *Business Week* (August 8, 1994), pp. 53–59.

45. For an in-depth, theoretical review of TQM and related topics, see the special issue of the *Academy of Management Journal* (July 1994), pp. 390–584.

46. See W. Edwards Deming, *Quality Productivity and Competitive Position* (Cambridge, Mass.: MIT Center for Advanced Engineering Study, 1982).

47. See W. Edwards Deming, "Improvement of Quality and Productivity Through Actions of Management," *National Productivity Review* (Winter 1981), pp. 12–22.

48. See, for example, Brian M. Cook, "Quality: The Pioneers Survey the Landscape," *Industry Week* (October 21, 1991), pp. 68–73.

49. *Ibid.*, p. 70.

50. For a review of some of TQM's Canadian success stories, see the special edition of the *Human Resource Professional*, (June/July, 1994).

51. Carla C. Carter, "Seven Basic Quality Tools," *HRMagazine* (January 1992), p. 81.

52. See, for example, Amit Majumdar, Megan Smolenyak, and Nancy Yenche, "Planting the Seeds of TQM," *National Productivity Review* (Autumn 1991), p. 492.

53. Ken Mark, "Dead Cert," *Human Resources Professional* (September, 1994), pp.13–15.

54. Frederick F. Reichheld and W. Earl Sasser, Jr., "Zero Defections: Quality Comes to Services," *Harvard Business Review* (September October 1990), p. 105.

55. See Morton Bahr, "Labor and Management…Working Together on Quality," *Journal for Quality and Participation*, Vol. 14, No. 3 (June 1991), pp. 14–17.

56. Edward E. Lawler III, "Total Quality Management and Employee Involvement: Are They Compatible?" *Academy of Management Executive*, Vol. 8, No. 1 (1994), pp. 68–76; and Richard Blackman and Benson Rosen, "Total Quality and Human Resources Management: Lessons Learned from Baldrige Award-Winning Companies," *Academy of Management Executive*, Vol. 7, No. 3 (1993), pp. 49–66.

57. Ken Mark., p. 15.

58. Sandra E. O'Connell, "Reengineering: Ways to Do It with Technology," *HRMagazine* (November 1994), p. 40.

59. Nancy K. Austin, "What's Missing from Corporate Cure-Alls," *Working Woman* (September 1994), pp. 16–19.

60. *Ibid.*

61. Sandra E. O'Connell, p. 40.

62. John A. Byrne, "Reengineering: What Happened?" *Business Week* (January 30, 1995), p. 16.

63. Julie Connelly, "Have We Become Mad Dogs in the Office?" *Fortune* (November 28, 1994), p. 197.

64. See for example, Debra Phillips, "The New Service Boom," *Entrepreneur* (August 1994), pp. 134–40.

65. Charles Handy, *The Age of Unreason*, (Harvard Business School Press: Cambridge, Mass.:, 1989).

66. Ann Crittenden, "Temporary," *Working Woman* (February 1994), p. 32.

67. Jaclyn Fierman, "The Contingency Work Force," *Fortune* (January 24, 1994), p. 32; "BOOM TIMES for Temporary Help Aren't Temporary, Experts Agree," *The Wall Street Journal* (October 25, 1994), p. A1; and Janet Novack, "Is Lean, Mean?," *Forbes* (August 15, 1994), p. 88.

68. Jamie Harrison, "Alternative Work Arrangements Not so Alternative Anymore," *Canadian HR Reporter* (March 8, 1998), p. 2.

69. Murray Campbell, "Part-Time Work Stats Questioned," The *Globe and Mail* (March 18, 1998), p. A2.

70. Johanna Powell, "Managing with Temps," *The Financial Post* (July 10, 1997), p. 49.

71. See, for instance, Audrey Freedman, "Human Resources Forecast 1995: Contingent Workers," *HRMagazine Supplement* (1994), pp. 13–14.

72. Maggie Mahar, "Part-Time: By Choice or By Chance," *Working Woman* (October 1993), p. 20.

73. Jaclyn Fierman, "The Contingency Work Force," p. 33.

74. Keith H. Hammonds, Kevin Kelly, and Karen Thurston, "The New World of Work," *Business Week* (October 17, 1994), p. 85.

75. Ann Crittenden, "Temporary," p. 33.

76. "Contracting Out White Collar Jobs Continues to Gain Steam," *The Wall Street Journal* (September 20, 1994), p. A1.

77. Ani Hadjian, "Hiring Temps Full-Time May Get the IRS On Your Tail," *Fortune* (January 24, 1994), p. 34.

78. For a fuller development of the portfolio perspective on HRM see, Andrew Templer and Tupper Cawsey, "The HRM Implications of Portfolio-Career Employees", *Paper Presented in the HRM Division at the Annual Conference of the Administrative Sciences Association of Canada* (June 1997, St. Johns, Newfoundland).

79. See, for example, Leon Rubis, "Benefits Boost Appeal of Temporary Work," *HRMagazine* (January 1995), pp. 54–58; and Anne Murphy, "Do It Yourself Job Creation," *Inc.* (January 1994), pp. 36–50.

80. Alana Mitchell, "He's a Trucker, She Types—1990s Just like the 50s," The *Globe and Mail* (March 18, 1998), pp. A1 & A6.

81. Marjorie Armstrong-Stassen, Norm Solomon, and Andrew Templer, "Telework and Job Security: A Case Study," In Izik Zeytinoglu (Chair), *Non-Standard Forms of*

Employment and Implication for Industrial Relations, (Symposium, St. Catherines, Ont.: Canadian Industrial Relations Association), May 1996.

82. For a current overview of telework in Canada, see Andrew Templer, Marjorie Armstrong-Stassen, Kay Devine and Norm Solomon, and Telework and Teleworkers, In Izik Zeytinoglu (editor), *Developments in Changing Work Relationships in Industrialized Economies* (Amsterdam, Holland: Kluwer Academic Publishers, 1998—in press).

83. KPMG Canada. (1997). *1997 telecommuting survey*. [On-line]. Available: HRRP://www.kpmg.ca/hr/tel_cmut.htm.

84. Frances Cairncross, "The Death of Distance," *The Economist* (September 13, 1997), p.87.

85. Commerce Clearing House, "Work at Home Increasingly Appealing to Employers, But Legal Pitfalls Abound," *Human Resources Management: Ideas and Trends* (February 16, 1994), pp. 25–26.

86. For a comprehensive overview of empowering employees, see Jay A. Conger and Rabindra N. Kanungo, "The Empowerment Process: Integrating Theory and Practice," *Academy of Management Review*, Vol. 13, No. 3 (July 1988), pp. 471–82.

87. See, for example, Jeffrey Pfeffer, "Producing Sustainable Competitive Advantage Through the Effective Management of People," *Academy of Management Executive*, Vol. 9, No. 1 (1995), pp. 55–72.

88. Keith H. Hammond, Kevin Kelly, and Karen Thurston, "The New World of Work," *Business Week* (October 17, 1994), p. 81.

89. See, for example, Jon L. Pierce, Stephen A. Rubenfeld, and Susan Morgan, "Employee Ownership: A Conceptual Model of Process and Effects," *The Academy of Management Review*, Vol. 16, No. 1 (January 1991), pp. 121–44.

90. *Ibid*, pp. 136–37; and Brian O'Reilly, "The New Deal: What Companies and Employees Owe One Another," *Fortune* (June 13, 1994), p. 44.

91. If you have found this chapter interesting, we encourage you to read David Ulrich, *Human Resource Champions*, (Boston: Harvard Business School Press, 1997).

92. Excerpted from, Bruce Livesey, "Heart of Steel," *Globe and Mail Report on Business Magazine* (August, 1997), pp. 20–27.

Chapter 3

1. "So Sensitive it Hurts," *Canadian Business*, Vol. 68, No. 1 (January 1995), p. 15.

2. *Ibid.*

3. *Ibid.*

4. *Ibid.*

5. Joanne. D. Leck and David. M. Saunders, "Achieving Diversity in the Workplace: Canada's Employment Equity Act and Members of Visible Minorities," *International Journal of Public Administration*, Vol. 19, No. 3, (1996), pp. 299–321; and *Employment Equity: A Guide for Employers*, (Ottawa, Ontario: Employment and Immigration Canada), 1991.

6. Victor M. Catano, Steven F. Cronshaw, Willi H. Wiesner, Rick D. Hackett, and Laura L. Methot, *Recruitment and Selection in Canada* (Scarborough, Ontario: ITP Nelson), 1997, pp. 31–73.

7. *Constitution Act*, 1982, being Schedule B of the *Canadian Act* (U.K.), 1982, c. 11.

8. *Equality: We All Have a Hand in It*, (Ottawa, Ontario: Canadian Human Rights Commission), 1996, p. 17; and Canadian Human Rights Commission, *Annual Report 1996*, (Ottawa, Ontario: Minister of Public Works and Government Services Canada), 1997, pp. 88–90.

9. Canadian Human Rights Commission, *Annual Report 1996*, (Ottawa, Ontario: Minister of Public Works and Government Services Canada), 1997, p. 58; *Large v. Stratford (City) Police Department*, 1995, 3 S.C.R. 733, and 24 C.H.R.R. D/1; and Shirish Pundit Chotalia, *The 1997 Annotated Canadian Human Rights Act*, (Scarborough, Ontario: Carswell Thomson Professional Publishing), 1996, pp. 65–68.

10. *Canadian Human Rights Act* R.S.C. 1985, c. 4–6, s.2; *Equality: We All Have a Hand in it*, (Ottawa, Ontario: Canadian Human Rights Commission), 1996; and *The Canadian Human Rights Act: A Guide*, (Ottawa, Ontario: Minister of Supply and Services Canada), 1993.

11. "Homosexual Rights Bill Clears Canadian Senate," *The New York Times* (June 6, 1996), p. A-18; and "Canada Bill Seeks to Shield Homosexual Workforce," *The Wall Street Journal* (April 30, 1996), p. B–2.

12. *Human Rights: A Daily Business*, Manitoba Human Rights Commission, 1998; and 29 C.H.R.R. D B 087.

13. *Canadian Human Rights Act 1985*, s.15. *The Canadian Human Rights Act: A Guide*, (Ottawa, Ontario: Minister of Supply and Services Canada), 1993.

14. Shirish Pundit Chotalia, *The 1997 Annotated Canadian Human Rights Act*, (Scarborough, Ontario: Carswell Thomson Professional Publishing), 1996, pp. 64–83; *Canadian Human Rights Act*, section 15(a); and Victor M. Catano, Steven F. Cronshaw, Willi H. Wiesner, Rick D. Hackett, and Laura L. Methot, *Recruitment and Selection in Canada* (Scarborough, Ontario: ITP Nelson), 1997, pp. 51–53.

15. *Bhinder v. Canadian National Railway*, 1985, 2 S.C.R. 561, and 7 C.H.R.R. D/3093.

16. *Patry v. Canada (Royal Canadian Mounted Police)*, (February 21, 1995), C.H.R.D. No.5 T.D. 5/95.

17. Victor M. Catano, Steven F. Cronshaw, Willi H. Wiesner, Rick D. Hackett, and Laura L. Methot, *Recruitment and Selection in Canada* (Scarborough, Ontario: ITP Nelson), 1997, pp. 77–119.

18. *Griggs v. Duke Power Co.*, 401 U.S. 424, 432, 91 (1971).

19. *Fact Sheet: Reasonable Accomodation*, Manitoba Human Rights Commission, 1998; The Canadian Human Rights Act: A Guide, (Ottawa, Ontario: Minister of Supply and Services Canada), 1993; and Canadian Human Rights Act 1985, s.15.

20. *Ibid.*

21. *Patry v. Canada (Royal Canadian Mounted Police)* (February 21, 1995), Canadian Human Rights Tribunal.

22. *Large v. Stratford (City) Police Department*, (1995), 3 S.C.R. 733, and 24 C.H.R.R. D-1; *Bell and Cooper v. Canada (Human Rights Commission)*, (1996), 3 S.C.R. 854; and "Age-Old Dispute Bias: County Orders Mandatory Retirement for Deputies and Firefighters Over 60. *The Los Angeles Times* (February 24, 1997), p. B1.

23. Supreme Court Allows Pilot Age Retirement Rule, *Time News Wire*, May 18, 1998; and *Bell and Cooper v. Canada (Human Rights Commission)* (1996), 3 S.C.R. 854; 140 D.L.R. (4th) 193.

24. The age sixty issue is currently being debated. For example, questions on who medical research was conducted on (e.g., private pilots, not commercial ones, and so forth) have raised many questions. However, at this time, mandatory retirement for pilots at age sixty is still in force.

25. Teacher's union claims discrimination, *Canadian Press Newswire*, August 17, 1994.

26. Canadian Human Rights Commission, *Annual Report 1996*, (Ottawa, Ontario: Minister of Public Works and Government Services Canada), 1997, pp. 57–58; and "Scrap Mandatory Retirement Age, Study Recommends," *The Winnipeg Free Press* (May 17, 1998), p. A–4.

27. Canadian Human Rights Commission, *Annual Report 1996*, (Ottawa, Ontario: Minister of Public Works and Government Services Canada), 1997, pp. 57–58.

28. *Equal Dollars Make Good Sense, A Booklet for Employees on Equal Pay for Work of Equal Value*, (Ottawa, Ontario: Canadian Human Rights Commission), 1991; Canadian Human Rights Commission, *Annual Report 1997*, (Ottawa, Ontario: Minister of Public Works and Government Services Canada), 1998, pp. 21–23; and Carole A. Reed, Contradictions and Assumptions: A Report on Employment Equity in Canada, *Resources for Feminist Research*, Vol. 24, No. 3–4, (1996), pp. 46–48.

29. *Equal Dollars Make Good Sense, A Booklet for Employees on Equal Pay for Work of Equal Value*, (Ottawa, Ontario: Canadian Human Rights Commission), 1991.

30. Robert S. Smith, "Comparable Worth: Limited Coverage and the Exacerbation of Inequality," *Industrial and Labor Relations Review*, Vol. 41, No. 2 (1998), pp. 227–239; and Jonathan Tompkins, "Comparable Worth and Job Evaluation Validity," *Public*

Administration Review, Vol. 47, No. 3 (May–June, 1987), pp. 254–258.

31. *Equal Dollars make Good Sense: A Booklet for Employees on Equal Pay for Work of Equal Value* (Ottawa, Ontario: Canadian Human Rights Commission), 1991; and *Guide to Pay Equity and Job Evaluation,* (Ottawa, Ontario: Canadian Human Rights Commission), 1997.

32. *Equality: We All Have a Hand in It,* (Ottawa, Ontario: Canadian Human Rights Commission), 1996, p. 11.

33. See for example, *Canada (Treasury Board) v. Tellier-Cohen,* (1982), 4 C.H.R.R. D-1169.

34. *A Guide to the Employment Standards Act,* (Victoria, British Columbia: British Columbia Ministry of Labour, 1996; and *Employment Standards—Fact Sheet: Pregnancy Leave,* (Toronto: Ontario Ministry of Labour), 1997.

35. Rosalie Silberman Abella, *Equality in Employment: A Royal Commission Report,* (Ottawa, Ontario: Minister of Supply and Services Canada), 1984.

36. *Working Towards Equality: The Discussion Paper on Employment Equity Legislation,* (Toronto: Ontario Ministry of Citizenship printer), 1991, pp. 5 B 9; *Employment Equity: The Federal Contractors Program,* (Ottawa: Minister of Supply and Services Canada), 1993; and Canadian Human Rights Commission, *Annual Report 1997,* (Ottawa, Ontario: Minister of Public Works and Government Services Canada), 1998, pp. 21–23.

37. *Disability is Normal,* (Saskatoon, Sask.: Saskatchewan Human Rights Commission), undated, p. 4; and Canadian Human Rights Commission, *Annual Report* 1997, (Ottawa, Ontario: Minister of Public Works and Government Services Canada), 1998, pp. 26–33.

38. Canadian Human Rights Commission, *Annual Report* 1997, (Ottawa, Ontario: Minister of Public Works and Government Services Canada), 1998, pp. 21–23.

39. Canadian Human Rights Commission, *Employment Equity: Fair Play at Work,* (Ottawa, Ontario: Minister of Supply and Services Canada), 1994.

40. Canadian Human Rights Commission, *Annual Report 1997,* (Ottawa, Ontario: Minister of Public Works and Government Services Canada), 1998, pp. 21–23; and Marguarite Keeley, "Employment Equity and the Canadian Human Rights Commission: A New Law for a New Decade of Change," *Human Rights Forum,* Vol. 5, No. 1 (Spring–Summer), 1995, pp. 2–4.

41. *Ibid.*

42. Marguarite Keeley, "Employment Equity and the Canadian Human Rights Commission: A New Law for a New Decade of Change," *Human Rights Forum,* Vol. 5, No. 1 (Spring–Summer), 1995, pp. 2–4; *Key Elements of the New Employment Equity Act and Regulations,* (Hull, Quebec: Human Resources Development Canada), 1996; and *Framework for Compliance Audits Under the Employment Equity Act,* (Ottawa, Ontario: Canadian Human Rights Commission), 1996.

43. Canadian Human Rights Commission, *Annual Report* 1997, (Ottawa, Ontario: Minister of Public Works and Government Services Canada), 1998.

44. *Chander and Joshi v. Canada (Department of National Health and Welfare),* (1996), C.H.R.D. No. 5 (Canadian Human Rights Tribunal); and "Ottawa Torques Up Its Racial Hiring Quota: Canadian Human Rights Commission Finds Discrimination in the Federal Department of Health," *British Columbia Report,* Vol. 8, No. 32 (April 7, 1997), pp. 8–9.

45. Action Travail des Femmes v. Canadian National Railways, (1987), 8 C.H.R.R. D-4210.

46. *Employment Equity – Facts and Fiction,* (Hull, Quebec: Human Resources Development Canada, Labour Operations), 1993.

47. Rosalie Silberman Abella, *Equality in Employment: A Royal Commission Report,* (Ottawa, Ontario: Minister of Supply and Services Canada), 1984.

48. Claudia H. Deutsch, "Don't Forget About the White Males," *The New York Times* (December 8, 1991), Section 3, p. 29.

49. *Ibid.*

50. *Employment Equity—Facts and Fiction,* (Hull, Quebec: Human Resources Development Canada, Labour Operations), 1993.

51. *Ibid.*

52. *Ontario (Human Rights Commission) and O'Malley v. Simpson-Sears Ltd.*, (1985), 2 S.C.R. 536, 7 C.H.R.R. D B 3102.

53. Jeffrey H. Greenhaus, Saroj Parasuraman, and Wayne M. Wormley, "Effects of Race on Organizational Experiences, Job Performance Evaluations and Career Outcomes," *Academy of Management Journal*, Vol. 33, No. 1 (1990), pp. 64–86.

54. Gary Dessler, *Personnel/Human Resources Management*, Fifth Edition (Englewood Cliffs, N.J.: Prentice-Hall), pp. 45–46.

55. Victor M. Catano, Steven F. Cronshaw, Willi H. Wiesner, Rick D. Hackett, and Laura L. Methot, *Recruitment and Selection in Canada*, (Scarborough, Ontario: ITP Nelson), 1997, pp. 77–119.

56. We must note here that the four-fifth rule, as established, does not recognize specific individual's requirements. That is, a minority could be any group. For example, when airlines hired only females as flight attendants, males were the minority.

57. *McDonnell-Douglas Corp. v. Green*, 411 U.S. 792, 80 (U.S. 1973).

58. Such a case is frequently referred to as a prima facie case. In such a situation, there is enough evidence to support the charge and will be considered sufficient evidence unless refuted by the organization.

59. *McDonnell-Douglas Corp. v. Green*, 411 U.S. 792, 80 (U.S. 1973); and Helen Creighton, "Age Discrimination," Nursing Management, Vol. 20, No. 2, (February, 1989), p. 21–22.

60. Cassandra Szklarski, "Firefighters Union Unfair to Women, Minority Applicants, Alleges Commission," *Canadian Press Wire*, December 16, 1997.

61. Canadian Human Rights Commission, *Annual Report* 1997, (Ottawa, Ontario: Minister of Public Works and Government Services Canada), 1998, pp. 53–55; and *Equality: We All Have a Hand in It*, (Ottawa, Ontario: Canadian Human Rights Commission), 1996, pp. 6–8.

62. *Filing a Complaint with the Canadian Human Rights Commission*, (Ottawa, Ontario: Canadian Human Rights Commission), 1994; Equality: We All Have a Hand in It, (Ottawa, Ontario: Canadian Human Rights Commission), 1996, pp. 14B15; and *The Canadian Human Rights Act: A Guide*, (Ottawa, Ontario: Minister of Supply and Services Canada), 1993.

63. *Filing a Complaint with the Canadian Human Rights Commission*, (Ottawa, Ontario: Canadian Human Rights Commission), 1993.

64. *Canadian Human Rights Tribunal: Origin and Role*, (Ottawa, Ontario: Canadian Human Rights Tribunal), undated.

65. Canadian Human Rights Commission, *Annual Report* 1997, (Ottawa, Ontario: Minister of Public Works and Government Services Canada), 1998.

66. *Equality: We All Have a Hand in It*, (Ottawa, Ontario: Canadian Human Rights Commission), 1996, pp. 14–15.

67. Ann B. Fisher, "Sexual Harassment, What to Do," *Fortune*, Vol. 128, No. 4 (August 23, 1993), pp. 84–88.

68. Clifford M. Koen, "Sexual Harassment Claims Stem from a Hostile Work Environment," *Personnel Journal*, Vol. 69, No. 8 (August 1990), pp. 84–88.

69. Canadian Human Rights Commission, *Annual Report* 1996, (Ottawa, Ontario: Minister of Public Works and Government Services Canada), 1997, pp. 50B51; and Shirish Pundit Chotalia, *The 1997 Annotated Canadian Human Rights Act*, (Scarborough, Ontario: Carswell Thomson Professional Publishing), 1996, pp. 59–64.

70. "U.S. Leads Way in Sex Harassment Laws, Study Says," *The Evening Sun* (November 30, 1992), pp. A–1, A–7.

71. Susan Webb, *The Webb Report: A Newsletter on Sexual Harassment*, (Seattle, Wash.: Premier Publishing Ltd. (January 1994), pp. 4B7; and (April 1994), pp. 2B5.

72. Gavin Souter, "EPL Suits Now Larger Concern in Canada," *Business Insurance*, Vol. 30, No. 43 (October 21, 1996), pp. 20–21.

73. Rick Coe, "The Real Story of Harassment at SFU," *CAUT Bulletin*, Vol. 45, No. 5 (May 1998), pp. 1, 3, 5.

74. "Charges Against Speaker Not Backed Up: All-Party Committee," *Canadian Press Newswire*, October 7, 1996.

75. Karen Prisciak, "Health, Safety, and Harassment," *OH & S Canada*, Vol. 13, No. 3 (April–May 1997), pp. 20–21.

76. *Canada Labour Code Part III* (Labour Standards), 1984.

77. Karen Prisciak, "Health, Safety, and Harassment," *OH & S Canada*, Vol. 13, No. 3 (April–May, 1997), pp. 20–21.

78. Jacqueline F. Strayer and Sandra E. Rapoport, "Sexual Harassment: Limiting Corporate Liability," *Personnel* (April 1986), pp. 30–31.

79. *Potapczyk v. MacBain* (1984), 5 C.H.R.R. D-2285, 84 C.L.L.C. 17,017 (Canadian Human Rights Tribunal).

80. *Clark v. Canada* (1994), 3 F.C.323, 3 C.C.E.L. (2d) 172, 20 C.C.L.T. (2d) 241.

81. *Robichaud v. Brennan* (1987), 2 S.C.R. 84; 40 D.L.R. (4th) 577.

82. Commerce Clearing House, *Human Resources Management: Ideas and Trends*, (March 5, 1992), p. 39.

83. "According to Royal Bank, Companies That Treat People with Dignity and Respect Will Prosper, and Those Who Don't Will Have Tough Time Competing for Customers and Employees," *Canada News Wire*, November 6, 1997.

84. Canadian Human Rights Commission, *Annual Report* 1997, (Ottawa, Ontario: Minister of Public Works and Government Services Canada), 1998, pp. 15–25; "Glass Ceiling Separates Women From Top," *Work-life Report*, Vol. 11, No. 1 (January 1997), p.15; and Ronald J. Burke, "Women in Corporate Management," *Journal of Business Ethics*, Vol. 16, No. 9, p. 1–3.

85. Tema Frank, "Opportunity Knocks," *CA Magazine*, Vol. 130, No. 2 (March 1997), pp. 24–28; and Jennifer Wells, "Stuck on the Ladder: Not Only is the Glass Ceiling Still in Place, But Men and Women Have Very Different Views of the Problem," *MacLean's–Toronto Edition*, Vol. 110, No. 42, (October 20, 1997), p. 60.

86. International Labour Organization, *Breaking the Glass Ceiling: Women in Management*, (Geneva, Switzerland: International Labour Office), 1997; and *Closing the Gap: Women's Advancement in Corporate and Professional Canada*, (Ottawa, Ontario: Conference Board of Canada), 1997.

87. Belle Rose Ragins, Bickley Townsend and Mary Mattis, "Gender Gap in the Executive Suits: CEOs and Female Executives Report on Breaking the Glass Ceiling," *Academy of Management Executive*, Vol. 12, No. 1, (1998), pp. 28–42.

88. Gene Epstein, "Low Ceiling: How Women Are Held Back by Sexism at Work and Child Rearing Duties at Home," Barron's, Vol. 77, No. 48, (December 1, 1997, pp. 35–40; Tema Frank, "Opportunity Knocks," *CA Magazine*, Vol. 130, No. 2 (March 1997), pp. 24–28; and Jennifer Wells, "Stuck on the Ladder: Not Only is the Glass Ceiling Still in Place, But Men and Women Have Very Different Views of the Problem," *MacLean's–Toronto Edition*, Vol. 110, No. 42, (October 20, 1997), p. 60.

89. Tema Frank, "Opportunity Knocks," *CA Magazine*, Vol. 130, No. 2 (March, 1997), pp. 24–28.

90. "Dismantling The Glass Ceiling," *HR Focus*, (May 1996), p. 12; and Jennifer Wells, "Stuck on the Ladder: Not Only is the Glass Ceiling Still in Place, But Men and Women Have Very Different Views of the Problem," *MacLean's-Toronto Edition*, Vol. 110, No. 42, (October 20, 1997), p. 60.

Chapter 4

1. This opening vignette comes from the following sources: McCarthy Tetrault, Alcohol and Drug Policies in Ontario: The Imperial Decision, 1996, Toronto, Ontario; Ontario Trucking Association, *Alcohol and Drug Policy Reviewed Under the Human Rights Code*, 1996, Toronto, Ontario; *Canadian Press Newswire*, "Human Rights Board Rules Imperial Drug Testing Illegal," September 17, 1996; Rick Bogacz, "Imperial's Drug Policy Ruled Unlawful," *Journal of Addictive Research Foundation*, Vol. 25, No. 6 (November–December 1996), p. 4; and "Mandatory Drug Testing Struck Down: Imperial Oil Policy Goes Too Far," *Toronto Star*, February 23, 1998, p. C3.

2. *Ibid.*

3. Margot Gibb-Clark, "Ruling Narrows Options for Drug Testing," *The Globe and Mail*, July 28, 1998, p. B. 11.

4. Stephanie Overman, "A Delicate Balance Protects Everyone's Rights," *HRMagazine*, Vol. 35, No. 1 (November 1990), pp. 36–37.

5. "Incompetence Led to Westray Tragedy," *OHS Canada*, Vol. 14, No. 1 (January–February 1998), p. 19; and Westray's Explosion: An Accident Waiting to Happen, *Our Times*, Vol. 17, No. 1 (January–February 1998), pp. 28–30.

6. Kevin Cox, "Westray Charges Stayed: Miners' Families Bitter at Learning Managers Won't Face Trial in Blast that Killed 26," *The Globe and Mail*, July 1, 1998, pp. A1, A4.

7. This example is taken from Carolyn Wiley, "Reexamining Perceived Ethics Issues and Ethics Roles among Employment Managers," *Journal of Business Ethics*, Vol. 17, No. 2 (January 1998), pp. 147–61.

8. This example is taken from Stratford Sherman, Levi's: "As Ye Sew, So Shall Ye Reap," *Fortune*, Vol. 139, No. 9, (May 12, 1997), pp. 104–16.

9. Victor M. Catano, Steven F. Cronshaw, Willi H. Wiesner, and Laura L. Methot, *Recruitment and Selection in Canada*, (Toronto, Ontario: ITP Nelson, 1997), pp. 23–24.

10. Bill Langdon, "Corporate Ethics Are Now a Mainstream Management Issue," *CMA Magazine*, Vol. 71, No. 6, (July–August 1997), p. 3.

11. William Cordeiro, "Suggested Management Responses to Ethical Issues Raised by Technological Change," *Journal of Business Ethics*, Vol. 16, No. 12–13 (September 1997), pp. 1393–1400.

12. Frank Navran, "12 Steps to Building a Best-Practices Ethics Program," *Workforce*, Vol. 76, No. 9 (September 1997), p. 117–22.

13. Minister of Public Works and Government Services, The Access to Information Act: A Critical Review, Ottawa, Ontario, 1994; and The Privacy Commissioner of Canada, *Annual Report 1997-1998*, Ottawa, Ontario, 1998.

14. Victor M. Catano, Steven F. Cronshaw, Willi H. Wiesner, and Laura L. Methot, *Recruitment and Selection in Canada*, (Toronto, Ontario: ITP Nelson, 1997), p. 329.

15. Victor M. Catano, Steven F. Cronshaw, Willi H. Wiesner, and Laura L. Methot, *Recruitment and Selection in Canada*, (Toronto, Ontario: ITP Nelson, 1997), p. 353; and Eugene Oscapella, Plunging Into the Gene Pool, OHS Canada, Vol. 13, No. 3 (April–May 1997), p. 54.

16. Richard M. Hodgetts, K. Galen Kroeck, and Michael E. Rock, *Managing Human Resources in Canada* (Toronto, Ontario: Dryden, 1995), pp. 171–74; David DeHaas, Morally Wrong, *OHS Canada*, Vol. 13, No. 6 (October–November 1997), p. 4; and Beverly Bell-Rowbotham and Kerri Ellis, "AIDS in the Workplace: Some Canadian Employers are Offering Innovative Programs to Employees Who Live, Work, and Cope with HIV/AIDS," *Benefits Canada*, Vol. 21, No. 5 (May 1997), pp. 69–74.

17. Lesley Young, "Workplace Violence: Beyond the Breaking Point," *OHS Canada*, Vol. 13, No. 7 (December 1998), pp. 38–40.

18. Vicki Gerson, "How Business is Dealing with the AIDS Epidemic," *Business & Health*, Vol. 15, No. 1 (January 1997), pp. 17–20; and "Employee Wins Right to Sue for HIV Test Disclosure," *Managing Office Technology*, Vol. 42, No. 3 (March 1997), pp. 8–9.

19. "Employee Wins Right to Sue for HIV Test Disclosure," *Managing Office Technology*, Vol. 42, No. 3 (March 1997), pp. 8–9.

20. Richard M. Hodgetts, K. Galen Kroeck, and Michael E. Rock, *Managing Human Resources in Canada* (Toronto, Ontario: Dryden, 1995), pp. 143.

21. Barbara Butler, "Alcohol and Drug Testing in Canada," *OHS Canada*, Vol. 13, No. 1 (January 1997), pp. 28–31; Substance Abuse in the Workplace, *HRfocus*, Vol. 74, No. 2 (February 1997), pp. 1–5;

22. *Ibid.*

23. Jane Easter Bahls, Drugs in the Workplace, *HRMagazine*, Vol. 43, No. 2 (February 1998), pp. 81–87; "Smoking Gun: Employers Have Been Joining the Battle to Help Employees Butt Out, but Are Their Efforts Worth the Time and Money?" *Benefits Canada*, Vol. 20, No. 10 (November 1996), p. 35–37; and Barbara Butler, Alcohol and Drug Testing in Canada, *OHS Canada*, Vol. 13, No. 1 (January 1997), pp. 28–31.

24. David DeHaas, "Finding the Boundaries," *OHS Canada*, Vol. 13, No. 1 (January–February 1997), p. 4; David Berman, Drug Testing? Just Say No, *Canadian Business*, Vol. 71, No. 4 (March 1998), pp. 24–25.

25. Eric Single, Lynda Robson, Xiaodi Xie, and Jurgen Rehm, "The Costs of Substance Abuse in Canada: Highlights of a Major Study of the Health, Social and Economic Costs Associated with the Use of Alcohol, Tobacco and Illicit Drugs," *Canadian Centre on Substance Abuse*, Ottawa, Ontario, 1997.

26. McCarthy Tetrault, "Alcohol and Drug Policies in Ontario: The Imperial Decision," 1996, Toronto, Ontario; Ontario Trucking Association, Alcohol and Drug Policy Reviewed Under the Human Rights Code, 1996, Toronto, Ontario; and Rick Bogacz, Imperial's Drug Policy Ruled Unlawful, *Journal of Addictive Research Foundation*, Vol. 25, No. 6 (November–December 1996), p. 4.

27. Jane Easter Bahls, "Dealing with Drugs: Keep it Legal," *HRMagazine*, Vol. 43, No. 4 (March 1998); and Victor M. Catano, Steven F. Cronshaw, Willi H. Wiesner, and Laura L. Methot, *Recruitment and Selection in Canada*, (Toronto, Ontario: ITP Nelson, 1997), p. 350–54.

28. Louisa Wah, Treatment vs. Termination, *Management Review*, Vol. 87, No. 4 (April 1998), p. 8.

29. Joseph G. Rosse, Deborah, F. Crown, and Howard D. Feldman, "Alternative Solutions to the Workplace Drug Problem," *Journal of Employment Counseling*, Vol. 27, No. 2 (June 1990), p. 62.

30. Dianna L. Stone and Debra A. Kotch, "Individuals' Attitudes Toward Organizational Drug Testing Policies and Practices," *Journal of Applied Psychology*, Vol. 74, No. 3 (June 1989), p. 521.

31. *Ibid*; and Micheal R. Carroll and Christina Heavrin, "Before You Drug Test," *HRMagazine*, Vol. 35, No. 6 (June 1990), p. 64–68.

32. Kevin R. Murphy, George C. Thornton III, and Kristen Prue, "Influence of Job Characteristics on the Acceptability of Employee Drug Testing," *Journal of Applied Psychology*, Vol. 76, No. 3 (June 1991), pp. 447–53.

33. "Did Whistle-Blower Blow His Job?" *Managing Office Technology*, Vol. 42, No. 12 (December 1997), pp. 10–11.

34. William Glenn, "Enforcement: Blowing the Whistle," *OHS Canada*, Vol. 13, No. 6 (October–November, 1997), pp. 14–16.

35. Jennie Walsh, "Tide to Turn in Favour of the Whistle-Blower," *People Management*, Vol. 3, No. 23 (November 1997), p. 9; and William Glenn, Enforcement: Blowing the Whistle, *OHS Canada*, Vol. 13, No. 6 (October–November, 1997), pp. 14–16.

36. Michael F. Rosenblum, "Security v. Privacy: An Emerging Employment Dilemma," *Employee Relations Law Journal*, Vol. 17, No. 1 (Summer 1991), pp. 81–101; and Alan Gahtan, Big Brother or Good Business, *WebWorld*, Vol. 2, No. 2 (March 1997), p. 24.

37. Peter Fitzpatrick, "CAW Union Says CN Spies on Workers," *Financial Post*, Vol. 91, No. 14 (April 6, 1998), p.10.

38. Kathleen Sibley, "The E-Mail Dilemma: To Spy or Not to Spy," *Computing Canada*, Vol.23, No. 7 (March 31, 1997), p. 14; and Alan Gahtan, "Big Brother or Good Business," *WebWorld*, Vol. 2, No. 2 (March 1997), p. 24.

39. Kathleen Sibley, "The E-Mail Dilemma: To Spy or Not to Spy," *Computing Canada*, Vol.23, No. 7 (March 31, 1997), p. 14.

40. Lee Smith, "What the Boss Knows About You," *Fortune*, Vol. 128, No. 3 (August 9, 1993), p. 89; Johanna Powell, "Keeping an Eye on the Workplace," *Financial Post*, Vol. 10, No. 36 (September 6, 1997), p. 24; and The Games We Play: Monitoring the Computer Habits of Your Employees, *Benefits Canada*, Vol. 21, No. 9 (October 1997), p. 11.

41. Kathleen Sibley, "The E-Mail Dilemma: To Spy or Not to Spy," *Computing Canada*, Vol. 23, No. 7 (March 31, 1997), p. 14.

42. William L. Kandel, "Employee Dishonesty and Workplace Security: Precautions Against Prevention," *Employer Relations Law Journal*, Vol. 16, No. 2 (Autumn 1990), pp. 217–31.

43. Jerry Collins, Rightful Dismissal: "What You Need to Know About Firing an Employee," *BC Business Magazine*, Vol. 26, No. 3 (March 1998), pp. 81–84; and Ellen E. Mole, *The Wrong Dismissal Handbook* (Toronto, Ontario: Butterworths, 1997).

44. Jerry Collins, "Rightful Dismissal: What You Need to Know About Firing an Employee," *BC Business Magazine*, Vol. 26, No. 3 (March 1998), pp. 81–84.

45. Losing Your Job, Public Legal Education Society of Nova Scotia, Halifax, Nova Scotia, 1997; Randall S. Echlin and Christine M. Thomlinson, Determining Reasonable Notice: An Exercise Which Involves More Art than Science, *Human Resources Professional*, Vol. 14, No. 4 (August–September 1997), pp. 10–11; and Randall S. Echlin, *Just Cause: The Law of Summary Dismissal in Canada* (Aurora, Ontario: Canada Law Books, 1992).

46. Jerry Collins, "Rightful Dismissal: What You Need to Know About Firing an Employee," *BC Business Magazine*, Vol. 26, No. 3 (March 1998), pp. 81–84; and *Losing Your Job*, Public Legal Education Society of Nova Scotia, Halifax, Nova Scotia, 1997.

47. *Cronk v. Canadian General Insurance Company*, Ontario Court of Appeal, September 21, 1995, Court File C19272.

48. Jerry Collins, "Rightful Dismissal: What You Need to Know About Firing an Employee," *BC Business Magazine*, Vol. 26, No. 3 (March 1998), pp. 81–84; and Ellen E. Mole, *The Wrong Dismissal Handbook* (Toronto, Ontario: Butterworths, 1997).

49. Termination Under the Employment Standards Act, Canadian Bar Association, British Columbia Branch, Vancouver, British Columbia, 1996.

50. Jerry Collins, "Rightful Dismissal: What You Need to Know About Firing an Employee," *BC Business Magazine*, Vol. 26, No. 3 (March 1998), pp. 81–84; and Losing Your Job, Public Legal Education Society of Nova Scotia, Halifax, Nova Scotia, 1997.

51. Jerry Collins, "Rightful Dismissal: What You Need to Know About Firing an Employee," *BC Business Magazine*, Vol. 26, No. 3 (March 1998), pp. 81–84.

52. Laura Ramsay, "Court Decision Lays Down the Law on Firings: Companies Can Expect to Pay Out Extra Compensation if Termination Procedure Ignores Employee's Vulnerability," *Financial Post*, Vol. 10, No. 45 (November 8, 1997), p. 41; and Michael Fitz James, Winnipeg Case Advances Law of Wrongful Dismissal, *Financial Post Daily*, Vol. 10, No. 155 (November 4, 1997), p. 16.

53. *Deildal v. Tod Mountain Ltd.*, (1997) S.C.C.A. No.338, 6 W.W.R. 239.

54. Howard A. Levitt, *The Law of Dismissal in Canada* (Aurora, Ontario: Canada Law Books, 1992).

55. *Farber v. Royal Trust Company*, (1986), (1997) 1S.C.R. 846, 145 D.L.R. (4th) 1.

56. Guy Dion, *Farber v. Royal Trust Company or the Notion of Veiled Dismissal*, Martineau Walker Bulletin, Vol. 2, No. 2 (Summer 1997), p. 7; James Carlisle, Supreme Court Sets Standard for Constructive Dismissal Suits, *Financial Post*, Vol. 10, No. 48 (April 29, 1997), p. 14; and Teresa Mitchell, SCC Defines Constructive Dismissal, *Law Now*, Vol. 22, No. 1 (August–September 1997), p. 5.

57. Wallace Wohlking, "Effective Discipline in Employee Relations," *Personnel Journal*, September 1975, pp. 491–492.

58. Martin Levy, "Discipline for Professional Employees," *Personnel Journal*, Vol. 69, No. 2 (December 1990), pp. 27–28.

59. Monica Belcourt and Phillip C. Wright, *Managing Performance Through Training and Development*, (Toronto, Ontario: ITP Nelson, 1996), pp. 154–55.

60. James G. Frierson, "How to Fire Without Getting Burned," *Personnel Journal*, Vol. 67, No. 9 (September 1990), pp. 44–48; Paul Falcone, "The Fundamentals of Progressive Discipline," *HRMagazine*, Vol. 42, No. 2 (February 1997), pp. 90–94; and Lauren M. Bernardi, Progressive Discipline: Effective Management Tool or Legal Trap? *Canadian Manager*, Vol. 21, No. 4 (Winter 1996), p. 9–10.

61. Walter Kiechel, "How to Discipline in the Modern Age," *Fortune*, Vol. 121, No. 10 (May 7, 1990), pp. 179–80.

62. Daniel P. Skarlicki and Robert Folger, Retaliation in the Workplace: The Roles of Distributive, Procedural, and Interactional Justice, *Journal of Applied Psychology*, Vol. 82, No. 3 (June 1997), pp. 434–43; and B.H. Sheppard, R.J. Lewicki, and J.W.

Minton, *Organizational Justice: The Search For Fairness in the Workplace*, (New York: Lexington Books, 1992).

63. It is true that two other disciplinary actions may be used—pay cuts or demotion—but they are rare. See for example: John P. Kohl and David B. Stephens, Is Demotion a Four Letter Word, *Business Horizons*, Vol. 33, No. 2 (March–April 1990), pp. 74–76.

64. Strict Code Urged for Fund Managers, *Canadian Press Newswire*, November 28, 1996.

65. Chimezie A.B. Osigweh YG and William R. Hutchinson, "To Punish or Not to Punish?" Managing Human Resources Through Positive Discipline, *Employee Relations*, Vol. 12, No. 3 (March 1990), pp. 27–32.

Chapter 5

1. Adapted from Sharon Lebrun, "People policies key to Sunoco turnaround," *Canadian HR Reporter* (February 10, 1997), pp. 1, 8.

2. See, for example, Max Messmer, "Strategic Staffing for the 90s," *Personnel Journal* (October 1990), p. 92.

3. Martin J. Plevel, Sandy Nells, Fred Lane, and Randall S. Schuler, "AT&T Global Business Communications Systems: Linking HR with Business Strategy," *Organizational Dynamics* (1994), pp. 59–71. See also, Randall S. Schuler, "Strategic Human Resources Management: Linking the People with the Strategic Needs of the Business," *Organizational Dynamics* (1992), pp. 18–32.

4. Messmer, p. 96.

5. As one reviewer correctly pointed out, strategic planning cannot be oversimplified to a two-page discussion. We agree but believe that a quick overview is in order. However, with respect to the strategic nature of business, for a comprehensive review of strategic planning we recommend, James Brian Quinn, Henry Mintzberg, and Robert M. James, *The Strategic Process* (Englewood Cliffs, N.J.: Prentice-Hall, 1988).

6. Taken from Bombardier's corporate profile (http://www.bombardier.com/ htmen/5_0.htm, (March14, 1998).

7. Goals that are established are a function of a number of factors. Such issues as the economy, government influences, market maturity, technological advances, company image, and location will factor into the analysis. See, for example, William J. Rothwell and Henry J. Sredl, *The ASTD Reference Guide to Professional Training Roles and Competencies*, Vol. 1 (Amherst, Mass.: HRD Press, 1992).

8. *Ibid.*, p. 95.

9. Joan E. Goodman, "Does Your HRS Speak English?" *Personnel Journal* (March 1990), p. 81.

10. See, for example, John Spirig, "HRIS," *Employment Relations Today*, Vol. 16, No. 54 (Winter 1989/1990), pp. 347–50.

11. Stephen G. Perry, "The PC Based HRIS," *Personnel Administrator* (February 1988), p. 60.

12. Even with fourth-generation languages, some glitches still exist. For example, generating reports still requires knowledge of computer lingo.

13. Jeffrey Knapp, "Trends in HR Management Systems," *Personnel* (April 1990), pp. 5657. See also John P. Polard, "HRIS: Time Is of the Essence," *Personnel Journal* (November 1990), pp. 42–43.

14. *Ibid.*, pp. 60–61.

15. Michael Meyer, Charles Fleming, Stryker McGuire, and Daniel McGinn, "Looking for Mr. Right," *Newsweek* (August 1, 1994), pp. 40–42.

16. See, for example, Michael Meyer, Stryker McQuire, Charles Fleming, Mark Millen, Andrew Murr, and Daniel McGuire, "Of Mice and Men," *Newsweek* (September 5, 1994), pp. 41–47; and "Disney Studios Chief Abruptly Resigns," *The Baltimore Sun* (August 25, 1994), p. 9D; 12D.

17. See *The Windsor Star*, March 16–18, 1998 and November 30, 1998.

18. Commerce Clearing House, "Sabbaticals: a Good Investment for McDonald's,"

Human Resources Management: Ideas and Trends (May 11, 1994), pp. 77, 84.

19. More detail on these resources can be found in *Making Career Sense of Labour Market Information*, Appendix A: Labour market resources essential for the practitioner (http://www.ceiss.org/randa/making/content/appen/appena/html), August 1998.

20. Richard Henderson, *Compensation Management: Rewarding Performance*, 6th ed. (Englewood Cliffs, N.J.: Prentice-Hall, 1994), p. 137.

21. For further detail, see Sidney A. Fine and Maury Getkate, *Benchmark Tasks for Job Analysis: A Guide for Functional Job Analysis (FJA) Scales*. Northvale, NJ: Lawrence Erlbaum Associates, 1995.

22. Henderson, p. 168.

23. See Wayne Cascio, *Applied Psychology in Personnel Management*, 4th ed. (Englewood Cliffs, N.J.: Prentice-Hall, 1991), p. 207; see also Stephanie K. Butler and Robert J. Harvey, "A Comparison of Holistic Verses Decomposed Rating of Position Analysis Questionnaire Work Dimensions," *Personnel Psychology*, Vol. 41, No. 4 (Winter 1988), pp. 761–71.

24. See, for example, Louis S. Richman, "America's Tough New Job Market," *Fortune* (February 24, 1992), pp. 52–61.

25. See, for example, John A. Byrne, "Why Downsizing Looks Different These Days," *Business Week* (October 19, 1994), p. 43.

26. Paul B. Carroll, "IBM Plans $3 Billion Charge and About 20,000 Jobs Cut," *The Wall Street Journal* (November 27, 1991), p. A–3.

27. Nancy Ursel and Marjorie Armstrong-Stassen, "The Impact of Layoff Announcements on Shareholders," *Relations Industrielles/Industrial Relations*, Vol. 50, No. 3 (1995), p. 638.

28. Marjorie Armstrong-Stassen, "Organizational Downsizing and Quality Management Programs: Can they coexist?" Paper presented at the Annual Meeting of the Academy of Management, Boston (August 1997); M. Cimons, "Federal Workers Cope, Yet Remain Resentful," *APA Monitor*, Vol. 27, No. 3 (1996), p. 9.

29. Armstrong-Stassen, op. cit.

30. John E. Gutknecht and J. Bernard Keys, "Mergers, Acquisitions, and Takeovers: Maintaining Morale of Survivors and Protecting Employees," *Academy of Management Executive*, Vol. 7, No. 3 (1993) p. 26.

31. John A. Byrne, "Why Downsizing Looks Different These Days," *Business Week* (October 19, 1994), p. 43.

32. Gayle MacDonald, "The Tough Task of Downsizing," *The Globe and Mail* (July 28, 1997), p. B11.

33. John A. Byrne, p. 43

34. Gayle MacDonald, p. B11.

35. This section is drawn from William Bridges, "The End of the Job," *Fortune* (September 19, 1994), pp. 62–74.

36. See John E. Gutknecht and J. Bernard Keys, pp. 26–35.

37. John A. Byrne, p. 43.

38. William Bridges, p. 72.

39. See, for example, Richard L. Bunning, "The Dynamics of Downsizing," *Personnel Journal* (September 1990), pp. 69–75.

40. See Dawn Walton, "Survey Focuses on Job Sharing," *The Globe and Mail* (June 10, 1997), p. B4.

41. Michael A. Verspej, "The New Workweek," *Industry Week* (November 1989), p. 14; Alan Deutschman, "Pioneers of New Balance," *Fortune* (May 20, 1991), p. 50.

42. Reported in Walton, op. cit.

43. Sharon Nelton, "A Flexible Style of Management," *Nation's Business* (December 1993), pp. 24–31, and Amy Saltzman, "Family Friendliness," *U.S. News and World Report* (February 22, 1993), pp. 59–66.

44. Jaclyn Fierman, "Are Companies Less Family Friendly?" *Fortune* (March 21, 1994), pp. 64–67.

45. Diane Bérard, "$\frac{1}{2} + \frac{1}{2} = 1$," *Commerce* (janvier 1997), pp. 20–24.

46. *Ibid.* p. 20.

47. Bunning, p. 73.

48. *Ibid.* see also Elaine M. Duffy, Richard M. O'Brien, William P. Brittian, and Stephen Cuthrell, "Behavioral Outplacement: A Shorter, Sweeter Approach," *Personnel* (March 1988), pp. 28–33.

49. Bunning, p. 73; see also Robert Volino, "Beyond Outplacement," *Information Week* (February 18, 1991), p. 24.

50. "Most Employers Laud Outplacement Firms, but Few Demur," *The Wall Street Journal* (October 1, 1991), p. A1.

51. Based on Ann Gibbon, "How the Bentalls Bowed Out," *The Globe and Mail* (September 17, 1996), p. B10.

Chapter 6

1. Based on Jeff Sallot, "Canada Wants a Few Good Women," *The Globe and Mail* (March 24, 1998), p. A3.

2. *Ibid.*

3. Andrew S. Bargerstock and Gerald Swanson, "Four Ways to Build Cooperative Recruitment Alliances," *HRMagazine* (March 1991), p. 49.

4. *Canadian Business* (May 1997), pp. 40–41.

5. Linda B. Robin, "Recruitment: Troubleshooting Recruitment Problems," *Personnel Journal* (September 1988), p. 94.

6. See, for example, Stephen J. Holoviak and David A. De Cenzo, contributing eds., "Service Industry Seeks Summer Help," *Audio Human Resource Report*, Vol. 1, No. 9 (October 1990), p. 5.

7. See, for example, Clyde J. Scott, "Recruitment: Employing a Private Employment Firm," *Personnel Journal* (September 1989), pp. 78–83.

8. See, for example, "The New Headhunters," *Business Week* (February 6, 1988), pp. 64–71.

9. *Ibid.*

10. Laura M. Graves, "College Recruitment: Removing Personal Bias from Selection Devices," *Personnel* (March 1989), p. 48.

11. http://www.careermosaic.com/cm/nortel/nortel7.htm

12. http://www.contraste.com

13. http://canada.careermosaic.com/

14. John Ross, "Effective Ways to Hire Contingent Personnel," *HRMagazine* (February 1991), pp. 52–53.

15. *Ibid.*, p. 53. See also Steve Bergsman, "Setting Up a Temporary Shop," *HRMagazine* (February 1990), pp. 46–49.

16. "The Temporary Help Business," *The Wall Street Journal* (February 25, 1992), p. A1.

17. Heather Hodgman, "The Next Office Temp Could be You," *Human Resources Professional* (May 1995), pp. 16–18.

18. See, for example, American Association of Retired Persons, *How to Recruit Older Workers* (Washington, D.C.: American Association of Retired Persons, 1993).

19. Lee Phillion and John R. Brugger, "Encore! Retirees Give Top Performance as Temporaries," *HRMagazine* (October 1994), pp. 74–77.

20. Reasons cited by the American Association of Retired Persons include the need to make money, to get health insurance coverage, to develop skills, to use their time more productively, to feel useful, to make new friends, to provide some structure to their daily lives, or to have a sense of achievement. See *How to Recruit Older Workers*, p. 27.

21. American Association of Retired Persons and the Society for Human Resource Management, *The Older Workforce: Recruitment and Retention* (Washington, D.C.: American Association of Retired Persons, 1993), p. 1.

22. Dorothy Lipovenko, "Job Bias Hits Older Workers: Study," *The Globe and Mail* (April 15, 1997), pp. A1, A10.

23. Caution is warranted regarding for whom an individual works. Generally, the employee is the responsibility of the leasing company, but under certain circumstances like longterm duration of the lease, the acquiring organization may be the employer of record, with the leasing company handling a variety of HRM associated paperwork. See Jane Easter Bahls, "Employees for Rent," *Nation's Business* (June 1991), p. 36.

24. Carole Howes, "Temping gains respect," *Calgary Herald* (March 29, 1997), p. H1.

25. Bargerstock and Swanson, p. 50.

26. Howes, p. 3

27. This story was influenced by an example in Arthur Sloan, *Personnel: Managing Human Resources* (Englewood Cliffs, N.J.: Prentice-Hall, 1983), p. 127.

28. James W. Thacker and R. Julian Cattaneo, *Survey of Personnel Practices in Canadian Organizations: A Report to Respondents.* Working paper W92-04, Faculty of Business Administration, University of Windsor, March 1993.

29. See discussion of this issue in Chapter 3.

30. See, for example, E. James Randall and Cindy H. Randall, "Review of Salesperson Selection Techniques and Criteria: A Managerial Approach," *International Journal of Research in Marketing*, Vol. 7, No. 2 (December 1990), pp. 81–95.

31. Thacker & Cattaneo, op. cit.

32. *Ibid.*

33. Sean A. Way and James W. Thacker, "Having a HR Manager in a Small Business: What difference Does it Make?" Paper presented at the annual meeting of the Administrative Sciences Association of Canada, Saskatoon, Sask. May 1998.

34. See, for example, "What Personnel Offices Really Stress in Hiring," *The Wall Street Journal* (March 6, 1991), p. A1.

35. "Responsible Background," ad in *HRMagazine* (February 1991), p. 50.

36. Adapted from Micelle Singletary, "Reference Gives Needed Wariness," *The Baltimore Sun* (October 28, 1991), pp. E1; E8; Commerce Clearing House, "Reference Checks/Lawsuits," *Human Resources Management: Ideas and Trends* (February 7, 1990), pp. 24–25; and "Management," *R&D Magazine* (April 1990), p. 95.

37. Margot Gibb-Clark, "Ruling Narrows Options for Drug Testing," *The Globe and Mail* (July 28, 1998), p. B11.

38. Colin Freeze, "TTC Rejects Drug-Test Proposal," *The Globe and Mail* (July 16, 1998), p. A8.

39. See, for example, Joyce Lain Kennedy and Dr. Darryl Laramore, Career Book (Lincolnwood, Ill.: National Textbook Company, 1988), Section 6; John L. Holland, Making Vocational Choices: *A Theory of Vocational Personalities and Work Environments*, 2nd ed. (Englewood Cliffs, N.J.: Prentice-Hall, 1985); John L. Holland, Gary D. Gottfredson, and Deborah Kimili Ogwawa, *Dictionary of Holland Occupational Codes: A Comprehensive CrossIndex of Holland's RIASEC Codes with 12,000 DOT Occupations* (Palo Alto, Calif.: Consulting Psychologists Press, Inc., 1982).

40. See David E. Bowen, Gerald E. Ledford, Jr., and Barry R. Nathan, "Hiring for the Organization, Not the Job," *Academy of Management Executive*, Vol. 5, No. 4 (November 1991), pp. 35–51.

41. See, for example, Sara L. Rynes, Robert D. Bretz, and Barry Gerhart, "The Importance of Recruitment in Job Choice: A Different Way of Looking," *Personnel Psychology*, Vol. 44, No. 3 (Autumn 1991), pp. 487–521.

42. See, for example, Charles A. O'Reilly III, David I. Caldwell, and Richard Mirable, "A Profile Comparison Approach to Person v. Job Fit: More Than a Mirage," in Jerry L. Wall and Lawrence R. Jauch, eds., *Academy of Management Best Papers Proceedings 1992*, Las Vegas, Nev. (August 9–12, 1992), pp. 237–42.

43. See, for example, Thomas F. Casey, "Making the Most of a Selection Interview," *Personnel* (September 1990), pp. 41–43.

44. See, for example, Wayne Cascio, *Applied Psychology in Personnel Management* (Englewood Cliffs, N.J.: Prentice–Hall, 1991), pp. 151–54.

45. See, for example, Richard Kern, "IQ Tests for Salesmen Make a Comeback," *Sales and Marketing* (April 1988), pp. 42–46.

46. A limitation of concurrent validity is the possibility of restricting the range of scores in testing current employees. This occurs because current employees may have been in the upper range of applicants. Those not hired were undesirable for some reason. Therefore, these scores theoretically should represent only the top portion of previous applicant scores.

47. A specific correlation coefficient for validation purposes is nearly impossible to pinpoint. There are many variables that will enter into the picture such as the sample size, the power of the test, and what is measured. However, for employment equity purposes, correlation coefficients must be indicative of a situation where the results are predictive of performance that is greater than a situation where chance alone dictated the outcomes.

48. Cut scores are determined through a set of mathematical formulae—namely, a regression analysis and the equation of a line. Any good introductory statistics text will show how these formulae operate.

49. Frank L. Schmidt and John E. Hunter, "Developing a General Solution to the Problem of Validity Generalization," *Journal of Applied Psychology*, Vol. 62, No. 5 (October 1977), pp. 529–39.

50. Lauress L. Wise, Jeffrey McHenry, and John P. Campbell, "Identifying Optimal Predictor Composites and Testing for Generalizability Across Jobs and Performance Factors," *Personnel Psychology*, Vol. 43, No. 2 (Summer 1990), pp. 355–66.

51. Stephen Cronshaw, *Industrial Psychology in Canada*, Waterloo Ont.: University of Waterloo Press, 1991.

52. This exercise was directly influenced by and adapted from Richard W. Beatty and Craig Eric Schneier, *Personnel Administration*. Reprinted with permission of Addison–Wesley Publishing Company, 1981.

Chapter 7

1. Based on Heather Scoffeld, "The Cult of the Cool Company," *The Globe and Mail* (April 15, 1998), p. B26.

2. See the Human Rights Code of Ontario, particularly subsection 10(1).

3. Jeff Sallot, "Canada Wants a Few Good Women," *The Globe and Mail* (March 24, 1998), p. A3.

4. Wayne F. Cascio, *Applied Psychology in Personnel Management* (Englewood Cliffs, N.J.: PrenticeHall, 1991), p. 265; see also Edson G. Hammer and Lawrence S. Kleinman, "Getting to Know You," *Personnel Administration*, Vol. 33 (May 1988), pp. 86–92.

5. Cascio, p. 265; See also Hammer and Kleinman, pp. 86–92.

6. See for example, Brooks Mitchell, "Bio Data: Using Employment Applications to Screen New Hires," *Cornell Hotel and Restaurant Administration Quarterly*, Vol. 29, No. 4 (February 1989), pp. 56–61.

7. Mitchell, p. 58. The seven specific items were not identified so that the competitive edge the hotel had in hiring practices would not be weakened.

8. Jack J. Kramer and Jane Close Conoley, supplement to *The Tenth Mental Measurements Yearbook* (Lincoln, Neb.: Buros Institute of Mental Measurements, 1990).

9. Fifty per cent in a 1992 study conducted by Thacker and Cattaneo (Survey of Personnel practices in Canadian Organizations: A Report to Respondents, Working paper W92-04, Faculty of Business Administration, University of Windsor, 1992) and 38 per cent in a follow-up survey conducted by Way and Thacker (Having a HR Manager in a Small Business: What Difference Does it Make, Paper presented at the Annual Meeting of the Administrative Studies Association of Canada, Saskatoon, 1998).

10. Thirty-two per cent in the 1992 Thacker and Cattaneo survey, 25 per cent in the Way and Thacker study.

11. Steve Mirsky, "Separate but EQ," *Scientific American* (April 1997); http://www.sciam.com/0497issue/0497scicit4.html

12. Mike Sadava, "Self-knowledge keyed to success," *The Edmonton Sunday Journal* (June 22, 1997). http://www.cadvision.com/Home_Pages/accounts/donaldja/Press970622.html and Paul Luke, "Emotional IQ: New Test Expected to be Big Measure of Job Applicants," *The Calgary Hearld* (January 11, 1997), p. G3.

13. http://www.erac.com/recruit/EQ.htm

14. For example, Steven F. Cronshaw, *Industrial Psychology in Canada* (Waterloo, ON: North Waterloo Academic Press, 1991), or Victor Catano, Steven A. Cronshaw, Willi Wiesner, Rick Hackett and Laura Methot, *Recruitment and Selection in Canada* (Toronto: ITP Nelson, 1997).

15. Windsor's Home Depot management was interviewed by Anil Risbud, April 1998.

16. See, for example, Walter C. Borman and Glenn L. Hallman, "Observation Accuracy for Assessors of Work Sample Performance: Consistency Across Task and Individual Differences Correlates," *Journal of Applied Psychology*, Vol. 76, No. 4 (February 1991), p. 11; see also Ivan T. Robertson and Sylvia Downs, "Work Sample Tests of Trainability: A Meta Analysis," *Journal of Applied Psychology*, Vol. 74, No. 3 (June 1989), pp. 402–10.

17. See, for example, Cynthia D. Fisher, Lyle F. Schoenfeldt, and James B. Shaw, *Human Resource Management* (Boston: Houghton Mifflin, 1990), p. 264.

18. See, for example, Jeffrey R. Schneider, and Neil Schmitt, "An Executive Approach to Understanding Assessment Center Dimension and Exercise Constructs," *Journal of Applied Psychology*, Vol. 77, No. 1 (February 1992), pp. 32–35.

19. Craig Russell, "Selecting Top Corporate Leaders: An Example of Biographical Information," *Journal of Management*, Vol. 16, No. 1 (March 1990), p. 74.

20. George Munchos III and Barbara McArthur, "Revisiting the Historical Use of Assessment Centers in Management Selection and Development," *Journal of Management Development*, Vol. 10, No. 1 (1991), p. 5.

21. Interview with George Shaffer, AT&T Assessment Director, March 12, 1992. Cost figures are not released according to company policy regarding proprietary information.

22. See, for example, Victor Dulewicz, "Improving Assessment Centers," *Personnel Management*, Vol. 23, No. 6 (June 1991), pp. 50–55.

23. David L. Kurtz, C. Patrick Flecnor, Louis E. Boon, and Virginia M. Rider, "CEOs: A Handwriting Analysis," *Business Horizons*, Vol. 32, No. 1 (January–February 1989), pp. 41–43.

24. Thacker and Cattaneo, op. Cit.

25. Terry Weber, "Scribblers Need Not Apply," *The Financial Post* (June 12, 1996), p. 14.

26. Thacker and Cattaneo, p. 21.

27. John F. Steiner, "Honesty Testing," *Business Forum*, Vol. 15, No. 2 (Spring 1990), p. 31.

28. Rom Zemke, "Do Honesty Tests Tell the Truth?" *Training*, Vol. 27, No. 10 (October 1990), pp. 7581; See also Robin Inwald, "Those Little White Lies of Honesty Vendors," *Personnel*, Vol. 67, No. 6 (June 1990), p. 52.

29. Jerry Beilinson, "Applicant Screening Methods: Under Surveillance," *Personnel*, Vol. 67, No. 12 (December 1990), p. 3.

30. Zemke, p. 75.

31. Vignettes based on Tom Washington, "Selling Yourself in Job Interviews," *National Business Employment Weekly* (Spring/Summer 1993), p. 30.

32. For a discussion on fit and its appropriateness to the interviewing process, see "The Right Fit," *Small Business Reports* (April 1993), p. 28.

33. See, for example, A.I. Huffcutt and W. Arthur, Jr., "Hunter and Hunter (1984) Revisited: Interview Validity for Entry-Level Jobs," *Journal of Applied Psychology* (April 1994), pp. 184–90; M.A. McDaniel, D.L. Whetzel, F.L. Schmidt, and S.D. Maurer, "The Validity of Employment Interviews: A Comprehensive Review and MetaAnalysis," *Journal of Applied Psychology* (August 1994), p. 599–616; and Herbert George Baker and Morris S. Spier, "The Employment Interview: Guaranteed Improvement in Reliability," *Public Personnel Management* (Spring 1990), pp. 85–87.

34. Thacker and Cattaneo; Way and Thacker.

35. Robert C. Dipboye, *Selection Interviews: Process Perspectives* (Cincinnati: Southwestern Publishing Co., 1992), pp. 6–9.

36. Adapted from Baker and Spier, p. 87; and Dipboye, Chapter 1.

37. Edward C. Webster, *Decision Making in the Employment Interview* (Montreal: Industrial Relations Centre, McGill University, 1964).

38. Dipboye, p. 8; and Baker and Spier, p. 87.

39. For a more detailed discussion of impression management, see Amy L. Kristof and Cynthia Kay Stevens, "Applicant Impression Management Tactics: Effects on Interviewer Evaluations and Interview Outcomes," *Academy of Management Best Papers Proceedings*, Dorothy P. Moore, ed. (August 14–17, 1994), pp. 127–31.

40. Reported in Robert E. Carlson, Paul W. Thayer, Eugene C. Mayfield, and Donald A. Peterson, "Improvements in the Selection Interview," *Personnel Journal* (April 1971), p. 272.

41. Dipboye, p. 201.

42. Michael P. Cronin, "Try Taping Those Interviews," *Inc.* (September 1994), p. 120.

43. See, for example, Wayne F. Cascio, *Applied Psychology in Personnel Management*, 4th ed. (Englewood Cliffs, N.J.: Prentice-Hall, 1991), p. 271.

44. Way and Thacker, op. cit.

45. *Ibid.*

46. See, for example, Cascio, p. 273; A. Phillips and R.L. Dipboye, "Correlation Tests of Predictions from a Process Model of the Interview," *Journal of Applied Psychology*, Vol. 74 (1989), pp. 41–52; M. Ronald Buckley and Robert W. Edner, "B.M. Springbett and the Notion of the 'Snap Decision' in the Interview," *Journal of Management*, Vol. 14, No. 1 (March 1988), pp. 59–67.

47. David S. Cohen, "Behaviour-based interviewing," *Human Resources Professional* (April/May 1997), pp. 29–36.

48. Way and Thacker, op. cit.

49. See, for example, Dipboye, pp. 39–45.

50. Michael W. Mercer, "Turnover: Reducing the Costs," *Personnel*, Vol. 65, No. 12 (December 1988), p. 36.

51. See, for example, Bruce M. Meglino, Angelo S. DeNisi, Stuart A. Youngblood, and Kevin J. Williams, "Effects of Realistic Job Previews," *Journal of Applied Psychology*, Vol. 79, No. 2 (May 1988), pp. 259–66.

52. See, for example, Robert J. Vanderberg and Vida Scarpello, "The Matching Model: An Examination of the Processes Underlying Realistic Previews," *Journal of Applied Psychology*, Vol. 75, No. 1 (February 1990), pp. 60–67.

53. See, for example, Gregory Service, "Keeping Out of Court," *Security Management Supplement* (July 1990), p. 11A.

54. See, for example, Michael A. McDaniel, "Biographical Constructs for Predicting Employee Suitability," *Journal of Applied Psychology*, Vol. 74, No. 6 (December 1989), pp. 964–70; and Michael Tadman, "The Past Predicts the Future," *Security Management*, Vol. 33, No. 7 (July 1989), pp. 57–61.

55. Commerce Clearing House, *Human Resources Management: Ideas and Trends* (May 17, 1992), p. 85.

56. Norman D. Bates, "Understanding the Liability of Negligent Hiring," *Security Management Supplement* (July 1990), p. 7A.

57. William T. Hill, "Getting Help from the Outside," *Security Management Supplement* (July 1990), p. 15A.

58. *Ibid.*

59. Commerce Clearing House, pp. 439–40.

60. Hazel Porter, "Police to Screen PSBGM Job Applicants," *The Gazette*, Montreal (June 27, 1997), p. A5.

61. "Michigan Man Charged as Fake Doctor," *Medserv* (http://www.medserv.dk/health/0698/11/story3.htm)

62. Madhavi Acharya, "23% of Job Seekers Lie on Résumés, Firm Finds," *The Toronto Star* (July 21, 1998), p. B4.

63. Dale E. Yeatts, Martha Hipskind, and Debra Barnes, "Lessons Learned from Self-Managed Work Teams," *Business Horizons* (July/August 1994), pp. 11–18.

64. "How to Form Hiring Teams," *Personnel Journal* (August 1994), pp. 14–17.

65. Based on several conversations between Cattaneo and Templer and members of Ford's Windsor Engine Plant management.

66. See, for example, Alexander Mikalachki, "Creating a Winning Team," *Business Quarterly* (Summer 1994), pp. 14–22.

67. "How to Form Hiring Teams," p. 14.

68. Based on Roy J. Lewicki, Donald D. Bowen, Douglas T. Hall, and Francine S. Hall, *Experiences in Management and Organization Behavior*, 3rd ed. (New York, NY: John Wiley & Sons, Inc., 1988), pp. 268–70. Used with permission.

69. This case is based on the article, Michael P. Cronin and Stephanie Gruner, "Hiring: The Devil You Know?" *Inc.* (April 1994), p. 109.

Chapter 8

1. This experience still brings an embarrassed flush to one of the authors as we write this.

2. Janet Wong, "Integrating New Executives: More Time at the Beginning Means Less Headache at the End," *Human Resources Professional* (December/January 1997/98), pp. 29–30

3. See, for example, Zandy B. Leibowitz, Nancy K. Schlossberg, and Jane E. Shore, "Stopping the Revolving Door," *Training and Development Journal*, Vol. 45, No. 2 (February 1991), pp. 43–50.

4. *Ibid.*

5. See, for example, Jitendra M. Mishra, and Pam Strait, "Employee Orientation: The Key to Lasting and Productive Results, Health *Care Supervisor* (March 1993), pp. 19–29; Henry L. Tosi, *Organizational Behavior and Management: A Contingency Approach* (Boston, Mass.: PWS Kent Publishing, 1990), pp. 233–35; also John Van Maanen, "People Processing: Strategies of Organizational Socialization," in Tosi's *Organizational Behavior and Management*, pp. 65–66.

6. See, for instance, R. L. Falcione and C. E. Wilson, "Socialization Process in Organizations," in G. M. Goldhar and G. A. Barnett (eds.) *Handbook of Organizational Communication* (Norwood, N.J.: Ablex Publishing, 1988), pp. 151–70; N. J. Allen and J.P. Meyer, "Organizational Socialization Tactics: A Longitudinal Analysis of Links to Newcomers' Commitment and Role Orientation," *Academy of Management Journal* (December 1990), pp. 847–58; V. D. Miller and F. M. Jablin, "Information Seeking During Organizational Entry: Influences, Tactics, and a Model of Process," *Academy of Management Review* (January 1991), pp. 92–120; and J. A. Chatam, "Matching People and Organizations: Selection and Socialization in Public Accounting Firms," *Administrative Science Quarterly* (September 1991), pp. 459–84.

7. Shirley A. Hopkins and Willie E. Hopkins, "Organizational Productivity 2000: A Work Force Perspective," *SAM Advanced Management Journal* (Autumn 1991), pp. 44–48.

8. See, for example, Timothy J. Fogarty, "Organizational Socialization in Accounting Firms: A Theoretical Framework and Agenda for Future Research," *Accounting, Organizations, and Society* (February 1992), p. 129–50.

9. Coy A. Jones and William R. Crandall, "Determining the Source of Voluntary Employee Turnover," *SAM Advanced Management Journal* (March 22, 1991), p. 16.

10. John Van Maanen and Edgar H. Schein, "Career Development," In J. Richard Hackman and J. Lloyd Suttle (eds.), *Improving Life at Work* (Santa Monica, Calif.: Goodyear, 1977), pp. 58–62; see also J. P. Wanous, A. E. Reichers, and S. D. Malik, "Organizational Socialization and Group Development," *Academy of Management Review*, Vol. 9 (1992), pp. 670–83.

11. D. C. Feldman, "The Multiple Socialization of Organization Members," *Academy of Management Review* (April 1981), p. 310.

12. For a thorough discussion of these issues, see Jennifer A. Chatman, "Matching People and Organizations: Selection and Socialization in Public Accounting Firms," *Administrative Science Quarterly* (September 1991), pp. 459–85.

13. For example, see Lisa K. Gundry, "Fitting Into Technical Organizations: The Socialization of Newcomer Engineers," *IEEE Transactions of Engineering Management* (November 1993), p. 335.

14. For an interesting viewpoint on selection fit and socialization, see Isaiah O. Ugboro, "Loyalty, Value Congruency, and Affective Organizational Commitment: An Empirical Study," *Mid-American Journal of Business* (Fall 1993), pp. 29–37.

15. *Ibid.*, p. 29.

16. "Youth Equity at Bank of Montreal," *Canadian HR Reporter* (October 20, 1997), p. 12.

17. Rabindra N. Kanungo and Jay A. Conger, "Promoting Altruism as a Corporate Goal," Executive (August 1993), pp. 37–48; Elizabeth Wolfe Morrison, "Longitudinal Study of the Effects of Information Seeking on Newcomer Socialization," *Journal of Applied Psychology* (April 1993), pp. 173–83; and Laurie K. Lewis and David R. Seinbold, "Innovation Modification During Intraorganizational Adoption, *Academy of Management Review* (April 1993), pp. 322–54.

18. Christopher Guly, "Tongue-Lashing: Starbucks Employee Lands in Hot Water over Jewelry", *The Globe and Mail: Report on Business Magazine* (August 1997), p. 6.

19. Cheri Ostroff and Steve W. J. Kozlowski, "Organizational Socialization as a Learning Process: The Role of Information Acquisition," *Personnel Psychology* (Winter 1992), pp. 849–74.

20. Tayla N. Bauer and Stephen G. Green, "Effect of Newcomer Involvement in Work-Related Activities: A Longitudinal Study of Socialization," *Journal of Applied Psychology* (April 1994), pp. 211–23.

21. See, for example, H. Eugene Baker III and Daniel C. Feldman, "Linking Organizational Socialization Tactics with Corporate Human Resource Management Strategies," *Human Resource Management Review*, Vol. 1, No. 3 (Fall 1991), pp. 193–202.

22. John Van Maanen and Edgar H. Schein, "Toward a Theory of Organizational Socialization," *In Research in Organizational Behavior*, ed. Barry M. Staw (Greenwich, Conn.: JAI Press, 1979), p. 210; see also "New Employee Orientation: Ensuring A Smooth Transition," *Small Business Report*, Vol. 13, No. 7 (July 1988), pp. 40–43.

23. Van Maanen, pp. 80–81.

24. Thomas J. Peters and Robert H. Waterman, *In Search of Excellence: Lessons from America's Best Run Companies* (New York: Harper & Row, 1982).

25. Adapted from Richard F. Federico, "Six Ways to Solve the Orientation Blues," *HR Magazine*, Vol. 36, No. 5 (May 1991), p. 69.

26. Andre Nelson, "New Employee Orientation: Are They Really Worthwhile?" *Supervision*, Vol. 51, No. 11 (November 1990), p. 6.

27. Allan Halcrow, "A Day in the Life of Levi Strauss," *Personnel Journal*, Vol. 67, No. 11 (November 1988), p. 14.

28. See, for example, Joseph F. McKenna, "Training: Welcome Aboard," *Industry Week*, Vol. 238, No. 21 (November 6, 1989), pp. 31–38.

29. Wong, pp. 29–31.

30. Marsha Kurman, "Customer Relations: The Personnel Angle," *Personnel*, Vol. 64, No. 9 (September 1987), pp. 38–40.

31. Paula Kulig, "When Training Meets Performance Support," *Canadian HR Reporter* (March 23, 1998), pp. 16–18.

32. Linda J. Bennett, "Why Benefits Communications Is Your Business," *Supervisory Management* (June 1993), p. 10.

33. Debra R. Comer, "Peers as Providers," *Personnel Administrator*, Vol. 34, No. 5 (May 1989), p. 84.

34. Sharon Lebrun, "Workers Teach Workers at Labatt Safety Day," *Canadian HR Reporter* (December 16, 1997) p. 20.

35. Paul Kulig, p. 18

36. Case written by Carolyn Baarda as part of an assignment for Professor Andrew Templer, University of Windsor, 1990.

Chapter 9

1. Jamie Harrison, "Stentor Learning Lab Provides Bottom-line Boost to Firm," *Canadian HR Reporter* (February 23, 1998), pp. 1,12.

2. Grant Buckler, "Canada's Stentor Alliance scaled Down," *Newsbytes News Network* (September 18, 1998) http://cnnfn.com/digitaljam/newsbytes/1118298.html.

3. Ronald Henkoff, "Companies that Train Best," *Fortune* (March 22, 1993), p. 62; and Commerce Clearing House, "Quality Challenge for HR: Linking Training to Quality Program Goals," *1994 SHRM/CCH Survey* (June 22, 1994), p. 1.

4. See, for example, Richard G. Zalman, "The Basics of In-House Skills Training," *HRMagazine* (February 1991), pp. 7478.

5. A case can also be built that development can also occur for a current job where, for example, a new skill is required because one will have greater responsibility. Nonetheless, we will differentiate these two primarily by time frames.

6. Kjersti Powell, "Learning Begins with Broad Perspective", *Learning for the Workplace* (May 19, 1997), p. L20.

7. Marilyn B. Gilbert and Thomas F. Gilbert, "What Skinner Gave Us," *Training*, Vol. 28, No. 9 (September 1991), pp. 42–48; see also B.F. Skinner, *Beyond Freedom and Dignity* (New York: Knopf, 1971).

8. Stephen P. Robbins, *Organizational Behavior: Concepts, Controversy, and Applications*, 6th ed. (Englewood Cliffs, N.J.: Prentice-Hall, 1993), pp. 111–12.

9. See, for example, J. Stewart Black and Mark E. Mendenhall, "The U-Curve Adjustment Hypothesis Revisited: A Review and Theoretical Framework," *Journal of International Business Studies*, Vol. 22, No. 2 (2nd Quarter, 1991), pp. 225–47; Linda Klebe Trevino and Stuart A. Youngblood, "Bad Apples in Bad Barrels: A Causal Analysis of Ethical DecisionMaking Behavior," *Journal of Applied Psychology*, Vol. 75, No. 4 (August 1990), pp. 378–85; Albert Bandura, *Social Learning Theory* (Englewood Cliffs, N.J.: Prentice-Hall, 1977).

10. See, for example, Howard J. Klein, "An Integrated Control Theory Model of Work Motivation," *Academy of Management Review*, Vol. 14, No. 2 (April 1989), pp. 150–72.

11. Norman Trainor, "Taking Lessons from the Royal Bank", *Canadian HR Reporter*. (March 9, 1998), p. 8.

12. Beth Rogers, "The Making of a Highly Skilled Worker," *HRMagazine* (July 1994), p. 62.

13. Lenore Buton, "Apprenticeship: The Learn-While-You-Earn Option," *Human Resources Professional* (February/March 1998), p. 25.

14. Leslie A. Bryan, Jr., "An Ounce of Prevention for Workplace Accidents," *Training and Development Journal*, Vol. 44, No. 7 (July 1990), p. 101.

15. William J. Rothwell and H. C. Kazanas, "Planned OJT Is Productive OJT," *Training and Development Journal*, Vol. 44, No. 10 (October 1990), pp. 53–56.

16. *Ibid.*, p. 55, Bryan, Jr., p. 102.

17. Richard P. Lookatch, "How to Talk to a Talking Head," *Training and Development Journal*, Vol. 44, No. 9 (September 1990), pp. 63–65.

18. Trainor, p. 8.

19. See, for example, Gene Bylinsky, "The Marvels of Virtual Reality," *Fortune* (June 3, 1991), p. 138.

20. Ken Mark, "Virtual Training—At Your Pace in Your Place," *Human Resources Professional* (February/March 1998), pp. 15–17.

21. Bob Filipczak, "Distance Teamwork," *Training* (April 1994), p. 71; Randall Johnson, "Alternative Methods: Technology, Good Client Relations Help Training to Thrive," *Training* (July 1992), p. B05.

22. *Ibid.*

23. Jane Pickard, "Training on Another Plane," *Personnel Management* (August 1992), pp. 45–47.

24. See for example, Michael Emery and Margaret Schubert, "A Trainer's Guide to Videoconferencing," *Training* (June 1993), pp. 5964; Bob Filipczak, "Distance Teamwork," *Training* (April 1994), p. 71.

25. *Virtual Conference on Telework*, scheduled for late 1998. Coordinator: Nava Fliskin, MCB Press, London, England.

26. See, for example, "Survival Training for Employees," *ABC World News Tonight/American Agenda* (July 21, 1993).

27. Johanna Powell, "How to Train for Business as Battle", *The Financial Post* (July 10, 1997), pp. 11–12.

28. Commerce Clearing House, "Should Your Company Encourage Mentoring?" *Human Resources Management: Ideas and Trends* (July 20, 1994), p. 122.

29. Sue Shellenbarger, "Corporate America Grooms Women Execs," *Working Woman* (October 1993), pp. 13–14.

30. Doug Burn, "Learning Organizations: A New Role for HR," *Human Resources Professional* (December/January 1997/8), pp. 21–23.

31. See, for example, James A. Wilson and Nancy S. Elman, "Organizational Benefits of Mentoring," *Academy of Management Executive*, Vol. 4, No. 4 (November 1990), pp. 88–94.

32. Michelle Neely Martinez, *HRMagazine*, Vol. 36, No. 6 (June 1991), p. 46.

33. George F. Dreher and Ronald A. Ash, "A Comparative Study of Mentoring Among Men and Women in Managerial, Professional, and Technical Positions," *Journal of Applied Psychology*, Vol. 75, No. 5 (October 1990), pp. 539–46.

34. For an excellent discussion of these issues, see William Whitely, Thomas W. Dougherty, and George F. Dreher, "Relationship of Career Mentoring and Socioeconomic Origin to Managers' and Professionals' Early Career Progress," *Academy of Management Journal*, Vol. 34, No. 5 (June 1991), pp. 331–51.

35. Daniel B. Turban and Thomas W. Dougherty, "Protégé Personality, Mentoring, and Career Success," in Jerry L. Wall and Lawrence R. Jauch (eds.) *Academy of Management Best Papers Proceedings 1992*, Las Vegas, Nevada (August 9–12, 1992), p. 419.

36. For a discussion of mentoring and minorities, see David A. Thomas, "The Impact of Race on Managers' Experiences of Developmental Relationships: An Intra Organizational Study," *Journal of Organizational Behavior*, Vol. 11, No. 6 (November 1990), pp. 479–92. For an opposing view of mentoring and women/race issues, see Belle Rose Ragins and Terri A. Scandura, "Gender and the Termination of Mentoring Relationships, *Academy of Management Best Papers Proceedings*, Dorothy P. Moore, ed., (August 1417, 1994), pp. 361–65.

37. Michael D. Esposito, "Affirmative Action and the Staffing Demands of the 1990s," *Journal of Compensation and Benefits*, Vol. 6, No. 4 (January February 1991), p. 41.

38. Cheryl McCortie, "Mentoring Young Achievers," *Black Enterprise*, Vol. 21, No. 11 (June 1991), p. 336.

39. See, for example, Stephen C. Bushardt, Cherie Elaine Fretwell, and B. J. Holdnak, "The Mentor/Protégé Relationship: A Biological Perspective," *Human Relations*, Vol. 44, No. 6 (June 1991), pp. 619–39.

40. See for example, Belle Rose Ragins and Terri A. Scandura, "Gender Differences in Expected Outcomes of Mentoring Relationships," *Academy of Management Journal* (1994), pp. 957–71.

41. John Lorinc, "The Mentor Gap—Older Men Guiding Younger Women: The Perils and Payoffs," *Canadian Business*, Vol. 63, No. 9 (September 1990), p. 93.

42. See Ronald J. Burke and Carol A. McKeen, "Mentoring in Organizations: Implications for Women," *Journal of Business Ethics*, Vol. 9, No. 4 (April May 1990), pp. 317–32.

43. Cy Charney, "Peer Mentoring: Using In-House Teams, Giving them Tools to Learn on their Own." *Canadian HR Reporter* (May 19, 1997), pp. L32–33.

44. David North, "Personal Business: Have Your Coach Call my Coach," *Canadian Business* (June 1997), p. 205.

45. Jerry Wisinski, "A Logical Approach to a Difficult Employee," *HR Focus* (January 1992), p. 9.

46. *Ibid.*

47. Gerald D. Cook, "Employee Counseling Session," *Supervision* (August 1989), p. 3.

48. Kurt Lewin, *Field Theory in Social Science* (New York: Harper & Row, 1951).

49. R. Wayne Pace, Phillip C. Smith, and Gordon E. Mills, *Human Resource Development* (Englewood Cliffs, N.J.: Prentice-Hall, 1991), p. 131.

50. *Ibid.*

51. Scott Kerr, "Managing Change Successfully," *Leadership and Organization Development Journal*, Vol. 12, No. 1 (January 1991), p. 2.

52. E. J. Muller, "How to Be an Agent of Change," *Distribution*, Vol. 90, No. 13 (1991), p. 24.

53. Elizabeth Church, "Circus Bends Over Backward for its People," *Globe and Mail, Report on Business* (April 21, 1997), p. B7.

54. Andrew Templer and Norm Solomon, "Factors Affecting Affecting the Successful Implementation of New Informational Technology in a Professional Union: A Research Note, "*Industrial Relations/Relations Industrielles* (Vol. 47, No. 2, 1992), pp. 325–32.

55. Sharon Lebrun, "T&D Becoming More Strategic," *Canadian HR Reporter* (February 10, 1997), pp. 1–2.

56. Monica Belcourt and Alan Saks, "Benchmarking Best Training Practices", *Human Resources Professional* (December/January 1997/1998), pp. 33–35.

57. Jacquelyn S. DeMatteo, Gregory H. Dobbins, and Kyle M. Lundby, "The Effects of Accountability on Training Effectiveness," *Academy of Management Best Papers Proceedings*, Dorothy P. Moore, ed. (August 417, 1994), p. 122; Ronald Henkoff, "Companies that Train Best," p. 62.

58. Ronald Henkoff, "Companies that Train Best," p. 62.

59. Sharon Lebrun, p. 2.

60. Doug Burn, "To Outsource Training or not to Outsource Training, That is the Question," *Human Resources Professional* (February/March 1998), p. 18.

61. Sean Way and James Thacker, "The HR Managers Impact on Human Resource Issues in a Small Business," Unpublished Paper (January 1998), p. 6.

62. See, for example, Joseph W. Weiss and Stanley Bloom, "Managing in China: Expatriate Experiences in Training," *Business Horizons*, Vol. 33, No. 3 (May–June 1990), pp. 23–29.

63. S. Ronen, "Training the International Assignee," in I.L. Goldstein & Associates (eds.), *Training and Development in Organizations* (San Francisco: JosseyBass, 1989), pp. 417–53.

64. From an undated Bristol-Myers handout.

65. M. Mendenhall and G. Oddou teaching note in "The Overseas Assignment: A Practical Look," *International Human Resource Management*, (Boston: PWS-Kent Publishing, 1991), pp. 259–69.

66. Adapted from Cy Charney, "Peer Mentoring: Using In-House Teams, Giving them Tools to Learn on their Own," *Canadian HR Reporter* (May 19, 1997), pp. L32–33.

Chapter 10

1. Sean Silcoff, "Go East, Young Man," *Canadian Business* (February, 1997), pp. 34–35.

2. Douglas T. Hall, *Careers in Organizations* (Santa Monica, Calif.: Goodyear Publishing, 1976); J. Van Maanen and E.H. Schein, "Career Development," in J.R. Hackman and J.L. Suttle (eds.), *Improving Life at Work: Behavioral Sciences Approaches to Organizational Change* (Santa Monica, Calif.: Goodyear Publishing, 1977), pp. 341–55.

3. Jeffrey H. Greenhaus, *Career Management* (New York: Dryden Press, 1987), p. 6.

4. See, for instance, E. P. Cook, "1991 Annual Review: Practice and Research in Career Counseling and Development, 1990," *Career Development Quarterly* (February 1991), pp. 99–131.

5. Paula Kulig, "Long Live Employee Loyalty", *Canadian HR Reporter* (April 20, 1998), p. 12.

6. Alanna Mitchell, "He's a Trucker, She Types—1990's Just Like the 50's," *The Globe and Mail* (March 18, 1998), pp. 1, 6.

7. Andrew Duffy, "21st Century Belongs to Women," *The Windsor Star* (April 15, 1998), pp. A1–A2.

8. Justin Martin, "Employees Are Fighting Back," *Fortune* (August 8, 1994), p. 12.

9. D. Yankelovich and J. Immerwahl, "The Emergence of Expressivism Will Revolutionize the Contract Between Workers and Employers," *Personnel Administrator* (December 1983), pp. 34–39, 114.

10. B. B. Grossman and R. J. Blitzer, "Choreographing Careers," *Training and Development* (November 1991), pp. 68–89; R. Chanick, "Career Growth for Baby Boomers," *Personnel Journal* (January 1992), pp. 40–44.

11. Julie Barlow, "Different Strokes," *The Globe and Mail Report on Business Magazine* (April 1997), pp. 88–92.

12. Van Maanen and Schein.

13. *Ibid.*

14. Hall.

15. Van Maanen and Schein.

16. M. London and S. A. Stumpf, *Managing Careers* (Reading, Mass.: Addison Wesley, 1982); A. S. Miner, "Organizational Evolution and the Social Ecology of Jobs," *American Sociological Review* (Fall 1991), pp. 772–85.

17. Cook, p. 99.

18. Greenhaus, p. 6.

19. See, for example, Donald E. Super, *The Psychology of Careers* (New York: Harper & Row, 1957); Edgar Schein, *Career Dynamics: Matching Individual and Organizational Needs* (Reading, Mass.: Addison Wesley, 1978); Daniel J. Levinson, C.N. Darrow, E.B. Klein, M.H. Levinson, and B. McKee, *A Man's Life* (New York: Knopf, 1978).

20. Andrew Templer and Tupper Cawsey, "Re-thinking the Contribution of HRM to Competitive Advantage in an Era of Portfolio Careers," *ASAC Annual Conference* (St. Johns, Nfld., June 1997).

21. Jaclyn Fierman, "Beating the MidLife Career Crisis," *Fortune* (September 6, 1993), p. 51.

22. Frederic M. Hudson, "When Careers Turn Stale," *Next* (Lakewood, Calif.: American Association of Retired Persons, 1994), p. 3.

23. Adele Scheele, "Moving Over Instead of Up, *Working Woman* (November 1993), pp. 75–76.

24. Marina Strauss and Paul Waldie, "Eaton's Chief Quits as Losses Deepen," *The Globe and Mail* (November 17, 1998), pp. A1, A7.

25. Kathy Blair, "Bay Ex-President Pursues Active 'Retirement'," *Canadian HR Reporter* (October 20, 1997), pp. 1–2.

26. D. E. Super, "A Lifespan Life Space Approach to Career Development," *Journal of Vocational Behavior*, Vol. 16 (Spring 1980), pp. 282–98; E. P. Cook, pp. 99–131; and M. Arthur, *Career Theory Handbook* (Englewood Cliffs, N.J.: Prentice-Hall, 1991); Louis S. Richman, "The New Worker Elite," *Fortune* (August 22, 1994), pp. 56–66.

27. John Holland, *Making Vocational Choices*, 2d ed. (Englewood Cliffs, N.J.: Prentice-Hall, 1985).

28. Julie Barlow, p. 89.

29. Ken Mark, "Virtual Training—At your Pace, in your Space," *Human Resources Professional* (February/March 1998), pp. 15–17.

30. Cheryl Granrose and James Portwood, "Matching Individual Career Plans and Organizational Career Plans and Organizational Career Management," *Academy of Management Journal*, Vol. 30, No. 4 (1987), pp. 699–720.

31. Trudy L. Somers, "A Study of Stress in Work–Family Relationships and Roles," Working paper, Towson State University, 1992; C. A. Higgins, L. E. Duxburey, and R. H. Irving, "Work–Family Conflict in the Dual–Career Family," *Organizational Behavior and Human Decision Processes* (January 1992), pp. 51–75.

32. N. Gupta and G. D. Jenkins, Jr., "Dual-Career Couples: Stress, Stressors, Strains, and Strategies," in T. A. Beehr and R. S. Bhagat (eds.), *Human Stress and Cognition in Organizations: An Integrated Perspective* (New York: John Wiley, 1985), pp. 141–75; Higgins, Duxburey, and Irving, pp. 51–75.

33. See, for example, Susan Caminiti, "What Happens to Laid-Off Managers," *Fortune* (June 13, 1994), pp. 68–78.

34. Employee Development Centres, "Variation on an Employability ," *Canadian HR Reporter: Special Edition on Learning for the Workplace* (May 19, 1997), p. L31.

35. H. P. Weisman and M. S. Leibman, "Corporate Scale Down: What Comes Next?" *HRMagazine* (August 1991), pp. 33–37; L. M. Laarman, "Cut Compensation Costs to Avoid Lay offs," *Employment Relations Today* (February 1991), pp. 137–42.

36. Jamie Harrison, "Greying Employees Feeling the Pinch", *Canadian HR Reporter* (February 9, 1998), p. 9.

37. See www.careerbridge.com.

38. Vinay Menon, "Internet Offers Job Seekers Chance to Surf to New Life," *The Toronto Star* (April 17, 1998), p. D3.

39. D. E. Berlow and D. T. Hall, "The Socialization of Managers: Effects of Expectations on Performance," *Administrative Science Quarterly*, 11 (1966), pp. 207–23; D.W. Bray, R.J. Campbell, and D.L. Grant, *Formative Years in Business: A Long-Term AT & T Study on Managerial Lives* (New York: John Wiley, 1974).

40. A. Cohen, "Career Stage as a Moderator of the Relationship Between Organizational Commitment and Its Outcomes: A Meta Analysis," *Journal of Vocational Psychology* (March 1991), pp. 253–68; T. W. Lee, S. J. Ashford, J. P. Walsh, and R. T. Mowday, "Commitment Propensity, Organizational Commitment, and Voluntary Turnover: A Longitudinal Study of Organizational Entry Processes," *Journal of Management* (January 1991), pp. 15–32.

41. *Ibid.*, pp. 85–86; J. P. Galassi, R. K. Croce, G. A. Martin, R. M. James, Jr., and R. L. Wallace, "Client Preferences and Anticipations in Career Counseling: A Preliminary Investigation," *Journal of Counseling Psychology* (January 1992), pp. 46–55.

42. James W. Walker, "Let's Get Realistic About Career Paths," *Human Resource Management* (Fall 1976), p. 6. F. Blau and M. Ferber, "Career Plans and Expectations of Young Women and Men," *Journal of Human Resources*, Vol. 26, No. 4 (April 1991), pp. 581–607.

43. Chris Knight, "Career Development: Part of Maritime Life," *Canadian HR Reporter* (July 14, 1997), pp. 10–11.

44. M. Knowles, *Andragogy in Action* (San Francisco: Jossey-Bass), 1984.

45. The three-step process in competencybased training includes an evaluation step to determine beginning skill levels, a training event to present only the skills which were assessed as deficient, and a validation or posttraining evaluation step.

46. H. G. Kaufman, *Obsolescence and Professional Career Development* (New York: AMACOM, 1974); J. R. DeLuca, "Strategic Career Management in NonGrowing Volatile Business Environments," *Human Resource Planning* (January 1988), pp. 49–61; B. Nussbaum, "A Career Survival Kit," *Business Week* (October 7, 1991), pp. 98–104; A. Gates, "Career Management: Hell No! I Won't Plateau," *Working Woman* (October 1990), pp. 100–05.

47. R. E. Hill and Trudy L. Somers, *The Transformation from Technical Professional to Technical Manager: Special Career Managerial Concerns* (Ann Arbor, Mich.: The Industrial Development Dominion), 1988.

48. Kathy Kolbe, "Avoiding a Mentor Mismatch," *Working Woman* (October 1994), pp. 66–69.

49. Kathleen O'Brien, "Grooming Women for the Top," *Working Woman* (July 1994), pp. 23–24.

50. For another view of mentoring and careers, see Hal Lancaster, "Managing Your Career: A Good Executive Is a Matter of Nature, Not Nurture," *The Wall Street Journal* (November 1, 1994), p. B1.

51. This categorization comes from G.A. Ford and Gordon L. Lippitt, *A Life Planning Workbook for Guidance in Planning and Personal Goal Setting* (Fairfax, Va.: NTL Learning Resources Corporation, 1972).

Chapter 11

1. Jennifer Myers, "Pizza Perks and Profit Sharing: To Keep Your Staff Happy and Productive, Try a Healthy Dose of Challenge, Reward and Fun," *PROFIT* (June 1996), pp. 93–94.

2. For a classic discussion, see Victor Vroom, *Work and Motivation* (New York: Wiley, 1964). A more recent discussion of the topic can be found in Rabindra N. Kanungo and Manuel Mendonca, *Compensation: Effective Reward Management*, 2nd ed. (Toronto: Wiley, 1997.)

3. Based on David Berman, "Carving up Cuddy," *Canadian Business* (March 27, 1998), pp. 39–44.

4. Our model is based on the expectancy theory of motivation as developed by Victor Vroom. For a complete review of expectancy theory, see Victor Vroom, *Work and Motivation* (New York: John Wiley, 1964).

5. Abraham Maslow's motivation theory is called "the hierarchy of needs." See Abraham Maslow, *Motivation and Personality* (New York: Harper & Row, 1954).

6. Douglas McGregor's motivation theory is called "Theory X; Theory Y." See Douglas McGregor, *The Human Side of Enterprise* (New York: McGrawHill, 1960).

7. Frederick Herzberg's motivation theory is called "the motivation-hygiene theory." See Frederick Herzberg, *Work and the Nature of Man* (New York: World Publishing, 1966).

8. David McClelland's motivation theory is called "the achievement, affiliation, and power motives theory." See David C. McClelland, *The Achieving Society* (New York: Van Nostrand Reinhold, 1961).

9. J. Stacey Adams's motivation theory is called "equity theory." See J. Stacey Adams, "Inequity in Social Exchanges," in Leonard Berkowitz (ed.), *Advances in Experimental Social Psychology*, Vol. 2 (New York: Academic Press, 1965), pp. 267–300.

10. Vroom, op. cit.

11. Myers.

12. "What Do Workers Want?" Inc., (June 1994), p. 12; Commerce Clearing House, "Employers: Employees Want Personal Satisfaction," *Human Resources Management: Ideas and Trends* (November 10, 1993), p. 181; Nancy K. Austin, "Motivating Employees Without Pay or Promotion," *Working Woman* (November 1994), pp. 17–18.

13. The model of motivation we present for HRM is directly influenced by two of the more contemporary theories of motivation—equity theory and expectancy theory.

14. Paul Simak, "Eureka! At Canada's Most Successful Mining Company, Even the Clerks Get . . . a Little Gold Dust," *Canadian Business* (June 1996), pp. 66–69.

15. Nadi Chiala and Suzanne Landry, "Compensation: Costs and opportunities," *CMA Magazine* (May 1997), pp. 23–27.

16. See, for example, David A. De Cenzo and Stephen J. Holoviak, *Employee Benefits* (Englewood Cliffs, N.J.: Prentice-Hall, 1990), Chapter 11.

17. Kenneth M. Dawson and Sheryl N. Dawson, "How to Motivate Your Employees," *HRMagazine* (April 1990), p. 79.

18. J. Richard Hackman and Greg R. Oldham, "Development of the Job Diagnostic Survey," *Journal of Applied Psychology* (April 1975), pp. 159–70.

19. See, for example, Shaul Fox and Gerald Feldman, "Attention State and Critical Psychological States as Mediators Return Job Dimension and Job Outcomes," *Human Relations*, Vol. 41, No. 3 (March 1988), pp. 229–45.

20. J. Richard Hackman, "Work Design," in *Improving Life at Work*, J.R. Hackman and J.L. Suttle (eds.) (Santa Monica, Calif.: Goodyear, 1977), p. 129.

21. J. Barton Cunningham and Ted Eberle, "A Guide to Job Enrichment and Redesign," *Personnel*, Vol. 67, No. 2 (February 1990), p. 57.

22. Based on input from Windsor Engine Plant management to course projects in courses taught by Drs. Cattaneo and Templer.

23. See, for example, "Job Characteristics Theory of Work Redesign," in John B. Miner, *Theories of Organizational Behavior* (Hinsdale, Ill.: Dryden Press, 1980), pp. 231–66; B. T. Loher, R. A. Noe, N. L. Moeller, and M.P. Fitzgerald, "A Metaanalysis of the Relation of Job Characteristics to Job Satisfaction," *Journal of Applied Psychology* (May 1985), pp. 280–89; M. G. Evans and D. A. Ondrack, "The Motivational Potential of Jobs: Is a Multiplicative Model Really Necessary?" in S. L. McShane (ed.), *Organization Behaviour*, ASAC Conference Proceedings, Vol. 9, Part 5, Halifax, Nova

Scotia (1988), pp. 31–39. It is important to note, however, that while these studies generally support the JCM, there still exists some debate about the dimensions used and the overlap of some of the dimensions. For an overview of that debate, see Y. Fried and G. R. Ferris, "The Dimensionality of Job Characteristics: Some Neglected Issues," *Journal of Applied Psychology* (August 1986), pp. 419–26.

24. Hackman, pp. 132–33.

25. See, for example, Cunningham and Eberle, p. 57.

26. See, for example, Norm Alster, "What Flexible Workers Can Do," *Fortune* (February 13, 1989), pp. 62–66.

27. Stephen J. Havolic, "Quality of Work Life and Human Resource Outcomes," *Industrial Relations* (Fall 1991), pp. 469–79.

28. Mitchell W. Fields and James W. Thacker, "Influence on Quality of Work Life on Company and Union Commitment," *Academy of Management Journal* (June 1992), p. 448.

29. Timothy D. Schellhardt, "Few Employers Give Job Rotation a Whirl," *The Wall Street Journal* (July 21, 1992), p. B1.

30. Also see Trisha McCallum, "Telecommuting: Managing Work-at-Home Personnel", *Human Resources Professional* (April/May 1997), pp. 45–49.

31. Alan Deutschman, "Pioneers of New Balance," *Fortune* (May 20, 1991) pp. 50–55.

32. Michael A. Verspej, "The New Workweek," *Industry Week* (Nov. 6, 1989) pp. 12–14.

33. "Flexible Work Arrangements—Gaining Ground," *Applied Research Bulletin*, Vol. 3 No. 1 http://www.hrdcdrhc.gc.ca/hrdc/corp/stratpol/arbsite/publish/bulletin/vol3n1/v3n1c3e.html.

34. David A. Ralston, "How Flextime Eases Work/Family Tension," *Personnel* (August 1990), pp. 45–48.

35. Helen Paris, "Balancing Work and Family Responsibilities: Canadian Employer and Employee Viewpoints," *Human Resource Planning*, Vol. 13, No. 2 (February 1990), p. 153.

36. Sun Life of Canada Actuarial Vacancies, http://www.infotechgroup.com/www.graduatelink.com/sun-life-of-canada.html, August 1998.

37. "Workplace Flexibilities: Flexible Work Arrangements," Royal Bank Financial Group (http://www.royalbank.com/english/hr/world/workplace.html), August 1998.

38. "Flexible Work Arrangements – Gaining Ground"

39. Margot Gibb-Clark, "Phase-Ins Offer Taste of Retirement," *The Globe and Mail* (August 20, 1998), p. B9.

40. Julie Cohen Mason, "Flexing More than Muscle: Employees Want Time on Their Side," *Management Review* (March 1992), pp. 78.

41. *Ibid.*, p. 8.

42. Adapted from Jeff Davidson, "Motivation Employees," *Restaurant Business* (May 20, 1990), p. 61.

43. Bob Nelson, "Appreciate Employees to Get the Best Results," *Canadian Manager* (Summer 1996), p. 11.

44. Charles Jaffe, "Management by Fun," *Nation's Business*, Vol. 78, No. 1 (January 1990), pp. 58–60.

45. See, for example, Louis S. Richman, "The New Worker Elite," *Fortune* (August 22, 1994), pp. 56–66; Ronald Henkoff, "Finding, Training, and Keeping the Best Service Workers," *Fortune* (October 3, 1994), pp. 110–22.

46. Myers.

47. Richman.

48. Based on Jerald Greenberg, "Employee Theft as a Reaction to Under Payment Inequity: The Hidden Cost of Pay Cuts," *Journal of Applied Psychology*, Vol. 75, No. 5 (October 1990), pp. 561–68.

1. This is an account of an event that has occurred in a fictitious company. Its sole purpose is to demonstrate the difficulties that can arise when performance evaluations are mishandled.

2. Bruce Livesey, "Provide and conquer: Husky Injection Molding Systems Is a Rarity," *The Globe and Mail, Report on Business Magazine* (March 1997), pp. 34–37.

3. See, for example, Joseph P. McCarthy, "A New Focus On Achievement," *Personnel Journal,* Vol. 70, No. 2 (February 1991), pp. 74–76.

4. Mike Deblieux, "Performance Reviews Support Quest for Quality," *H.R. Focus,* Vol. 68, No. 11 (November 1991), pp. 34.

5. See, for example, Jeffrey A. Bradt, "Pay for Impact," *Personnel Journal,* Vol. 70, No. 5 (May 1991), pp. 76–79; Kathleen A. Guinn and Roberta J. Corona, "Putting a Price on Performance," *Personnel Journal,* Vol. 70, No. 5 (May 1991), pp. 72–77.

6. James M. Jenks, "Do Your Performance Appraisals Boost Productivity?" *Management Review,* Vol. 80, No. 6 (June 1991), p. 45.

7. Sandra O'Neal and Madonna Palladino, "Revamp Ineffective Performance Management," *Personnel Journal* (February 1992), pp. 93–102.

8. Robert J. Sahl, "Design Effective Performance Appraisals," *Personnel Journal* (October 1990), pp. 56–57.

9. Mary Mavis, "Painless Performance Evaluations," *Training and Development* (October 1994), p. 40; Herbert H. Meyer, "A Solution to the Performance Appraisal Feedback Enigma," *Academy of Management Executive* (February 1991), p. 68.

10. See, for example, Maria Castanda and Afsaneh Nahavandi, "Link of Manager Behavior to Supervisory Performance Rating and Subordinate Satisfaction," *Group and Organizational Studies* (December 1991), pp. 357–66.

11. *Ibid.*

12. Gary English, "Tuning Up for Performance Management," *Training and Development Journal* (April 1991), pp. 56–60.

13. Donald W. Myers, Wallace R. Johnston, and C. Glenn Pearce, "The Role of Human Interaction Theory in Developing Models of Performance Appraisal Feedback," *SAM Advanced Management Journal* (Summer 1991), p. 28.

14. Barry R. Nathan, Allan M. Mohrman, Jr., and John Milliman, "Interpersonal Relations as a Context for the Effects of Appraisal Interviews on Performance and Satisfaction: A Longitudinal Study," *Academy of Management Journal* (June 1991), pp. 352–63.

15. Robert J. Nobile, "The Law of Performance Appraisals," *Personnel* (January 1991), p. 7.

16. Larry L. Axline, "Ethical Considerations of Performance Appraisals," *Management Review* (March 1994), p. 62.

17. Richard Henderson, *Compensation Management: Rewarding Performance,* 6th ed. (Englewood Cliffs, N.J.: Prentice-Hall, 1994), p. 433.

18. Ahron Tziner and Richard Kopelman, "Effects of Rating Format on Goal-Setting: A Field Experiment," *Journal of Applied Psychology* (May 1988), p. 323.

19. See, for example, Dennis M. Daley, "Great Expectations, or a Tale of Two Systems: Employee Attitudes Toward Graphic Rating Scales and MBO-Based Performance Appraisal," *Public Administration Quarterly* (Summer 1991), pp. 188–201.

20. Henderson, 1994, p. 433.

21. Mary L. Tenopyr, "Artificial Reliability of ForcedChoice Scales," *Journal of Applied Psychology* (November 1988), pp. 749–51.

22. Kevin R. Murphy, "Criterion Issues in Performance Appraisal Research: Behavioral Accuracy Versus Classification Accuracy," *Organizational Behavior and Human Decision Processes* (October 1991), pp. 45–50.

23. H. John Bernardin and Richard W. Beatty, *Performance Appraisal: Assessing Human Behavior at Work* (Boston: Kent Publishing, 1984), p. 86.

24. James W. Thacker and R. Julian Cattaneo, "Survey of Personnel Practices in Canadian Organizations: A Summary Report to Respondents." Working Paper No. W92-04, Faculty of Business Administration, University of Windsor, March 1993.

25. Sean A. Way and James W. Thacker, "Strategic Human Resources Management Can Provide a Sustained Competitive Advantage: Are Canadian Organizations Prepared?" Paper presented at the annual meeting of Administrative Sciences Association of Canada, Saskatoon, May 1998.

26. See, for example, Kevin R. Murphy and Virginia A. Pardaffy, "Bias in Behaviorally Anchored Rating Scales: Global or Scale Specific," *Journal of Applied Psychology* (April 1989), pp. 343–46; Michael J. Piotrowski, Janet L. Barnes-Farrell, and Francine H. Esris, "Behaviorally Anchored Bias: A Replication and Extension of Murphy and Constans," *Journal of Applied Psychology* (October 1988), pp. 827–28.

27. *Ibid.*

28. For an overview of MBO, see Peter F. Drucker, *The Practice of Management* (New York: Harper & Row, 1954).

29. Thacker & Cattaneo, Way and Thacker. In the latter survey, 51 per cent of companies reported using Work Planning and Review (WP&R), considered by many to be a variation on MBO.

30. Henderson, p. 428–29.

31. See, for example, William H. Bommer, Jonathan L. Johnson, and Gregory A. Rich, "An Extension of Heneman's Meta-Analysis of Objective and Subjective Measures of Performance," *Academy of Management Best Papers Proceedings*, Dorothy P. Moore (ed.), (August 14–17, 1994), pp. 112–16.

32. Bernardin and Beatty, p. 140.

33. *Ibid.*, p. 270.

34. *Ibid.*, p. 139.

35. David Kipuis, Kari Price, Stewart Schmidt and Christopher Stitt, "Why do I Like Thee: Is it Your Performance or My Orders?" *Journal of Applied Psychology* (June 1981), p. 324.

36. Ibid., pp. 324–28.

37. See, for example, Sandy J. Wayne and K. Michele Kacmar, "The Effects of Impressive Management on the Performance Appraisal Process," *Organization Behavior and Human Decision Processes* (February 1991), pp. 7088. Sandy Wayne and Robert Liden, "Effects of Impression Management on Performance Ratings: A Longitudinal Study,"*Academy of Management Journal* (February 1995), Vol. 38, No. 1, pp. 232–260.

38. See, for example, Bernardin and Beatty, pp. 271–76.

39. See, for example, Hannah R. Rothstein, "Interrater Reliability of Job Performance Ratings: Growth to Asymptote Level with Increasing Opportunity to Observe," *Journal of Applied Psychology* (June 1990), pp. 322–27; Mary D. Zalesny, "Rater Confidence and Social Influence in Performance Appraisals," *Journal of Applied Psychology* (June 1990), pp. 274–89.

40. Ted H. Shore, Lynn McFarlane, and George C. Thornton III, "Construct Validity of Self and Peer Evaluations of Performance Dimensions in an Assessment Center," *Journal of Applied Psychology* (February 1992), pp. 42–54.

41. Catherine M. Petrini, "UpsideDown Performance Appraisals," *Training and Development Journal* (July 1991), pp. 15–22.

42. See for example, Martin L. Ramsey and Howard Lehto, "The Power of Peer Review," *Training and Development* (July 1994), pp. 38–41.

43. Jiing-Lib Farh, Albert A. Cannella, and Arthur G. Bedian, "Peer Ratings: The Impact of Purpose on Rating Quality Acceptance," *Group and Organization Studies* (December 1991), pp. 367–86.

44. Marilyn Moats Kennedy, "Where Teams Drop the Ball," Across the Board (September 1993), p. 9.

45. Irene H. Buhalo, "You Sign My Report Card-I'll Sign Yours," *Personnel* (May 1991), p. 23.

46. Jerry Baumgartner, "Give It to Me Straight," *Training and Development* (July 1994), pp. 49–51.

47. John F. Milliman, Robert A. Zawacki, Carol Norman, Lynda Powell, and Jay Kirksey, "Companies Evaluate Employees from All Perspectives," *Personnel Journal* (November 1994), p. 99.

48. "Companies Where Employees Rate Executives," *Fortune* (December 27, 1993), p. 128, Ann Fisher, "Hey, Hotshot, Take a Good Look at Yourself," *Fortune* (November 11, 1996).

49. Examples can be found at such Web sites as //www.insoc.co.uk, //www.zigonperf.com/performance.htm, //www.lookgood.demon.co.uk/mva.html.

50. Brian O'Reilly, "360 Degree Feedback Can Change Your Life," *Fortune* (October 17, 1994), p. 96.

51. *Ibid.*

52. See for example, Dianne Nilsen, "Self-Observer Rating Discrepancies: Once an Overrater, Always an Over-rater," *Human Resource Management* (Fall 1993), pp. 265–82; Walter W. Turnow, "Perceptions or Reality: Is Multi-Perspective Measurement a Means or an End?" *Human Resource Management* (Fall 1993), pp. 221–30; Manuel London and Richard W. Beatty, "360-Degree Feedback as a Competitive Advantage," *Human Resource Management* (Fall 1993), pp. 353–73; and Robert E. Kaplan, "360-Degree Feedback PLUS: Boosting the Power of CoWorker Rating for Executives," *Human Resource Management* (Fall 1993), pp. 299–315.

53. Roland Nagel, "The 360-degree feedback avalanche," http://www.ipma-hr.org/global/360au.html (June 1998), and the Iconoclast, "An uneasy look at 360-degree feedback," *HR Monthly* (June 1996).

54. W.C. Borman, "The Rating of Individuals in Organizations: An Alternative Approach," *Organizational Behavior and Human Performance* (August 1974), pp. 105–24.

55. Beverly Dugan, "Effects of Assessor Training on Information Use," *Journal of Applied Psychology* (November 1988), pp. 743 48; Clinton O. Longenecker, Dennis A. Gioia, and Henry P. Sims, Jr., "Behind the Mask: The Politics of Employee Appraisal," *Academy of Management Executive* (August 1987), p. 191.

56. Charles Lee, "Poor Performance Appraisals Do More Harm than Good," *Personnel Journal* (September 1989), p. 91.

57. *Ibid.*

58. Peter J. Dowling, Randall S. Schuler, and Denice E. Welch, *International Dimensions of Human Resource Management*, 2d ed. (Belmont, Calif.: Wadsworth, 1994), pp. 10320; G. Oddou and M. Mendenhall, "Expatriate Performance Appraisal: Problems and Solutions," in M. Mendenhall and G. Oddou, eds., *Readings and Cases in International Human Resource Management* (Boston: PWS Kent Publishing, 1991), pp. 364–74.

59. Oddou and Mendenhall, p. 366.

60. J.S. Solomon, "Employee Relations Soviet Style," *Personnel Administrator*, Vol. 30, No. 10 (October 1985), pp. 79–86.

61. Dowling, Schuler, and Welch, pp. 113–15; Oddou and Mendenhall, pp. 372–74.

62. *Ibid.*

63. Case adapted from Brian O'Reilly, p. 100.

Chapter 13

1. Tricia McCallum, "The compensation catwalk," *Human Resources Professional* (June/July 1998), pp. 21–25, and Sean Silcoff, "Secrets of a best seller," *Canadian Business* (June 26/July 10, 1998), pp. 91–93.

2. Susan Sonnesyn Brooks, "Noncash Ways to Compensate Employees," *HRMagazine* (April 1994), p. 43.

3. Stephenie Overman, "How Hot Is Your Reward System?" *HRMagazine* (November 1994), p. 51.

4. Clifford J. Mottaz, "Determinants of Organizational Commitment," *Human Relations* (June 1988), pp. 467–82.

5. Philip A. Rudolph and Brian H. Kleiner, "The Art of Motivating Employees," *Journal of Managerial Psychology* (May 1989), pp. i–iv.

6. The authors are indebted to Professor Gloria Miller of St Francis Xavier University for this example.

7. Status of Women Canada, *Economic Gender Equality Indicators*. Ottawa: 1997.

8. "Pay Equity," *Executive Female* (March-April 1991), p. 9.

9. Shawn McCarthy, "Pay equity bill at least $3-billion," *The Globe and Mail* (July 30, 1998), pp. A1, A3; Kathryn May, "PSAC wins pay equity battle," *The Windsor Star* (July 30, 1998), pp. A1, A3.

10. *The Globe and Mail* (September 2, 1998), p.A1

11. Daniel Leblanc, "Bell Pay-equity Ruling a Setback for Ottawa," The Globe and Mail (November 18, 1998), pp. A1, A14.

12. Richard Henderson, *Compensation Management: Rewarding Performance*, 6th ed. (Englewood Cliffs, N.J.: Prentice-Hall, 1994), p. 223.

13. *Ibid.*

14. *Ibid.*

15. John D. McMullen and Cynthia G. Brondi, "Job Evaluation Generate the Numbers," *Personnel Journal* (November 1986), p. 62.

16. A discussion of the Factor Evaluation System (FES) can be found in Rabindra N. Kanungo and Manuel Mendonca, *Compensation: Effective Reward Management* (Toronto: Wiley, 2nd ed., 19997), pp. 257–259.

17. See, for example, Henderson, p. 266.

18. David W. Belcher, *Compensation Administration* (Englewood Cliffs, N.J.: Prentice-Hall, 1974), p. 157.

19. Richard D. Arvey, "Sex Bias in Job Evaluation Procedures," *Personnel Psychology* (Summer 1986), pp. 316–18.

20. For a thorough mathematical discussion of various methods of determining the pay structure, see Henderson, Chapter 11, "Design a Base Pay Structure."

21. Henderson, pp. 315–16.

22. Jack C. O'Brien and Robert A. Zawacki, "Salary Surveys: Are They Worth the Effort?" *Personnel* (October 1985), pp. 70–73.

23. See the URL, http://www.kpmg.ca/abc/vl/surveys/salary.htm.

24. See, for example, Rosabeth Moss Kanter, "The Attack on Pay," *Harvard Business Review* (March-April 1987), pp. 60–67.

25. Stephen H. Applebaum and Barbara T. Shapiro, "Pay for Performance: Implementation of Individual and Group Plans," *Journal of Management Development* (July 1991) pp. 30–40.

26. Cheryl Stepan, "Bottom-line compensation," *The Montreal Gazette* (September 22, 1997), p. C14.

27. Luis R. Gomez-Mejia and David B. Balkin, "Effectiveness of Individual and Aggregate Compensation Strategies," *Industrial Relations* (1989), pp. 431–45.

28. Kate Beatty, "Pay and Benefits Break Away from Tradition," *HRMagazine* (November 1994), p. 64.

29. *Ibid.*, p. 20.

30. Hoyt Doyel and Thomas Riley, "Incentive Plans," *Management Review* (March 1987), pp. 36–37; and K. Dow Scott, Steven E. Markham, and Richard W. Robers, "Compensation," *Personnel Journal* (September 1987), pp. 114–15.

31. Darcy Toms and Jan Bowland, "Pay for performance: An incentive pay program," *Directions in Transportation* (Summer 1995),
http://www.kpmg.ca/trans/vl/d95sum5.htm.

32. Thomas B. Wilson, "Group Incentives: Are You Ready?" *Journal of Compensation and Benefits* (November 1990), pp. 25–29.

33. Cheryl Stepan, op. cit.

34. Henderson, p. 461.

35. *Ibid.*, p. 462.

36. *Ibid.*, pp. 455–58.

37. *Ibid.*, p. 457; and Charles R. Gowen III, "Gainsharing Programs: An Overview of History and Research," *Journal of Organizational Behavior Management* (1990), pp. 77–99.

38. "Union and Management are partners in 'Heart'", *Scanlon News* (Summer 1997).

39. Roger T. Kaufman, "The Effects of IMPROSHARE on Productivity," *Industrial and Labor Relations Review* (January 1992), p. 311.

40. *Ibid.*

41. *Ibid.*, pp. 319–22.

42. "Profile: Pittsburgh Township, On. Manages Costs," http://www.cyberus.ca/~ppp/profiles/pittsbur.html.

43. "WCB and Compensation Employees' Union reach tentative agreement on new contract," http://newswire.ca/releases/December1997/11/c3194.html.

44. See John Greenwald, "Workers: Rules and Rewards," *Time* (April 15, 1991), pp. 42–43.

45. Spragins, p. 79.

46. Towers Perrin, "Competency-Based Pay: Paying People, Not Jobs," presented at The National Conference on Using Competency-Based Tools and Applications to Drive Organizational Performance (Boston, Mass.: November 2–4, 1994), p. 8.

47. Marc E. Lattoni, and Andrée Mercier, "Developing Competency-Based Organizations and Pay Systems," *Focus: A Review of Human Resource Management Issues in Canada* (Calgary, Canada: Towers Perrin, Summer 1994), p. 18.

48. *Ibid.*, pp. 1–4.

49. Sandra O'Neal, "Competencies: The DNA of the Corporation," *ACA Journal* (Winter 1993/94), pp. 6–12.

50. Lattoni and Mercier, p. 7.

51. Aileen Baird and Real St-Amand, *Trust Within the Organization, Part 2-Building* Trust. Public Service Commission of Canada, October 1995.

52. See http://www.oil.ca/~twalker/Bio.html.

53. See Howard Gleckman, Sandra Atchison, Tim Smart and John A. Byrne, "Bonus pay: Buzzword or Bonanza?" *Business Week* (November 14,1994), pp. 62–64.

54. Henderson, p. 407.

55. See Stephen P. Robbins and David A. De Cenzo, *Fundamentals of Management* (Englewood Cliffs, N.J.: Prentice-Hall, 1995), p. 262.

56. "Fifty CEOs who made between $27.4-million and $2.0-million," *The Globe and Mail* (April 18, 1998), p. B6.

57. John Partridge, "Options spell pay dirt," *The Globe and Mail* (April 18, 1998), pp. B1, B6, B7.

58. John Partridge, op. cit., and Sophie Cousineau and Gilles Lajoie, "Les salaires des PDB," *Commerce* (July 1997), pp. 24–35.

59. "Canadian CEOs earn 37% of what their U.S. counterparts do", *Canadian HR Reporter* (June 2, 1997), p. 9.

60. "Pay, perks and performance," *Profit* (December–January 1998), pp. 26–27.

61. Rob Norton, "Making Sense of the Boss's Pay," *Fortune* (October 3, 1994), p. 36.

62. "Canadian CEOs earn 37% of what their U.S. counterparts do".

63. John A. Byrne and Lori Bongiorno, "CEO Pay: Ready for Take-off: Is anybody worth this much?" *Business Week* (April 24, 1995), p. 88.

64. "Fifty CEOs..."

65. David Berman, "Do they deserve it?" *Canadian Business* (September 27, 1997), pp. 31–33.

66. KMPG, Executive Compensation Practices in the TSE 300 Companies 1997. May be downloaded from KMPG's Web site, http://www.kpmg.ca/abc/vl/surveys/TSE300.htm.

67. Current tax laws require tax to be paid on that amount of premium paid on life insurance over $50,000. Furthermore, Section 89 of the IRS Tax Code requires that those perks offered to the higher paid employees, that are not given to the average employee, to be considered taxable income to the recipient.

68. See, for example, Felix Kessler, "Executive Perks Under Fire," *Fortune* (July 22, 1985), pp. 29–30.

69. Richard Waters, "Stock-based incentives may soon face first real test," *The Financial Post* (January 6, 1998), p. 22.

70. For further reading on international compensation, see Peter J. Dowling, Randall S. Schuler, and Denice E. Welch, *International Dimensions of Human Resource Management*, 2nd ed, Belmont, Calif.: Wadsworth, 1994), Chapter 6.

71. Anne V. Corey, "Ensuring Strength in Each Country: A Challenge for Corporate HQ Global HR Executives," *Human Resource Planning*, Vol. 14, No. 1 (1991), pp. 1–8.

72. Calvin Reynolds, "Compensation of Overseas Personnel," in *Handbook of Human Resources Administration*, 2d ed., Joseph J. Famularo, (ed.) (New York: McGraw-Hill, 1986), pp. 56–2, 56–3.

73. Based on Bruce Livesey, "Provide and conquer: Husky Injection Molding Systems is a rarity," The Globe and Mail *Report on Business Magazine* (March 1997), pp. 34–37, and Nadi Chlala and Suzanne Landry, "Compensation: costs and opportunities," *CMA Magazine* (May 1997), pp. 23–27.

Chapter 14

1. "The Sounds of Satisfaction," *Salute! Celebrating the Progressive Employer*, pp. 12–15.

2. A more detailed coverage of this subject can be seen in Rabindra N. Kanungo and Manuel Mendonca, *Compensation: Effective Reward Management*, 2nd edition (Toronto: Wiley, 1997), and Richard J. Long, *Compensation in Canada* (Toronto: ITP Nelson, 1998).

3. Frederick Herzberg, *Work and the Nature of Man* (New York: World, 1.)

4. Kanungo and Mendonca, p. 326.

5. As discussed in Chapter 3, government regulations have a major impact on the increase in employee benefits; so have management practices and labour union demands.

6. Roland Thériault, *Mercer Compensation Manual: Theory and Practice* (Boucherville, Quebec: Gaétan Morin, 1992), p. 415.

7. "Merit WCB Plan for Ontario Small Business," *Canadian HR Reporter* (January 12, 1998), p. 3.

8. A discussion of the then-pending legislation is in Michael D. Failes, "WCB Reform Nears Completion," *Human Resources Professional* (February/March 1997), pp. 42–43.

9. "Canadian Provincial Health Benefits," Benefits Interface (http://www.benefits. org/interface/benefit/prov-body.htm).

10. For details, consult the CanPay Web site, http://www.canpay.com/payinfo.

11. Pay Research Bureau, *Benefits and Working Conditions*—1990 (Ottawa: Public Service Staff Relations Board, 1990).

12. Paula Kulig, "Employees Give Thumbs-Down to Benefit Drug Formularies," *Canadian HR Reporter* (March 23, 1998), pp. 1, 9.

13. Pay Research Bureau, op. cit.

14. Human Resources Development Canada, *Canada Pension Plan* (http://www.hrdc-drhc.gc.ca/isp/common/cppind_e.shtml), July 1998.

15. "The Canada Pension Plan—Brave New World?" *Mercer Bulletin* (Canada) (January 1998).

16. HRDC, Current CPP Payment Rates (http://www.hrdv-drhc.gc.ca/isp/cpp/rates_e.shtml, revised March 1998). The maximum benefit under the QPP was $750.69 per month.

17. Stephen Bindman, "Widow's Pension Fight Goes To Supreme Court," *Vancouver Sun* (January 19, 1998); Nancy Law v. Minister of Human Resources Development, Supreme Court File No. 25374).

18. Details in HRDC, *Canada Pension Plan.*

19. HRDC, *Current CPP Payment Rates.*

20. A more detailed discussion, very useful for overall concepts, if a little out of date, can be found in Thériault, pp. 424–37.

21. "Proportion of Labour Force and Paid Workers Covered by Registered Pension Plans (RPP) by Sex," http://www.statscan.ca/english/Pgdb/People/Labour/labor26.html, July 1998.

22. Kevin Marron, "Group Plans Offer Competitive Advantage," *The Globe and Mail* (February 10, 1998), p. C15.

23. "Many Canadians Working Beyond Age 65." *The Financial Post* (January 22, 1998), p. R12.

24. Thériault, pp. 438–39.

25. Innis Christie, *Employment Law in Canada* (Toronto: Butterworths, 1980).

26. This discussion is based on Labour Canada's summary of vacation legislation, *Annual Vacations with Pay* (http://labour-travail.hrdc-drhc.gc.ca/policy/leg/e/stand9-e1.html), July 1998

27. Human Resources Development Canada, *Employment Standards Legislation in Canada* (http://labour-travail.hrdc-drhc.gc.ca/policy/leg/e/index.html), July 1998.

28. Doug Ross, "Corporate Culture at Loggerheads with Family-Friendly Workplace Policies," *Canadian HR Reporter* (December 16, 1996), pp. 29–30.

29. Kanungo and Mendonca, p. 335.

30. Bev Cline, "Rewarding Employees Through Non-Monetary Compensation," *Human Resources Professional* (August/September 1997), pp. 19–23.

31. Details of leaves required by statute can be found on the CanPay Web site, http://www.canpay.com/payinfo.

32. Kanungo and Mendonca, p. 333.

33. Robert Wilson, "Therapy Gets Wired," Benefits Canada (April 1998); http://www.benefitscanada.com/ Content/1998/04-98/ben049802.html.

34. Personal communication of London Life HR management with Drs. Cattaneo and Templer.

35. Wilson, op. cit.

36. Frederick Weston, "Cough Up or Butt Out," Wellness and Health Promotion http://www.chp-ca.com/wellness2.html), July 1998.

37. "Benefits: Evolving for the Future," Benefits Canada http://www.benefitscanada.com/electric/ health/ healthier.html) July 1998.

38. *University of Windsor Undergraduate Calendar* 1997–1998, p. 449.

39. Joanne Chianello, "The Office as Utopia," *Montreal Gazette* (March 7, 1998), p. I8.

40. *Ibid.*

41. Margaret Cannon, "Taking Care of Business: Private Medical Care, the Latest Office Perk for Executives Who Don't Have Time to be Sick, is Poised for Takeoff." *Report on Business Magazine* (November 1997), pp. 146–8.

42. Robert J. McKay, *Canadian Handbook of Flexible Benefits* (Toronto: Wiley, 1996).

43. *Ibid.*

44. *Ibid.*

45. "Are Employers Required to Provide Same-Sex Spousal Employee Benefits?" *Mercer Bulletin* (Canada), Vol. 47 No. 8 (August 1997).

46. *Leshner v. Ontario (Deputy Attorney General)*, (1992) 10 O.R. (3d) 732, 96 D.L.R. (4th) 41. *Dwyer v. Toronto (Metropolitan)*, (1997) O.H.R.B.I.D. No. 33 Decision No. 96-0033, Board File No. B1-0056-93.

47. *Moore v. Canada (Treasury Board)* (1997) C.H.R.D. No. 4, No. T.D. 4/97. and *Niels Lassoe v. Air Canada.* (1996) C.H.R.D. No 10, no. T.dD. 10/96.

48. Kathy Blair, "Same Sex Benefits for Manitoba Civil Servant," *Canadian HR Reporter* (January 12, 1998), p. 1.

49. "Same Sex Spousal Benefits: The CUPE Ontario Court of Appeal Decision," *Mercer Bulletin (Canada)* Vol. 48 No. 2 (February 1998).

50. Elaine Carey, "Sharing a Job 'the Best of Both Worlds'," *The Toronto Star* (June 10, 1997, pp. A1, A24.

51. Doug Ross, op. cit.

52. *Ibid.*

53. Personal visits of Drs. Cattaneo and Templer to London Life.

54. Helen LaFountaine and Greg Kodzrowski, "Today's Workplace: A United Nations of Needs," *Canadian HR Reporter* (July 14, 1997), pp. 15, 17, 18.

55. Jim Murta, "Benefits Under Review," *Benefits Canada* (May 1998); http://www.benefitscanada.com/ Content/1998/05-98/ben059803.html.

56. "Communications Awards: Electronic," *Benefits Canada* (June 1998) http://www.benefitscanada.com/ Conent/1998/06-98/ben069801c.html.

57. "Communication Awards: Overall Strategy," *Benefits Canada* (June 1998) http://www.benefitscanada. com/Content/1998/06-98/ben069801a..html.

58. "Vacations Are Shorter in the US and Japan than in Europe," *The Wall Street Journal* (June 2, 1992), p. A-1; Anita Bruzzese, "Workers Getting More Say in When, How They Take Time Off," *Carroll County Times* (July 23, 1993), p. B-5; Bill Leonard, "The Employee's Favourite, the Employer's Quandary," *HRMagazine* (November 1994), p. 53.

59. This framework is based on Long, pp. 314–23.

60. Sonya Felix, "The Ins and Outs of Outsourcing," *Benefits Canada* (February 1998), p. 41–46.

61. Felix, p. 43, and "Towers Perrin Unveils Benefits Centre," *Benefits Canada* (December 1997), pp. 79, 83.

62. Felix, p. 43

63. Sonya Felix, "Wellness Workout," *Benefits Canada* (January 1998), http://www.benefitscanada.com/ Content/1998/01-98/ben019801.html)

64. "Performance 2000," *Canadian Business* (June 26/July 10, 1998), p. 135 ff.

Chapter 15

1. *Westray Mine Public Inquiry, The Westray Story: A Predictable Path to Disaster*, Report of the Westray Mine Public Inquiry, Justice K. Peter Richard, Commissioner (Halifax, NS: Province of Nova Scotia, 1997), p. ix.

2. Kelly Toughill, "Westray Disaster: Charges Dropped," *The Toronto Star*, July 1, 1998, p. A1, A9; and "At Last, Compensation for Coal Mine Staff," *The Toronto Star*, October 23, 1998, p. A6.

3. Nicole Eve Lidell, "Developing a Health and Safety Culture: A Case Study of Dupont's Kingston Site," *Workplace Gazette: An Industrial Relations Quarterly* (Fall 1998), p. 58.

4. *Ibid.*, p. 83.

5. *Ibid.*

6. Adapted from Ministry of Labour, *A Guide to the Occupational Health and Safety Act* (Toronto: Queen's Printer for Ontario, June 1996), pp. 2–4.

7. *1998 Canadian Master Labour Guide*, 12th edition (Toronto: CCH Canadian Limited, 1998), p. 1017.

8. *Safety Act*, R.S.N.W.T. 1988, c. s-1, asam. *Safety Act* S.N.W.T. 1994, c.15, ss.2-3.

9. *1998 Canadian Master Labour Guide*, 12th edition (Toronto: CCH Canadian Limited, 1998), p. 1018.

10. Cited in Marjo Cusipag, "A Healthy Approach to Managing Disability Costs," *Human Resources Professional* (June-July 1997), p. 13.

11. B.C. Reg. 296/97, effective April 15, 1998, cited in *Canadian Employment Safety and Health Guide* (Toronto: CCH Canadian Limited, April 1998), pp. 40, 462.

12. *Ibid.*

13. John D. Thompson, "Employers Should Take Measures to Minimize Potential for Workplace Violence," *Commerce Clearing House: Ideas and Trends* (December 20, 1993), pp. 201–03; 208.

14. Adapted from Randall S. Schuler, "Definition and Conceptualization of Stress in Organizations," *Organizational Behavior and Human Performance* (April 1980), p. 189.

15. This information is adapted from a newswire report by Mari Yamaguchi as cited in "Stress in Japanese Business," *Audio Human Resource Report,* Vol. 2, No. 2 (March 1991), pp. 6–7.

16. Randall S. Schuler, op.cit., pp. 200–5; see also Kenneth E. Hart, "Introducing Stress and Stress Management to Managers," *Journal of Managerial Psychology* (February 1990), pp. 9–16.

17. Cited in Marjo Cusipag, "A Healthy Approach to Managing Disability Costs," *Human Resources Professional* (June-July 1997), p. 15.

18. Nick Mykodym and Katie George, "Stress Busting on the Job," *Personnel* (July 1989), p. 293.

19. *Ibid.*; see also Patti Watts, "Are Your Employees Burnout Proof?" *Personnel* (September 1990), pp. 12–14; and Philip J. Dewe, "Applying the Concepts of Appraisal to Work Stresses: Some Explanatory Analysis," *Human Relations* (February 1992), pp. 114–15.

20. Donald F. Parker and Thomas A. DeCotiis, "Organizational Determinants of Job Stress," *Organizational Behavior and Human Performance*, 32 (1983), p. 166.

21. Whiton Stuart Paine, *Job Stress and Burnout* (Beverly Hills, CA: Sage, 1982), p. 19.

22. Canadian Mental Health Association, "Depression in the Workplace" (Toronto: Canadian Mental Health Association, 1995).

23. Kevin J. Williams and George M. Alliger, "Role Stressors, Mood Spillover, and Perceptions of Work-Family Conflict in Employed Parents," *Academy of Management Journal*, Vol. 37, No. 4 (1994), p. 837.

24. "EAPs Evolve to Health Plan Gatekeeper," *Employee Benefit Plan Review* (February 1992), p. 18.

25. Diane Kirrane, "EAPs: Dawning of a New Age," *HR Magazine* (January 1990), pp. 30–34.

26. Deborah Shalowitz, "Employee Assistance Plan Trends," *Business Insurance* (June 24, 1991), p. 24.

27. Michael M. Harris and Mary L. Fennell, "Perceptions of an Employee Assistance Program and Employees' Willingness to Participate," *Journal of Applied Behavioral Science*, Vol. 24, No. 4 (1988), p. 423.

28. Gary Johns, "The Effective Management of Employee Attendance," *Human Resources Professional* (June/July 1997), p. 37.

29. Shari Caudron, "The Wellness Payoff," *Personal Journal* (July 1990), p.55.

30. "What Happened at Bhopal," *Time* (April 1, 1985), p. 71, and "India's Bhopal Suit Could Change All the Rules," *Business Week* (April 22, 1985), p.38.

31. Can be consulted on the World Wide Web at http://www.dfait-maeci.gc.ca/travel/report/menu_e.htm.

32. Peter Shawn Taylor, "Two Dead, No Answers," *Canadian Business*, Vol. 71, No. 3 (February 27, 1998), pp. 16, 18.

Chapter 16

1. Alanna Mitchell, "Co-op Looks for Love in Strange Places," *The Globe and Mail Report on Business* (March 27, 1998), p. B22.

2. Mary V. Williams, "Managing WorkPlace Diversity: The Wave of the '90s," *Communication World* (January 1990), p. 16.

3. Eric Roher, "Forever Tango in the Workplace: Developing a Policy Handbook," *Canadian HR Reporter* (November 18, 1996), p. 19.

4. Sharon Lebrun, "People Policies Key to Sunoco Turnaround," *Canadian HR Reporter* (February 10, 1997), pp. 1, 8.

5. Thomas A. Stewart, "The Search for the Organization of Tomorrow," *Fortune* (May 18, 1992), pp. 91–92.

6. Claudine Kapel, "Xerox Canada's Empowerment Strategy Takes the Blueprint from its Global Comparators," *Human Resources Professional* (August1994), pp. 17–18.

7. Quoted by Elizabeth Hunt, Communicating in the Information Age, *Canadian Business Review* (Vol. 23, No. 2, Summer 1996), pp. 23–5.

8. Brian Coleman and Gregory White, "War Room Shapes DaimlerChrysler Future," *The Globe and Mail* (November 13, 1998), p.B10.

9. Richard G. Charlton, "The Decade of the Employee," *Public Relations Journal* (January 1990), p. 26.

10. *Ibid.*

11. Julie Foehrenback and Steve Goldfarb, "Employee Communication in the '90s: Great(er) Expectation," *Communication World* (May June 1990), pp. 101–06.

12. Alvie L. Smith, "Bridging the Gap between Employees and Management," *Public Relations Journal* (November 1990), p. 20.

13. Jerry Beilinson, "Communicating Bad News," *Personnel* (January 1991), p. 15.

14. Paula Kulig, "The Importance of Being a Good Listener," *Canadian HR Reporter* (April 20, 1998), pp. 15, 19.

15. Ann Welsh, "The Give and Take of Recognition Programs," *Canadian HR Reporter* (September 22, 1997), pp. 16–17.

16. *Ibid.*

17. James V. O'Connor, "Building Internal Communications," *Public Relations Journal* (June 1990), p. 29.

18. Pamela K. Cook, "Employee Communications in the United States: What Works, and Why," *Benefits and Compensation International* (June 1991), pp. 25.

19. Adapted from David K. Lindo, "They're Supposed to Know," *Supervisor* (March 1992), pp. 1417.

20. David N. Bateman, "Communications,"" *Human Resource Management: Ideas and Trends* (Chicago: Commerce Clearing House, Inc., July 26, 1988), p. 128.

21. Smith.

22. Bateman.

23. Bateman.

24. Kulig, "The Importance of Being a Good Listener," p. 19.

25. Roher, p. 18.

26. Roderick Wilkinson, "All Purpose Employee Handbook," *Supervision* (January 1992), p. 5.

27. Lori Block, "Texas Utility Effort Shines among Benefit Handbooks," *Business Insurance* (November 18, 1991), p. 63.

28. *Ibid.*

29. Commerce Clearing House, "Handbooks: Should Your Business Have One?" in *Topical Law Reports* (Chicago: Commerce Clearing House, Inc., May 1989), p. 54–60.

30. See, for example, Robert J. Nobile, "Leaving No Doubt About Employee Leaves," *Personnel* (May 1990), pp. 54–60.

31. *Ibid.*

32. *Ibid.*

33. Paula Cohen and Robert J. Nobile, "Confessions of a Handbook Writer, Say It Legally," *Personnel* (May 1991), p. 9.

34. Randall G. Hesser, "Watch Your Language," *Small Business Reports* (July 1991), pp. 45 49.

35. Cohen and Nobile; Elliot H. Shaller, "Avoiding the Pitfalls in Hiring, Firing," *Nation's Business* (February 1991), pp. 51–54; Pamela R. Johnson and Susan Gardner, "Legal Pitfalls of Employee Handbooks," *Advanced Management Journal* (Spring 1989), pp. 42–46.

36. Roher, p. 19.

37. Wilkinson.

38. Marilyn Melia, "Mergers, New Laws Spur Rewrites of Employee Handbooks," *Savings Institutions* (April 1992), p. 47.

39. Cohen and Nobile.

40. This format is adapted from the compilation of data presented in Commerce Clearing House, "What Should Be in the Handbook?" *Topical Law Reports* (Chicago: Commerce Clearing House, Inc., October 1990), pp. 545–176.

41. Karen Matthes, "Corporate Television Catches Employees' Eyes," *Personnel* (May 1991), p. 3.

42. The following intranet examples are drawn from: Al Czarnecki, "HR Takes Flight on the Intranet," *Canadian HR Reporter* (April 7, 1997), pp. G6–G7; Catherine Gibson, "Building an Intranet on the Cheap," *Canadian HR Reporter* (October 6,1997), pp. G20–G21; Joyce Hampton, "The 500-Channel Intranet," *Canadian HR Reporter* (March 23, 1998), pp. 19–20.

43. Linda Lee Brubaker, "Six Secrets for a Great Employee Newsletter," *Management Review* (January 1990), pp. 47–50.

44. Art Durity, "Confessions of a Newsletter Editor," *Personnel* (May 1991), p. 7; see also Brubaker.

45. Paula Kulig, "HR Grudgingly Turns to E-Mail," *Canadian HR Reporter* (May 4, 1998), p. 8.

46. Sharon Lebrun, p. 1.

47. Suellyn McMillian, "Squelching the Rumor Mill," *Personnel Journal* (October 1991), pp. 95–101.

48. Kathleen Sibley, "Communications Overload is Hindering Work: Study", *Computing Canada* (Vol. 23, No. 11, May, 1997), p. 6.

49. Paula Kulig, "HR Grudgingly Turns to E-Mail," p. 8.

50. Denis Detzel, "Their Employees Tend to Report that Management Listens to 'Problems and Complaints,'" in *Human Resources Management: Ideas and Trends* (Chicago: Commerce Clearing House, Inc., February 21, 1990), p. 39.

51. *Ibid.*

52. Based on Ken Mark, "On Track with Safety Self-Regulation," *Human Resources Professional* (June-July 1997), pp. 21–26.

Chapter 17

1. J. M. Weiler, "The Role of Law in Labour Relations," in *Labour Law and Urban Law in Canada*, I. Bernier and A. Lajoie, eds. (Toronto: University of Toronto Press, 1986).

2. R.P. Chaykowski and A. Verma, eds., *Industrial Relations in Canadian Industry* (Toronto: Dryden, 1992).

3. For a comprehensive review of Canadian labour and employment law, see H.W. Arthurs, D.D. Carter, J. Fudge, H.J. Glasbeek and G. Trudeau, *Labour Law & Industrial Relations in Canada*, 4th ed. (Markham, ON: Butterworths, 1993).

4. S.C. 1907, c. 20.

5. Conciliation (or mediation) is a non-binding process whereby an outside party assists the employer and union in their efforts to reach a negotiated resolution to their dispute. This is in contrast to arbitration where the third party has authority to resolve the dispute. A central feature of our modern labour relations system is its reliance on both the mediation and arbitration processes.

6. [1925] A.C. 396 (Judicial Committee of the Privy Council); 2 D.L.R.5.

7. 49 Stat. 499 (1935).

8. B.C. Labour Relations Code, R.S.B.C. 1996, c. 244, section 23.

9. S.C. 1966-67, c. 72.

10. *Constitution Act*, 1982, Schedule B.

11. (1986) 33 D.L.R. (4th) 174 (S.C.C.).

12. Re *Public Service Employee Relations Act* (Alberta) (1987) 1 S.C.R.313, 38 D.L.R. (4th) 161 (S.C.C.); Saskatchewan v. R.W.D.S.U. (1987) 38 D.L.R. (4th) 277 (S.C.C.); P.S.A.C. v. The Queen (1987) 38 D.L.R. (4th) 249 (S.C.C.).

13. *Levigne v. O.P.E.U.* (1991) 2 S.C.R. 211 81 D.L.R. (4th) 545.

14. K. Wm. Thornicroft, Case Comment: *Lavigne v. O.P.S.E.U. et al., Canadian Bar Review* 71(1), March 1992, pp. 155–66.

15. It is important to note that the AFL-CIO and the CLC are not labour unions; rather, they are federations comprised of a number of national and international unions.

16. Edwin F. Beal and James P. Begin, *The Practice of Collective Bargaining* (Homewood, Ill.: Richard D. Irwin, 1982), p. 107.

17. Y. Reshef and K. Stratton-Devine, "Long-Range Planning in North American Unions: Preliminary Findings," *Industrial Relations/Relations Industrielles* 48(2), Spring 1993, pp. 250–66.

18. R.E. Walton and R.B. McKersie, *A Behavioral Theory of Labour Negotiations* (Ithaca: ILR Press, 1965) called this phenomenon "intraorganizational bargaining." For an excellent example of "intraorganizational bargaining" at work, see the National Film Board video production, "Final Offer" which concerns the breakaway of the Canadian arm of the United Auto Workers to form the Canadian Auto Worker. For more information on this latter topic, see S. Ginden, *Canadian Auto Workers: The Birth and Transformation of a Union* (Toronto: Lorimer & Company, 1995).

19. Negotiation committees and shop stewards oversee the collective bargaining process (i.e., contract negotiation and administration). Some overlap between the former and the executive committee may exist.

20. In most cases, union dues are collected by a dues "checkoff" process whereby the employer deducts the appropriate amount of union dues from the employees' pay and, in turn, remits this directly to the union local.

21. Across Canada, managerial employees are generally excluded from collective bargaining legislation.

22. For a Canadian view of the factors affecting certification success, see F. Martinello, "Correlates of Certification Application Success in British Columbia, Saskatchewan and Manitoba," *Relations Industrielles* 51(3), Fall 1996, pp. 544–62.

23. Jim Wimberly, "Union Elections," *Human Resources Management: Ideas and Trends* (February 15, 1990), p. 35.

24. Some of the most commonly used tactics simply involve taking a very adversarial approach before the labour board such as challenging the nature of the bargaining unit or seeking management exclusions from the unit. See R. Holmes and R. Rogow, "Time to Certification of Unions in British Columbia," *Industrial Relations/Relations Industrielles* 49(1), Winter 1994, pp. 133–51.

25. Some recent evidence suggests, contrary to accepted wisdom, that Canadian managers are just as opposed to unions as their US counterparts. On the other hand, Canadian legislation more severely limits management's ability to implement anti-union strategies and tactics. See I. Saporta and B. Lincoln, "Mangers' and Workers' Attitudes Toward Unions in the U.S. and Canada," *Industrial Relations/Relations Industrielles* 50(3), Summer 1995, pp. 550–66.

26. D. Taras, "Why Non-Union Representation is Legal in Canada," *Industrial Relations/Relations Industrielles* 52(4), Fall 1997, pp. 763–86.

27. P. Kumar and L. Acri, "Unions' Collective Bargaining Agenda on Women's Issues: The Ontario Experience," *Industrial Relations/Relations Industrielles* 47(4), Fall 1992, pp. 623–53.

28. "Japan Report," The Wall Street Journal (April 23, 1991), p. A1.

29. Peter J. Dowling and Randall S. Schuler, *International Dimensions of Human Resource Management* (Boston: PWS-Kent Publishing, 1990), pp. 138–57.

30. Weiler, op cit.

31. R.B. Freeman and J.L. Medoff, *What Do Unions Do?* (New York: Basic Books, 1984), ch. 3.

32. P. Laporta and A. Jenkins, "Unionization and Profitability in the Canadian Manufacturing Sector," *Industrial Relations/Relations Industrielles* 51(4), Fall 1996, pp. 726–55.

33. The right-to-work states are concentrated in the south and far Midwest. Is it a coincidence that most Japanese automobile "transplants" have located in right-to-work states?

34. R. Chaykowski and A. Giles, "Globalization, Work and Industrial Relations," *Relations Industrielles* 53(1), Winter 1998, pp. 3–12.

35. T.A. Kochan, H.C. Katz, and R.B. McKersie, *The Transformation of American Industrial Relations* (New York: Basic Books, 1986).

36. J. Rinehart, C. Huxley, and D. Robertson, "Worker Commitment and Labour Management Relations under Lean Production at CAMI," *Industrial Relations/Relations Industrielles* 49(4), Fall 1994, pp.750–75.

37. Robert E. Cole and Donald R. Deskins, Jr., "Racial Factors in Site Location and Employment Patterns of Japanese Auto Firms in America," *California Management Review* (1988), pp. 9–22.

38. G.M. Saltzman, "Job Applicant Screening by a Japanese Transplant: A Union-Avoidance Tactic," *Industrial and Labour Relations Review* Vol. 49(1) October 1995, pp. 88-104; T. Besser, *Team Toyota: Transplanting the Toyota Culture to the Camry Plant in Kentucky* (New York: State University of New York Press, 1996).

39. H. Slomp, *Between Bargaining and Politics: An Introduction to European Labour Relations* (Westport, Conn.: Praeger, 1996).

40. Peter Dowling, Randall S. Schuler, and Denice E. Welch, *International Dimensions of Human Resource Management*, 2d ed. (Belmont, CA: Wadsworth, 1994), pp. 201–3.

41. Brooks Tigner, "The Looming Crunch," In M. Mendenhall and G. Oddou, eds., *Readings and Cases in International Human Resource Management* (Boston: PWS-Kent Publishing, 1991), pp. 412–17.

42. "Workers Want Their Piece of Europe Inc.," *Business Week* (October 29, 1990), p. 46.

Chapter 18

1. Opening vignette based on Alan Adams, "NHLPA Furious at League," *Globe and Mail* (August 9, 1994), p. C6; Gare Joyce, "Mending the Fabric of Shredded Season in the NHL," *The Globe and Mail* (January 16, 1995), p. D5.

2. Craig, A. and N. Solomon, *The System of Industrial Relations in Canada* (Toronto: Prentice-Hall, 1996).

3. D.C. Bok and J.T. Dunlop, "Collective Bargaining in the United States: An Overview," in W. Clay Hammer and Frank L. Schmidt (eds.), *Contemporary Problems in Personnel* (Chicago: St. Clair Press, 1977), p. 383.

4. An international union, in this context, typically refers to a national union in Canada with links to a union in the US.

5. If we take into account public sector collective bargaining, then we have another exception—the public. The taxpaying voting public can influence elected officials to act in certain ways during negotiations.

6. Readers should recognize that although the closed shop (compulsory union membership before one is hired) was declared illegal by the Taft-Hartley Act, a modified form still exists today. That quasi-closed shop arrangement is called the hiring hall and is found predominantly in the construction and printing industries. However, a hiring hall is not strictly a form of union security because it must assist all members despite their union affiliation. Additionally, the hiring hall must establish procedures for referrals that are non-discriminatory.

7. Michael R. Carroll and Christina Heavrin, *Collective Bargaining and Labor Relations* (New York: Merrill/MacMillan Publishing, 1991), pp. 310–11.

8. Adapted from Stephen P. Robbins, *Supervision Today* (Englewood Cliffs, N.J.: Prentice-Hall, 1995), p. 533.

9. One must be aware, however, that in some organizations where participative management styles exist, the minority does not make the decisions.

10. Other factors can affect a settlement such as political infighting, unreasonable legislation, efforts to bust the union, and so on.

11. To be accurate, a strike vote is generally held at the union local level in which the members authorize their union leadership to call the strike.

12. Sharon Lebrun, "Ontario to Ban Right to Strike Across Public Sector," *Canadian HR Reporter* (July 14, 1997), pp. 1–2.

13. Gord Henderson, "University Picked the Wrong Place to Draw the Line," *The Windsor Star* (March 20, 1997), p. 8.

14. "The Strike Weapon Remains Highly Troublesome for Unions," *The Wall Street Journal* (February 26, 1991), p. A–1.

15. Sharon Lebrun, "Finding Common Interest: Companies Move Past Labour-Management Squabbles," *Canadian HR Reporter* (May 19, 1997), p. 6.

16. Eugene C. Hagburg and Marvin J. Levine, *Labor Relations: An Integrative Perspective* (St. Paul, Minn.: West Publishing, 1978), p. 8.

17. *Ibid.*

18. Alison Rogers, "Now Playing in Peoria," *Fortune* (July 12, 1993), p. 11.

Conclusion

1. Andrew Templer and Tupper Cawsey, "Rethinking the Contribution of HRM to Competitive Advantage in an Era of Portfolio Careers," Paper presented at *ASAC Annual Conference* (St. Johns, Newfoundland: June, 1997)

2. David Foot and Daniel Stoffman, *Boom, Bust and Echo* (Toronto: Macfarlane, Walter & Ross, 1996)

3. Tom Redman and Brian Matthews, "Service Quality and Human Resource Management: A Review and Research Agenda," *Personnel Review* (Vol. 27, No. 1, 1998), p. 58–77.

4. David Ulrich, Michael Losey, and Gerry Lake (eds.), *Tomorrow's* ᴴᴿ *Management* (New York: John Wiley & Sons, 1997).

5. *Ibid*, p. 354.

6. See Scott Adams, *The Joy of Work: Dilbert's Guide to Finding Happiness at the Expense of Your Co-workers.* New York: HarperBusiness, 1998.

7. Andrew J. Templer and R. Julian Cattaneo, "A Model of Human Resources Management Effectiveness," *Canadian Journal of Administrative Sciences* (Vol. 12, No. 1, 1997), pp. 77–88.

8. See, for example, the classic study Luis Gomez-Mejia, "Dimensions and Correlates of the Personnel Audit as an Organization Assessment Tool," *Personnel Psychology* (Vol. 38, 1985), p. 293–308; and the more recent study M. Patterson, R. Lawthom, and S. Nickell, *Impact of People Management Practices on Business Performance* (London: Institute for Personnel and Development, 1997).

9. Monica Belcourt, Arthur Sherman, George Bohlander, and Scott Snell, *Managing Human Resources: Canadian Edition* (Toronto: Nelson Canada, 1996) p. 689.

10. Hermann Schwind, Harri Das, and Terry Wager, *Canadian Human Resource Management: A Strategic Approach,* (Toronto: McGraw-Hill, 1998), pp. 689–90.

11. Templer and Cattaneo, p. 87.

12. David Ulrich, 1997, pp. 3–4.

13. James Peters, "A Future Vision of Human Resources," in David Ulrich, Michael Losey, and Gerry Lake (eds.), *Tomorrow's* ᴴᴿ *Management* (New York: John Wiley & Sons, 1997), pp. 250–58.

14. M. Armstrong, "Personnel Director's View from the Bridge," *Personnel Management* (Vol. 21, June 1986), p. 54.

Appendix A

1. See, for example, Julia Hawlon "Scanning Resumes: The Impersonal Touch," *USA Today* (October 7, 1991), p.7B.

2. Terry Mullins, "How to Land a Job," *Psychology Today* (September/October 1994), pp.12–13.

Appendix B

1. Kirsten Schabacker "Tips on Making a Great First Impression," *Working Woman* (February 1992), p.55.

2. See Jundra Woo, "Job Interviews Pose Risk to Employees," *The Wall Street Journal* (March 11, 1992), p.B1; and Joann Keyton and Jeffrey K. Springston, "What Did You Ask Me?" *National Business Employment Weekly* (Spring 1991), p.32.

3. Stephen M. Pollon and Mark Levine, "How to Ace a Tough Interview," *Working Woman* (July 1994), p.49.

4. *Ibid.*

Glossary

(Number in parentheses indicates the page in which term first appeared)

360-Degree Appraisal

360-Degree Feedback (367) Performance appraisal process in which supervisors, peers, employees, customers, and the like evaluate the individual.

Absolute Standards (351) Measuring an employee's performance against some benchmark.

Adjective Rating Scale (352) A performance appraisal method that lists a number of traits and a range of performance for each. Also known as graphic rating scale.

Adverse (Disparate) Impact (77) A consequence of an employment practice that results in a greater rejection rate for a minority group than it does for the majority group in the occupation.

Adverse (Disparate) Treatment (78) An employment situation where protected group members receive different treatment than other employees in matters like performance evaluations, promotions, etc.

Advertisement (170) Materials informing the general public that a position in a company is open.

Affirmative Action (77) A practice in organizations that goes beyond discontinuance of discriminatory practices, including actively seeking, hiring, and promoting minority group members and women.

AFL-CIO (492) The American Federation of Labor and the Congress of Industrial Relations; the U.S.-based labor federation with which some Canadian unions are affiliated.

Annual Vacation (419) A period of several days or weeks when employees are away from work and which are intended to be used for rest and recreation.

Apathy (318) Significant dysfunction tension resulting in no effort being made.

Application Form (180, 200) Company-specific employment forms used to generate specific information the company wants.

Apprenticeship Training (259) Putting the trainee under the guidance of a master worker; common in the skilled trades.

Assessment Centres (208) Facilities where performance simulation tests are administered. These are made up of a series of exercises and are used for selection, development, and performance appraisals.

Attitude Survey (270) Data gathering questionnaires used to elicit responses or interviews from employees regarding how they feel about their jobs, work groups, supervisors, and the organization.

Attribution Theory (362) A theory of performance evaluation which differentiates between what the employee can and cannot control.

Attrition (155) A process in which the jobs of incumbents who leave for any reason are not filled.

Auditing Process (76) The CHRC inspects whether and ensures that companies covered under the EEA comply with this law.

Baby Boom Echos (36) Those individuals born between 1980 and 1995.

Baby Boomers (36) Those individuals born between 1947 and 1966.

Baby Busters (36) Those individuals born in 1967 and 1979.

Background Investigation (181) The process of verifying information job candidates provide.

Bargaining Unit (488) The particular group of employees that is represented by a single trade union in negotiations with the employer; the structure of the unit is determined by the labour relations board.

Behavioural Description Interview (BDI) (217) A type of structured interview in which the interviewee is asked questions about what he or she actually did in specific work-related situations.

Behavioural Symptoms (450) Symptoms of stress characterized by decreased productivity, increased absenteeism and turnover, and possibly even substance abuse.

Behaviourally Anchored Rating Scales (BARS) (354) A performance appraisal technique that generates critical incidents and develops behavioural dimensions of performance. The evaluator appraises behaviours rather than traits.

Behaviour-Based Interview (217) A type of structured interview that is based on inquiring about actual behaviours needed on the job.

Best Practices (104) A series of principles or "proven" strategies in implementing an ethics program.

Blind-box Ad (170) An advertisement in which there is no identification of the advertising organization.

Bona fide occupational qualifications (BFOQ)
Bona fide Occupational Requirement (BFOR) (70, 166) A particular discriminatory practice that is reasonably necessary to assume the efficient safe, and economical performance of the job.

Broadbanding (395) Grouping together several grades into wider bands, thus encouraging growth in personal competencies.

Bulletin Board (472) A means a company uses to post information of interest to its employees. This can be a traditional physical board or an electronic one.

Burn-out (450) Chronic and long-term stress can lead to emotional and/or physical exhaustion and a decline in work productivity.

Business Necessity (86) Certain employment requirements are reasonably necessary to meet the normal and safe operation of an organization.

Canada Health Act (416) An act of Parliament specifying the conditions that provincial health and hospital insurance plans must meet in order to receive assistance from the federal government.

Canada Pension Plan (CPP) (416) Public pension plan that operates throughout Canada (excluding Quebec), providing pensions for workers upon retirement.

The Canadian Labour Congress (CLC) (492) The Canadian equivalent of the U.S.-based AFL-CIO; approximately 60% of Canadian unions are affiliated with the CLC making it the largest Canadian labour federation.

Career (283) The sequence of positions that a person holds over his or her life.

Career Counselling (300) Assisting employees in setting directions and identifying areas of professional growth.

Career Development (284) A process designed to assist workers in managing their careers.

Career Stage (289) Steps in the development of an individual's career.

Central Tendency (360) The tendency of a rater to give average ratings to everyone, good and bad alike.

Certification (496) The exclusive right, granted by the labour relations board, authorizing a union to represent a particular group of employees.

Change Agent (271) Individuals responsible for fostering the change effort and assisting employees in adapting to the changes.

Checklist Appraisal (352) A performance appraisal approach in which a rater checks off those attributes of an employee that apply.

Classification Method (386) Method of job evaluation that involves placing jobs into pre-determined classes based on skills, knowledge, and abilities required.

Co-Determination Stage (524) A labour-management relationship characterized as separate but equal.

Collaboration Stage (524) A labour-management relationship characterized as working together for a common cause.

Collective Bargaining (486, 509) The employment agreement reached between the union and employer setting out the bargaining unit employees' terms and conditions of employment.

College and University Placements (174) An external search process focussing recruiting efforts on college and university campuses.

Communication (461) The transference of meaning and understanding.

Communications Programs (18) HRM programs designed to provide information to, and receive feedback from employees.

Company Newsletter (472) A means of providing information for employees in a specific recurring periodical.

Company-Wide Meetings (474) Meetings used to inform employees of various company issues.

Comparable Worth (72) Equal pay for similar jobs, jobs similar in skills, responsibility, working conditions, and effort.

Compensation Management (381) The process of managing a company's compensation program in a cost-effective manner.

Competency-Based Compensation (394) Organizational pay system that rewards the employee's skills, knowledge, and behaviours.

Complaints Procedure (475) A formalized procedure in an organization through which an employee seeks resolution of a work problem.

Comprehensive Interview (181) A selection device in which in-depth information about a candidate can be obtained.

Comprehensive Selection (184) Applying all steps in the selection process before rendering a decision about a job candidate.

Concurrent Validity (187) Validating tests by using current employees as the study group.

Conditional Job Offer (182) An offer of employment that is firm except for the requirement that the applicant must pass a medical or physical examination.

Confrontational Stage (523) A labour-management relationship characterized as fighting one another until one or the other ultimately wins.

Constitution Act (66) Supreme law of Canada enacted in 1982.

Constraints on Recruiting (165) Factors that can affect or limit the effectiveness of external recruiting.

Construct Validity (187) The degree to which a given test successfully measures an abstract trait or property (the construct).

Constructive Dismissal (118) The employer unilaterally changes the conditions of employment to the effect that employees are demoted without their consent.

Content Validity (187) The degree to which the content of the test is representative of the phenomenon that it is intended to measure.

Contingent Workforce (46) The part-time, temporary, and contract workers used by organizations to fill peak staffing needs, or perform work unable to be done by core employees.

Continuous Process Improvement (42) A Total Quality Management concept whereby workers continue toward 100 per cent effectiveness on the job.

Contract Administration (516) Implementing, interpreting, and monitoring the negotiated agreement between labour and management.

Controlling (4) A management function concerned with monitoring activities.

Cooperation Stage (523) A labour-management relationship characterized as working together on a few specific issues.

Core Employees (46) Workers who hold full-time jobs in organizations.

Correlation Coefficients (188) A statistical function that shows the strength of the relationship between two variables (in this case, between the score on a test and job performance).

Criterion-Related Validity (187) The degree to which a particular selection device accurately predicts the important elements of work behaviour (e.g., the relationship between a test score and job performance).

Critical Incident Appraisal (351) A performance appraisal method that focuses on the key behaviours that make the difference between doing a job effectively or ineffectively.

Cultural Environments (34) The attitudes and perspectives shared by individuals from specific countries that shape their behaviour and how they view the world.

Culture (236) The rules, jargon, customs, and other traditions that clarify acceptable and unacceptable behaviour in an organization.

Cumulative Trauma Disorder (447) An occupational injury that occurs from repetitively performing similar physical movements.

Cut Score (187) A point on the scoring of a test at which applicants scoring below are rejected.

Decline Stage (289) The final stage in one's career, usually marked by retirement.

Delegation (56) A management activity in which activities are assigned to individuals at lower levels in the organization.

Deprivation (318) A state of having an unfulfilled need.

Diary Method (144) A job analysis method requiring job incumbents to record their daily activities.

Dictionary of Occupational Titles (144) A US government publication that lists more than 30,000 jobs.

Dismissal (114) A disciplinary action that results in the termination of an employee

Documentation (345) The record of the performance appraisal process outcomes.

Downsizing (38, 150) An activity in an organization aimed at creating greater efficiency by eliminating certain jobs.

Dual-career Couple (297) A situation in which both partners have distinct careers outside the home.

Dues Checkoff (516) The employer withholds union dues from union members' pay-cheques.

Duty of Fair Representation (496)   The union's duty to ensure that it represents all of the bargaining unit employees in good faith and without discrimination.

Dysfunctional Tension (318)   Tension that leads to negative stress.

Early Retirement (154)   A downsizing effort that gives employees close to retirement some incentive to leave the company earlier than expected.

Economic Strike (521)   A work stoppage that results from labour and management's ability to agree on the wages, hours, terms, and conditions of a new contract.

Effort (318)   Outward action of individuals directed towards some goal.

Effort-performance Relationship (320)   The likelihood that putting forth the effort will lead to successful performance on the job.

Electronic Media (470)   Technological devices such as radio, TV, and computer networks that enhances communication.

E-mail (474)   Electronic mail that can be sent or received over the Internet or private networks.

Employee Assistance Programs (EAPs) (421, 451)   Plans intended to help employees deal with issues such as stress, depression, anxiety, family and marital problems, and substance abuse.

Employee Benefits (410)   Membership-based, non-financial rewards, such as insurance, pensions vacations, and other services designed to attract and retain employees.

Employee Counselling (267)   A process whereby employees are guided in overcoming performance problems.

Employee Development (252)   Future-oriented training, focusing on the personal growth of the employee.

Employee Handbook (466)   A central information source outlining the important aspects of employment an employee needs to know.

Employee Involvement (56)   Techniques that aim at including employees in decision-making processes.

Employee Leasing (176)   The hiring of personnel through a leasing firm for long periods of time.

Employee Monitoring (112)   An activity whereby the company is able to keep informed of its employees' activities.

Employee Referral (169)   A recommendation from a current employee regarding a job applicant.

Employee Rights (101)   A collective term dealing with varied employee protection practices in an organization.

Employee Surveys (477)   Systematic study of the attitudes and perceptions of employees to ascertain how they feel about various aspects of their work and their environment.

Employee Training (252)   Present-oriented training, focusing on individual's current jobs.

Employment Equity Act (EEA) (74)   Aimed to remove employment barriers and achieve equality in the workplace so that no qualified individual (woman, aboriginal people, visible minority, or a person with a handicap is denied employment opportunities.

Employment Insurance (415)   Administered by the federal government, it is intended to provide temporary income support to the unemployed while they search for jobs.

Employment Legislation (15)   Laws that directly affect the hiring, firing, and working conditions of individuals.

Employment Test (205)   Any selection examination that is designed to determine if an applicant is qualified for the job.

Encounter Stage (233)   The socialization stage in which individuals confront the possible contradiction between their organizational expectations and reality.

Environmental Influences (9)   Those factors outside the organization that directly affect HRM operations.

Equal Pay Legislation (381)   Laws that require that men and women be paid the same if they are performing identical or substantially similar work, and in some jurisdictions, if they are performing work of equal value.

Ergonomics (447)   The process of matching the work environment to the individual.

Essay Appraisal (351)   A performance appraisal method in which an appraiser writes a narrative about the employee.

Establishment Stage (289)   A career stage in which one begins to search for work. It includes getting one's first job.

Ethical Codes and Standards (104)   Ethical codes or standards guide HR managers in their decision making on ethical matters that they may confront in their job.

Ethics (101)   Going beyond the law in employment decisions designed to protect employee rights and dignity.

Executive Perquisites Perks (423)   Benefits made available to executives and managers but not to lower-level employees.

Executive Search Firm (174)   Private employment agency specializing in middle and top management as well as hard-to-fill positions.

Expatriates (167) Individuals who work in a country in which they are not citizens or permanent residents.

Exploration Stage (289) A career stage that usually ends in one's mid-twenties as one makes the transition from school to work.

External and Internal Careers (287) Career value and success as defined externally and internally to the individual.

Extinction (255) Removing reinforcement of a behaviour so that individuals eventually cease doing it.

Extrinsic Rewards (379) Rewards one gets from the employer, usually money, a promotion, or benefits.

Fact-finding (523) A process conducted by a neutral third party individual who conducts a hearing to gather evidence and testimony from the parties regarding the differences between them.

Factor Comparison Method (386) A method of job analysis in which job factors are compared to determine the worth of the job.

Family-Friendly Benefits (154, 426) Flexible benefits that support care for the employee's family.

Federal Contractors Program (75) Companies that bid for goods or services contracts with the federal government (valued at 200,000 or more a year) must comply with the *EEA*.

Flexible Benefits (424) Benefits programs that allow employees to pick the benefits that best meet their needs.

Flextime (331) A scheduling system in which employees are required to work a number of hours per week but are free, within limits, to vary the hours of work.

Forced-Choice Appraisal (353) A type of performance appraisal in which the rater must choose between two specific statements about an employee's work behaviour.

Four-Fifths Rule (78) A rough indicator of discrimination, this rule requires that the number of minority members that a company hires must be at least 80 per cent of the majority members in the population hired.

Functional Job Analysis (FJA) (144) A job analysis process developed on the basis of the US Department of Labor's methodology.

Functional Tension (318) Positive tension that creates the energy for an individual to act.

Gainsharing (393) Plant-wide incentive plans in which workers share in the organization's financial gains.

Glass Ceiling (91) The invisible barrier that blocks females minorities from ascending into upper levels of an organization.

Glass Walls (93) Discrimination in the assignment of particular jobs that in effect limit people's (women and visible minorities) access to special and critical jobs that are necessary to promotion.

Global Village (32) The world considered as a single interdependent community linked by telecommunications.

Golden Parachute (400) An approach to protecting executives in the case of a hostile turnover by providing either severance pay or guaranteed positions.

Good Faith and Fair Dealing (118) In the process of dismissal, the employer should treat the employee with respect and dignity.

Graphology (211) Handwriting analysis which purports to disclose personality characteristics.

Grievance (Rights) Arbitration (519) The final step in the grievance procedure when an external arbitrator resolves the dispute.

Grievance (494) A formal protest filed by the union alleging that the employer has violated a provision of the collective bargain.

Grievance Procedures (517) A complaint-resolving process contained in union contracts.

Griggs v. Duke Power (70) Landmark US Supreme Court decision stating that tests must fairly measure the knowledge or skills required for a job.

Group Interview Method (144) Meeting with a number of employees to collectively determine what their jobs entail.

Group Life Insurance (418) A life insurance policy covering a group of people (in particular, the employees of an organization).

Group Order Ranking (354) A relative standard of performance characterized as placing employees into a particular classification such as the "top one-fifth."

Halo Error (360) The tendency to let our assessment of an individual on one trait influence our evaluation of that person on other specific traits.

Harshness Error (359) Rating performance lower than it should be.

Hawthorne Studies (14) A series of studies that provided new insights into group behaviour.

Health and Safety Duties (441) Specific duties that the law assigns to employers, managers, and workers to help ensure a safe and healthy workplace.

Health Insurance (415) An insurance policy intended to provide individuals with the means to pay for medical services, hospital care, and the like.

Holland Vocational Preferences Model (293) A model that relates personality characteristics to preferred occupational choices.

Host-Country National (HCN) (167) A citizen or permanent resident of a given country, hired by a multinational firm to work in that country.

Human Resources Inventory (137) A roster that describes the skills that are available within the organization.

Human Resources Management (9) Function in the organization concerned with the staffing, training and development, motivation, and maintenance of employees.

Human Resources Management System (135) A computerized system that assists in the processing of HRM information.

Impasse (521) A situation where labour and management cannot reach a satisfactory agreement.

Impression Management (215, 362) Influencing the interview by portraying an image that is desired by the interviewer.

IMPROSHARE (393) "Improving Productivity through Sharing," an incentive plan that allocates employee bonuses through a mathematical formula based on cost or other savings.

Independent Contractors (178) Temporary employees offering specialized services to an organization.

Individual Interview Method (143) Meeting with an employee to determine what his or her job entails.

Individual Needs (317) A basic want or desire.

Individual Performance-Organizational Goal Relationship (321) The expectation that achieving individual goals will lead to the attainment of organizational goals.

Individual Ranking (356) Listing employees' performance in order from highest to lowest.

Initial Screening (179) The first step in the selection process whereby inquiries about a job are screened.

Interactive Video Disks (IVD) (261) Videos that permit the user to make changes/selections and see the effects of their decisions in real time.

Interest Arbitration (523) An impasse resolution technique used to settle contract negotiation disputes, where the arbitrator hears testimony and render a decision.

Interest Dispute/Arbitration (490) An interest dispute is a dispute about the terms and conditions of employment; interest arbitration is the process whereby a third party neutral issues a binding decision regarding the dispute.

Internal Search (168) Seeking to fill a position with current employees of the organization.

Internal System of Responsibility A system that relies on the people in the workplace to identify health and safety problems and develop solutions.

Internet (261) The international network of computers that allows communication via electronic mail and the World Wide Web.

Interview (212) A selection method that involves a face-to-face meeting with the candidate.

Intranet (470) An organization-specific information network often including an Internet-based set of Web pages.

Intrinsic Rewards (379) Rewards one receives from the job itself, such as pride in one's work, a feeling of accomplishment, or being part of team.

ISO 9000 (43) Set of global quality standards established by the International Standards Organization in Geneva.

Job Analysis (142) Provides information about jobs currently being done and the knowledge, skills, and abilities that individuals need to perform the jobs adequately.

Job Characteristics Model (328) A framework for analysing and designing jobs. JCM identifies five primary job characteristics and their interrelationship.

Job Description (146) A written statement of what the job holder does, how it is done, and why it is done.

Job Enrichment (330) The process of expanding the depth of the job by allowing employees to plan and control their work more.

Job Evaluation (148, 380) The process of determining the value of each job in relation to the other jobs in the organization.

Job Instruction Training (JIT) (259) A systematic approach to on-the-job training consisting of four basic steps.

Job Rotation (263) Moving employees horizontally or vertically to expand their skills, knowledge, or abilities.

Job Specification (148) Statements indicating the minimal acceptable qualifications incumbents must possess to successfully perform the essential elements of their jobs.

Job-Related Criteria (86) Criteria that predict on the job performance.

Labour Relations Board (488) The quasi-judicial administrative tribunal charged with administering and enforcing collective bargaining legislation.

Labour Trilogy (491)   The three 1987 decisions issued by the Supreme Court of Canada all holding that collective bargaining and the right to strike were not constitutionally protected activities.

Late-Career Stage (289)   A career stage in which individuals are no longer learning about their jobs, nor is it expected that they should be trying to outdo levels of performance from previous years.

Lay-off (152)   Temporary or permanent dismissal of workers from their jobs.

Leading (4)   A management function concerned with directing the work of others.

Learning Curve (256)   Depicts the rate of learning.

Leaves of Absence (153)   Permission to be absent from one's job.

Leniency Error (359)   Rating performance higher than it should be.

Loaning (153)   Permitting employees to work for not-for-profit organizations, where the employer pays a portion of the employee's salary.

Local Union (494)   Typically, the union that is certified to represent a particular group of employees; provides the grassroots support for union members in their daily interactions with the employer.

Lockout (521)   A situation in labour-management negotiations whereby management prevents union members from returning to work.

Management (4)   The process of efficiently getting activities completed with and through other people.

Management by Objectives (MBO) (356)   A performance appraisal method that includes mutual objective setting and evaluation based on the attainment of the specific objectives.

Management Rights (515)   Items that are not part of contract negotiations, such as how to run the company, or how much to charge for products.

Management Thought (14)   Early theories of management that promoted today's HRM operations.

Mandatory Retirement (71)   The age that is considered "normal" for the kind of work involved.

Medical or Physical Examination (182)   An examination to determine whether an applicant is medically or physically fit to perform the job.

Membership-Based Rewards (380)   Rewards that go to all employees regardless of performance.

Mentor (266)   A senior employee who supports the career development of a junior employee.

Mentoring or Coaching (265)   The active guidance of a junior employee by a more senior one.

Merit Pay (391)   An increase in pay based on some overall measure of individual performance, usually awarded at regular periods such as annually or bi-annually.

Metamorphosis Stage (233)   The socialization stage in which the new employee must work out any inconsistencies discovered during the encounter stage.

Mid-Career Stage (289)   A career stage marked by a continuous improvement in performance, leveling off in performance, or the beginning of deterioration of performance.

Mission Statement (132)   A declaration of the reason an organization is in business.

Motivating Potential Score (329)   A predictive index suggesting the motivation potential of a job.

Motivation (316)   The willingness to do something, conditioned by the action's ability to satisfy some need.

National Labour Relations Board (488)   Established to administered and interpret the *Wagner Act*, the NLRB has primary responsibility for conducting union representation elections in the US.

National Occupational Classification (144)   Published by Human Resources Development Canada, it includes over 10,000 job descriptions.

National or international union (493)   The national or international union body that charters local unions and provides institutional support for collective bargaining and contract administration.

Negative Reinforcement (255)   Removing a response to a behaviour so that the behaviour is more likely to be repeated.

Norms (236)   Tell group members what they ought or ought not do in certain circumstances.

Observation Method (142)   Watching employees at work (directly or on film) to determine what their jobs entail.

Occupational Health and Safety Legislation (439)   Standards set to ensure safe and healthy working conditions and provide stiff penalties for violators.

Open Shop (515)   Employees are free to choose whether or not to join the union, and those who do not are not required to pay union dues.

Operant Conditioning (254)   A type of conditioning in which behaviour leads to a reward or prevents punishment.

Organizational Development (OD) (269)   A process in the organization that helps employees adapt to change.

Organizational Goal (316)   An objective that the organization seeks to achieve.

Organizational Goal-Individual Goal Relationship (323)   The expectation that achieving organizational goals will lead to the attainment of individual goals.

Organizing (4)   A management function that deals with what jobs are to be done, by whom, where decisions are to be made, and the grouping of employees.

Organizing Drive (495)   The process whereby a union seeks to be designated as the employees' bargaining agent; usually, the union will solicit employees' signatures on union membership cards which in turn will be presented to the labour relations board for verification.

Outdoor Training (264)   Specialized training that occurs outdoors and focuses on building self-confidence and teamwork.

Outplacement (155)   The process of assisting company employees to search for jobs outside the organization.

P.C. 1003 (488)   The 1944 emergency wartime regulations that established Canada's first collective bargaining regime.

Paired Comparison (356)   Ranking individuals' performance in relation to all others on a one-on-one basis, and counting the number of times any one individual is the preferred member.

Parent-Country National (PCN) (167)   A citizen or permanent resident of the country where a multinational firm has its headquarters, assigned to work for the company as an expatriate in another country.

Participative Management (56)   A management concept giving employees more control over the day-to-day activities on their job.

Pay in Lieu of Notice (116)   Rather than giving the employee reasonable notice, the organization offers the employee a lump sum of money that would have been earned over the reasonable notice period.

Pay Secrecy (400)   The practice of keeping information on pay strictly confidential.

Pay-for-Performance (325)   Rewarding employees based on their performance.

Peer Evaluations (366)   A performance evaluation approach in which co-workers provide input into the employee's performance.

Peer Orientation (245)   Co-workers assist in orienting new employees.

Performance Appraisal Process (343)   A formal process in an organization whereby each employee is evaluated to determine how he or she is performing.

Performance Simulation Tests (207)   Tests that require the applicant to perform tasks that are part of the job, as in work sampling tests and assessment centres.

Performance-Based Rewards (380)   Rewards that are based on the job performance of individuals or teams.

Perquisites (400)   Benefits that are made available to executives; commonly called "perks."

Physiological Symptoms (449)   Characteristics of stress such as increased heart and breathing rates, higher blood pressure, and headaches.

Piecework Plan (392)   A compensation plan whereby employees are typically paid for the number of units they actually produce.

Planning (4)   A management function focusing on setting organizational goals and objectives.

Plant-Wide Incentives (393)   Incentive system that rewards all members of the plant based on how well the entire group performed.

Plateauing (291)   A condition of stagnating in one's current job.

Point Method (387)   Breaking down jobs based on identifiable criteria then allocating points to each.

Portfolio Focused HRM (49)   HRM activities organized around the skill sets or portfolios of employees in an organization.

Position Analysis Questionnaire (PAQ) (144)   A job analysis method that allows analysts to quantitatively group interrelated job elements into dimensions.

Position-Focused HRM (49)   HRM activities, organized around specific jobs on positions in an organization.

Positive Discipline (124)   A form of discipline that tries to eliminate the punitive nature from the discipline process and instead treats discipline as an education process.

Positive Reinforcement (255)   Providing a response to a behaviour that makes it more likely for the behaviour to be repeated.

Post-Training Performance Method (273)   Evaluating training programs based on how well employees can perform their jobs after they have received the training.

Pre-Arrival Stage (232)   The socialization process stage that recognizes individuals arrive in an organization with a set of organizational values, attitudes, and expectations.

Pre-Boomers (36)   Those individuals born before 1947.

Predictive Validity (187)   Validating tests by using prospective applicants as the study group.

Pre-Post-Training Performance Method (273) Evaluating training programs based on the difference in performance before and after employees receive training.

Pre-Post-Training Performance with Control Group (273) Evaluating training by comparing pre- and post-training results with individuals who did not receive the training.

Privacy Act (106) Requires federal government agencies to make available information in an individual's personnel file.

Private Employment Agency (173) A private firm specializing in recruiting workers.

Private Health Insurance (416) A health insurance plan that supplements public health and hospital insurance coverage and is administered through private insurance companies.

Private Pension Plans (417) Pension plans that supplement the CPP/QPP.

Problem Solving Style (295) The way in which a person goes about gathering and evaluating information in solving problems and making decisions.

Professional Organizations (174) Organizations whose members share a common profession or occupation, such as labour unions, engineering societies, and the like. These organizations frequently provide placement services for their members.

Programmed Instruction (260) Material is learned in a highly organized, logical sequence, that requires the individual to respond.

Progressive Disciplinary Action (121) The discipline process generally follows a sequence from less to more severe punishment or discipline.

Protected Group Members (78) Any individual who is afforded protection under employment discrimination laws.

Psychological Symptoms (450) Characteristics of stress such as tension anxiety, irritability, boredom, and procrastination.

Public Employment Service (171) Government-funded agencies, such as Canada Employment Centres, that assist employers to find workers and individuals to find jobs.

Public Health Insurance (416) Health insurance available to all residents of Canada through programs administered by the provinces and territories, with assistance from the federal government.

Public Service Staff Relations Act (490) The first major public sector bargaining law enacted by the federal government in 1967.

Punishment (119, 255) Penalizing an employee for undesirable behaviour.

Quebec Pension Plan (QPP) (416) Public pension plan that operates in Quebec providing pensions for workers upon retirement. The QPP is coordinated with the Canada Pension Plan, and they operate virtually as one plan.

Rand Formula (515) An arrangement in which all workers pay union dues.

Ranking Method (385) A method of evaluating jobs by placing them in order, from most to least valuable.

Realistic Job Preview (RJP) (218) A selection device that allows job candidates to learn negative as well as positive information about the job and organization.

Reasonable Accommodation (71) Making adjustment to the work or workplace so that individuals with particular needs can effectively perform their job.

Reasonable Notice (114) The employer has to let the employee know, and offer a specific and reasonable time frame, that he or she will be dismissed.

Reduced Work Hours (154) A staff reduction concept where by employees work fewer than forty hours and are paid accordingly.

Re-engineering (44) Radical, quantum change in an organization.

Registered Pension Plans (417) Private pension plans must be registered with Revenue Canada for tax purposes(hence the name.

Registered Retirement Savings Plans (RRSPs) (418) Personal retirement savings plans in which any individual may contribute.

Relative Standards (354) Measuring an employee's performance by comparing it to other employees' performances.

Reliability (186) A selection device's consistency of measurement

Repetitive Strain Injuries (RSIs) (447) Injuries caused by continuous and repetitive movements, usually of the hand and arm as in typing.

Representation Vote (487) The vote conducted by the labour relations board to determine if a union has majority support among bargaining unit employees.

Replacement Charts (136) HRM organizational charts indicating positions that may become vacant in the near future and the individuals who may fill the vacancy.

Restricted Policy (80) An HRM policy that results in the exclusion of a class of individuals.

Reverse Discrimination (77)   People, in particular White males, feel the victim of *EEA* programs and claim that as a result of these programs they are now discriminated against.

Rightsizing (150)   Bringing the number of employees in line with the organization's strategy and needs.

Roles (237)   Sets of behaviours that job incumbents are expected to display.

Scanlon Plan (393)   An organization-wide incentive program that distributes cost savings and productivity gains among all employees and emphasizes cooperation between management, union, and employees.

Scientific Management (14)   A set of principles designed to enhance worker productivity.

Selection Process (179)   The process of selecting the best candidate for the job.

Sexual Harassment (88)   Anything of a sexual nature that results in a condition of employment, an employment consequence, or creates a hostile or offensive environment.

Shared Responsibility (440)   A system where employers and employees share the responsibility for health and safety in the workplace.

Shared Services (22)   Sharing HRM activities among geographically dispersed divisions.

Shop Steward (494)   The union representative, typically elected, who is responsible for administering the collective agreement at the level of the shop floor.

Sick Buildings (446)   An unhealthy work environment caused by harmful materials such as airborne chemicals, asbestos, or other indoor pollutants.

Similarity Error (360)   Evaluating employees based on the way evaluators perceive themselves.

Simulation Exercises (264)   Training techniques which try to recreate an environment which closely mirrors actual managerial problems.

Situational Interview (217)   Structured interview designed to see how the applicants handle themselves under pressure.

Skill Deficiencies (38)   The gap between required and available skills.

Smoke-Free Policies (447)   Organization policies that reduce or prohibit smoking on company premises.

Social Learning Theory (255)   Theory of learning that views learning as occurring through observation and direct experience.

Socialization (230)   A process of adaptation that takes place as individuals attempt to learn the values and norms of work roles.

Standard Occupational Classification (144)   Based on the National Occupational classification it provides a structure that allows analysts to categorize jobs.

Statutory Holidays (420)   Days for which time off must be given with pay as specified by the appropriate jurisdiction's laws (statutes).

Stock Options (400)   An incentive plan that permits executives to purchase company shares at some time in the future at the price set at the moment the option is granted, thus encouraging them to work towards increasing the value of the company's shares.

Strategic Goals (133)   Organization-wide goals setting direction for the next five to twenty years.

Strategic Human Resources Planning (132)   The process of linking human resources planning efforts to the company's strategic direction.

Stress (448)   A condition in which you have either the opportunity to gain something that is important to you but the outcome is uncertain or you are prevented from gaining something by constraints and demands placed on you.

Stress Interview (212)   An interview designed to see how the applicants handle themselves under pressure.

Stressors (449)   Anything that causes stress in an individual.

Structured Interview (215)   An interview in which there are fixed questions that are presented to every applicant.

Structured Questionnaire Method (144)   A specifically designed questionnaire on which employees rate tasks they perform on their jobs.

Succession Planning (136)   Ensuring that there are individuals ready to move into positions of higher responsibility.

Successorship (498)   The process whereby the labour relations board declares that new employer, say a purchaser of the business, is bound by the former employer's certification and collective bargaining agreement.

Suggestion Program (476)   A process whereby employees have the opportunity to tell management how they perceive the organization is doing.

Supplemental Unemployment Benefits (SUBs) (415) Payments available to laid-off workers in certain industries (particularly the automotive industry) that supplement the payments they receive from Employment Insurance.

Systemic Discrimination (77) A seemingly neutral employment practice discriminates (unintentionally) against one or more protected groups.

Team-Based Rewards (395) Rewards based on how well the team, not the individual employee, performed.

Technical Conference Method (144) A job analysis technique that involves extensive input from the employee's supervisor.

Telework (52) Work performed at a distance, outside of the organization's central office environment.

Temporary Employees (176) Employees hired for a limited time to perform a specific job.

Third Country National (TCN) (370) An employee of a multinational company who is not a permanent resident of the country where the corporation has its headquarters, and who is assigned to work as an expatriate in a country different from that of his or her permanent residence.

Total Quality Management (TQM) (41) An organization-wide perspective on quality and broad interventions aimed at its improvement.

Undue Hardship (70) The accommodating an employee's disability or needs does not exceed reasonable costs (e.g. financial costs, disruption of collective agreement, or work scheduling).

Unfair Labour Practices (488) A violation by the employer or the union of the rules set out in the collective bargaining legislation; the violation can be remedied in a variety of ways by the labour relations board.

Union (485) An organization that exists to represent, and bargain on behalf of, a group of employees as their agent with respect to the employees' terms and conditions of employment.

Union Density Rate (485) The percentage of the workforce represented by union members and employees covered by collective bargaining agreements.

Union Membership Card (487) A card signed by an employee authorizing the union to act on his or her behalf; relied on by the union when applying to be certified an exclusive bargaining agent.

Union Security Arrangements (515) Labour contract provisions designed to attract and retain dues paying union members.

Union Shop (515) Employers can hire nonunion workers, but they must become dues-paying members within a prescribed period of time.

Upward Appraisal (367) An employee appraisal process whereby employees evaluate their supervisors.

Validity (186) The proven relationship of a selection device to some relevant criterion.

Validity Generalization (191) The extent to which the validity of a test can be statistically extended across several different situations.

Virtual Reality (261) A process which simulator actual activities allowing the individual to refine his or her skills.

Voluntary Recognition (498) The process whereby an employer recognizes a union as the bargaining agent for a group of employees even though that union has not been officially certified by the labour relations board.

Wage and Salary Curves (389) The result of the plotting of points of established pay grades against wage or salary base rates to identify the general pattern of wages or salaries and find individuals whose wage or salaries are out of line.

Wage and Salary Structure (390) Organizing jobs into pay grades and assigning wages or salaries to each grade. Frequently each grade is assigned a pay range.

Wage and Salary Survey (389) The process of gathering and interpreting information regarding the wages or salaries paid in the relevant labour market.

Wagner Act (488) Also known as the US *National Labour Relations Act* of 1935, the *Wagner Act* gave employees the legitimate right to form and join unions and to engage in collective bargaining.

Walk-Ins (175) Unsolicited applicants for employment maybe a prospective source for recruitment depending on their particular circumstances.

Weighted Application Blank (WAB) (181, 203) An application form in which several elements have been statistically related to job outcomes.

Wellness Programs (422, 452) Programs designed to help employees maximize their physical well-being.

Whistle-Blowing (111) A situation in which an employee notifies authorities of wrongdoing in an organization.

Wildcat Strike (521) An unauthorized and illegal strike that occurs during the terms of an existing contract.

Work Sampling (208) A selection device requiring the job applicant to actually perform a small segment of the job.

Work Sharing (153)   A work concept whereby two or more individuals share one full-time job with the remaining time spent on individual pursuits.

Work Teams (56)   Formal work groups made up of interdependent individuals who are responsible for attainment of a specific goal.

Workers' Compensation (415)   Payment to workers (or their heirs) for death or disability resulting from job-related activities.

Workers' Rights (440)   The employer's right to direct workers and control the production process must be counterbalanced by rights for the employees. Basic rights include the right to participate, the right to know, the right to refuse work, and the right to stop work.

Workforce Diversity (35)   The varied personal characteristics that make the workforce heterogenous.

Workplace Hazardous Materials Information System (WHMIS) (441)   This process plays a key role in educating employees about handling material controlled by the federal *Hazardous Products Act.*

Written Test (205)   An organizational selection tool designed to indicate whether an applicant will be successful on the job if hired.

Wrongful Dismissal (116)   The employee has been given an insufficient length of notice.

Organization Index

Subject Index